Exiles Traveling
Exploring Displacement, Crossing Boundaries in German Exile Arts and Writings 1933-1945

Edited by
Johannes F. Evelein

Amsterdam - New York, NY 2009

Die 1972 gegründete Reihe erscheint seit 1977 in zwangloser Folge in der Form von Thema-Bänden mit jeweils verantwortlichem Herausgeber.

Reihen-Herausgeber:

Prof. Dr. Norbert Otto Eke
Universität Paderborn
Fakultät für Kulturwissenschaften, Warburger Str. 100, D - 33098 Paderborn, Deutschland, E-Mail: norbert.eke@upb.de

Prof. Dr. Martha B. Helfer
Rutgers University
172 College Avenue, New Brunswick, NJ 08901
Tel.: (732) 932-7201, Fax: (732) 932-1111, E-mail: mhelfer@rci.rutgers.edu

Prof. Dr. Gerhard P. Knapp
University of Utah
Dept. of Languages & Literature, 255 S. Central Campus Dr. Rm. 1400
Salt Lake City, UT 84112, USA
E-Mail: gerhard.knapp@m.cc.utah.edu

Prof. Dr. Gerd Labroisse
Sylter Str. 13A, 14199 Berlin, Deutschland
Tel./Fax: (49)30 89724235 E-Mail: Labroisse@t-online.de

Cover illustration:
Criss Cross (Universal Pictures 1948).
Universal Studios Home Video 2004.

All titles in the Amsterdamer Beiträge zur neueren Germanistik (from 1999 onwards) are available online: See www.rodopi.nl
Electronic access is included in print subscriptions.

The paper on which this book is printed meets the requirements of "ISO 9706:1994, Information and documentation - Paper for documents - Requirements for permanence".

ISBN: 978-90-420-2540-0
©Editions Rodopi B.V., Amsterdam – New York, NY 2009
Printed in The Netherlands

Exiles Traveling
Exploring Displacement, Crossing Boundaries in German Exile Arts and Writings 1933-1945

AMSTERDAMER BEITRÄGE ZUR NEUEREN GERMANISTIK

68 2009

Herausgegeben von

Norbert Otto Eke
Martha B. Helfer
Gerhard P. Knapp
Gerd Labroisse

Table of Contents

List of Contributors   7

Preface   9

Johannes F. Evelein (Hartford CT, USA): Traveling Exiles, Exilic Travel – Conceptual Encounters   11

I. Topographies and Chronotopes of Exile   33

Wulf Koepke (Roslindale MA, USA): On Time and Space in Exile – Past, Present and Future in a No-Man's Land

Thomas Pekar (Tokyo, Japan): Jüdisches Exil in Ostasien, vor allem in Japan (1933–1945)   51

Hubert Roland (Louvain-la-Neuve, Belgium): German and Austrian Exile Literature in Belgium (1933–1945). Topography and Perspectives   73

Henrike Walter (Hamburg, Germany): Fern-Weh. Wolfgang Hildesheimer's Novels *Tynset* and *Masante* as Topographical Reflections of Exile Experience   99

Donald G. Daviau (Riverside CA, USA): Paul Zech's Exotic Travels in South America   115

Reinhard Andress (St. Louis MO, USA): The German Exile Experience in Brazil from the Perspective of Arnold van Gennep's *Les rites de passage*   133

Susanne Utsch (Berlin, Germany): Chronotopoi und Kindheitserinnerung: Europareisen im amerikanischen Exilwerk von Klaus Mann   153

II. Crossing Borders

Jörg Thunecke (Cologne, Germany): Definitions of Exile. *Unwilling Tourist* (1941–1942): Adolf Hoffmeister's Odyssey into Emigration (1939–1940)   177

Laura Heins (Charlottesville VA, USA): Criss-Crossings of Robert Siodmak: The Time and Space of Cinematic Exile   201

W. Scott Hoerle (Belmont MA, USA): The Nazi Envoy: Travel Experiences of the Poet Hans Friedrich Blunck in Great Britain and France, 1935 and 1937   223

Primavera Driessen Gruber (Vienna, Austria): Traveltalks in Music. Von Mahlers *Lieder eines fahrenden Gesellen* zu Eislers *Hollywooder Liederbuch* und darüber hinaus   239

Lisa Hooper (Bloomington IN, USA): Themes of Exile in the Music and Public and Private Writings of Arnold Schoenberg (1930–1945)   265

III. Narrating Exilic Travel

Patrick B. Farges (Saint Denis, France): Transit/Transfer/Transgression: Das Erzählen von "Ent-Ortung" in Anna Seghers' Erzählungen (1924–1980)   283

Birgit Maier-Katkin (Tallahassee FL, USA): "Kahl und wild wie ein Mondgebirge" – Exile and Mind Travel in Anna Seghers' *The Excursion of the Dead Girls*   297

Helga Schreckenberger (Burlington VT, USA): Aimless Travels: Deromanticizing Exile in Irmgard Keun's *Kind aller Länder* (1938)   313

Margot Taureck (Paris, France): Exil und Reisen im Geiste – Rudolf Leonhards *Traumbuch des Exils*   329

Karina Lindeiner-Stráský (Aberystwyth, Wales): "Jetzt stocke ich in zwei Zungen" – The Influence of Exile and Travel on Themes, Language and Literary Style in the Writings of Members of *Das Jüngste Deutschland*   347

Jacqueline Vansant (Dearborn MI, USA): Involuntary and Voluntary Travel in Egon Schwarz's *Unfreiwillige Wanderjahre* and *Die japanische Mauer*   369

Index   385

List of Contributors/
Anschriften der Autorinnen und Autoren

Prof. Dr. Reinhard Andress
Dept. of Modern and Classical
  Languages
Ritter Hall 336
St. Louis University
220 North Grand Blvd.
USA – St. Louis, MO 63103

Prof. Dr. Donald G. Daviau
University of California, Riverside
Markt 230
A – 2880 Kirchberg am Wechsel

Dr. Primavera Driessen Gruber
Exilmusikforscherin
A – Vienna
orpheustrust@chello.at
www.orpheustrust.at

Prof. Dr. Johannes F. Evelein
Dept. of Language and Culture
  Studies
Trinity College
300 Summit Street
USA – Hartford, CT 06106

Prof. Dr. Patrick Farges
Université de Paris 8 /
  EHESS – Paris
3 rue Franklin
F – 93200 Saint Denis

Prof. Dr. Laura Heins
Dept. of Germanic Languages and
  Literatures
P.O. Box 400125

509 New Cabell Hall
University of Virginia
USA – Charlottesville, VA 22904

Prof. Dr. W. Scott Hoerle
University of Massachusetts at
  Lowell
38 Poplar St.
USA – Belmont, MA 02478

Ms. Lisa Hooper
Indiana University
1955 North College # 26
USA – Bloomington, IN 47401

Prof. Dr. Wulf Koepke
50 Winton Street
USA – Roslindale, MA 02131

Prof. Dr. Birgit Maier-Katkin
The Florida State University
316 A Diffenbaugh
Dept. of Modern Languages
USA – Tallahassee, FL 32306-1540

Prof. Dr. Thomas Pekar
Gakushuin University
1-5-1 Mejiro Toshima-ku
J – Tokyo 171-8588

Dr. Hubert Roland
FNRS / Université Catholique de
  Louvain
Collège Erasme, Place Blaise
  Pascal 1
B – 1348 Louvain-la-Neuve

Prof. Dr. Helga Schreckenberger
Dept. of German and Russian
University of Vermont
Waterman Bldg Rm 418-A
USA – Burlington, VT 05405

Dr. Karina Lindeiner-Stráský
Dept. of European Languages
Aberystwyth University
6 Y Lanfa
Trefechan
UK – SY23 1AS Aberystwyth, Wales

Dr. Margot Taureck
Ecole Polytechnique
91 rue de la Santé
F – 75013 Paris

Prof. Jörg Thunecke
Marsiliusstr. 20
D – 50937 Köln

Dr. Susanne Utsch
Berliner Festspiele
Schaperstraße 24
D – 10719 Berlin

Prof. Dr. Jacqueline Vansant
Dept. of Modern and Classical
   Languages
University of Michigan-Dearborn
4901 Evergreen Rd
USA – Dearborn, MI 48128

Dr. Henrike Walter
Walter A. Berendsohn-
   Forschungsstelle für deutsche
   Exilliteratur
Universität Hamburg
Holstenplatz 10
D – 22765 Hamburg

Preface

However presumptuous it may be to call this volume of essays a "first", there is some truth to it. While one will find any number of books on the subject of exile or travel literature, one has to search long and hard to find a serious study devoted to the interface between exile and travel: their connectedness as critical categories, human experiences, or (post)modern practices. This is remarkable, as the tension between these two critical terms abundantly yields new, powerful questions and opens up uncharted territory to explore. The nineteen essays in this volume, some more theoretical, others more text-immanent, show just how fertile the subject is and from how many different angles it can be approached. This volume, then, is first and foremost an invitation to take a closer look at the connection between exile and travel as two well-weathered generators of meaning and framers of human experience, and to show how open this field of inquiry is and how much work can and still needs to be done.

This book is the result of a collaborative effort for which I have to thank many. I am grateful for the advice received from the editorial board of "Amsterdamer Beiträge zur neueren Germanistik": Martha Helfer, Gerd Labroisse, Norbert Eke, and Gerhard Knapp. Rodopi's editorial assistant, Esther Roth, deserves praise for her patience and guidance in preparing the manuscript. I would furthermore like to thank all contributors for the care with which they wrote their essays and for the many stimulating conversations as this project grew from idea to finished volume. Thanks in particular to John Alcorn, my colleague at Trinity College and masterful juggler of words and ideas, and Julia Goesser for her editorial assistance. Furthermore, I am indebted to the *DAAD* for its generous support of an international conference at Trinity College in 2006, which prompted me to assemble this volume of essays. Finally, I am grateful for the support and funding received from the Dean of Faculty at Trinity College. This book is dedicated to Isabel, Thomas and Alice, in part to make up for the many hours not spent together while finishing this project.

Johannes F. Evelein
Hartford, CT

Johannes F. Evelein

Traveling Exiles, Exilic Travel – Conceptual Encounters

"Exile and Travel": the title of this collection of essays seems straightforward enough. Both terms are well-weathered critical categories and a closer look at their interface should yield new insights into two perennial "practices of displacement", to borrow Caren Kaplan's term. And yet, even the most cursory study of the critical literature shows that "exile" and "travel" are highly problematic tropes: unstable, approximate at best, suffering both from non-specificity and semantic overcharge. Isn't it fair, then, to ask why such problematic categories are still maintained despite their inherent tension and social, historical and political contingencies? What is the benefit of retaining a terminology that appears to require an explanation every time it is used? It may be too easy to suggest that all terminologies eventually suffer from semantic slipperiness, no matter how carefully they have been delineated. All terms are anchored in time and space, they have origins and contexts and hence cannot be transplanted without either carefully carrying over or losing their contextual references. As such, they are "translations", a term James Clifford applies to "all broadly meaningful concepts". They are "built from imperfect equivalences. To use comparative concepts in a situated way means to become aware, always belatedly, of limits, sedimented meanings, tendencies to gloss over differences. Comparative concepts – translation terms – are approximations, privileging certain 'originals' and made for specific audiences".[1]

Following Clifford's reading of the inherent tentativeness of comparative concepts, this study uses "exile" and "travel" as translations of broad experiences and practices whose translatedness underscores both their rich meaning and obvious limitations. As Clifford points out, "all translation terms used in global comparisons – terms like 'culture', 'art', 'society', 'peasant', 'mode of production', 'man', 'woman', 'modernity', 'ethnography' – get us some distance *and* fall apart".[2] It seems, then, that the terms at the center of this volume, exile and travel, are no more and no less provisory than any other concept, but this offers limited relief. It does call for a careful analysis of both categories to see how much distance one can travel with them and at what point they collapse into meaninglessness. Not surprisingly, many investigations into the nature of exile begin with the *Königsfrage*, which is never answered sufficiently enough

---

[1] James Clifford: *Routes. Travel and Translation in the Late Twentieth Century.* Cambridge: Harvard University Press 1997. P. 11.
[2] Ibid. P. 39.

to keep others from asking it all over again: "What does it mean to be an exile?" André Aciman inquires in *Letters of Transit*: "How does exile alter someone? How does it reinvent one? What is exile? When does it go away? Does it ever go away? What is the difference between, say, a refugee, and an expatriate, or between an immigrant and an emigrant, or between the uprooted and the unrooted, the displaced, the *dépaysés*, the evicted, the *émigrés*?".[3] Likewise, the Bangladesh-born British scholar Syed Manzurul Islam frames the question that propelled him to write *The Ethics of Travel*: "I have often asked myself: What does it mean to travel? How is it possible to travel? What is travel, anyway? Am I really a traveller?".[4] Clearly, there is a considerable definitional desideratum, or rather, everyone pitches his or her semantic tent somewhat differently and demarcates the territory to be explored accordingly. Take William H. Gass's philosophically bold statement – in which he is far from alone – that "life is itself exile, and its inevitability does not lessen our grief or alter the fact. It is a blow – *un coup de destin* – from which only death will recover us, and when we are told, as we lie dying, that we are going home, we may even be ready to welcome the familiar darkness, the slumberous emptiness of the grand old days when days were nothing but nights".[5] To be fair to Gass, he then continues to qualify his term beautifully and convincingly, but the definitional net has been cast wide and is allowed to catch all kinds of ontological fish. Similarly, the novelist and ethnographer Amitav Ghosh suggests that man's wanderlust is so pervasive that in the end we are all travelers, whether actively or receptively, as each one of us belongs to a culture that is in large part the result of encounters with other cultures. "Everyone's on the move, and has been for centuries: dwelling-in-travel".[6] Following such broad existential definitions, our very humanity positions us squarely within the time-space continuum of exilic travel: we *are* because we are practitioners of displacement, sailors on Sebastian Brant's "ship of fools", until our exile loses its charge upon the arrival at *stasis*, non-being.

Such are the outer boundaries of exile and travel, as wide as mankind itself. But even if we subscribe to such an Olympian definition, it doesn't offer us much help in negotiating the numerous 20th-century discourses of exile and

---

[3] André Aciman: Editor's Foreword: Permanent Transients. In: *Letters of Transit. Reflections on Exile, Identity, Language, and Loss*. Ed. by André Aciman. New York: The New York Press 1999. Pp. 9–14. Here: p. 9.
[4] Syed Manzurul Islam: *The Ethics of Travel. From Marco Polo to Kafka*. Manchester: Manchester University Press 1996. P. 1.
[5] William H. Gass: Exile. In: *Finding a Form*. New York: Knopf 1996. Pp. 213–236. Here: p. 214.
[6] Clifford: *Routes* (n. 1). P. 2.

travel that employ highly nuanced categories, designations and tropes, all of which have evolved over time, respond to specific contexts, and are anchored historically. "All displacements are not the same", Caren Kaplan points out in *Questions of Travel*:

> Yet the occidental ethnographer, the modernist expatriate poet, the writer of popular travel accounts, and the tourist may all participate in the mythologized narrativizations of displacement without questioning the cultural, political, and economic grounds of their different professions, privileges, means, and limitations. Immigrants, refugees, exiles, nomads, and the homeless also move in and out of these discourses as metaphors, tropes, and symbols but rarely as historically recognized producers of critical discourses themselves.[7]

For terms such as travel and exile to remain meaningful, they must be rehistoricized, set up against the axes of real time and space, and reclaimed as specific instances and practices. And yet, the fact that such terminological slippage has happened is quite telling in itself: in particular the modernist erosion of specificity that resulted in the use of exile and travel largely as aesthetic terms points to a desire to adopt an exilic position and consider exile (or travel as intellectual mobility) to be an apt metaphor for a generally perceived, even aspired sense of estrangement and distance thought to be at the heart of the modern condition.

Exile

The semantic field of exile has indeed expanded greatly, making for strange fellow travelers. In its original meaning, of course, exile connoted banishment, separation as punishment, rejection by the community or the collective; a forced severance of organic ties to a place called home, a place without which life lost its meaning. William H. Gass's initial bird's eye view of universally applicable exile quickly focuses in on the individual, using Socrates – choosing death over exile – as a case in point: "Above all, exile is amputation, a mutilation of the self, because the society Socrates lives in is an essential part of his nature, a nature he cannot now divide".[8] Exile is a rupture with oneself, a terrible loss synonymous with, possibly even worse than, death. Eva Hoffman recalls that for centuries it was considered the ultimate retribution:

> In medieval Europe, exile was the worst punishment that could be inflicted. This was because one's identity was defined by one's role and place in society; to lose that was to lose a portion of one's self. After being banished from Florence, Dante lived less

---

[7] Caren Kaplan: *Questions of Travel. Postmodern Discourses of Displacement*. Durham: Duke University Press 1996. P. 2.
[8] Gass: Exile (n. 5). P. 218.

than a hundred miles from his city-state – and yet he felt that his expulsion was a kind of psychic and social death [...]. Real life, for Dante, was in Florence; it could not exist fully anywhere else.[9]

In this narrow, classical sense, exile signifies the separation from one's home that inflicts unmitigated pain upon its sufferer and holds no redemptive qualities.

But truth be told: however painful the conditions of exile might have been, and no matter how barren the exilic landscape proved, it didn't keep exiles from imagining, thinking, and writing. It was in Tomis, a place bordering with the great unknown and well beyond the reach of Rome, that the Roman poet Ovid wrote his *Tristia*: "I have been silenced. But will not be stilled". In his splendid novel, *An Imaginary Life*, David Malouf portrays the exiled poet, Rome's "Nose", sniffing up newness, transforming himself in the process from a man sentenced to social death into a rebellious imaginer revivified by new sensations and a new tongue. "How I have changed! What a very different self has begun to emerge in me! ... Seeing the world through this other tongue I see it differently. It is a different world. ... I feel the ice of myself cracking. I feel myself loosen and flow again, reflecting the world. That is what spring means".[10] Malouf's fictional account of Ovid's final years banished from Rome suggests that exile allows the poet to see afresh, freeing him from convention and liberating his essential self. Exile can be a window of opportunity for self-discovery.

Of course we know next to nothing about Ovid's life in Tomis, but Malouf's ultimately positive portrayal of expulsion connects with a radically different understanding of exile that turns its original configuration on its head. Death by exile is transcended into a bold re-affirmation of life from which exile – or the distance it provides – washes away all dullness, conventional restrictions, societal expectations, rendering it fresh. Exile, then, yields a different perspective, a new way of seeing. Of course such an epistemological shift isn't procured without a cost, and frequently the cost is high, but its advantages may outweigh the pain that exile indubitably inflicts. Framed as a departure from familiarity, exile begins to show some conceptual overlap with travel, albeit only a certain kind of travel, as the American travel writer Paul Theroux is quick to point out: "Homesickness is part of this kind of travel. In these circumstances, it is possible to make interesting discoveries about oneself and one's surroundings. Travel has less to do with distance than with insight: it is, very often, a way of seeing".[11] But more about that later.

---

[9] Eva Hoffman: The New Nomads. In: *Letters of Transit*. Ed. by André Aciman. New York: The New York Press 1999. Pp. 35–64. Here: p. 40.
[10] David Malouf: *An Imaginary Life*. New York: Vintage 1996. P. 65.
[11] Paul Theroux: Stranger on a Train. In: *Sunrise with Seamonsters*. Boston: Houghton Mifflin 1985. Pp. 126–136. Here: p. 131.

Gradually the notion of exile solely as political punishment through one's removal from society begins to give way to a more metaphorical understanding, turning exile into a voluntary practice. This paradigm shift manifests itself most noticeably in the post-enlightenment era, when an entire generation of poets and artists grew increasingly antagonistic toward a world that worshipped man's intellect and rational powers, whose attitude toward nature was instrumental rather than inspirational, and that sought to control rather than celebrate human emotions. British poets such as Wordsworth and Coleridge both employed exilic motifs in their poetry, most notably in works such as Wordsworth's "A Poet's Epitaph" or Coleridge's "Ancient Mariner". And of course, they spent prolonged periods of time away from England, whether with the intent to dodge the draft – in the case of Wordsworth, as has been suggested – or to be liberated from a country deemed both too damp and too conservative, as Coleridge saw things. To be sure, exile was still mostly negatively charged, often associated with poetic death, isolation and suffering, but as a *Stilfigur* it was becoming part of a poetic language, widening its semantic field and showing a deepening partiality toward exile as a necessary and aesthetically empowering and enriching experience. German Romanticism, too, contributed greatly to this lexical, conceptual and psychological expansion of exile, as it was fueled by a shared imagination of another, better or at least more exciting world, in search of which many poets rebelled against utilitarian society, capitalized on uniqueness, personality, individuality, and called into being a host of literary heroes representing the spirit of non-conformism. They displayed a pronounced dislike of stability and tradition, time and again taking leave of hearth and home to find meaning, either in the great "elsewhere" or in the painful sensation of separation. Exile as a voluntary practice was in vogue.

Of course, metaphorical exile was frequently compounded by political banishment. The 19th century witnessed an unprecedented number of poets, artists, and intellectuals forced to seek asylum from their hostile homeland. It is safe to say that some of the most significant works were created while in exile, informed by the distance and isolation that exile imposes, or grants, depending on one's perspective. Whether it is Karl Marx's London-based poverty-stricken exile from Prussia that produced his major political writings, Richard Wagner's revolutionary dreams during his twelve-year stay in Zurich as one of Prussia's most prominent *personae non gratae*, or Heinrich Heine, Germany's exile poet *par excellence* whose poetry evokes the pains of separation from home, one's center of belonging: exile is conceptually wound up with creativity, a widening perspectival horizon, and a self-transcendence through intellectual or aesthetic effort. It is not surprising, then, that exile assumed a noble, even heroic quality, turning it gradually into a condition that, albeit painful, could yield rich rewards. Exile transforms into an act of ennobling, solitary, stoic suffering, and as such it begins to show affinity with the "grand narratives" of exile: Abraham's forced departure from Ur, Jeremiah's prophetic guidance of the Jewish people in Babylonian exile, Boethius' expulsion to Pavia where he, out of despair, sits down to compose his marvelous *The Consolation of Philosophy*. And the list can be easily expanded.

Importantly, what all exiles have in common is distance from a place of connection, a distance that affords a view from outside, unperturbed by proximity or participation. With the emergence of modernism in the 1880s, this outsider position became the preferred intellectual stance. After all, modernism, in its various manifestations and movements, sought to break away from tradition, create radically new aesthetic languages, and emancipate itself from any kind of fixed notions of self, society, art, or class. Malcolm Bradbury writes,

> Much Modernist art, has taken its stance from, gained its perspectives out of, a certain kind of distance, an exiled posture – a distance from local origins, class allegiances, the specific obligations and duties of those with an assigned role in a cohesive culture. [...] The writer may hold on to locality, as Joyce did on to Dublin, Hemingway the Michigan woods; but he perceives from the distance of an expatriate perspective of aesthetic internationalism. [...] Thus frequently it is emigration or exile that makes for membership of the modern country of the arts, which has been heavily travelled by many great writers – Joyce, Lawrence, Mann, Brecht, Auden, Nabokov. It is a country that has come to acquire its own landscape, geography, focal communities, places of exile – Zürich during the First World War, New York during the second. The writer himself becomes a member of a wandering, culturally inquisivity group – by enforced exile (like Nabokov's after the Russian Revolution) or by design and desire".[12]

Even though Bradbury continues to differentiate between "enforced exile" and exile "by design and desire", the term begins to lose much of its existential weight as it is now placed within the same taxonomical sphere as "emigration", "expatriation", or "wandering". Exile is becoming synonymous with perspective, non-affiliation, and uncompromising intellectual inquisitiveness. Moreover, exile now affords acceptance into a new kind of intellectual community that Bradbury describes as a "country". Ironically it is exile, the very act of disconnection from one's center, that facilitates reconnection. With relative ease, exile is turned into a modern *modus vivendi* with a distinct urban, cosmopolitan signature. Caren Kaplan maintains that in the modernist era, the exilic posture became normative, propelling

> a discourse of authorship that has come to be expressed in literary criticism as an imperative of displacement. [...] When detachment is the precondition for creativity, then disaffection or alienation as states of mind becomes a rite of passage for the

---

[12] Malcolm Bradbury: The Cities of Modernism. In: *Modernism. A Guide to European Literature 1890–1930*. Ed. by Malcolm Bradbury and James McFarlane. London: Penguin 1991. Pp. 96–104. Here: p. 100–101.

"serious" modern artist or writer. The modernist seeks to recreate the effect of statelessness – whether or not the writer is, literally, in exile. As a result, even those writers who do not find themselves actually exiled may easily extend the metaphor.[13]

The problem is, of course, that these exiles – James Joyce, Gertrude Stein, Ernest Hemingway, Ezra Pound – were still in possession of their passports and could return home, to put it crudely, as soon as they ran out of money. Hence, to use the word "exile" for the modernist expatriate tradition seems cavalier at best, as it deliberately ignores the human cost of "real" exile. But the use of "exile" goes well beyond the literary, artistic, and intellectual expatriation with Paris, London, and Berlin as its main centers of gravity. Nico Israel maintains that "exile, broadly understood, could be said to inform most of the significant strands of modern social and philosophical thought, from Marxian alienation to the Freudian unconscious, from Nietzsche's transvaluation of values to Heidegger's thrownness – each of which involves a particular kind of banishment or "leaping out", conceived spatially, temporally, linguistically, or ideologically".[14] Employed to cover such a vast territory, exile as a critical category loses definition and is increasingly removed from its original meaning.

Kaplan considers the mythologization of the "artist in exile" a production of a *style* that emulates exile's effects, yet she shies away from employing moral categories, "true" or "false" exile, to distinguish between both phenomena. Mary McCarthy's term "faux exiles", referring to American expatriates in Paris, may indeed be better, but moral adjectives aside: it is imperative to anchor exile historically and to disallow conceptual obfuscation or mythologization. That said, if one adheres to a separation of terms – voluntary versus involuntary, privileged versus forced, political versus aesthetic – the modernist concept of exile as cosmopolitan, instrumental, goal-oriented distancing shows remarkable affinity with another "privileged practice": travel.

With the emergence of 20th century totalitarianism and dictatorial rule reigning in Spain, Italy, Germany and the Soviet-Union, many exponents of modernism found themselves quickly isolated, confronted with a palpable need to take leave of their home, and increasingly cut off from their language, publishing venues, intellectual centers. "The shock of exile",[15] as Peter Nicholls captures modernist estrangement and cultural contrast, was now compounded with political exile, yet their intellectual exilic stance had scarcely prepared them for exile in the flesh. However true it may be that someone like Heinrich Mann con-

---

[13] Kaplan: *Questions of Travel* (n. 7). P. 36.
[14] Nico Israel: *Outlandish. Writing between Exile and Diaspora*. Stanford: Stanford University Press 2000. P. 5.
[15] Peter Nicholls: *Modernisms. A Literary Guide*. Berkeley: University of California Press 1995. P. 165.

sidered himself spiritually estranged from Germany and felt more kinship with, and received more recognition in, France, it was without a doubt a terrible blow to find himself quickly rejected by the New Germany, removed from the *Preußische Akademie der Künste*, his apartment ransacked, his assets frozen and his citizenship revoked. Now he, along with so many others, had to exercise what Breyten Breytenbach calls the "dur métier de l'exil, to be climbing up and down other people's staircases, to be changing countries more often than changing your shoes, despairing whether the revolt can ever bring injustice to an end".[16] Stefan Zweig, in the preface to his autobiography *Die Welt von Gestern*, appears to embrace his new exilic fate, suggesting that it may render him free to pursue truth uncompromisingly and finally bound to no one and no place:

> Sie haben mir dreimal Haus und Existenz umgeworfen, mich von jedem Einstigen und Vergangenen gelöst und mit ihrer dramatischen Vehemenz ins Leere geschleudert, in das mir schon wohlbekannte "Ich weiß nicht wohin". Aber ich beklagte das nicht: gerade der Heimatlose wird in einem neuen Sinne frei, und nur der mit nichts mehr Verbundene braucht auf nichts mehr Rücksicht zu nehmen. So hoffe ich, wenigstens eine Hauptbedingung jeder rechtschaffenen Zeitdarstellung erfüllen zu können: Aufrichtigkeit und Unbefangenheit.[17]

Zweig, too, draws parallels between his new exile, thrice removed, and a sensation of non-belonging with which he had been well acquainted for years, if not decades. His exile bears resemblance to a broader sense of alienation, or figurative exile, fueled by his pacifism and Jewishness to be sure, but also the result of an acquired modernist position of difference. "Writers", Michael Seidel points out, "are more at home in the conjured spaces of their works than in their actual homelands".[18] Exile for Zweig manifests itself ironically as a kind of homecoming, a heightened awareness of self: "Denn losgelöst von allen Wurzeln und selbst von der Erde, die diese Wurzeln nährte, – das bin ich wahrhaftig wie selten einer in den Zeiten".[19] But who can ultimately survive in such thin air? Zweig himself could not, even though he had no financial worries, and even though his fame granted him easy access to travel papers, resident permits, publishing venues; considerable obstacles for many of his fellow exiles.

In *Die Welt von Gestern*, Zweig contributes to a mythologizing exile discourse in which exile is presented as an elevated position, granting freedom, unchaining potential, and allowing new and true insight. In an often-quoted

---

[16] Breyten Breytenbach: You Are an Outsider. In: *The Oxford Book of Exile*. Ed. by John Simpson. Oxford: Oxford University Press 1995. Pp. 207–277. Here: p. 229.
[17] Stefan Zweig: *Die Welt von Gestern. Erinnerungen eines Europäers*. Stockholm: Fischer 1944. P. 7.
[18] Michael Seidel: *Exile and the Narrative Imagination*. New Haven: Yale University Press 1986. P. 2.
[19] Zweig: *Die Welt von Gestern* (n. 17). P. 7.

passage, Edward Said warns against such a romanticizing depiction of what he describes as an eventually debilitating experience:

> Exile is strangely compelling to think about but terrible to experience. It is the unhealable rift forced between a human being and a native place, between the self and its true home: its essential sadness can never be surmounted. And while it is true that literature and history contain heroic, romantic, glorious, even triumphant episodes in an exile's life, these are no more than efforts meant to overcome the crippling sorrow of estrangement. The achievements of exile are permanently undermined by the loss of something left behind forever.[20]

Said is responding to an ontological deflation of exile that disregards its human consequences. His criticism of a pattern of overly glib metaphorizations applies to modernism and postmodernism alike: Whereas modernism regards notions of "home", "belonging", or "center" with distrust, it still operates within a sphere that includes nation-states, borders, and clearly delineated spaces, cultures, and languages. Postmodernism no longer subscribes to such fixed entities as it emphasizes flux, pluralism, global dwelling, non-affiliation, decenteredness, and a breakdown of binary systems such as here vs. there. The postmodern posture is nomadic and as such defined by movement from place to place, not between home and away-from-home. In this "nomadic" configuration, Eva Hoffman observes,

> exile loses its charge, since there is no place from which one can be expelled, no powerful notion of home. [...] Instead, home is conceived of mostly as a conservative site of enclosure and closure, of narrow-mindedness, patriarchal attitudes, and dissemination of nationalism. And, indeed, the notion of "home" may have been, in recent times, particularly overcharged, as the concepts of "country" and "nation" have been superimposed on each other with a seeming inevitability. "France", for the French, is both la belle France and la patrie. Such overlapping is not a necessary one. We have seen, for example, in the unhappy case of the former Yugoslavia, that a geographic territory can abruptly change its national identity. But the nostalgia of exiles for their birthplace has undoubtledly often been augmented by this conjunction of geographic and patriotic longing.[21]

Indeed, in our global world the orthodox notion of "home" as a locus of belonging and meaning has been challenged, and its gradual fading has coincided with a fading desire for an identifiable, frameable place or center. But are we now all rootless, cosmopolitan, frictionless practitioners of displacement, nomads? Wouldn't such an attitude of profound detachment spell the death of community or of any kind of shared project that, in the end, needs to be

---

[20] Edward Said: *Reflections on Exile and Other Essays*. Cambridge: Harvard University Press 2002. P. 173.
[21] Hoffman: The New Nomads (n. 9). P. 58.

anchored in locality – even internet dwellers need a place to stay – and hands-on commitment? People who appear to be moving effortlessly through modernity still hold, it seems, considerable reserves of "home" without which their mobility, transcultural crossings and global purview would render them perpetually liminal. And though liminality, as with distance, may be given privileged status, it would be a cold place to dwell indeed. "Home", then, remains an important currency. And with it exile, fueled by the very absence of "home" in its many hues, retains its critical significance.

Travel

Like exile, travel is an expansive "translation term" that needs to be anchored in specific historical contexts and practices if it is to yield meaning as a critical category. In *Abroad. British Literary Traveling Between the Wars*, Paul Fussell contends that there once was "real" travel, a practice that, sadly, has all but disappeared in the age of tourism. Such genuine travel involves work, endurance, and pain, all of which are inscribed in the orthodox meaning of the term: "Etymologically a traveler is one who suffers *travail*, a word deriving in its turn from Latin *tripalium*, a torture instrument consisting of three stakes designed to rack the body".[22] To travel, then, is to suffer or at least to experience profound discomfort which, if one believes Fussell, eventually has its epistemological rewards. To stay with Fussell: "Your true traveler will not feel that he has had his money's worth unless he brings back a few scars".[23] Of course, Gregor Samsa in Franz Kafka's *Die Verwandlung*, a professional "Reisender", suffers greatly, yet his pains bear little fruit. In fact, Gregor's metamorphosis appears to be in part the consequence of his travels, which bring the fragility of his humanity to the fore: "Tag aus, Tag ein auf der Reise. Die geschäftlichen Aufregungen sind viel größer, als im eigentlichen Geschäft zu Hause, und außerdem ist mir noch diese Plage des Reisens auferlegt, die Sorgen um die Zuganschlüsse, das unregelmäßige, schlechte Essen, ein immer wechselnder, nie andauernder, nie herzlich werdender menschlicher Verkehr. Der Teufel soll das alles holen!".[24] True, Gregor's travels numb the mind in their repetitiveness, whereas "genuine" travel grants new insights, it lavishes rich rewards on the traveler intrepid enough to endure its hardship. True travel teaches you if you are a good student: Before the development of tourism, travel was conceived to be like study, and its fruits were considered to be the adornment of the mind and the formation of

---

[22] Paul Fussell: *Abroad. British Literary Traveling Between the Wars.* New York: Oxford University Press 1980. P. 39.
[23] Ibid. P. 40.
[24] Franz Kafka: Die Verwandlung. In: *Sämtliche Erzählungen.* Ed. by Paul Raabe. Frankfurt/Main: Fischer 1987. Pp. 56–57.

judgment. Written into travel as a practice of displacement is a clear epistemological hierarchy, giving the notion of "true" travel an unmistakable ring of elitism. It is no surprise, then, that genuine travelers, including most modernist travelers, shared a deep distrust of popular travel, felt to be an undesired democratization of a practice better left to the initiated.[25]

Starting in the 19th century, travel came to be regarded as an almost certain instrument of transformation provided the traveler – more often than not young men, especially in the Anglo-American tradition of the Grand Tour – had an open mind and set himself clear learning goals made easy by a growing number of travel guides. As such, Wiliam Stowe maintains, travel quickly collapsed into convention,

> controlled at one level by the layout of transportation networks and a list of canonical sights, at another level by the socially sanctioned purposes of travel, and at a third, most intimate level by the appropriate responses to individual sights suggested (and repeated) by cultural authorities and previous visitors. It was, in other words, a kind of secular ritual, complete with prescribed actions, promised rewards, and a set of quasi-scriptural writings.[26]

19th century travel removed itself more and more from earlier explorative modes of travel and resulted in the establishment of sites and agencies. Travel had become an industry, the traveler a consumer of prepared goods, and tourism was born, deplored as it may have been by Henry James and other writers in the "habit of flux": "Tourists are vulgar, vulgar, vulgar".[27]

Does the traveler who is forced into a corset of conventions and adheres to strict guidelines of mobility travel at all? After all, the travel industry is bent on reducing any travel pains or nuisances to a minimum to facilitate quick transfers and a feeling of comfort one might expect at one's own home. Asked differently: is modern travel still authentic? In travel literature and critical studies on the subject, the answer is frequently a counter-question: which travel? A closer look at the entire travel spectrum reveals two extreme positions, one being undubitably "genuine" whereas the other is largely synonymous with non-movement or epistemological *stasis*. In his travel essay, "Stranger on a Train: The Pleasure of Railways", Paul Theroux – who claims to engage in the

---

[25] See also Peter Hulme and Tim Youngs: *The Cambridge Companion to Travel Writing*. Cambridge: Cambridge University Press 2002. P. 79.
[26] William W. Stowe: Going Abroad. *European Travel in Nineteenth-Century American Culture*. Princeton: Princeton University Press 1994. P. 18–19.
[27] Henry James quoted in: Philip Pearce and Gianna Moscardo: The Concept of Authenticity in Tourist Experiences. In: *Australian and New Zealand Journal of Sociology*. Vol. 22. Pp. 121–32. Here: p. 121.

"purest form of travel, a combination of flight and suspended animation" – proposes the following dichotomy:

> There are those whom we instantly recognize as clinging to the traditional virtues of travel, the people who endure a kind of alienation and panic in foreign parts for the aftertaste of having sampled new scenes. On the whole travel at its best is rather comfortless, but travel is never easy: you get very tired, you get lost, you get your feet wet, you get little co-operation, and – if it is to have any value at all – you go alone. [...] The second group of travelers has only appeared in numbers in the past twenty years. For these people travel, paradoxically, is an experience of familiar things; it is travel that carries with it the illusion of immobility. It is the going to a familiar airport and being strapped into a seat and held captive for a number of hours – immobile; then arriving at an almost identical airport, being whisked to a hotel so fast it is not like movement at all. [...] In this sort of travel, you take your society with you: your language, your food, your styles of hotel and service.[28]

Whereas Paul Fussell claims that travel is hardly possible anymore – all that's left is tourism that makes a mockery of travel – Theroux is less radical in his assessment, arguing that one can still make "discoveries in a glorious solitary way". True travel, then, must comprise three basic elements: alienation, solitude, and feats of learning. Travel is teleological, its ultimate goal is to enrich mind and soul, and it has transformative powers both in failure and success. It is no surprise that, imbued with such epiphanic potential, the act of travel needs to be executed alone; a singularity that adds to its quasi-religious connotations. It also exposes a tense relationship with modernity, as its proponents are highly skeptical of mass mobility, tourism, in short a "democratic" kind of travel. The genuine traveler savors his experiences, or in the words of Paul Bowles in *The Sheltering Sky*: "The difference is partly one of time … Whereas the tourist generally hurries back home at the end of a few weeks or months, the traveler, belonging no more to one place than to the next, moves slowly, over periods of years, from one part of the earth to another".[29]

Framed as an imperative of "solitary mobile learning", real travel is ultimately an ethical act as it draws its legitimacy from enabling genuine encounters with otherness. Those who are attentive to the alterity to which travel exposes them have heeded the inherent call for engagement between self and environment. In *The Ethics of Travel*, Syed Manzurul Islam realizes, however, that very few people, including the most intrepid travelers he encountered in reading numerous travel books, "despite moving so much and so far in space, did not seem to have travelled at all".[30] Like Theroux, he too arrives at a conceptual dichotomy, though his definition turns travel into an even more elevated experience that

---

[28] Theroux: Stranger on a Train (n. 11). P. 131.
[29] Paul Bowles: *The Sheltering Sky*. New York: Ecco Press 1949. P. 14.
[30] Islam: *The Ethics of Travel* (n. 4). P. vii.

occurs at a level few can attain. Islam differentiates between sedentary and nomadic travel:

> Nomadic travel is to do with encounters with otherness that fracture both a boundary and an apparatus of representation: it is a performative enactment of becoming-other. In the ethical sense, only nomadic travel deserves the name 'travel'. And on the cross-cultural plane, nomadic travel also impels one to come face to face with the other, without the paranoia of othering that represents the other in relation to oneself. From an ethical perspective, sedentary travel hardly deserves to be called 'travel' at all. Of course, it involves a movement across geographical and textual space, but it settles for a representational practice that scarcely registers an encounter with the other. [...] Inevitably, then, sedentary travellers, burdened as they are by the need to establish essential difference on a binary frame and to capture otherness in knowledge, obsessively bring into existence a rigid boundary which separates them from the other.[31]

The genuine traveler, then, needs to transcend boundaries separating self and other, as it is the act of traversing thresholds that lends travel its proper weight. If these boundaries are drawn too rigidly, travel may not be possible at all and any representational practice will remain shallow, ill-informed. Clearly, given the strict perimeters bounding Islam's concept of travel, most practices of displacement amount but to pseudo-travel, never really able to burst the bubble of solipsism.

Given the rich promises of genuine travel, its potential for transcending self and other, and the hard work it necessarily involves, it seems only logical that travelers often feel compelled to document their experiences, challenges, and lessons learned. Whereas tourism is associated with taking pictures – Susan Sontag claimed that "today everything exists to end in a photograph"[32] – travelers write. In fact, travel has been among the most common motifs for as long as people have written fiction or other literary accounts. "Writing and travel", Peter Hulme observes, "have always been intimately connected. The traveller's tale is as old as fiction itself. [...] The biblical and classical traditions are both rich in examples of travel writing, literal and symbolic – Exodus, the punishment of Cain, the Argonauts, the *Aeneid* – which provide a corpus of reference and intertext for modern writers".[33] Literary modernism in particular was a traveling movement, as the majority of European and American writers spent considerable time abroad, traveled widely, and made significant contributions to travel writing as a genre that in many cases bordered on ethnography. Travel was considered a medium for observation for which the perennial motifs of road, journey, pilgrimage, odyssey, search, wandering, departure and return provided powerful

---

[31] Ibid. Pp. vii–viii.
[32] Susan Sontag: *On Photography*. Harmondsworth: Penguin 1979. P. 24.
[33] Hulme and Youngs: *The Cambridge Companion to Travel Writing* (n. 25). P. 2.

structures. In the modern imagination, then, the traveler/writer gave the trope of travel yet another dimension of exclusivity, in which travel – as a practice anchored firmly in high culture – is transformed into high art seeking in turn audiences equipped to appreciate the lessons and aesthetic rewards it holds.

The narrowly defined boundaries of genuine travel exclude many practices of displacement and exposes fields of tension between the various forms of mobility. But is the line that separates tourism from travel demarcated unambiguously? Might the social, cultural, and economic navigations of a *Gastarbeiter* in a foreign society, whether absorbing or rejecting otherness, show some affinity with travel as a translation term? Any attempt to establish tight categories that fall either within or outside the practice of travel raises problems, as James Clifford notes:

> Alexander von Humboldt obviously did not arrive on the Orinoco coast for the same reasons as an Asian indentured laborer. But although there is no ground of equivalence between the two "travelers", there is at least a basis for comparison and (problematic) translation. […] The project of comparison would have to grapple with the evident fact that travelers move about under strong cultural, political, and economic compulsions and that certain travelers are materially privileged, others oppressed. These specific circumstances are crucial determinations of the travel at issue – movements in specific colonial, neocolonial, and postcolonial circuits, different diasporas, borderlands, exiles, detours, and returns. Travel, in this view, denotes a range of material, spatial practices that produce knowledges, stories, traditions, comportments, musics, books, diaries, and other cultural expressions.[34]

Problematized as such, how do exiles travel, if indeed they do? What marks their spatial practice and how does it translate into cultural expression? Can someone exiled from Nazi Germany at all be considered a "practitioner of displacement", a "traveler"? When "exile" is superimposed onto "travel", what areas overlap and where does one fall outside the other?

Interfacing Exile with Travel

Erich Maria Remarque, the Manns, Hans Sahl, Irmgard Keun, Alfred Döblin, Bruno Frank, Anna Seghers, Lion Feuchtwanger, Henry William Katz: it seems difficult to consider their exilic itineraries to be travel. To be sure, there are many commonalities: roads, places, trains, passports, new friends and experiences, maps. But how does an exile look at a map? Having fled Nazi Germany and finding temporary shelter in Finland, Bertolt Brecht's well-known poem *1940* reads:

VIII
Auf der Flucht vor meinen Landsleuten
Bin ich nun nach Finnland gelangt. Freunde

---

[34] Clifford: *Routes* (n. 1). Pp. 35–36.

> Die ich gestern nicht kannte, stellten ein paar Betten
> In saubere Zimmer. Im Lautsprecher
> Höre ich die Siegesmeldungen des Abschaums. Neugierig
> Betrachte ich die Karte des Erdteils. Hoch oben in Lappland
> Nach dem Nördlichen Eismeer zu
> Sehe ich noch eine kleine Tür.[35]

Does his gaze at the map bear any resemblance to the traveler/explorer's gaze? Is his curiosity fueled by adventure? Can 'flight' at all be considered travel? Of course these questions steer toward a fairly unambiguous "no", which has everything to do with the weight and charge of words. "Travel" seems light and is by and large positively charged, *travails* and all. We benefit from travel despite, or *because*, of the difficulties that accompany it. More than anything else it holds the power to widen one's horizon and build character. Travel, certainly in Fussell's understanding of serious, genuine travel, is "good" for you. Moreover, our desire to travel is ultimately a search for authenticity, the source of which tends to be elsewhere, beyond the boundaries of the place we call home. Our engagement with difference, with otherness, makes us look at the world afresh and may fill a void that is the sum of all the normalcies in our lives. Travel is anomalous, extraordinary, and if one can adopt a nomadic rather than a sedentary posture – following Syed Islam's distinction – one stands to benefit lastingly from the insights it yields.

Compared to the positively charged term travel, exile is heavy, and dark. Obviously, one is by and large voluntary whereas the other is not, but there is more to it. The "true" traveler, to stay with Fussell, is determined to experience fully the strange surroundings that he has sought out. As such, his posture is defined by openness, he invites otherness. He looks ahead for what's to come; for the traveler, the future and the new experiences it holds are his for the taking. The exile, on the other hand, rarely displays such orientation toward an open future. In Milan Kundera's magnificent testament to exile, *The Book of Laughter and Forgetting*, one of the main characters – Tamina – is forced to leave her native Bohemia and finds herself in Paris as a waitress, yet in a state of mind that doesn't allow her to see or feel her new environment. Rather, she looks back, her eyes fixed on her world of memories, which, no matter how hard she resists, have started to fade. This is how the narrator sees Tamina: "I imagine Tamina's present [...] as a raft adrift on the water, with her on that raft looking back, looking only back".[36] Tamina, like so many exiles, experiences loss that magnifies the importance of her past life *because* it is out of reach.

---

[35] Bertolt Brecht: 1940. In: *Deutsche Literatur im Exil 1933–1945*. Ed. by Michael Winkler. Stuttgart: Reclam 1977. Pp. 96–98. Here: p. 98.

[36] Milan Kundera: *The Book of Laughter and Forgetting*. New York: Harper Perennial 1996. P. 116.

Jean Baudrillard asserts that only the exiles have a land, made concrete by the impossibility of their return.[37] Desire demarcates home. One may disagree with the depiction of the exile as backward looking, and true: it certainly does not apply to everyone. Yet it is a posture encountered in many narratives of exile. Stefan Zweig, for instance, describes how he, leaving fascist Austria for good, averts his eyes when his train arrives at Salzburg, the city where he lived for many years: "Ich blickte nicht hin. Wozu auch? – Ich würde es doch nie wieder bewohnen. Und in dem Augenblick, wo der Zug über die Grenze rollte, wußte ich wie der Urvater Lot der Bibel, daß alles hinter mir Staub und Asche war".[38] Lot knows that he cannot turn around, for the site/sight of Sodom and Gomorra will turn him to stone, as of course happens to his wife. He is ordered to look forward as a guide and leader for his family and his people. But does not his inability to see the physical space amplify his urge to *think* about the city he used to call home? Likewise, Stefan Zweig may not look, as a willful act of closure, but the very title of his memoir, *Die Welt von Gestern*, reveals that it is the pastness of yesteryear that occupies his mind. The term "traveler" doesn't seem to apply to Stefan Zweig the exile.

Yet can it really be suggested that exiles, unlike travelers, are unable to see their new surroundings? That they, having been uprooted, are no longer equipped to distill meaning from the environment in which they now find themselves? The words of the Palestinian poet Mahmoud Darwish resonate with this rather bold proposition: "We travel like other people, but we return to nowhere. As if traveling/is the way of the clouds". And he continues, "We travel in the carriages of the psalms/sleep in the tents of the Prophets/and come out of the speech of the gypsies". Darwish captures travel in words, in the traditions that are the fabric of his people. "Speak, speak", he writes, "so we may know the end of/this travel".[39] And this is essential: the traveler's desire is to perpetuate his journey and avoid home; the exile longs for his journey to end, as it coincides with his homecoming. The traveler's return home marks the end of his explorations and with that the end of his authentification process, whereas for the exile the return home signifies the end of *dis*placement and the beginning of place, of meaning. As such, the exile is nostalgic in the truest sense of the word: yearning for "nostos", the great return, which dims the light cast on the here and now.

Of course, exiles aren't predestined to be epistemologically impaired the moment they leave their country. Alfred Kerr, the sharp-tongued, satirical theater

---

[37] For a broader discussion of Baudrillard's views on exile and travel, see Kaplan: *Questions of Travel* (n. 13). Pp. 68–82.
[38] Zweig: *Die Welt von Gestern* (n. 17). P. 367.
[39] Mahmoud Darwish: We Travel Like Other People. In: *Unfortunately, It Was Paradise*. Berkeley: University of California Press 2003. P. 11.

critic of the Weimar Republic, composed a poem in 1937 entitled, "Exil", in which he makes "ein offenes Geständnis" about his own painful departure:

VI
[...]
Manchmal fühlt das Herz sich sehr erheitert
(Trotz der zugeschlagenen deutschen Tür):
Weil die Flucht den Horizont erweitert,
Ja, du dankst den Jägern fast dafür!
War dir noch so lausiges Leid geschehn – :
Wenn du (gleichviel, wo du her bist)
Ein Ulysses oder Ahasver bist
Kriegst du zur Belohnung was zu sehen!
Bei der Dummheit aller Lebensschlachten
Ist ein solches Plus nicht zu verachten.[40]

The exile's "reward", Kerr writes, is that he can go places and see things. In other words, the exile gets to travel. Kerr's sincerity in wanting to thank the Nazi perpetrators for this fringe benefit is of course anything but sincere. What's more, his analogy of the exile to the *travails* of Odysseus and Ahasuerus suggests that the word "travel" doesn't really apply here either. Exile seems too heavy a concept to allow conflation with travel, which is what explains the typical usage of a more elevated set of terms: the exile is on a voyage, an odyssey, a journey; he wanders, or roams, rather than travels. The exilic travels of the main protagonists in Oskar Maria Graf's New York-based novel, *Die Flucht ins Mittelmäßige*, are paradigmatic: "Alle hatten eine langjährige, abenteuerliche, oft lebensgefährliche Odyssee durch viele Länder des Exils hinter sich".[41] And the "Emigrant W.M", the comically tragic hero in Robert Neumann's, *Marcus oder die Emigration*, even contemplates writing an "Odysseus-Roman", which proves to be yet another symptom of his worsening illness diagnosed as "emigratio communis primaria".[42]

As much as such literary or mythical comparisons, paired with a more elevated register, lend themselves to the plight of the exile, such analogies are highly problematic. The ahistoricity of exilic metaphors may lead to ahistorical readings of a phenomenon that should remain rooted in time and place. As mentioned, modernism claimed exile or displacement as a necessary and privileged practice in any aesthetic or critical pursuit, and as such stripped exile of

---

[40] Alfred Kerr: Exil. In: *Exil. Literarische und politische Texte aus dem deutschen Exil 1933–1945*. Vol. 2. Ed. by Ernst Loewy. Frankfurt/Main: Fischer, 1982. P. 588.
[41] Oskar Maria Graf. *Die Flucht ins Mittelmäßige. Ein New-Yorker Roman*. Frankfurt/Main: Nest 1959. P. 19.
[42] Robert Neumann: *An den Wassern von Babylon*. München: Deutscher Taschenbuch Verlag 1987. P. 217.

its political, religious, or ethnic contexts. What's more, the modernist metaphors used, fraught with heroism and individualism, and the images of unhoused travelers have turned exile into a singular, private experience even though the modern phenomenon of exile is widespread, diverse, and affecting hundreds of thousands of people. For politically forced mass movements we have reserved the word "refugees"; exile, as it is used most often, is a private predicament. In addition, exile within the postmodern context is by and large a positive designation as it connotes inquisitiveness, detachment, cosmopolitanism, a global and polyglot awareness of the world. Exile has become an instrument by which to position and/or redefine oneself, in particular the writer.

Exile and travel as aesthetic and critical postures, despite the differences referred to earlier, do overlap in various ways. This is particularly the case with regard to the singularity of their character. The "true" traveler is an eccentric loner, but his eccentricity is respectable. Tourists flock, there is undeniably something silly about them as they take their snapshots to show back home, and as they "do" Amsterdam in one day en route to Paris with the Eiffel Tower as their prime destination. The tourist is the product of consumerism, whereas the traveler dwells in higher regions of consciousness. Think only of the 19th century British gentleman traveler exploring the vastness of Her Majesty's empire. His attitude borders on aloofness, he is different from the rest of the crowd and is bent on keeping the boundaries between them and him sharply defined. In fact, he cultivates his difference, his class. Cast in this way – which, granted, borders on caricature – the image of the exile, part of an aesthetic tradition, bears remarkable resemblance to the traveler's. He, too, stands out in a crowd as he radiates – or maybe creates – foreignness, present but not really a participant, giving him an almost noble quality. Comsider John Freccero's portrait of Leo Spitzer, the exiled Austrian Romanist and boldly personal literary scholar, at Johns Hopkins University:

> We sometimes wondered if [h]is filial piety toward the continental tradition, contrasting so sharply with his generally polemical relationship to his colleagues, were not simply another way to distance himself from the rest of us, like the opera cape he wore when it rained, or the Homburg set rakishly on a mane of white hair. In those days of crew cuts and white bucks, the figure of the continental virtuoso challenged every canon of male decorum.[43]

Spitzer's foreignness feels orchestrated, opera cape and all, and corresponds with a role that the exile either plays – with varying degrees of consciousness – or is

---

[43] Quoted in: Emily Apter: Comparative Exile. Competing Margins in the History of Comparative Literature. In: *Comparative Literature in the Age of Multiculturalism*. Ed. by Charles Bernheimer. Baltimore: Johns Hopkins University Press 1995. Pp. 86–96. Here: p. 89.

expected to perform. Well known is Theodor Adorno's embrace of difference, which he regarded as the only posture the exile could assume: to remain "suspendiert", "unverbindlich",[44] never allowing oneself to become comfortable. The exile poet and essayist Hans Sahl clearly cultivated his exilic eccentricity, though with considerable self-irony and theatrical playfulness, as his poem *Nachwort* shows:

> So treten wir vor euch hin
> mit dem Lächeln, das ihr von uns
> erwartet, die Baskenmütze keck
> auf dem Ohr oder die Yarmalka,
> mit dem Daumen die Stationen
> des Exils einritzend
> in die bereits abgegriffene Landkarte,
> Genauigkeit mit Poesie verbindend,
> Leben einhauchend den Gebeinen,
> bevor sie uns fortschwimmen
> im Spülicht der Erinnerung,
> spurlos dahin auf Immerwiedersehen.[45]

Whether "Baskenmütze" or continental virtuosity, pronounced non-belonging – often manifested in eccentricity – is inscribed into the émigré character, condensing over time into a mythology of exile. Both traveler and exile, then, are part of the same modernist stuff of legends that renders them stoic, heroic: members of a group apart somehow, strangely outside of time and place.

Some critics have called attention to the masculine nature of travel, in particular pilgrimages, explorations, and the 19th century travel-to-grow phenomenon. Eric Leed even coins the term "spermatic journey", referring to the male-dominated Victorian travel ritual that bears resemblance to certain male initiation rites.[46] So-called "genuine" travel indeed has a distinctly male feel to it, as it is supposed to be without comfort, harsh, solitary, and even potentially dangerous: supposedly not the stuff women are drawn to. Exile, or at least exile mythology, shows a similar leaning toward maleness, and the great majority of works written in and about exile portray male heroes. Of course there are important exceptions: Gertrude Stein (a self-proclaimed exile), Hilde Spiel, Irmgard Keun, to name just a few. Yet it is telling that Anna Seghers, in her partly autobiographical novel, *Transit*, chooses a male protagonist (the first-person

---

[44] Theodor Adorno: *Minima Moralia. Reflexionen aus dem beschädigten Leben*. Berlin: Suhrkamp 1951. P. 57.
[45] Hans Sahl: *Wir sind die Letzten. Der Maulwurf. Gedichte*. Frankfurt/Main: Luchterhand 1991. P. 67.
[46] See Stowe: *Going Abroad* (n. 26). P. 22; Eric J. Leed: *The Mind of the Traveler. From Gilgamesh to Global Tourism*. New York: Basic Books 1991. P. 217.

narrator) to relive many of her own experiences as an exile in Marseilles attempting to obtain proper travel papers. *Transit* is certainly not devoid of female presence; in fact, the hardship of exile frequently comes to the fore in brief depictions of women in traditionally feminine roles:

> Als ich mir einen Schlafplatz suchte im Bahnhof von Toulouse, kletterte ich über eine liegende Frau, die zwischen Koffern, Bündeln und zusammengelegten Gewehren einem verschrumpften Kind die Brust gab. Wie war die Welt in diesem Jahr gealtert. Alt sah der Säugling aus, grau war das Haar der stillenden Mutter, und die Gesichter der beiden kleinen Brüder, die über die Schulter der Frau sahen, waren frech, alt und traurig.[47]

Yet all this is seen through the eyes of a male hero who navigates consulates and customs, domains of male domination, and is shown as a *homo faber* – a mechanic – equipped, it seems, to endure the trials of exile. As aesthetic discourses, both exile and travel are male-dominated and unwittingly contribute to a skewed mythology of male heroes enduring a male fate, following patterns of malehood, and rendering the terms "exile" and "travel" themselves male.

There are "faux travelers" (tourists that fake it, imposters) and there are "faux exiles" (Mary McCarthy's term for American expatriates in Paris and other such hedonists). Alfred Kerr's Ahasuerus, aimlessly and tragically roaming the earth, must indeed be called a true exile, as would the Flying Dutchman, both of whom have so frequently been invoked in narratives of exile. But are they really travelers? Siegfried Kracauer, himself an exile since 1933, has a little-known essay on *Ahasver oder das Rätsel der Zeit*, in which he gives the following depiction of this tragic shoemaker:

> Er wüßte über die Entwicklungen und Übergänge in der Tat aus erster Hand Bescheid, denn er allein in der gesamten Geschichte hatte unfreiwillig Gelegenheit, den Prozeß des Werdens und Vergehens an sich zu erfahren. (Wie unaussprechlich schrecklich er aussehen muß! Gewiß, sein Gesicht litt nicht durch Altern, aber ich denke es mir zusammengesetzt aus vielen Gesichtern, deren jedes einen der Zeiträume spiegelt, die er durchzog und die alle ewig neue Muster ergeben, während er ruhelos und vergeblich auf seiner Wanderung versucht, aus den Zeiten, die ihn formten, jene Zeit zu rekonstuieren, die er zu inkarnieren verdammt ist.)[48]

In Kracauer's conception, time doesn't progress, flow, or march. It simply exists. As such, Ahasuerus captures the essence of time as being, in that he does

---

[47] Anna Seghers: *Transit*. Berlin: Aufbau 1993. P. 36. See also Johannes F. Evelein: Männergedanken? Anna Seghers' *Transit* and the Portrayal of Gender. In: *Selecta*. Ed. by Craig W. Nickisch. Portland: Pacific Northwest Council for Languages 1998 (Journal of the NCFL 19). Pp. 12–25.

[48] Siegfried Kracauer: Ahasver oder das Rätsel der Zeit. In: *Schriften 4. Geschichte. Vor den letzten Dingen*. Frankfurt/Main: Suhrkamp 1971, Pp. 133–151. Here: Pp. 148–149.

not grow, alter, or age as he wanders through the ages. Rather, while his face records the times he traverses, he "is" the seismographer of time, but he does not "become". His travels, or better, travails, are a condition, not a process, and this applies to the fate of the exile as well. Exile of course frequently involves moving great distances, setting up temporary shelter, negotiating new surroundings lest one succumb to their perils. And yet all these movements take place within a confined mental structure, a kind of waiting room. Interestingly, Lion Feuchtwanger aptly named his exile trilogy – comprising *Erfolg*, *Die Geschwister Oppermann*, and *Exil* – "Die *Wartesaal*-Trilogie".

Exile, then, is a place, a frame of mind, not a movement. What keeps the exile waiting in this place of inner *stasis* is the hope that, one day, his circumstances will change, allowing him to leave the stagnant waters of his banished existence and reconnect with the flow of meaningful life. Such a reading would render the Flying Dutchman an exile but not a traveler. Or to be more precise: the 17th century Dutch sailor Bernard Fokke, suspected of having made a pact with the devil which granted him superhuman speed on his voyages between Java and Amsterdam, can certainly be called a bold traveler, though his mercantilism outweighed his educational strivings. However, Fokke's mythic rendition – if it was indeed Fokke who modelled for the Flying Dutchman – has ceased to travel and is entirely exilic as he is rendered forever unable to distill meaning from his everlasting cursed voyage. Whereas the traveler's travails may transform him, the exile's plight disallows growth, transformation, or redemption. This goes hand in hand with André Aciman's observation: "What makes exile the pernicious thing it is is not really the state of being away, as much as the impossibility of ever *not* being away – not just being absent, but never being able to redeem this absence".[49] Hence it is the permanence of the exile condition, the permanence of unredeemable absence, that distinguishes it from travel. The exile may *want* to travel, yet he can't because for him, travel is not an end unto itself but a deflection from the real end, which is the – forever elusive – end of exile. The traveling exile: a contradiction in terms? Not quite, but the relationship between exile and travel as critical categories is tense. Distance, Adorno writes, is not a safety zone but a "Spannungsfeld".[50] It is this very tension through distance that provides fuel for the contrastive analysis central to this collection of essays.

---

[49] Aciman: Editor's Foreword: (n. 3). P. 10.
[50] Adorno: *Minima Moralia* (n. 44). P. 127.

I. Topographies and Chronotopes of Exile

Wulf Koepke

On Time and Space in Exile – Past, Present and Future in a No-Man's Land

While a traveler has a home to which he can return, exile is a voyage of no return. This was the fundamental shock for the German-speaking exiles after 1933. This essay studies how exile also alters the experience of time and space. A hasty and unprepared escape gives no opportunity to experience the surroundings, except for signs of danger. The arrival in a new land is mostly a non-arrival. The refugee is not welcome. He is told to wait. Waiting rooms, ugly, unfamiliar, unpleasant, are typical for the new condition. Exile turns into a "waiting room" period without real hope for an ending. Whereas the European countries such as France, Czechoslovakia, Italy, and Switzerland were known to the exiles from previous visits and many were familiar with the languages spoken there, the real exile began overseas, in America. It is not surprising that few of the exiles wrote about the Americans and life in the United States, and when they did, it was about their own circles. Most writers in Los Angeles-Hollywood considered their years there a lost time in an empty space, with nothing to fill the present. While the exiles in Latin America seemed to be far more receptive to their new environment, they seized more upon the exotic features, such as Indian myths, than on the realities of the present. One of the favorite genres of the exiles was the historical novel. When they were accused of escapism they justified their choice by pointing out that it was history that made the present comprehensible. However, it took many years before they were ready to confront the problems of recent German history. In their "waiting rooms", they hoped against hope for a "turning point", a real peace after the war that would allow a return to a "Heimat". Yet the years after 1945 turned into a cold war, and the exiles continued their existence in an in-between-space with an endless time, as exterritorial people waiting for a utopia that never became a reality.

Departure without Return

Stefan Zweig's autobiography *Die Welt von Gestern* begins and ends with the journey into exile. An inveterate traveler, he realized the fundamental difference between traveling and being forced into exile. The traveler has a home awaiting his return, a center, a safe and definite place of his/her own. This home provides the structure for the journey, for the time and space of travel. Such temporal and spatial proportions and sequences make traveling productive and enjoyable, an experience of enrichment, new insights and a fresh look at oneself and one's home. Homecoming provides closure, a welcome rest, and a readiness for new experiences, a rhythm that is the essence of a creative life. Even failed journeys and negative experiences can contribute to a full life and a deeper understanding of reality and oneself.

For the "journey" into exile, Stefan Zweig is at a loss for adequate words. He calls it "Gejagtsein", hunted down, and he feels "ins Leere geschleudert, in das mir schon wohlbekannte 'Ich weiß nicht wohin'".[1] The future appears as "Leere", as an empty space, a giddiness and disorientation without a chance of reaching a solid ground. As soon as one thinks, one "hat Fuß gefasst" (443), one may be pushed away and expelled. When Stefan Zweig lived in London between 1934 and 1938, he was always free to return to Austria, although he was depressed by the threatening signs of a catastrophic future. What was more, he was respected as a lawful citizen of another country. But this country ceased to exist with the "Anschluss" of 1938, and that made him "rechtlos", a refugee whose residence permit could be revoked at any moment. Many exiles envied Stefan Zweig's privileged status; he was rich and famous, and his books sold well in translations into many languages. But it was this acute feeling of the loss of past security, that his world was "von Gestern", of being thrown into emptiness, of being a nobody in the eyes of authorities, without a valid passport, of a future in a world that was not his own, that haunted him until his voluntary death in Brazil. Zweig's "case" is a telling example for the involuntary departure, the non-arrival and the non-return that characterizes the tragedy of exile.

It seems to be unavoidable to describe exile with words from the travel vocabulary, since exile is characterized by a frequent change of place, by a sequence of departures, by movement, displacement without stability. Words like "Lebensreise", "Abfahrt", "Aufenthalt", even "Rückkehr" are commonly used in the autobiographies of the exiles; but at a closer look, "Abfahrt" usually means "Flucht" (escape), and "Rückkehr" (return) remains an unfulfilled dream. Equally problematic are terms like "Auswandern", "Fuß fassen", "neue Heimat": exile and emigration are not the same, although many exiles felt that, over time, their escape turned into a genuine emigration to a new land with new attachments. It is understandable that exiles, after a final return to Europe, wanted to present their life, to others and to themselves, as a well-rounded and meaningful "journey", and to reduce the period of exile to just one episode or period of their lives with a definitive closure. It was Carl Zuckmayer who realized more than others that this was the ultimate and possibly fatal illusion.

> Die Fahrt ins Exil ist 'a journey of no return'. Wer sie antritt und von der Heimkehr träumt, ist verloren. Er mag wiederkehren – aber der Ort, den er dann findet, ist nicht mehr der gleiche, den er verlassen hat, und er ist nicht mehr der gleiche, der fortgegangen ist. Er mag wiederkehren, zu Menschen, die er entbehren mußte, zu Städten, die er liebte und nicht vergaß, in den Bereich der Sprache, die seine eigene ist. Aber er kehrt niemals heim.[2]

---

[1] Stefan Zweig: *Die Welt von Gestern. Erinnerungen eines Europäers*. Frankfurt/Main: S. Fischer 1990. P. 7. The following quotes are from this edition.
[2] Carl Zuckmayer: *Als wär's ein Stück von mir. Horen der Freundschaft*. Frankfurt/Main: S. Fischer 1997. P. 539.

Zuckmayer had the need and the best talent to create a "home" for himself, wherever he had to go: in Henndorf, near Salzburg, on his farm in the Green Mountains of Vermont, and then in Switzerland. Hollywood, however, offered no place to him "um Wurzeln zu schlagen", and Zuckmayer left after a short time in spite of financially attractive offers. But notwithstanding his efforts, Vermont did not become a new "Heimat", at least as he saw it in his later memory. It was a space that took him out of the flow of history: "Die Jahre rollten dahin, im Wechsel der Jahreszeiten". He himself felt he had disappeared in the woods: "Mein eigenes Leben in dieser Zeit, je mehr mir die Härten seiner Realität zu schaffen machten, wurde immer unwirklicher, abseitiger, verwunschener".[3] The work on the goat farm did not take him back to reality, his life turned into a fairytale, "verwunschen", outside of real time and space. Yet faraway Europe kept intruding, it never left his mind: "Man war von Toten umgeben, man fühlte sich vom großen Sterben bedrückt".[4] His friend Carlo Mierendorff, the Social Democratic politican who took part in the conspiracy of the 20th of July, 1944, was among those dead that he mourned, and so was Ernst Udet, the flyer and organizer of the German airforce whose death gave the spark for Zuckmayer's play *Des Teufels General*. As long as the war went on, Zuckmayer had to wait "und sich ins Unvermeidliche fügen". [5] But then in 1945 a return to the old country seemed to be possible. However, it was at this point that Zuckmayer realized: wherever he would go, his exile would be with him. The waiting time turned into an endless "Zwischenzeit", an "in-between-time" without ending, except death. It is indeed wrong and misleading to speak of an exile " between 1933 and 1945". For many writers at least, their real exile was just beginning in 1945: the awareness of an extraterritorial existence without end, wherever they tried to settle down – Switzerland, Italy, Israel for instance; even Austria and Germany remained "fremd".

An Exile's Perception of Reality

Many exiles feel impelled to leave an account of their lives and thoughts. The numerous autobiographies of the exiles of 1933 and 1938, as diverse as they are in structure, style, perspective and purpose, agree on some significant points. Their departures, 1933 from Germany, 1938 from Austria and Czechoslovakia, and 1940 from France, were unprepared psychologically and in their practical aspects; departure, "Abreise", turned into "Flucht", flight, escape, it transformed the traveler into a refugee. Their travels were characterized by danger, anxiety, shock, trauma, disorientation, loss of human dignity, starvation and a general feeling of degradation. A telling (counter-)example is provided by the

---

[3] Ibid. P. 615 and 621.
[4] Ibid. P. 625.
[5] Ibid. P. 630.

account of Alma Mahler-Werfel who refused to feel and be treated as a refugee. In her memoirs she complains about the awful conditions of the hotels and the trains, the difficulties in finding taxis, and this, for instance in Lourdes, at a time when her companion Franz Werfel felt so desperate that he made the famous vow to write the story of Bernadette Soubirous, should he ever get out alive. Alma insisted on the transportation of her eight suitcases, containing her hats! (besides handwritten scores of symphonies by Gustav Mahler).[6] She was indignant when she had to walk and climb across the Pyrenees at night to reach the safety of Spain. Alma Mahler still considered herself a lady of the Austrian high society and did not accept being what she really was at that moment, a "rechtloser Flüchtling". And indeed, she was still privileged, not being imprisoned in an internment camp, and traveling with a sufficient amount of money.

Others had a very different perspective. A keen analysis of the gradual descent into the status of a nobody is given by Alfred Döblin in his *Schicksalsreise*. He is departing from Paris on an official train as a member of the French Department of Public Information, but when the train stalls and does not seem to reach any destination, Döblin, like others, tries to strike out on his own. His goal is to reach his wife and son in Le Puy. To be able to travel by bus and train, he has to get rid of much of his luggage; and when he is finally stuck in a refugee camp in Mende, he seems to have lost his last suitcase. Even though he finds it again, he loses most of his material possessions and his civil and social status (albeit lucky to be a French citizen), which brings about a mental crisis. This is when he encounters Jesus Christ in the cathedral of Mende. In the end, the contact with his wife is restored, and he is able to proceed to Toulouse and Marseilles and escapes to the United States. Yet the experience of a "Robinson in Frankreich" would never leave him and was decisive for his state of mind for the rest of his life. When he later recalls these events, from the distance of time and space in America, he recognizes:

> Wenn ich jetzt, in Amerika, jenseits des großen Wassers, an der Pazifischen Küste, an diesen Tag und die folgenden Wochen denke, an Flucht und Umherirren, an die endlose Spannung, das Warten und Drängen, das bald kam, so erscheint mir dieser ganze Abschnitt meines Lebens unwirklich. Ich erinnere mich nicht, je zu irgend einer Zeit meines Lebens so wenig 'ich' gewesen zu sein. Ich war weder 'ich' in den Handlungen (meist hatte man nicht zu handeln, man wurde getrieben oder blieb liegen), noch war meine Art zu denken und zu fühlen die alte.[7]

---

[6] Alma Mahler-Werfel: *Mein Leben*. Frankfurt/Main: S. Fischer 1960. See in particular pp. 302–316. She characterizes the hotel in Port-Bou after the border by the expressions "ein primitives Speisezimmer" und "drei oder vier schäbige Schlafzimmmer" (318). The crossing of the Pyreneees requires "zwei Stunden steilsten Klimmens" (316). Still, even she feels: "ceterum censeo – Die Emigration ist eine schwere Krankheit" (299).
[7] Alfred Döblin: *Schicksalsreise*. Olten/Freiburg: Walter Verlag 1980. P. 116.

Again, the self is turned into a mere object; a non-person incapable of acting, condemned to a passive state of waiting, like the anonymous mass of other refugees, alienated from a normal way of thinking and feeling, deprived not only of possessions, but of one's identity. "Es ist die Zeit der Beraubung. Mein Ich, meine Seele, meine Kleider wurden mir weggenommen".[8] It was not just a trip from one geographic place in France to another: "Wenn ich es genau und rundheraus sagen soll: es war keine Reise von einem französischen Ort zu einem andern, sondern eine Reise zwischen Himmel und Hölle. Von Anfang bis Ende hatte die Reise einen – ich möchte sagen: traumhaften, imaginären Charakter; ich meine, einen nicht nur realen Charakter". In his particular case, Döblin feels that there was a higher purpose: "Die Reise verlief zugleich an mir, mit mir und über mir".[9] Not reaching any earthly destination, he found a transcendent goal. But most exiles did not find such a path to salvation.

For the refugee, life is reduced to a struggle for physical survival, but often enough the mental survival is threatened in an equal measure. Instead of a normal open environment, the refugee's world is reduced to places of confinement: internment camps, prisons, hiding places, waiting rooms in administrative offices and train stations, at best in hotels and temporary shelters. None of these places provides comfort or security. The refugee is a victim, if not of persecution, then at least of arbitrariness, administrative, bureaucratic, legal, military hassles and stumbling stones. The exile has no rights, he depends entirely on the good graces of foreign authorities and unexpected friendly helpers. Human relations are dominated by fear, anxiety, suspicion, self-pity, and the general awareness of being the undignified loser. Refugees are either fleeing, running away, or endlessly waiting. A normal walk, "Spazierengehen", seems impossible under these circumstances. Therefore, the gaze around the environment is interrupted. The goal, the destination seems always uncertain and unexpected, life is a sequence of surprises, most of them unwelcome. In Franz Werfel's "comedy of a tragedy", *Jacobowsky und der Oberst*, the attempts of the colonel to keep controlling their destinies and to ignore the danger and degradation, seem preposterous and funny, if not grotesque. Jacobowsky and the colonel are just running away, and it is the surprise of a comedic and fairytale's happy ending that leads them to survival in a safe place, after all their bravery and cunning are exhausted.

The two modes of fleeing and waiting have their specific temporal aspects: time that races by as opposed to an endless empty present. In both cases, the past and the future seem to be forgotten, history and the purpose of human life are obliterated. The immediate concerns crowd out any long-term planning and deeper reflections. People and events are either friendly and helpful, or

---

[8] Ibid. P. 203.
[9] Ibid. P. 150.

threatening. One feels like an animal in the wild, always watchful and suspicious. As Brecht puts it in his great poem *An die Nachgeborenen*, "der Lachende/ Hat die furchtbare Nachricht/ Nur noch nicht empfangen".[10]

Escape into History

It is only an apparent contradiction to this condition that, after the initial accounts of what happened in 1933 – for instance Lion Feuchtwanger's *Die Geschwister Oppermann*, Wolfgang Langhoff's *Die Moorsoldaten*, H. W. Katz' *Schloßgasse 22*, Ferdinand Bruckner's *Die Rassen*, to be followed by Friedrich Wolf's *Professor Mamlock*, Brecht's *Furcht und Elend des Dritten Reiches*, and eventually by Irmgard Keun's *Nach Mitternacht*, Klaus Mann's *Mephisto* and Anna Seghers' *Das siebte Kreuz* – the exiles turned to the genres of the historical novel, the biography and the historical play. Kurt Hiller denounced this at the time as harmful escapism, and it generated the first controversy among and around the exile writers, initiated by the Dutch writer Menno ter Braak, who looked in vain for a political response to Hitler in the writings of the exiles.[11] Historical novels and biographies were popular in many countries during the thirties: the audience needed relief from the pressing and depressing conditions of the day. Absorbing oneself into history provided a new foothold of "reality" for writers who were deprived of the day-to-day contact with their own environment, as Alfred Döblin noted. Biographies and historical novels (there was only a gradual difference) also offered a view of history and human life that could take the refugees beyond their present helplessness. For example, Lion Feuchtwanger could discover in past times of historical transitions and revolutions the confirmation that it was "Vernunft" (reason) that ultimately governed human history, and not blind fate and violence. Ludwig Marcuse has observed that there was no real difference between Feuchtwanger's historical novels and

---

[10] Bertolt Brecht: *Gesammelte Werke. Werkausgabe.* Vol. 9: Gedichte 2. Frankfurt/Main: Suhrkamp 1969. P. 722. This is followed by the famous line on the "Gespräch über Bäume" being "fast ein Verbrechen" (723), because it implies silence about the horrible crimes of the age – a line that sparked so many differing responses.
[11] Ludwig Marcuse, one of the participants in the dispute, put it this way: "Seine ideale Forderung lautete: diese Literatur soll mehr sein als eine Fortsetzung. Da er erwartet hatte, daß dem Thomas Mann und dem Alfred Döblin nach Überschreiten der Grenze übermenschliche Kräfte zugewachsen waren, enttäuschte es ihn, daß sie alle nur weiter waren, was sie auch schon vorher gewesen sind. Er umgab die Schriftsteller der Emigration mit einem Strahlenkranz, der sie ganz häßlich machte; sie stachen, wie er richtig herausfand, elend ab gegen den verklärenden Rahmen". *Mein zwanzigstes Jahrhundert.* Zürich: Diogenes 1975. Pp. 178–179. This is one aspect, but the problem was much more complex and cannot be explained without understanding the tradition of "Geist und Macht".

his "Zeitromane" – they both were based on the same principles: looking at life from a distance, filtering out the essential truths from the contingent facts, presenting what was relevant for the present, and illuminating the cumbersome progress of reason. Heinrich Mann told the story of the French king Henri IV as an "ordinary" man who came at the right time to help his people,[12] the counter-image of all those more or less charismatic and demonic "Verführer" of Heinrich Mann's own day, as a reminder of the true human values: "Vernunft", goodness, tolerance, love of peace, a sense of enjoyment and happiness, and above all, "Menschlichkeit".

It is worth considering, however, that the exiles, at that stage, were unable to confront the history of Germany and the Germans. Later, in the United States, during World War II and after, they were harshly reminded of the negative and ugly aspects of their history; of personalities like Martin Luther, the Prussian king Friedrich II, and Bismarck, not to mention anti-Semites like Richard Wagner. The years around 1945 would be the time for reflection on the German past, in works like Thomas Mann's *Doktor Faustus*, Alfred Döblin's *November 1918*, Leonhard Frank's *Deutsche Novelle*, Anna Seghers' *Der Ausflug der toten Mädchen* and Hermann Kesten's *Die Zwillinge von Nürnberg*. In the 1930's, the exiles preferred to write about "their own", for example Heinrich Heine, Gotthold Ephrain Lessing, and Georg Büchner.

This is remarkable since, by contrast, the German-speaking writers from the former Austro-Hungarian monarchy were then heavily engaged in a debate about their heritage and the downfall of the Habsburg empire. Robert Musil, Joseph Roth, Hermann Broch, Max Brod, Ernst Lothar, F. C. Weiskopf and Ludwig Winder are only a few names that come to mind. It is true that the Germans would have had to write against a massive tradition and nationalist propaganda of glorification of the Hohenzollern and praise of the German nation, exemplified by Gustav Freytag's *Die Ahnen* and *Bilder aus deutscher Vergangenheit* and his many imitators, not to mention idealizing images like Friedrich Schiller's *Wilhelm Tell*, whose Swiss heroics were eagerly appropriated by the Germans.

Typically, the historical imagination of the exiles identified with writers and artists, with outsiders – for which they were chided by Georg Lukacs. Bruno Frank wrote on Cervantes, Lion Feuchtwanger on Flavius Josephus, Klaus Mann on Tchaikovsky, Ludwig Marcuse on Plato (albeit focusing on his political

---

[12] See Heinrich Mann's letter to Ludwig Marcuse, 16 September 1935: "Henri Quatre hat auch nur darum Erfolg gehabt, weil infolge des Vorangegangenen ein Aufatmen durchaus notwendig geworden war. Persönlich ist er ein mittlerer Mensch von schnellem, gesundem Geist, aber ohne Dämonie und ähnliche Herrlichkeiten; ich hoffe, daß es bei mir herauskommt". *Briefe von und an Ludwig Marcuse*. Ed. by Harold von Hofe. Zürich: Diogenes 1975. P. 20.

adventure in Syracuse), Franz Werfel on Verdi, Hermann Broch on the dying Virgil. Even Thomas Mann's "historical" novel *Lotte in Weimar* deals with Goethe and his entourage. This is very different from the panoramas of Walter Scott, Leon Tolstoy, Victor Hugo or Emile Zola.

Disorientation and Non-arrival

It goes without saying that the elements of persecution: threat, arrest, imprisonment, and (attempted or successful) escape are constitutive for the works of the exiles and appear even in unexpected places. Besides the obvious examples, like Anna Seghers' *Das siebte Kreuz* and *Transit*, we find them in Bruno Frank's *Cervantes*, Lion Feuchtwanger's *Josephus*, Irmgard Keun's *Nach Mitternacht*, Brecht's *Der kaukasische Kreidekreis* and *Galilei*, in Stefan Zweig's *Schachnovelle* and Thomas Mann's *Joseph und seine Brüder*. They determine the structure of the documentary and literary accounts about the defeat of France in 1940, as seen in Hans Habe's *Ob Tausend fallen*, Arthur Koestler's *Scum of the Earth*, Franz Werfel's *Jacobowski und der Oberst*, Lion Feuchtwanger's *Der Teufel in Frankreich*, Hans Sahl's *Das Exil im Exil* und Alfred Döblin's *Schicksalsreise*, each in a different way and from a different perspective. If the sometimes miraculous liberation from a seemingly hopeless impasse seems to provide a happy ending for these crises, it masks the fact that escape did not mean "arrival". After the happy moment of crossing the border and saving one's life, after the first days of euphoric reception in a new country, the awareness of reality sets in. Where am I? The refugee arrives as a nobody whose past fame is more of a burden than an asset. He is a person without a name, most unwanted and not welcome, a "Störenfried" with dubious claims. Franz Kafka's novel *Das Schloß* comes to mind where a pretended land surveyor K. arrives from nowhere, who claims that he has been called and hired by the authorities, but that will never be confirmed. When he tries to get a foothold in the "village", he is unable to find his own space, spending his time in waiting rooms and sleeping in rooms not meant for personal living. Günther Anders and Hannah Arendt noticed the surprising similarities with their own situation as exiles at that time.[13] The protagonists of *Der kaukasische Kreidekreis* decide at the end to "disappear" for a while, we don't know where Georg Heisler and the couple in *Nach Mitternacht* go, but we know that the exile in the *Schachnovelle* will just disappear in a foreign land. The narrator of Anna Seghers' *Der Ausflug der toten Mädchen* seems to make it back home, but shortly before she reaches the house of her parents she wakes up and finds herself in a lonely part of Mexico, in a scenery of death. Still, these stories are

---

[13] Günther Anders: *Franz Kafka – Pro und Kontra*. München: C. H. Beck 1951. It was reedited a number of times.

not final, non-closure is the typical "last word". The future is there, it is "eine Aufgabe", it needs to be learned and mastered, Anna Seghers' narrator needs to write her account of the fate of the dead girls.

Yet death seems so often to be the real point of arrival for the restless wanderers, and the ultimate closure for the text. Erich von Kahler called Thomas Mann's *Doktor Faustus* a book "des Endes".[14] Death is the final completion of the story in Klaus Mann's *Symphonie Pathetique*, as it is in Alfred Döblin's *November 1918* and *Amazonas*, and of course in Hermann Broch's *Der Tod des Vergil* Death concludes Heinrich Mann's haunting "last story" *Der Atem*. Even Lion Feuchtwanger's *Josephus* ends at that point, with the protagonist disappearing in a no-man's land between the fronts in Palestine.

Waiting for the Impossible Return

As long as the exiles stayed in Europe, they remained close to Germany, to the idea of "Heimat" and a foreseeable return. Their geographic focus was on Germany, their thinking about the future concentrated on the moment of return. With the flight to other continents, from India and China to Argentina and the United States, the perspective changed decisively. Authors like Stefan Zweig and Heinrich Mann had considered themselves "Europeans", the farewell from Europe proved to be "überaus leidvoll", as Heinrich Mann put it in his memoirs *Ein Zeitalter wird besichtigt*. The departure from Europe was for them the journey into real exile. Whereas the exiles' experience of Latin America was characterized by the encounter with an unknown exotic world, the writers in the United States felt little affinity with the new life and environment, least of all with Los Angeles-Hollywood, where a considerable number of them found their refuge. Most writers had little previous knowledge of this new environment and had to learn a new language. Their cultural space had been continental Europe, especially the countries around the Mediterranean Sea. This affinity with France and Italy could not be transferred to the Anglo-Saxon world, certainly not to the United States.[15] Prejudices against and negative experiences with the capitalistic system of the USA, most drastically told in

---

[14] Erich von Kahler: Secularization of the Devil: Thomas Mann's 'Doctor Faustus'. In: *The Orbit of Thomas Mann*. Princeton (NJ): Princeton University Press 1969. Pp. 20–43. The original study, in German, appeared in 1948. The translation calls these novels "*terminal* books, apotheoses of the narrative form" (20), and mentions James Joyce's *Ulysses, Der Mann ohne Eigenschaften* by Robert Musil, Herman Broch: *Der Tod des Vergil*, André Gide, *Les Fauf-Monnayeurs*, Sartre's *La Nausee*, Camus' *L'Etranger*, and of course the novels by Franz Kafka.

[15] See my study: Innere Exilgeographie? Die Frage nach der Affinität zu den Asylländern. *Exile across Cultures – Kulturelle Wechselbeziehungen im Exil*. Ed. by Helmut Pfanner. Bonn: Bouvier 1986. Pp. 13–24.

Hans Marchwitza's *In Amerika*, made the situation worse. Whereas New York, with all its drawbacks, remained a fascinating city, Los Angeles seemed to be solely a space of emptiness and non-reality, a cultural and social "desert". The non-reality and make-believe of Hollywood seemed to pervade the life in the city, and even the mild climate was felt as hostile to creative activities. It was Leonhard Frank who most vehemently complained about the lost years of Hollywood. "Was sollte er, ein deutscher Schriftsteller, in Amerika".[16] The entire country impressed him by its monotony: "Während der Fahrt nach Hollywood sah Michael ein paar hundertmal ein und dasselbe Städtchen, alle mit Benzinstation, Drugstore und Kino". While he lived in Hollywood, he felt constantly tired, "infolge des blutverdünnenden tropisch warmen, weichen Klimas".[17] Bert Brecht equally complained about the climate and claimed he had to take vitamins to feel fit for work. And this was the main complaint of Leonhard Frank: "Er verlor in Hollywood viel Zeit, kostbare Zeit, unwiederbringliche Jahre". He lost time, and time lost him. Time in this unreal place was empty. "Die Zeit, nicht ausgefüllt mit wirklichem Leben, das es in der Filmstadt für niemand geben kann, verflog, als wäre sie ein vorbeizuckender farbloser Vogel".[18] One of Frank's strongest impressions was the ritual of funerals, especially the funeral receptions with the made-up corpse placed in the middle of the room.[19]

It is in keeping with this perception of an empty time that vanishes into an empty space, when other exiles characterized their condition as a "Wartesaal", a waiting room. Lion Feuchtwanger called the "trilogy" of his Zeitromane *Erfolg, Die Geschwister Oppermann* and *Exil* the "Wartesaal-Trilogie", and in the epilog of *Exil* he had expressed confidence that he would be able to add a fourth novel, "Die Rückkehr". But this was not to be. Thomas Mann spoke of the "Wartesaaltag"; Ernst Lothar, Franz Schoenberner, and Ludwig Marcuse all used the term to express their sense of time. "Wartesaal" is still a euphemism; while it expresses the sense of spending (or losing) an empty time in an environment that is not one's own, usually ugly, hostile, uncomfortable, there is a schedule indicating an end to the waiting period: the arrival of the train, bus or plane one is waiting for, the appointment with the official, the doctor or the dentist. Yet the exiles linger between hope and no-hope – is it Dante's (another exile's!) hell or purgatory? Can there be a train taking them to their destination?

---

[16] Leonhard Frank. *Links wo das Herz ist*. Berlin: Aufbau-Verlag 1957. P. 595. Although Frank labeled the book as "Roman" and narrated it in the third person, calling the protagonist "Michael", it is evidently an autobiography and recounts his own experiences.
[17] Ibid. Pp. 597, 600.
[18] Ibid. Pp. 600, 605.
[19] Ibid. Pp. 601–602.

It was possible for some to transform the waiting room into a protected space outside the money-grabbing "hell", as Brecht defined it.[20] Lion Feuchtwanger, who had spent the previous years in Sanary-sur-Mer, the idyllic French fishing village where the exiles were able to shield themselves temporarily from the devastating onslaught of the brutal times, acquired a villa in Pacific Palisades, which to him seemed like a gigantic version of Sanary. But Feuchtwanger's "castle" above the ocean, or Thomas Mann's home nearby, was founded on sufficient funds of money, together with the attitude of self-worth that legitimized Feuchtwanger to immerse himself into past ages, staying away from, above and beyond the emptiness of the other exiles' waiting rooms.

The end of the war in Europe was the beginning of a permanent crisis. Was it possible or advisable to return to a Europe in its darkest hour? Hans Sahl, from a later perspective in New York, observed that those who were ready to return were politicians and political writers and artists committed to an ideology and the discipline of a political party. "Zurück blieben die Zauderer, die Zweifler, die Unentschlossenen, die auf die Frage: 'Was ist die Antwort?' mit Gertrude Stein antworteten: 'Was ist die Frage?'".[21] He himself emigrated "von einer Ungewißheit in die andere".[22]

Franz Carl Weiskopf concluded his survey of exile literature of 1947, *Unter fremden Himmeln*, with a section where he declared: now that the period of exile was over, the writers had the duty to return and do their part for the reconstruction of their native countries.[23] There were also other reasons for an attempted return: Actors who had not been able to find a new voice in another language; writers like Alfred Döblin who were unable to make a living in the American environment; and, last but not least, "Heimweh", the longing for the old country, particularly strong among the Austrians. Most stories of return do not have a good ending, however: even politically committed writers did not find "home". Erich Arendt would be a prime example of this non-adjustment in his home region. He found his poetic voice again only when he was traveling in Greece. Carl Zuckmayer had spoken the truth, and when Oskar Maria Graf presented a panorama of the disintegration of intellectual exile in New York, in his vast novel *Die Flucht ins Mittelmäßige*, he ended with examples for the futility of attempted returns. Even Erich Maria Remarque, if one believes his novel

---

[20] Bertolt Brecht: Nachdenkend über die Hölle. *Gesammelte Werke. Werkausgabe.* Vol. 10. P. 830. See also his "Hollywood-Elegien". Pp. 849–850.
[21] Hans Sahl: *Das Exil im Exil*, Frankfurt/Main: Luchterhand 1990. P. 154.
[22] Ibid. P. 156.
[23] F. C. Weiskopf: *Unter fremden Himmeln. Ein Abriß der deutschen Literatur im Exil 1933–1947*. Berlin: Dietz 1947. Weiskopf's book is much more than a mere "Abriß"; it offers basic insights into the literary exile, it is remarkably well informed and relatively unbiased.

Schatten im Paradies, did not see a happy solution for this conflict.[24] The "Provisorium" of the exile proved to be a permanent one.

Confrontation With an Exotic World

Whereas the encounter with the United States is largely characterized by the refusal to engage with the reality of the new country and to "appropriate" its idioms, Latin America offered another challenge. The exile writers arrived in Mexico, Colombia, and Argentina at a time when the cultural elites of those countries turned against the domination by their European, mostly Spanish, heritage, and went back to "native" roots, the Pre-Colombian past. The Mexican artists collected Pre-Colombian art, and the murals in the public buildings of Mexico tell the story of Spanish oppression and the innocence of the native Indios. The German writers were familiar with Diego Rivera, Tamayo and Siqueiros, and it was this aspect of Mexican life that attracted them in several ways: as a pre-industrial idyl, as the voice of a genuine Volk, the common people, but also in its foreignness, in its uncanny, incomprehensible, mythical otherness. Anna Seghers, Bodo Uhse, Ludwig Renn, Erich Arendt in Colombia, and Paul Zech in Argentina all had models for writing about this world and its people. There was a tradition of "colonial" stories from Joseph Conrad to Rudyard Kipling and Jack London, but the immediate point of reference was the mysterious German writer B. Traven, who had shaped the "socialist" image of Mexico since the 1920s. Although there seems to have been no personal contacts with this elusive writer, the impact of his style and approach is unmistakable in Bodo Uhse and Anna Seghers' stories.[25] It is remarkable that the exiles emphasized the otherness, those aspects that did not conform to Western civilization, not only for ideological reasons. It was the search for authentic roots, "das Ursprüngliche", that comes through in the writings of Anna Seghers, Gustav Regler, Paul Zech and Erich Arendt, the encounter with the mythical world of the Indio.[26] This search also led them into a search for a "heile Welt",

---

[24] See the account of the various attempts for a life after Hitler in my "Gibt es eine Rückkehr aus dem Exil?". In: *Deutschsprachige Exilliteratur seit 1933*, Part III: USA. Vol. 5. Ed. by John M. Spalek, Konrad Feilchenfeldt, and Sandra Hawrylchak. München: K. G. Saur 2002. Pp. 334–363.

[25] See my study: B. Traven and the Exiles in Mexico. In: *B. Traven. Life and Work*. Ed. by Ernst Schürer, Phillip Jenkins. University Park: Pennsylvania State University Press 1987. Pp. 296–306.

[26] See my essay: The Indio as Seen by the European Exile Writers, with an Emphasis on Exile Legend. In: *Latin America and the Literature of Exile*. Ed. by H. B. Moeller. Heidelberg: C. Winter 1983. Pp. 151–179. This volume, little noticed since it was published in Germany but in English, contains a number of very significant studies.

an idyl before the arrival of the evil Western conquerors, and a time in congruence and agreement with the change of seasons, with the natural life of plants, animals, and human beings, with life and death. While the exiles were aware that this world of the traditional Indian communities was disappearing in Latin American societies, they hoped to find in this natural rhythm the foundation for a renewal of life in the modern societies, aware of the danger of escapism and exoticism. The "timeless" life of the Indios in their protected spaces might very well be a life of an irretrievable past and not a key to a better life in the future. Lastly, a contradiction: while the communist party loyalists focused on the planning for the future after National Socialism, they also experienced the waiting time in the manner of the Indios, living in a present without history.

The Dilemma Without Solution

The longer exile goes on, the more acutely it leads to a dilemma: is it possible to preserve one's identity, or will the exiled person be changed, transformed by the new environment? How can a writer and artist survive under such drastically changed conditions? Even Lion Feuchtwanger, a master in protecting his "inner space", stated in his speech "Arbeitsprobleme des Schriftstellers im Exil"[27] that the foreign environment intruded on the mind and the style of a writer in a major way. Exile and the new perspectives became essential elements of writing. The foreign language around him forced the writer to be much more aware of his own language and made his style more precise and forceful. Only at first sight is it surprising that so few exile writers in America became bilingual or switched languages: language was the identity that the writers tried at all cost to preserve. In the United States, very few authors went beyond using English for "Sachprosa", "American" novelists like Stefan Heym were rare even among the young generation – Stefan Heym's promising American career, however, was cut short by the anti-Communist wave after 1945.

In some cases, the language problem with all its implications proved to be a fatal dilemma. The tragic death of Klaus Mann offers the most telling example. In 1945 Klaus Mann was at a crossroad of his career. His political engagement as an anti-fascist writer and editor had come to an end, the return to Europe seemed possible once again, but where could he go? He had identified with the protagonist Tchaikovsky of his *Symphonie Pathetique*, whom he described in

---

[27] Arbeitsprobleme des Schriftstellers im Exil, first printed in 1943 in the *Proceedings* of the conference on the problems of writers in exile reprinted several times, first in *Das Goldene Tor*, edited by Alfred Döblin, then in *Centum Opuscula*, later published with the title *Ein Buch nur für meine Freunde*. Frankfurt/Main: Fischer Taschenbuch 1984. Pp. 533–538.

these terms: "Er war ein Emigrant, ein Exilierter, nicht aus politischen Gründen, sondern weil er sich nirgends zu Hause fühlte, nirgends zu Hause war".[28] Klaus Mann, at least as he claimed in his autobiography, *Der Wendepunkt*, had not considered the initial years in Europe as an "exile", as he was equally at home in Amsterdam, Zurich and Paris. Yet the verdict remained: "Die Emigration war nicht gut".[29] And in 1945, when he came back to Germany and had to confront his hometown Munich as a reporter for "Stars and Stripes", he felt a deep shock: "War dies die Heimkehr? Alles fremd, fremd, fremd".[30] And he realized: "Die alte Heimat findest du nicht mehr, auch eine neue ist dir nicht beschieden. Die Welt ist deine Heimat. Eine andere hast du nicht". But "die Welt" can only be "Heimat" if it is a whole world where one is welcome and can feel at home: "Die ganze Welt wird meine Heimat sein, gesetzt, es gibt noch eine ganze Welt nach diesem Kriege".[31] His problems, however, were more specific and immediate: would he try to be once more a German writer, or an American? Which was his world, Europe or America? Could he go on as a permanent restless wanderer? Klaus Mann could not find the answer. Like quite a few liberal and independent socialist intellectuals, he was squeezed into a position between the two powers and ideologies of the Cold War, making him a political outsider, if not outcast.

In this he was not alone. Hans Sahl's *Das Exil im Exil* describes the position of a permanent outsider and offers a chronicle of the writers and artists whose place he referred to as "exterritorial". Exterritorial means a life without a home, without a true space of one's own, without a fatherland, without loyalty to a political party and institution, yet with a belief in "Menschlichkeit", with moral principles and the adherence to the identity of one's way of expression and aesthetic values. In contrast to Klaus Mann, Hans Sahl was able to live (and make a living) as a mediator, a translator of American plays into German, a correspondent for major German newspapers, and as the voice and witness for the cultural exile, in his poems and his autobiography *Das Exil im Exil*.

It is this space "in-between" and this time "in-between", the "Zwischenraum" and "Zwischenzeit", that turned out to be the typical destination of the exiles after 1945. Hans Sahl voiced the conviction that the exiles had provided continuity, a kind of a bridge, for the German literature from the days of the Weimar Republic to the "rebirth" of German letters with Ingeborg Bachmann, Martin Walser and *Die Blechtrommel*, connecting it with Kafka,

---

[28] Klaus Mann. *Symphonie Pathétique*. Amsterdam: Querido 1935. P. 383.
[29] Klaus Mann. *Der Wendepunkt. Ein Lebensbericht*. München: Edition Spangenberg 1976. Pp. 343 and 383.
[30] Ibid. P. 551.
[31] Ibid. P. 496.

Lasker-Schüler and Döblin.[32] Maybe. But the fact remains that the exiles were "outside" and that the expectation of a "Heimkehr" remained a Fata Morgana, symbolized in a poignant way by the ending of Anna Seghers' story *Der Ausflug der toten Mädchen*. It is an ending of death and disappearance that characterizes the works of the exiles after 1945, much more than the idea of a new beginning. The crisis of 1945 did not find a "solution".[33]

The Nazi regime and mentality had unhinged all previous conditions. The Jewish writers remained in doubt whether it was really possible to be a German Jew, Jewish and German at the same time. The German-speaking writers from Prague lost their home. Even committed communists like Egon Erwin Kisch and F. C. Weiskopf were not welcome in the new Czech environment. Weiskopf survived as a diplomat for Czechoslovakia in foreign countries, a telling sign for his exterritorial existence. Was there anything more that the exile writers could provide than the memory of the past and the awareness of the values and tradition of a previous literary and artistic tradition in the German-speaking countries?

It sounds ironic that one of the major works and legacies of the German exile is *Das Prinzip Hoffnung* by Ernst Bloch. The legacy of the exiles has not yet been adequately understood, and it may just fade away in the turmoils of the "postmodern" mentality of the 21st century. Yet the perception of time and space of the "exterritorial man" is so close to the life and mind of the present age that it cannot and should not be ignored.

---

[32] Hans Sahl: *Das Exil im Exil. Memoiren eines Moralisten II*. München: Deutscher Taschenbuch Verlag 1994. P. 198. Sahl sees the decisive merit of exile literature in that it "die verlorengegangene Einheit von Mensch und Werk wiederherstellte" (197). Sahl stressed that exile literature was no "Sonderfall", but "ein Bestandteil der deutschen Literatur" (198), a point still not generally accepted.

[33] See my study: Eine Krise ohne Ausgang. Das Exil im Jahr 1945 und der Blick in die Zukunft. In: *Literarisches Krisenbewußtsein im 20. Jahrhundert*. Ed. by Keith Bullivant and Bernhard Spies. München: Iudicium 2001. Pp. 128–141.

Thomas Pekar

Jüdisches Exil in Ostasien, vor allem in Japan (1933–1945)

While there are a host of publications concentrating on the theme of exile in Shanghai, other areas of East Asia, in particular Japan, are still to be regarded as a desideratum of research into the field of exile. Although Japan was known as a collaborating force with Nazi Germany, many people including the philosopher Karl Löwith, who was himself exiled in Japan from 1936 until 1941, speak of 'German emigrants in Japan'. Within the field of power of Japan and Germany there were a multitude of factors, many of which little researched, which decided the fate of the emigrants. In this essay, firstly, I give an overview of research activities in exile studies relevant to Japan; secondly I analyze the specific problem of Japan as an exile country, and thirdly I present an unknown report of a journey into exile via Japan and some relatively unknown poems about Japan from an emigrant.

Mit diesem Beitrag sollen zwei Bereiche der Exilforschung angesprochen werden: Zum einen die 'klassische' Exilforschung, als eine positivistisch orientierte Forschung, die sich um bestimmte Fakten, Personen und Ereignisse kümmert; in dieser Hinsicht geht es hier um das sicherlich problematische 'Exilland' Japan. Zum anderen soll dieser Ansatz mit einem Thema verbunden werden, welches in den gegenwärtigen Diskussionen um die Kulturwissenschaften breiten Raum einnimmt, nämlich das Thema der kulturellen Begegnung, der Kulturkontakte, der inter- und transkulturellen Austauschprozesse, der, kurzgesagt, Reisethematik. Die leitende Frage hier ist, inwieweit die kulturelle Mobilität der Émigrés, die oft gezwungen waren, von Europa über Asien in die USA zu flüchten, zu einer differenzierten Wahrnehmung der ihnen fremden Kulturen – und hier soll es um die asiatischen Kulturen bzw. insbesondere um die japanische Kultur gehen – beitrug. Weiter wäre zu fragen, ob es besondere, aus der spezifischen Situation des Exils herrührende Formen (bzw. Strategien) der Wahrnehmung, der Lesbarkeit und der Vertextung dieser fremden – in diesem Fall ostasiatischen – Kulturen gibt. Es wäre in dieser Hinsicht von Kultur-Texten des Exils zu sprechen, die eine durchaus auch gesellschaftliche bzw. kulturelle Wirklichkeit erzeugende ('performative') Kraft haben.[1]

---

[1] Einen 'Kultur-Text' definiere ich mit Neumann/Weigel so: "Ein [...] Kultur-Text wäre als ein Bedeutungsgewebe aufzufassen, das durch Sprache, Handeln, Symbolbildungen und Artefakte, namentlich aber durch einander stützende wie einander widerstreitende Codes, durch Rede-, Schreib- und Bildordnungen, allererst gesellschaftliche Wirklichkeit erzeugt [...]". Gerhard Neumann/Sigrid Weigel: Einleitung. In: *Lesbarkeit der Kultur. Literaturwissenschaft zwischen Kulturtechnik und Ethnographie*. Hg. von Gerhard Neumann/Sigrid Weigel. München: Fink 2000. S. 349–364. Hier: S. 11.

Bevor ich am Ende dieses Beitrages mögliche Beispiele von solchen Kultur-Texten des Exils vorstelle, seien einige Bemerkungen zum Stand der Exilforschung in Hinsicht auf Japan und/oder Ostasien vorausgeschickt: In dem 1998 erschienenen *Handbuch zur deutschsprachigen Emigration 1933–1945*, in dem Aufsatz *Ostasien*, heißt es: "Japan stellt ein Desiderat der Exilforschung dar".² Solche 'Desiderate' gibt es in diesem Forschungsbereich fast nicht mehr, vor allem seitdem in den letzten Jahren zu einem der letzten dieser Desiderate, nämlich dem jüdischen Exil in Shanghai, eine ganze Reihe von Arbeiten publiziert worden sind.³ Diese Untersuchungen sind für den

---

² Patrik von zur Mühlen: Ostasien. In: *Handbuch der deutschsprachigen Emigranten 1933–1945*. Hg. von Claus-Dieter Krohn u.a. Darmstadt: Wissenschaftliche Buchgesellschaft 1998. S. 336–349. Hier: S. 346.

³ Vgl. dazu vor allem die Literaturangaben in dem genannten Artikel Patrik von zur Mühlens, die den Forschungsstand bis 1997 angeben; an wichtigen Arbeiten, die danach zu diesem Thema erschienen sind, wären u.a. zu nennen: Ammon Barzel: *Leben im Wartesaal. Exil in Shanghai 1938–1947*. Berlin: Jüdisches Museum 1997; *Zwischen Theben und Shanghai. Jüdische Exilanten in China – Chinesische Exilanten in Europa. Almanach zum V. Else-Lasker-Schüler-Forum "Flucht in die Freiheit"*. Hg. von Hajo Jahn. Berlin: Oberbaum 1998; Pamela Rotner Sakamoto: *Japanese Diplomats and Jewish Refugees: A World War II Dilemma*. Westport, Conn.: Praeger 1998; Antonia Finnane: *Far from where? Jewish Journeys from Shanghai to Australia*. Carlton South: Melbourne University Press 1999; Frieda Miller: *Shanghai: a Refuge During the Holocaust: A Teacher's Guide*. Vancouver: Vancouver Holocaust Education Centre 1999; Avraham Altman/Irene Eber: Flight to Shanghai, 1938–1940. The Larger Setting. In: *Yad Vashem Studies* 28 (2000). S. 51–86; *Exil Shanghai. Jüdisches Leben in der Emigration (1938–1947)*. Hg. von Georg Armbrüster/Michael Kohlstruck/Sonja Mühlberger. Teetz: Hentrich & Hentrich 2000; Astrid Freyeisen: *Shanghai und die Politik des Dritten Reiches*. Würzburg: Königshausen & Neumann 2000; Ira Epstein: *Shanghai Sanctuary: A Story of Survival in the Midst of the Holocaust for Twenty Five Thousand Jews Who Fled to Shanghai, China*. New Haven (CT): Southern Connecticut State University 2002; Weijian Liu: Shanghai aus Sicht der deutschsprachigen Literatur zwischen 1920 und 1949. In: *Ostasienrezeption im Schatten der Weltkriege. Universalismus und Nationalsozialismus*. Hg. von Walter Gebhard. München: Iudicium 2003. S. 187–216; *Passagen nach Fernost. Menschen zwischen Bremen und Ostasien*. Hg. von Peter Kuckuk. Bremen: Edition Temmen 2004; *Shanghai Remembered: Stories of Jews Who Escaped to Shanghai from Nazi Europe*. Hg. von Berl Falbaum. Royal Oak (MI): Momentum Books 2005. Neben dieser wissenschaftlichen Forschung wurden in den letzten Jahren viele biographische Erinnerungsbücher Betroffener über ihre Zeit in Shanghai veröffentlicht; vgl. z.B.: Anna Lincoln: *Escape to China (1939–1948)*. New York: Manyland Books 1982; Alfred W. Kneucker: *Zuflucht in Shanghai. Aus den Erlebnissen eines österreichischen Arztes in der Emigration 1938–1945*. Bearbeitet und hg. von Felix Gamillschaeg. Nachwort von Kurt R. Fischer. Wien: Böhlau 1984; Chaim U. Lipschitz: *The Shanghai Connection: Based*

Themenkomplex 'Jüdisches Exil und Japan' deshalb von höchstem Interesse, da Japan als Besatzungsmacht in Shanghai direkt involviert war.[4]

Nur wenige Untersuchungen gibt es hingegen, die sich auf die jüdisch-japanischen Beziehungen selbst in diesen Kriegsjahren konzentrieren. Hier wäre, neben Birgit Pansas Buch *Juden unter japanischer Herrschaft*,[5] welches sich zu wesentlichen Teilen auf das Standardwerk zu diesem Themenbereich,

---

on the Hebrew "Nes Hatzalah". New York: Maznaim Publ. 1988; Rena Krasno: *Strangers Always: A Jewish Family in Wartime Shanghai*. Berkeley (CA): Pacific View Press 1992; Ernest G. Heppner: *Shanghai Refuge: A Memoir of the World War II Jewish Ghetto*. Lincoln: University of Nebraska Press 1993; Evelyn Pike Rubin: *Ghetto Shanghai*. New York (NY): Shengold 1993; Betty Grebenschikoff: *Once My Name Was Sara: A Memoir*. Ventnor (NJ): Original Seven Publishing Co. 1993; Ya'acov Liberman: *My China: Jewish Life in the Orient. 1900–1950*: Berkeley (CA): Gefen Pub. House Ltd. 1998; Sigmund Tobias: *Strange Haven: A Jewish Childhood in Wartime Shanghai*. Urbana: University of Illinois Press 1999; Ursual Bacon: *Shanghai Diaries*. Seattle (WA): Hara Pub. 2002; Vivian Jeanette Kaplan: *Ten Green Bottles: Vienna to Shanghai: Journey of Fear and Hope*. Toronto: Robin Brass Studio 2002; Horst Eisfelder: *Chinese Exile: My Years in Shanghai and Nanking*. Caulfield South (Vic.) Australia: Makor Jewish Community Library 2003.

1997 wurde der Film *Exil Shanghai* von Ulrike Ottinger bei der Berlinale (beim *Internationalen Forum des Jungen Films*) uraufgeführt. 2002 entstand der amerikanische Dokumentarfilm *Shanghai Ghetto* von Dana Janklowicz-Mann und Amir Mann.

[4] Nach dem Ersten Japanisch-Chinesischen Krieg (1894 bis 1895), in dem Japan Korea annektiert hatte, und dem Russisch-Japanischen Krieg (1904 bis 1905), durch den sich Japan großen Einfluß in der Mandschurei sichern konnte (Japan übernahm z.B. von Rußland die für den Rohstofftransport wichtige Südmanschurische Eisenbahn), kam es seit Anfang der 1930er Jahre immer wieder zu Kämpfen zwischen Japanern und Chinesen. Japan hatte zum Schutz dieser Eisenbahn eine Armee, die Guandong Armee, in der Mandschurei stationiert, die immer wieder für Unruhe sorgte (Mukden-Zwischenfall 1931; Mandschurei-Krise 1931, die zur Gründung des japanischen Marionettenstaates Mandschuko führte, erster Angriff Japans auf Shanghai 1932 u.a. mit Flächenbombardements). 1937 kam es zwischen Soldaten der Guandong Armee und chinesischen Soldaten zu einem erneuten Zwischenfall an der Marco-Polo-Brücke in Peking, der zum Ausbruch des Zweiten Japanisch-Chinesischen Krieges (1937 bis 1945) führte (in Japan 'Japanisch-Chinesischer Krieg', Nichū Sensō, in China 'Antijapanischer Krieg' genannt). Im November 1937 wurde Shanghai schließlich von den Japanern, nach einem verbittert geführten Kampf gegen die von der Kuomintang geführten Chinesen, erobert, wobei allerdings die exterritorialen Gebiete (International Settlement und French Concession) respektiert wurden, die erst nach dem 7.12.1941 (Angriff Japans auf die USA, Pearl Harbor) besetzt wurden.

[5] Vgl. Birgit Pansa: *Juden unter japanischer Herrschaft. Jüdische Exilerfahrungen und der Sonderfall Karl Löwith*. München: Iudicium 1999. Diese Untersuchung entstand als Magisterarbeit am Japanologischen Seminar der Universität Heidelberg.

David H. Kranzlers Buch *The Japanese, the Nazis, and the Jews* (1976),[6] stützt, die Bonner Dissertation *Japan und die Juden* von Heinz Eberhard Maul zu nennen.[7] Erwähnt werden sollten auch einige Spezialarbeiten auf diesem Gebiet, nämlich das Buch von Marvin Tokayer und Mary Swartz über den Fugu-Plan, d.h. den Plan bzw. die Pläne der japanischen Regierung, in der japanisch besetzten Mandschurei einen Judenstaat zu errichten,[8] sowie die umfangreiche Untersuchung über stereotype Vorstellungen der Japaner über Juden von David G. Goodman und Miyazawa Masanori und Arbeiten des Historikers Gerhard Krebs, der verschiedene Aufsätze zur Judenpolitik der Japaner und zu ähnlichen Themen veröffentlicht hat.[9]

Was könnten die Gründe dafür sein, daß Japan ein solches 'Desiderat' ist? Ich denke, der wichtigste und offensichtlichste Grund ist der, daß es überhaupt fraglich ist, *ob* Japan überhaupt ein 'Exilland' war. Als Bündnispartner Nazi-Deutschlands erscheint Japan als 'Exilland' eigentlich disqualifiziert; andererseits aber gab es – zumindest in einer bestimmten Phase des Zweiten Weltkriegs – in Japan selbst einige jüdische und politische Flüchtlinge, prominente wie unbekannte, von denen einer, nämlich Karl Löwith, durchaus von "deutschen Emigranten in Japan" sprach.[10] Und zudem befanden sich in Shanghai über 20.000 jüdische Emigranten, die spätestens ab 1941 vollständig den Japanern ausgeliefert waren.

Angesichts dieser widersprüchlichen Situation, daß ein Verbündeter Nazi-Deutschlands dennoch ein Exilland war, wäre von Japan als einem *problematischen* Exilland zu sprechen – und diese Problematik soll hier zunächst unter

---

[6] Vgl. David H. Kranzler: *The Japanese, the Nazis, and the Jews: the Jewish Refugee Committee of Shanghai 1938–1945*. New York: Yeshiva University 1976.

[7] Vgl. Heinz Eberhard Maul: *Japan und die Juden. Die Judenpolitik des Kaiserreiches Japan während der Zeit des Nationalsozialismus (1933–1045)*. Bonn: Univ. Diss. 2000. URL: http://hss.ulb.uni-bonn.de/diss_online/phil_fak/2000/maul_heinz_eberhard.

[8] Vgl. Marvin Tokayer/Mary Swartz: *The Fugu Plan: the Untold Story of the Japanese and the Jews During World War II*. New York: Paddington Press 1979.

[9] Vgl. David Goodman/Masanor Miyazawa: *Jews in the Japanese Mind: the History and Uses of a Cultural Stereotype*. New York: Free Press 1995 und z.B. Gerhard Krebs: Die Juden und der Ferne Osten. In: *Nachrichten der Gesellschaft für Natur- und Völkerkunde Ostasiens (NOAG)* 175–176 (2004). S. 229–270; japanischsprachige Arbeiten zu diesem Thema, wie z.B. Bandō Hiroshis Untersuchung über Japans Politik gegenüber den Juden (vgl. *Nihon no Yudaya jin seisaku. 1931–1935. Gaikō Shiryokan bunsho*. Tōkyō: Miraisha 2002), wurden von mir für diesen Beitrag nicht systematisch ausgewertet.

[10] Vgl. Karl Löwith: *Mein Leben in Deutschland vor und nach 1933. Ein Bericht*. Mit einem Vorwort von Reinhart Koselleck und einer Nachbemerkung von Ada Löwith. Stuttgart: Metzler 1986. S. 115.

drei Aspekten diskutiert werden, nämlich a) dem Aspekt des Verhältnisses Japans zu Deutschlands, b) dem des Images der Juden in Japan und c) dem der historischen Gegebenheiten selbst.

Zunächst zum japanisch-deutschen Verhältnis in den Jahren 1933 bis 1945. Ganz grundsätzlich läßt sich dazu sagen, daß Japans Einstellung zu Deutschland in dieser Zeit ganz und gar *nicht* eindeutig war, sich laufend änderte – und daß von diesen permanenten Veränderungen des Verhältnisses, bei allerdings immer vorhandenen Ambivalenzen, auch die Behandlung der sich im japanischen Machtbereich befindlichen jüdischen Emigranten abhängig war.[11]

Welche Ambivalenzen prägten diese Beziehung zwischen Japan und Nazi-Deutschland? Zunächst gab es auf deutscher Seite aus politisch-strategischen Überlegungen heraus Vorbehalte gegenüber einer zu engen Partnerschaft mit den Japanern; zum anderen existierten auch rassische Vorbehalte.[12] Die beiden Länder waren auch ganz einfach geographisch zu weit voneinander entfernt, um Nachrichten und Waren unproblematisch austauschen oder anderweitig eng miteinander kooperieren zu können. Und so wurde auch, trotz einer ganzen Reihe von Bündnissen, von denen der im September 1940 geschlossene Dreimächtepakt das wichtigste war,[13] zwischen Deutschland und Japan die Kriegsführung nie richtig miteinander koordiniert, weshalb der Historiker

---

[11] So betont z.B. Bernd Martin die 'Vielschichtigkeit dieses Bündnisses', seine 'Wechselfälle' und die 'Rivalitäten und Mißverständnisse', die hier zu finden waren. Vgl. Bernd Martin: *Deutschland und Japan im Zweiten Weltkrieg 1940–1945. Vom Angriff auf Pearl Harbor bis zur deutschen Kapitulation*. Hamburg: Nikol 2001. S. 14.
[12] Als die britische Kolonie Singapore von Hitlers Verbündeten Japan erobert wurde, soll dieser 'die schweren Verluste des weißen Mannes in Ostasien' bedauert haben. Vgl. Martin (wie Anm. 11). S. 70. "Als Rassist war Hitler weit davon entfernt, die Japaner als gleichwertig anzusehen. Er billigte ihnen einen Zwischenstatus als 'kulturtragendes' Volk zu, anders als die 'kulturschöpferischen' Arier, aber immer noch besser als die 'kulturzerstörenden' Juden". Gerhard Krebs: Antisemitismus und Judenpolitik der Japaner. In: Armbrüster/Kohlstruck/Mühlberger (wie Anm. 3). S. 58–73. Hier S. 62. Es gab auch Diskriminierungen von Japanern und von Kindern aus deutsch-japanischen Ehen in Deutschland. "Die Japaner befürchteten, als 'Farbige' selbst Opfer des deutschen Rassewahns zu werden, und äußerten sich wiederholt voller Sorge gegenüber Deutschland". Krebs (wie Anm. 3). S. 241. Erst die Nürnberger Gesetze von 1935 beruhigten die Japaner etwas, da in ihnen ausschließlich die Juden als 'Nicht-Arier' definiert wurden; trotzdem blieb natürlich der deutsche Rassismus im Alltag bestehen. Ähnlich war es aber auch auf japanischer Seite; auch hier gab es Vorbehalte gegenüber der 'weißen Rasse'. Vgl. Martin (wie Anm. 11). S. 47.
[13] Zwischen Deutschland, Italien und Japan.

Bernd Martin zu der grundsätzlichen Einschätzung kommt: "Der Weltkrieg wurde von Deutschland und Japan getrennt geführt".[14]

Diese Uneindeutigkeiten, Distanzen und Ambivalenzen, die für das deutsch-japanische Kriegsbündnis kennzeichnend waren, lassen es verständlich erscheinen, daß Japan keineswegs in Hinsicht auf die Umgehensweise mit jüdischen Emigranten als Erfüllungsgehilfe Nazi-Deutschlands anzusehen ist, sondern einen eigenständigen Kurs hatte, der nicht zuletzt auch von dem traditionellen Image der Juden in Japan bestimmt war.

Versucht man dieses Image zu ergründen, so ist zunächst festzustellen, daß es in Japan, anders als etwa in China, keine 'alteingesessenen' Juden gab;[15] erst nach der erzwungenen Öffnung des Landes in der Mitte des 19. Jahrhunderts ließen sich einige jüdische Kaufleute in japanischen Hafenstädten nieder, doch traten diese in den Augen der Japaner nicht als eine besondere Gruppe in Erscheinung.[16]

Das Image der Juden in Japan wurde wesentlich durch ein Ereignis im Zusammenhang mit dem japanisch-russischen Krieg von 1904/05 geprägt: Damals kaufte ein amerikanischer Kaufmann jüdischer Herkunft, der in Deutschland geborene Jacob H. Schiff (1847–1920), der u.a. als Direktor für New Yorker Banken arbeitete, japanische Kriegsanleihen im Wert von rund zweihundert Millionen Dollar, die den Krieg Japans gegen Rußland, der für Japan siegreich enden sollte, finanzierten; er war über antijüdische Pogrome im zaristischen Rußland erzürnt und unterstützte deshalb Japan.[17] Er erhielt später als erster Ausländer überhaupt eine Einladung zu einem Essen im kaiserlichen Palast in Tokio und eine hohe japanische Auszeichnung.[18] Dieser

---

[14] Martin (wie Anm. 11). S. 15. An anderer Stelle schreibt er: "Wie die Deutschen, so verfolgten auch die Japaner nur ihre eigenen Pläne und übersahen dabei die Chance, einen Weltkrieg zu führen und möglicherweise zu gewinnen". S. 110. Darüber kann man ja nur froh sein! Deutlichster Ausdruck für diese unkoordinierte Vorgehensweise ist die sogenannte 'Teilung der Welt' entlang des 70 Grades östlicher Länge, die im Anschluß an den Dreimächtepakt in einer Militärkonvention ein Jahr später zwischen Italien, Deutschland und Japan vorgenommen wurde. Der politische Zweck dieser militärischen Teilung der Operationsbereiche lag auf Seiten der Japaner in der Schaffung einer 'großasiatischen Wohlstandssphäre', aus der die Weißen – eben auch die Deutschen – möglichst herausgehalten werden sollten.

[15] In China tauchten bereits im 7. Jahrhundert, vielleicht auch schon eher, Juden auf, vor allem als Händler. Ihre größte Gemeinde war in Kaifeng (wahrscheinlich im 10. Jahrhundert gegründet). Vgl. Krebs (wie Anm. 9). S. 231.

[16] Die ersten Japaner, die deutschsprachige Literatur und Kultur rezipierten, unterschieden nicht zwischen jüdischen und nicht-jüdischen deutschsprachigen Autoren und Künstlern.

[17] Vgl. Krebs (wie Anm. 9). S. 237.

[18] Vgl. Geoffrey Wigoder: *Dictionary of Jewish Biography*. New York: Simon & Schuster 1991. S. 461.

Kaufmann begründete den Ruf, den die Juden in Japan hatten – und eigentlich bis heute haben, daß sie nämlich finanziell und politisch äußerst mächtig seien. Aber im täglichen Leben hatte man in Japan kaum mit Juden zu tun; zwar siedelten sich in einigen Hafenstädten wie Nagasaki, Yokohama und Kobe im Laufe der Zeit einige Juden an, die dort auch Synagogen gründeten.[19] Aber das fiel nicht weiter auf, lag doch "die Gesamtzahl der in Japan lebenden Juden […] um 1930 bei [nicht] mehr als fünfhundert".[20]

Trotz dieser verschwindend geringen Zahl beschäftigten aber Juden das japanische Denken auf ganz merkwürdige Weisen, so z.B. in der Vorstellung, daß das japanische Volk vom jüdischen abstamme. Dies hatte der schottische Geschäftsmann Norman McLeod 1879 behauptet;[21] eine Idee, die von einigen Japanern aufgegriffen wurde und sich bis heute erhalten hat,[22] wie z.B. Internet-Seiten zum Stichwort *Jewish Japan* zeigen, auf denen diese Idee sehr ernst genommen wird.[23]

Demgegenüber gab es aber in Japan, vor allem in Kreisen des Militärs, antisemitische Denkweisen, die man aus Europa und vor allem aus Rußland übernommen hatte. Ein Beispiel dafür ist der japanische General Shiōden Nobutaka (1878–1962), der seit einem Aufenthalt in Frankreich antisemitisch eingestellt war und enge Kontakte mit Nazis in Deutschland pflegte.[24] Shiōden gründete 1937,

---

[19] Die erste Synagoge in Japan wurde von russischen Juden um 1861 in Nagasaki gegründet (vgl. *Encyclopedia of Zionism and Israel*. Vol. 1. Ed. by Raphael Patai. New York: Herzl Press/Mc Graw-Hill 1971. S. 603).
[20] Pansa (wie Anm. 5). S. 17.
[21] Vgl. Norman McLeod: *Epitome of the Ancient History of Japan*. Nagasaki: Printed at the Rising Sun Office 1879 und dazu: Renate Giacomuzzi-Pütz: Abenteuer in Japan (1938) von Max Brod. In: *Ostasienrezeption im Schatten der Weltkriege. Universalismus und Nationalismus*. Hg. von Walter Gebhard. München: Iudicium 2003. S. 161–186. Hier: S. 176ff.
[22] Hier sind die Aktivitäten des Theologen und Kirchengründers Nakada Jūjis (1870–1939) zu nennen (vgl. Pansa (wie Anm. 5). S. 21). Diese Vorstellung schlug zuweilen aber in Antisemitismus um, wenn etwa Sakai Katsuisa (1870–1939), der allerdings umgekehrt die Abstammung der Juden von den Japanern postulierte, daraus folgerte, daß die Japaner die Juden bekämpfen und beherrschen müßten, um ihnen dann gewissermaßen eine Kooperation aufzuzwingen (vgl. Isaiah Ben-Dasan: *The Japanese and the Jews*. New York: Weatherhill 1972).
[23] Vgl. z.B. URL: http://www.haruth.com/Jews.Japan.html. In diesem Zusammenhang wird oft die These variiert, daß die Japaner Nachkommen einer der verlorenen zehn Stämme Israels seien, Juden und Japaner also gemeinsame Vorfahren haben sollen.
[24] 1936 übersetzte er die *Protokolle der Weisen von Zion* ins Japanische; 1938 besuchte er den Reichsparteitag in Nürnberg, wo er u.a. mit Alfred Rosenberg und Julius Streicher zusammentraf. Shiōden bezeichnete sich selbst als 'Streicher von Asien' (vgl. Louis W. Bondy: *Racketeers of Hatred: Julius Streicher and the Jew-Baiters' International*. London: Newman Wolsey Limited 1946. S. 245). Nach dem Zweiten Weltkrieg wurde Shioden als Kriegsverbrecher eingestuft, aber nicht bestraft.

mit Unterstützung des japanischen Außenministeriums, eine antisemitische Vereinigung, die *Studiengruppe für Internationale Politik und Wirtschaft (Kokusai Seikei Gakkai)*.[25] Jedoch wurde dieser größtenteils importierte Antisemitismus oft durch japanische Ambivalenzen gefiltert, was ich gleich an einem Beispiel zeigen möchte.

Die Frage des japanisch-jüdischen Verhältnisses stellte sich in den 1930er Jahren immer dringlicher, waren doch durch die japanischen Besetzungen der Mandschurei 1931/32, Nordchinas und vor allem Shanghais 1937 ca. 70.000 Juden in den japanischen Machtbereich gekommen, zu denen dann auch noch die jüdischen Emigranten zu zählen sind, die nach Shanghai oder dann eben direkt nach Japan – und dann zumeist weiter in andere Länder – flohen.[26] Japan wurde nach den antisemitischen Ausschreitungen in Deutschland im November 1938 mit einer Emigrantenwelle aus Deutschland konfrontiert, da deutsche Staatsbürger – und zu dieser Zeit wurden deutsche Juden noch als deutsche Staatsbürger angesehen – für Japan kein Visum benötigten.[27] Juden, die in sogenannter 'Schutzhaft' waren, wurden entlassen, wenn sie nachweisen konnten, z.B. nach Shanghai auswandern zu können.[28]

---

[25] Vgl. Ebd. S. 246 und Maul (wie Anm. 7). S. 47; wie Maul hier schreibt, hatte diese Vereinigung auch Büros im Ausland, z.B. in Shanghai, wo ein 'Büro für Jüdische Angelegenheiten' 1940 eröffnet wurde.

[26] In der Mandschurei und Nordchina lebten rund 27.000 Juden, meist kamen sie aus Rußland; in Shanghai lebten rund 18.000 Juden, hinzukamen rund 20.000 Flüchtlinge während des Zweiten Weltkrieges.

[27] Das 'Reichsbürgergesetz' vom 15. September 1939 (zu den sogenannten 'Nürnberger Gesetzen' gehörend) führte zwar den Unterschied zwischen 'Staatsangehörigen minderen Rechts' (Juden) und 'Reichsbürgern' (Ariern) ein, entzog den deutschen Juden jedoch noch nicht die deutsche Staatsangehörigkeit. Mit der 'Elften Verordnung zum Reichsbürgergesetz' vom 25. November 1941 wurde Juden, die ihren 'gewöhnlichen Aufenthalt im Ausland' hatten, die deutsche Staatsangehörigkeit aberkannt; die 'Zwölfte Verordnung' zu diesem Gesetz (vom 25. April 1943) aberkannte Juden generell die deutsche Staatsbürgerschaft (vgl. URL: http://www.verfassungen.de/de/de33-45/reichsbuerger35-v11.htm und http://www.verfassungen.de/de/de33-45/reichsbuerger35-v12.htm. "Japan wollte die überwiegende Mehrheit der Juden von seinem Machtbereich fernhalten, hatte aber keine juristischen Mittel, den Zuzug völlig zu verhindern (...). Noch bekannte sich die [japanische] Regierung zu dem Beschluß der Nichtdiskriminierung von Juden, wie Außenminister Arita im Februar 1939 vor dem Parlament erklärte". Krebs (wie Anm. 9). S. 66.

[28] Ein Beispiel dafür ist Hugo Burkhard, der nach siebenjähriger Haft 1940 aus Buchenwald entlassen wurde und nach Shanghai emigrierte. Vgl. Hugo Burkhard: *Tanz mal Jude! Meine Erlebnisse in den Konzentrationslagern Dachau, Buchenwald, Getto Shanghai 1933–1948*. 2. Aufl. Nürnberg: Reichenbach 1967. S. 141.

Diese ambivalente, unentschieden zwischen Philo- und Antisemitismus pendelnde japanische Haltung gegenüber den Juden möchte ich kurz an einem Beispiel veranschaulichen: Es geht um einen Obersten der japanischen Armee, Yasue Senkō (auch unter dem Namen Yasue Norihiro bekannt) (1888–1950), der in den 1920er Jahren in Sibirien stationiert war, um antikommunistischen Russen, die zugleich ausgesprochen antisemitisch eingestellt waren, im Kampf gegen die Bolschewisten zu helfen. Nach seiner Rückkehr nach Japan setzte Yasue seine antisemitischen 'Studien', wenn man das so nennen will, fort und übersetzte die *Protokolle der Weisen von Zion* aus dem Russischen ins Japanische, dieses bekannte fiktive antisemitische Pamphlet, welches eine jüdische Weltverschwörung behauptet und von dem man sagt, daß seine Autoren in den Kreisen der zaristischen Geheimpolizei zu suchen seien.[29] Erstaunlicherweise war – und ist! – die Rezeption der *Protokolle* in Japan allerdings nicht durchweg antisemitisch. Immer wieder wird berichtet, daß Japaner die in den *Protokollen* behauptete 'jüdische Weltverschwörung' als ein positives Modell aufgefaßt hätten, dem man sogar nacheifern sollte, um weltweit Einfluß zu gewinnen.[30]

Yasue galt durch diese Übersetzung eines antisemitischen Machwerkes in den Kreisen der japanischen Politik und des japanischen Heeres als Fachmann für Judenfragen und wurde in dieser Eigenschaft 1926 nach Palästina geschickt, wo er wichtige Führer der zionistischen Bewegung traf und sogar eine Zeitlang in einem Kibbuz lebte. 1938 wurde Yasue dann Verbindungsmann zwischen der japanischen Regierung und dem *Fernöstlichen jüdischen Rat*, der 1937 von Juden in der Mandschurei gegründet worden war. Dieser *Jüdische Rat* veranstaltete drei Konferenzen, und auf der dritten Konferenz in der nordchinesischen Stadt Harbin trat Yasue als Redner auf und wurde von dem jüdischen

---

[29] Ein anderer einflußreicher japanischer 'Experte' für Judenfragen war Kapitän zur See Inuzuku Koreshige (1890–1965).
[30] So erzählt Hadassa Ben-Itto in seinem Buch über die *Protokolle* eine Anekdote, die Professor Ben-Ami Shillony, dem Leiter der Ostasiatischen Studien der Hebräischen Universität Jerusalem (und Autor grundlegender Bücher und Aufsätze über das japanisch-jüdische Verhältnis. Vgl. vor allem sein Buch *The Jews and the Japanese. The Succesful Outsiders*. Rutland, VT/Tokyo: Charles E. Tuttle Company 1992), widerfuhr: Als dieser 1978 nämlich einmal japanische Gäste hatte, Geschäftsleute und Professoren, überreichten ihm diese eine gebundene Fassung der *Protokolle* als wohlgemeintes Gastgeschenk. Die Japaner hatten, in Vorbereitung ihrer Israel-Reise, dieses Buch gelesen und "sie waren voller Bewunderung für die Juden, weil sie den in dem Buch dargelegten anspruchsvollen Plan mit so großem Erfolg in die Tat umsetzen". Hadassa Ben-Itto: *Die Protokolle der Weisen von Zion. Anatomie einer Fälschung*. Berlin: Aufbau Verlag 1998. S. 372.

Vorsitzenden des Rates, Dr. Abraham Kaufman (1885–1971), "öffentlich für seine Hilfe den Juden gegenüber gelobt".[31] Kaufman waren natürlich die antisemitischen Aktivitäten und Denkweisen Yasues nicht bekannt.[32]

Diese Haltung Yasues erscheint mir ganz symptomatisch für die japanische Einstellung überhaupt gewesen zu sein, die sich dadurch kennzeichnen läßt, daß sie versucht, etwas miteinander zu verbinden, was aus anderer Perspektive schlechthin unvereinbar ist, nämlich, wie in diesem Fall, Antisemitismus mit Philosemitismus.[33]

Diese merkwürdige Haltung zeigte sich auch an einer wichtigen Konferenz japanischer Minister, die nach den Pogromen, die in Deutschland am 9./10. November 1938 stattgefunden hatten (sogenannte 'Reichskristallnacht') und nach dem deutsch-japanischen Kulturabkommen (vom 25.11.1938), abgehalten wurde.[34] Thema der Konferenz war, wie Japan nun mit den Juden umgehen sollte, vor allem auch mit denjenigen Juden, die nach Japan emigrieren wollten. Einige der Minister traten für einen jüdischen Staat unter japanischer Herrschaft in der Mandschurei ein; das war der sogenannte 'Fugu Plan', genannt nach dem japanischen Fugu-Fisch, der als Delikatesse gilt, aber tödlich sein kann, wenn er nicht richtig zubereitet ist. Schon diese Bezeichnung zeigt die japanischen Ambivalenzen, die sich mit dieser Idee verbanden: Einerseits erhoffte man sich Aufschwung für die japanische Wirtschaft durch einen solchen wahrscheinlich prosperierenden jüdischen Staat; auch erwartete man reiche Investitionen amerikanischer Juden dort und überhaupt das Wohlwollen der USA, die man als weitgehend von den Juden kontrolliert ansah; andererseits fürchtete man, daß die Juden sich in die japanische Wirtschaft und Politik einmischen und die Herrschaft übernehmen

---

[31] Pansa (wie Anm. 5). S. 29.

[32] Kaufmann wurde dann, durch Vermittlung Yasues nach Tokio eingeladen und von japanischen Politikern empfangen, die ihm noch Ende der 1930er Jahre alle versicherten, "daß Japaner antisemitisches Gedankengut ablehnten und daß der japanische Staat vielmehr eine philosemitische Politik betreibe". Birgit Pansa (wie Anm. 5). S. 29. Es war nun nicht etwa so, daß Yasue durch den Kontakt mit 'wirklichen' Juden seine antisemitischen Einstellungen abgelegt hätte – nein, keineswegs, denn auch während seiner Zeit der guten Zusammenarbeit mit jüdischen Organisationen schrieb er unter einem Pseudonym weiterhin antisemitische Hetzschriften.

[33] Die Unvereinbarkeit dieser beiden Haltungen *in concreto* bleibt auch dann bestehen, wenn man eine gemeinsame Wurzel beider Haltungen anerkennt. Vgl. zu diesem Problem u.a. Frank Stern: *Im Anfang war Auschwitz. Antisemitismus und Philosemitismus im deutschen Nachkrieg*. Gerlingen: Bleicher 1991; und *Gerüchte über die Juden. Antisemitismus, Philosemitismus und aktuelle Verschwörungstheorien*. Hg. von Hanno Loewy. Essen: Klartext 2005.

[34] Diese Konferenz trägt den Namen 'goshō kaigi'/'Fünf-Minister-Konferenz'. Vgl. Pansa (wie Anm. 5). S. 48ff.

würden – Lektürenfolgen der "Protokolle"! Die Konferenz endete damit, daß man diese Ansiedlungspläne weiter verfolgen wollte, ohne sie jedoch zu konkretisieren. Als Konsens wurde folgendes festgehalten:

> Unsere diplomatischen Verbindungen zu Deutschland und Italien machen es nötig, eine Distanz zum jüdischen Volk zu wahren, da dieses von unseren Alliierten abgelehnt wird [...], aber wir sollten die Juden nicht in der Form ablehnen, wie es unsere Alliierten tun [...]. Dies ist von besonderer Bedeutung angesichts unseres Wunsches, Amerika nicht zu verärgern und ausländisches Kapital nach Japan zu holen.[35]

Dieser Wunsch – und damit auch der Fugu-Plan – wurde dann mit der Veränderung der japanischen Politik, die im Angriff auf Pearl Harbor kulminierte, obsolet. Diese historischen Entwicklungen sollen jetzt noch kurz erörtert werden.

Betrachtet man die historische Entwicklung, so ist dieses Datum, der 7.12.1941, der Tag des japanischen Angriffs auf Pearl Harbor, von entscheidender Bedeutung: Man kann die japanische Einstellung zu den jüdischen Emigranten ganz klar in ein *vor* und *nach* Pearl Harbor einteilen, d.h. nach Pearl Harbor verschlechterte sich die japanische Einstellung zu den Juden und zu anderen Emigranten und eben auch ihre konkrete Behandlung ganz erheblich. Dieser Kriegseintritt Japans kam für die Ausländer in Japan ganz überraschend.[36]

Für die japanische Haltung zu den Juden *vor* Pearl Harbor mag ein Bericht vom März 1939 des Pressebeirates der deutschen Botschaft in Tokio kennzeichnend sein, in dem sich deutsche Diplomaten über die Japaner beklagten. Es heißt da in diesem Bericht,

> dass das Judenproblem in Japan relativ neu sei und ihm noch nicht mit ausreichenden Maßnahmen begegnet würde. Am stärksten seien die Juden unter Künstlern – vor allem Musikern – und Gelehrten vertreten, unter Lehrern, Professoren und Ärzten. Die am meisten gelesenen Bücher in deutscher Sprache seien Erzeugnisse von Juden und Judengenossen, besonders Schnitzler, Wassermann, Feuchtwanger sowie Thomas und Heinrich Mann.[37]

Man kann sagen, daß in dem, wenn auch relativ kurzen Zeitraum, 1938 bis 1941, Japan viele jüdische Emigranten aufnahm bzw. ihnen ermöglichte, den Nazis zu

---

[35] Zit. nach Pansa (wie Anm. 5). S. 50.
[36] Klaus Pringsheim jun. (1923–2001) beschreibt dies so: "Über Nacht veränderte sich das Klima in Tokio. Aufruhr und Entsetzen herrschte unter der ausländischen Bevölkerung. Von einem Tag auf den anderen wurden Bewohner des Landes zu Kriegsgegnern. Amerikaner, Briten und Kanadier wurden als erste eingesperrt oder interniert und dann auf der schwedischen *Gripsholm* oder anderen Schiffen abgeschoben". Klaus Pringsheim jun.: *Wer zum Teufel sind Sie? Lebenserinnerungen.* Bonn: Weidle 1995, S. 49.
[37] Krebs (wie Anm. 9). S. 63.

entkommen. Vielleicht nur für diesen kurzen historischen Zeitraum verdient Japan die Bezeichnung 'Exilland'. In diesem Zusammenhang sind auch die Aktivitäten des japanischen Konsuls in Litauen, Sugihara Chiune (1900–1986),[38] zu nennen, der vielen jüdischen Flüchtlingen besonders aus Polen ab 1940 Ausreisevisa erstellte (es sollen täglich über hundert gewesen sein), mit denen sie vor allem in die japanische Hafenstadt Kobe gelangen konnten.[39]

Es gibt viele Berichte von dem doch relativ guten Empfang der jüdischen Flüchtlinge in Kobe, wo sie auch von jüdischen Organisationen, wie dem *National Council of Jews in East Asia* und dem *Jewish Committee of Kōbe*, unterstützt wurden. Kobe funktionierte deshalb als gute Anlaufstation, da sich dort seit dem Ende des 19. Jahrhunderts einige Juden aus Harbin und Shanghai niedergelassen und eine kleine jüdische Gemeinschaft gegründet hatten. Sie organisierte sich unter dem Namen JEWCOM und half den Emigranten.[40]

Ich denke, daß 'Kobe' gewissermaßen für die japanische 'Exilpolitik' beispielhaft ist: 'Kobe' bedeutete kein Ziel, wie die USA, sondern nur eine 'Transitstation': Bis November 1941 waren so gut wie alle Flüchtlinge, die

---

[38] Es mag hier erwähnenswert sein, daß der gegenwärtige japanische Kaiser Akihito Sugihara ausdrücklich würdigte und damit in dem engen Rahmen, der ihm für politische Aktivitäten ermöglicht ist, doch deutlich andere Akzente setzt als etwa der gegenwärtige japanische Premierminister Abe Shinzō: Während Abe eine revisionistische Politik pflegt, die die japanische Kriegsvergangenheit in einem verklärenden, von allen problematischen und kriegsverbrecherischen Aktivitäten gereinigten Licht darzustellen versucht (vgl. dazu z.B. den kritischen Artikel von Francis Fukuyama: Abe needlessly fans the flames. In: *The Japan Times*. March 29, 2007. URL: http://search.japantimes.co.jp/print/eo20070329a2.html), ehrte Kaiser Akihito bei seinem Besuch in Litauen im Mai 2007 Sugihara, indem er und Kaiserin Michiko ein Monument zum Gedenken an Sugihara in Vilnius besuchten (vgl. Yasuhiko Shima: Emperor honors 'Japan's Schindler'. In: *Asahi Shinbun*. May 28, 2007. URL: http://www.asahi.com/english/Herald-asahi/TKY200705280065.html). Dies bedeutet eine späte Anerkennung der Aktivitäten Sugiharas, der immerhin nach dem Krieg aus dem Außenministerium, wohl wegen seiner unerlaubten Visaausstellungen, entlassen wurde.

[39] Diese Visa waren Transitvisa für Japan, mit dem offiziellen Ziel Curaçao, einer karibischen Insel, die kein Einreisevisum forderte. Es war aber klar, daß niemand zu dieser Insel weiterreisen würde. Obwohl das japanische Außenministerium diese Ausgabepraxis Sugiharas kritisierte, wurden von Japan die von ihm ausgestellten Visa akzeptiert, d.h. viele Flüchtlinge konnten durch die Sowjetunion nach Kobe reisen (was bis etwa Ende 1941 ging; durch Hitlers Angriff auf die Sowjetunion wurde den Flüchtlingen dieser Weg abgeschnitten), von dort weiter in die USA oder nach Palästina oder mußten in Japan bleiben und wurden dann später nach Shanghai deportiert, wo sie zwar unter sehr schlechten Lebensbedingungen leben mußten, aber nicht verfolgt und getötet wurden.

[40] Der Präsident dieses Hilfskomitees war der russische Textilhändler Anatol Ponve (Poniversky).

nach Kobe gekommen waren, weitergereist. Bot diese 'Transitstation' den Flüchtlingen zwar keinen sicheren Daueraufenthalt, so doch immerhin die Möglichkeit des Weiterreisens.[41]

Pearl Harbor bedeutete dann einen Einschnitt: Die Ausweitung des Krieges zum Weltkrieg und auch die Tatsache, daß Japan und Deutschland nun, mit dem Kriegseintritt der USA, einer erdrückenden Übermacht gegenüberstanden, schloß diese so ungleichen Bündnispartner nach Pearl Harbor und der kurz danach, am 11.12.1941, ergangenen deutschen Kriegserklärung an die USA noch einmal enger zusammen. Da diese Zusammenarbeit aber auf Grund der geographischen, militärischen und technischen Gegebenheiten auf diesen Gebieten kaum zu verwirklichen war, war dieser Zusammenschluß vor allem ein ideologischer, betraf also auch die japanischen Einstellungen zu den Juden.[42] Nach Pearl Harbor kam es zur Verhaftung von Ausländern generell und von Juden im besonderen. Berichtet wird von menschenunwürdigen Zuständen und auch von Folterungen.[43] Obwohl sich die Lage für die deutschjüdischen Emigranten in Japan z.B. in beruflicher Hinsicht verschlechterte, wurden sie jedoch nicht nach Deutschland ausgeliefert, da es zwischen Deutschland und Japan kein Auslieferungsabkommen gab.

Allerdings versuchten deutsche Stellen immer wieder auf die Japaner Druck in Hinsicht auf die Diskriminierung und Verfolgung der Emigranten auszuüben: Für diesen verschärften Kurs ist die Entsendung des sogenannten Polizeiattachés – in Wirklichkeit: Gestapo-Attachés – Josef Meisingers (1899–1947) von Deutschland nach Japan im Jahre 1941 bezeichnend.[44] Meisinger, Oberst der deutschen Polizei und SS-Standartenführer, nach dem

---

[41] Vgl. Pansa (wie Anm. 5). S. 61.

[42] Zu den ideologisch-kulturellen Beziehungen zwischen Japan und Nazi-Deutschland vgl. Thomas Pekar: Fatale Interkulturalität. Nationalsozialistische deutsche Heldenideologie und der japanische Bushido-Diskurs. In: *Ostasienrezeption im Schatten der Weltkriege. Universalismus und Nationalsozialismus.* Hg. von Walter Gebhard. München: Iudicium 2003. S. 109–128.

[43] Die Gefängniszellen waren oft überbelegt und ansteckende Krankheiten, wie Typhus, grassierten. Über Torturen in japanischen Gefängnissen berichtet z.B. Burkhard: "Der Gefangene hatte sich in der vorgeschriebenen Weise, mit gekreuzten Beinen, auf den kalten Zementboden zu setzen, ohne daß ihm während des Tages nur einmal erlaubt gewesen wäre, sich aufzurichten oder die abgestorbenen Gliedmaßen etwas zu strecken". Vgl. Burkhard (wie Anm. 28). S. 152. Ähnlich schreibt Klaus Pringsheim, der in Tokio inhaftiert war, über den "Zwang, den ganzen Tag aufrecht dasitzen zu müssen" (vgl. Klaus Pringsheim jun. (wie Anm. 36). S. 76) und darüber, nicht genügend Essen zu bekommen.

[44] 1943 wurde dann auch der gemäßigte deutsche Botschafter General Eugen Ott (1889–1977; ab 1938 Botschafter in Japan) durch den Parteigenossen Heinrich Georg Stahmer abgelöst. Vgl. Martin (wie Anm. 11). S. 122ff.

Krieg 1947 in Warschau als Kriegsverbrecher hingerichtet, wurde auch 'Schlächter von Warschau' genannt, da er in Polen Massenerschießungen hatte durchführen lassen.

Seine Aufgaben waren die Überwachung der Deutschen in Japan und die Intervention bei japanischen Stellen, um gegen Juden vorzugehen. Dazu reiste er u.a. nach Shanghai.

Wenn ein Historiker über ihn heute so urteilt – "Er bewirkte allerdings kaum etwas, abgesehen von der gläubigen Aufnahme deutscher Propagandathesen in einigen isolierten Zirkeln".[45] – so halte ich dies für ein krasses Fehlurteil, denn einmal verloren viele Emigranten, wie z.B. Löwith, nach 1941 ihre berufliche Stellung und waren gezwungen, Japan zu verlassen; zum anderen richteten die Japaner dann am 18.5.1943 in Shanghai ein jüdisches Ghetto ein. Sie verfügten, daß alle nach 1937 eingewanderten 'Flüchtlinge' in einen 'ausgewiesenen Bezirk' (die Japaner vermieden in ihrer Proklamation, mit der sie dies verfügten, sowohl das Wort 'Jude' als auch das Wort 'Ghetto', obwohl es sich bei den 'Flüchtlingen' fast ausschließlich um Juden handelte und der 'Bezirk' faktisch zum 'Ghetto' gemacht wurde) umziehen mußten, der im chinesischen Stadtteil Hongkou lag. In diesem etwa 2,5 km^2 großen Ghetto, welches man nur mit Genehmigung der japanischen Militärbehörden verlassen durfte, mußten bis zum Kriegsende ca. 20.000 jüdische Flüchtlinge unter menschenunwürdigen Bedingungen leben.[46] Parallel zur Ghettoisierung wurden auch neue Pässe für Juden ausgestellt, "in denen ein 'yu' für 'yudayajin', Jude, vermerkt wurde".[47] Immer wieder wird von Augenzeugen in diesem Zusammenhang auf den japanischen Leiter der Paßausgabeabteilung, einen Offizier namens Goya, verwiesen, der sich selbst 'König der Juden' nannte und eine Art Willkürherrschaft in Hinsicht auf die überlebensnotwendige Paßausgabe ausübte.

---

[45] Krebs (wie Anm. 9). S. 71.
[46] Ein Augenzeuge, Hugo Burkhard, schreibt darüber: "Wir bekamen Ausweise, auf denen die Zeit verzeichnet war, wann wir das Ghetto verlassen konnten und wieder zurück sein mußten. Außerdem hatten wir, sichtbar an unseren Kleidern, ein kleines rundes, medaillonartiges Abzeichen zu tragen (…). Wir waren also wieder einmal gekennzeichnet. Diesmal nicht mit dem Davidstern, dafür mit einer Blechmarke". Burkhard (wie Anm. 28). S. 155. Auf diesen Blechmarken befindet sich, wie die Abbildung bei Burkhard (S. 165) zeigt, das sinojapanische Zeichen, welches zum japanischen Verb *tōru* bzw. *tōsu* gehört, was 'hindurchgehen' bzw. 'passieren lassen' bedeutet. Im Unterschied zum sogenannten 'Judenstern' in Deutschland war diese Blechmarke also keine explizit 'rassische' Markierung.
[47] Pansa (wie Anm. 5). S. 73.

Es gab auch immer wieder Gerüchte, daß eine Ermordung aller Juden anstehe, die nun allerdings nicht stattfand. Wenn sich die Lebensbedingungen im Shanghaier Ghetto gegen Kriegsende auch drastisch verschlimmert hatte, so entgingen die Menschen dort doch ihrer Ermordung und konnten dann nach Kriegsende zumeist in die USA ausreisen.[48]

So viel wird man sagen können: Es gab immerhin in Japan einflußreiche Kreise, bei denen ein solcher ‚hardliner' wie Meisinger, der mit dem Hauptgrund nach Japan geschickt wurde, dort bzw. in Shanghai die Ermordung der Juden durchzusetzen, offene Ohren fand. Ob diese Japaner dann aber auch bereit gewesen wären, die Ermordung der Shanghaier und anderer Juden in Ostasien, die der japanischen Herrschaft unterstanden, wirklich durchzuführen, wenn der Krieg noch länger fortgedauert hätte – darüber kann man natürlich nur spekulieren. In den von Nazi-Deutschland kontrollierten Gebieten Europas war es jedenfalls so gewesen, daß die Ghettoisierung der Juden *immer* ihrer Deportation und Ermordung vorausgegangen war.[49]

Es sollen nun einige konkrete Emigrantenschicksale in Japan unter der anfangs entwickelten Fragestellung nach den 'Kultur-Texten des Exils' thematisiert werden.

Bekanntere Emigranten in Japan waren zunächst einmal Musiker wie z.B. der Violinist Robert Pollak (1880–1962),[50] der Komponist, Dirigent und

---

[48] "Die Situation im Shanghaier Judenghetto verschlechterte sich [gegen Kriegsende] zunehmend, immer mehr ähnelte sie den Verhältnissen in den Konzentrationslagern jener Zeit. Die Menschen liefen in Säcken durch die überfüllten Straßen und kämpften gegen Hunger, Kälte und Seuchen ums nackte Überleben". Ebd. S. 75ff.
[49] Nach dem Zweiten Weltkrieg verhielten sich die Antisemiten in Japan zunächst einmal recht unauffällig. Wer während der Kriegsjahre sich öffentlich pro-nationalistisch und antisemitisch geäußert hatte, wurde in den ersten Jahren nach dem Krieg weitgehend gemieden. Mitte der 1980er Jahre erlebte Japan jedoch einen regelrechten Boom an antisemitischer Literatur – und zwar dies im Zusammenhang mit wachsenden wirtschaftlichen Spannungen zu den USA. Daran sieht man, daß im Grunde immer noch dieses alte Image in Japan vorherrscht, daß die Juden politisch und finanziell so einflußreich seien, daß sie also gewissermaßen einen Wirtschaftskrieg gegen Japan anzuzetteln in der Lage seien. Trotz alldem – ich besuchte vor einigen Monaten einmal die sehr kleine jüdische Gemeinde in Tokio und konnte dort mit einem älteren Gemeindemitglied, mit Ernest Salomon, dem ehemaligen Präsidenten der Jüdischen Gemeinschaft in Japan sprechen, der seit den 1950er Jahren in Tokio lebt – und er sagte mir, daß er in all diesen Jahren, also in rund 50 Jahren, keinen einzigen antisemitischen Zwischenfall in Japan erlebt habe. Dies ist doch ein recht beruhigendes Zeichen.
[50] Der in Wien geborene Violinist Pollak lebte und lehrte u.a. in Genf, Lausanne, Moskau, Wien und San Francisco, bevor er nach Japan ging. Später lebte er dann in den USA.

Pianist Leonid Kreutzer (1884–1954)[51] und Dirigenten wie Joseph Rosenstock (1895–1985)[52] oder Klaus Pringsheim (1883–1972).[53]

Weiter waren Emigranten Gelehrte, die zum Teil, zumindest zeitweilig, an japanischen Universitäten angestellt waren, wie z.B. der Philosoph Karl Löwith (1897–1973), der sich 1928 bei Martin Heidegger habilitiert hatte und von 1936 bis 1941 in Japan lebte; dort lehrte er in Sendai, an der damals kaiserlichen, heute staatlichen Tōhoku-Universität, Philosophie.[54] In dieser Zeit konnte Löwith in Sendai sein wichtiges, epochemachendes Buch *Von Hegel zu Nietzsche. Der revolutionäre Bruch im Denken des 19. Jahrhunderts* beenden.[55] 1941 mußte er, aufgrund von Interventionen deutscher Nazis in Tokio,[56] zusammen mit seiner Frau Japan verlassen und emigrierte weiter in die USA.[57] Löwith ging dann zunächst in die USA, nach Hartford, wo er am Theologischen Seminar unterrichtete,[58] dann, 1949 nach New York, wo er eine Stelle bei der *New School for Social Research* fand. Nach dem Krieg kehrte Löwith als einer der wenigen Emigranten nach Deutschland zurück und wurde Professor für Philosophie in Heidelberg. Löwith ist wohl, wie dies Birgit Pansa in ihrer Arbeit über ihn

---

[51] Der in St. Petersburg als Sohn deutsch-jüdischer Eltern geborene Kreutzer war seit 1938 in Japan, wo er dann auch, in Tokyo, verstarb.

[52] Rosenstock war von 1936 bis 1946 Dirigent des Staatlichen Japanischen Symphonieorchesters, dem heutigen NHK-Sinfonieorchester.

[53] Klaus Pringsheim sen., Schwager von Thomas Mann, der mit Pringsheims Zwillingsschwester Katia (1883–1980) verheiratet war, wurde in München geboren. 1931 ging er als Dirigent ans Kaiserliche Konservatorium nach Tokio. 1937 mußte er diesen Posten verlassen, lebte dann erst in Thailand, um dann 1939 nach Tokio zurückzukehren, wo er sich mit Unterricht an kleineren Musikhochschulen und Privatunterricht über die Kriegsjahre rettete; vgl. dazu auch die schon oben erwähnten Aufzeichnungen von Klaus Pringsheim jun. der allerdings nicht sein leiblicher Sohn war.

[54] Löwith hatte, nach seiner Habilitation, bis 1933 einen Lehrauftrag in Marburg. 1934 ging er mit einem Stipendium der *Rockefeller Foundation* nach Italien. 1935 wurde ihm sein Marburger Lehrauftrag entzogen. Er war aus seiner Marburger Zeit mit dem japanischen Professor Kuki Shūzō (1888–1941) bekannt, der ihn nach Japan holte. Vgl. Pansa (wie Anm. 5). S. 80ff.

[55] Dieses Buch erschien 1941 in Zürich.

[56] Hierbei tat sich ein gewisser Dr. Donat, als selbsternannter nationalsozialistischer 'Kulturwart', unrühmlich hervor. Walter Donat (1898–1970), ein Japanologe, der sich 1937 mit einer Arbeit über den *Heldenbegriff im Schrifttum der älteren japanischen Geschichte* in Hamburg habilitiert hatte – einem Thema also, welches völlig auf der Linie der nationalsozialistischen Ideologie lag -, wurde 1943 für seine Linientreue belohnt und zum Direktor des von der Berliner Universität und der SS getragenen Ostasieninstituts in Berlin-Dahlem ernannt.

[57] Schon vorher hatte es immer wieder Interventionen des Nationalsozialistischen Lehrerbundes in Japan gegen Löwith gegeben, z.B. beim Rektor der Universität in Sendai, doch hatte man diesem Druck bis 1941 standgehalten.

[58] Freunde wie Paul Tillich und Reinhold Niebuhr hatten ihm zu dieser Stelle verholfen.

schreibt, als 'Sonderfall' aufzufassen,[59] da die guten Lebensbedingungen, die er bis 1941 in Japan hatte, nicht zu vergleichen waren mit den harten und oft unwürdigen Lebensbedingungen der anderen jüdischen Emigranten.

Löwith wurde natürlich allerdings auch nicht als ein solcher Emigrant nach Japan berufen, sondern als ein vielversprechender deutscher Philosoph, zudem Schüler Heideggers. Von Löwith wollte man in Japan, wie er dies selbst ganz richtig erkannte, allein 'europäische Geistesart lernen".[60] Löwith folgte dieser Vorgabe unversehens, ja begrüßte die Möglichkeit, sich *nicht* auf die japanische Welt einstellen zu müssen, durchaus.[61] Wenn man es kritisch sehen will, verpaßte Löwith im Grunde die Chance zu einer inter- oder auch transkulturellen Begegnung mit Japan. Er kam – und ging als Fremder! Als er nach immerhin viereinhalb Jahren Aufenthalt in Japan von dort abreist, schreibt er erleichtert: "Schon auf dem Schiff fällt von uns alles Japanische ab, als hätte man nie damit intensiv zu tun gehabt".[62] Zu fest verwurzelt war er in der westlichen Kultur und Philosophie, zu gesichert war seine Position in Japan, um sich der japanischen Welt wirklich öffnen zu können.[63]

Neben Löwith ist als weiterer ‚Sonderfall' der Schriftsteller und Nationalökonom Kurt Singer (1886–1962) zu nennen, der schon 1931 ganz

---

[59] Vgl. Pansa (wie Anm. 5).
[60] Karl Löwith: Curriculum vitae (1959). In: Karl Löwith (wie Anm. 10). S. 146–157. Hier: S. 152.
[61] Wenn er z.B. schreibt: "Ich hatte (...) in Sendai das unwahrscheinliche Glück, vor japanischen Studenten dort fortfahren zu können, wo ich in Marburg abbrechen mußte" (Ebd. S. 151), so wird er gewiß nicht zunächst die Kenntnisse und die Aufnahmemöglichkeiten dieser japanischen Studenten eruiert haben, sondern er wird einfach seine Vorlesung fortgeführt haben, d.h. wahrscheinlich an den Studenten vorbeigesprochen haben – was man allerdings oft bei japanischen Professoren als eine für ihre Studenten anscheinend notwendige 'Initiation' in 'europäische Geistesart' durchaus schätzt.
[62] Karl Löwith: *Von Rom nach Sendai. Von Japan nach Amerika. Reisetagebuch 1936 und 1941*. Hg. von Klaus Stichweh und Ulrich von Bülow. Mit einem Essay von Adolf Muschg. Marbach: Deutsche Schillergesellschaft 2001. S. 101.
[63] Ich sehe den Hauptgrund für Löwiths Nicht-Annäherung an Japan in seiner dauernden Bezugnahme von japanischen Phänomenen auf die europäische Antike. Dafür ein Beispiel: Löwith schreibt über die japanischen Religionen, Buddhismus und Shintoismus, und führt aus: "Ich habe angesichts der volkstümlichen Konsekration aller natürlichen und alltäglichen Dinge (...) zum ersten Mal auch etwas von dem religiösen Heidentum und der politischen Religion der Griechen und Römer verstanden". Löwith: Curriculum vitae (wie Anm. 10). S. 151. Von Anfang an stand im übrigen sein Japan-Aufenthalt unter dieser *europäischen* Perspektive. So schreibt Löwith anläßlich seiner Abreise von Italien nach Japan emphatisch über Rom, daß ihm dort "Antike und Christentum" beständig vor Augen ständen – und fügt dann bedauernd und sich doch tröstend hinzu: "Aber nun soll alles anders werden – im 'fernen Osten', dessen Ferne einem 'Europa' vielleicht erst wieder nahebringt". Löwith (wie Anm. 62). S. 8.

freiwillig nach Japan reiste, um als außerordentlicher Professor für Nationalökonomie an der kaiserlichen – heute staatlichen – Universität Tokyo zu lehren; 1933 wurde ihm, da er jüdischer Herkunft war, von der Universität Hamburg, wo er sich habilitiert hatte, in Abwesenheit die Lehrbefugnis aberkannt, und in eben diesem Jahr entließ ihn zudem die Universität Tokyo bzw. verlängerte seinen zunächst auf 2 Jahre geschlossenen Vertrag nicht. Auch dafür war, wie bei Löwith, der Druck der *Nationalsozialistischen Lehrervereinigung* und anderer Nazi-Organisationen auf das japanische Kultusministerium entscheidend.[64]

Singer fand dann eine Anstellung als Deutschlehrer an einer Oberschule in Sendai, in eben der Stadt, in der auch Löwith lebte, aber beide hatten kaum Kontakt zueinander. Löwith hielt Singer – obwohl Singer eben auch jüdischer Herkunft war – schlichtweg für einen Faschisten.[65] Singer blieb bis 1939 in Sendai, ging dann nach Australien und starb später vereinsamt in Athen.[66]

Stellvertretend für die viele unbekannten Japan-Emigranten will ich hier auf den 'Emigrations-' und 'Reisebericht' von Ernest R. Stiefel eingehen,[67] der 1921 in Frankfurt/Main geboren wurde und 1940 über Rußland und Japan in die USA emigrierte und später als Soldat gegen Nazi-Deutschland kämpfte.

Stiefel entschloß sich 1940 zu emigrieren und besorgte sich in Berlin eine Broschüre des Norddeutschen Lloyd, datiert vom 25.5.1940, in der die Reiseroute von Berlin nach Tokio, via Sibirien und Mandschurei, genau beschrieben war. Mit Hilfe des 'Jüdischen Hilfsvereins' in Berlin konnte sich Stiefel die verschiedenen Transitvisa und ein Schiffsticket von Yokohama nach San Francisco besorgen. Am 4. Juli 1940 verließ er mit der Eisenbahn Berlin-Charlottenburg, Richtung Moskau. Am 7. Juli ging es von dort aus mit der Transsibirischen Eisenbahn weiter. Am 13. Juli erreichte der Zug die russisch-mandschurische Grenze, an der das japanisch kontrollierte Gebiet begann. Immer wieder notierten Reisende den Unterschied dieses Gebietes zu Rußland; auch Stiefel, der schreibt: "What a difference between Russia and Manchuria [...]. What a hustle and bustle in comparison to the slow, phlegmatic Russians".[68]

Weiter heißt es:

Manchuria, and especially Manchuli, impressed me; the cleanliness, the rush and the activities of the Japanese. The difference between Manchuria and Russia was like day and night.[69]

---

[64] Vgl. Krebs (wie Anm. 9). S. 63.
[65] Vgl. das bei Gerhard Krebs genannte Löwith-Zitat. Krebs (wie Anm. 9). S. 244.
[66] In Australien schrieb Singer ein kenntnisreiches Buch über Japan überhaupt, nämlich *Mirror, Sword and Jewel*; dieses Buch wurde aber erst posthum 1973 in englischer Sprache veröffentlicht – erst 1991 erschien die erste deutschsprachige Ausgabe.
[67] Er befindet sich als Typoskript im New Yorker Leo Baeck Institut (Sigel ME 208; MM 75).
[68] Ebd. S. 91.
[69] Ebd. S. 92.

The train [in Manchuria] and the railroad stations were clean; the train had ventilation and the dining car was appetizing. The countryside looked attractive and one could see that this was a much richer country. The Japanese were well dressed; this was the first time that I saw ladies in kimonos.[70]

Am 15. Juli ging die Fahrt weiter in die Stadt Harbin. Unterwegs traf Stiefel im Zug mandschurische Soldaten: "When they found out that we came from Germany they said 'our friends' ".[71]

Stiefel fiel auf: "I noted that the second class cars on the train looked like the second class cars of the Berlin 'Stadtbahn' (city train)".[72]

In Harbin kümmerte sich ein jüdisches Komitee um die Ankommenden, welches sogar eine Stadtrundfahrt arrangiert hatte, die aber, weil es stark regnete, ausfallen mußte.

Von Harbin wurde die Fahrt dann weiter nach Pusan, der koreanischen Hafenstadt, fortgesetzt, wo er am 18. Juli ankam. Hier hatte er etwas Aufenthalt und schaute sich, zusammen mit anderen Mitreisenden, die Stadt an: "At that time Fusan[73] […] was a very small fishing village. Again the 'natives' [die Koreaner] looked at us as if we had just arrived from Mars".[74]

Am Abend fuhr er mit dem Schiff von Pusan nach Shimonoseki, Japan, von wo es direkt mit dem Zug nach Yokohama weiterging: "Now I was in Japan […]. Our train ride took us along the Japanese riviera, most beautiful scenery. On one side we saw the clear blue Sea of Japan and on the other side mountains, Japanese houses, rice fields under water. I had a very good impression of Japan".[75]

In Kobe, wo Stiefel kurz Aufenthalt hatte und im *Jewish community house* übernachten konnte, traf er einen Frankfurter Bekannten, Dr. Werner Hochheimer, der wohl während des gesamten Krieges in Kobe blieb und später in San Francisco lebte.

Auch in Kobe schilderte er knapp einige Eindrücke:

Japanese children appeared well behaved; they hardly cried even when they were in pain. Traffic in Japan was on the left side, as in England. I also saw billboards with the swastika, the Japanese and Italian flags together. I could not read the contents, they were in Japanese.[76]

Am 22. Juli kam er in Yokohama an, wo er sich gleich auf ein Schiff, die *Hikawa Maru*, einschiffen konnte. Er erreichte dann am 2. August Kanada und wenig später sein endgültiges Reiseziel in den USA.

---

[70] Ebd. S. 94.
[71] Ebd. S. 93f.
[72] Ebd. S. 94.
[73] 'Fusan' ist die japanische Aussprache von 'Pusan'.
[74] Ebd. S. 95.
[75] Ebd. S. 96.
[76] Ebd. S. 98.

Das Erstaunliche an dieser Emigrationsgeschichte ist m.E. eigentlich der relativ unkomplizierte, ja gewissermaßen professionell organisierte Verlauf, der durchaus für diesen Zeitabschnitt typisch war. Die Emigranten waren fast immer froh, nach Rußland japanisch kontrolliertes Gebiet zu erreichen; sie hatten also keineswegs das Gefühl, hier wieder in ein ihnen feindlich gesonnenes Land zu kommen, allenfalls ein Plakat, auf dem die Fahnen der Bündnispartner Japan, Italien und Deutschland zu sehen waren – und dann eben auch das Hakenkreuz – irritierten.

Immer wieder wird auch Freundlichkeit der Einheimischen und natürlich auch das Staunen der Chinesen, Koreaner und Japaner, mit denen sie zu tun hatten (wobei man allerdings nur selten zwischen diesen Völkern differenzierte), beschrieben. Die Reaktion der mandschurischen Soldaten, die die deutschen Emigranten begeistert als ihre 'deutschen Freunde' begrüßten, ist ein Indiz dafür, daß die wenigsten Menschen in Japan und Ostasien über die deutsche Politik der Juden-Diskriminierung informiert waren.

Man könnte in diesem freundlichen, alltäglichen Japan einen Gegendiskurs zum heldenhaften Japan der offiziellen deutsch-japanischen Kriegspropaganda sehen, d.h. also einen 'Kultur-Text des Exils', wenn es auch gewisse Überlappungen dieser Diskurse gibt, wenn z.B., wie zitiert, Stiefel einmal behauptete, daß die japanischen Kinder auch bei Schmerz gar nicht weinen würden – eine Behauptung, die vielleicht doch eher in das kriegerisch-heroische Japan-Bild der Kriegspropaganda gepaßt hätte.[77]

In einer ganz anderen Weise wäre von einem solchen 'Kultur-Text des Exils' zu sprechen, nämlich in den Gedichten des jüdisch-deutschen Juristen und Schriftstellers Kurt Bauchwitz, alias Roy C. Bates (1890–1974), die unlängst durch eine Publikation von Johannes Evelein neu 'entdeckt' wurden.[78] Bauchwitz emigrierte 1939 mit seiner Familie von Deutschland nach Japan, von wo aus er weiter in die USA reisen wollte, was er dann auch, allerdings erst nach einer fast anderthalb jährigen Wartezeit in Japan, tun konnte. Diese Zeit in Japan nutzte er, um dort umher zu reisen und sich besonders mit japanischen Gedichten vertraut zu machen.[79]

Diese Besonderheit seiner Lage, insbesondere als Exilant zwischen drei Sprachen zu stehen, nämlich dem Deutschen, welches seine Muttersprache ist, die er aber, so wie Deutschland überhaupt, ablegen und loswerden möchte, dem Englischen, in welches er, wie in seine neue Heimat USA, überwechseln

---

[77] Vgl. hierzu z.B. Thomas Pekar: 'Bushido-Diskurs' und 'Totale Mobilmachung' bei Ernst Jünger: Eine fatale interkulturelle Beziehung. In: *Neue Beiträge zur Germanistik/Doitsu Bungaku*. Bd. 1 (2002) H. 109. S. 243–251.

[78] Kurt Bauchwitz: *Heim-Findungen. Lebensbuch eines Emigranten*. Hg. von Johannes Evelein. Bonn: Weidle 2006.

[79] Vgl. Evelein: Einführung. In: Ebd. S. 5–24.

möchte, und dem Japanischen, welches die unbekannte Sprache ist, mit der er aktuell in dem ihn faszinierenden Land Japan konfrontiert wird, entbindet komplexe Gedichte, die gängige Denkweisen und Begrifflichkeiten durchbrechen und die inter- bzw. transkulturelle Verfaßtheit seiner Lebenssituation auf den Punkt bringen. Dafür einige Beispiele:

Die 'Babelisierung' seiner sprachlichen Situation, den Sprachverlust, aber auch einen gleichsam 'transgressiven' Sprachenwechsel ironisiert Bauchwitz in dem Gedicht *Gute Erziehung*:

Ich begrüße mit
Ohayo gozaimasu! den chief officer.
Hätte auch good morning! sagen können,
Mein Englisch ist beinah
So schlecht wie mein Nippongo,
Und er versteht mich weder
Noch.
———
Dō shite dame deshō ka? (Ist das unmöglich zu tun?)

25.IV., seit heute,
In this year of grace '39,
Tauschen wir Sprache.
Der chief officer verlernt Japanisch
Und ich Deutsch.[80]

Deutlich weist die Verwendung der englisch- und japanischsprachigen Wörter und Ausdrücke in einem – noch! – mehrheitlich deutschsprachigen Gedicht auf das Flüssigwerden der Sprachen hin. Mimetisch gleichsam, durch bloßes – und nicht 'verstehendes' – Nachsprechen bzw. Nachschreiben versucht Bauchwitz sich hier dem Japanischen anzunähern, wobei die paradoxe (sicherlich ironisch aufzufassende) Pointe des Gedichtes im 'Verlernen' der jeweiligen Muttersprache (beim japanischen 'chief officer' und ihm) besteht, was dann, allerdings unausgesprochen, die Möglichkeit eines vielleicht gemeinsamen Lernens einer 'dritten' Sprache, des Englischen, eröffnen könnte.

So wie die Sprachen ins Trudeln geraten, so auch bislang verläßliche Koordinanten, wie 'Heimat' und 'Fremde/Exotik':[81] Die deutsche Lieder singende Japanerin in Kobe wird zur ‚engsten Landsmännin';[82] 'Fremdheit'

---
[80] Bauchwitz (wie Anm. 78). S. 58.
[81] Diese spätere englischsprachige Aufzeichnung Bauchwitz' läßt sich als Quintessenz zu dieser (ja doch nur angenommenen) Dichotomie von 'fremd' und 'eigen' lesen: "My one and a half years in Japan, after traveling in India and China, have convinced me that the mysterious East is as mysterious as the mysterious West". Ebd. S. 188.
[82] Ebd. S. 59.

hingegen manifestiert, konkretisiert sich – in ihm selbst, ist er selbst doch am exotischen Ort:

Wo der Pfeffer wächst,
Im Paradiese,
Bin ich.[83]

Wie aber diese Redewendung, "wo der Pfeffer wächst", zeigt, die ja als Zielangabe für lästige Menschen verwendet wird, hat das 'Paradies' durchaus auch seine Schattenseiten, wie dies dann in Bauchwitz' späteren Gedichten, vor allem den beiden Zyklen *Tokyo Gedichte* und *Der Zitronenbaum* deutlich wird, in denen negative Stimmungen wie Langeweile, Schicksalsergebenheit, Trauer, ja Resignation überwiegen. Hier aber ist es die östliche Philosophie und Religion, vor allem der Zen-Buddhismus, den Bauchwitz rezipiert und zur Bewältigung dieser schwierigen Zeit des Heimatverlustes und der Isolation aufbietet. Wenn er immer wieder nach dem 'Sinn' seines Lebensweges und seines Leidens fragt,[84] so zerstreut sich ihm aber allmählich diese Kategorie des 'Sinns' immer mehr durch die Einbeziehung von zen-buddhistischen Zentralvorstellungen wie 'Entzug', 'Leere' und 'Nichts'.[85]

Diese Annäherung an östliche Denkweisen kulminiert in der Übernahme von japanischen Gedichtformen (Haiku und Tanka), die Bauchwitz die Möglichkeit geben, seine prekäre Lebenssituation des Exils auf künstlerisch gelungene Weise – und damit bleibend – Ausdruck zu geben: Als Beispiel dafür – und zugleich als Beispiel für einen äußerst gelungenen 'Kultur-Text des Exils' – möchte ich abschließend ein Haiku-Gedicht Bauchwitz' zitieren, eine Impression anläßlich eines Steingartens, den man in japanischen Zen-Tempeln, wie dem berühmten Ryōan-ji in Kyōto, finden kann:

Sand, wellig gefegt,
Steine, blumenlos Garten.
Leere lehrt Fülle.[86]

---

[83] Ebd. S. 60.
[84] Beispielhaft in den beiden Gedichten *Sinn des Weges* und *Sinn des Leidens* aus dem Zyklus *Der Zitronenbaum*. Ebd. S. 88f.
[85] Angesichts von chinesischen Schriftzeichen, die er nicht lesen kann, bemerkt Bauchwitz:
"Ich bin halt verliebt in Charaktere, / Die sich entziehn". Ebd. S. 65. Die mit Zen in Verbindung stehende 'Leere' wird positiv erfahren: Sie "durchstillt" beispielsweise, so wie das 'Nichts' ihn "umfängt". Ebd. S. 64 und S. 90.
[86] Ebd. S. 122 (Gedicht Nr. 126).

Hubert Roland

German and Austrian Exile Literature in Belgium 1933–1945. Topography and Perspectives

This essay is devoted to a survey of German and Austrian exile literature in Belgium from 1933 to 1945, a field that has been unexplored so far. Belgium happens to be quite a difficult case study, because of the provisional and transitory character of exile for writers attracted largely by the neighboring countries of France and the Netherlands. However, it is possible to organize a significant volume of materials outlining a topography of exile following, on the one hand, the geographical principle of settlement (Brussels, Antwerp, Ostende), and on the other hand, the principle of political networks (communist, "humanist"). Particular attention will be paid to the Austrian presence following the Anschluss *in 1938, including not only Jean Améry but also the forgotten* roman à clef *of Hertha Ligeti,* Die Sterne verlöschen nicht *(1959). At another level the Belgian case, and especially Améry and Ligeti's works, will help contribute to a reflection on shifting identities and boundaries in literature of the exile in contrast to travel literature.*

With the exception of Hans Mayer/ Jean Améry, and some other Austrian exiles after 1938, we know very little about the position of Belgium as an exile country. This particular geographical focus has so far been quite neglected by the *Exilforschung*.[1] Considering the geographical border situation of Belgium, it is nevertheless quite obvious that it was a destination to be considered by many political emigrants from the first days following the *Machtübernahme*, even though it was somewhat of a transitory destination in the expectation of better days. Belgium also functioned as a *Drehscheibe*, where German emigrants coming from other countries met from time to time and from which they were expected to travel further. In this respect, Belgium may not be as important as countries like France, and especially the Netherlands, where well-known exile publishers were active, but it certainly deserves attention.

This provisional character of exile for many political refugees, who subsequently often crossed other borders, certainly made any investigation into Belgium's status as an exile country difficult, and may also explain why German and international research had problems in seizing it as a coherent object of study. Furthermore, the lack of attention to this question from a

---

[1] Compare Ursula Langkau-Alex ("Belgien als Exilland ist weitgehend ein Stiefkind der deutschsprachigen Forschung") in her article and bibliographical survey: *Handbuch der deutschsprachigen Emigration*. Darmstadt: Wissenschaftliche Buchgesellschaft 1998. Pp. 168–173.

Belgian perspective may have also had its reasons. These are possibly related to a form of historical amnesia, arising from the fact that in the 1930s Belgium did not prove equal to its reputation of treating famous political opponents from neighbouring countries as well as it had Victor Hugo and Karl Marx in the 19th century.

In the fall of 1938,[2] some 5,000 officially registered German and Austrian refugees needed assistance. Some of them were connected to each other through networks and collective organizations, which I shall try to sketch out in this introductory survey of German-speaking exile in Belgium. This will also include an overview of the writers who left some trace, if only sometimes in the literary form, of a travel experience.

In the process of this analysis, the case study of Belgium as a particularly transitory destination will also be an opportunity to reflect on the concept of frontier and its status in exile literature, which contrasts significantly with its function in travel literature. This eventually implies a distinct space of consciousness, as well as a specific conception of uncertain identities.

The Precarious Situation of German Emigrants in Belgium

In order to characterize the situation of Jewish emigrants in Belgium after 1933, the historian Frank Caestecker coined the term "uninvited guests" (*ongewenste gasten*). These "uninvited guests" were often relegated by the Belgian authorities to the status of illegal aliens.[3] This is also true for German emigrants and exiles, who, in principle, were not welcome in Belgium in those years. This cool reception of German refugees, whether they were outwardly politically active or Jewish, was primarily due to the economic crisis and fear of competition between these emigrants and the Belgian workers and unemployed. Nor should one underestimate the fact that the reputation of Hitler's Germany was at this point not as unfavorable as one should retrospectively expect. The persistent climate of economic and political crisis had led certain circles to envisage alternatives to the democratic model of society. This is confirmed by the interesting account of the German journalist Kurt Grünebaum, who recapitulated in an interview with the German-speaking *Belgischer Rundfunk* (13th October, 1982) the reasons why the first German emigrants

---

[2] Ibid. Pp. 169–170.
[3] Frank Caestecker: *Alien Policy in Belgium, 1840–1940. The Creation of Guest Workers, Refugees and Illegal Aliens*. New York – Oxford: Berghahn Books 2000, as well as *Ongewenste gasten. Joodse vluchtelingen en migranten in de dertiger jaren in België*. Brussels: VUB Press 1993.

were, from his perspective, "coolly" and "neutrally" received by the Belgian population in 1933:

> Man darf aber nicht vergessen, dass in weiten Kreisen der belgischen Öffentlichkeit eine Stimmung vorherrschte, die, ohne direkt Hitler-freundlich zu sein, doch Hitler eine Chance geben wollte, weil man der Ansicht war, Hitler bringe in die zerfahrene Wirtschaft der Weimarer Republik wieder Ordnung hinein und Hitler sei unter Umständen der Mann, mit dem man ungefähr so auskommen könne, wie man auch mit Mussolini auskommt.[4]

Grünebaum refers particularly to the situation of German-speaking Belgium, which needs to be explained briefly. The Treaty of Versailles attributed the Eastern territories of Eupen/Malmedy to the Belgian State, which had belonged to Germany before World War I.[5] In the 1920s, it was painful and difficult for this population to feel that they belonged to the Belgian nation. Many still remained faithful to the German linguistic and cultural community, even after the pseudo-referendum that made them an official part of the Belgian state. This did not, of course, mean that they all became faithful adherents of Hitler after 1933. In fact, the relationship to Germany was particularly tense and contradictory, all the more so since it actually became an outpost of Nazi organizations abroad.

As a whole, Belgium became a place of great strategic importance in the early 20th century, largely because of its policy redefining the country's traditional neutrality dating from the 19th century. In the years 1936–1937, Belgian King Leopold III and Prime Minister Paul-Henry Spaak strongly reaffirmed

---

[4] Unpublished interview of Hubert Jenniges with Kurt Grünebaum ("Gespräch mit Kurt Grünebaum") for the *Belgischer Rundfunk*, 13th October 1982. The German Social-Democrat journalist Kurt Grünebaum (1910–1988) arrived in Belgium early in 1933 because members of his family had already been threatened by the National-Socialist authorities. It was the chief editor of the German-speaking paper *Grenz-Echo* (which clearly took position against Hitler) who gave him the chance to launch a career in journalism. After the Second World War, Grünebaum and his wife decided to remain in Belgium. He continued working for the *Grenz-Echo* and for other French-speaking papers and even became an informal cultural ambassador for German-speaking Belgium in Brussels (see Roland Baumann: Kurt Grünebaum, entre l'Allemagne et la Belgique. In: *Carl-Einstein-Kolloquium 1998. Carl Einstein à Bruxelles: Dialogues par-dessus les frontières/ Carl Einstein in Brüssel: Dialoge über Grenzen*. Hg. von R. Baumann & H. Roland. Frankfurt/Main [a.o.]: Peter Lang 2001. Pp. 169–197; Klaus Pabst: Kurt Grünebaum. In: *Geschichte im Westen. Halbjahres-Zeitschrift für Landes- und Zeitgeschichte*. 4.1 1989. Pp. 113–115.

[5] See Philippe Beck's survey of the cultural and political history of this region in *Landeskunde Belgien*. Ed. by Johannes Koll. Münster: Aschendorff 2007. Pp. 203–223.

the principle of Belgian independence in foreign matters (*politique des mains libres*), whose purpose was to prevent the country from getting involved in a possible war. The country's neutrality was formally recognized and guaranteed by Hitler on September 30, 1937.[6] This also meant that Belgium had to treat Germany carefully at a diplomatic level, which indirectly made the situation of German emigrants even more precarious, and hardly allowed for an alternative image of *Das andere Deutschland*.

Moreover, a real symbolic rivalry between different images of Germany was at work to garner support and sympathy from the population, especially among the younger intellectuals. The most active cultural mediators between Germany and Belgium eventually worked in the field of cultural propaganda, as did, for instance, Friedrich Sieburg, who held a position at the German Embassy in Brussels in 1939.[7] They were eager to promote a positive image of a "new communitarian Germany," in which the German people, especially the German youth, would show solidarity and stick together in support of the country's new leader. This promotion campaign enjoyed relative success among younger intellectuals, who, although they did not really show frank enthusiasm for it, were nevertheless curious and wanted to analyze the situation unprejudiced. They were in search of alternatives to the permanent state of crisis, to which they not only assigned a social and political meaning, but which they also interpreted as a crisis of moral values.[8]

In this context, the situation of German political emigrants was necessarily one of an extremely precarious nature. In his memoirs, the future Social-Democrat premier of Nordrhein-Westphalen, Heinz Kühn, who had lived in Brussels since 1936, remembers their marginal situation. He and his collaborators on the paper *Freies Deutschland* were threatened with expulsion by the Belgian authorities if they did not stop the paper's publication. The German

---

[6] See Gustaaf Janssens: De l'indépendance à la neutralité. Léopold III et la politique extérieure de la Belgique. In: *Léopold III*. Ed. by M. Dumoulin, M. van den Wijngaert & V. Dujardin. Bruxelles: Complexe 2001. Pp. 83–84.
[7] Albrecht Betz: *Exil und Engagement. Deutsche Schriftsteller im Frankreich der dreißiger Jahre*. München: edition text + kritik 1986. Pp. 169–174.
[8] This was especially true among the younger generation of Catholic students and graduates who wrote for the review *La Cité chrétienne* and wanted to combine in a new program Catholicism and social action. The German Embassy in Brussels offered its services to organize a study travel to Germany:"Rappelons également qu'un groupement d'*Amis de la Cité chrétienne* a décidé de faire en Allemagne, un voyage d'études d'une huitaine de jours. Il en coûterait un millier de francs environ: ce qui est pour rien. Des mesures seraient prises avec la légation d'Allemagne pour rendre le voyage le plus instructif possible" (*La Cité chrétienne*. 20 October 1935).

Embassy considered it a violation of Belgium's principle of *geistige Neutralität*, a surprising stance after the outbreak of the War in 1939.[9]

A new study by Belgian historians of the Centre for Historical Research and Documentation on War and Contemporary Society (CEGES/SOMA) points out[10] that the behaviour of the Belgian authorities and population toward Jewish refugees wavered between tolerance and prejudice according to the political situation of the day. Moreover, any tolerance shown the Jewish refugees was not based on legal rights, which the refugees did not enjoy – as the Belgian legislation offered no solution for the concept of racial prosecution, the newcomers were not granted the status of political refugees – but essentially on favors and assistance principally offered by Jewish committees and organizations. As far as the political refugees were concerned, some people did feel solidarity with the victims of Nazism, but they also had to counter proto-fascist currents within Belgian society, which tried to influence the position of the conservative parties. Above all, as has been shown, the state's interests had to be preserved, even at the cost of the refugees.[11]

The main feature of German-speaking exile in Belgium after 1933 thus lies in its transitory character, and Belgium has to be considered as an extension of the larger European networks of neighboring countries. This is why Walter Landauer regularly visited Brussels on behalf of the publisher Lange; Klaus Mann also occasionally visited colleagues in Brussels and Ostende; Erika Mann and the *Pfeffermühle* performed in Antwerp and Brussels to try to gain sympathy for German opponents, etc. It is therefore necessary to establish a precise chronicle of German exile in Belgium, as Albrecht Betz did for France in his work *Exil und Engagement*.[12]

---

[9] Kühn draws a historical parallel between the attitude of the Belgian authorities threatening Karl Marx' position (because they feared the French authorities) and his own situation: "so wie Marx den Ausweisungsbefehl aus Furcht vor den annexionistischen Absichten Napoleons III. und aus Furcht der belgischen Regierung vor Repressialien des kaiserlichen Frankreichs erhielt, so wurde auch uns nach Kriegsbeginn 1939 die Ausweisung angedroht, wenn wir nicht unmittelbar die Herausgabe des *Freien Deutschland* in Brüssel einstellten, aus Furcht der belgischen Regierung vor den diplomatischen Drohungen des hitlerischen Deutschlands". Heinz Kühn: *Widerstand und Emigration. Die Jahre 1928–1945*. Hamburg: Hoffmann und Campe 1980. P. 183.

[10] This book is the result of a research project that was recently commissioned by the Belgian Senate and supported by the Belgian federal government to establish the possible responsibility of the Belgian authorities in the prosecution and deportation of the Jewish population in the years 1940–1944.

[11] R. Van Doorslaer, E. Debruyn, F. Seberechts, N. Wouters: *Gewillig België. Overheid en jodenvervolging tijdens de tweede wereldoorlog*. Antwerpen – Amsterdam: Meulenhoff/ Manteau en Soma 2007. Pp. 108–110.

[12] Betz: *Exil und Engagement* (n. 7). Pp. 281–327.

In the meantime, I shall establish a topography of exile in Belgium, which could lay the foundations for such a chronology. This topography will be structured in accordance with two principles that partially overlap: the geographical and that of international networks.

The Geographical Principle

A quick overview identifies three centers of the German-speaking exile in Belgium: the first, unsurprisingly, is Brussels, followed by Antwerp, the Flemish city that served as an open door to the Netherlands. Included is also Bredene/Ostende, on the Belgian coast, where the famous faces of the German and Austrian exile met several times. Their traces in the city's memory were only rediscovered a few years ago.

Bredene/Ostende

Curiously enough, as was also the case with Sanary-sur-Mer,[13] it was not an established scholar, but a *freier Schriftsteller*, who first recalled the memory of the *lieu de mémoire* Bredene. As late as 2001, the Flemish-speaking journalist Mark Schaevers recounts the story of German exiles in Bredene, a suburb of Ostende, in the semi-literary publication *De zomer van 1936 (The Summer of 1936)*.[14] The author clearly identifies Bredene as a smaller Sanary-sur-Mer, where some of the most famous German and Austrian writers regularly met in 1936/1937: Irmgard Keun (living in Ostende since 1935), Egon Erwin Kisch (living part-time in a Ghent), Joseph Roth, Hermann Kesten, Stefan Zweig, Arthur Koestler and Ernst Toller (possibly also Willi Münzenberg), all of whom visited Belgium more or less regularly.

We are indebted to Schaevers for putting together an important documentary work, drawing on an exhaustive and reliable bibliography of correspondences, memories, autobiographies, and fictional texts. Some may be critical of the "poetics of exile" he uses in telling the story of Bredene, which is a mix between historical, biographical research and creative writing. *The Summer of 1936* does contain many ingredients that constitute such a poetics. The initial framework of the story is built around the destiny of Irmgard Keun, and more

---

[13] Manfred Flügge: *Wider Willen im Paradies: deutsche Schriftsteller im Exil in Sanary-sur-Mer*. Berlin: Aufbau-Taschenbuch Verlag 1996.

[14] Mark Schaevers: *Oostende, de zomer van 1936*. Antwerpen – Amsterdam: Atlas 2001. This work comprises earlier publications of John Gheeraert: *Bericht uit Bredene. Vermaarde joodse emigranten in Vlaanderen*. Antwerpen – Amsterdam: de Vries-Brouwers 1987; *Stefan Zweig. Een Weense flaneur in Vlaanderen*. Antwerpen – Amsterdam: de Vries-Brouwers 2000.

specifically, her love affair with Joseph Roth. The historical marker of 1936 therefore fits perfectly with the larger purpose of integrating this smaller story into European history: the success of the *Front populaire* in France, the Civil War in Spain, the Olympic Games in Berlin, the first Moscow Trials. The narrative, which is richly illustrated by photographic materials, alternately focuses on the individual exiles and on the intertwining between them.

Despite the presence of communist activists like Kisch, the image conveyed by the "colony" of Bredene is not principally that of politically committed writers, but rather of individualistic bourgeois writers waiting for the world to collapse. The latter is evidenced by such "decadent" traits as the alcoholism of Roth and the brief homosexual affair of Klaus Mann in Ostende. This schema neatly corresponds to the motif of travelling as *Scheitern*; some of the writers are pictured as being doomed to death and suicide, as they did not survive the coming catastrophe (or lost hope in the future of humanity after the end of the war, as in the case of Klaus Mann). Schaever's work may be interpreted as a kind of poetic-aesthetic compensation for the status of being "wrecked," inspired by the genre of travel literature and applied to the tragic destiny of the exiles. The best literary testimony issuing from this context was written from the perspective of the ten-year old child Kully, in Irmgard Keun's *Kind aller Länder*.[15]

Brussels

The famous faces of Ostende notwithstanding, it is also a group of individual artists living in a very isolated, marginal position in Brussels, such as the famous painter Felix Nussbaum, who was arrested and later died in a concentration camp during the war, that deserves more critical attention. At first glance, they hardly seem to have come into contact with one another. Even if some networks were constructed, as will be described later, many did not cooperate, and chose to search out their own allies and support within Belgian society.

The most famous representative of German literary life was the former Expressionist Carl Sternheim, who resided in Belgium between 1912 and 1918, and again settled in Brussels in 1930, initially with his third wife Pamela Wedekind. The aging Sternheim had become physically ill and psychologically very unstable; he lived in great isolation in the shadow of his earlier literary career. Some Belgian friends, like the writers Franz Hellens and Albert Ayguesparse, helped him gain the status of a political refugee as he was denied

---

[15] First published in 1938 by the publisher Querido. Reedited in 2004 by List/Ullstein.

Belgian nationality.[16] In a conference he gave about Sternheim at the Goethe-Institut in Brussels many years later, Kurt Grünebaum openly regretted that Sternheim, who died during the war in 1942 and is buried in Brussels, did not seek contact with the circles of German political exiles.[17]

It is therefore a matter of conjecture whether Sternheim was acquainted with the activities of the pacifist writer Ernst Friedrich (1894–1967) in Brussels. Friedrich's Documentation Center about World War I had been founded in Berlin-Mitte in 1925, following the publication of *Krieg dem Kriege! War against War!*, which had been reviewed by Kurt Tucholsky in the *Weltbühne*.[18] After this Anti-War Museum had been destroyed and made into a SA-*Sturmlokal* in March 1933, Friedrich had to spend several months in prison and eventually fled with his family to Czechoslovakia at the end of the year. From Prague they then continued on to Switzerland, where they were welcomed by Quaker friends active for the League of Nations. Because of the publication in Geneva of the militant book *Vom Friedens-Museum zur Hitler-Kaserne*,[19] Friedrich was officially expelled from Switzerland "wegen Beleidigung eines befreundeten Staatsmannes (Hitlers)".[20] Yet he had international connections – this new publication was edited simultaneously in German, French, Dutch and Swedish – and reached political exile in Belgium with the help of Belgian trade unions and the Belgian Socialist Party. Moreover, Friedrich managed to reopen his Peace Museum in Brussels with archival materials preserved during his flight.

---

[16] Interesting is Ayguesparse's tactics to try to help Sternheim gain the Belgian nationality. The Interior Minister required for this an uninterrupted stay of ten years on Belgian territory, to which Sternheim could not attest, because he had left the country in 1918. In an interview with Ayguesparse published in the literary review *Le Rouge et le Noir*, he simultaneously reminded of earlier Belgian acquaintances during World War I and suggested that he had never left the country since then. Albert Ayguesparse: Rencontre avec Carl Sternheim. In: *Le Rouge et le Noir.* 26 April 1934. Pp. 1–2.

[17] See the posthumous text of the conference which I edited and commented: Kurt Grünebaum: Carl Sternheim in Belgien. In: *Archiv für das Studium der neueren Sprachen und Literaturen*. Vol 234. 1/1997. Pp. 89–96.

[18] *Krieg dem Kriege! Guerre à la Guerre! War against War! Oorlog aan den Oorlog* was first published by Friedrich in 1924. 50000 copies of the book had been distributed until 1930. A pocket edition reedited in 1980 had a still much greater success. Tommy Spree, Friedrich's grandson, rebuilt a museum in Berlin-Wedding (Brüsseler Straße 21) in 1982 and made of it again a cultural and political center in the pacifist spirit of his grandfather. For this project he managed to gain the interest of Willy Brandt.

[19] *Vom Friedens-Museum... Zur Hitler-Kaserne. Ein Tatsachenbericht über das Wirken von Ernst Friedrich und Adolf Hitler.* Ed. by Internationales Komitee für die Wiedererrichtung des ersten internationalen Anti-Kriegs-Museums. Genf 1935.

[20] Tommy Spree: *Ich kenne keine 'Feinde'. Der Pazifist Ernst Friedrich. Ein Lebensbild.* Berlin: Anti-Kriegs-Museum 2000. Pp. 91–95.

The reopening of this museum in the trade union house on October 4th 1936, covered by the Belgian press, proves that despite the caution of the Belgian government toward the German problem, it was actually possible to be informed about the lies of Hitler's peace propaganda in neutral countries. In his opening remarks, Friedrich showed the audience weapons belonging to the ordinary rucksack of members of the *Hitlerjugend*, a dagger and a grenade:

> Etwas 'Kostbares' hatte ich bei mir. Zwei Dokumente vom 'Friedenswillen' Hitlers: Einen Hitler-Dolch und eine Übungsgranate. Diese Mordwaffen benutzt die Hitler-Jugend bei ihren friedlichen Kriegsübungen.Der gesamten Weltöffentlichkeit will ich sie zeigen, diese untrüglichen Beweise der wahren 'Friedensliebe' Adolf Hitlers [...]. Es gilt, die Völker Europas zu warnen vor Hitlers Friedensreden, vor diesen Hitlerdolchen, damit sie wachsam sein mögen... damit nicht eines Tages ihr Blut an den Hitlermessern klebt.[21]

In 1936, a series of events highlighted the political prosecution in Hitler's Germany. I shall later comment on the conference for political prisoners in Germany, which was organized at the *Palais d'Egmont* in Brussels in July 1936. The *Palais des Beaux-Arts* had become a place that quite systematically fostered the representatives of German exiles supporting a humanist conception of commitment. The review *Le Rouge et le Noir* informed its readership that Friedrich, after escaping the concentration camps in Germany, was settled in Brussels and that the German pacifist had held a literary conference there on January 24th 1936. Assistance for this conference was strongly encouraged to express solidarity with exiles living in material privation as well as in danger:

> Pour ceux qui imaginent cependant les difficultés matérielles que rencontre aujourd'hui l'exilé, ils réaliseront immédiatement que ce n'est pas simplement un souci esthétique qui les appellera vendredi prochain au Palais des Beaux-Arts, mais encore un devoir de solidarité envers un écrivain banni de son pays.[22]

The event was repeated one month later, and Mil Zankin again tried to move the readership to attend Friedrich's talk.[23] At the beginning of March, it was Hermann Kesten's turn to be invited and give his view of exile literature before his fellow exiles. The reporter André Claudet suggests that the condition of

---

[21] Quoted from Ibid. P. 97.
[22] Ernst Friedrich parle.... In: *Le Rouge et le Noir*. 22 January 1936.
[23] Mil Zankin: Ernst Friedrich parle. In: *Le Rouge et le Noir*. 26 February 1936. On that occasion Friedrich read among other things scenes from Ernst Toller's play *Hinkemann*. Zankin also covered the opening of the Peace Museum later (Un musée anti-guerre à Bruxelles. In: *Le Rouge et le Noir*. 14 October 1936).

being exiled favours a poetics born of anger, but that it contributes to the elevation of the writer. Claudet claims:

> L'exil lui fut un stimulant et un catalyseur. La colère le souleva au-dessus de lui-même et cet art, né de la haine et de la virulence, eut des accents uniques pour fustiger la violence et la barbarie, et l'infamie arbitraire, la dictature et l'oppression.[24]

Kesten, whose works were published in Holland by Langen, defended exiled authors against the reproach of escapism levelled against them due to their proclivity for writing historical novels or literary biographies:

> Parallèlement à ce courant historique, qui n'est au fond que la transposition de la lutte contre le régime dictatorial sur un plan plus large et plus humain, les exilés écrivent des œuvres actuelles, libres, volontaires, où vit le dernier souffle de la justice et la farouche ardeur de ceux qui ne se rendent pas. Il [i.e. Kesten] dira que le roman historique est pour lui un pamphlet, et que l'imagination retrouve, dans ces luttes et dans ces révoltes, les affres du temps présent et la volonté de vaincre.[25]

Serving as an earlier testimony of solidarity with the German exiles at the *Palais* was Erika Mann's 1935 cabaret troupe, *Die Pfeffermühle*, although the reporter Olivier Meurice did not sympathize with the aesthetic approach of Thomas Mann's daughter, qualifying it as vulgar:

> La troupe du Pfeffermühle excelle à éveiller les appétits grossiers d'une foule à laquelle le snobisme seul donne un semblant de délicatesse. [...] Les huit cabotins qui font partie de la troupe sont d'une médiocrité définitive. Quant à Erica Mann, elle est insupportable de prétention mais il faut lui rendre cette justice qu'elle a réalisé une parfaite communion entre la salle et la scène. La communion dans la vulgarité![26]

On the other hand, this "communion" of the audience must suggest an alliance of the Brussels audience against Hitler's policy.[27] However, the mood of the

---

[24] André Claudet: Hermann Kesten à Bruxelles. In: *Le Rouge et le Noir*. 4 March 1936.

[25] Ibid. About this question of the historical novel, which was quite in vogue among exiles but also among writers of the *Innere Emigration*, see the contrastive approach of Annette Schmollinger: *"Intra muros et extra". Deutsche Literatur im Exil und in der Inneren Emigration. Ein exemplarischer Vergleich.* Heidelberg: C. Winter 1999. Pp. 82–107.

[26] Olivier Meurice: Le cabaret littéraire de Erica Mann. In: *Le Rouge et le Noir*. 29 May 1935.

[27] The *Pfeffermühle* also performed in Antwerp at that time but did not seem to have had a great success. See Carlos Tindemans: Exiltheater und Rezeption in Antwerpen 1933–1940. In: *Zur deutschen Exilliteratur in den Niederlanden*. Ed. by Hans Würzner. Amsterdam: Rodopi 1977. Pp. 175–186. Here: p. 181 (Amsterdamer Beiträge zur Neueren Germanistik. Vol. 6).

Belgian reviews, and possibly of the Belgian audience, was uneven at best. While some commentators of *Le Rouge et le Noir* backed the German political refugees at the time, the sheer plurality of reviews revealed both progressive and conservative tendencies.

Ernst Friedrich had no other income than the money he received as gifts for his museum and as compensation for his conferences; he lived like most German and Austrian exiles in precarious material conditions. Worse still was the lack of confidence of the Belgian authorities after the outbreak of the war on May 10th 1940. Together with other suspect German and Belgian sympathizers of National-Socialist Germany, exiles like Friedrich, Kurt Grünebaum and Jean Améry were arrested and deported to the camps Gurs and Saint-Cyprien in southern France.[28]

Brussels/Antwerp: the Austrian Presence

A similar fate was bestowed on many members of the better-structured and more organized Austrian settlements in Antwerp and Brussels following the *Anschluss* in 1938.[29] Its most famous writer was, of course, the young Jean Améry, who first arrived among approximately 50,000 other Jews in Antwerp, and lived there with the aid of the local Jewish Help Committee until May 1940.[30] Améry's notes for preparing a 1975 radio program about the way stations of his exile years for *Deutschlandfunk* show how far removed he is from idealizing and romanticizing the experience of exile. He writes

---

[28] The administrative arrest of a still unknown number of people was indeed carried out in chaos and improvisation on the following days. Approximately 7000 to 10000 male citizens from Germany, Austria and Czechoslovakia in age of being mobilized – most of them Jews – were considered as mere "enemy subjects". *Gewillig België* (n. 11). Pp. 236–238.

[29] Antwerp, the open door to the Netherlands, was a town with a particular status for the exiles because they enjoyed the protection of its Social-Democrat mayor, the Minister Camille Huysmans, who even had problems with the Belgian Ministry of Justice because of this benevolence. See Frank Caestecker: Het reëel bestaande socialisme in West-Europa en de vlucht uit Nazi-Duitsland, 1933–1934. Een oefening in private internationale solidariteit. In: *Cahiers d'Histoire du Temps présent*. 15 (2005). P. 107–122. The presence of well organized Jewish networks and organizations enabled welcoming refugees like the Free Mason writer Hans-Henner Bendgens who was arrested and executed during the War. See the exhaustive study of Joris Duytschaever: Zur Asylpraxis in Holland und Belgien: Der Fall Hans Bendgens-Henner (1892–1942). In: *Zur deutschen Exilliteratur* (n. 27). Pp. 69–117.

[30] See the biography of Irene Heidelberger-Leonard: *Jean Améry. Revolte in der Resignation*. Stuttgart: Klett-Cotta 2004. Pp. 70ff.

about the *Station Antwerpen* (from the beginning of 1939 until the outbreak of war):

> [...] Exil: ganz anders als das, was wir aus der Exilliteratur kennen – keine literarisch-politischen Klubs, dafür: endlose und kreisende Gespräche der Emigranten über Auswanderungsmöglichkeiten nach den USA, Australien, Neuseeland, Brasilien, China, nach der fernsten Ferne – Warten auf den Krieg: nur er konnte Erlösung bringen – alle Emigranten waren in tiefster Seele bellizistisch – Stadtbilder: der Hafen mit seinen Hurenhäusern hinter dem Stadthaus – flämische Renaissance im Stadtzentrum und Brooklyn – Atmosphäre im Judenviertel – [...].[31]

Améry's considerations confirm the individualistic character of exile. No emigrant searched out social contact, be it with the local, suspicious population, or with fellow exiles.[32] We may, however, ask if Améry's retrospective memories do not tend to exaggerate this solitude, as he was dependent on the help of the Jewish Committee for which he also gave courses devoted to German Romanticism, the Realist novel, etc.[33] This seems to suggest some degree of integration into a community or, at least, an ambivalent relation to the collective body.

At the outbreak of war, which plunged him into a state of ideological confusion, Améry was even eager to join any committee or organization ready for action. He undersigned different "declarations of loyalty", and was even expecting the mobilization of an imaginary Jewish Brigade within the Belgian Army.[34] Hence the example of Améry illustrates a contradictory feeling between solitude and belonging to a community. The helplessness and confusion of German and Austrian refugees may also be explained by the manifest tension amongst organizations in search of their official, legitimate, representation to Belgian authorities. As will be addressed later, this rivalry considerably weakened the community of refugees.

---

[31] Jean Améry: *Werke. Band 2: Jenseits von Schuld und Sühne. Unmeisterliche Wanderjahre. Örtlichkeiten.* Ed. by Gerhard Scheit. Stuttgart: Klett-Cotta 2002. P. 820.

[32] Améry later expressed some resentment against exiles who had lived in a better situation than him and, in his judgment, far from the political and social reality. See the recently published article of Jürgen Doll: Weit von Sanary – Jean Amérys Auseinandersetzung mit der Exilliteratur und den Exilliteraten. In: *Lion Feuchtwanger und die deutschsprachigen Emigranten in Frankreich von 1933 bis 1941/ Lion Feuchtwanger et les exilés de langue allemande en France de 1933 à 1941*. Ed. by Daniel Azuélos. Bern: Peter Lang 2006. Pp. 527–537. See also Rosemarie Müller: Jean Améry in Belgien. In: *Germanistische Mitteilungen* 31. 31 (1990). Pp. 37–48.

[33] Améry: *Werke* (n. 31). Pp. 806–807.

[34] Ibid. P. 809.

After escaping from Gurs and returning to Brussels at the end of 1941, the circumstances of the occupation drove Améry to an unambiguous commitment against the oppressor. Through the mediation of the German refugee Marianne Brandt, he became involved in a resistance network, the *österreichische Heimatsfront* (a member of the Independence Front), which systematically favored subversion in the occupied country. They wrote and disseminated tracts calling for insubordination among German and Austrian soldiers, and published an anonymous clandestine paper, *Die Wahrheit*. Améry and Brandt were arrested in July 1943, following a so-called *Flugzettel-Affäre*. They were caught by soldiers while engaged in propaganda work, were first tortured in the Belgian camp of Breendonck, and eventually deported to Auschwitz. Marianne Brandt did not survive.

Even if concrete material proof of this connection has yet to be found, Améry was most probably a member of the same organization as Hertha Ligeti.[35] She is the author of a forgotten work *Die Sterne verlöschen nicht*, an impressive keystone novel based on the experience of the Austrian activists in Brussels after 1938 and during World War II. Ligeti and her companions' memories may in all points be compared to Améry's: first the struggle for survival before the war, then the organized resistance to the occupying forces, scenes of arrest, torture, and the eventual deportation to Auschwitz and Birkenau in the last years of the war.

The context of this novel's publication is quite important for an adequate aesthetic and ideological interpretation. *Die Sterne verlöschen nicht* was actually published (in German) in Rumania in 1959, to which Ligeti had moved after the war. The novel may be considered as an historical account of the time, even if its reliability has to be measured against the genre to which it belongs, and which it perfectly illustrates: Socialist Realism. The author's intention is indeed strongly didactic, as she tells the story of exemplary characters living according to the principles and values of the revolution. This is put into contrast with ordinary characters, whose political consciousness and courage had to be awakened out of the slumber of weakness and compromises with the occupiers. As I have already provided a more detailed analysis of this novel in a former publication,[36] I shall only emphasize two aspects here.

---

[35] See the article on Hertha Fuchs-Ligeti in the *Lexikon der österreichischen Exilliteratur*. Wien – München: Franz Deuticke 2000. P. 233.
[36] Hubert Roland: Hertha Ligetis Roman *Die Sterne verlöschen nicht* (1959): Ein vergessenes Werk der Exilliteratur in Belgien. In: *Langues à niveaux multiples. Hommage au Professeur Jacques Lerot*. Ed. by Heinz Bouillon. Peeters: Louvain-la-Neuve 2004. Pp. 217–227 (Bibliothèque des Cahiers de l'Institut de Linguistique de Louvain 112).

The first is the positive image of women who actively participate in the struggle against fascism. Although they act together with men, they do so through highly subversive and dangerous activities. Gender questions thus also belong to political activism. Whereas young men are responsible for spreading illegal papers and leaflets, young women have to sympathize with occupying soldiers in order to demobilize them in a subtle way; this is the so-called *Mädelarbeit*, highly risky of course, and the cause of the arrest of the main protagonist. The responsibility of mothers in matters of education is also stressed, echoing Brecht's play *Die Mutter*. The character Berta Tannenbaum wishes she could address all soldiers with the following words:

> [D]aß sie sich nicht zur Schlachtbank treiben lassen dürfen, daß sie den eigenen und fremden Müttern nicht so großes Leid antun, daß sie doch Mitleid mit sich selbst haben sollen. Oh! Sie könnte sie schon davon überzeugen, daß sie sich gegen das Verbrechen wehren müssen; ein Mutterherz bringt viel zustande. "Wenn wir Mütter uns zusammenschlössen, könnte keine Macht der Welt uns widerstehen!" dachte sie versonnen. Aber das wissen ja diese Jungen nicht, das können sie auch nicht wissen. Auch die Männer wissen das nicht, und selbst von uns Müttern lange nicht alle. Vielleicht ist dies das Unglück der Welt? Ich kann mir vorstellen, daß wir Mütter ihre Erlösung bringen könnten, und ich glaube, daß auch dann, wenn die Freiheit befreit sein wird, noch viele Dummheiten gemacht werden, wenn die Politiker nicht auf die Mütter hören.[37]

The second aspect of Ligeti's novel I wish to highlight here is the significance of the "vitalist" component of Socialist Realism. All characters must adhere to the imperative of remaining faithful to life and its regenerating process, even in the face of suffering and life's unbearable aspects, which are not hidden, but on the contrary, exposed to be denounced. The novel's title hints at this necessity, and one may even observe that faith in life reaches its peak in particularly painful and unbearable moments. After a companion has been sentenced to a cruel death, the narrator adds: "Der Baum fällt nicht mit den Blättern, und die Sterne verlöschen nicht, wenn auch Wolken sie verdecken".[38] I will finally quote from a conversation between a young man, Lois, and his older companion who fought during the Spanish War; beyond courage, bravery and readiness to sacrifice, it is love for life that is defined as the most important value characterizing a good Communist:

> Auch ein Faschist kann mutig, tapfer und sogar aufopferungsfähig sein. Die Christen waren es auch, und das Bürgertum hat auch diese Eigenschaften besessen, als es noch revolutionär war, ich kenne Bibelforscher, die vielleicht mutiger sind als

---

[37] Hertha Ligeti: *Die Sterne verlöschen nicht*. Bukarest: Espla Staatsverlag für Kunst und Literatur 1959. Pp. 399–400.
[38] Ibid. P. 472.

viele Kommunisten. – Weißt du, was meiner Meinung nach den Kommunisten auszeichnet? Seine unbedingte Liebe zum Leben und sein Glaube an den Triumph des Guten im Menschen.[39]

Ligeti's voice constitutes an original literary testimony in the polyphony of the exile experience in Belgium, although, of course, it is much closer to the traditional pole of exile literature as *littérature engagée* rather than *littérature pure* if we consider the controversial criteria intensely discussed in the historiography of the *Exilliteratur*. In her very instructive survey on the *Forschungslage* of this question, Bettina Englmann recalls the political framework of this quarrel, which exacerbated the polarization between works suspected of escapism (*Realitätsflucht*), like those of Hermann Broch or Joseph Roth, and politically committed works.[40]

The intention to soften this dichotomy may be characteristic of a younger generation of scholars.[41] There is no such contradiction between *Exilrealität* and exile as a metaphor that evokes the existential difficulties of isolation in displacement, sometimes with the help of some tropes possibly used elsewhere by travel literature.[42] A further exploration of exile literature in Belgium should bear this evolution in mind. All the more so, as it enables a broader contextualization, enlarging the exile experience to encompass not only all aspects of its protagonists' exilic memories, despite significant temporary distance (Ligeti, Améry) but also its heritage as a collective memory of the guest society (Schaevers).

Uncertain Borders and Identity Confusion

In her survey on modernism and travel (1880–1940), which focuses on Anglophone literature, Helen Care points to a "new consciousness of cultural heterogeneity" registered in modernist texts. She asserts that in both imaginative and travel writing, "modernity, the meeting of other cultures, and change"

---

[39] Ibid. P. 239.
[40] Bettina Englmann: *Poetik des Exils: die Modernität der deutschsprachigen Exilliteratur*. Tübingen: Niemeyer 2001. Pp. 1–11.
[41] In my opinion it is also complementary with Annette Schmollinger's comparative approach between literary texts from the exile and texts from the *Innere Emigration* (see n. 25).
[42] "Exilrealität und Exilmetapher vermischen sich in vielen literarischen Texten" states Englmann (ibid. P. 6) referring explicitly to Anna Seghers' *Transit*. The comparison with travel literature is mine. It may in this respect be relevant to study the case of Salamon Dembitzer, which could not be taken in consideration in this survey. Dembitzer was an exile in Belgium during the years 1935–1940, before leaving for Portugal and the United States. See *Lexikon der österreichischen Exilliteratur* (n. 35). Pp. 149–150.

have become inseparable.[43] In the three stages of travel writing she distinguishes within this period, Care situates a strong popularity and a climax of the genre in the interwar years, during which many travel writing texts were published by authors who were equally, or better, known for their fiction.[44]

Such successful assimilation of cultural heterogeneity does not characterize German-speaking exile literature during those same years. The circumstances of the meeting between cultures are heavy with distrust and even reproach, as Jean Améry later recalls in *Örtlichkeiten* ("Aber warum habt ihr eigentlich gegen diesen Hitler keine Revolution gemacht?"[45]). The daily press and contact with people regularly reminds him of his status as someone who is *unerwünscht*. There were even some public murals that urged refugees to show their worthiness of the host country's "welcome":

> Réfugiés!! Zeigt Euch der Gastfreundschaft, die ihr in Belgien geniesst würdig! Führt Euch stets in mustergültiger Weise auf. Achtet die Sitten des Landes. Macht Euch nicht bemerkbar. Vermeidet es, in den Strassen und an öffentlichen Orten laut zu sprechen. Wahret Disziplin! Es handelt sich um Euer eigenes Interesse.[46]

Such condescending instructions – formulated in the "Du"-form and translated into French to ensure that the message of implied distrust reaches everyone – deny the right to exist if one does not adapt, or even if one speaks too loud!

Not knowing where he may find "bleibende Bleibe," the exile is reduced to the existential condition of waiting without any kind of resolution. Furthermore, he loses the hope of a real social exchange based on the recognition of his identity and dignity. As Améry recalls in a manuscript he wrote thirty years later for German radio:

> Sowieso verlangte es keinen Emigranten nach gesellschaftlichem Anschluss. Wer auch die minimalste Chance zu haben glaubte, betrieb energisch seine Emigration nach einem Wirtsland, das Aussicht auf dauernde Gastfreundschaft bot.[47]

The only country in which the exile can hope to regain status is the "promised land," a country in which cultural and ethnic identity should play no role, i.e. the United States.

---

[43] Helen Carr: Modernism and Travel (1880–1940). In: *The Cambridge Companion to Travel Writing*. Ed. by Peter Hulme & Tim Youngs. Cambridge: Cambridge University Press 2002. Pp. 70–86. Here: p. 74.
[44] Ibid. P. 75.
[45] Améry: *Werke* (n. 31). P. 390.
[46] The photograph of this mural, which was subsequently destroyed, was taken in the center of Brussels in the 1980's.
[47] Améry: *Werke* (n. 31). P. 805.

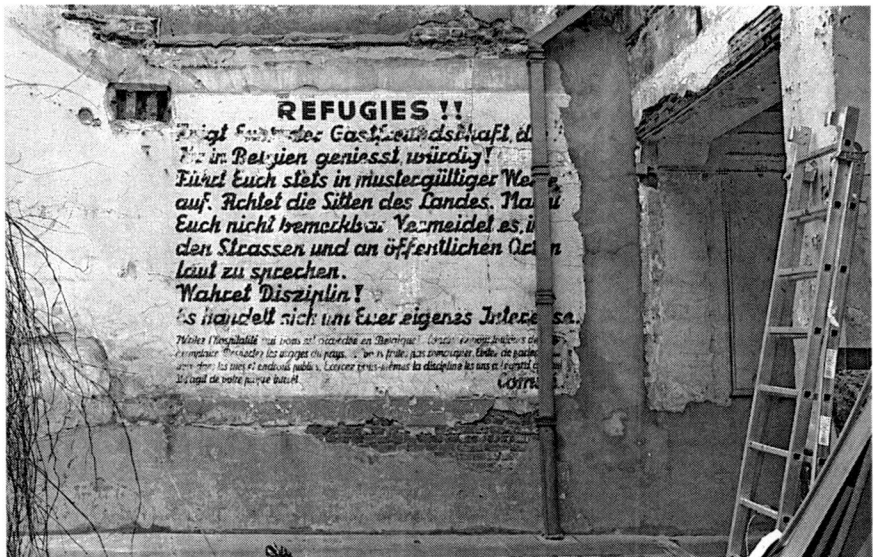

Ill. 1: "Refugies!!" Mural photographed by Christian Carez. The wall used to stand in the Rue Philippe de Champagne, Brussels. © Christian Carez Photographie. Laarheidestraat 40. 1650 Beersel, Belgium.

The exile's fundamental state of uncertainty and unhappiness is, of course, due to the historical conditions of an exile differing markedly from the experiences of authors simply travelling abroad. The latter are not especially threatened by the risk of identity loss. On the contrary, confrontation with other cultures under the circumstances of travel may even strengthen the consciousness of oneself.

As far as the exile experience is concerned, we may also envisage the troubled relationship to space and frontiers it contains. Commenting on "the notion of boundary" in his standard study *Universe of the Mind*, Yuri M. Lotman first postulates that "[e]very culture begins by dividing the world into 'its own' internal space and 'their' external space" and that the interpretation of this binary division "depends on the typology of the culture".[48] In other words, every culture organizes itself in the form of a special space-time grid upon which its existence rests. Within this framework, the notion of boundary is an "ambivalent" one, which "both separates and unites". It works as a "mechanism for translating

---

[48] Yuri M. Lotman: *Universe of the Mind. A Semiotic Theory of Culture*. London – New York: Tauris 1999. P. 131.

texts of an alien semiotics into 'our' own language, it is the place where what is 'external' is transformed into what is 'internal' [...]".[49]

The structure of Lotman's approach presupposes clear cultural spheres and identities that help conceptualize a relationship to the other and its space. It is very helpful for the analysis of travel literature, especially from the imperial period. But it seems less appropriate for the situation of the exiles, as their relationship to space and boundaries is disturbed and troubled. After all, the exile has lost his home, his "internal space," and is cut off from it for political reasons. For many German-speaking exiles this trauma would never be healed, and the loss of *Heimat* proved definitive. This feeling may also explain the many suicides among them (Carl Einstein, Ernst Toller, Joseph Roth, Stefan Zweig, etc.). And even for those exiles who survived, the way back was not taken (Jean Améry), or proved unsatisfactory and thus temporary (Alfred Döblin).

The exile has been expelled from his culture and is unable to find a substitute for it. This is due to his being perceived abroad as a potential threat, and being continually reminded not to disturb the political and social order of his guest country. Furthermore, geographical boundaries have lost their function as markers of clarity and distinction, because of the ideological factor. The "internal space" of *Heimat* has turned to the "external space"; even if some support may be expected from allies in the exile country, the latter remains a place of strangeness, even danger, because of the presence of enemies. The German-Belgian border in these historical circumstances particularly lacked clarity, as people spoke the same language on both sides of the frontier, and because National-Socialist propaganda was very active in eastern Belgium. Améry remembers his own situation as a disoriented *Grenzgänger*:

> [...] – eine Grenzstation in Kaltherberg in der Eifel – Kantone Eupen-Malmédy – dem Grenzgänger, der dort seinen Weg ins Landinnere sucht, prägt ein Satz aus dem "Völkischen Beobachter" sich ein: "Am St. Niklasplatz in Eupen schlägt das deutsche Herz" – die politische Machtausstrahlung des Dritten Reiches war spürbar – wer Abwehrbereitschaft in Belgien erwartete fand dort zunächst Wohlwollen gegenüber dem Hitlerstaat, denn "dieser hatte es geschafft", er hatte die Arbeitslosigkeit beseitigt.[50]

Yet reality actually proved to be even more contradictory: the German-speaking Belgian paper *Grenz-Echo*, for which the exile Kurt Grünebaum wrote, demonstrated its commitment against National-Socialist Germany. Nevertheless, Améry's perception indicates how unsure exiles felt in this particular region of diluted boundaries.

---

[49] Ibid. P. 137.
[50] Améry: Werke. P. 819.

Such uncertainty also offered material for a chapter of Hertha Ligeti's novel, in which the motif and character of the *Grenzgänger*, who helps the refugees cross the border through the woods, refers to his own ambivalence in regard to idealism and opportunism. The misleading, deceptive aspect of the boundary ("Trügerisch ist die Ruhe des Waldes") is also associated with the hybrid character of the inhabitants' identity. It is indeed impossible to define the nation to which the child Henri belongs:

> Keiner verlangt von ihm einen Grenzübertrittausweis. Er ist ein Kind beider Nationen, wohnt auf belgischem Gebiete, ist belgischer Staatsbürger, seine Muttersprache aber ist Deutsch, und da der nächste Ort eine halbe Tagreise entfernt ist, geht er in Aachen zur Schule […]. Welches ist sein Heimatland? "Du bist Belgier deutscher Nationalität", sagt sein Vater, aber in der Schule lehrt man ihn: "Du bist Deutscher. Die Belgier sind deine Feinde, du mußt sie hassen". Doch er versteht von diesen Dingen noch nichts. Seine Heimat ist die Eifel, dieser herrliche Wald mit seinen uralten Eichen, Linden und Buchen […]. Daß mitten durch sein Fleckchen Heimatland die Grenze verläuft, verursacht ihm kein Kopfbrechen. Er spaziert tagtäglich darüber hin, ganz ohne Ehrfurcht, trällernd und vor sich hinpfeifend […].[51]

Clearly Ligeti, as an Austrian citizen who had moved to Rumania at the time she wrote her novel, was sensitive to questions of transient belonging, and uncertain or changing identities. Perhaps she compared them to her own unclear position. However, although undoubtedly based on historical accounts, the key features of her novel, like the story of Henri, are (most probably) fictitious anecdotes.

The destiny of the German-speaking Belgian Joseph Neumayer illustrates many of these themes and motifs with great irony. At the very beginning of the war, before the German invasion of Belgium, Neumayer is drafted into the Belgian Army for a couple of days. On that occasion he receives the identity card of his French-speaking fellow countryman Dumont, who has just died, enabling Neumayer to escape German mobilization after Neumayer's hometown of Eupen is returned to the *Reich*. Neumayer's situation becomes completely absurd after he volunteers for a work camp in Austria, not realizing in advance that he will eventually desire to escape from such living conditions. In order to return to his *Heimatstadt*, Neumayer/ Dumont switches identities with the young Austrian resistance fighter Ottl, who himself needs to hide in his own country. This leaves Neumayer to return home as an Austrian refugee.

With this anecdote, Ligeti brings together the motifs of the *Grenzgänger* and the exile, suggesting that the question of their official citizenship actually makes little sense. They may temporarily be faithful to one nationality or

---

[51] Ligeti: *Sterne* (n. 37). Pp. 112–113.

another, but above all they will retain their independence, like Neumayer's friend, who profits from the woods and the frontier:

> In Wahrheit war er niemandem treu ergeben, nur dem Walde, und deshalb fiel es ihm auch nicht schwer, mal dem einen Staat Treue zu schwören, mal dem anderen, und es bereitete ihm auch keine Gewissensbisse, sie zu hintergehen – sein wahrer Brotgeber war der Wald, dem schon seine Vorfahren gedient. Ihn betrachtete er als seine richtige Heimat und fühlte sich ihm gegenüber als Untergebener und Herrscher zugleich.[52]

Like the *Grenzgänger*, the exile is attached to his independence. But unlike the former, he has to pay the price for this independence with the burden of feeling a deep *Heimatlosigkeit* and solitude. However, Ligeti may tend to underestimate the solitude that the exile suffers in her novel, for as an exile, he has also lost the use of his own language. In contrast, this theme is intimately associated with homelessness by Améry: "Wir waren aus der deutschen Realität ausgesperrt und darum auch aus der deutschen Sprache" (*Jenseits von Schuld und Sühne*). In his assessment of Améry's autobiographical writings, Peter Süss points out how often the writer makes use of specific expressions and word creations derived from the concept of *fremd*.[53]

Fremdheit is inherent to the condition of the exile, and this more permanently than in the experience of the traveller. The former has tragically lost the marker of his culture of origin. The only alternative for him is a sort of hybrid identity, which may bring him the advantages of additional independence, but also much suffering if the status of homelessness is prolonged, be it involuntarily or deliberately, as in the case of Améry.

The Principle of Networks and Reviews

At the beginning of his exile, Améry was reluctant to be labelled as a member of a community. After his arrival in Antwerp, his comrades quickly directed him to the Jewish solidarity network, but the refugee was at first unwilling to integrate this way, as he recalls in *Örtlichkeiten*:

> Er [Der Unerwünschte] hat so manchen Schicksalsgenossen in Antwerpen, der ihm Rat erteilen möchte. Aber alle verweisen ihn immer wieder auf das jüdische Viertel, "de joodse wijk". Gerade dort will er nicht hin. Er weiß nun schon manches über die Antwerpener Verhältnisse, hat vernommen, daß es sehr viele reiche Diamantenhändler gibt, die in vornehmen neuen Buildings am Stadtrand wohnen.[54]

---

[52] Ibid. P. 545.
[53] Peter Süss: "Autobiographische Essayistik bei Jean Améry". In: *Germanistische Mitteilungen* 32 (1990). Pp. 6–7.
[54] Améry: *Werke* (n. 31). Pp. 389–390.

However, isolation and living in a marginal position become unbearable in the long run. Adhesion to collective organizations and networks proved a necessity, also for the young Améry, who revised his stereotypes and participated in community work.

From a political viewpoint it is possible to identify two principal networks organized and integrated at a supranational level, which show international connections at work in the field of political and literary exile. They were committed to some of the activities already mentioned above, and actually also overlap.

The Communist Network

The most active network appears to have been the Communist one, even though there had never been a well-established Communist tradition in Belgium. Hence, party representatives had to participate more or less secretly with leftist Social-Democrat organizations and publications. Nico Rost, a Dutch journalist and a friend of Egon Erwin Kisch, managed to do so very well. Having lived in Berlin and travelled in the circle of important members of the avantgarde, such as Gottfried Benn and Carl Einstein, Rost was forced to leave Germany in 1933. He moved to Brussels, and while there, numerous emigrants and exiles like Hermann Kesten felt welcome in his house.

Rost's biographer Hans Olink discovered a report regarding his activities for the party in the archive of the *Parti Communiste de Belgique*.[55] Rost was put in charge by the German party authorities of establishing a Belgian chapter of the *Schutzverband deutscher Schriftsteller*, which organized, among other things, a commemoration event after the death of Carl von Ossietzky in the *Maison des huit heures* in Brussels.[56] In June of 1939, he also organized an exhibition devoted to "le livre libre allemande," and on that occasion invited Paul Westheim and Bruno Frei, both of whom belonged to the international network of Münzenberg, to give a conference. Because these speeches were directed

---

[55] Nico Rost: Kort exposé van mijn partijbedrijvigheid. Archive of the *Parti Communiste de Belgique*.
[56] This was most probably also the place where Ernst Friedrich opened his Peace Museum. In collaboration with the Belgian *Comité de vigilance des intellectuels antifascistes*, whose member Rost was with the Dutch writer Jan Greshoff, the *Schutzverband* would have organized monthly reading conferences with such speakers as Rudolf Leonhard, Arthur Koestler, Gustav Regler and Alfred Kantorowicz. Kesten's conference at the *Beaux-Arts* was also an initiative of this *Comité*. See Hans Olink: *De man die van Duitsland hield*. Amsterdam: Nijgh & Van Ditmar 1997. Pp. 99–118.

against Hitler's Germany, the Belgian Minister of Justice tried to ban the conference. Nevertheless, it took place, as Rost reported in the *Neue Weltbühne*.[57]

Furthermore, Rost wrote regularly for the Social-Democrat Flemish newspaper *Vooruit*, and for other leftist organs such as *Combat*. He was attentive to all cultural events where German culture and literature were represented, such as the *Festival des Lettres flamandes* at the end of 1937, which most European literary delegations attended. Rost denounced the fact that Italian and German literatures were represented only by "official writers" (instead of exiles), who left the delegation while the French President of the international PEN-Club, Jules Romains, was holding a courageous speech. The poet Rudolf Alexander Schröder and the publisher Anton Kippenberg were already well-known in Belgium, especially in Flemish literary circles. During World War I, they had actively contributed to the German cultural propaganda due to their important translation work of Flemish writers into German. Such cultural mediation was integrated into German political efforts in order to promote a strong Flemish autonomy, the so-called *Flamenpolitik*. Twenty years later, the Dutch journalist Rost, writing for *Combat*, warns against the continuation of this translation enterprise aimed at favouring Flemish authors fitting the *Blut und Boden* aesthetics:

> Schröder et Kippenberg ont séjourné longtemps en Belgique pendant la guerre et ont tâché de faire connaître en Allemagne la littérature flamande moderne. Dans quel dessein? Voulaient-ils par ces traductions effacer toutes les cruautés des Allemands pendant la guerre en Belgique et créer l'illusion d'une Allemagne qui était toujours le pays "der Dichter und Denker"? Maintenant, sous Hitler, le même phénomène se présente. N'avez-vous pas remarqué, combien de romans flamands modernes, soit de Streuvels, de Teirlinck, de Roelants, de Pillecyn et de Walschap, ont été traduits en allemand au cours des dernières années? […]. Toutes ces œuvres peuvent paraître en Allemagne parce que leur caractère n'est pas en contradiction avec l'idéologie du fascisme et beaucoup d'entre elles correspondent aux postulats de la Blubo de Hitler.[58]

The reality of the situation may be more intricate, since publishers such as Kippenberg were concerned with quality rather than with propaganda, and as the promotion of "regional" authors like Felix Timmermans cannot simply be labelled *Blut und Boden*, even if it was implemented as such by the official German state. Nevertheless, Rost is right in the sense that such representatives

---

[57] Nico Rost: Von Proudhon bis Westheim. In: *Die Neue Weltbühne*. 8 June 1939. This review from "the intellectual left" was financed by Münzenberg and was simultaneously published in Prague, Zurich and Paris.

[58] Nico Rost: À propos du festival des Lettres flamandes. In: *Combat*. 4 December 1937.

of official German culture consciously overshadowed, and even excluded, German exiles at an international delegation.

The "Humanist" Network

Yet another network still deserves to be better delimited and identified in regard to its Belgian and international permanent members. To that end, I will now focus on the "left intellectual Humanism" gathering of liberal and socialist personalities. It is most likely that this network organized Kesten's and Friedrich's conferences at the *Palais des Beaux-Arts* in cooperation with the already mentioned *Comité de vigilance des intellectuels antifascistes*.

However, the main highlight was the Amnesty Conference for German political prisoners, which took place at the *Palais d'Egmont* in July 1936 and was organized, among others, by Jeanne Vandervelde, the wife of Belgian Social-Democrat Minister Emile Vandervelde. The press reported that many German emigrants were in attendance, and also commented on a parallel exhibition of documentary books, pictures and engravings illustrating the tragic situation of German prisoners. The painter Karl Schwesig and two other young Germans gave a public account of their torture in German prisons:

> Successivement, trois jeunes Allemands, sortis de geôles allemandes, viennent narrer au congrès les circonstances de leur arrestation et les tortures qui leur furent infligées [...]. M. Armand Abel, traduisant ces dépositions en français, s'écrie: 'J'ai honte d'avoir du sang aryen dans mes veines, quand je vois quelles ignominies on commet près de nous, dans les geôles du régime hitlérien'.[59]

Letters of support written by Thomas Mann and Romain Rolland were also publicly read. Presumably the same sympathizers of the emigrant cause invited Heinrich Mann to talk about "the peace" at the Universal Congress for Peace (*Rassemblement universel pour la Paix*), which also met in Brussels at the very beginning of September 1936.[60]

The Exile Press

The German-speaking exile press published in Belgium showed a great diversity, yet, at the same time, did not adequately reflect the outlined networks; a

---

[59] Quoted from archive materials of CEGES/SOMA devoted to the German painter Karl Schwesig (CEGES/SOMA, class mark AA 873). Reports of the event were published in the daily papers *Le Soir*. 6 July 1936 and *Le Peuple* 5 July 1936.
[60] See Heinrich Mann: Der Friede. In: *Die neue Weltbühne*. 3 September 1936. I am grateful to Wolfgang Klein, who is currently preparing the critical edition of Heinrich Mann, for communicating this information to me.

true polyphony of minor reviews and papers claimed to represent the collective voice, the "wir" of Germany in exile.

Only five editions of the *Brüsseler Zeitung*, the so-called *hebdomadaire belge politique et littéraire de langue allemande* ("Contre l'hitlérisme. Pour la défense des droits de la liberté"), were published between July 4th and August 2nd 1936. The chief editor of this paper was Jan Tassin,[61] who stressed that it was supported by "young people" (*junge Menschen*), the collective voice of the exiles:

> Wir wissen, dass wir schwach sind, aber in dem Worte 'wir' liegt eine Gemeinsamkeit, die verpflichtend für heute und immer ist. Gemeinsames Los und Schicksal schweisste uns auf fremdem Boden zusammen, ein fremder Boden, der uns lieb wurde, da die Menschen uns mit Achtung, ja sogar mit Liebe begegnen. Wir sind umsorgt, wenn wir auch unsere Sorgen haben, aber neben den Sorgen entsteht schüchtern eine Blume, die von Tag zu Tag grösser wird, die Hoffnung. Ja wir hoffen, noch; wir hoffen auf den Anbruch der Freiheit für uns, noch mehr aber für unsere bedrängten Brüder und Schwestern in Deutschland. Mögen 'wir' die Erfüllung unserer Hoffnung 'nicht' erleben, wir wissen aber, unsere 'Kinder' werden 'frei' sein.[62]

One article, entitled "Bagatellisierung der Emigration," clearly shows signs of rivalry and discord with other exile organizations in Brussels.

The theme of youth, which seems quite unusual for exile literature – a prominent personality like Heinrich Mann, on the contrary, embodied the authoritative voice of experience – is again emphasized in the review *Kameradschaft. Schriften junger Deutscher*, which was published in Brussels from November 1937 until at least mid-1939, appearing monthly at the beginning, then more irregularly.[63] The first editorial sounds like a manifest:

> Wir stehen im Kampfe, wir jungen Deutschen. Was unsere Sehsucht in Jahren reichen Jugendlebens war, was wir für uns und unser Volk erträumten und ersehnten, ist ferner denn je. Was wir uns schufen, ist zerstört oder tödlich bedroht. Unser Wollen ist verfehmt, unsere Gemeinschaft verboten. Die braune Pest herrscht in Deutschland. Der Tyrannen Willkür zerstört unsere Heimat. Schwer stöhnt das Volk in den Ketten der Unfreiheit, dunkel und bedroht ist seine Zukunft, für die gerade wir, die Jugend dieses Volkes, Verantwortung tragen.[64]

---

[61] I did not manage to identify most of the editors of these papers, using pseudonyms.
[62] *Brüsseler Zeitung. Hebdomadaire belge politique et littéraire de langue allemande* Nr. 1. Verlag, Redaktion und Inseratenannahme: Édition de la Toison d'or, Bruxelles, 94–96 rue de la Senne. 4 July 1936.
[63] This review was supervised by Hans Ebeling and Theo Hespers. Four successive chief editors are mentioned: E. Van den Driessche, Fernand Lefebvre, V. Borne and Fernand Rousseau.
[64] Anonymous: Kameradschaft. In: *Kameradschaft. Schriften junger Deutscher*. November 1937. P. 1.

This motif, which, as we know, was also characteristic of National-Socialist propaganda, is associated with the idea of companionship arising from the memory of common experiences during World War I. This sounds quite contradictory to the identity of a collective "youth," as a former fighter of the Great War would have been, at least, over 35 years old at the time the review was published:

> Manche von uns waren noch im Kriege. Die romantische Kameradschaft der Horde wurde zur harten Kameradschaft der Front. Da wuchs Mensch zu Mensch. Da blieb uns in Stahlgewittern nur noch die Gewissheit der treuen Kameradschaft als Stütze. Da aber brach das Wissen in vielen auf, dass eine neue Zeit vor der Tür stehe und dass die Jugend sich ein Neuland zu schaffen habe, in der die neuerlebten Werte Wirklichkeit für alle, für das ganze Volk werden müssten. So wurde der feldgraue "Wandervogel" zum Revolutionär und zum politischen Menschen.

The allusion to Ernst Jünger's *In Stahlgewittern* is certainly not characteristic of the exile press, and *Kameradschaft* rather resembles a paper whose aggressive rhetoric is pleading for the spirit of martial community (though born during the carefree years of the *Wandervögel*): "Kameradschaft hatten wir, weil unser Leben immer eine harte Kampfgemeinschaft war"; "Kameradschaft fordert eiserne Zucht";

> Kameradschaft ist aber auch nur dann, wenn das trennende Nebeneinander überwunden ist durch zuverlässige Führung und zuverlässige Gefolgschaft. So wie die Kameradschaft des Führers die Gefolgschaft ermöglicht, fordert es sie auch. Wir sind eine Kampfgemeinschaft. Wir können gehorchen.

The programmatic text of the first edition ends with an open call to initiative, to unity, and to battle: "Jetzt gilt es zu beweisen, dass es uns mit unserem Wollen, blutiger, heiliger Ernst war und ist [...]. Jetzt ergeht der Ruf zur Einheit, zur Sammlung. Das Vaterland und des Volkes Zukunft ist in Gefahr".[65]

Other isolated initiatives show how scattered the exile press truly was, and how there existed an open lack of dialogue between these organs: Hans Bendgens Henner's *Das andere Deutschland. Zeitschrift der Kultur-Gemeinde 'Das andere Deutschland'*; Heinz Kühn's *Freiheitsbriefe an die deutsche Wehrmacht*; Max Sievers' *Informationsbrief*. One wonders to what extent this absence of communication happened fortuitously, or if it was principally due to ideological divergences.

---

[65] Ibid. Pp. 2–3.

Conclusion and Perspectives

This briefly sketched panorama of the exile press should be completed and deepened,[66] as well as contrasted with other published sources, such as the very interesting German-language Belgian paper *Grenz-Echo*.

The study of the Belgian case could prove fruitful, because it fundamentally relies on its integration into the international context, beyond the specificities worked out above. The relation of a more or less voluntary concurrence between the exile reviews may contribute to the reflection on German exile as a literary field, an approach favored at the moment in the research seminar "Dominants et marginaux dans le champ intellectuel allemand exilé (1933–1945)".[67]

Let us, however, not overlook the fact that the intellectual field of exile is certainly not autonomous or closed, and that all exiles primarily had to fight for recognition in foreign societies against tyranny and oppression. People abroad were not well informed about the tragic situation of the exiles, whether due to a lack of objective information, or because they were unwilling to perceive it due to its threatening of official, Belgian "neutrality". It should finally be mentioned that National-Socialist propaganda was particularly active in neighboring countries and regions concerned with muffling the voice of the exiles.[68]

---

[66] A good basis is offered by the survey of Thomas Biene: Exilpublizistik in den Niederlanden, Belgien und Luxemburg. In: *Presse im Exil. Beiträge zur Kommunikationsgeschichte des deutschen Exils 1933–1945*. Ed. by H. Hardt, E. Hilscher, W. B. Lerg. München: K.G. Saur 1979. Pp. 181–222.

[67] This seminar (see http://www.seminaireexil.blogspot.com/) is led by Nathalie Raoux and Valérie Robert.

[68] This was especially true in Eastern German-speaking Belgium, a border frontier in which National-Socialist propaganda extended very easily.

Henrike Walter

Fern-Weh. Wolfgang Hildesheimer's Novels *Tynset* and *Masante* as Topographical Reflections of the Exile Experience

This essay analyzes Hildesheimer's twin novels, Tynset *and* Masante, *in the context of exile and travel as coherent metaphors of existence. The metaphor of travel as a transformed exile is central to both novels, although there is a crucial difference in the mobilization of that metaphor. While* Tynset *seems to be dominated by the narrator's oppressive immobility and his infinite longing to move,* Masante *is striking for the protagonist's manic restlessness, which finds its only possible resolution in the endless expanses of the desert into which the narrator eventually (and successfully?) tries to disappear. The deep trauma of exile is revealed as an everlasting stain: "Unbehaustheit" is the exile's fatal condition.*

1.

The writer and artist Wolfgang Hildesheimer began his creative production comparatively late and under unusual circumstances. Born in Germany in 1916, his childhood was shaped by the continual relocations required of his father's profession; leave-taking and the subsequent re-orientation in unfamiliar environments thus formed an essential part of the boy's socialization, and as such, did not bear the stain of threat or trauma. Even when sent to England in the early 1930s, Hildesheimer did not perceive the separation from his parents, mother country, and culture as unsettling. On the contrary, he states (with hindsight and perhaps some idealization) that "when I first came to England, one of my sensations must have been that I was nearer to my aim".[1] His exile experience began in England, where his parents fled in 1933 with their son on their way to Palestine, and at first it appears as though the family's move to England is nothing more than a continuation of their itinerant life previous to 1933.[2]

Yet a key difference arises, owing to the fact that this move occurred under the conditions of persecution and threat. Even though Hildesheimer consistently denies that "emigration" would in any way be an adequate term to describe his experiences ("Ich fühle mich auch gar nicht emigriert"[3]), traces of the particular

---

[1] Wolfgang Hildesheimer in: Volker Jehle: *Wolfgang Hildesheimer. Werkgeschichte*. Frankfurt/Main: Suhrkamp 1990. P. 116.
[2] For a complex and detailed presentation of Hildesheimer's life and work in the context of questions of cultural as well as personal identity, see Henry A. Lea: *Wolfgang Hildesheimers Weg als Jude und Deutscher*. Stuttgart: Hans-Dieter Heinz 1997.
[3] Wolfgang Hildesheimer in: Hanjo Kesting, *Dichter ohne Vaterland. Gespräche und Aufsätze zur Literatur*. Berlin – Bonn: Dietz 1982. P. 58.

conditions of his migration are manifest in the structure and topics of his works. His neologism, "Häscher," denoting those who represent persecution and threat, as well as the constant fear of those doomed to be on the 'wrong side' – is a term meant to deflate the intensity of that fear: "der Furcht den Stachel rauben, sie in jene Bereiche der kindlichen Angst ziehen, in denen man schließlich heimisch wird".[4] "Heimischwerden" in the realm of fear is the only form of belonging to which Hildesheimer ever commits himself; a profound sense of disconnect with people or places is acute in his prose and comments, repeatedly culminating in the statement "ich mag nicht dazugehören".[5] However, in a paradox characteristic of his work, it is this deliberate "Heimatlosigkeit" that connects Hildesheimer to Judaism.[6] (Of course, a constraint must be mentioned: in contrast to orthodox Jews, Hildesheimer opposes the idea of "Heimat" not only on earth, but in heaven as well.) It appears that Hildesheimer saw himself neither as an emigrant, nor as a Jew, nor even as a German: the English language and culture seem to have attracted him more, or, at least as deeply, as the German. His cultural background as reflected in his prose spans the entire middle-European intellectual landscape – evidently, Wolfgang Hildesheimer exceeds the categories of traveler and exile, drawing experientially upon both but belonging to neither.[7]

We should, therefore, take a closer look at the works in which he reveals his own self-understanding most explicitly, and in which the questions of "Heimischsein" and "Dazugehören" are granted a particularly striking expression in the dichotomy of "here" and "there". Movement and travel, the fundamental aspects of his biography, are transformed artistically into images of immense emotional and associative power. The topic of "traveling" is highly present and of central significance in his work, particularly in his novels, even though the outer setting often remains static or somehow disconnected from the narrator throughout the plot.[8] Read as a state of being, "travel" is the most adequate metaphor to understand the various narrators' dispositions. Being

---

[5] Wolfgang Hildesheimer: *Masante*. Frankfurt/Main: Suhrkamp 1973. P. 211.

[5] Wolfgang Hildesheimer in: Jan Süselbeck: *Nicht dazugehören. Wolfgang Hildesheimers zweite Emigration*. In: Literaturkritik.de (April 2005).

[6] Critics have had fewer doubts categorizing Hildesheimer as an artist and individual: Lea (n. 2) portrays him as a "Jew and German", Marcel Reich-Ranicki mentions him in the context of German-Jewish writers as well, whose common characteristic would be the subversive power of their writing. Cf. Marcel Reich-Ranicki: *Über Ruhestörer. Juden in der deutschen Literatur*. München: Piper Verlag 1973.

[7] Also see John M. Spalek and Robert F. Bell: *Exile: The Writer's Experience*. Chapel Hill: University of North Carolina Press 1982. Pp. 333–339.

[8] While in *Tynset* and *Masante*, the narrator tells his story from a position fixed in time and space and merely wanders through time and space in his mind, Hildesheimer's biographical novels *Mozart* and *Marbot* stand as documentations of the protagonists' 'real' way through life. Although there is a precise description of the

underway is the exile's fate: the original flight from persecution is a fundamental loss of home – a return to the point of origin is impossible. Even a return to their home after exile will reveal a different perception from that of before their flight. As aimless as this flight may have been (even if there was, as in the case of the Hildesheimers, a particular place set as a kind of transitory homeland), the exiles flounder in a constant limbo, never knowing if the place they currently inhabit is permanent, or if the next decampment is just about to come. The abundance of places visited, present in memories and images of different kinds, is at odds with the utter lack of geographical permanence, of a home in which to feel safe. This continuous state of movement, as well as the constant fear of losing what, or whom, one loves, hinders the refugee from building up deeper relations: the spatial trauma is reflected in the relational. In most of Hildesheimer's prose, a first-person narrator evokes not only a particular closeness between author and work, but also a closeness between reader and text. The narrator wanders between landscapes and villages, houses and paths: between diverse dimensions of 'reality'. Mythological, psychological, realistic, and historical layers condense in an overall-contingency of life, reflected in Hildesheimer's thinking and writing, and reveal themselves to be beyond comprehension, logic or sensibility.

2.

The novels *Tynset* and *Masante* (I shall use the term 'novels' although the question of their genre has not yet been decided by scholars of his work and would deserve an analysis of its own) express the author's distance to any concept of a closed, coherent, consistent or logical world order. Both revolve around the topic of travel, the first in an unfulfilled, the second in a somewhat exaggerated sense. The first-person narrator of *Tynset* is stuck in an apparently self-imposed solitude; he has retreated from human society into a farmhouse in the Italian Alps, where his only companion is an old, alcoholic, Catholic factotum. Night after night the narrator studies an expired timetable of Norwegian train connections, envisioning traveling to Tynset and finding peace. The whole nightmare of his story evolves out of the contrast between this envisioned redemption to be found in a small Norwegian town, and his immobility, even confinement, due to trauma and fear, in a nameless nowhere. In *Masante*, the same narrator appears as a deeply restless traveler, forever doomed to constant

---

places they live and the roads they travel, the outer movement is but a mere reflection of the protagonists' inner disposition. Particularly in *Mozart*, where the author had to follow the biographical facts at least to a certain degree, the artful interlacing of external 'truth' and internal state gives a good example of Hildesheimer's specific 'aesthetic of space'. See Wolfgang Hildesheimer: *Mozart*. Frankfurt/Main: Suhrkamp 1980; Wolfgang Hildesheimer: *Marbot*. Frankfurt/Main: Suhrkamp 1984.

movement and unable to reach his destination. As the use of the term "Behausung" suggests, this destination is a metaphysical one: a home, a place in which to feel safe and comfortable.

The backdrop of both novels is the trauma of the Nazi era. In light of the unimaginable that has become, or rather broken into, reality, the author can no longer maintain any idea of 'meaning' or 'reason' in what occurs. The absurd thus replaces the idea of order – and for Hildesheimer it becomes a fundamental principle, "die Wirklichkeit so darzustellen, als sei sie absurd, obwohl ja eigentlich das Absurde das Wirkliche ist" – which leads to his characteristic strategy to mount "absurde Parallelsituationen, die nun wirklich erfunden sind, die aber ebenso gut wahr sein können".[9] The borders between reality and phantasm dissolve; imagination and experience coexist in equal measure and effect, and can – at least sometimes – hardly be differentiated from one another. This diffusion has been interpreted in two directions. The first interpretation, as, for example, in the work of Volker Jehle,[10] sees this diffusion as the expression of man's directionless search. The second interpretative direction, which proceeds from the postulate of the absurd character dominating Hildesheimer's prose, sees the diffusion of reality and phantasm as the mode of representing man's strangeness in the world.[11] Both interpretations are in some way convincing, but remain, in my opinion, directed too far into the metaphysical sphere, and thus fail to grasp the more basic, existential dimension of Hildesheimer's texts, which manifests itself through the use of well-established existentialist symbols: the desert, boulders, and black night sky.

Tynset and *Masante* are not only connected by a narrator who deliberately presents himself as the same person at different stages, but also through similarities in structure, images or topics. Günter Blamberger[12] has argued that their main coherence lies in a shared "Realität des Absurden", insofar as their stories serve as examples of its omnipotence. In both works, the first-person narrator reports on his experience of isolation in the face of incomprehensible chaos. Since the connection between the novels is established clearly by several details, we may assume that on the basis of their interconnection an analysis should

---

[9] 'Ich kann über nichts anderes schreiben als über ein potentielles Ich'. Gespräch mit Wolfgang Hildesheimer. In: Manfred Durzak: *Gespräche über den Roman*. Frankfurt/Main: Suhrkamp 1976. Pp. 271–295. Here: p. 290. Also see Dietmar Goll-Bickmann: *Aspekte der Melancholie in der frühen und mittleren Prosa Wolfgang Hildesheimers*. Münster: Lit Verlag 1989.
[10] See Jehle: *Wolfgang Hildesheimer* (n. 1).
[11] Stephan Reher: *Leuchtende Finsternis. Erzählen in Callots Manier*. Wien: Böhlau 1997.
[12] Günter Blamberger: Der Rest ist Schweigen. Hildesheimers Literatur des Absurden. In: *Text und Kritik* 89/90. München 1986. Pp. 33–44.

follow the same patterns for both works. By focusing upon the great degree of subtlety with which the author transforms individual and historical biographic experience into artistic structures, we will find that certain dimensions of meaning are interwoven, adding to or even opposing the denotative layer of the text. The topographic structure of the two novels is most significant in this respect, since it forms an important part of the complex imagery. I will show that by the particular artistic use of different *loci*, the narrator reveals his own position as being somewhere 'in between'. In a paradoxical reflection on the multiplicity of imaginative and reported movements and travels, he is inescapably fixed to this state of being. The double meaning of travel as flight and hope reflects dimensions of the past (the flight away from one's origin) and the future (longing for something that might be found). The narrative loci, as we will see, are deliberately staged as images of this dichotomy, and the motif of traveling corresponds in a characteristic paradox with the particular narrator's inability to move at all.

3.

The topographical structure in both texts appears, at first glance, to be quite clear and strictly ordered. The narrator's point of view, the formal 'here', is easily identifiable. In *Tynset*, it is an old farmhouse probably located somewhere in the Italian part of the Alps, where the narrator's only living company is the pious-alcoholic householder Celestina. In *Masante*, it is the miserable settlement at the edge of a desert called Meona, where the narrator has taken up quarters in 'La Dernière Chance,' a hostel-pub as worn out as its owners. In spite of their prominence as titles of the novels, both Tynset and Masante do not appear as concrete places visited or inhabited by the narrator, but rather as absent images of his longing. As stated before, the two novels share the same narrator, who is only represented in different states of his search or at different points of time. This deduction is evoked explicitly in the text: "Eine Zeitlang rieb ich mich in Sucht und Suche nach möglichen Zielen auf, eines war im Norden und hieß Tynset, das Ypsilon hatte es mir angetan, dann war auch das vorbei, und ich wählte Masante".[13] This also implies that the place from which *Tynset* is told is not Masante itself! I would not, for many reasons, follow this assumption all too easily: the travels and outer restlessness of the narrator in *Masante* contrasts too sharply with the *Tynset* narrator's seclusion and immobility. We should, however, concentrate on a second level of meaning in order to understand the significance of this obviously similar symbolic structure of places. The 'here': the actual position of the narrator somewhere-nowhere, the 'there': the places predominating the novels in structure and reception, Tynset and Masante, and the images they evoke.

[13] Hildesheimer: *Masante* (n. 3). P. 321.

Tynset

The old house in which the narrator of *Tynset* lives, works – growing and selling herbs in different mixtures – and sleeps (or rather: not sleeps) is nowhere explicitly described. Yet the reader gets a very specific impression, which is dominated mainly by two interconnected aspects: the house's labyrinthine structure and the presence of the past. The narrator explains how he came to live in the house, and deliberately connects the necessary movement from somewhere outside into the house with an emphatic and repeated image of a standstill: "Aber seit ich nun hier bin, bin ich nur noch hier, immer ausschließlicher, der Kreis, in dem ich mich bewege, wird immer kleiner".[14] At the same time, he points out that he has somehow grown into a life that has been there before: "Das Haus ist das gleiche geblieben, ich habe wenig hinzugefügt, habe wenig verändert, ich habe das Haus übernommen, einschließlich Celestina".[15] The former owner strolled through the house at night in the never ending effort to measure the world: "Er war ganz damit beschäftigt, die äußerlichen Offenbarungen der Welt und ihres Laufes und des Lebens in ihr zu registrieren, zu messen, was es zu messen gibt, aufzuzeichnen, was es aufzuzeichnen gibt".[16] The narrator himself continues these somnambulate expeditions, strolling through his inner universe of memories, nightmares and longings. In contrast to his uncle (the former owner) he has given up the effort to measure and report his perceptions in the scientific way of numbers and forms. Confronted with the omnipresence of chaos, and with the futility of reason in a world of arbitrariness and anarchy, he has substituted the traditional concept of 'reality' with a universe of contingent stories, thereby dispensing with any idea of 'truth.' Consequently, his world is one of frightening abundance: literary and historical figures all somehow connected with stories of love, loss and murder (Hamlet's father, Goethe's Erlkönig, Dante's Paolo and Francesca and, of course, the artful narrative compositions of love and death in summer- and winterbed), blend with vague memories of women once loved, friends once lost, or persecutors once – and still – deeply feared. The house is, as we see, not at all empty. Likewise, the narrator is not captured within the walls he has chosen as a retreat, but cannot bring himself to stay in – and, despite his deliberate seclusion, does not even want to do so:

> so weit komme ich, bis zu diesem obersten, äußersten Winkel meines Hauses, weiter nicht, weiter will ich auch nicht, jedenfalls nicht auf meinen Beinen, wohl aber mit meinen Augen und Gedanken, hier stehe ich still, mein Körper schlägt Wurzel, als

---

[14] Wolfgang Hildesheimer: *Tynset*. Frankfurt/Main: Suhrkamp 1989. P. 140.
[15] Ibid. P. 140.
[16] Ibid. P. 141.

stehe er hier von nun ab für immer und ewig [...]. Hier stehe ich und bohre mich tief ins ewig Unvorstellbare.[17]

We find such spatial images of redemption throughout the novel, in places where the narrator's restlessness and fear vanish under the illusion of a sense of belonging, of liberation from fear and threat. These are places wherein an inner peace appears as possible as relations with others: places that are free from the constant threat of loss predominating the narrator's relations (and memory of relations) thus far. While the house reflects the narrator's captivity in his sinister recollections – closeness and isolation, the labyrinthine structure of involuted rooms, stairs, and chambers all add to the impression of a haunted, sinister and tortured mind – there are two places set in opposition to all that is frightening and depressing. The night sky is one, and the telescope set under the roof of the house allows the narrator to dream himself up into the blackness where he hopes to find the particular spot, "an dem nichts ist und nichts sein kann und nie etwas gewesen ist". This wish is unsurprising when considering the crowded memories plaguing him night after night! Most significantly, this shall be "der leere Raum, durch den man hindurchsieht *auf Etwas*".[18] We see that it is not really nothing, the complete "Nichts" so often conjured up throughout the novel as the ultimate aim of his longing, but rather that there is something that can be seen and felt through it: "Etwas". Behind the empty space something new may be expected: a metaphor for the need to forget the past, to clear one's mind in order to enter new spheres of experience and feeling. The pointlessness of this dream is obvious and inevitable, since it takes its start from within the house, that is, from within the haunted mind. Even while gazing at the sky, the narrator remains in the loft of the house where his telescope is erected. Again, the description of this particular setting is in itself significant: "Hier oben bin ich in einem umgekippten, ausgehöhlten Schiffsleib, einer Arche umgedreht [...] das Regenwasser tropfenweise [aufgefangen], wo der Schiffskörper leck ist".[19] The arch, originally the symbol of rescue and shelter, is *turned* into an image of shipwreck, of "Unbehaustheit", a vision that remains part of, and intermingles with, his trauma.

The character of Tynset, the second of the two spatial counterparts to the house and the presence of past experiences, is in some way different, since the particular character of the longing projected onto it is conveyed more openly. It becomes evident through the course of the narrator's monologue that his actual travel there is as futile a project as is his search for the night sky "Nichts". Yet since Tynset is a place at least somehow founded in 'reality,' we at first follow

---

[17] Ibid. P. 177.
[18] Ibid. P. 181.
[19] Ibid. P. 176.

the narrator's dreams with more optimism. Its first mention already indicates the relational character that strikes and fascinates the narrator: "Die Buchstaben sind gut gewählt, sie passen zueinander [...] Zerlege ich das Wort in seine beiden Silben, so habe ich zuerst das 'Tyn', einen hohen Gongschlag, Beginn eines Rituals in einem Tempel [...] habe also das Tyn, das sich alsbald, jäh aus seinen Vibrationen gerissen, mit dem 'set' setzt [...] Tynnn-Settt".[20] The promise of Tynset is kept deliberately vague, and grows out of the unknown as the main and, in some ways, most comforting attribute: "Von Elverum und Tynset dagegen weiß ich nichts, aber auch sie verheißen etwas. Vielleicht weniger Elverum, das die Endung eines Neutrums hat, als Tynset. Ja, Tynset, wegen des Ypsilons. Wo ein Ypsilon ist, da steckt nicht selten ein Geheimnis".[21] The escape into the unknown is explicitly revealed as the only possible destination the narrator can still imagine for himself, and it is fundamentally connected to the vision of redemption constantly flickering through the evocations of Tynset: " – ich sollte nach Tynset fahren. Das wäre ein Wagnis, wie? Nach so vielen Jahren das Haus verlassen, sich abstoßen, und dann im Unbekannten schwimmen, oder im nicht mehr Bekannten. Es wäre ein Ziel, das einzig mögliche, das einzig denkbare".[22] Detachment from the familiar also means detachment from past experiences, and it is obvious that these experiences are the shackles binding the narrator to the lonely house full of ghosts.

There are moments in which a vague impression of homeliness flashes up even in the context of the house, as if the outward distance to human society, the almost total seclusion into which the narrator has fled, suffices to reduce the actual threats at least to a minimum. In these moments, the narrator may smell the scent of herbs he grows and harvests and may remember "Dinge, die es noch gibt, es gibt Minuten, Viertelstunden, in denen das Aroma dieser Dinge Trost verbreitet, Fremdheit vergessen lässt".[23] In this moment a moving impression of belonging emerges, a positive memory that catches the narrator's attention among the dense composition of frightening, unsettling, irritating images otherwise dominating his thoughts. The same striking ambivalence, the simultaneity of comfort or homeliness in the face of "Fremdheit" and threat, is conveyed by the image of the narrator's sole companionship with the housekeeper Celestina. Their relation begins with the silent "Vorwurf, dass ich ein Mörder sei" in conjunction with moments,

> in denen unsere gegenseitige Anhänglichkeit begann, ausgehend von beiden Teilen gleichzeitig, Vorwurf auf der einen, Einsicht auf der anderen Seite, unsere

---

[20] Ibid. P. 27.
[21] Ibid. P. 15.
[22] Ibid. P. 75.
[23] Ibid. P. 125.

Loyalitäten tasteten sich gegeneinander vorwärts, Zugehörigkeit entstand, schmiedete sich ineinander, unzertrennlich aber noch uneingestanden.[24]

In contrast to these very limited images of human contact are the vast number of threatening scenes that convey fear, and the threatening irritation of society that is condensed in the narrator's odyssey through the labyrinths of human settlement. Here he is most bluntly confronted with the fact of his strangeness and non-belonging: "dazwischen ich, der ich nicht wusste, wohin ich gehörte".[25] Underlying the narrator's entire odyssey is his memory of the labyrinth at Villa Barbarigo in Valsanzibio, where the eyes of those who hardly escaped from the maze are "von einem kurzen Schrecken getrübt, als hätten sie dem Tod ins Angesicht gesehen. Wahrscheinlich hatten sie genau das getan".[26]

Tynset is deliberately and artfully set up against these images as a vision of redemption, especially because of 'the unknown' attributed to it. Since the narrator obviously feels that he has never experienced even a moment of fearless, harmonious safety in human company, it is this aspect of the unknown that constitutes Tynset's particular attraction. Its image is filled with all his hopes and visions, which remain as vague as their meaning for the narrator is strong, due to the extreme individuality of his vision, undeterred by the threat of human interference: "keiner von ihnen weiß von mir, keiner weiß, was mir Tynset ist. Ich weiß es ja schließlich selbst nicht. Ein Ankerplatz in einem Meer von Irrtum".[27] Tynset represents a home, an orientation. It is Tynset that rescues the narrator from the never ending loops of terror and confusion: " [...] los von dieser Hand im Spiel, los von dem Spiel! Was wollte ich noch? Was wollte ich vorher? Ich wollte nach Tynset fahren, richtig".[28] Through one significant detail his vision becomes concrete; he imagines the teacher of Tynset, and in imagining and following his thoughts, he envisions deep, emotional sympathy: "Das denkt der Lehrer von Tynset, *mein Freund*".[29] This vision of an understanding friend, of someone whose thoughts may be shared and understood, contrasts with the images of telephone contact with those who do not listen, of the dumb factotum who does not understand, of the fierce persecutors who lie, betray and kill.

While the setting (the narrator's 'here' of the secluded house in the Italian Alps) remains on the outer level of meaning throughout the novel, the narrator's inner position is much more complex and vague. He appears to hover in a

---

[24] Ibid. P. 217.
[25] Ibid. P. 117.
[26] Ibid. P. 98.
[27] Ibid. P. 135.
[28] Ibid. P. 110.
[29] Ibid. P. 137.

sphere that can best be described as 'between'; bound to, and burdened with, the traumatic memories of the past that are, unequivocally, experiences of persecution and exile, of homelessness and strangeness, of suspicion and fear, he is unable to move on and develop further. He is aware that these experiences belong to the past in a temporal sense, but since they are still present in his perception, accompanying him in the house in crude manifestations and stories, he seems to be preoccupied in maintaining them night after night rather than ever coming to terms with them. These are his only companions, threatening as they are. As strong as the wish to leave might be (indicated by the constant repetition of the wish to travel to Tynset and liberate himself from the house and the past it secludes), the fact that he eventually stays (as he did all the nights before) proves that this particular "being in between" is in fact not a state, but rather a fatal consequence of the exile experience. As long as the past is the refugee's closest companion, any other relation will, figuratively speaking, be perceived in its shadow. The result is isolation, but the complete seclusion as envisioned by the narrator – "das Nichts" as a state of total liberation – is not actually the redemption for which he longs. On the contrary, it is the space *between* the threat and a promising "Etwas", a kind of relation unexperienced before that no longer stands under the auspices of persecution. This is "there," the ideal locus Tynset represents, in the harmony of its sound, the integration of the individualistic Epsilon into the whole of the letters' company – an ideal that, at the end of the night, the narrator has to acknowledge as unreachable. It is not because of the distance or the snow that he does not go, but rather because *Tynset* is a future state not (yet?) open for him. Fettered by the past, he remains inescapably 'in between'.

Masante

As in *Tynset*, the setting of *Masante* is characterized by seclusion and strangeness. But while the massive stone walls of the old farmhouse in some way reflect the protective shell the narrator has tried to erect around his vulnerable inner self, the dilapidated settlement at the edge of the desert conveys the futility of these efforts. The restlessness of a refugee unable to feel at home anywhere finds its symbolic expression in the houses that do not offer shelter, and the settlement that promises no hope to the lonely wanderer on his search for redemption. The company in Meona is as rotten as the houses themselves. Maxine has lost her self in a devilish pact with alcohol and isolation, which perhaps springs from a peculiar source of sympathy leading her to sleep with any wanderer passing by. She hopes all the while that the act of sexual merging will somehow bring about recognition of souls. However, instead of finding herself in the other, she absorbs strange identities: stories of lives perhaps invented, perhaps led, and buries herself under the compilation of possible vitae she has blended with her own, memories and dreams alike. Consequently, she is the main counterpart for the narrator who tries to enter her game, re-inventing and expanding her stories and yet not giving up the idea that there is, somewhere in this mosaic of stories, one that is true. The recognition of this might allow a different kind of understanding: deeper, more honest, free from doubt and irritation.

Also present is her husband Alain, whose indifference only adds to his baneful character, and his dark, fateful role in the narrator's story: " 'Heute gehen Sie gewiss nicht mehr hinaus. Es wird dunkel, und Sie kennen sich nicht aus. Aber morgen vermutlich'. Das ist eine Feststellung, keine Frage. Er bestimmt es, er schickt mich in die Wüste".[30] The third individual in the strange triangle so deliberately set in this fatal place is the Irishman, whose sheer weirdness in the eyes of the narrator develops into the threatening association of the very "Häscher" the narrator is trying to escape (now that the physical threat might be overcome, the mental persecution turns out to be even more torturing). It is he who delivers the formal counterpoint to *Tynset*: "Sie sind in Meona, sagte oder vielmehr sang er, Meona, ein Frauenname, den man singt", and the narrator agrees: 'Me-' der Auftakt, Vorhalt, ein bescheidenes Versprechen. Die Betonung liegt auf dem langen O, ein Omega, nur offener. Das Na ist kurz, es hüpft hinterher und stellt den Namen in Frage".[31] The same attention has been given to the sound of Tynset, but the result is absolutely contradictory. While *Tynset* promises peace, seclusion in harmony and silent company, meditation, a ritual consoling and confirmation of a social self, Meona's promise is an explicitly modest one, jeopardized by the open ending.

The narrator's position in this setting is that of a wanderer, and he insists that his stay is caused by sheer coincidence, another vagary of a fortune to which he has completely surrendered.

> Ein Punkt am Rand der Wüste, an den einer wie ich nur zufällig gelangt, das entspricht genau meiner Ordnung, so hatte ich es mir vorgestellt, so weit so gut. Ein blinder Stich mit dem Bleistift auf die Landkarte: Meona. Meona, beinah verlassen, Siedlung eines Volkes aus der Vorzeit, genannt Karumäer, das klingt wie eine Erfindung, ist es vielleicht auch.[32]

Here he is, "ein unzufriedener, ewig bestürzter Unheld, ein flüchtiger Gast, doch harmlos und für andere nicht schwierig".[33] Meona is apparently only one in a long sequence of places to which the narrator has traveled on his search for redemption from the past: haunted by memories, restlessly striving to find the

---

[30] Hildesheimer: *Masante* (n. 3). P. 249.
[31] Ibid. P. 22.
[32] Ibid. P. 19.
[33] Ibid. P. 45.

place where a start – a new start, beginning with the effort of writing in order to come to terms with his own and the collective memory – would be possible: "In Masante, da dachte ich: nur woanders sein, irgendwo wo nichts ist, und dort wird es sich abspulen. Nicht in Masante zwischen Schönheit sitzen, die sich seit Horaz nicht geändert hat, und es geht. Aber was soll eigentlich gehen?"[34] What he finds, then, is not peace, but the tragic certainty that escape through flight is as impossible as escape through seclusion (which the *Tynset*-narrator prefers):

> Denn auch hier werden sie kommen, die bösen Stunden des Nachmittags. Überall sind sie gekommen, unweigerlich, in Masante und unterwegs auf Reisen, in Hotelzimmern, an fremden Orten waren sie noch böser; ich war mit dem Nichtzuhause-sein so beschäftigt, dass ich es nicht fertiggebracht hätte, mich auch noch mit anderem zu beschäftigen als dem Dortsein, dem Fernsein als aktivem Vollzug; Jedes Erlebnis, auch das erhoffteste, misslang; der Versuch, mich auf Reisen abschiednehmend zu delektieren, war müßig, dieses Schema war schon veraltet.[35]

Yet, in spite of this insight, the narrator cannot calm his desire. On the contrary, he re-projects it onto the place he once lived in and subsequently left, Masante – this individual house with a name, secluded again from the settlement that is nearby, and in this aspect closely corresponding with the narrator's character. It is significant that Masante was only a second choice for him, since the house he originally wanted was not available: "Es gab in Urbino ein schönes Haus, ich hätte es gern gehabt. Es trägt keinen Namen wie Masante, ist mit anderen Häusern zusammengewachsen, hinter ihm türmt sich die Stadt […] Vor dem Haus fällt die Stadt ab zur zentralen Ader".[36] This unnamed house represents integration, contact, and being part of an organically organized whole of human company. The needs and dreams of a homeless refugee could hardly be expressed more clearly, and yet he himself knows that this would have been the "wrong" house for him, as unreliable a home as Maxine's stories are for her in her search for truth. In the distance, this house – a home, a place to return to – grows in beauty and chance. It seems as if the narrator needed this distance, the confrontation with worse places in which to live, in order to be able to acknowledge what Masante might be: "Ich bin nur hier, um mir Masante von fern heranzuträumen, erst die Distanz ergibt die Proportionen und den Wert".[37] Deep inside he knows that his restlessness and quest will not allow him to gain inner peace wherever he is. In the face of past and omnipresent threats conveyed through memory and his own mental life, the secluded beauty of Masante grows

[34] Ibid. P. 140.
[35] Ibid. Pp. 36f.
[36] Ibid. P. 128.
[37] Ibid. P. 134.

into a vision of "home". The narrator resembles a fairytale knight, burdened with a challenging task he has to perform before he is expected to return to happiness and glory: "Ich werde nach Masante zurückkehren – die Rückkehr leuchtet vor mir auf – sobald ich nur einen einzigen Faden gefunden habe, den weiterzuspinnen es sich lohnt".[38] As if trying to transfer his vision into more realistic realms, he points out his own and his travels' specific character and his rational motifs:

> ich bin nicht auf der Flucht, bin auch kein Märtyrer, auch suche ich keine Gefahren […] Es hält mich nicht an einem Ort, wo eine unbekannte Hand Kultgegenstände verteilt, böse Kerne in Idyllisches verpackt; einen Punkt, der einbezogen ist in das Netz der Planer und Vermesser, die ihre Grenzen dauernd auswärts treiben […] und so den Boden vorbereiten für das Entsetzliche: Weihnachtsbaum – Singen unter dem Baum – Hausmusik – Hausordnung – Zuchtundordnung – Verhör und Folterung – Mord – Motschmann, Globotschnik, Perchtl.[39]

The constant ambivalence in differentiation between the phantastic and the possible, the real and the schizophrenic, terror and hope, is condensed in the grotesque setting of Meona. The obviously existentialist composition, represented by the desert, the stones, and the sandstorm, only add to its perception as a landscape "of soul" rather than of geographical order. It is contrasted with the ancient beauty, the *arcadia* envisioned in Masante.

Like the "Nichts" of the black night sky in *Tynset*, there is another vision woven into the outward "here" – Meona – and the place projected as hope and redemption, "there" – Masante: "Saloniki: einer der Orte, an denen der Schrecken lang nicht in Erscheinung trat, allem Geschehen entrückt, noch lange konnte man sich dort wohl fühlen und beinahe sicher".[40] The name 'Saloniki' conveys its meaning; it is here where the narrator met Niki, the girl, or woman, with whom love seemed possible, at least for some time and also as an idea: "Ich traf sie in einem Museum, unter dem Bild der Simonetta Vespucci, erfand für sie eine Geschichte über das Bild, die ihr gefiel. Es kamen weitere Bilder, eine Bindung entstand, eine Liebe, so glaubten wir, und ich folgte ihr nach Haus –".[41] A trust in love and the invented stories of phantasy are connected by a created world. Yet Niki keeps silent about her mad uncle, who believes he is a dog – an image closely connected with the torture practices in concentration camps. Thus, complete confidence between them, which the narrator envisions as the condition of redemptive love, is impossible. The chance of healing through love is implied by the image of Salo-Niki, the place without fear. However, both place and opportunity are tragically distorted by the experience of imperfection.

---

[38] Ibid. P. 134.
[39] Ibid. Pp. 177f.
[40] Ibid. P. 317.
[41] Ibid. P. 152.

Although the narrator's constant incantation of a return to Masante subverts, rather than underlines, the probability of such an ending, his way out into the desert is prepared from the very beginning. Facing the intensity and urgency of the narrator's hopes, as well as his ardent consciousness of never-ending flight and restless search, his way out into the desert seems inevitable. The end that awaits the wanderer in the heart of the desert is a promise and a threat at the same time: "Wüste, sollte man meinen, ist nicht abgesteckt, eine weiße Fläche auf der Jagdkarte aller Verfolger und Häscher, eine große weite Masche in ihrem Netz, wer hineingerät, verendet in der Mitte".[42] Furthermore, both refugee and persecutor are equal in the desert's indifferent face: "Die Wüste ist neutral – ein elender Standpunkt – sie trägt keine Verantwortung, lädt nicht ein, warnt nicht, droht nicht, aber sie wartet eben".[43] Its existentialist potential is demanding, resting at its edge *La dernière chance* for the wanderer to give his life the decisive turn. If he does not succeed in liberating himself here and restarting his life in different terms, he will not succeed anywhere. Yet it remains highly questionable whether there really is any chance for these wanderers. It might just as well be the case that, if it exists at all, their liberation lies in an undisguised confrontation with their fate. They must either accept their situation and live as wanderers until the end of their lives, or evade it entirely by vanishing into the emptiness: "Hier draußen in der Leere verloren gehen, – was bliebe? [...] Man wird aus dem Wenigen, das man hier findet, kein Bild aufbauen können".[44] A life led in constant fear of hiding one's traces, of recognition, may dissolve here. It should be added that Hildesheimer, although influenced by the philosophy of Schopenhauer, did not consider suicide "als eine Flucht ins Nicht-Sein, und damit als den Ausdruck einer Haltung zur Welt [...], sondern als Verweigerung dessen, was die grausame Natur mit uns einzelnen Individuen treibt oder vorhat".[45] The self-determined ending of a life that he presents in *Masante*, and refines in his later fictive biography *Marbot*, is part of human existence, and may as well become the object of creative potential. Shaping and inventing one's life does not exclude its ending.

Upon entering the desert, the narrator realizes that both the concepts of love (Niki) and home (Masante), and thus the prospect of redemption as such, vanish into an insurmountable distance ("Niki, die ist ziemlich fern. Masante noch ferner"[46]). He himself becomes part of the desert's paradox. Instead of the emptiness he had hoped to find, and which should, as the redemptive "Nichts",

---

[42] Ibid. P. 117.
[43] Ibid. P. 118.
[44] Ibid. P. 365.
[45] Wolfgang Hildesheimer: Schopenhauer und Marbot. In: Jehle: *Wolfgang Hildesheimer* (n. 1). P. 191.
[46] Hildesheimer: *Masante* (n. 3). P. 375.

erase the traces of the past and offer at least a notion of the "Etwas" lying beyond, the desert has turned out to be full. Like the empty house in Tynset, here, in the endless space, memories and traumata emerge unobstructed. In the face of their presence he recognizes that there is no other option left than to dissolve in the emptiness. There is no "there", no point at which to arrive for someone who has never been "here".

4.

In summary, the two novels operate similarly, conveying the tragic dilemma of an exile in an impressive way, completely lacking inappropriate pathos. For reasons of time and precision, I have left out all the intermediate places and images of travel integrated into the novels that complement the novels' reception, and fuel the tension between remembered and unresolved traumata, and unfulfillable longings. They correspond to the opposition of "here" and "there" as worked out above, and contribute to the strong impression of the narrators' non-belonging and restlessness. However, I hope to have shown that there is a strong connection between the geographic places described in the novels, and the inner states of each particular narrator. Hildesheimer's aesthetics of space and traveling thus give a clear impression of the way in which the exile experience forms and determines a migrant's life: a subtle and highly artistic mode of transforming the rupture of exile into the language and images of art.

Donald G. Daviau

Paul Zech's Exotic Travels in South America

The article examines Paul Zech's diaries of the travels he claimed to have made throughout South America. In the aggregate these informative and entertaining writings, a combination of Dichtung und Wahrheit, *would have provided an excellent overview of the life, landscapes and history of the major countries for German readers in the 1930s, but for unknown reasons they were never published. That Zech did not personally visit all the places he describes may reflect on him but does not discredit the works. These highly readable texts still possess value for their portrayal of conditions in South America at that time and serve as important sources for anyone who wants to fully understand Paul Zech.*

"Als ich im Spätsommer 1933 zum ersten Mal den Südamerikanischen Kontinent mit leeren Taschen, aber quälender Gedankenfracht betrat, war ich bereit, in dieses Land einzudringen, es zu begreifen, um vielleicht hier ein verlorenes Heimatgefühl zu finden". Thus does Paul Zech begin the "Nachwort" that accompanies his collection of Indian Love Stories entitled *Die grüne Flöte vom Rio Beni*.[1] He believed that one must not view South America with European eyes and claims that he finally called upon the services of an old Indian "nature healer" to rid him of his European spirit: "Der gute Mann war fest der Meinung, in mir stecke der böse Geist Europas und gab mir seltsame Ingredienzen zur Besserung. ... Die Kur dauerte reichlich ein halbes Jahr, bis ich mich wesentlich besser fühlte und von dem bösen Geist geheilt war".[2] This, of course, is pure fantasy, simply titillation for his readers. In fact, Zech never overcame his European orientation, primarily because he never intended to stay in South America but, like most exiles everywhere, lived for the day when he would be able to return home. However, practical realist that he was, he turned his attention to South American themes when he had difficulties publishing his anti-Fascist political writings and ultimately wrote more about South America than any other German writer.

The aim of this essay is to show the various ways by which Zech entered into the spirit of his new country, concentrating primarily on the works ostensibly describing his travels throughout South America and touching briefly on the closely related collections of Indian fairy tales, legends and sagas. In his early writings he had often described natural phenomena, particularly in his volumes of poetry, so it does not represent any change of direction or interest when he undertook the task of depicting the wonders of various South American countries

---

[1] Paul Zech: Nachwort. In: *Die grüne Flöte von Rio Beni. Indianische Liebesgeschichten.* Hamburg: Fischer Taschenbuch Verlag 1982. P. 149.
[2] Ibid.

and the exotic customs of the Indios. He intended these travel books for German readers in South America as well as for his countrymen, who had little information at that time beyond Kasimir Edschmid's novel *Glanz und Elend Südamerikas* (1931). I will first discuss how Zech came to find himself in exile in Buenos Aires, provide a brief overview of the various accounts of travels throughout South America and conclude with an examination of the controversy surrounding these purported first-hand diaries, which have never been published but still languish in various archives in Germany,[3] a fate Zech pleaded to be spared: "Nur bestrafe mich nicht in Museen zu verstauben".[4]

That Zech could never rid himself of his European thinking can be seen in the presence of the same strong socialist viewpoint in these diaries that is to be found in his earlier writings in Germany. Although he featured the opulence and exotic magnificence of the South American landscape and the unusual customs of the Indios, at the same time Zech, whose ideals were based on his model Karl Marx, always retained his strong sense of human dignity, equality and social justice, which he readily reveals in his condemnation of the treatment of the Indios, the Blacks and the impoverished European immigrants. Some of the diaries deal with past history such as the destruction of the Inca and Aztec Empires and the Great War between Paraguay, Bolivia and Argentina in the Gran Chaco, while others portray the economic and political conditions of the country in that day as well as the starkly contrasting lives of the upper and lower classes. Thus in the 1930s these writings presented in an entertaining way substantive commentaries and insights that were not yet readily available in German either in South America or in Europe. And yet, apart from the essay "Buenos Aires", which appeared in 1933,[5] none of the travel diaries found a publisher, possibly because he did not submit them anywhere. This entire aspect of Paul Zech's career, important because it represents the most substantial portion of his writings in exile and reveals so much about him, escalates into an extremely complex, convoluted matter, about which, despite the excellent contributions of Arnold Spitta and Alfred Hübner,[6] the last word has yet to be spoken. And now to begin.

---

[3] For locations see Ward B. Lewis: *Poetry and Exile. An Annotated Bibliography of the Works and Criticism of Paul Zech*. Frankfurt/Main: Peter Lang 1975. Pp. 119–127. It should be noted that all published bibliographies of Zech's works are outdated by thirty or more years and do not reflect the current holdings of the archives.

[4] Paul Zech: Über mich. In: *Schwarzer Greif – Ein Almanach auf das Jahr 1925*. Ed. by Karl Dietz. Rudolstadt: Greifenverlag 1925. Pp. 13–18. Here: p. 18.

[5] Paul Zech: Buenos Aires. In: *Die Sammlung*, 2. Jg. Vol. 8 (1935). Pp. 427–436. Reprinted in: P. Walter Jacob: *Ein Theatermann im Exil*. Hamburg: Ernst Kabel-Verlag 1985. Pp. 84–91.

[6] Arnold Spitta: *Paul Zech im südamerikanischen Exil 1933–1946*. Berlin: Colloquium Verlag 1978 deals with the prose works; Alfred Hübner: *Das Weltbild im Drama Paul Zechs*. Frankfurt/Main: Peter Lang 1975 with the dramas.

After Hitler's accession to power on 30 January 1933, life began to grow complicated for Paul Zech in Berlin because he sympathized with the Communists and stood in opposition to the Nazis. However, not his politics but illegal activities such as a charge of plagiarism and using the title of doctor falsely brought him under police scrutiny.[7] In addition, after a house search in March 1933, he was dismissed from his job as *wissenschaftlicher Hilfsarbeiter* in the Berlin Stadtbibliothek in April for misappropriating rare books. In June he was held for questioning for three days in Spandau prison, and after another house search in August 1933, he fled unceremoniously into exile, taking only a typewriter, all of his unfinished manuscripts and a few personal items.[8]

Not finding Prague congenial, he traveled to Paris, where he received an invitation from his brother Roberto to come live with him in Buenos Aires. Roberto, who had emigrated in 1929, had been alerted about Paul's difficulties by Hilde Herb, the life companion Zech truly loved and from 1925 called his wife in Berlin. The lengthy trip carried Zech from Marseilles to Naples and then to the ports along the Eastern coast of South America, Bahia, Rio de Janeiro, Porto Allegro, Sao Paulo, Montevideo and Buenos Aires, to each of which he devoted a chapter in his diaries, as will be seen.

Initially Paul Zech hated his life in Buenos Aires, which he called the *Lärmstadt*. In a letter to his old friend Stefan Zweig, whom he was able to meet during the International PEN Club meeting in Buenos Aires in 1936, Zech notes the salutory affect on him of Zweig's visit but reports about his life in the darkest terms: "Es ist manches wieder aufgerührt worden, was diesen Zustand der Fremde als grauenhaft und eine Plage erscheinen läßt. Ich werde hier nie heimisch werden können. Man lebt wie ein Tier, das angeschossen ist und sich im Gebüsch verkrochen hat".[9] Given that he was living modestly well, supported by his brother, and earned pocket money from a few publications, it is clear that he exaggerated his condition to arouse his friend's sympathy and gain his support. Together with his brother, who was fluent in Spanish, Zech had translated Jorge Icasa's political novel *Huasipungo*, but no publisher could be found. Zech asked Zweig if he could place it, mentioning as a possibility the Malik Verlag of his friend Wieland Herzfelde. Zweig had no better luck, because all publishers feared anything "was auch nur aufrührerisch oder kommunistisch angesehen werden konnte".[10] Even Herzfelde was afraid to touch it.

---

[7] *Paul Zech. Ausgewählte Werke.* Ed. by Bert Kasties and Dieter Breuer. Five volumes. Aachen: Shaker 1999. Here Vol. 1. P. 31.
[8] Paul Zech: Ursache und Weg meiner Reise nach Südamerika. In: *Der Greifenalmanach*. Rudolstadt: Greifenverlag May 1954. P. 273.
[9] *Stefan Zweig – Paul Zech Briefe 1910–1942.* Ed. by Donald G. Daviau. Frankfurt/Main: Fischer Taschenbuch Verlag 1986. P. 103.
[10] Ibid. P. 106.

A main cause of Zech's discontent and unhappiness was his inability to bring Hilde Herb to Buenos Aires or contribute to her support in Berlin. He finally broke with his brother in 1937 because Roberto would not cover the costs of her trip. It was a severe blow, when Zech was notified by Hilde's brother-in-law, Erich Meurer, one of his best friends, that she had been killed in a bombing attack, a story Meurer possibly concocted to spare Zech from the unpleasant truth. For actually Hilde, in despair when her lover in Berlin abandoned her, carried out a carefully planned suicide in a hotel room in Berlin.[11] During the years 1937–1941 Zech had a difficult time living on his own, but he enjoyed a reasonably comfortable existence for the last 4 1/2 years of his life living in the home of Elsa Z. de Kusch and her son Roberto, who revered him. Indeed, her name appears on Paul Zech's death certificate as his wife. However, in a letter of 26 September 1970 to Rudolf and Hella Zech she insists they were never married. She was horrified when she discovered this error: "Wie dieses Irrtum entstanden ist, weiss ich bis heute noch nicht...

Ich ging zum deutschen Konsulat und hab nun die Bestätigung, dass ich **nicht** mit Paul Zech verheiratet war, sondern nur mit mir und meinem Sohn wohnte".

Zech began his new life auspiciously, for he had the good fortune of being hired by Ernesto Allemann to contribute items to his newspaper *Argentinisches Wochenblatt*. Allemann, who liked Zech and was impressed by his reputation as a writer, even provided him with a train ticket to explore the regions in the North and West of Argentina. However, he would only accept a poem a week and none of the diary entries or Indian prose tales and most certainly not any of his anti-Nazi writings. There was a strong Nazi presence in Buenos Aires, and in 1935 after Zech published a hard-hitting "Antifaschistische Glaubensbekenntnis" that alienated readers, Allemann had to fire him, despite his admiration. The Nazis also showed the power they wielded by blocking all plans to perform Zech's anti-Fascist plays in Bueno Aires. A scheduled performance of "Nur ein Judenweib" by a theater in Montevideo had to be cancelled after bomb threats were received.[12] Zech bowed to expediency, and, "durchschauert von der hitzigen Bewegung exotischer Dinge und bunter Abenteuer, in einer Stadt, wo man nach dem Ende gewisser Räume in seinem Leben wieder von vorn anfangen muß, ohne selber auch gleich ein ungeschickter Anfänger zu sein" determined to make a new beginning with South American themes, as he announced in the essay "Buenos Aires".[13] His enthusiasm shows through in a letter to Zweig

---

[11] Unpublished letter of Hella Zech to Else de Kusch dated 7 September 1970 in possession of the author.
[12] See Donald G. Daviau: Paul Zech's Anti-Fascist Drama "Nur ein Judenweib". In: *Exile and Enlightenment. Festschrift for Guy Stern*. Ed. by Jerry Glenn. Detroit: Wayne State University Press 1987. Pp. 171–180.
[13] Zech: Buenos Aires (n. 5). P. 427.

describing his travels: "Ich habe drei Monate im Norden des Landes gelebt, drei Monate in Uruguay und Brasilien, immer auf Haciendan und Estancien. Was ich sah war absolute Wildnis. Ein erlebter Gewinn, vielleicht auch einmal zu realisieren. Aber kaum von hier aus".[14] Zweig encouraged his friend to complete his book on South America, for such a work would have little competition: "Ich weiß ja selbst, daß es außer Edschmid gar nichts gibt, und der ist heute für unser Gefühl schon zu amüsierlich und außerdem von der Zeit überholt".[15] Ironically Zech had already completed the long work "Südamerika. Alles und Nichts. Eine nicht ganz einfache Reise ins Blaue hinein" in December 1935[16] but failed to admit it to Zweig. Through a quirk in his nature, truthfulness was not one of Paul Zech's basic qualities, but rather he always tried to keep his private life secret by confusing his friends with different stories of his activities. In this case it is strange that he did not solicit Zweig's help in finding a publisher for this manuscript, since he displayed such enthusiasm about its chances. There are multiple typed versions of the various journeys, for Zech, an indefatigable worker, kept revising these texts until his death and generously gave copies to various friends, one of his pleasures.

Rudolf had to expend a great deal of energy and effort to gather and gain possession of the *Nachlaß*. As Else Z. de Kusch explains in her letter of 26 September 1970, because he had not had any contact with his family in Berlin throughout his years of exile, Paul Zech instructed her to ship the *Nachlaß* to Kurt Erich Meurer, who had contacted him right after the end of the war. With the assistance of Albert Theile, Zech's colleague on the Deutsche Blätter, she followed his wishes and sent the shipment weighing 38 kilograms to Meurer. At the same time, Emma Barta-Mickl, a close friend of Paul Zech and Else Z. de Kusch, sent other texts and letters, including those of Stefan Zweig, to the son Peter Meurer. In both instances Rudolf had to initiate lawsuits to force them to surrender all the materials they had received. In addition, Rudolf methodically requested the return of manuscripts from his father's friends who had been given them. Rudolf deserves great credit for his efforts to gather 80 manuscripts of the *Nachlaß* and also for serving as the impetus to publish enough manuscripts to create a postwar renaissance of Paul Zech's literary reputation, including a number of dissertations in the 1960s and 70s.

Initially, Rudolf, who was a professional printer, planned to publish all of these works in his own Rudolf R. Zech Verlag. He edited 17 manuscripts, including four of the travel diaries, but he discovered that he did not possess

---

[14] *Zweig – Zech Briefwechsel* (n. 9). P. 104.
[15] Ibid. P. 106.
[16] Paul Zech: Südamerika Alles und Nichts. Eine nicht ganz einfache Reise ins Blaue hinein (1935). Two volumes, 483 and 553 pages respectively. Unpublished manuscript in the Paul Zech Archive, Akademie der Künste, Berlin.

either the finances or the energy to carry out such an ambitious program. The work of editing and publishing proved to be too great a strain on his health, and he made arrangements with the Greifenverlag in Rudolstadt, Paul Zech's former publisher, to bring out the works in the *Nachlaß*. That no travel diaries were included in the small program does not indicate that they were considered unimportant, but rather that other works such as the *Nachdichtungen* of the Indian legends and the timely novel *Deutschland, Dein Tänzer ist der Tod* were given a higher priority as being more salable. It was also the case that the travel diaries still required considerable editing in addition to the efforts that Rudolf had made.

Writing about nature was nothing new to Paul Zech, as can be readily seen by the numerous volumes of poetry and tales among his pre-exile writings. He was a keen observer both of natural phenomena as well as of human social and political behavior. At the same time he was a writer and not a trained naturalist, anthropologist or sociologist. He was not striving to record new discoveries for the scientific community like Alexander von Humboldt, whose accounts he had read. On the other hand, he was also no Karl May, who had never seen any of the country he was portraying. Rather, like all good authors, it was Zech's dual aim to entertain and inform his readers, in this case to introduce them to the wonders, the majesty and mystery, of a world few Europeans knew much about at that time. Nevertheless, while his travel diaries, like his novels and collections of tales, portray the exotic natural phenomena, they also provide researched information about the past history and critical commentaries about the political and social conditions of the countries he describes. The wonders of this new land outstripped one's imagination, and Zech had no need to embellish on exotic natural phenomena that he considered indescribable. Several times in the different accounts he remarks that the forms and colors of the landscapes are paintings that no artist could duplicate, not even Cézanne. Only Rimbaud or Mallarmé or an Oriental fairy-tale teller would be able to capture these views in words. On the whole, the diaries are generally straightforward, and at times the writing can be rather flat and prosaic, resembling drafts to be fleshed out later, in contrast to the retellings of the Indio legends and fairy tales, where he can give free rein to his imagination. Yet on occasion, as will be seen, Zech in the diaries indulges in descriptions of Indio customs that match the exoticism of the legends and stretch his credibility and the credulity of the reader to the limit.

Clearly these travel books would have found publishers and readers in Europe and America under normal circumstances, but not in wartime. In any event his books were banned in Germany because of his flight into exile. The collections of legends, fables and sagas published in Germany in the postwar period were all well received. Zech managed to publish a few texts in

Spanish – *Bäume am Rio de la Plata,*[17] *Neue Verse aus der Emigration,*[18] *Ich suchte Schmied ... und fand Malva wieder*[19] – but he did not include any of the diaries.

Among Zech's close friends was James I. Friedmann, who regarded him highly as the most prominent German exile in South America and a leading voice of the anti-Nazi group. Friedmann operated a bookstore and a lending library and also founded the journal Editorial Cosmopolita or Freier deutscher Buchverlag, the largest publishing house in Buenos Aires. In his manuscript "Muttersprache. Das Vaterland der Heimatlosen – Erinnerungen und Dokumentation eines Verlegers in der Emigration" (1966), which to this day remains unpublished,[20] he reports that Zech, despite his financial plight, refused offers by book firms in the USA and Israel eager to publish writings of the man they considered as the most eloquent, idealistic defender of the real humanistic Germany and the author they expected to be a leading moral force in Germany after the war. However, they wanted political writings, not works about South America. In any event nothing could move the *Dickschädel* Zech, as he called himself, to release any manuscripts, which he now insisted he wanted to save as the means to reestablish his literary position in Germany when he returned. Throughout the years of exile Zech was sustained by the belief that he would be recalled after the war to help revitalize Germany. However, no such call ever came before his death on 7 September 1946.

Zech worked steadily throughout the years, producing a large number of typed manuscripts in multiple copies. He also kept editing his writings, so that many of the unpublished manuscripts in the archives established at the urging of Rudolf Zech and his wife Hella – the Akademie der Künste in Berlin, the Schiller Nationalmuseum at Marbach am Neckar, the Stadt- und Landesbibliothek in Dortmund and the Deutsche Bibliothek in Frankfurt am Main – contain his hand-written emendations. Rudolf devoted years to obtaining the *Nachlaß* from South America as well as gathering manuscripts and letters from friends. It is solely due to the initiative and impetus of Rudolf and his wife Hella that the various archives were established on the basis of the materials they provided.

---

[17] Paul Zech: *Bäume am Rio de la Plata*. Buenos Aires: Verlag Alemann y Cia 1935. A number of short excerpts from the diaries were published in German journals in the 1930s. See Lewis: *Poetry and Exile* (n. 3). Pp. 75–77. Some of these texts have now been included in: Paul Zech: *Ausgewählte Werke*. Vol. 4. *Prosa*. Ed. by Bernd Kasties and Dieter Breuer. Aachen: Shaker 1999.
[18] Paul Zech: *Neue Verse aus der Emigration*l. Buenos Aires: Quadriga Verlag 1939.
[19] Paul Zech: *Ich suchte Schmied ... und fand Malva wieder*. Buenos Aires: Editorial Estrellas 1941.
[20] Manuscript in possession of the author. Rudolf Zech intended to publish Friedmann's text under the title *Der einsame Gringo in Südamerika* but failed to do so.

The accounts of the various trips may or may not have been written in any sequential order. Each account can stand alone, and as a result there is considerable overlap in the descriptions of the natural phenomena and of the lives of the colonists and the Indios. In preparing volumes of the diaries for publication, Rudolf designates them as "Aus den südamerikanischen Tagebüchern", but he did not follow the exact arrangement of "Südamerika Alles und Nichts". As a result, travel accounts and Indio legends and tales may be found in the same volume.

In the first manuscript "Orangen und harte Schwielen. Erste Schritte in eine neue Welt",[21] Zech describes his trip to Buenos Aires and his first travels in Argentina. In the opening chapter "Grau ist der Abend in der Eisenbahn" his mind is filled with "grauen Gedanken als ein Verjagter, ein Emigrant", while sitting on the train from Paris to his ship in Marseilles. He travels to Naples, where he describes the eruption of Vesuvius that destroyed Pompeii, and then begins the long journey to Buenos Aires. He is disappointed when the ship does not stop at Algiers as anticipated. He mentions stopping at Rio de Janeiro but not at other ports along the way, although in the subsequent account "Schwarzes Gold von Patagonien" he discusses stops at Bahia, Rio, Santos, Sao Paulo, and Montevideo, as will be seen.

In "Einfahrt in Buenos Aires" Zech remarks that he was the last person to leave the ship. And here the account deviates from what one would anticipate. Since his brother was expecting him, it is logical to assume that he would have met the ship. But Zech does not mention anything of his brother, but instead relates how he hired a taxi to take him to a boarding house, where he takes a room. This indicates that he does not intend these "diaries" to be completely factual documents but narratives on the order of Goethe's *Dichtung und Wahrheit*. Although he feels an outsider in these new surroundings, Zech at the same time recognizes that he has the freedom to find his happiness here.

Zech's introduction to his new environment begins with a university professor, who informs him that there are 60,000 Germans in Buenos Aires, but the children assimilate and do not retain their language. The women marry Argentine men, and the men study to become doctors and lawyers and achieve more than they ever could in their homeland. Some Germans own large estates and cattle farms but never see them, just reap the profits at long distance. Zech is fascinated by the *Urwald* and discusses the lives of German immigrants, who founded a colony in 1924 and carved farms out of the massive forest and survive by fighting a continuous battle with the ants, locusts, droughts and the difficulty of getting their products to market. These 18 families, many of them

---

[21] Paul Zech: *Orangen und harte Schwielen. Erste Schritte in die neue Welt*. Manuscript of 130 pages edited by Rudolf Zech. Manuscript in possession of the author.

professional men, endure a hard life in their new adopted world. In another area, which has no name beyond Kilometer 210, he meets Alejandro Zinn, a former editor in Berlin, who had enough of civilization and bought a piece of land in this remote area and earns a living with hard work.

In his travels Zech passes colonies of Hungarians, Poles and Jews. Now the government has passed laws against colonies of single nationalities, because they can cause trouble. They must assimilate and be comprised of different nationalities. The Poles, according to Zech, are born into debt and die in debt, which is passed on to the children. Zech's humaneness shows in his sympathy for these people who have to endure such hard lives from which they can never escape. Their fate is completely dependent on the weather, on the attacks of locusts and on the prices they can obtain for their crops. The big estates can diversify their crops and also keep cattle, but the small farmer can only grow one crop, The big estates can get the government to build roads to the markets, and often own outlets in the city. There are no roads to the small farms, and they have to accept whatever prices buyers offer. The small farmers show the signs of their hard life: "Aus den Gesichtern hatte die Sonne ein borkiges Stück Holz gemacht, ihre Hände waren eine einzige blutige Schwäre".[22] One needs 50,000 orange trees or 14,000 cows to do well. Otherwise you work like an "Ochs im Joch".[23]

Paul Zech's father and grandfather had both been socialists, and his own strong socialist orientation – he was a great admirer of Karl Marx – can be seen in his early works portraying the coal miners as well as in his Expressionist works. He believed that all literature should be political, a view he defended under the pseudonym Timm Bora in a debate about the role of the author in "Die neue Gaucho Literatur".[24] Zech was always a defender of the underdog and the exploited poor people. Thus it would have represented a major change of attitude if he had not been a staunch defender of these immigrant farmers and of the oppressed and persecuted Indios. His interest took two forms: on the one hand, he never fails to mention their brutal repression and mistreatment, their exploitation and eradication, with caustic criticism of the governments that do nothing to aid, educate or protect them; and, on the other hand, he attempts to preserve their heritage and legacy by recording their customs, legends and myths. He mentions that the Creoles and Indians were forced to fight the war for the independence of Argentina, but the history books do not mention this fact nor do the survivors benefit in any way from their contribution. It appears that South America had its own version of the American concept of

---

[22] Ibid. P. 105.
[23] Ibid. P. 116.
[24] In: Paul Zech: *Menschen der Calle Tuyut'. Erzählungen aus dem Exil*. Rudolstadt: Greifenverlag 1982. Pp. 215–225.

"Manifest Destiny" used to eradicate the Indians. The Whites feel that the Indios have no place in the new society and take the land they have cleared, driving the Indios further and further into the *Urwald* and systematically eliminating them. The universities study them but do nothing to alleviate their mistreatment or eradication.

Zech quite likely traveled to the Pampas Southwest of Buenos Aires with the ticket Allemann provided for him. In a chapter entitled "Argentinisches Land, Argentinisches Leben" he stops at a train station designated simply as Kilometer 180 or "Ingeniero Irrituburro Azcuénaga", an arid area that stands in complete contrast to the lushness of the primeval forest. The Pampas can go for several months without rain, and the winds carry the dust for many kilometers. Yet one rainfall can bring it suddenly to life and turn it into fertile grazing land for herds of cattle.

In the manuscript entitled "Das Dorf der roten Spinnen. Eine kleine Reise nach dem Amazonas",[25] Zech describes a trip to and along the Amazon River, experiencing many wonders that one would not have considered possible. He begins the opening chapter "Mit dem 'San Pedro' den Rio Madeira hinab" with a long quotation providing factual information about the Amazon River, so that one has an idea of its size and geography, an example of how he incorporated research into these diaries. He also relates the early history of the Amazon women, who were warriors, like Kleist's *Penthesilea*, and captured men they used for reproduction and then killed. He travels with a group of tourists, mostly Americans who soon depart out of boredom, while he does not tire of viewing the dolphins that swim around the boat, the deadly piranha fish, the alligators and the scenery on both sides of the river. The stop at Manaos, which reached its highpoint between 1908 and 1913 because of the discovery of how to make rubber, but now a dead city like Bruges, gives him an occasion to relate its rich history. For hundreds of years the town was nothing more than a sleepy gathering place for the Indios until the need for rubber brought in large international companies and made it an important trading center and a very wealthy, wide-open city, not unlike the gold rush towns in the USA and sharing the same fate when the great demand subsided.

Learning of an island called Icaca Yupú, where three Indians who are 100 years old reside, he plans a visit, declining an interpreter because he claims to know a dozen Indian languages. However, when he arrives, he meets a German doctor, who acts as interpreter, making it unnecessary for Zech to communicate with the inhabitants directly. Despite the boastful claims of knowing Indian languages, he maintains the integrity of the accounts on the linguistic level by always finding an intermediary to assist him with the language.

---

[25] Paul Zech: *Das Dorf der roten Spinnen. Eine kleine Reise nach dem Amazonas*. Manuscript of 253 pages edited by Rudolf Zech. In possession of the author.

Zech relates that the village on the "Insel der Seligen" is holding a celebration, and he and the doctor are invited to take part. A young girl is assigned to him, and she brings him roasted monkey meat, which she first chews and then feeds to him by making a spoon of her tongue. She also cracked Brazil nuts with her teeth and made a paste of the nut to feed him the same way. It was evident that she was intended to remain his companion for the night, but he politely declined. Zech adds more exoticism in "Wie Ipaca Yupú entsteht", describing another trip with the doctor up the Rio Purus to a big island in a large lake. The doctor used the occasion to measure the skulls of the Indians, while Zech listened to the legend of how the island was formed. He describes the people, who were adept at fishing and weaving baskets, and notes that the women here are shameless and take men whenever it pleases them. According to Zech, no white man could ever become interested in these dirty "rote Spinnen" with stringy hair. When the Chief's son falls ill, 100 women dance around him naked. The doctor treats him for malaria, but the chief, not seeing any immediate improvement, summons the witch doctor, who performs his tricks. The boy is cured, but it is not clear by whose treatment. The diary concludes with Zech retelling the new legend that he learned there: "Die Legende vom Orion, Sirius und der Taube".[26] This diary with its fanciful descriptions of the unusual customs of this group of Indios is fascinating to read, but here the travel accounts closely resemble the tales and legends and cause one at times to wonder about the reliability of the information.

The third installment of the travel diaries that Rudolf edited, "Schwarzes Gold von Patagonien",[27] contains the account of his visits to the port cities on his initial voyage. He is awed by the spectacular sights that he sees in this new world. He finds the unique, exotic city Pernambuco so full of contrasts that it is difficult to describe. At best he can only give snapshots of highlights such as the colorful plants and birds. Above all Zech is struck by the presence of so many Blacks. He reports that in 1870 there were 1.8 million slaves from Africa working on plantations and in the mines producing gold, all of which went to Europe. On the basis of what he sees, he comments that although the Black slaves were declared free in Brazil by the end of the 19th century, their lives have not improved.

Bahia has a population of 360,000 people, three-quarters of whom are Black, one of the detailed statistics about the city he provides, showing that he supplemented his observations with research. He notes that the city has 365 churches, and its basic exports are tobacco, coffee, cocoa beans, semi-precious stones, pelts, bananas and oranges. Zech remembers smoking choice

---

[26] In: Ibid. Pp. 238–253.
[27] Paul Zech: *Schwarzes Gold von Patagonian*. Manuscript of 165 pages. In possession of the author.

Dannemann cigars in Berlin in 1912. Here they are much cheaper, and he can enjoy the experience again. Most of the Blacks live in squalor, and lice are everywhere, causing everyone, including him, to scratch. Like the Indians of Peru and Ecuador, they are treated as if they were still slaves, grow poorer and receive no aid from the government. With no education available to them, they retain their belief in the gods like their forbears in Africa. By contrast, the successful Blacks associate with whites and marry white women. Money is the standard by which one is judged, not color. There is no democracy here under President Vargos, who rules with ruthless force, and the "Mischlinge" control the power, because they hold the bureaucratic offices and have the wealth.

Zech is rapturous in his eloquent enthusiasm for "Rio de Janeiro", a wonder that makes an indelible but inexpressible impression. It is one of his greatest experiences in South America, and he believes the travel guide, who tells him that one day in Rio is worth a month anyplace else. Here Zech realizes that he must adjust and adapt to South America and stop judging what he sees in European terms. Such a comment suggests that this visit and those to the other port cities were made during his initial crossing. This idea is reinforced by the comment in "Santos", a suburb of Sao Paulo, the second largest port of Brazil, that his clothes are totally impractical for the weather, for he is dressed for October in Berlin while here Spring has arrived, turning the trees green. What he experiences gives him a great deal to contemplate, but he still has his Berlin haste and view of things. He spends seven nights in Santos, the major coffee exporting port of Brazil, and has time to visit Sao Paulo, Brazil's second largest city, with a million people, a third of which are Italians, with 20,000 Germans, slightly more Hungarians and a substantial number of Japanese. All have the European attitude toward money and are out to get rich as quickly as possible. One Italian named Matarozzo arrived with nothing and grew rich and powerful, and he serves as the model showing that it can be achieved. The city is surrounded by splendid trees and coffee plantations. There are not so many Blacks and *Mischlinge* in evidence. The Whites form the aristocracy and bring in everything expensive from North America and Europe: paintings, operas and ballets. The orchestras play European music and the bookstores stock English, French and German authors.

In the manuscript "Die Ruinen von Tiahuanaco. Reise durch Chile und Peru",[28] Zech records the travels that he most likely never made, except in his mind. Yet one cannot detect any difference in these accounts that were doubtlessly based on conversations with people familiar with these countries, supplemented by research, from the reports comprised of first-hand experiences

---

[28] Paul Zech: *Die Ruinen von Tiahuanaco. Reise durch Chile und Peru*. Manuscript of 165 pages. In possession of the author.

and observations also supplemented by research. He even mentions reading travel brochures and is struck by the contrast between the glowing descriptions the flyers present to lure immigrants from Europe and the harsh reality of the colonists he has witnessed. At the same time he wonders if the primitive life in the *Urwald* is not preferable to the *Scheinkultur* of the big cities in Europe.

Zech begins by asserting that anyone who spends a night in the harbor of Rio de Janeiro experiences a miracle of nature that will never be forgotten. Valparaiso cannot compare with this, but it is the most beautiful harbor on the Pacific Coast, adding that he has, of course, not yet seen California. The title of the first chapter "Chile: Stadt Land und Schneeberg" provides a capsule description of the contents. Chile was the poorest of the old Inca Imperium, but the discovery of gunpowder brought great wealth to the country because of the abundance of Saltpeter. Foreigners come to get rich, and he feels that in time Europeans will swap the Riviera for the beaches of Valparaiso. Germans and Italians have developed agriculture that has brought prosperity. He describes his trip north and portrays the picturesque landscapes he saw from the train. He remarks that the colonists endure a hard life at first carving fields out of the primeval forest, but eventually they become successful, and when they do, they in turn exploit the Indios with poor wages for hard labor.

Zech relates his visits to a German, who owns a large herd of cows, each of which wears a Bavarian bell, his trip by car and mule to the top of the snow-capped mountain of Llaima, which has a glacier and is also an active volcano, and his tour of the Sewell copper mine. He continues on to see the ruins of the Jesuit colony at San Ignacio, pausing to see the Iguazu Falls, which he calls the greatest wonder of the world. Zech is usually hostile to clerics and the church, but he shows empathy for these Jesuits because they were the only ones who ever tried to help the Indios. The Jesuit colony did not find favor with the big farm and mine owners, who, angry at losing their workers, persuaded the church in Rome that the Jesuits were enemies and traitors. These stories were believed, and the Jesuit order was disbanded.

San Ignacio existed under the Spanish crown from 1604 to 1767 with 300 brothers overseeing 18,000 Indians. Zech marveled at the design of the facilities, with the grand cathedral at the center and the other buildings constructed in a square around it like a fort. Everything was built of stones, which had to be brought a long distance. A German designed the original plans, which still exist. Zech insists that one has to acknowledge and appreciate the social accomplishments of the Jesuits. The small farmers plundered the buildings in 1895, and Zech wonders why the government did not protect and preserve this unique monument. He himself saw items such as baptismal fountains and friezes at various farms he visited. In one village, where Russians had a perfume factory because every kind of exotic flower grew in the vicinity, he noticed that the main gate was that of San Ignacio.

A visit to Cuzco, the former residence of the Incas, leads to Zech relating Pizarro's ruthless slaughter of the Inca prince Atahualpa and 5000 of his people on 16 November 1532 in his quest for gold and precious stones.[29]

The Indians in Puno, Bolivia were the dirtiest Zech has ever encountered and the most lice-ridden. He was bitten and needed help from a disgusting, foul-smelling person to be cured. The natives wear green and red-striped ponchos and go barefoot. They have boats that somewhat resemble Hawaian canoes and use llamas as pack animals. North American scholars dig up artifacts, draw conclusions, build museums, write thick books and with their findings build a bridge across the Pacific.[30] The regime welcomes the scholars, who give the country validation and bring in money to buy artifacts, as well as the big companies that pay royalties for oil and other resources. But what of the Indios, "die einstigen Arbeitstiere des Inka-Reiches, die noch atmender menschlichen Ruinen dieses Erdteils", who work in the fields and in the tin mines, but do not share in any of the wealth they help produce: "Sie kauen coca und tragen das grosse Absterben ihrer Rasse in den Augen herum".[31]

As he has repeatedly done in all of the texts, Zech once again repeats his sorrowful description of the Indios and Blacks, the "Lasttiere" that are badly paid and treated worse. He also finds that the Slovakian and Polish immigrants, who stay in the cities, are treated no better. The workers have no benefits and no rights. They are treated worse here than in the sugar fields of Pernambico. But this treatment is not a matter that one can discuss with the locals. While on the dock, he watches the workers being exhorted to strike. The harbor goes quiet, until the soldiers wearing helmets that resemble *Pickelhauben* arrive.

Two other unpublished manuscripts also relate to Zech's travels. One is an untitled series of chapters in which Zech presents himself as a reporter in Rio de Janeiro, who writes about the daring escape of H. F. Poole from the prison at Cayenne and hides in the jungle. Zech pursues him throughout South America and Mexico and writes newspaper stories of his escapades.[32] The second manuscript, written in three different handwritings, is entitled "Ergänzungen und Erläuterungen zu Aleijadhino" and describes the life of this architect, who lived and worked in Ouro Preto, Brazil.[33]

I do not have the space to also discuss the collections of Indian tales, but, unlike the travel diaries, they are published and available. In the *Nachwort* to *Die grüne Flöte von Rio Beni. Indianische Liebesgeschichten*, Zech gives free

---

[29] Zech also used this historical episode as the basis of his unpublished drama *Der letzte Inka*.
[30] Zech: *Ruinen* (n. 28). P. 104.
[31] Ibid. P. 105.
[32] Unpublished typescript of 97 pages. In possession of the author.
[33] Unpublished handwritten manuscript of 51 pages. In possession of the author.

reign to his imagination in recounting his travels to gather these fairy tales, sagas and fantasies: "So zog ich jahrelang weiter, befuhr den Amazonas, besichtigte Sonnentor und die Ruinen von Tiahuanaco, auf einem Binselboot berauschten mich die Sonnenuntergänge auf dem Titicacasee, ich erlebte die Wasserfälle des Iguazu und sah immer dabei den Indios auf den Mund".[34] The publisher goes along with this account and acknowledges these travels, even including as a frontispiece a map showing the various regions Zech visited. Similarly the editor of the book *Das rote Messer. Begegnung mit Tieren und seltsamen Menschen*, containing examples of the most exotic people, places, animals and plants that Zech ever encountered, praises the author's gift of observation:

> Paul Zech schildert den harten, zuweilen dramatischen Kampf von Tieren und Menschen in der unbändigten oder erst teilweise unterworfenen Wildnis, fängt die Farbensattheit jener exotischen Welt in all ihrer Vielfalt und phantastischen Fülle ein und fesselt durch genaue Naturbeobachtung…Zechs "wesentliches Talent der poetischen Vermittlung konkreter Wahrnehmung" machen diese Texte zu Kabinettstücken deutscher Prosa.[35]

Finally it is necessary to examine the validity and importance of the travel diaries, to which Zech devoted so much of his life in exile. To what extent did Zech actually take the trips he claims to have made? To date no proof has surfaced to prove the matter definitively one way of the other. Certainly he visited the port cities where his ship stopped on his original trip, and it is evident that he traveled around Argentina on the train ticket Allemann provided. The more distant trips to Bolivia, Ecuador, Chile and Peru and up the Amazon in Brazil are questionable, because it is doubtful that Zech ever had the finances for such trips. After 1937 his health was also a factor to be considered. Arnold Spitta, who has investigated this matter most closely, flatly dismisses the notion that Zech took any of those longer trips on the basis of conversations with people who knew Zech.[36] Yet there are friends such as James I. Friedmann, who claims that Zech did make these travels, for he would disappear for lengthy periods and then return without providing any explanation of his absence. This was typical behavior for Zech, who behaved the same way when he lived in Berlin. He was always secretive about his life even to his family and close friends. On the basis of Friedmann's manuscript, Rudolf Zech readily believed that his father made these trips and spread this colorful information about the travels and about knowing Indian languages. He even persuaded Kurt Pinthus to include

---

[34] Zech: *Grüne Flöte* (n. 1). P 151.
[35] Paul Zech: *Das rote Messer. Begegnung mit Tieren und seltsamen Menschen*. Frankfurt/Main: Fischer Taschenbuch Verlag 1984. Frontispiece.
[36] Spitta: *Paul Zech im südamerikanischen Exil* (n. 6). P. 129.

this information in the 2nd edition of *Menschheitsdämmerung*. Pinthus did so[37] but put the account in quotation marks attributed to Rudolf, because he himself was not persuaded of its truthfulness. Rudolf also included this information in the program notes to the "Indio Spiele", which the Haller Studios staged successfully in Heidelberg and Marbach in 1960 and which were subsequently broadcast on the radio with favorable newspaper reviews.

One aspect of this controversy is clear: Zech did not learn any Indian languages. Indeed, he never became fluent in Spanish because he feared it would be harmful to his German. He employs common names and terms in his diaries for realism, but on his travels he invariably meets a German speaker, who can act as a translator for him.

As for the travel accounts, in my view they should not be discredited or dismissed just because there is doubt about whether he actually saw all of the places he described. He would have had to carry out research on the various topics he covered whether he visited them personally or not. For how else could he provide factual information about populations, number of immigrants, weather conditions, exports, slavery, the dimensions of the Amazon River, the destruction of the Inca and Aztec empires, the war in the Gran Chaco and the exploitation of the people and the land by the big foreign oil companies? True, he claims these are first-hand experiences, but that makes the question a moral issue, which may reflect on Zech's character but has no bearing on the value and quality of the travel diaries any more than the knowledge that his collections of legends and fairy tales are *Nachdichtungen* of existing texts. Many of his best and most enduring works in Germany are *Nachdichtungen*, one of his favorite forms. In both cases the writings should be judged in literary terms on their merits, not on the basis of the author's character. The main point is that on the whole the information he presents in these diaries is accurate because of the research he carried out. In his situation he can hardly be blamed for trying to make these works as exotic and salable as possible. Thus I subscribe to the sensible response of Luis Borges, who knew Zech, when he expressed his reaction to this matter by saying: "Wenn Zech behauptet, er sei da und dort gewesen, so war er da und dort, ganz gleich ob er die Reise realiter unternommen hat oder im Geist".[38]

The more important question concerns the value and importance today of these diaries that Paul Zech devoted years of his life to writing and editing. Clearly these works would have informed and entertained readers if they had been published at the time they were written, and these rich, diverse accounts,

---

[37] See Kurt Pinthus: *Menschheitsdämmerung*. Reinbek bei Hamburg: Rowohlt 1955. Pp. 370–371.

[38] Quoted in: Wolfgang Minety: Der schwarze Baal von den Hochöfen. In: *Die Welt*. 19 February 1981. P. 15.

which present a reasonably comprehensive overview of conditions in South America in the 1930s, still possess historical value today for readers interested in that era. Stefan Zweig praised Zech for the unique manner in which he captured the essence of South America:

> Meines Wissens bist Du der erste, dem es gelungen ist, aus dem Südamerikanischen das Exotische, das uralt Autochthone herauszuholen. Hinter der realistischen Erscheinung – der vielleicht allzu realistischen dieses Erdteils – das Geheimnisvolle fühlen zu lassen, dies Geheimnisvolle, das vielleicht jetzt schon in Auflösung begriffen ist und der Organisation zum Opfer fällt, diese Organisation, auf die man hierzulande so stolz ist, ohne zu wissen, wie sie entfärbt und entsaftet. Und wir Europäer wissen überdies noch, wohin es führt, wenn man Völker in Dynamos und Präzisionsmaschinen verwandelt. Manchmal habe ich das Gefühl, wir werden die Letzten sein, die wir Südamerika gesehen haben. ... Daß es Dir gelungen ist, noch diese letzten Tropfen rein aus der verwässerten Substanz herauszuholen, ist ein großes Verdienst, und welche Freude war es für mich zu sehen, daß Deine Sprache die alte formende und gelegentlich auch neuformende Kraft hat.[39]

Ultimately Zech wrote more than any other German author in South America and more accurately about South America even than Zweig, who refused to say anything critical about the treatment of the lowly workers in his book *Brasilien, ein Land der Zukunft* (1941). Wolfgang Kiessling adds his critical view of the value of these writings: "Zech brachte als erster bedeutender antifaschistischer Schriftsteller – noch vor Anna Seghers, Egon Erwin Kisch, Bodo Uhse und Erich Arendt – die Landschaft und die Menschen Lateinamerikas in die deutsche Exilliteratur ein und bereicherte sie damit thematisch wie künstlerisch".[40]

One should consider how Zech's collections of Indian tales entertained readers and spread information about South America to many readers in German-speaking countries. I believe that certainly in the 1930s and in the postwar era the travel diaries would have enjoyed the same success had they been published. Today in addition to their value as documents of an important period of South American development, these texts are also significant for the biographical information they contain, material that is indispensable for anyone who wishes to investigate and fully understand Paul Zech's complex and controversial life in South American exile.

---

[39] *Zweig – Zech Briefwechsel* (n. 9). P. 113.
[40] Wolfgang Kiessling: Nachwort. In: *Paul Zech. Menschen der Calle Tuyuti. Erzählungen aus dem Exil.* Ed. by Wolfgang Kiessling. Rudolstadt: Greifenverlag 1982. P. 320.

Reinhard Andress

The German Exile Experience in Brazil from the Perspective of Arnold van Gennep's *Les rites de passage*

This paper examines German exiles of National Socialism who emigrated to Brazil from all walks of life and captured their experiences in autobiographical texts. In order to organize their exile experience, the comments draw upon Arnold van Gennep's anthropological study of 1909, Les rites de passage, *in which the author sees life as a series of passages connected to three phases of rites: "separation"* (séparation), *"transition"* (marge), *and "incorporation"* (agrégation). *By applying van Gennep's classification, the paper shows that travel is intimately connected with these rites of transition. The remarks serve to shed light on the exile experience of those who fled National Socialism for a country which, on the South American continent, absorbed the second largest number of emigrants after Argentina.*

In his study of 1909, *Les rites de passage*, the Belgian anthropologist Arnold van Gennep (1873–1957) describes an individual's life in any society as "a series of passages from one age to another and from one occupation to another".[1] He sees these passages as connected to three phases of rites: "separation" (*séparation*), "transition" (*marge*), and "incorporation" (*agrégation*), also referring to them as "preliminal", "liminal" and "postliminal".[2] Van Gennep then goes on to apply his classification of rites of passage to, for example, pregnancy and childbirth, childhood, initiation, betrothal and marriage, and funerals, in the process coming to the following conclusion: "Their [the rites'] position may vary [...], but the differences lie only in matters of detail. The underlying arrangement is always the same. Beneath a multiplicity of forms, either consciously expressed or merely implied, a typical pattern always recurs: *the pattern of the rites of passage*".[3] Although written early in the 20th century and structuralist in approach, van Gennep's classification of rites remains current; its seminal significance is still referenced today.[4] It can also,

---

[1] Arnold van Gennep: *Rites of Passage*. Translated by Monika B. Vizedom and Gabrielle L. Caffee. Chicago: University of Chicago Press 1960. Pp. 2–3.
[2] Ibid. Pp. 10–11.
[3] Ibid. P. 191.
[4] An Internet search reveals a host of references to van Gennep's study. See <anthro.palomar.edu/social/soc_4.htm>;<www.wilderdom.com/rites/> or <ccat.sas.upenn.edu/bmcr/2000/2000-06-34.html>.

for example, be traced in the work of another important anthropologist, Victor Turner (1920–1983).[5]

Van Gennep invited the reader to check his classification "by applying the conceptual scheme of *The Rites of Passage* to data in his own realm of study".[6] This is precisely what Jane Wilkinson undertook with regard to travel in her essay, "Passports and the German border: who holds the key to the door?". She writes:

> The traveller as ritual participant must first 'separate' from his/her home country. He/she then enters the second phase of 'transition rites', which Van Gennep terms the 'liminal' phase. This expression is taken from the Latin word 'limen', meaning 'threshold'. The liminal phase of travel is the phase during which the traveller is between the point of exit from his/her home country and the point of entry into the destination country, Germany. The traveller is at the border or 'threshold' of Germany. 'Rites of transition' or liminal rituals, Van Gennep believes, prepare the participant for the third and final phase of 'rites of incorporation', during which the traveller is granted entry to and thus 'incorporated' into Germany. At this point the traveller gains a new identity, such as that of tourist, 'foreign' businessperson, migrant worker or exchange student.[7]

Accepting van Gennep's invitation, I would like to apply his rites of separation, transition and incorporation to the German exile experience after 1933 by looking at autobiographical texts written by some of those who lived through that exile. Since this would include a corpus of texts too vast to consider here, I will limit my remarks to the German exile experience connected with Brazil and as reflected in an anthology project which Marlen Eckl edited and in which I collaborated: *"... auf brasilianischem Boden fand ich eine neue Heimat". Autobiographische Texte deutscher Flüchtlinge des Nationalsozialismus, 1933–1945* (2005). Although restricted in this way, the texts under consideration nonetheless represent writings by Germans from many walks of life: artists, lawyers, professors, doctors and housewives. I will show that van

---

[5] Turner used van Gennep's rites of passage as a point of departure for his own thoughts on "social dramas", which he defined as "units of aharmonic or disharmonic process, arising in conflict situations". See *Dramas, Fields and Metaphors: Symbolic Action in Human Society*. Ithaca: Cornell University Press 1974. P. 37. For him, social dramas have four main phases: "breach", "crisis", "redressive action", and "reintegration" (see pp. 38–41). Upon closer inspection, we can see that breach and crisis correspond to van Gennep's rite of separation, redress to transition, and reintegration to incorporation.

[6] van Gennep: *Rites of Passage* (n. 1). P. xxv.

[7] Jane Wilkinson: Passports and the German border: who holds the key to the door? In: *Contemporary German Cultural Studies*. Ed. Alison Phipps. London: Arnold 2002. Pp. 17–39. Here: p. 21.

Gennep's classification of rites functions as a productive way to break down and better understand the German exile experience. In addition, it will become clear that travel within exile figures prominently in the rites of transition. Finally, I will elaborate briefly on the limits of van Gennep's classification as applied to exile when he tries to establish the rites of passage as a "cosmic conception".[8]

Van Gennep characterizes separation or preliminal rites as making "the break gradual rather than abrupt".[9] This was indeed the case for German Jews who saw themselves exposed to a process of being ostracized. Klaus Oliven, born in 1918 as a Jew and son of the famous librettist and poet Fritz Oliven, writes of the formal restrictions and laws that made up a part of that process:

> Von nun an [after Hitler was named Chancellor on January 30, 1933] folgten hintereinander die Zwangsmaßnahmen und Gesetze gegen die politischen Feinde und vor allem die Juden, wie etwa der Boykott der jüdischen Geschäfte am 1. April 1933, die Bücherverbrennung am 10. Mai desselben Jahres, die Entfernung der jüdischen Beamten aus dem Berufsleben, die infamen Nürnberger Rassengesetze von 1935 etc., etc. Das Leben in Nazideutschland wurde somit für die Juden immer unerträglicher.[10]

Whereas Oliven takes a historical approach in describing the increasing marginalization of Jews, other texts capture personal moments. Eva Sopher, a Jew born in 1923 in Frankfurt am Main, experienced alienation when her sister came home one day from school in tears because a schoolmate had said her father would not allow her to sit next to a Jewish girl any longer. For Karl Lieblich (1895–1984), an up-and-coming German-Jewish writer and established lawyer in the Weimar Republic, it is the official notification by the *Reichsschrifttumskammer Berlin* forbidding any further literary activity that defines a personal moment and rite in the process of being separated from Germany as a Jew.

An initial reaction by German Jews was often a ritualistic denial of the National Socialist anti-Semitic intentions of separation from society. In the case of Hans Hamburger (1891–1953), a World War I veteran and judge in the Weimar Republic, it took the form of disbelief. Would he not be exempted from official sanctions against Jews as a decorated and severely wounded officer who had given so much to the fatherland? Another form of denial was, as Karl

---

[8] van Gennep: *Rites of Passage* (n. 1). P. 194.
[9] Ibid. P. 36.
[10] *"... auf brasilianischem Boden fand ich eine neue Heimat". Autobiographische Texte deutscher Flüchtlinge des Nationalsozialismus 1933–1945*. Ed. by Marlen Eckl (with colloboration by Reinhard Andress). Remscheid: Gardez! Verlag 2005. P. 73. All further quotes from this source will be referenced with the page number in parenthesis.

Lieblich describes it, blind optimism and Glaube an den endgültigen Sieg der Legalität.[11] In any case, for the time being, he was set on practicing "Zurückhaltung"[12] in the hopes that the National Socialist regime would fail, a sentiment Klaus Oliven also expresses: "Sie [the Jews] dachten, dass die Sache sich wieder 'einrenken' oder das System mit der Zeit 'abwirtschaften' würde".[13]

It is, however, Oliven who then writes of the general defining historical moment that made it clear that Jews were to be permanently separated from Germany, namely the *Kristallnacht*: "Nach den furchtbaren Ereignissen des 9. Novembers [1938] wurde es allen Juden, die sich damals noch in Deutschland befanden, völlig klar, dass das Leben dort für sie ein Ende genommen hatte und sie das Land schnellstens verlassen müssten".[14] That frightful event certainly plays a role for Hans Hamburger as well, although his wife Charlotte Hamburger (1899–1977), writing on his behalf, speaks of a more personal moment when he receives the official letter of dismissal from state service as a judge: "Das Versprechen Hindenburgs, an das Hans in seinem Innersten doch noch geglaubt hatte: 'Der Dank des Vaterlandes ist Euch (den kriegsbeschädigten Offizieren) gewiss', fiel in Nichts zusammen".[15] For Karl Lieblich it is a confrontation with the Gestapo that makes emigration a "beschlossene Sache".[16]

What is interesting to explore are the psychological consequences of ostracism as a rite of separation and as seen from the distance of many years when those who had to endure it wrote their autobiographical texts. For the Hamburgers it is like living in two worlds:

> Die eine war die des Alltags, erfüllt mit den Freuden und Sorgen der Kinder; der Trauer um Mutters zunehmend sich verschlechternde Gesundheit; mit dem Ergehen der Geschwister und mit Hansens Berufsproblemen; die andere Welt, die immer an Bedeutung zunahm, war die Politik und, von ihr abhängig, die Planung unseres zukünftigen Lebens mit der Hauptfrage: Auswanderung, ja oder nein?[17]

Although Hans Hamburger feels a high degree of "Bitterkeit"[18] towards Germany for being treated so poorly as a war veteran, taking leave "von allem Deutschen"[19] is nonetheless very painful, the result a "innere und äußere

---

[11] van Gennep: *Rites of Passage* (n. 1). P. 43.
[12] Ibid. P. 47.
[13] Ibid. P. 82.
[14] Ibid. P. 83.
[15] Ibid. P. 342.
[16] Ibid. P. 51.
[17] Ibid. Pp. 334–335.
[18] Ibid. P. 341.
[19] Ibid. P. 338.

Zerrissenheit".[20] There is a profound sense of loss expressed most clearly by Trudi Landau, a Jew born 1920 in Cologne, in her poem entitled "Fragmentos de currículo", which serves as a prologue to *"... auf brasilianischem Boden fand ich eine neue Heimat"* and in which the incantation of "perdi" (I lost) functions as a *leitmotif*:

> Com vinte e poucos anos
> perdi a pátria.
> perdi a cidadania,
> perdi o meu lar.
> Perdi os direitos
> civis e humanos.
> Perdi os estudos
> e as perspectivas.
> Perdi o rasto de minha mãe.
> Perdi meu pai querido
> em campo de concentracão.
> Perdi as medidas,
> Perdi os pertences,
> perdi os parentes,
> perdi os documentos,
> perdi os amigos,
> perdi as lembranças,
> perdi minhas malas
> na fuga precipitada.[21]

The emotional impact of loss leaves a permanent scar. In this regard, the title of Eva Sopher's text, "Dieser Riss bleibt für immer...",[22] is emblematic.

Alice Brill-Czapski, born 1920 in Hamburg as the daughter of the Jewish journalist and writer Marte Brill, is an exception in this context. Also hoping that the Nazi regime will not last, her mother takes her out of school in March 1933 and to the Spanish island of Majorca, then still in Republican hands before the Spanish Civil War begins in July 1936. On the island, we observe the perspective of a 13-year-old child who spends her days experiencing a very different life: "Nie in meinem Leben war ich so frei gewesen zu tun, was ich wollte, und ich habe es ausgiebig genossen".[23] However, later in Brazil, she,

---

[20] Ibid. P. 341.
[21] Ibid. P. 21. Translation: At the age of 20 some years / I lost my homeland, / lost my citizenship / lost my home. / I lost my rights / civil and human. / I lost my education / and perspectives. / I lost all traces of my mother, / lost my beloved father / in a concentration camp. / I lost all measure, / lost my possessions, / lost my relatives, / lost documents, / lost friends, / lost memories, / lost my baggage / on the hasty flight.
[22] Eckl: *"... auf brasilianischem Boden"* (n. 10). P. 128.
[23] Ibid. P. 151.

too, is exposed to the harsher side of exile as the title of her text indicates: "Das waren bittere Jahre".[24]

Already during the rites of separation, characterized by a process of ostracism, denial and the psychological and emotional impact of loss, transition or liminal rites set in. On the one hand, they involve very practical considerations. For the Hamburger family and Karl Lieblich, for example, there is the issue of converting possessions and assets into a form that could be taken abroad as the basis for a new material existence. On the other hand and of more central concern is the question: whither? Who will take in these German Jews and other Germans persecuted by the Nazis? The Hamburger family considers New Zealand and Israel before Brazil turns out as the best alternative. Karl Lieblich has a vision: "Was mir vorschwebte, war Neuland, Fruchtbarkeit, Wirkung ins Größe, hingedehnte Ebenen, gewaltige Bergketten, Wälder, in denen noch die Urkraft der Erde brauste".[25] He tries finding this romantic vision during a visit to Colombia but realizes he is not made for that type of life and needs to adjust his plans. Since his education in German law is impractical in a foreign country, he quickly learns the printing trade in Basle, which ends up serving him relatively well later in São Paulo. Klaus Oliven initially decides that he wants to emigrate to Israel and learns gardening and farming to prepare himself for life in a *kibbuz*.

The most significant transition rite leading to exile is, however, the daunting task of taking care of the necessary paperwork, above all procuring a visa for the country of destination. This is the principal focus of Herman Görgen's efforts. Born a Catholic in 1909 in the Saarland, Görgen's name will forever be connected with saving the so-called *Gruppe Görgen*, 48 Nazi refugees (45 adults and three children, 38 of them Jews according to Nazi law), for whom in Switzerland he arranges emigration to Brazil. Görgen himself also goes into exile there but returns in 1954 to the Saarland where he is politically involved in the failed movement to europeanize the Saar region as a first step toward the construction of a united Europe. During the Konrad Adenauer era, he is so successfully dedicated to improving German-Latin American relations, especially with Brazil, that he receives the *Cruzeiro do Sul*, the highest award the Brazilian state grants. In his text he encapsulates most succinctly the difficulties of getting the necessary documentation together for the group:

> Zugleich wuchsen die ungelösten Probleme meiner in Zürich sich ständig vergrößernden Flüchtlingsgruppe auf allen Gebieten: Aufenthaltserlaubnis für die Schweiz, Passfragen, Arbeitsmöglichkeiten, die Internierung in den schweizerischen Arbeitslagern, Finanzierung des Aufenthalts in der Schweiz und der

---

[24] Ibid. P. 149.
[25] Ibid. P. 52.

Ausreise, die entsprechenden Gesuche an die verschiedenen Hilfsorganisationen, an kirchliche, staatliche und private Stellen, Verhandlungen mit neun Ländern um Einreisevisa, Konflikte mit den schweizerischen Behörden, Bemühungen bei Reiseagenturen um Schiffsverbindungen nach Übersee, ständige Berichte an die starken Druck ausübenden schweizerischen Behörden über den Stand der Aktion, Übereinkommen mit dem Lagerkommandanten der schweizerischen Arbeitslager zur Beurlaubung vom Arbeitsdienst für Besprechungen oder Umschulungen – jeder einzelne Flüchtling brachte zusätzlich zahlreiche persönliche Sonderprobleme mit sich, die einen großen Zeit- und Arbeitsaufwand und vor allem Finanzmittel erforderten.[26]

After negotiations with various countries, Brazil finally comes through thanks to the help of the Brazilian Consul in Geneva, Milton Cesar Weguelin de Vieira, who quietly circumvents the anti-semitically laced emigration laws of Brazil. It is a *jeito* that does the trick and that Görgen describes as follows:

Jeito ist das Zauberwort im brasilianischen Alltag mit vielerlei Bedeutung. Es ist unübersetzbar und besagt, einen Ausweg für ein schwieriges Problem, eine Lösung zu finden. Das klingt sachlich und kühl. *Dar um jeito* – "einen *jeito* geben" ist aber auch mehr als Auswege und Lösungen finden. Es ist die menschliche Bewältigung einer – oft auch juristisch – schwierigen Situation, es ist ein fast ritueller Dialog zwischen Bittenden und Gebenden, es ist die humane Interpretation des Gesetzes und der Vorschrift bis zur letzten Dehnbarkeit, es ist der zutiefst vom Gefühl her motivierte Wille, in einer schwierigen ausweglosen Lage – in großen und kleinen Dingen des Lebens – dem Bedürftigen, Bittenden noch einmal zu einem Anlauf zu verhelfen [...]. Er zeigt die profunde Fähigkeit des Brasilianers, sich aus spontan menschlichen Gründen souverän dem Zwang von Reglements und Gesetzen mit einer gefühlvollen und zugleich intelligenten – keineswegs illegalen – Variante, eben dem *jeito*, zu entziehen.[27]

In the case of the *Gruppe Görgen*, the *jeito* involved quickly making the Jews of the group into Catholics with a certified baptism so that the Consul could sign off on their visa applications since he would not have been able to do so if they had declared themselves as Jews.

Although the focus here has been on Görgen's text, almost everyone in *"... auf brasilianischem Boden fand ich eine neue Heimat"* has a visa story to tell. Together with his parents, Klaus Oliven was also trying to reach the shores of Brazil:

Wir erhielten diese Visen am 3. März 1939. So unglaublich es klingt, ein einfacher Gummistempel mit dem Visum im Pass konnte in jenen Jahren den Unterschied zwischen Leben und Tod bedeuten. Der brasilianische Konsul in Marseille hat mit der Erteilung dieser Visen unser Leben gerettet. Zweifellos hat er dies aus rein

---
[26] Ibid. P. 136.
[27] Ibid. Pp. 136–137.

humanitären Gründen getan, denn außer den vorgeschriebenen geringfügigen Gebühren für die Ausstellung der Visen verlangte er keinerlei Bezahlung.[28]

What becomes visible in both Görgen's and Oliven's texts is that human decency in unexpected moments and often just plain luck played decisive roles in making emigration possible.

As van Gennep pointed out, travel plays a significant role as a part of transition rites; it is a "neutral zone" where the individual "wavers between two worlds"[29] before being incorporated into a new set of existential circumstances. This is most certainly true for the exile experience, and almost every text in the anthology being discussed here contains an aspect of travel. In no text, however, does it figure more prominently than in the one by Ilza Czapska (1896–1983), a baptized Jew and German-speaking native of Silesia who married the Pole Fryderyk Czapski, which made her a Polish citizen as well. When the Nazis turn Silesia into the Warthegau in September 1939, she and her three children (Fryderyk is not present at the time) are driven from their landed estate to be resettled in the Nazi *Generalgouvernement* of eastern Poland. What ensues is a 21-month trek with seemingly insurmountable difficulties as Fryderyk, from afar in France, tries to make arrangements for his family to get out of Poland and eventually to Brazil.

Intermediary stops and stages include various smaller villages in eastern Poland and a long train trip through Hungary, Yugoslavia and Italy to Vichy, France where they are reunited briefly with Fryderyk who, back from a trip to Brazil to inspect land he had bought there, is now serving as an officer in the exiled Polish army. When Hitler's *Wehrmacht* invades France in June 1940, the family is forced to separate again. Ilza Czapska and the children fail in an attempt to cross the Spanish border in order to transit to Portugal in hopes of catching a ship to Brazil from Lisboa. They find refuge in southern France before finally embarking for South America from Marseille in January 1941. What should have been a three-week passage is interrupted by an unwanted sojourn as the *Alsina* is detained for over four months in Dakar, Senegal by English authorities because of contraband. Early in June, the ship is allowed to set sail for Morocco and Casablanca where the passengers are unceremoniously left to fend for themselves. The Czapskis end up having considerable luck, unlike many of the other *Alsina* passengers, since they are able to make their way to Cádiz, Spain where they board another ship, the *Cabo de Buena Esperanza*, and set sail for Rio de Janeiro, arriving there in July 1941. A week later they are reunited again with Fryderyk.[30]

---

[28] Ibid. P. 92.
[29] van Gennep: *Rites of Passage* (n. 1). P. 18.
[30] The trials and tribulations of the *Alsina* made their way into Anna Seghers novel of exile, *Transit* (1944). In the fourth chapter, she describes the fate of the "Alesia", which very closely parallels that of the *Alsina*.

The arduous journey is characterized by flight, constant restlessness and exhaustion. Of her son Janek and the other children, Ilza Czapska writes:

> Er hat aus dieser Zeit eine lebhafte Erinnerung bewahrt an gehetztes Aufgewecktwerden und Jagen nach einem Zug, den man doch noch in letzter Minute erreicht, in Angst, ob es auch uns allen gelingen würde einzusteigen. Es war dies wohl ein häufig sich wiederholender Vorgang in diesen bewegten Tagen. Ihr Kinder alle hattet es schwer auf dieser Reise: Immer unausgeschlafen, immer sehr wenig zu essen, immer in Hetze das Gepäck hin und her schleppen.[31]

Mortal dangers, at times human solidarity, coincidences and good and bad luck play a further role during the rite of transition in Ilza Czapska's case. It is all framed by the constant question of whither next and the attending visa problems already discussed above:

> Ich betrieb inzwischen unsere Ausreise weiter, und es wollte nie gelingen, alle drei Visen gleichzeitig zu haben; das spanische und portugiesische Durchreisevisum und das französische Ausreisevisum. Immer war bereits eines verfallen, wenn das andere eintraf. Endlich schien es so weit, wir packten unsere Koffer und machten uns auf den Weg, aber kamen am selben Tag zurück, denn inzwischen galt das französische Visum nicht mehr für die Grenze, über die wir fahren mussten. Davon hatte man uns am Tage vorher nichts gesagt![32]

Aside from the practical considerations of securing a material existence, we have explored the role that travel plays in the transition rites of exile. We have now reached the phase of incorporation or postliminal rites which, according to van Gennep, are like those of separation in that they are "also carried out in stages".[33] Broadly speaking, they consist of an encounter with the language, culture, society, nature and climate of a very different country, of persisting visa problems and work as a further element of incorporation. In a word, the exiles must deal with their alterity. It is a process of considerable adjustment requiring great inner motivation before Brazil becomes a new *Heimat* for the exiles.

The rite of passage of learning Portuguese merits detailed attention because of its key function regarding incorporation. Although Hilde Wiedemann (1900–1981), born into a family of Protestant pastors on the mother's and a Jewish banker's family on the father's side, settles with her family among other German settlers and refugees in Terra Nova where they establish a farm in 1935, they move on to the cities of Curitiba and Recife a couple of years later for the better economic opportunities there. Seriously learning Portuguese at

---

[31] Eckl: *"... auf brasilianischem Boden"* (n. 10). P. 118.
[32] Ibid. P. 122.
[33] van Gennep: *Rites of Passage* (n. 1). P. 36.

this point becomes vital since they are no longer among Germans to the same extent as before. Charlotte Hamburger mentions learning Portuguese as well, especially the difficulties her husband Hans had:

> Hans nahm gleich portugiesische Stunden, erst bei einer Studentin, dann bei Godinho, einem ausgezeichneten Portugiesisch-Lehrer, der auch viel über Land und Leute wusste und Hans darüber erzählte. Hans sprach die erste Zeit sehr wenig. Er ließ mich in meinem unzureichenden Portugiesisch radebrechen und fing erst an zu sprechen, als er sicher war, keine Fehler zu machen. Hans behielt trotz allen Bemühens einen ausländischen Akzent bei. Der brasilianische Stil, reich an Höflichkeitsphrasen und schmückenden Beiwörtern, lag ihm nicht sehr. Es war ein ständiges Ringen mit der Sprache und im Grunde konnte er sein Herkommen nicht verleugnen. Er behielt die für Preußen charakteristische, knappe, klare und kurze Ausdrucksweise bei. In späteren Jahren fragte er wohl die Tochter oder die Söhne über stilistische Feinheiten um Rat. Dabei zeigte sich, dass fast immer sein Wortschatz der sehr viel reichere war, im Gebrauch der üblichen Umgangssprache war die jüngere Generation ihm jedoch überlegen.[34]

Klaus Oliven also emphasizes the easier time he had in learning certain aspects of Portuguese in comparison to his father.

These examples of learning Portuguese address the advantage of youth in the incorporation process of adjusting to the new environs. Eva Sopher alludes to it when she observes the difficulties her grandmother has as a former "Frau Kommerzienrat"[35] in her new, more proletarian existence in Brazil. The younger generation also has less cultural baggage brought along from Europe. Mathilde Maier (1897–1999), a Jew of middle class origins educated as a chemist, writes: "Für die jüngere Generation der Emigranten und ihre Kinder gelten diese Bindungen an Europa nicht im gleichen Maße. Sie sind stärker im Lande integriert, auch hinsichtlich der gesamten geistigen Haltung".[36] In part, the younger generation turns away from its parents, certainly not an unusual phenomenon the world over, but perhaps heightened within the context of emigration. Karin Schauff (1902–1999), a Catholic born in the Rhineland whose husband Johannes Schauff saw himself persecuted as an opponent of National Socialism, writes about how her children leave the farm near remote Rolândia and go to the cities. Occasionally returning, they enjoy the peace and tranquility of rural life, but also see the "Traumland" their parents have built up, "einen Parsifal-Garten, der mit der echten rauen brasilianischen Wirklichkeit wenig übereinstimmte".[37] They insist on finding "ihre echte eigene Verwirklichung in diesem Lande und gemeinsam mit den Menschen, zu denen wir sie geführt hatten […]".[38]

[34] Eckl: *"... auf brasilianischem Boden"* (n. 10). P. 346.
[35] Ibid. P. 173.
[36] Ibid. P. 202.
[37] Ibid. P. 215.
[38] Ibid. P. 215.

Although the strong presence of darker-skinned Brazilians as descendents of slaves – today roughly 50% of the Brazilian population – is initially a strong socio-cultural difference for the exiles, it is also a *leitmotif* in the process of easing incorporation. The perceived lack of racial discrimination is seen as a relief after the experiences of anti-Semitism in Nazi Germany. Mathilde Maier writes: "Die große Völkervermischung Brasiliens hat Rassengegensätze sehr gemildert. Bei Schulfesten im Städtchen sieht man das blondeste Kind Hand in Hand mit einem krausen, dunkelhäutigen Kerlchen in einer Reihe marschieren".[39] The issue of racial equality also appears in the text by Paul Rosenstein (1875–1964), a Jewish doctor and well-known surgeon before being forced to emigrate, who sees Afro-Brazilians as "in keiner Weise diskriminiert" although somewhat backward in "Bildung und Kultur".[40] He also emphasizes the progress being made to rectify this situation. There are even moments of humor when Hilde Wiedemann writes of her daughter Dorothea's first direct encounter with a dark-skinned man: "Auch die Menschen besah sie sich kritisch: 'Schwarzer Mann, warum bist du so schwarz?' fragte sie auf dem Postamt vorwurfsvoll einen baumlangen Soldaten, der ihr freundlich zulächelte. 'Du solltest dich mal tüchtig waschen!'"[41] In Rosenstein's statement and the incident Wiedemann relates, there may be some culturally hegemonic thinking present, perhaps a covert or indirect form of discrimination. Yet, what predominates is the thankfulness that race is not an issue, at least from the naïve perspective of the exiles.

Their view is credulous because the facts in Brazil speak a very different language. Although blacks and whites may be equal before Brazilian law and there was not the kind of segregation that prevailed in the USA, there has always been economic discrimination against Afro-Brazilians. In addition, back then, when the exiles arrived, and even today they are not represented in Brazilian government corresponding to their numbers.[42] However, these are problems not seen critically by the exiles. One cannot help but think that the overly negative experience of racial discrimination in Germany clouded a more objective view of the issue of race in Brazil.

Maintaining German and European cultural values in Brazil, especially among the older generation of exiles, was certainly also a rite of incorporation and may very well have served as a way of negotiating the alterity of their situation, that is the entirely different cultural values they encountered, making their impact less severe. On their farm near remote Rolândia, the Maiers and

---

[39] Ibid. P. 196.
[40] Ibid. P. 306.
[41] Ibid. P. 250.
[42] See Neil Callender's article on 'Protests by Afro-Brazilians and Indigenous Indians' at www.raceandhistory.com/worldhotspots/braziliansprotest.htm.

many other German exile families in the area read and discussed Goethe and Thomas Mann together. In his texts, Max Hermann Maier (1891–1976), Mathilde Maier's husband and a lawyer in Frankfurt before leaving Germany, mentions an eight-volume edition of Goethe's letters brought along to Brazil, and quotes extensively from them, including the master's conversations with Eckermann. For Max Hermann Maier, Goethe is "ein guter Tröster und ein meisterhafter Lehrer, der mir gerade in der Fremde ein Begleiter mit überreichen Gaben auf vielen Gebieten wurde".[43] He ends one of his texts with the following quote from Goethe's diaries:

> Wir stolpern wohl auf unserer Lebensreise
> Und doch vermögen in der Welt, der tollen,
> Zwei Hebel viel auf's irdische Getriebe:
> Sehr viel die Pflicht, unendlich mehr die Liebe.[44]

It must, however, be noted that at least in the case of the Hamburgers, the cultural differences apparently remained so large that they became an obstacle to more extensive cultural incorporation. Hans Hamburger's difficulties in learning Portuguese, mentioned earlier, no doubt played a role in this regard. Of one of their trips, Charlotte Hamburger writes: "Nur auf einer Reise, und zwar auf unserer ersten, kamen wir in Kontakt mit Brasilianern".[45]

Aside from cultural differences, there were extreme ones related to nature and climate that also required considerable adjustment, especially for those who ended up in Rolândia. Located in the Brazilian state of Paraná, the *Gesellschaft für wirtschaftliche Studien* had reserved a very large tract of land near there in 1932 through the *Companhia de Terras Norte do Paraná*, a subsidiary of the London-based *Paraná Plantation Ltd*. German settlement of the land was encouraged as part of an official program to alleviate the high unemployment in the Weimar Republic. After 1933, however, it also became a refuge for Germans fleeing the Nazi regime who were able to circumvent the very strict currency regulations and pay for the land indirectly. This was possible because the *Companhia de Terras Norte do Paraná* owned the majority of stock in a railway company, and in exchange for German railway tracks purchased by the exiles, they received land near Rolândia and even the necessary visa in order to settle there.[46] These exiles were often intellectuals who now saw themselves exposed to the most severe of natural elements as they tried to establish new lives as coffee farmers.

---

[43] Eckl: *"... auf brasilianischem Boden"* (n. 10). P. 203.
[44] Ibid. P. 203.
[45] Ibid. P. 353.
[46] See Vorwort. In: Eckl: *"... auf brasilianischem Boden"* (n. 10). Pp. 23–25.

Karin Schauff writes of the confrontation with a vastly different insect and animal world of strange spiders, bats, opossums, lizards and poisonous snakes of various types. Mosquitos are another problem. Mathilde Maier describes the arrival on their piece of land near Rolândia and being greeted by a friend: "Aber wie war sie von Moskitos und Boraschuten zerstochen! Die Stiche dieser Plagegeister waren angeschwollen und vereitert. Sie trug es mit Humor und Geduld, wir sollten bald ihrem Beispiel folgen".[47] For others, as Karin Schauff adds, the required adjustment was just too great both in terms of nature and culture:

> Größtenteils waren unsere Nachbarn Menschen, die aus geistigen Berufen oder aus dem Beamtenstand kamen und deshalb in den Anfangsjahren an der Umstellung auf die tropische Landwirtschaft über das normale Maß hinaus litten. Sehr viele zeigten sich den Anstrengungen seelisch und körperlich nicht gewachsen. Sie siechten nach wenigen Jahren dahin. Viele setzten ihrem Leben auf gewaltsame Weise ein Ende. Es gab für sie keine Hoffnung, je aus dem Tiefstand herauszukommen. Und das waren nicht nur ältere Menschen, auch eine Reihe von verzweifelten jungen Männern war darunter, die den Glauben an ein sinnvolles Weiterkommen in der Wildnis verloren hatten. Einige Farmer wurden von ihren brasilianischen Arbeitern umgebracht, weil sie nicht in der Lage waren, sich den Gepflogenheiten und Gesetzen des Landes und der Mentalität des Volkes gegenüber richtig einzustellen.[48]

In spite of all the difficulties, Mathilde Maier also speaks of the advantages of living in a warmer climate because "in einem warmen Klima auf reichem Boden lebt auch der Besitzlose ein leichteres Leben".[49]

Just as many exiled families retain cultural ties to Germany and Europe, Karin Schauff does the same in terms of nature by planting the seeds of various types of fruit trees she had brought along in Brazilian soil. For her, they are invested with a symbolic meaning:

> Ihr Schicksal war dem unsren gleich: Auch sie waren Einwanderer auf fremdem Boden. Inzwischen sind sie sich selbst, ihrem Urbild, unähnlich geworden unter der grellen Sonne. Dennoch lieben wir sie immer noch wie treue Freunde und ziehen ihre Früchte oft aus reiner Anhänglichkeit den viel saftigeren und aromatischeren Fruchtsorten des Landes vor.[50]

Having arrived in Brazil, visa problems persist and thus also constitute a part of the rite of incorporation. It is the time of the dictatorial, pro-fascist, corporatist regime of Getúlio Vargas with strong nationalistic underpinnings. This led to an immigration policy not free of anti-Semitic tendencies. Thus, for

---

[47] Ibid. P. 188.
[48] Ibid. P. 213.
[49] Ibid. P. 192.
[50] Ibid. P. 234.

example, a *Circular Secreta* issued in 1937 by the Brazilian Foreign Ministry theoretically excluded the immigration of all foreigners of semitic origin. At the end of 1938, a system of quotas was installed that gave preference to farmers, a group in which Jews were not strongly represented. Although this was only an indirect form of discrimination, in the second half of 1940 a new measure was adopted that required that all immigrant applicants show proof of baptism.[51] Klaus Oliven gives us insight into what he experienced:

> Da wir nach Brasilien nur mit sechs Monate gültigen Touristenvisen eingewandert waren, versuchten wir nach unserer Ankunft, eine permanente Aufenthaltserlaubnis zu erhalten. Jedoch lehnte es die brasilianische Regierung ab, uns und allen anderen auf diese Art eingereisten Emigranten eine solche zu erteilen. Die nazifreundliche Regierung hatte diesbezüglich strenge Richtlinien erlassen. Inzwischen war der Krieg ausgebrochen, und man konnte niemanden mehr ausweisen, denn kein anderes Land wollte mehr Flüchtlinge aufnehmen. Deshalb erteilte die brasilianische Regierung ab 1941 provisorische Aufenthalts- und Arbeitserlaubnis *a t'tulo precário* für als Touristen eingereiste Emigranten, die jeder Zeit widerrufen werden konnten. Damit wollte die Regierung sich ihre Optionen für die Zeit nach Ausgang des Krieges offen halten.[52]

With great *tour de force* persistence and acumen, Klaus Oliven is able to arrange to have his fiancée Seldi join him, emphasizing above all her agricultural training. Ironically, she ends up receiving permanent visa status before he does. Although he is able to argue rationally for her visa, it must be emphasized that corruption, bribes and occasionally human decency, the aforementioned *jeito*, played a role in undercutting the anti-Semitic policies set by the government and in turning tourist visas into the highly desired permanent visas.

Again, there are many stories to tell here. Suffice it to add Paul Rosenstein's case. In his text he describes how, with the help of high-level connections that even involved President Vargas, he is able to establish legal residency for himself and his family in Brazil. However, he never receives the permission to practice as a doctor, something that may very well have been due to the subliminal anti-Semitism in Brazil during that time. It embitters him terribly; he feels sorry for the many cancer patients he was unable to help. Although he

---

[51] See Hans-Albert Walter: *Deutsche Exilliteratur 1933–1950. Band 2: Europäisches Appeasement und überseeische Asylpraxis.* Stuttgart: J.B. Metzlerische Verlagsbuchhandlung 1984. Pp. 312–22; Vorwort. In: Eckl: *"... auf brasilianischem Boden"* (n. 10). Pp. 15–21. Regarding the zigzag course of Brazilian immigration policy during this time, particularly for Jews, see Jeffrey Lesser: Immigration and Shifting Concepts of National Identity in Brazil during the Vargas Era. In: *Luso-Brazilian Review* 25/2 (1988). Pp. 45–58.
[52] Eckl: *"... auf brasilianischem Boden"* (n. 10). P. 282.

remains thankful to Brazil for giving him a new home, his text is characterized by an ambivalence also reflected in its title: "Zwischen Enttäuschung und Dankbarkeit".[53]

The texts further show work as a rite of passage to economic incorporation. Charlotte Hamburger sees her husband's position on the supervisory board of a paper factory in São Paulo as "der Anfang seiner wirtschaftlichen Einordnung"[54] although the cultural incorporation remains limited as mentioned above. Klaus Oliven ends up establishing a successful import business that lasts for over 50 years, a business that allows him to steadily improve the material quality of his life in Brazil: in 1948 he and his wife buy a piece of property and build a good-sized house on it, in 1949 they purchase their first car. That is not to say, however, that economic integration goes without a hitch in a country where other values of business interaction also point to cultural differences. Ilza Czapska describes the problems she and her husband had in this regard:

> Wir hatten in den vier Jahren in São Paulo viel gelernt: Wir wussten nun, dass die Mentalität der Brasilianer so anders als die der Europäer ist, dass man sich bescheiden muss und keine vergleichenden Maßstäbe anlegen darf. Es regieren hier andere Ideale. Zuverlässigkeit, Wahrheitsliebe, Fleiß und Pünktlichkeit sind keine Ziele (wenn sie wohl auch gelegentlich beim Partner geschätzt werden), hingegen tritt man überall auf Höflichkeit, Hilfsbereitschaft, Anspruchslosigkeit und ein Sichzurechtfinden in allen Situationen.[55]

Aside from objective economic integration, successful work makes the exiles feel subjectively incorporated into the new society and gives meaning to life. For Karin Schauff, the difficulties of working Brazilian land and converting the "Chaos des Urwaldes"[56] into productive soil is a source of great satisfaction and new roots. Beyond the coffee plantation itself, her private garden is a "schöpferische Aufgabe" which she has transformed into "ein Stück Paradies für uns alle und die vielen Freunde und Besucher".[57] Looking back, she writes: "Und so unglaublich es im Gedanken an unsere anfängliche Heimatlosigkeit und die in jeder Hinsicht entbehrungsreichen ersten Jahre klingt, im Rückblick erscheint es, als habe gerade damals das eigentliche Glück unseres Lebens begonnen, die für Leib und Seele sinnvoll ausgefüllte Zeit, die das Recht gibt zu sagen, dass man wirklich gelebt habe".[58]

---

[53] Ibid. P. 298.
[54] Ibid. P. 348.
[55] Ibid. P. 262.
[56] Ibid. P. 225.
[57] Ibid. P. 226.
[58] Ibid. P. 230.

Starting in 1960, Eva Sopher dedicates herself tirelessly to promoting culture in Porto Alegre in southern Brazil. Successfully organized cultural events or public recognition of her cultural work are what make her feel that Brazil is her new home:

> Aus diesem Grund gibt es vier Momente, die mehr noch als die brasilianische Einbürgerung unauslöschlich in mein Gedächtnis eingeschrieben sind – der Tag, an dem ich die Ehrenbürgerschaft von Porto Alegre erhielt; der Abend vom 7. September 1972, an dem auf meine Anregung hin der Abschluss der Unabhängigkeitsfeiern mit einem Konzert des Israeli Philharmonic Orchestra unter der Leitung von Zubin Mehta begangen wurde, meine Teilnahme an dem Karnevalsumzug auf der Straße, bei dem mir das Volk von beiden Seiten zujubelte und meinen Namen rief, und schließlich der glorreiche Abend der Wiedereröffnung des Theatro São Pedro im Juni 1984.[59]

As well integrated or incorporated as Eva Sopher becomes into Brazilian life and as much as this is generally the case among the exiles in these texts, it must be emphasized once again that the process is by no means an easy one. The ambivalent attitude of Paul Rosenstein somewhere between thankfulness and disappointment vis-à-vis Brazil has been touched upon previously. Also mentioned earlier is Alice Brill-Czapski's text with its apt title, "Das waren bittere Jahre…",[60] by which she refers to the early years in Brazil, years under the shadow of war and the threat of fascism, an uncertain future, the existential fight to survive from one day to the next and the tragedy of her father, who perishes in a concentration camp. The loss of loved ones in the Holocaust accompanies many of the exiles during the incorporation phase. For Eva Sopher, it is part of the "Riss"[61] that stays forever; for Klaus Oliven and his wife Seldi, it is what motivates their commitment to keeping the memory of the Holocaust alive in order to prevent it from happening again.

What keeps all the exiles going is the inner motivation Hilde Wiedemann talks about, a further rite of incorporation:

> Zum Aufbau eines Lebens auf Neuland und in fremder Umgebung gehört neben der praktischen Befähigung vor allem irgendein zwingender innerer Grund. Ob das ein soziologisches Ideal, eine politische Überzeugung oder ein religiöser Glaube ist, in jedem Fall muss die Triebkraft stark genug sein, um durch Jahre hindurch Mut und Geduld allen Widerwärtigkeiten zum Trotz nicht erlahmen zu lassen.[62]

It is precisely the Jewish faith that features prominently in Paul Rosenstein's text: "Würde ich nicht einen so unbeirrbaren Gottesglauben haben, hätte ich

---
[59] Ibid. Pp. 176–177.
[60] Ibid. P. 149.
[61] Ibid. P. 170.
[62] Ibid. P. 254.

niemals bestehen können vor den großen Dingen und den Wundern der Natur und hätte niemals herausfinden können aus der Wirrnis und der Willkür der letzten Zeit".[63] Catholicism plays a similar role for Karin Schauff. A child is baptized, a festival that culminates in the erection of a cross on their farm:

> Die Taufe war das erste größere fröhliche Fest im Haus und auf der ganzen Farm, die am gleichen Tag ebenfalls ihren Namen, Santa Cruz, zu Deutsch: Kreuzhof, erhielt. Aus dem Kreuzhof eines tausendjährigen rheinischen Dorfes stammten Vorfahren der Familie. Ein hohes, schweres Kreuz aus Perobaholz, dessen Balken von den gesamten männlichen Mitgliedern des Hauses behauen worden waren, wurde an jenem Tag auf der Hügelkuppe errichtet. An einer hervorragenden Stelle des Gartens, die weithin für uns alle und das Tal zu unseren Füßen sichtbar war [...]. Zum ersten Mal läutete die neue Fazendaglocke, die die Umschrift trug: "Im Kreuz sind wir getröstet und erlöst".[64]

The cross as a symbol of Jesus's passion consoles and is a symbol as well for the burden that the Schauffs and their fellow Catholic exiles, too, have to bear. The obstacles are many, but their faith in Christ lets them persevere.

Ultimately, Brazil becomes a new home for all the exiles quoted here. When the Czapskis travel to Germany and Poland in 1970, their return to Brazil is a "Heimkehr".[65] In spite of his difficulties of being able to practice as a doctor, Paul Rosenstein has the same sentiment when, after visiting Europe, he boards the Italian ship *Conde Grande*, "das mich in meine neue Heimat Brasilien zurücktrug": "Ich war wieder zu Hause. Selten habe ich so voller Glück und Geborgenheit meine neue Heimat begrüßt".[66] Earlier, Trudi Landau's poem was quoted within the context of the rites of separation and may be considered here again with regard to the rites of incorporation and Brazil becoming a new home:

> Com trinta e poucos anos,
> em terra brasileira
> achei uma pátria nova
> e nova cidadania.
> Fundei um novo lar.
> Com minha mãe me reencontrei.
> Pranteei meu pai querido e
> mandei gravar seu nome na pedra.
> Fiz novos amigos,
> comprei novas malas
> e tratei de minha saúde.
> [...]
> Sou diferente, machucada

---

[63] Ibid. P. 313.
[64] Ibid. Pp. 225–226.
[65] Ibid. P. 277.
[66] Ibid. P. 312.

porém sou forte, compenetrada,
judia consciente de uma missão.
Salvei dos escombros o essencial:
a minha integridade.[67]

The rites of an incorporation Landau has achieved are most clearly expressed through the preterite verb forms she employs in the first-person singular such as "achei" (I found), "fundei" (I founded), "reencontrei" (I reunited), "pranteei" (I mourned), "comprei"(I bought) or "salvei" (I rescued). They speak of reestablishing one's existence materially, reuniting with relatives, reconnecting with identity, and, at the same time, mourning loss. Brazil is the new home where all this occurs: "em terra brasileira / achei uma pátria nova".[68] It was these words that gave *"... auf brasilianischem Boden fand ich eine neue Heimat"* its title.

The "missão" that Landau talks about also becomes a kind of rite in many of the texts. Klaus Oliven writes of the commitment he feels to tell the story of the Holocaust:

> Seldi und ich glauben, dass die Tatsache, dass wir beide überlebt haben und in der Lage waren, eine glückliche Familie in einem neuen Lande zu gründen, für uns eine Verpflichtung bedeutet. Wir müssen gegen die Assimilation und für den Weiterbestand des jüdischen Volkes kämpfen und dafür, dass der Holocaust nie wieder vorkommen kann. In diesem Sinne müssen wir uns bemühen, die neue Generation zu erziehen. Schon der Prophet Jo'l hat uns treffend dazu ermahnt:
> Saget euren Kindern davon,
> und lasset's eure Kinder ihren Kindern sagen,
> und diese Kinder ihren Nachkommen.[69]

Less politically and religiously charged, Ilza Czapska, Hilde Wiedemann and Charlotte Hamburger are saying something similar when they indicate they are writing their stories down for their grandchildren.

Returning to van Gennep's classification of the rites of passage as related to the Brazilian exile experience, we have seen that they let us organize that experience. The rites of separation include ostracism (especially for Jews), denial on their part of the gravity of the situation, and the psychological and emotional

---

[67] Ibid. P. 32. Translation: At the age of 30 some years, / I found a new homeland / on Brazilian soil / and a new citizenship. / I founded a new home. / I reunited with my mother, / mourned my beloved father and / had his name / engraved in stone. / I found new friends, / bought new suitcases / and treated my illness. / [...] / I'm different now, hurt, / but I'm strong, confident, / a Jew, conscious of my mission. / From the ruins I rescued what's essential: / my integrity.
[68] Ibid. P. 32.
[69] Ibid. P. 291.

impact of separation and loss. The rites of transition evolve around practical matters of arranging emigration such as securing assets, finding a country willing to accept the exile, and procuring all-important documentation, above all a visa. Travel as an element of transition frequently consists of a difficult trek containing elements of flight, constant restlessness, exhaustion, mortal danger, coincidences, and good and bad luck. Finally, the rites of incorporation may be characterized by a confrontation of the exiles with their own alterity in Brazil and of partially overcoming it by adapting and embracing the new culture with, for example, its distinct language and racial composition, while still holding on to European values. For those exiles who led a rural existence, there is an adjustment to the untamed nature of Brazil with its vastly different climate and animal world. Procuring a valid visa also still plays an important role during the phase of incorporation. Mourning and remembering the loss of loved ones in the Holocaust, and work as the prime factor of economic integration are further rites. What caps it all is the inner and often religious motivation that keeps the exiles going in the face of so much adversity.

Van Gennep concludes *Les rites de passage* with the following statement: "Finally, the series of human transitions has, among some peoples, been linked to the celestial passage, the revolutions of the planets, and the phases of the moon. It is indeed a cosmic conception that relates the stages of human existence to those of plant and animal life and, by a sort of pre-scientific divination, joins them to the "great rhythms of the universe".[70] This is an attempt to turn the rites of passage into a grand metaphysical narrative and to place it implicitly beyond the possibility of human intervention. For if we accept van Gennep's rites of passage as a "cosmic conception" and as part of the "great rhythms of the universe", we are giving into something that is inevitable. As helpful as van Gennep's rites have been in organizing the German exile experience in Brazil, we must resist what he is implying here when projecting his rites of passage onto the exile condition. Exile has root causes that can be extirpated through the implementation of the political, economic and social policies that create a truly democratic society. If anything, we would hope that the clarity van Gennep adds in investigating the exile experience makes its trauma all the more apparent and worthy of concerted efforts to prevent its causes.

---

[70] van Gennep: *Rites of Passage* (n. 1). P. 194.

Susanne Utsch

Chronotopoi und Kindheitserinnerung: Europareisen im amerikanischen Exilwerk von Klaus Mann

In the course of his travels to Europe between 1943 and 1946 as a soldier and independent writer, Klaus Mann – after years of silence on the topic – reengaged again directly with Germany. Interestingly, both his essays and works of fiction bracket out Germany and Europe which he had left only few years prior, in 1938. Even the years before 1933, in fact even the Weimar Republic in general, are hardly mentioned. Mann's travels to Europe shortly before and after the end of the war, however, evoke memories of his childhood. This can be demonstrated through an analysis of the experience of Bakhtin's "chronotopos" and the merging of temporal and spatial characteristics. Mann's journeys through Europe and especially his visits to Germany evolve into journeys of memory, which in turn impress and influence both his experience of the present and his exile identity. Foremost, his memories are concerned with specific places, but also with travels during his childhood. By examining texts such as the narrative fragment, Reunion Far From Vienna *(1944), his essays* You Can't Go Home Again *(1945), and* An American Soldier Visiting His Former Homeland *(1947), different levels and performative functions of memory can be mapped. They lead to new insights on Klaus Mann's concept of memory in exile and shed light on his first journey to postwar Germany and Europe.*

"The baby carriage is the paradise lost. [...] There is no happiness where there is memory. To remember things means to yearn for the past. Our nostalgia begins with our consciousness", schrieb Klaus Mann in *The Turning Point. Thirty-five Years in This Century*, seiner 1942 in den USA veröffentlichten Autobiographie.[1] Er beschäftigte sich in diesem Lebensbericht intensiv mit Funktion und Wesen der Erinnerung, ausgehend von einem Rückblick auf die eigene Vergangenheit. Bis dahin hatte der Topos 'Kindheitserinnerung' nicht zu den Themen gehört, die Klaus Mann im Exil behandelte. Ende 1941 veränderten sich jedoch die außenpolitischen Parameter: Noch während er *The Turning Point* verfasste, ließ der Eintritt der USA in den Zweiten Weltkrieg die gefühlte Distanz zwischen dem europäischen und dem amerikanischen Kontinent schrumpfen und eröffnete erstmals seit Kriegsbeginn die – zumindest theoretische – Option, im Rahmen der Army nach Europa zu reisen. Für Klaus Mann erfüllte sich Ende 1943 dieser lang gehegte Wunsch, als er, nun amerikanischer Staatsbürger und ordentliches Army-Mitglied, mit einem Truppentransport nach Europa verschifft wurde und dort vorerst bis 1946

---

[1] Klaus Mann: *The Turning Point. Thirty-five Years in This Century*. New York: Fischer 1942. S. 4.

blieb. Im Rahmen dieser Reise lässt sich, ausgelöst durch die Wiederbegegnung mit dem europäischen Kulturkreis, in fiktionalen und nichtliterarischen amerikanischen Exiltexten Klaus Manns ein vergleichsweise intensives Erinnern an die europäische Herkunft und Kindheit nachweisen, besonders eindrücklich im Erzählfragment *Reunion Far From Vienna* (1944). Über den Titel der Autobiographie *The Turning Point* sagte Klaus Mann in einem Interview: "It refers to a juncture in my personal life, the beginning of a new phase in my personal career – and also, above all, the general situation".[2] Wie die Veränderung der persönlichen Erinnerungslandschaft zeigt, birgt die Kategorie 'Wendepunkt' hier auch eine erinnerungsspezifische Dimension, die sich an der eingangs zitierten Äußerung festmachen lässt: Diese markiert gewissermaßen den Beginn einer revidierten Wahrnehmung und Bewertung von erlebter Vergangenheit und Erinnerung, die sich diametral von bis dato nachweisbaren Erinnerungsäußerungen Klaus Manns unterscheidet.

Erinnerungsfunktionen im Exil

Um die Signifikanz dieser Veränderung sichtbar zu machen, ist es notwendig, vorab Erinnerung und Erinnerungsfunktionen Klaus Manns im Exil bis 1942 zu umreißen, vor allem Deutschland betreffend. In diesem Zusammenhang kommt auch dessen grundsätzliches Reise- und Exilverständnis zum Tragen, das in direktem Zusammenhang mit selbstverortender Erinnerung steht. Im Vorwort zu *Escape to Life*, dem 1939 erschienenen, essayistischen Gemeinschaftswerk von Erika und Klaus Mann, formulierte er:

> Das Reisen, das zu Anfang Abenteuer gewesen war, wurde bald zum gewohnten Lebenszustand. Ich lebte, schon 'vor Hitler', mehr im Ausland als in München oder Berlin, und ich habe mehr Zeit in einem Hotelzimmer zugebracht als im Haus meiner Eltern. […] Ich lebe in vielen Ländern – in Frankreich, in der Schweiz, in Holland, am meisten in den Vereinigten Staaten von Amerika. Ich habe nicht das Gefühl, heimatlos zu sein; erstens, weil die deutsche Heimat, als innerer Besitz, unverlierbar ist; dann aber auch, weil ich niemals nur Deutschland als meine Heimat empfunden habe.[3]

Neben dem Lebensentwurf 'Unterwegssein' klingt hier ein implizites Zugehörigkeitsgefühl an, das Klaus Mann nach der Flucht aus Deutschland im März 1933 wiederholt thematisiert hatte: "[W]ir werden niemals aufhören, Deutsche zu sein. Zu einer bestimmten Nation zu gehören, ist ein Schicksal

---

[2] Klaus Mann: Reader's Almanac. Radio-Interview vom 14.12.1942. Unveröffentlichtes Typoskript. In: Stadtbibliothek München. Monacensia. Literaturarchiv. KMA. KM 59. S. 1. Ich danke Uwe Naumann für die freundliche Genehmigung zum Abdruck der unveröffentlichten Zitate Klaus Manns.
[3] Klaus Mann: *Escape to Life. Deutsche Kultur im Exil*. München: Edition Spangenberg 1991. S. 24 und 26.

von besonders komplizierter, nicht immer heiterer Art. Ein solches Schicksal wird nicht dadurch von einem genommen, daß ein 'autoritärer Staat' einen 'ausbürgert' ".[4] Diese Beschreibung einer schicksalhaften, quasi unkündbaren Verbindung erinnert an das allumfassende Sprachgemeinschaftskonzept von Leo Weisgerber, der in den zwanziger Jahren begann, eine unlösbare Bindung an die muttersprachliche Gemeinschaft zu postulieren.[5] Wie Klaus Mann formulierten auch andere Exilschriftsteller wiederholt ihre enge Bindung an Deutschland und die deutsche Sprache – in ähnlichem Tenor wie Weisgerber, ja bisweilen fast im gleichen Wortlaut.[6] So schrieb Klaus Mann, er sei "mit irgendeiner sehr tiefen Schicht" mit dem Land verbunden, "an dessen reicher Kultur wir erzogen sind und in dessen Sprache wir die ersten Worte unseres Lebens gebildet haben".[7] Es liegt geradezu auf der Hand, dass eine dergestalt enge Bindung Erinnerungsformen wie Heimweh und Sehnsucht evoziert. So sind es in *Escape to Life* "Heimatlaute", die positive Empfindungen und Erinnerungen hervorrufen:[8] "Er spricht Deutsch zu uns", wird der fiktive Interviewer im Prolog charakterisiert, "mit dem Akzent unserer bayrischen Heimat. Das stimmt uns zutraulich".[9] Heimat wird hier über den bairischen Dialekt definiert, wenngleich diese Mundart für Erika und Klaus Mann kein muttersprachliches

---

[4] Klaus Mann: A Family Against a Dictatorship (Oktober 1937). In: Ders.: *Das Wunder von Madrid. Aufsätze, Reden, Kritiken 1936–1938*. Hg. von Uwe Naumann und Michael Töteberg. Reinbek: Rowohlt 1993. S. 247–261. Hier: S. 260.
[5] Vgl. dazu Susanne Utsch: *Sprachwechsel im Exil. "Die linguistische Metamorphose" von Klaus Mann*. Köln u.a.: Böhlau 2007. Besonders die Kapitel A.1.5. Muttersprache. Annäherung an ein problematisches Konstrukt und A.4.3. Der Essay *Die Sprache* (1947): Leo Weisgerber und die Sprachbewahrer.
[6] Vgl. Susanne Utsch: Übersetzungsmodi. Zur Komplementarität von Sprachverhalten und transatlantischem Kulturtransfer bei Klaus Mann. In: *Exilforschung. Ein Internationales Jahrbuch* 25 (2007). S. 134–151 (Übersetzung als transkultureller Prozess).
[7] Klaus Mann: unveröffentlichtes Vortragsmanuskript "Thanksgiving Day" (Dezember 1936) (KM 552/KMA). S. 1.
[8] Mann: *Escape to Life* (wie Anm. 3). S. 230. Es ist teilweise kaum rekonstruierbar, welche Teile Erika und welche Klaus Mann verfasst hat. Vgl. auch Irmela von der Lühe: *Erika Mann. Eine Biographie*. Frankfurt/Main: Fischer 2001. S. 224. Insgesamt kann mit Michel Grunewald davon ausgegangen werden, dass der Anteil Klaus Manns größer war, vgl. Ders.: *Klaus Mann 1906–1949. Eine Bibliographie*. München: Edition Spangenberg im Ellermann Verlag 1984. S. 145. Die hier zitierten Äußerungen aus dem Kapitel "Aktivität in Europa" stammen definitiv von Klaus Mann, vgl. den unveröffentlichten Tagebucheintrag vom 3.8.1939 (Heft 12/KMA): "Arbeit an 'Escape to Life' (grosser Abschnitt: 'Aktivität in Europa' usw.)".
[9] Klaus Mann: *Escape to Life* (wie Anm. 3). S. 15.

Idiom war.[10] Im Kompositum 'Heimat' drückt sich jedoch ein über die dialektale Umgebung wahrgenommenes, erinnertes Zugehörigkeitsgefühl aus. Die positive Bewertung der Mundart beruht also auf Erinnerungen an die Vergangenheit und sie ist, daraus resultierend, in die Zukunft gerichtet, wenn es im Abschnitt über den Nobelpreisträger Erwin Schrödinger heißt: "Nun klingen um ihn die Heimatlaute der süddeutschen Sprache, denen unsere Sehnsucht gilt, und er klettert auf Berge, die wir in unseren Träumen sehen".[11] Die Berge haben übertragene Bedeutung: Sie versinnbildlichen nicht nur die im Exil selten gewordene Unbeschwertheit früherer Freizeitbeschäftigungen, sondern auch den freien Zutritt zu (Sprach-) Regionen, die aus politischen Gründen nach 1933 verwehrt waren. Landschaft bildet hier also einen räumlichen Erinnerungsrahmen, die, wie Jan Assmann es formuliert, "die Erinnerung auch noch und gerade in absentia als 'Heimat' festhält".[12]

Die Erinnerungsdarstellung hatte in den ersten Jahren des US-amerikanischen Exils bei Klaus Mann demnach unterschiedliche Textfunktionen: Sie diente der Untermauerung des Gemeinschaftsgefühls der Exilanten, der Illustration des einschränkenden Exilerlebnisses oder dem antifaschistischen Aufruf, sich am Kampf gegen Hitler zu beteiligen – je nachdem, ob sich der Text an Exilanten, deutschamerikanische oder amerikanische Leser richtete. Unabhängig von dieser textinhärenten Erinnerungsfunktion lässt sich eine weitere Form herausarbeiten, die ebenfalls in direktem Zusammenhang zu der engen Bindung an Deutschland steht: Von Exilbeginn an betrachtete sich Klaus Mann als Repräsentant der deutschen Kulturgemeinschaft, deren kulturelles Gedächtnis er schützen wollte. Die Besinnung auf die deutsche humanistische Tradition, das gemeinsame Erbe und einen zu bewahrenden Kanon können als Ausdruck einer erinnerten, gegenwärtig und auch künftig erhofften geistigen Gemeinschaft mit den sogenannten 'anderen Deutschen' gelesen werden, jenen, die – wie Klaus Mann bis Kriegsbeginn 1939 vergeblich annahm – vermeintlich die Revolution gegen Hitler vorbereiteten.[13] Wie Jan Assmann

---

[10] Erika Mann konnte als einzige in der Familie bairisch sprechen. Vgl. Irmela von der Lühe: *Erika Mann. Eine Biographie.* S. 22. Vgl. zur sozialen Komponente des Heimatbegriffs auch Andrea Bastian: *Der Heimat-Begriff. Eine begriffsgeschichtliche Untersuchung in verschiedenen Funktionsbereichen der deutschen Sprache.* Tübingen: Niemeyer 1995. S. 40.
[11] Mann: *Escape to Life* (wie Anm. 3). S. 230.
[12] Jan Assmann: *Das kulturelle Gedächtnis. Schrift, Erinnerung und Identität in frühen Hochkulturen.* München: Beck 1999. S. 38.
[13] Vgl. dazu: Das 'andere Deutschland'. Zur Nationalcharakteristik im Exil. In: *Unbehauste. Zur deutschen Literatur in der Weimarer Republik, im Exil und in der Nachkriegszeit.* Hg. von Thomas Koebner. München: text und kritik 1992. S. 197–219.

gezeigt hat, sind konkrete Ereignisse, Personen oder Bilder notwendig, um Erfahrungen und Ideen des kulturellen Gedächtnisses zu vergegenständlichen; er nennt diese Hilfskonstrukte Erinnerungsfiguren.[14] Erinnerungsfiguren beziehen sich durch kulturelle Formung und institutionalisierte Kommunikation konkret auf bestimmte Menschen, Räume und Zeiten.[15] Wegen dieses Zeit-, Raum- und Gruppenbezugs ist das kulturelle Gedächtnis nicht übertragbar, sondern immer Ausdruck einer bestimmten Zugehörigkeit und damit identitätskonkret. Und es ist verbindlich: Durch den Bezug auf ein normatives Selbstbild der jeweiligen Gruppe ergibt sich "eine klare Wertperspektive und ein Relevanzgefälle".[16] Bei Klaus Mann lässt sich dies an einem selbst zusammengestellten Kanon geistesgeschichtlicher Persönlichkeiten festmachen, einem gemeinschaftsbildenden Wissensspeicher der 'anderen Deutschen', in dem er Luther,[17] Goethe, Lessing, Nietzsche und Rilke versammelte, deren normativen, vorbildlichen und maßstabgebenden Charakter er im Exilkontext zu konservieren und rekonstruieren versuchte.[18] "Wir müssten an Deutschland verzweifeln", schrieb er, "wenn wir nicht Stimme und Zeugnis einiger großer Deutscher hätten".[19] Während Jan Assmann Erinnerungsfiguren als Träger des kulturellen Gedächtnisses in einer nicht mehr von Zeitzeugen erinnerten quasimythischen Vorvergangenheit jenseits aller konkreten Erinnerungen verortet, zieht Klaus Mann als solche auch Nietzsche und Rilke heran, die nach Assmanns Definition streng genommen dem kommunikativen Gedächtnis zugeordnet werden müssten, das den maximalen Erinnerungsrahmen über individuelle Biographien definiert, also rund 80 Jahre umfasst und als Zeithorizont "mitwandert".[20] Der übergeordnete, entscheidende Aspekt ist jedoch, wie erinnert wird und wofür die Erinnerung steht, denn die genannten

---

[14] Assmann: *Das kulturelle Gedächtnis.* (wie Anm. 12). S. 37–38.
[15] Vgl. Assmann: *Das kulturelle Gedächtnis* (wie Anm. 12). S. 37–42. Vgl. auch Ders.: Kollektives Gedächtnis und kulturelle Identität. In: *Kultur und Gedächtnis.* Hg. von dems. und Tonio Hölscher. Frankfurt/Main: Suhrkamp 1988. S. 9–19, S. 12.
[16] Assmann: Kollektives Gedächtnis (wie Anm. 15). S. 14.
[17] Interessant ist die sukzessive Negativbewertung Luthers nach Kriegsbeginn, vgl. dazu Susanne Utsch: *Sprachwechsel im Exil. "Die linguistische Metamorphose" von Klaus Mann.* Kapitel A. 4. 1. Veränderte Wahrnehmung von Sprachvorbildern: Martin Luther.
[18] Vgl. dazu auch die Überlegungen von Herbert Grabes und Margit Sichert: Literaturgeschichte, Kanon und nationale Identität. In: *Gedächtniskonzepte der Literaturwissenschaft. Theoretische Grundlegung und Anwendungsperspektiven.* Hg. von Astrid Erll und Asgar Nünning. Berlin u.a.: de Gruyter 2005. S. 297–314.
[19] Klaus Mann: Eine schöne Publikation (Februar 1939). In: Klaus Mann: *Zweimal Deutschland. Aufsätze, Rede, Kritiken 1938–1942.* Hg. von Uwe Naumann und Michael Töteberg. Reinbek: Rowohlt 1994. S. 70–71. Hier: S. 71.
[20] Vgl. Assmann: *Das kulturelle Gedächtnis* (wie Anm. 12). S. 48–56.

Schriftsteller werden hier nicht konkret-historisch, sondern als Teil des kulturellen Kanons erinnert, der sich in der absoluten Vergangenheit konstituiert hat und Hoffnung auf die postnationalsozialistische Epoche ausdrückt: "Es ist dieses Deutschland, das die Welt seit Jahrhunderten mit so viel Herrlichkeiten beschenkt hat, dessen Überlieferung wir fortzusetzen versuchen [...]. Mit den bescheidenen Kräften, die uns gegeben sind, kann man für seine großen Werte sich allerorts einsetzen – auch in den USA, oder *gerade* in den USA".[21] Um sie von dort aus, so Klaus Mann Anfang 1938, "schließlich einmal wieder zurückzutragen in unsere endlich befreite Heimat".[22] Diese Wiederbegegnung mit Deutschland, die Konfrontation des realen Raums, der realen Landschaft mit der Erinnerung, fand für Klaus Mann im Zuge der Reisen nach und in Europa zwischen 1944 und 1946 statt. Für die Erinnerungsfunktion Klaus Manns in den Jahren bis 1939 kann festgehalten werden, dass Erinnerungsäußerungen über Deutschland und die deutsche Sprache weniger persönliche als vielmehr strategische Dramaturgiefunktion in Texten hatte, auch, weil Klaus Mann sich dezidiert von einem singulären Heimatbegriff distanzierte. In der Hoffnung auf die Rückkehr konnte Heimat mittelfristig überall sein. Die private Erinnerungsfunktion bestand im Bewahren des gemeinsamen Kulturerbes und war vorrangig positiv-optimistisch besetzt. Nach 1939 finden sich in dessen Texten kaum mehr Äußerungen mit Erinnerungs- oder Gedächtnischarakter: Nachdem die erhoffte Revolution gegen Hitler durch das 'andere Deutschland' ausgeblieben war, distanzierte sich Klaus Mann von Deutschland. Vor diesem Hintergrund geht es nun um die thematische Auswirkung der Europareisen zwischen 1943 und 1945/1946 auf das Erinnern sowie um die direkte Konfrontation der Erinnerung mit der europäischen bzw. deutschen Realität, sowohl in den fiktionalen als auch in nichtliterarischen Texten.

Chronotopos und die Inszenierung von Erinnerung in *Reunion Far From Vienna*

Besonders deutlich lässt sich dies im 13-seitigen Erzählfragment namens *Reunion Far From Vienna* (1944) aus dem Nachlass herausarbeiten, das nach Ansicht von Michel Grunewald im Jahr 1944 verfasst wurde – zu dem Zeitpunkt also, als Klaus Mann gerade in Marokko bzw. Italien stationiert worden war.[23] Hauptfigur des Fragments ist der Exilant Max Berman, der 1939 im

---

[21] Klaus Mann: Deutsche in Amerika (Juni 1937). In: *Das Wunder von Madrid* (wie Anm. 4). S. 198–202. Hier: S. 199.
[22] Klaus Mann: Kultur und Freiheit (Januar 1938). In: Ebd. S. 297–309. Hier: S. 306.
[23] Klaus Mann: *Reunion Far From Vienna* (ca. 1944). KM 268/KMA. Hier zitiert nach dem Erstabdruck des Fragments in Utsch (2007). S. 419–431. Vgl. auch Michel Grunewald: *Klaus Mann 1906–1949. Eine Biographie*. München: Edition Spangenberg 1984. S. 198.

Alter von neunzehn Jahren gemeinsam mit der Mutter aus Österreich in die USA emigriert ist und sich dort zum – nicht näher definierten – Zeitpunkt der Erzählhandlung bereits sprachlich und ökonomisch erfolgreich integriert hat. Er dient in der Armee und ist am Vortag der eigentlichen Handlung gemeinsam mit seiner Kompanie in der französischen Kolonie Marokko eingetroffen. Der fiktionale Text beschreibt zunächst die vermeintlich gelungene Anpassung des Exilanten, um sie dann sukzessive zu dekonstruieren. Dabei kommt der Erinnerungsdarstellung eine zentrale Erzählfunktion zu: Die Reise nach Europa ruft gleich mehrere verdrängte Erinnerungsebenen hervor. Diese Reise über den Atlantik wird beschrieben als "a long nightmare of boredom and seasickness",[24] wobei die tiefere Bedeutung der lakonischen Beschreibung von Dauer ("long") und pejorativen Erlebens ("nightmare") erst im Zuge der späteren Ereignisse deutlich wird.[25] Zu Beginn der Erzählung wird der Protagonist für einen Ausflug in die nächstliegende Stadt freigestellt, deren Besichtigung mit einigen Kollegen den äußeren Handlungsrahmen bildet. Die erzählte Zeit umfasst exakt den Zeitraum von ein Uhr mittags bis 21 Uhr abends.

Während die Figur Max Bermans auf den ersten Fragmentseiten über die Selbst- und Fremdwahrnehmung innerhalb der amerikanischen Gesellschaft – bzw. als deren Pars pro Toto innerhalb der Army – charakterisiert wird, gewinnt dessen Reaktion auf das marokkanische Umfeld zunehmend an Bedeutung. "Max had been in this part of the world before",[26] heißt es bereits knapp auf der ersten Seite – eine Randbemerkung, die im Rahmen der Stadtbesichtigung größeres Gewicht bekommt. Dort sind es zunächst die amerikanischen GIs, die die Andersartigkeit des Ortes wahrnehmen und daran scheitern, die fremden Eindrücke mit bestehenden räumlichen und zeitlichen Bewertungskategorien zu erfassen: "Unreal, not quite from this world", "the precious grace of past ages".[27] Einziges Beschreibungsvokabular liefern ihnen literarische Werke: beim Anblick der altertümlichen Kutschen Flauberts *Madame Bovary*, beim Besuch des Sultanspalastes die Märchensammlung *1001 Nacht*, "the taste of the Arabian Nights".[28] Wie diese Verweise belegen, nehmen die amerikanischen Besucher im Text Marokko ausschließlich als exotisch und lebensfern wahr.

---

[24] Mann: *Reunion* (wie Anm. 23). S. 420.
[25] In dieser Beschreibung setzte Klaus Mann offenkundig seiner eigenen Schiffspassage ein Denkmal. Vgl. Brief an Katia Mann vom Neujahrsabend 1944: "That journey from Virginia to Casablanca was probably the worst experience of my Army life". In: *Briefe und Antworten. 1922–1949*. Hg. von Martin Gregor-Dellin. Reinbek: Rowohlt 1991. S. 531.
[26] Mann: *Reunion* (wie Anm. 23). S. 420.
[27] Ebd. S. 423.
[28] Ebd. S. 424.

Ihre Unfähigkeit, die Fremderfahrung zu entschlüsseln, mündet schließlich in dem Vorhaben, "an old hysterical monkey"[29] als Kompaniemaskottchen zu kaufen. Der Affe steht in diesem Zusammenhang als Symbol der Torheit für die nutzlose Kaufidee selbst und die sich darin manifestierende touristische Oberflächlichkeit.[30] Dieser klischeehaft dargestellte Umgang mit der marokkanischen Kultur kann als Kritik am sogenannten Fremdenverkehr gelesen werden, "ein von religiösen, erzieherischen und Erwerbszwecken entlastetes Reisen, welches vornehmlich dem Zeitvertreib und Gewinn von 'Erlebnissenë dient. [...] Die betreffenden Fremden hatten weiße Hautfarbe und einen gewöhnlich höheren Status als die Einheimischen", wie Justin Stagl zusammengefasst hat.[31] Diese Form des Reisens war an der Wende vom 19. zum 20. Jahrhundert ein Breitenphänomen geworden und sie lässt sich auch im postkolonial-imperialistischen Impetus nachweisen, der im Fragment *Reunion Far From Vienna* den amerikanischen Soldaten unterstellt wird. Dieses kritische Amerikabild hat textinhärent die Funktion einer kontrastiven Folie für die Entwicklung der Figur Max Bermans, der als einziger im übertragenen und konkreten Sinne nüchtern bleibt und für den die Begegnung mit der marokkanischen Stadt zurückliegende, vertraute Ereignisse wachruft: "He had been in a peculiar mood for the past two or three hours. For one reason or another, the sightseeing got on his nerves [gestrichen: it made him feel pensive, nostalgic]. Maybe it was just that the city reminded him of his father who had once pointed out to him its monuments and curiosities – inconceivably long ago".[32]

Beim Erleben der marokkanischen Stadt verbinden sich für den Protagonisten die Dimensionen Zeit und Raum, ja die räumliche Erfahrung wird in eine zeitliche übersetzt, wie Michail M. Bakhtin es anschaulich für das Phänomen des Chronotopos beschrieben hat:

> Im künstlerisch-literarischen Chronotopos verschmelzen räumliche und zeitliche Merkmale zu einem sinnvollen und konkreten Ganzen. Die Zeit verdichtet sich hierbei, sie zieht sich zusammen und wird auf künstlerische Weise sichtbar; der Raum gewinnt Intensität, er wird in die Bewegung der Zeit, des Sujets, der Geschichte hineingezogen. Die Merkmale der Zeit offenbaren sich im Raum und der Raum wird von der Zeit mit Sinn erfüllt und dimensioniert.[33]

---

[29] Ebd. S. 424.
[30] Vgl. Eintrag: Affe. In: *Lexikon der Tiersymbole. Tiere als Sinnbilder in der Malerei des 14.–17. Jahrhunderts*. Hg. von Sigrid und Lothar Dittrich. Petersberg: Imhof 2004. S. 22–37. Hier: S. 24.
[31] Justin Stagl: Grade der Fremdheit. In: *Furcht und Faszination. Facetten der Fremdheit*. Hg. von Herfried Münkler et al. Berlin: Akademie Verlag 1997. S. 85–114. Hier: S. 86.
[32] Mann: *Reunion* (wie Anm. 23). S. 425.
[33] Michail M. Bakhtin: *Formen der Zeit im Roman. Untersuchungen zur historischen Poetik*. Frankfurt/Main: Fischer 1989. S. 8.

Es handelt sich beim Chronotopos also um eine Form-Inhalt-Kategorie, und obwohl Bakhtin sein Konzept zunächst für die Romanforschung entwickelt hat, bietet es sich auch für die Interpretation von kürzeren Texten an, insbesondere der Exilliteratur, wegen des häufig engen Zusammenhangs vom Ort, der Erinnerung auslöst, und der dargestellten Erinnerung als zeitlicher Rückwendung in einen symbolischen Raum. "[D]ie Sujetereignisse werden im Chronotopos konkretisiert", heißt es bei Bakhtin: "Von einem Ereignis kann man Mitteilung machen, über ein Ereignis kann man informieren, man kann dabei Ort und Zeit seines Verlaufs exakt angeben. Doch wird das Ereignis nicht zum Bild. Der Chronotopos liefert nun die entscheidende Grundlage, auf der sich die Ereignisse zeigen und darstellen lassen".[34]

Indem der Chronotopos dergestalt die künstlerische Einheit des literarischen Textes bestimmt, schließt er immer zugleich ein "Wertmoment" ein.[35] Es äußert sich in *Reunion Far From Vienna* in der engen Verflechtung der historischen bzw. sozialen Wirklichkeit mit privaten, ja intimen Erfahrungen, die der Raum wachruft. Denn die Umgebung, die marokkanische Stadt und ihre Sehenswürdigkeiten, also die Ebene der Basiserzählung, erinnern den Protagonisten an seine Kindheit, an die eingangs erwähnte Reise mit den Eltern: "The corporal remembered this journey as one of the great adventures of his pre-American life. What a glorious time they had – Dad, Ma, and he – in those strange, fabulous cities".[36] Die durch den Kulturkontakt evozierte Erinnerung an die frühere Reise löst ein in die Vergangenheit gerichtetes Heimweh nach den "good old days"[37] aus. Das erwähnte Wertmoment tritt hier in Form der Adjektive "great", "glorious" und "good" auf. Durch die emotionale Wertschätzung kommt dem Chronotopos in diesem Zusammenhang wesentliche Erzählfunktion zu, weil die durch ihn hervorgerufene zweite Erinnerungsebene die Gegenwart kontrastiert: Der Vater lebt nicht mehr, der väterliche Wohlstand ging verloren, Max Berman kennt Unbeschwertheit nur noch aus der Erinnerung und der gegenwärtige Besuch Marokkos hat nicht mehr den Charakter eines vergangenen "pleasure trip",[38] sondern er dient dem Kampf gegen Hitler. Zeitadverbien wie "ages ago",[39] "once" und "inconceivably long ago"[40] dienen dazu, die Erlebnisdifferenz der erinnerten Vergangenheit und der erzählten Gegenwart auch formal zu betonen. Die Unbestimmtheit der Zeitwörter unterstützt dabei die Schwere der zurückliegenden Ereignisse.

---

[34] Mann: *Reunion* (wie Anm. 23). S. 200.
[35] Ebd. S. 191.
[36] Ebd. S. 420.
[37] Ebd. S. 427.
[38] Ebd. S. 420.
[39] Ebd. S. 420.
[40] Ebd. S. 425.

Neben dieser konkreten Erinnerung an die Kindheit und die tatsächlich stattgefundene Reise eröffnet die chronotopische Umdeutung des Raums 'Marckko' in *Reunion Far From Vienna* eine zusätzliche, symbolische Dimension der Erinnerung, die die Peripetie der Handlung einleitet:

> Or was there something else that intrigued him? The atmosphere of the French colonial seaport was laden with memories full of familiar rhythms [...]. He sensed Europe – its misery, its charm, its tradition, its tragedy. Wherever he looked, he recognized the marks of suffering and struggle [...] – the proudly concealed symptoms of poverty and decay; the shabiness [!] under the surface of elegance; the weariness behind a smile, the nervous tension behind a polite phrase or gesture. How could he help being sensible to these inconspicuous, yet unmistakable nuances?[41]

Die in der marokkanischen Stadt beobachteten Verhaltensweisen, Gebräuche und Kodices ("familiar rhythms") erzeugen beim Protagonisten unbewusst ein vertrautes Zugehörigkeitsgefühl. Er erlebt sie als Elemente des sozialen Gedächtnisses, die Harald Welzer als "die Gesamtheit der sozialen Erfahrungen der Mitglieder in einer Wir-Gruppe" beschreibt.[42] Im Spiegel kolonialfranzösischer Begegnungen rückt Europa in greifbare Nähe, sowohl aus kultureller wie geographischer Sicht. Der dergestalt umgedeutete Raum erinnert den Protagonisten mit "unconspicious, yet unmistakable nuances"[43] an dessen Herkunftsregion, und das Bewusstwerden darüber stellt schließlich auch die Identifikation mit der amerikanischen Gesellschaft in Frage. Das zuvor im Text dargelegte Zugehörigkeitsgefühl, die Selbstwahrnehmung einer gelungenen Integration in den USA, stellt sich in Folge des sukzessiven Entfremdungsprozesses als einseitig heraus, als, wie Alois Hahn es formuliert, Verstehensfiktion: "Wir unterstellen Gemeinsamkeit des Erlebens und Urteilens ohne diese Gemeinsamkeit jeweils ständig zu überprüfen".[44] Die daraus resultierenden Gefühle entsprechen dem sozialen Heimwehbegriff, den Ina-Maria Greverus geprägt hat: "Nicht die affektive Bindung an einen Wertraum 'Heimat' verursacht das 'Heimweh', sondern die Unfähigkeit des Sich-Einordnens in neue Gegebenheiten, die zu einer subjektiven Überbewertung

---

[41] Mann: *Reunion* (wie Anm. 23). S. 425.
[42] Vgl. Das soziale Gedächtnis. In: *Das soziale Gedächtnis. Geschichte, Erinnerung, Tradierung.* Hg. von Harald Welzer. Hamburg: Hamburger Edition 2001. S. 9–20. Hier: S. 9–10.
[43] Mann: *Reunion* (wie Anm. 23). S. 425.
[44] Alois Hahn: Die soziale Konstruktion des Fremden. In: *Die Objektivität der Ordnungen und ihre soziale Konstruktion. Für Thomas Luckmann.* Hg. von Walter M. Sprondel. Frankfurt/Main: Suhrkamp 1994. S. 140–166. Hier: S. 146.

eines gehabten Satisfaktionsraums führt".[45] Der formale Aufbau der Vergangenheitsreflexion unterstreicht mit Parallelkonstruktionen diese subjektive, für die anderen Soldaten nicht wahrnehmbare Umdeutung des Raums: "While his American friends were fascinated by the gaudy facade [...] he sensed behind it a drama which they were not aware".[46] Und wenige Zeilen später heißt es: "Not that he wanted to notice all those melancholy, disquieting things, [...] which were ignored by his naive compagnions". Eine kontaktbedingte Erlebnistiefe wie diese bleibt den – erneut pejorativ ("naïve") gezeichneten – amerikanischen Kollegen zwangsläufig verschlossen. Die Erinnerung lässt sich nicht steuern ("not that he wanted") und bleibt emotional präsent ("the sightseeing got on his nerves [gestrichen: it made him feel pensive, nostalgic]").

Der Versuch, für eine erfolgreiche Integration in den USA die europäische Vergangenheit zu verdrängen, scheitert in *Reunion Far From Vienna* spätestens an der geographischen Nähe zum Herkunftsland, eine direkte Folge auf die Marokkoreise. Die indirekte Wiederbegegnung mit der alten Heimat und die subjektive Entfremdung von der amerikanischen Identifikationsgruppe lösen beim Protagonisten eine Identitätskrise aus, die auch formal deutlich wird. Auf den letzten Satz des Reflexionsabsatzes: "He was a child of the tragic continent whose proximity now disconcerted him",[47] folgt eine Leerzeile, die den inneren Konflikt veranschaulicht. "No, he had nothing to do with Europe; the troubles [gestr. and splendors] were none of his business. He was an American citizen and an American soldier, having chow with a bunch of boys [...] in a restaurant full of US uniforms".[48] *Reunion Far From Vienna* veranschaulicht damit das komplexe Ausmaß eines exilbedingten Verdrängungsprozesses, den erst die Reise nach Europa und der damit verbundene Ortswechsel aufdeckt. Die alptraumhafte Überfahrt ist vor diesem Deutungshintergrund wörtlich, als noch im Schlafzustand befindlich, zu verstehen: Erst in Marokko kommt der Protagonist zu sich, erst jetzt wird er sich der zurückliegenden, unterdrückten Ereignisse bewusst. Damit bediente sich Klaus Mann des Schemas "Vergessens-Schlaf und Erinnerungs-Erwachen", das Aleida Assmann als eine der wesentlichen zeitlichen Gedächtnis-Metaphern anführt.[49] Es ist die unerwartet

---

[45] Ina-Maria Greverus: *Der territoriale Mensch*. München: Beck 1972. S. 34.
Michael Basseler und Dorothee Birke: Mimesis des Erinnerns. In: *Gedächtniskonzepte der Literaturwissenschaft. Theoretische Grundlegung und Anwendungsperspektiven.* Hg. von Astrid Erll und Asgar Nünning. Berlin u.a.: de Gruyter 2005. S. 121–147. Hier: S. 136.
[46] Mann: *Reunion* (wie Anm. 23). S. 425.
[47] Ebd. S. 425.
[48] Ebd. S. 425.
[49] Aleida Assmann: *Erinnerungsräume. Formen und Wandlungen des kulturellen Gedächtnisses*. München: C.H. Beck 2003. S. 170.

hervorgerufene Erinnerung an die ungetrübte Vergangenheit, die ihn außerdem veranlasst, sich die schmerzvolle Zwischenzeit zwischen Damals und Heute zu vergegenwärtigen: "So many things had happened since – apocalyptic events, disasters which changed the face of the world and upset millions of innocuous individual lives"[50].

Insgesamt lassen sich in *Reunion Far From Vienna* aus der Perspektive des Protagonisten also drei Erinnerungsebenen unterscheiden, die mit Identitätsentwürfen, Gegenwartsdeutung und Geltungsansprüchen verknüpft sind. Der Chronotopos ist dabei erfahrungsrelevant: Die empfundene Vertrautheit mit der marokkanischen Stadt lässt sich auf die Reise im Kindesalter zurückführen. Diese räumlich konkretisierbare Erinnerung löst als zweite Erinnerungsebene die Rückbesinnung auf die intakten Familienverhältnisse im österreichischen Kulturkreis aus. Diese ersten beiden Erinnerungsdimensionen veranschaulichen an konkreten Beispielen, dass Raum ein Speicher von Zeit sein kann: Der Text lebt geradezu von einem "gleichzeitige[n], gleichwertige[n] und gleichberechtigte[n] Nebeneinander mehrerer Zeitebenen", und hebt damit die lebensweltlichen Grenzen zwischen erinnerter und tatsächlicher Vergangenheit auf.[51] Die französische Kolonialstadt verweist zudem auf Europa und steht symbolisch für einen dezidiert nicht-amerikanischen Verhaltens- und Wertekodex. Vor allem diese dritte, symbolische Erinnerungsdimension löst eine Identitätskrise des Protagonisten aus: Der Text suggeriert, dass die verdrängte europäische Herkunft unvermindert großen Einfluss auf dessen Selbstwahrnehmung und Identitätsentwurf hat. Damit verweist er auf die Grenzen von Anpassung und Integration, als Ergebnis erinnerungsbedingter Gegenwarts- und Selbstdeutung, die sich auf Textebene in der Begegnung mit einem gleichsprachigen Jugendfreund manifestieren. Denn auf dem Höhepunkt des existentiellen Identitätsdilemmas verbindet sich in *Reunion Far From Vienna* die erinnerte Vergangenheit mit der Gegenwart in der zufälligen Begegnung der Hauptfigur mit einem Jugendfreund: Otto Stössinger, der als französischer Soldat in Marokko stationiert ist. Dessen Erscheinung versinnbildlicht die Zwischenzeit, die beide getrennt erlebt haben: Der erwachsene Mann ("tall and lean, and he wore a strange kind of beard"[52]) ist für den Protagonisten nicht "at once" identifizierbar. Erst die Stimme stellt den vertrauten Bezug her: "It was Otto, all right. This was the familiar voice – the voice of the good old days, of brotherly affection"[53]. Die Figur Otto Stössinger personifiziert im Text aber nicht nur die Erinnerung an die intakte Kindheit in Österreich, sondern auch die verdrängte

---

[50] Mann: *Reunion* (wie Anm. 23). S. 420.
[51] Vgl. Basseler und Birke: Mimesis des Erinnerns (wie Anm. 45). S. 136.
[52] Mann: *Reunion* (wie Anm. 23). S. 429.
[53] Ebd. S. 426–427.

europäische (Sprach-)Identität. "'Why, Otto!'... Max's voice sounded shaky and his eyes were full of tears. 'Bist Du's wirklich...' he said – laughing now and already in the arms of his friend".[54] Während dieser wie selbstverständlich Französisch spricht ("Mais c'est bien moi, mon vieux, [...]. C'est moi, Otto"[55]), wechselt jener zwischen der englischen und der deutschen Sprache. Dieses Code-Switching legt nahe, dass das differierende Sprachverhalten als eine Konsequenz des Reflexionsprozesses betrachtet werden muss, den der Kulturkontakt beim Protagonisten ausgelöst hat. Infolge ihrer neuen Exilidentität ist die Kommunikation der beiden Ex-Österreicher quasi unmöglich:

> Should they speak German? It seemed the natural thing to do, no doubt – and yet it would have been utterly out of place, indeed, almost scandalous. Otto's English was fair – considerably better than Max's French. Courteous and ambitious, Otto tried to express himself in the unfamiliar tongue. But somehow it did not work; he was handicapped, irritated by the limitations of his vocabulary and the awkwardness of his accent. Should Max make an effort to be more fluent, in French? But if Otto, definitely the more brilliant one of the two – had failed in this kind of experiment, how could Max hope to succeed? It would be a waste of time. And they had only half-an-hour before the café would close.[56]

Die auf zwei Seiten ausgeführten erfolglosen Versuche, die Zweitsprache des anderen zu verwenden, dienen im Text als Beweisführung: Kein Idiom außer der deutschen Muttersprache kann die emotionalen Inhalte der Freunde transportieren und ihre frühere Vertrautheit wieder herstellen. Der Gebrauch der deutschen Sprache als Sprache des Feindes wäre – zumal im Beisein alliierter Soldaten – jedoch ein Skandalon.[57] Was bleibt, gleicht im Text babylonischer Sprachverwirrung, denn die Freunde, die im Fragment zuvor ihre Mehrsprachenkompetenz ausgezeichnet hat, entpuppen sich im Zwiegespräch als kommunikationsunfähig. Diesem Erleben von Sprachverlust und Sprachlosigkeit steht diametral die problemlose, nonverbale Verständigung der französischen und amerikanischen Soldaten gegenüber: "While the boys understood each other, although one half of their party didn't know what the other half was talking about, Max and Otto found it difficult to choose the idiom in which to open their conversation".[58] Die Erzählung bricht schließlich ab, bevor ein Gespräch der Jugendfreunde entsteht bzw. eben weil sich gezeigt

---

[54] Ebd. S. 427.
[55] Ebd. S. 426.
[56] Ebd. S. 429.
[57] Bereits während der Begrüßungsszene überspielt Max die ungewollte Verwendung der deutschen Sprache mit der amerikanischen Bemerkung: "'Why Otto...' This was Max again – slightly embarrassed after his emotional outburst". S. 8.
[58] Mann: *Reunion* (wie Anm. 23). S. 429.

hat, dass keines entstehen kann. Der fragmentarische Charakter der Erzählung unterstreicht damit auch formal das Kommunikationsproblem, das die jeweils neue (Sprach-)Identität auslöst.

Diese abschließende Begegnungsszene steht im Text für die sprachliche Dimension des erinnerungsbedingten Identitätskonflikts. Sie symbolisiert, dass Sprache identitätskonkret ist und als solche nicht nur negativ besetzt sein kann. Das Fragment suggeriert also, dass nur die Mutter- bzw. Erstsprache als hörbarer Ausdruck gewachsener sozialer Beziehungen eine kathartische Auseinandersetzung mit der Vergangenheit ermöglicht und damit ein neuerliches Bekenntnis zur Herkunftskultur. Die gescheiterte Kommunikation am Ende des Textes ist also nicht nur ein deutliches Indiz für die Identitätskrise des Protagonisten Max Berman, sondern auch als Kritik am hyperkorrekten Anpassungsverhalten der beiden Freunde zu lesen: Die dogmatische Anpassung an die Normen der Exilländer, das Aufgeben von Herkunftskultur und -sprache sowie das Verdrängen jeglicher Erinnerung an die europäische Vergangenheit verhindern im Text die erfolgreiche *Reunion Far From Vienna*. Diese Erkenntnis ist ein Resultat der fiktiven Europareise, der Wiederbegegnung mit dem "tragic continent" und eine Folge der dadurch ausgelösten, vielschichtigen Rückschau des Protagonisten. Der Chronotopos hat in Klaus Manns Erzählfragment also eine wesentliche dramaturgische und inhaltliche Erzählfunktion: Er dient der Entfaltung der Problematik und strukturiert den Text durch das Moment der Peripetie mittels der konzentriert-verdichteten Erinnerungsdarstellung. Erst das gleichzeitige Erleben der gegenwärtigen und vergangenen Zeit in der Raumerfahrung Marokko, zumal deren unterschiedliche Bewertung, unterstreichen in *Reunion Far From Vienna* die Endgültigkeit des unwiederbringlich Verlorenen und lösen die Identitätskrise aus. Weitreichende chronotopische Erfahrungen wie diese kennzeichnen in den Jahren nach 1942 jedoch nicht nur diesen fiktionalen Text von Klaus Mann, sondern letztlich auch sein nicht-literarisches Schreiben: Er blickte – nicht nur im europäischen Kontext – verstärkt auf die eigene Kindheit und thematisierte wiederholt die Vergangenheit.

Heimat der Kindheit: Imagination und Konfrontation

Während Klaus Mann das Erzählfragment *Reunion Far From Vienna* im Rahmen seiner durch die Armee veranlassten Europareise schrieb, hatte er sich bereits im Herbst 1943 – noch aus der sicheren Distanz des amerikanischen Exils – in einer Artikelserie mit der Bombardierung einzelner deutscher Städte befasst. Sie gehören zu den ersten Texten, in denen er sich nach 1939 erstmals wieder dezidiert mit der Situation in Deutschland auseinandersetzte. Bei dem Gedanken an die Trümmer in Hamburg, an die "unwiederbringliche Fülle an Traditionen und Energien" empfand er Trauer, wenngleich kein Mitleid für die

Bevölkerung.[59] "Wie merkwürdig, sich jetzt – wie viele Jahre ist das wohl her? – an meine einsamen Spaziergänge zu erinnern, entlang der engen Kanäle, 'Fleete' genannt, die sich quer durch die Altstadt ziehen".[60] Ein Jahr später, als Klaus Mann dann über Casablanca und Tunis nach Italien gereist war, bereitete er sich dort mental auf die erste Begegnung mit Nachkriegsdeutschland vor. Die dort verfassten Texte spiegeln nun jedoch nicht mehr Orte oder Menschen der Lebenswirklichkeit von 1933 wieder, sondern eine zeitlich und räumlich viel länger zurückliegende: Er dachte vor allem an das München seiner Kindheit. "Who is living now in my room with the beautiful view?", schrieb er im Sommer 1944 an Katia Mann, "I am looking forward to the day when I shall requisition personally good old Poschi – throwing out with the utmost brutality, its present inhabitants and moving right into my own old room".[61] In diesem Zusammenhang ist zwar nicht die Rede von Heimweh – dies galt nur Paris[62] – oder Heimkehr, aber die Attribute zeigen, dass Klaus Mann die der Heimat zugeschriebenen Empfindungen wie Ruhe, Geborgenheit und Zugehörigkeit mit dem Wohnhaus der Eltern in München verband.[63] Irmela von der Lühe hat dies bestätigt: Die "Poschi", also das Elternhaus in der Poschinger Straße, sei für Erika und Klaus Mann Ausdruck einer "behüteten, wenngleich aufregenden Kindheit" und "heilen Welt" gewesen.[64] Daneben riefen bei Klaus Mann kurz vor Kriegsende Städtenamen wie München, Innsbruck und Kitzbühel nostalgische Gefühle hervor: "My whole childhood comes back, with the sound of these familiar names. They remind me of my first skiing lessons, of mountain-climbing, of swimming in beautiful lakes …".[65] Ähnlich der fiktiven Erinnerungsdarstellung im Erzählfragment *Reunion Far From Vienna* hatte die geographische Nähe zu Deutschland, die europäische Umgebung, also offensichtlich auch Einfluss auf Klaus Manns persönliches

---

[59] Klaus Mann: Cities in the News (1): Hamburg (September 1943). In: Ders.: *Auf verlorenem Posten. Aufsätze, Reden, Kritiken. 1942–1949.* Hg. von Uwe Naumann und Michael Töteberg. Reinbek: Rowohlt 1994. S. 74–78, S. 75. Der Artikel wurde – wie die anderen, im Folgenden zitierten Texte dieser Serie – ursprünglich von Klaus Mann auf Englisch verfasst.
[60] Ebd. S. 76.
[61] Klaus Mann, unveröffentlichte Briefe an Katia Mann vom 28.6.1944 und vom 22.8.1944 (beide KMA). Mit "Poschi" ist die Poschingerstr. 14 gemeint, die Adresse der Mann-Villa in München-Bogenhausen.
[62] Vgl. Klaus Mann: Cities in the News (7): Paris (Oktober 1943). In: Ders.: *Auf verlorenem Posten.* S. 99–103. Hier: S. 100.
[63] Vgl. Jakob und Wilhelm Grimm: *Deutsches Wörterbuch.* Bd. 10. München: dtv 1984 (=Nachdruck von 1877). S. 864–865. Sie nennen das elterliche Haus bzw. dessen Besitz als dritte von sieben Bedeutungsmöglichkeiten von 'Heimat'.
[64] von der Lühe: *Erika Mann* (wie Anm. 10). S. 21.
[65] Klaus Mann: "Interview mit Grant Parr" (14.4.1945). KM 360/KMA. S. 2.

Erinnern: Im Unterschied zur strategischen Funktion der Erinnerungsdarstellung in früheren Texten beschäftigte er sich nun – weiterhin öffentlich – intensiv mit der eigenen Vergangenheit und äußerte Erinnerungen an deutsche bzw. österreichische Orte. Der empfundene Heimatradius des Weltbürgers Klaus Mann erstreckte sich in Italien jedoch allein auf den Horizont eines Kindes, wie die Erwähnung des eigenen Zimmers und des Sportunterrichts veranschaulichen. Berlin, wo Klaus Mann 1933 gelebt hatte, erwähnte er in Italien mit keinem Wort, auch nicht dort lebende ehemalige Freunde und Bekannte.

Diese – für Klaus Mann bis dato untypisch nostalgische – Rückbesinnung auf die Kindheit war zugleich ein exilspezifisches Phänomen: Walter Benjamin beschrieb Kindheitsbilder als diejenigen, "die im Exil das Heimweh am stärksten zu wecken pflegen".[66] Ohne Rückkehrhoffnung rief er sie bewusst im Ausland hervor – ein Verfahren, das er als heilsam empfand und "Impfung" nannte: "Das Gefühl der Sehnsucht durfte dabei über den Geist ebensowenig Herr werden wie der Impfstoff über einen gesunden Körper".[67] Benjamin selbst plante, die sinnlich-emotionalen Erlebnisse auf diese Weise von ihren biographischen Zügen zu trennen und als Exempel einer Großstadtkindheit zu statuieren, was sich etwa in dem methodischen Imperativ äußerte, "das Wort 'ich' nie zu gebrauchen".[68] Trotz dieses Vorhabens bleibt der Verlust der als Kind erfahrenen Geborgenheit als Grundtenor in *Berliner Kindheit um neunzehnhundert* allgegenwärtig. Während sich Walter Benjamin also intensiv damit beschäftigte, die hervorgerufenen Bilder seiner Kindheit auf ihren präformierenden Gehalt hin zu untersuchen, lässt sich bei Klaus Mann – zumindest in öffentlichen Texten – eine grundsätzliche Skepsis gegenüber erinnerten Bildern als autobiographischen Indikatoren feststellen. Im ersten Kapitel von *The Turning Point*, das bezeichnenderweise mit "The Myths of Childhood" überschrieben ist, heißt es:

> What, then, do I remember? [...] Our unconscious responds to certain tokens, secret cues and signs that come to us from nobody-knows-where. There is an aroma, faint and yet intense; a fusion of rubber and a particular sort of linen and lacquered wood, with a touch of flannels and calico, the material of which curtains are made: the curtain of a baby carriage. But is it *my* baby carriage whose soft, swinging rhythm I now feel rocking me, once again? Or is this another delusion?[69]

---

[66] Walter Benjamin: *Berliner Kindheit um neunzehnhundert*. Frankfurt/Main: Suhrkamp 1996. S. 9.
[67] Ebd.
[68] Walter Benjamin: Berliner Chronik. In: *Gesammelte Schriften*. Unter Mitwirkung von Theodor W. Adorno und Gershol Sholem. Hg. von Rolf Tiedemann und Hermann Schweppenhäuser. Bd. I-VII. Frankfurt/Main: Suhrkamp 1972–1989. Hier Bd. IV. S. 475.
[69] Mann: *The Turning Point* (wie Anm. 1). S. 4.

Im Kontext des Autobiographie-Schreibens betonte Klaus Mann mehrfach die Relativität von Erinnerung, nicht zuletzt auch, um die Verfremdung, ja Fiktionalisierung der eigenen Vita quasi präventiv zu legitimieren.[70] Der Umgang mit Kindheitserinnerungen steht damit bei Walter Benjamin und Klaus Mann in diametralem Gegensatz: Während jener die schmerzhaften Kindheitsbilder bewusst hervorrief und ihre Physiognomien herauslöste, um eine "Antiautobiographie" zu schreiben, wie Nicolas Pethes es genannt hat, wollte Klaus Mann "the truth, the whole truth and nothing but the truth" seines eigenen Lebens erzählen.[71] Dazu gehörte trotz aller Erinnerungszweifel auch die im Exil stark ausgeprägte Sehnsucht nach dem frühen "Paradies vollkommener Wunschlosigkeit", und die ersten Kapitel von *The Turning Point* bzw. *Der Wendepunkt* geben eindringlich dessen prägende Wirkung wieder.[72] In diesem Zusammenhang sind auch die Rückbesinnungen auf das München der Kindheit zu verstehen, ähnlich dem, wie es Theodor W. Adorno formuliert hat: "Ich wollte einfach dorthin zurück, wo ich meine Kindheit verbracht hatte, wodurch mein Spezifisches bis ins Innerste vermittelt war".[73] Denn die Rückbesinnung auf die Kindheit barg die ungetrübte Hoffnung auf eine eigentlich gute Welt im Sinne Ernst Blochs: "Was allen in die Kindheit schien und worin noch niemand war: Heimat".[74] Diese heimatlichen Gefühle bezogen sich bei Klaus Mann kurz vor Kriegsende in Italien allein auf den geographisch klar abgrenzbaren Raum sinnlicher, auch sprachlicher Erfahrungen einer bürgerlich-behüteten Kindheit.[75]

Umso größer war die Fallhöhe: Am fünften Mai 1945, kurz nach der Kapitulation der deutschen Truppen in Italien, trat Klaus Mann als Korrespondent der US-amerikanischen Armeezeitung *Stars and Stripes* von

---

[70] Vgl. dazu Susanne Utsch: Fiktionalisierte Vita: Das autobiographische Gedächtnis Klaus Manns in "The Turning Point" (1942) und "Der Wendepunkt" (1949). In: *Klaus Mann zum 100. Geburtstag. Tagungsband.* Hg. von Irmela von der Lühe und Wiebke Amthor. Frankfurt/Main: Lang (im Druck).
[71] Nicolas Pethes: *Mnemographie. Poetiken der Erinnerung und Destruktion nach Walter Benjamin.* Tübingen: Max Niemeyer 1999. S. 276. Vgl. Klaus Mann: *The Turning Point, Klappentext.*
[72] Klaus Mann: *Der Wendepunkt. Ein Lebensbericht.* Frankfurt/Main: Fischer 1952. S. 20.
[73] Theodor W. Adorno: Was ist deutsch? Rundfunkgespräch (1965). In: Ders.: *Stichworte. Kritische Modelle.* Frankfurt/Main: Suhrkamp 1969. S. 102–112. Hier: S. 107.
[74] Ernst Bloch: *Das Prinzip Hoffnung.* Bd. 3. Frankfurt/Main: Suhrkamp 1967. S. 1628.
[75] Vgl. Michael Neumeyer: *Heimat. Zu Geschichte und Begriff eines Phänomens.* Kiel: Geogr. Institut der Universität Kiel 1992. S. 89. Die Sehnsucht nach Heimat steht auch für die Sehnsucht nach einer positiv erlebten Lebenswelt.

Rom aus die erste Deutschlandreise nach Exilbeginn an. Erste Eindrücke schilderte er in Briefen und Zeitungsartikeln, besonders aufschlussreich sind die Texte "You Can't Go Home Again" (1945) und, zwei Jahre später, "An American Soldier Revisiting His former Homeland" (1947), den er mit den Worten einleitete: "You can't go home again...: These words were in my mind – haunting me like a nostalgic tune, a melancholic leitmotiv, while I was touring occupied Germany, in 1945 and 1946".[76] Die erste Reise im Mai 1945 diente vorrangig dem Besuch der Heimatstadt München, dem bereits erwähnten Elternhaus und dem Besuch einiger als integer erinnerter Freunde. "Approaching Munich I expected to find a mutilated, half-destroyed town; reality turned out to be worse. Munich is dead. It does not exist anymore. What used to be the fairest town of Germany, one of the most attractive European cities, has been transformed into a vast cemetery [...]. It was like an evil dream".[77]

Das Bild des Alptraums wählte Klaus Mann wiederholt, um diese erste Besichtigung Nachkriegs-Münchens zu beschreiben, das der erinnerten Stadt seiner Kindheit in nichts mehr glich: "What a strange, nightmarish experience! – to walk through those once-familiar streets, now reduced to masses of ruins and rubble...".[78] Die ruinenbedingt reduzierte Orientierung löste wider Erwarten ein großes Entfremdungserlebnis aus, das Klaus Mann in *Der Wendepunkt* 1948/1949 literarisch stilisiert – und verstärkt hat: "War dies die Heimkehr? Alles fremd, fremd, fremd... Und doch auch wieder nicht! Fremd und vertraut zugleich... Die ur-vertraute Landschaft wild-fremd geworden; das Wild-Fremde mit Spuren von Ur-Vertrautheit: dies kommt nur in bangen Träumen vor".[79] Diese pseudo-dichotomischen Äußerungen belegen den vagen, unbewussten Charakter von Heimat, vielleicht auch des Heimwehs, von dem der Exilant Vilém Flusser gesprochen hat: "Es sind zumeist geheime Fasern, die den Beheimateten an die Menschen und Dinge der Heimat fesseln. Sie reichen über das Bewusstsein des Erwachsenen hinaus [...] ins nicht gut artikulierte, kaum artikulierte und unartikulierte Gedächtnis".[80] Der irreale

---

[76] Klaus Mann: An American Soldier Revisiting His Former Homeland. In: *The Turning Point. Thirty-five Years in This Century.* Hg. von Shelley Frisch. New York: Markus Wiener 1984. S. 367–372. Hier: S. 367.
[77] Klaus Mann: You Can't Go Home Again, S. 4 (KMA, KM 406). Vgl. auch Ders.: Brief an Thomas Mann vom 16.5.1945. In: *Briefe* (wie Anm. 25). S. 535. Vgl. außerdem die Briefe an Thomas Mann vom 16.5.1945. In: *Briefe* (1991), S. 539: "It's all very confusing and somewhat depressing, even though fascinating"; und an Ferdinand Bruckner vom 5.10.1945: "The old continent is sad, morbid and messy, yet not without a certain absurd attraction" (unveröffentlicht, KMA).
[78] Mann: An American Soldier (wie Anm. 76). S. 368.
[79] Mann: *Der Wendepunkt* (wie Anm. 72). S. 513.
[80] Vilém Flusser: Wohnung beziehen in der Heimatlosigkeit. In: *DU* (Dezember 1992). Heft 12. S. 12–14. Hier: S. 12.

Eindruck der Ruinenlandschaft München, jener Stadt, die Klaus Mann zuvor als "schöne Stadt, eine der elegantesten des Kontinents", als "heiter und vornehm" gerühmt hatte,[81] berührte ihn existentiell, wie es besonders beim Besuch der elterlichen Villa deutlich wird: "[T]he sense of estrangement and profound complexity which I had already experienced in the ruined streets overcame me again, almost intolerably intensified. To look at these broken walls and empty windows was like facing a sinister caricature of my own past. I made haste to get out".[82] Die durch das nahezu personifiziert erlebte Haus ausgelöste Befremdung Klaus Manns, die der Kontrast der erinnerten, belebten und möblierten Zimmer mit dem kargen und umgebauten Hausinnern evozierte, verstärkte die Information, dass die Nationalsozialisten das Elternhaus als Lebensborn-Zentrum missbraucht hatten: "our poor mutilated, polluted house! [...] [F]or one reason or other, it didn't quite look like home to me...".[83] Mit diesem makabren Wissen schrieb Klaus Mann schließlich fast erleichtert an Thomas Mann: "I am only happy that I am not with P.W.B. [Psychological Warfare Branch, d. Verf.] anymore and don't have to stay here and become an editor of the revived *Münchener Neuesten Nachrichten*".[84] Der ursprüngliche Wunsch, persönlich am Neuanfang Deutschlands im Dienst der Alliierten mitzuwirken, relativierte sich also bei Klaus Manns erster Deutschlandreise durch die Konfrontation der Kindheitserinnerung mit der nachkriegsdeutschen Gegenwart im Frühsommer 1945, auch deshalb, weil die ersten persönlichen Begegnungen mit Deutschen einen "bitteren Nachgeschmack" hinterließen.[85] Klaus Manns Deutschlandbild schwankte deshalb zwischen Anklage und Selbstmitleid: "terrible old Germany", "our depraved, ravaged, disfigured former fatherland", "pitiful, fearful Old Country" und "sad country", wobei sich en gros mitfühlende, also positive Äußerungen auf die zerstörten Städte und pejorative auf deren Bewohner

---

[81] Klaus Mann: Cities in the News (6): München (Oktober 1943). In: Ders.: *Auf verlorenem Posten*. S. 96–99. Hier: S. 96.
[82] Mann: You Can't Go Home Again (wie Anm. 77). S. 4–5.
[83] Klaus Mann: Brief an Thomas Mann vom 16.5.1945. In: *Briefe* (wie Anm. 25). S. 536 und Ders.: An American Soldier Revisiting his Former Homeland. S. 4. In Lebensbornhäusern zeugten sogenannte arische Männer und Frauen den Nazi-Nachwuchs. "Lebensborn was a place where racially qualified young men and equally well-bred young women collaborated in the interest of the German nation". Ebd. S. 4. Vgl. zum Lebensborn etwa Georg Lilienthal: *Der "Lebensborn e.V.". Ein Instrument nationalsozialistischer Rassenpolitik*. Frankfurt/Main: Fischer 2003.
[84] Klaus Mann: Brief an Thomas Mann vom 16.5.1945. In: *Briefe* (wie Anm. 25). S. 539.
[85] Klaus Mann: Ein Mann guten Willens. Begegnung mit Dr. Hermann Brill (Juli 1945). In: *Auf verlorenem Posten*. S. 248–251. Hier: S. 248.

bezogen.⁸⁶ "It is terrible to be in Germany, but not without a certain sinister fascination", schrieb Klaus Mann Anfang Juli 1945, als er von seinem ersten Deutschlandbesuch zurückkam.⁸⁷

Die Konfrontation der realen Orte und Menschen mit den erinnerten, zumal jenen der Kindheit, führte zu Irritation, Enttäuschung und Verärgerung Klaus Manns. "Die Vergangenheit erträgt alles, nur nicht den Augenschein von dem, was aus ihr geworden ist", hat Günther Anders diese Erfahrung beschrieben.⁸⁸ Bei Klaus Mann verstärkten gesamtgesellschaftliche Phänomene wie die allgemeine Schuldabwehr diesen Eindruck: "Well-fed, well-clad, well-organized, they appeared as cocky as ever. Surely there was nothing humble about them", schrieb er im Mai 1945.⁸⁹ Diese Wahrnehmung verstärkte sich in den folgenden Jahren, als er eine Stagnation im Entnazifizierungsprozess beobachtete: "[Q]uite a few of them [Deutsche, d. Verf.] have remained faithful to him up to the present day and would be only too happy if they could have him back…"⁹⁰ Die Alptraum- und Friedhofsmetaphern, mit denen er 1945 München als leblose, menschenleere Stadt dargestellt hatte, dienten schließlich auch der Beschreibung ehemaliger Berliner Bekannter im Jahr 1948:

> [A] ghost parade, a procession of shadows, a band of materialized, if somewhat undernourished, memories. Like the hero in Marcel Proust's psychological saga À la Recherche du Temps Perdu, I had to face my own 'Past Recaptured': There it was – smiling at me, beckoning me […]. Their voices sounded strange, for all the intriguing, cream-like familiarity of their features. I knew that I would not feel at home in their midst any more.⁹¹

Geister und Schatten, eine Übertragung des physischen Ausdrucks von Unterernährung, die materialisierte Erinnerung sowie das Ritual der Prozession stehen für die endgültige Historisierung einer Vergangenheit, die sich nicht mehr zurückholen ließ. Andererseits hatten diese ruhelosen

---

⁸⁶ Klaus Mann: Briefe an Fritz H. Landshoff vom 28.7. und vom 4.9.1945. In: Ders.: *Briefe*. Hg. von Friedrich Albrecht. Berlin u.a.: Aufbau 1988, S. 500–501 und 509; Ders.: Brief an Hermann Kesten vom 11.8.1945. In: *Briefe* (wie Anm. 25). S. 545.
⁸⁷ Klaus Mann: Brief an Fritz H. Landshoff vom 1.7.1945. In: *Briefe* (wie Anm. 86). S. 495.
⁸⁸ Vgl. Günther Anders: *Die Schrift an der Wand. Tagebücher 1941–1966*. München: Beck 1967. S. 150–160.
⁸⁹ Vgl. Mann: You Can't Go Home Again (wie Anm. 77). S. 2: Vgl. auch Ders.: "Deutschland und seine Nachbarn" (unveröffentlichter Vortrag, April 1948). KM 120/KMA. S. 8: "Selbst-Mitleid statt Reue…Man will von 'kollektiver Schuld' nichts hören…".
⁹⁰ Mann: An American Soldier (wie Anm. 78). S. 367.
⁹¹ Klaus Mann: Lecture in Europe on American Literature. In: *Vogue* (Dezember 1948). S. 193–196. Hier: S. 196.

Scheintoten auch beunruhigende ("disquieting"), befremdliche ("strange") und sogar bedrohliche Wirkung, wie Klaus Mann mit militärischen Vokabular deutlich machte: "They beleaguered the platform before and after my lecture, they bombarded me with letters, wires and telephone calls; they invaded my hotel room".[92] Argumentiert man mit Freud, lassen sich daraus auch Anklänge einer unbefriedeten Vergangenheit Klaus Manns herauslesen.[93] Dieser war aber nicht nur über den Umgang der Deutschen mit der jüngsten Vergangenheit befremdet, er vermisste auch ein Interesse an seiner Person.

Die Deutschlandreisen von 1945 und den folgenden Jahren sind also von diversen Enttäuschungen geprägt: der Desillusionierung bei der Suche nach der Heimat seiner Kindheit, dem Desinteresse an seiner Person von deutscher Seite aus und der ausbleibenden Veränderung der Deutschen auf der Grundlage eines umfassenden Schuldeingeständnisses. Trotz der Distanz, die Klaus Manns GI-Identität bot, hinterließ der Besuch der zerstörten Nachkriegsstädte München und Berlin das Gefühl des irreparablen Verlustes von Erinnerungsorten, wie die Rückkehrmetaphorik in Form von Alptraum- und Totenbildern veranschaulicht. Diese Gedächtnisorte, um es mit Aleida Assmann zu formulieren, waren für ihn unlesbar geworden.[94] Die Trivialität dieser Bewusstwerdung, die unter Exilanten verbreitet war, lag für Jean Améry darin, dass "niemals der Wiedereintritt in einen Raum auch ein Wiedergewinn der verlorenen Zeit ist", auch deshalb, weil der Heimkehrer sich verändert habe.[95] Klaus Manns Erinnerungsorte waren jedoch ohnehin unwiederbringlich, da er bereits vor der Rückkehr nach Deutschland im Mai 1945 die "nahe Zukunft mit ferner Vergangenheit" vermischte, weil er die unbeschädigten Orte seiner Kindheitserinnerungen und nicht etwa jene der Flucht im Jahr 1933 wiederzusehen hoffte.[96] "Die Heimat ist das Kindheits- und Jugendland. Wer sie verloren hat, bleibt ein Verlorener", hat Jean Améry diesen Heimatverlust von Exilanten beschrieben.[97] Der Verlust der Erinnerungsorte verstärkte bei Klaus Mann die Entfremdung von den Dagebliebenen, die für die Zerstörung

---

[92] Ebd. S. 196.
[93] Für Sigmund Freud haben Totenbilder diese Funktion. Vgl. zur Metaphorik der Geisterbeschwörung; Assmann: *Erinnerungsräume* (wie Anm. 49). S. 171–178.
[94] Vgl. dazu Assmann: *Erinnerungsräume* (wie Anm. 49). S. 314–322.
[95] Jean Améry: Wieviel Heimat braucht der Mensch? In: *Bewältigungsversuche eines Überwältigten*. Stuttgart: Klett Cotta 1980. S. 74–101. Hier: S. 75. Vgl. auch Carl Zuckmayer: *Als wär's ein Stück von mir*. Frankfurt/Main: Fischer 1967. S. 461: "Er mag wiederkehren, aber der Ort, den er dann findet, ist nicht mehr der gleiche, den er verlassen hat, und er selbst ist nicht mehr der gleiche, der fortgegangen ist".
[96] Vgl. Mariela Sartorius: Lebenslügen. Die Rückkehr. In: *Süddeutsche Zeitung* 9.6.1998.
[97] Améry: Wieviel Heimat braucht der Mensch? (wie Anm. 95). S. 84.

verantwortlich schienen bzw. es offenkundig waren: Die anfängliche Bereitschaft zu Kontaktaufnahme und Auseinandersetzung innerhalb Deutschlands nahm in Relation zum Ausbleiben der Vergangenheitsbewältigung der Gesprächspartner ab. Alexander und Margarete Mitscherlich haben diese Unfähigkeit zum Schuldeingeständnis, "die Abwehr gegen Schuld, Scham und Trauer", als eine Entlastungstechnik des deutschen Kollektivbewusstseins diagnostiziert.[98] Klaus Mann vermisste den Freudschen Prozess des Erinnerns, Wiederholens und Durcharbeitens in der deutschen Gesellschaft als Schuldeingeständnis und Bewältigung der NS-Vergangenheit. Er selbst befand sich, ausgelöst durch die Konfrontation mit vertrauten Menschen und Orten, bereits in diesem Prozess, wenn auch auf der anderen, der Opferseite. Hannah Arendt hat dieses "Wiedererkennenserlebnis" der Remigranten – im Sinne der griechischen Tragödie – als "Drehpunkt der Handlung" betrachtet.[99] Ein neuerlicher Wendepunkt also? Festzuhalten bleibt, dass die Europa- und Deutschlandreisen nach 1943 Klaus Manns Erinnerung an Deutschland veränderten, und damit zusammenhängend seine Selbstdarstellung vom Repräsentanten des kulturellen Gedächtnisses hin zu einem Individuum mit sehr persönlichen, von Sehnsucht und Heimweh geprägten Kindheitserinnerungen. Die Wiederbegegnung mit den Erinnerungsorten kann mit Hannah Arendt in der Tat als neuerlicher Dreh- bzw. Wendepunkt verstanden werden. Denn bei den Deutschlandbesuchen durchlebte Klaus Mann eine Enttäuschung, die jener über den ausbleibenden Widerstand bei Kriegsbeginn vergleichbar ist. Daneben stand die Trauer über die verlorenen Orte, wodurch sich bestätigte, was Klaus Mann bereits 1942 – noch vor der großen Reise nach Europa – als ein wesentliches Charakteristikum des Erinnerns in *The Turning Point* festgehalten hatte: Das Paradies des Kinderwagens war unwiderbringlich. "No matter how hard we try to capture the bliss of paradise, it is only our own longing for the paradise lost we succeed in finding".[100]

---

[98] Alexander und Margerete Mitscherlich: *Die Unfähigkeit zu trauern. Grundlagen kollektiven Verhaltens*. München: Piper 1969. S. 27.
[99] Vgl. Hannah Arendt: Was bleibt? Es bleibt die Muttersprache. In: *Zur Person. Porträts in Frage und Antwort*. Band 1. Hg. von Günter Gaus. München: Feder 1964. S. 13–32. Hier: S. 26.
[100] Mann: *The Turning Point* (wie Anm. 1). S. 4.

II. Crossing Borders

Jörg Thunecke

Definitions of Exile. *Unwilling Tourist* (1941–1942): Adolf Hoffmeister's Odyssey into Emigration (1939–1940)

Adolf Hoffmeister's (1902–1973) travelogue The Animals Are in Cages *(1941)/*The Unwilling Tourist *(1942) is a semi-fictitious account of the protagonist Jan Prokop's (i.e. Adolf Hoffmeister's) escape (1939–1941) from Prague – via Paris, Bordeaux, Casablanca, Tangier, and Lisbon – to New York. While the account of the actual events: occupation of Czechoslovakia in March 1939, exile and internment in France (1939–1940), escape from Europe to the USA via North Africa and Lisbon after the fall of France in June 1940, was quite a typical refugee experience, Hoffmeister's humorous-ironic style – accompanied by some two dozen illustrations – is anything but typical compared with similar (semi-) fictitious accounts in exile literature covering the period 1939–1940.*

Also unusual – and pivotal to Hoffmeister's travelogue – is the attempt half-way through the book at defining what constitutes a 'refugee': an analysis of 14 'definitions' given by various passengers aboard the S.S. Lorient, sailing from France to North Africa, leads to the conclusion that a refugee is an unwilling tourist (the title of the English edition), barely surviving the present, and concerned about the future only in so far as it would lead to a revival of the past. This, in fact, was quite a unique – and highly critical – assessment, rarely officially shared by fellow exiles, but nonetheless in many ways probably closer to the truth than many refugees were willing to admit.

> "To travel hopefully is a better thing than to arrive".
> Robert Louis Stevenson: *Virginibus Puerisque and other Papers* (1881).

Adolf Hoffmeister (1902–1973),[1] probably best known as the librettist of Hans Krasa's (1899–1944) children's opera *Brundibar* (1935),[2] first performed in a Jewish orphanage in Prague in 1941, and later, in 1942, some 50 times in the

---

[1] See Miroslav Lamač: *Výtvarné Dílo – Adolfa Hoffmeistera*. Prague 1966; *Schiffe des Kolumbus. Adolf Hoffmeister: Karikaturen – Collagen – Illustrationen*. Ed. by Harald Olbrich. Berlin: Eulenspiegel Verlag 1986, especially pp. 133ff; *Adolf Hoffmeister*. Ed. by Karel Srp. Prague: Gallery 2004; Karel Srp: Svét Jako Smutek (= Die Welt als Trauerspiel). Ibid. Pp. 176–205; *Sto Let České Karikatury*. Ed. by Adolf Hoffmeister. Prague: Státní Nakladatelství, Krásné Literatury Hudby a Aumění 1955. Pp. 444–70; and Karel Srp: Adolf Hoffmeister v. Knihách. Soupis Knižní Tvorby 1917–2003. Ibid. Pp. 362–75. (All Czech translation thanks to Ulli Rink [Cologne], to whom I herewith would like to extend my gratitude).

[2] *Brundibar*. New York: Michael di Capua Books/Hyperion Books 2003. Adapted by Tony Kushner, with illustrations by Maurice Sendak.

Terezin (Theresienstadt) concentration camp. The son of an attorney, he studied law at Charles University in Prague (since 1921) and earned a doctorate (1925), after which he joined his father's law firm, thus achieving financial independence to pursue his varied interests in the field of arts. At the early age of 18, prior even to graduating from high school in 1921, he became a founding member of 'Devětsil' (= Neunkräfte, Pestwurz), an avant-garde group devoted to primitive art,[3] while at the same time writing poetry.[4] He spoke fluent German and was acquainted with most of the Prague-German writers during the 1920s and 1930s. Among others he knew Franz Kafka (in 1968–1969 he designed a stamp of the author), and, being quite a connoisseur himself, drew various sketches for an anniversary volume of the Prague wine merchant Jos. Oppelts Neffe entitled *Wein. Anthologie. Aus Anlass der 110jährigen Bestandsfeier und zu Ehren des Weines für ihre Freunde und Gönner* (1933), to which numerous well-known German-speaking authors from Prague contributed, like Oskar Baum, Rudolf Fuchs, Rudolf Haas, Heinz Politzer, Walter Seidl, Richard von Schaukal, Friedrich Torberg, Johannes Urzidil, Ernst Weiss, Franz Werfel, Oskar Wiener, and Ludwig Winder, most of whom later emigrated. Hoffmeister traveled a lot, spent a term at Selwyn College (Cambridge) in 1924,[5] regularly visited Paris, where he made the acquaintance of such famous people as Čapek, Masaryk, Joyce, Picasso, Max Ernst, Majakowski, Ehrenburg. In London (1926) he met Chesterton and Shaw, both of whom he sketched (see e.g. *Podoby* [= *Gestalten* 1961], *Visages écrits et dessinés* [1964]). In Paris, during the early 1930s, he also became acquainted with the surrealist movement and arranged a major exhibition, 'Poesie 1932', in Prague at the gallery Manes. In 1928 he became a member of P.E.N. and was increasingly active as a caricaturist (see e.g. his cooperation with Vlasta Burian in illustrating Swift's *Gulliver's Travels* [*Guliverovy cesty*] in 1929). Numerous publications followed in quick succession: *Kalendář* (1930), *Piš jak slyšíš* (= *Schreib, wie du bist* 1931), *Svě za mřízerni* (= *Die Welt hinter Gittern* 1933) jointly with J. Voskovec and J. Werich, *Povrch pětiletky* (= *Die Oberfläche des Fünfjahresplanes* 1931) following a trip to the USSR, and *Americké Houpačky* (= *Amerikanische Wippen* 1937) following a fact-finding touring through the United States of America in 1936.

---

[3] Other founding members were Jaroslav Seifert (1901–1986), who was awarded the Nobel Prize for Literature in 1984, and Karel Teige (1900–1951).
[4] See Matthew S. Witkovsky: *Avant-garde and Center: Devětsil in Czech Culture 1918–1938*. Philadelphia: Ph.D. Diss. Pennsylvania University 2002, esp. p. 534. See also *Devětsil: Czech Avant-garde – Architecture and Design of the 1920's and 1930's*. Ed. by Rostislav Švacha. Oxford – London – Prague: Museum of Modern Art 1990.
[5] See Adolf Hoffmeister: *Kaleidoskop*. Dědivocé: Labyrint 2004. Pp. 13ff.

After the rise to power by the Nazis in Germany in 1933 Hoffmeister increasingly focused on political caricatures,[6] which were mainly published in the Prague-based anti-Fascist magazine *Simplicus*, in the wake of the forced closure of its German counterpart *Simplicissimus*. He also arranged a major exhibition of caricatures and humor at the Gallery Manes in Prague in 1934. Hoffmeister's anti-Fascist engagement was, however, also the reason for his departure from Czechoslovakia (Protectorate) in late April 1939. He initially went to Paris where he had good contacts; but following the outbreak of World War II in September 1939 he was arrested and kept for 7 months in La Santé prison (see *Vězení* [1969] *La Prison* [1969]) until finally released in 1940,[7] only to be interned again in various French camps following the defeat of France in June 1940. He eventually made his escape by boat to Casablanca in Morocco later that year, and from there to Lisbon via Tangier, finally arriving in New York (via Havana) at the beginning of 1941. After a brief stay there he toured the US and stayed for 5 months in Hollywood, where *The Animals Are in Cages* (1941)[8] was written, which a year later – with a more suitable title – was also published in England as *The Unwilling Tourist* (1942),[9] a fictitious – though highly autobiographical – account of an artist's escape from Prague in spring 1939, via France, Morocco, Portugal to the United States (also published in Czech immediately after the war as *Touristou proti své vůli* [1946]).

Hoffmeister gradually managed to gain a professional foothold in the United States, he collaborated with the 'Voice of America' in 1942, and after 1944 ran its Czech section.[10] He had exhibitions in the Museum of Modern Art in New York in 1943, inaugurated by none less than Edvard Beneš, and in London (1944).[11] However, following the end of World War II he almost immediately returned to Czechoslovakia (in August 1945), joined the KSČ (in September 1945) and the Czech diplomatic service as ambassador to Paris (1948–51). In

---

[6] See some early examples of Hoffmeister's anti-Fascist caricatures.
[7] The subtitle in the French translation states: "Écrit en 1940 à Paris, dans la prison de La Santé, illustré par les codétenus de l'auteur. Traduit du Tchèque par Dominique Grandmont".
[8] Adolf Hoffmeister: *The Animals are in Cages*. New York: Greenberg 1941. No translator is stated, but the translation quite obviously was done by Don Perris (all citations and illustrations from this edition [page numbers follow in brackets] unless otherwise stated).
[9] Adolf Hoffmeister: *Unwilling Tourist*. London: John Lane The Bodley Head 1942. Transl. Don Perris. The two versions are not completely identical, and spelling and expressions in the English version have been anglicized. Citations and illustrations from this edition unless otherwise stated.
[10] See Srp: Svět Jako Smutek (n. 1). P. 190.
[11] See Lamač: Biographique Notice. Ibid. (appendix, no page ref.).

addition, he also became the ČSSR's representative to UNESCO (in 1947), a post which he kept for many years and which took him to numerous countries worldwide, especially following his dismissal from the diplomatic service in 1951, being demoted to professor at an insignificant art academy (FAMU). As Czechoslovakia's UNESCO representative he traveled to Mexico, China, Japan, and many European countries while at the same time pursuing his artistic career. In 1958 he contributed to the Czech pavilion at the Expo in Brussels, in November 1964 he became – against the wishes of the KPČ – president of the Czech artists' confederation and eventually joined the 'Prague Spring' movement in 1968, only to be ousted from all positions following the suppression of the liberal Czech regime under Dubček by Warsaw Block forces in August 1968. Apart from visits to France – lecturing in Vincennes in 1968–1970 – he spent the rest of his life in total isolation near Prague, never – like e.g. Kundera – considering renewed emigration. He died a 'non-person' in late Juli 1973, and his reputation was only restored in the early 1990s after the fall of the Iron Curtain. Hoffmeister visited the United States at least twice prior to his forced emigration to the US in 1941: once in 1929 on the occasion of a cartoon exhibition in Louisville, KY, and – as mentioned earlier – in the autumn of 1936 when – judging by his account in *Americké Houpačky* – he visited New York, Pittsburgh, Chicago, Santa Fe, parts of California (Los Angeles/Hollywood and San Francisco), Denver, and Washington, DC, before returning to Europe via New York. Consequently, Hoffmeister was no stranger to the host country which offered him refuge for four and a half years, though it must be borne in mind that in 1941 he came involuntarily, that is to say, his earlier visits took place under completely different circumstances.[12] He was a multi-talented artist, often simultaneously a painter, caricaturist, illustrator, stage designer, writer, dramaturge, translator, journalist, radio commentator, teacher, art critic, political pundit, diplomat, cultural administrator, and – last not least – a passionate traveler. This passion for traveling, which took Hoffmeister to virtually every part of the globe, is also reflected in his semi-fictitious travelogue *Unwilling Tourist* – similar to fellow-countryman Egon Hostovsky's account in *Listy z vyhnanství* (*Letters from Exile* [1942][13]) – even though, as the title of the British version suggests, in this instance it was an involuntary sojourn, an 'Irrweg', which took Jan Prokop, a left-wing anti-Fascist activist, from Prague to New York in 1939–1941. Yet unlike Lion Feuchtwanger (*Unholdes Frankreich* [1942]), Anna Seghers (*Transit* [1944]), Alfred Döblin (*Schicksalsreise* [1949]), Albert Drach (*Unsentimentale Reise* [1966]), Fred Wander (*Hotel Baalbek* [1991]), Peter Fürst (*Der Zigarettentöter* [1994]), and Soma Morgenstern

---

[12] See Srp: Svét Jako Smutek (n. 1). P. 176.
[13] Egon Hostovsky: *Letters from Exile*. London: Allan & Unwin 1942. See also Egon Hostovsky: *Cizinec hledlá byt*. Prague: Melantrich 1947.

(*Flucht in Frankreich* [1998]),[14] Hoffmeister's narrative is deceptively light-hearted, with an ongoing ironic undercurrent,[15] to which digressions – mainly reflections on the exile conditions in the respective host country, not to mention his own illustrations (47 in all) – greatly contribute. The travelogue is structured along the various staging posts of his itinerary into exile, starting in his hometown Prague, via Paris, two French internment camps (Sanglière and Cresson), Bordeaux, Bayonne (all these trips by train), Casablanca, Tangier, Lisbon, and finally New York (the latter journeys by boat).

Definitions

Prior to entering into a detailed discussion of Hoffmeister's travelogue, a few words about the genre seem to be in place, followed by a brief analysis of the concept of 'involuntary travel'.

As far as the genre is concerned, there has been at least one recent publication on the topic in German: *Der Reisebericht*,[16] a collection of essays edited by Peter Brenner. In his introduction Brenner points out that 'Reiseberichte' are reports about authentic journeys,[17] adding that – since the genre in the past tended to lack credibility with the reading public – it is essential to properly assess the relationship between 'Eigenem' and 'Fremdem', the borderlines of the two approaches being fluid.[18] Important is also – as Wolfgang Neubert emphasized – that "[d]as Moment der Selbstreflexion der beobachtenden Vernunft mit dem Ziel einer philosophischen Synthese des empirischen Materials Raum für die Wiedergabe von Eindrücken, Schilderungen oder Reflexionen [schafft] und den Reisebericht in neuer Weise [strukturiert], indem der narrative Determinismus der fortschreitenden Chronologie zwar nicht aufgehoben, doch aufgelockert wird".[19] The genre of the travelogue – according to Neubert, who in turn refers back to Manfred Link's 1963 dissertation[20] – consists of an interplay of various disciplines.

---

[14] See Jörg Thunecke: Im Niemandsland der Parias. Von Soma Morgensterns *Flucht in Frankreich* zu Fred Wanders *Hotel Baalbek* – eine Geschichte in Fortsetzungen. In: *Exil* 21 (2001). Pp. 82–87.

[15] A contemporary review of *Unwilling Tourist* (R.P.: Gruss aus Amerika. In: *Einheit* 4 (17.7.1943), 15. P. 20) confirms this impression: Immer wieder muss man bei den humorerfüllten, menschlichen, jedem romantischen Klimbim abholden Schilderungen des Autors an unseren Kisch denken".

[16] Peter J. Brenner: *Der Reisebericht*. Frankfurt/Main: Suhrkamp 1988.

[17] Peter J. Brenner: Einleitung. In: *Der Reisebericht* (n. 16). Pp. 7–12. Here: p. 9.

[18] Peter J. Brenner: Die Erfahrung der Fremde. In: *Der Reisebericht* (n. 16). Pp. 14–49. Here: pp. 15 and 18.

[19] Wolfgang Neuber: Zur Gattungspoetik des Reiseberichts. In: *Der Reisebericht*. Pp. 50–67. Here: p. 60.

[20] Manfred Link: Der Reisebericht als literarische Kunstform von Goethe bis Heine. Köln: Dr. Phil. Diss. 1963. Here pp. 7–11.

In connection with such narrative interactions Neubert notes an increasing "Subjektzugewandtheit des Reiseberichts bei abnehmender Sachorientierung"[21] and reminds the reader to be wary that "der Reisebericht nicht zur Darstellung von subjektiver Innerlichkeit übergeht, sondern seine Sachorientierung bewahrt".[22] This is an issue also aired by Joseph Strelka, whose definition puts travelogues into the category 'Reisenovelle' and 'Reiseroman',[23] stressing, however, that all depends on the "persönlichen Haltung des Autors", on his "künstlerische Gestaltungskraft" and his "Sprachkraft".[24] In light of above statements I would therefore like to assert – even prior to an actual analysis of the text – that Hoffmeister's travelogue strikes a neat balance between authenticity and fictionality, and that his kind of 'unfreiwilliger Tourist' – a term coined by Strelka[25] – never veers far from a middle-road of the two possible extremes of the genre.

A completely different issue, raised by Hoffmeister's travelogue *Unwilling Tourist*, is the question of tourism. Hans Magnus Enzensberger, in a seminal essay entitled 'Eine Theorie des Tourismus' way back in 1958, sketched the development of 'travel' from 'Zweckhaftigkeit'[26] – 'Reisen' being a 'notwendiges Übel'[27] – to 'Zwecklosigkeit' and 'Selbstzweck'[28] in the course of two centuries, pointing out that modern tourism amounts to nothing less than a "Fluchtbewegung aus der Wirklichkeit".[29] He also maintained that the freedom modern tourists seek from social pressures at home is highly deceptive – he speaks of "das betrügerische Wesen einer Freiheit"[30] and a sort of "Massenbetrug"[31] by the tourist industry – refering to tourism as a kind of Pyrrhic victory, especially for members the Western bourgeoisie, who had hoped to escape – at least temporarily – their normal humdrum existence in a 'Gegenwelt'.[32]

---

[21] Wolfgang Neuber: Zur Gattungspoetik des Reiseberichts (n. 19). P. 51.
[22] Ibid. P. 60.
[23] Joseph Strelka: Der literarische Reisebericht. In: *Jahrbuch für Internationale Germanistik* 3 (1971). Pp. 63–75. Here: p. 65. See also Joseph Strelka: Der literarische Reisebericht. In: *Prosakunst ohne Erzählen*. Ed. by Klaus Weissenberger. Tübingen: Max Niemeyer Verlag 1985. Pp. 169–84.
[24] Ibid. P. 63.
[25] Ibid. P. 75.
[26] Hans Magnus Enzensberger: Eine Theorie des Tourismus. In: Enzensberger: *Einzelheiten I: Bewußtseins-Industrie*. Frankfurt/Main: Suhrkamp 1964. Pp. 179–205. Here: p. 187.
[27] Ibid. P. 188.
[28] Ibid. Pp. 186 and 196.
[29] Ibid. P. 204.
[30] Ibid.
[31] Ibid. P. 205.
[32] See Konrad Köstlin: Reisefieber – Massentourismus. In: *Reise-Fieber*. Ed. by Margit Berwin and Konrad Köstlin. *Regensburger Schriften zur Volkskunde* 2 (1984). Pp. 9–16. Here: p. 10.

Seen in this context, Enzensberger's analysis of modern tourism, and his strictures of the supposed 'freedom' proffered by it, throws quite a different light on Adolf Hoffmeister's account of his protagonist's involuntary flight from the Nazis halfway across Europe. For while the mere idea of an 'unwilling tourist' amounts to an oxymoron *par excellence*, the irony of the situation is further highlighted by a comparison of the refugee's predicament in 1939/40 to that of a contemporary tourist, one traveling involuntarily to freedom, the other voluntarily accepting all kinds of constraints during his sojourn. Oxymorons are traditionally employed to create humor, and this is undoubtedly also the case in Hoffmeister's travelogue whose very title points to nothing less than a contradiction in terms, stirring the potential reader's interest. However, the title additionally aims at a more subtle textual substrata; for the very concept of an 'unwilling tourist' also has disparaging implications – strictly speaking reserved for today's 'willing tourist' – drawing attention, specially with hindsight, to the domain of contemporary sociological disputes raised by Enzensberger's essay, surreptitiously criticizing a widely accepted term by reference to an apparently nonsensical one.

Prague

Jan Prokop, the protagonist of Hoffmeister's *Unwilling Tourist*, was forced to leave Prague almost immediately after the German invasion in March 1939[33] on account of his anti-Fascist activities in the 1930s. For suddenly "[e]veryone who loved his country [i.e. Czechoslovakia; JT] and his people was in danger" (5), a reference indicative of the autobiographical nature of this travelogue; because, like in Hoffmeister's case, the Gestapo was in possession of a dossier on Prokop, which would have led to his arrest had he not fled the country. The file read as follows: " 'Prokop, Jan. Not very important. A writer and cartoonist. 5 1/2 feet tall, weight 170, age 37, Catholic, bachelor, residing at – [...] Satirical verses, books and utterances, mostly of an anti-fascist nature' " (see Ill. 1). And the comments of an accomplice – whom Prokop met in Prague zoo (undoubtedly the origin of the book's US title *The Animals Are in Cages*)[34] – corroborate this impression: " 'Sh! No allusions, please. Now listen' ", this helper says: " 'Your dossier at Gestapo headquarters contains three yellow pages. These pages list five cases of libel against the Fuehrer, both in words and in pictures. They also mention help to German refugees and relations with anti-fascist elements' " (11). And so, despite the fact that he is not Jewish, a point emphasized in one of the numerous satirical

---

[33] Page references – from the US edition *The Animals are in Cages* – follow citations in brackets.
[34] See Srp: Svét Jako Smutek (n. 1). P. 192: "Zatímco tehdy ve svých liternárních dílech rušil hranice, mezi vězením či klecí a okolním světem, nyní zavíral některé obzvláště nebezpečne jedince jako Adolfa Hitlera do zoo jako na svéř".

passage, "[t]he humble applicant swallowed his fury and presented his birth certificate, and the certificates of his mother, his father, two grandmothers, and two grandfathers" to obtain "an immensely important official document", the so-called *Unbedenklichkeitsbescheinigung* ("Certificate of Unsuspiciousness") (15).

Thus Jan Prokop, a Czech writer and artist, had to flee Prague on account of his political background, travelling by train to Paris, via Pilsen, Kehl and Strasbourg. With gleeful irony the narrator enumerates the limited number of items the protagonist is allowed to take on his journey into exile:

One small suitcase, with stockings and shirts
Two English Pounds
Some dreams and plans
The germs of homesickness and longing
A clear, rock-firm world outlook (27).

Ill. 1. In: Adolf Hoffmeister: *Unwilling Tourist*. London: John Lane The Bodley Head 1942. P. 6.

Paris

Like Hoffmeister himself, Jan Prokop had visited the capital of France repeatedly during the 1920s and 1930s and remembers the city fondly: "*My sweet France*" – he says on his arrival, "*I loved you so much, dear Mademoiselle*" [italics in the original; JT]. Yet Paris has nothing but endless disappointments in store for him. Whereas German and Austrian refugees (since the beginning of 1933 and spring 1938 respectively) enjoyed a fair amount of freedom of movement until the end of the decade, Prokop, like Hoffmeister a latecomer, benefited from this freedom only a relatively short time, as reported by the protagonist:

> Clouds of two wars were gathered on the horizon. The first was declared on the third of September 1939. The second war had already begun. The first one did not much interest the masters of France. The second war haunted them day and night. It was the war against those who saw it clearly. "Scoundrels! Troublemakers! Throw them in jail!". [...] The newspapers, the radio stained the name of Peace, distorted the meaning of the war. Blind to the warnings, blind to the struggle of the courageous people, ready to fight if only there were something to fight for, the masters began the war against labor. Tanks were not ranked on the battlefield. They stood at the factory gates. French rifles were aimed at the French workers. By that second war the Frenchmen lost their first. I loved you so much, frivolous secrets of Paris. Yes, you were certainly beautiful, dear Mademoiselle, already undressed by your seducers. I knew it. But I was one of the poor, who couldn't afford to buy your love [...]. I loved you so much, my sweet France! Oh you bankrupt beauty-parlor! You trollop! [...] You betrayed me [...] will you ever be the same sweet France again? (31–32).[35]

The result was that "cockeyed, slap-happy French summer of 1939", when all "[t]hose who loved the tiny fatherland left it to serve those who had sold them out at Munich. Lie followed lie. A terrible doubting seeped into every event. Mankind moved in the web of the spider. The budding traitors used the hysterical fear of a fifth column to take revenge on all who would not believe their lullaby of appeasement" (32). By September 1939, however, when Britain and France declared war on Germany following the invasion of Poland, things changed radically: Prokop – once again echoing Hoffmeister's personal fate – was arrested and thrown into La Santé prison,[36] where he was kept for seven

---

[35] See Julian Jackson: *France: The Dark Years 1940–1944*. Oxford: Oxford University Press 2001. Especially I/6: The Debacle. Pp. 112–36.

[36] In a kind of dedication, preceding the text proper of *La Prison*, Hoffmeister stated: "Réfugié en France après l'occupation de la Tchécoslovaquie par les nazis, porté sur la liste noire de la Gestapo, j'ai été arrêté et mis en tôle à Paris pendant la drôle de guerre pour mes opinions trop avancées et trop libres à cette triste époque de l'histoire. C'est à la prison de la Santé que j'ai écrit, pendant sept mois, en confinement solitaire, ce journal et ces dialogues de détenus". (See n. 19).

months, as reported by the author himself in *La Prison* (the French translation of *Vězení. Napsal roku 1940 ve vězení La Santé v Paříž*): "Le 24 septembre 1939, se refermait sur moi la porte de la cellule numéro douzième section de la prison de la Santé. [...] C'était un dimanche à Paris. Le temps était clair, et un peu frais".[37] As so often in this travelogue, the first-person narrator reports with biting irony on the life inside this notorious Paris jail:

> The prison of La Santé, as the name indicates, is one of the healthiest resorts in France. High walls of black stone cut off the pleasant quiet of the prison from the noisy Paris without. Through the massive gate we enter the majestic hall with its guard-tower in the center. From this hall radiate several drafts, with corridors to match. These drafts reach to the large, three-storied wings, which are connected by suspension bridges. As you will notice, everything in the prison, with the negligible exception of the space behind doors or under pieces of furniture, fairly shines with cleanliness. Pretty colored signal-lights – red, green, orange – pierce the bluish halfdark created by the air-defense paint smeared on the skylight. Very few of the panes are broken, so that very little snow gets in. To a prisoner without prejudice, the prison brings to mind the shadowy glamour of a huge, darkened theatre. With reverent silence, the lesser criminals launder and wait on table for the bigger criminals, who are not allowed to leave their cells. Chatter among the prisoners, which disturbs the cathedral-like calm of the prison, is, of course, discouraged. [...] Leaving the physical culture division, we pass to the first floor cells. These are reserved for the more serious cases, such as Deputies, writers, philosophers, refugees, and others who have sinned by spreading inflammatory truths, or the historical principles of the Revolution. During these gray days we have simply turned one wing into a sort of branch office of the Parliament, and are playing host to an entire political party. Although the government has found it necessary to employ strict measures, even those persons placed in solitary confinement have never been deprived of their God-given right of freedom of speech. Here are the upper-story cells, reserved for the lesser criminals – murderers, kidnappers, arsonists, and the like. In these solitary confinement cells the prisoners may meditate upon the transience of worldly joy. Here, for example, is one Jan Prokop, held on remand. A kind of writer or something (44–47).

As mentioned earlier, it took seven months of ongoing interrogation by police and army before Prokop (and Hoffmeister for that matter) finally regained his freedom, seven boring months punctuated only by the 'excitement' of the daily food ration:

> The prison week has seven days, which get their names from the afternoon soup. Monday is Peasday, Tuesday is Lentilsday. Wednesday is Potatoesday; Thursday, Riceday; Friday, Beansday. Saturday is Potatoesday again and Sunday is Ricewithbeefflavorsday. The convicts measure time by the length of their beards, or by the number of pounds they have lost. They scratch crude calendars on the silt-covered wall. The vast wall diary of prisoners speaks a sensitive, poetic language full of mistakes in grammar, telling their large and small miseries (51–52).

---

[37] Adolf Hoffmeister: *La Prison*. Paris: Gallimard 1969. P. 11.

In spring 1940 Prokop was finally released only to be re-arrested in June of the same year, in the wake of the German attack on France, and interned in Stade de Colombes (see Ill. 2), previously a world-famous sports stadium, now a concentration camp, along with many other German, Austrian and Czech refugees (63–64). Subsequent to the advance of German troops towards Paris, Prokop is transferred by train to an internment camp – the narrator refers to it as a concentration camp – in the West of France called Sanglière, the next staging post of the protagonist's itinerary into exile: "In three days there was another journey, this time in a long, sad train which drew them for hour upon hour through sweet landscapes in France. It was late in the evening when the tired, bedraggled bunch of prisoners and guards arrived […]" (64–65).

Ill. 2. In: Adolf Hoffmeister: *Unwilling Tourist*. London: John Lane The Bodley Head 1942. P. 62.

Sanglière & Cresson

Sanglière[38] was neither a transit camp like Drancy nor a concentration camp like Riversaltes or Gurs; it was more like one of the internment camps on the Isle of Man in Britain, and camp life was accordingly. Jan Prokop was assigned to barracks number nine, made up of a highly international mix of prisoners:

> In two tiers of wooden berths, sixty-six prisoners were stored. Of these, only one was really dangerous to the Republic. He was a tall, immaculately dressed German, the attorney of the Nazi embassy in Paris. This man was made to monitor over his fellow-prisoners and given the leadership of twenty-eight Slovaks, one Bulgarian, twelve Czechs, ten Austrians, and fifteen Germans (71).

As mentioned, camp life at Sanglière, on the whole, bore little semblance to conditions in camps like Gurs or Riversaltes:

> The Czechs and the Slovaks became the champion shirkers of the camp. Close on their heels came the Viennese. The shrewd painters dazzled the commandant with the perfect bad taste of their watercolors of camp life, and offered him diligently terrible pictures of his staff that far surpassed even the masterpieces of the four-for-a-dime photographer (83).

In due course, Jan Prokop too managed to become a member of this group of artist, erstwhile "dandies of the Vienna, Berlin, and Prague boulevards" (84), who, at the end of each day, gathered idly at the western boundary of the camp on a "promenade of the disinherited" called 'Boulevard de la Paresse'/'Lazy Street' (85). However, such idyllic conditions did not prevail for long, since the rapid advance of the German armies forced the French authorities to transfer even those refugees to camps who so far had been exempted:

> One day Jan Prokop was yanked out of line and placed at a table in the dining hall. Here, aided by his knowledge of languages, he was supposed to fill out the questionnaires for the newcomers who poured into the camp. The most hardened painter cannot imagine a procession so apocalyptic as that which passed by Jan's desk, for through the gates of the camp boiled and plunged an army of miserable cripples – one-legged men leading blind comrades, one-armed men pushing the little carts of the legless, feeble-minded convicts sustaining the old. They had been left at large till now because of the wounds they had received on the battlefields of war and life.

---

[38] Some of the geographical details in *Unwilling Tourist* are incorrect. See especially Denis Peschanski: *La France des Camps. l'Internement 1938–1946*. Paris: Gallimard 2002. Especially Ch. III: Une 'drôle de guerre'. Pp. 72–94; Ch. IV: L'urgence. Pp. 98–107; Ch. VI: Le camp dans son environment. Pp. 121–147; Ch. VII: La débâcle. Pp. 152–74; Ch. VIII: L'occupation allemande et l'internement administratif. Pp. 175–207. On a map of all French internment camps (Camps de rassemblement et d'internement français pour étrangers [1939–1940]. Ibid. P. 79) neither Sanglière nor Cresson is mentioned.

Now they were herded from their lairs and hospitals by the brainless police, who saw in every foreigner a parachutist. The stage manager, Death, aligned his cast in a mob scene of monsters that would have made Goya pale with envy. The terrible clack of crutches on the pavement, the groans of the frightened and abandoned, the smell of the old, the odor of rags and bandages accompanied the march of the prisoners through the mud of the camp square. Laughing at humanity, the shy began to cry, and rain dropped from heaven upon the hellish army (89 and 91).

Thus, living in a world of their own, away from normal people, "[the internees'] character [was] crippled, their human dignity undermined, a new destructive class of the disinherited was born" (98). Eventually, when the rumbling of the German guns was already audible in the distance, orders were given to evacuate the camp (98) and the inmates moved even further West:

The train, with war slogans and cartoons of Hitler on its sides, moved slowly through the stations clogged with retreating armies. The rail-road angels, the young misses of the Red Cross, fed the hungry with bouillon cubes and tinned sardines. After three days' journey, lying on straw in a cattle car, the tired gang arrived at Cresson, near Bordeaux, where the new camp was located in a ruined A.E.F. [American Expeditionary Force during WWI; JT] dynamite factory (99).

Finally, in late June 1940, the prisoners were permanently set free: "The breakdown of the French front was faithfully reflected in the camp. German raids on Bordeaux banished sleep, and discipline fell apart. One day the frightened commandant called the camp together and announced that the German army was near and that all the prisoners would be released that evening" (102).

Left to his own devices, Jan Prokop and a couple of friends headed for Bordeaux:

Over them, airplane motors roared menacingly. In the darkness, the rusty cranes loomed like dinosaurs along their way. The small bundles on their shoulders were all they took with them. Everything they owned lay abandoned in the camp. Somewhere lay mountains of pigskin trunks full of beautiful suits, coats – provisions stored by human squirrels – and now they wrung their hands at the thought of leaving behind such lovely things. On the highway sounded the muffled footsteps of the thousands who could play no part in the war-drama, who suddenly were placed in then open jaws of hunger in the helltime of destruction and chaos (102).

From Bordeaux – since he could not find anybody to help him escape by boat – Prokop made his way by train towards the Spanish border via Bayonne, St. Lean de Luz, and Hendaye, and finally succeed in persuading the port authorities in Bayonne to get him a passage on the S.S. Lorient, sailing on June 23, 1940 for an unknown destination (104).[39]

---

[39] The statement that the S.S. Lorient sailed down the Gironde is obviously wrong (Bayonne is located on the confluence of Adour and Nive), unless Hoffmeister meant the ship to sail from Bordeaux.

Ill. 3. In: Adolf Hoffmeister: *Unwilling Tourist*. London: John Lane The Bodley Head 1942. P. 106.

Passage to Africa

The ship's journey to Casablanca, which took five days (109), was not as tranquil a trip as the fugitives might have hoped for; for the cargo of the S.S. Lorient – unknown to all but the crew and Jan Prokop – consisted of torpedoes; in other words, "[t]he sons of war, the children of flight, slept unknowing on their explosive pillow" (108–109), while German submarines patrolled the Bay of Biscay. And while still on the high seas the captain informed the exiles that France had capitulated and that an armistice had been signed: "It was the necrology of France" (109), the narrator commented. Meanwhile the refugees cynically argued among themselves what their exact status was, searching for the best suitable definition of 'refugee'. This debate, which roughly occurs in the middle of Hoffmeister's travelogue (and therefore, in a manner of speaking, forms the axis of the book), is of crucial interest for the story in question and beyond, since it lists no less than fourteen essential traits which characterize a potential refugee, features which above all delineate their attitude to past, present and future. Pivotal in this context is the fact that virtually all definitions put forward by the passengers on the S.S. Lorient are linked to either their present condition or their past existence, while hardly any refer to their future other than expressing hope for a restoration of past conditions. In other words: past and future merge in their current aspirations.

Consequently, almost half of these definitions refer exclusively to the present:

> "The refugee is the one honest man whose papers can never be in order, and, therefore, the police constantly demand that he shows them" (109).
> "A refugee is a man who embarrasses only those who have not yet been refugees" (109).
> "Being a refugee is the occupation of the patriot, for the time being" (110).
> "A refugee is an unwilling tourist" (110).[40]
> "The refugee is a man with a center of gravity outside his body" (110).
> "The refugee is a being without money or fatherland, but with, alas, a body" (110).

A couple of definitions do happen to point towards the future, but in these instances the future invariably invokes the past, i.e. hope for a restoration of conditions which once existed but have since been lost:

> "A refugee is one who runs from country to country with but one desire – to sit quietly at home" (110).
> "The refugee is the man forever on his way home" (110).

The remaining definitions establish a firm link between past and present:

> "A refugee is one who runs away because he has done something good. So each port he enters suspects, *a priori*, that he will do something bad" (110).
> "The refugee is a homeless man who searches everywhere he goes for that which he has lost in some far-distant place [...]" (109).
> "The refugee is the poor relative who likes to tell over and over how rich he was" (110).
> "The refugee is the too-faithful lover, who, fleeing through the world, loses each new love when he calls her by the name of his beloved wife" (110).
> "A refugee is a lover who abandons his love, wanting her only the way she used to be" (110).

The one exception to the overall pattern is the final definition, which, by maintaining that "[t]he refugee is the man who cannot stay at home because he belongs sometimes to yesterday, sometimes to tomorrow, but never to today" (110), firmly places refugees in a kind of no-man's land.

---

[40] A definition which lend the title to the English edition of Hoffmeister's travelogue.

In summary, Hoffmeister defines 'refugees' as individuals forced to travel against their will, often without passport and/or visa, at worst even stateless, i.e. as 'unwilling tourist' compelled to be forever on the move while desiring nothing more than a haven of refuge. Though opposed to the authoritarian regime of their native country, abroad they are often suspected of being criminals. Focussed more on the outside world than on their inner life, they are usually more patriotic than the indigenous population of the country of refuge, thus being the cause of embarrassment and guilt complexes among the locals. Their relationships with other people, particularly the opposite sex, are often marred by the fact that they constantly hanker after their lost love (either their former husband/wife or boy/girl friend), unable to desist from expecting their new partner to emulate the previous one. In other words, by living in a physical and mental 'no-man's land' whence they cannot escape, the place of refugees is a kind of modern-day limbo. And since they permanently long for the past, and would like nothing better than its restoration in the future, their life, here and now, is dominated by the yearning for what once was and the hope to regain what was lost. There was a reason, of course, for this outpouring of memory, as pointed out in a different context by Robert Hewison. It was not simply that these refugees found it difficult to deal with the immediate present, but "[t]he probing back into the past was in search of some explanation for the crisis of the times".[41] Here applies what Robert Neumann in the chapter 'Marcus, or, Exile' of his novel *By the Waters of Babylon* (1939–1945) defined as one of the criteria of a disease called 'emigratio communis primaria', namely that "[t]he more consumptive space grew, the more splendid became the patient's wealth of time".[42]

Casablanca

When the S.S. Lorient arrived in Casablanca, "[w]ounded by flights from Germany to Austria, from Austria to Czechoslovakia, from Czechoslovakia to Paris, from Paris to the South of France, from France at last to Africa, many of the refugees fell exhausted on their bunks" (111). For the Moroccan authorities initially refuse them to disembark since "[t]he law prescribes that refugees must live in a space 'between sea and land', in a constant state of arrival and departure, in a time that was neither the present nor the past, and even less the future" (113). Finally they interned the refugees, "first on a hospital ship, and later in a real concentration camp" (111). To that end, they at last were put ashore, "only

---

[41] Robert Hewison: *Under Siege. Literary Life in London 1939–1945*. London: Weidenfeld & Nicolson 1977. P. 91.
[42] Robert Neumann: *By the Waters of Babylon*. London: Dent 1939. P. 249. See also Robert Neumann: *An den Wassern von Babylon*. Oxford: East and West Library 1945. P. 243: "Hatte der Raum die Schwindsucht – desto herrschaftlicher verfügte der von der Emigration Befallene über die Zeit".

to be stuffed into buses and rocketed inland to a concentration camp at Ain-Chock,[43] on the edge of the desert" (113); for "[w]ith the flood-tide of refugees came the flood-tide of sorrow for the Moroccan authorities. They simply did not know what to do with all of them" (113). Following registration, the refugees were eventually released, not without clear distinctions being made:

> There are two kinds of refugees. There are those who have been running enough to save their fortunes, and who bring with them everything they own. And there are those who have had to sell all their possessions and live on the tiny sum that grows smaller day by day, until at last they join the penniless thousands. The rich have a much easier time of it, and in Ain-Chock, too, the rich got away first. A long time after them the others began to leave (117–118).

After obtaining their release, "[l]ike a brood of mangy vultures (classified by nations) the liberated refugees circled about, ready to swoop down and carry off a visa. In their language visa meant heaven" (118):

> Time tore to pieces the little society of refugees. Jealous, insincere toward each other, hungry for favors, the furtive denied that they had gotten visas and refused to tell how they secured berths on the ships. But since ships didn't leave anyhow, that didn't make any difference [...]. The refugees threw away the day in the cafés, listening to the latest intrigues. Suspicion broke up the community. Hate of the consuls mounted with every refusal (136).

This went on until eventually German soldiers – Rommel's Africa Corps – were approaching and the refugees' departure from Casablanca once again became a matter of life and death. Jan Prokop was one of the lucky ones who succeeded – with the help of the local Moroccan prefect – to escape on a tiny lobster boat called Volupté destined for Portugal (see Ill. 4), though not until the Tangier representative of the Jewish Aid Committee offers him some remarkable insights into the European refugee situation; for it was Loew's contention that the refugees "believe the stories they have made up about themselves, for, having told them so many hundred of times to different customs and border officials, they have lost their feeling for lying and their feeling for the possible. They live in a land of visas and they haven't the slightest idea what they will do if the ever *go* anywhere. They have become used to flight, and rush ever forward, haunted by restlessness, from one temporary life to another" (123).

Tangier

However, due to a sudden storm the lobsterman was compelled to make an emergency stop at international port of Tangier, which meanwhile had been occupied by Spanish troops of General Franco's. Consequently, Jan Prokop,

---

[43] The proper name of the camp was Ain Qurak.

Ill. 4. In: Adolf Hoffmeister: *Unwilling Tourist*. London: John Lane The Bodley Head 1942. P. 139.

and twenty-seven fellow-refugees, became marooned once again, and a feeling of resignation took hold of Hoffmeister's protagonist:

> For eight hours the captain struggled to enter the harbor of Tangier, the nearest place of safety. At last, at three in the afternoon, he managed to slip in beside the lighthouse and drop anchor just before the post-card city. [...] But look! On the white tower of the international port building waves but one single flag – the banner of Gestapo-ridden Franco Spain. Well, if it had not been this, it would have been something else. The motor-boat of the harbor police came alongside: the officer told the captain that Franco had taken over the port and declared it Spanish territory. As he spoke, the yellow-red flag fluttered and started down and the arms of the soldiers snapped to salute. But this single caraway in a seething stew of events didn't impress the hardy sea-travelers. Idly they wondered what would happen next to them now. Another scene in the drama was unfolding. You know the actors. The play can begin (143–44).

This interlude, a sketch in 14 scenes entitled 'Lobster and Almonds' – Time: The summer of 1940 (i.e. July 1940; JT); Place: The harbor of Tangier

(145, 147–148, 150–154 and 156) – covers, with biting irony, the circumstances of their eventual rescue and departure on the steamer for Portugal as originally planned: "The *Santa Maria* winged through the quiet afternoon sea toward Lisbon", the narrator informs us, "[p]ast the shining white cabins and the brilliant foliage of the Portuguese coast she sailed, and dropped anchor at last in the mouth of the Tajo" (157), beyond the ancient Torre de Belem where ships from the entire world rode at anchor, Brazilian, Greek, Argentine, British, French, Spanish, Portuguese, Panamanian, American: "The refugees gaped at the display, the pattern made by the colors of departure. They saw the gates of the world swing wide to let them through" (158).

Lisbon

For the first time since his initial arrival in Paris from Prague, well over a year ago, Jan Prokop is able to breathe the air of freedom: "Forgetting everything, he wandered in his peace-delirium, whispering to himself the enchanted words: 'Butter, cheese, sausages, meat, game. ...' [...] Carefree, Jan found a hotel and slept his first night – on credit". (159) For five months – i.e. from August till December 1940 – he walked the streets of what arguably is one of the most beautiful cities in Europe (160), forbidden to work, permanently hard up, and constantly trying to obtain an overseas visa:

> He sat with the Portuguese in tiny side-street bars, afraid of the main thoroughfares crowded with foreigners. Each passer-by, it seemed to Jan, had evil intentions. And he was nearly right. The big cafés on the Rossio echoed with the tongues of every conquered nation, German dominating them all. When Jan sat down at his table in the Café Chaave d'Ouro he could be sure that with him sat a British agent, a Nazi spy, a Portuguese Secret Service man, and at least one refugee. Worn out by the everlasting hiding, the endless waiting for overseas visas, the mass of the refugees became shapeless, formless things, no longer men. The money of the rich opened for them the backdoors of the consulates. The poor crowded the waiting-rooms of HICEM, the enormous Jewish organization that fed multitudes with loaves and fishes like Jesus on the lake. In their offices Jew and Gentile alike squabbled over steamer-tickets in perfect harmony (160–161).

These fellow-refugees cause Jan Prokop to reflect upon the multitudes of refugees that had poured into Prague from Germany following Hitler's rise to power, and later from Austria and the Sudetenland, and he recalls how he had tried to help them. But he also now wonders whether he had really assisted them at the time. One way or the other: "Now he knew how they must have felt" (162).

Came the winter of 1940–1941, which, even in a southern country like Portugal, was rather inclement:

> Times grew harder. There was no money at all. Winter forced a new way of life on Jan. He spent most of the day in bed, for when he got up at noon he was saved the

expense of breakfast, and when he arose in the afternoon he didn't eat breakfast or lunch either. And sometimes in the evening he would meet a friend who would buy him a dinner or a seat at the cinema or a glass of wine (166).

Jan Prokop – as many refugees like him – gradually becomes a cynic and increasingly doubts his own abilities:

> He climbed the five flights of stairs to his little attic, talking derisively to himself. "After all, my dear Jan Prokop, what difference does it make? So you *have* lost everything. Does it really matter? Did you ever care whether you had things or not? You have lost love and home and fatherland. But didn't you dream, even when you were a schoolboy, of world-citizenship, of the free life of the vagabond, of exotic love? You wrote books. Fifteen books, Jan Prokop! What could you write about for fifteen books? Did you have so many experiences then? Did you know so much about life that it took that long to tell it all? They must have been pretty bad ones, Jan. But now you can write, Jan Prokop. Now you know that there is no one to read you. Now that nobody understands your language. You sat with the Shaws, the Wellses, the Capeks. You amused yourself by sketching them. And where are you now? Sitting with sailors, newsboys, grocers, fishermen, with the shipwrecked. Their faces are lined with sorrow, but they are beautiful faces, Jan. What has changed? Tell me, Jan Prokop, what has changed?" (166–67).

But there is no reply to this question; for meanwhile the 'unwilling tourist' has also become an 'unwilling author', suffering from writer's cramp, unable to document his own experiences. Standing at the open window of his tiny room at night, overlooking Lisbon, he trembles at the thought that even these last peaceful lights on the westernmost fringe of Europe might eventually be extinguished: "Down there blinked the lights of Paris, London, Vienna. There died away the last echoes of Europeanism, there the high romance of the past was fading" (167). And while reflecting upon what he considers to be a 'sideshow of old Europe', Prokop also contemplates the fate of many prominent cultural representatives from central Europe, whom he met in the streets of Lisbon, now stranded in the Portuguese capital in late 1940:

> The silent spokesmen of Art and Science reluctantly recognizing their fellow-delegates to this unsummoned convention of genius. All of them had to pass through this stopover on the road to salvation. All of them had to sit in one of the pastry shops on Rossio Square and enviously read the shipping news of the *Diario de Noticias*, the largest daily paper of Portugal, which they nicknamed "Diarrhea of News" [...]. Colleagues of the French concentration camps were meeting here again, happy and at penniless liberty once more. Hidden behind a newspaper and behind an alias sits Lion Feuchtwanger. Right behind him is Wladimir Pozner, the young French-Russian. And there are the legendary Ignace Paderewski, the Austrian storyteller Roda-Roda, Alfred Polgar, witty interpreter of rumor and gossip, originator of cultures, wars, and wrecked marriages, the German movie star Oscar Karlweiss – one heart of the *Zwei Herzen im Dreivierteltakt*, a mixture which doesn't blend. In the café Chaave d'Ouro Prokop met his countrymen. Jan knew most of those who gathered on the terrace for

their daily chat – the emotional and disheveled Franz Werfel, the skinny poet-pessimist Egon Hostovsky, the easy-going skeptic Friedrich Torberg (all of them writers), and the heavy, melancholy eyelids of the great comedian Hugo Haas. Caricaturists Sors and Adolf Hoffmeister doodled on the tablecloths (168–169).

Like himself – the above reference to a character called Adolf Hoffmeister is an important acknowledgement of the fact that *Unwilling Tourist* is indeed semi-autobiographical – all these

> writers and artists lacked strength to work out the inexhaustible tangle of ideas and stories. In their uncertain, harried state of mind they were incapable of writing. Each day they came together and exchanged imaginary excuses for wasted hours, days, months. [...] And great poets, sitting down on the benches of the Botanical Garden of Lisbon, memorized: 'I pledge allegiance to the flag of the United States of America, and to the republic ... for which it stands ... one nation, indivisible ... with liberty and justice for all' (169 and 171).

Ill. 5. In: Adolf Hoffmeister: *Unwilling Tourist*. London: John Lane The Bodley Head 1942. P. 170.

After months of waiting and many futile attempts at obtaining an overseas visa, Jan Prokop finally is granted a Mexican visa and scheduled to depart on December 18, 1940 (172), only to be frustrated yet again when the ship's departure is delayed. For once though this delay proves to be a blessing in disguise, since Prokop is almost simultaneously granted a US visa, departs from Lisbon in late December and arrives in New York at the beginning of 1941. Prior to disembarking he is interrogated by a US emigration office, who inquiries why he has come to the United States of America. "There are official answers to such questions, expected answers", the narrator comments: "Jan made them. But in Jan's heart there surged the real reason, the reason that cried to be uttered" (173). And consequently, almost euphorically, he informs the official why he is so pleased to be finally able to set foot in the 'land of the free':

> "Why have I come [Jan Prokop tells an immigration officer; JT]? I have come because the Nazis drove me from my home. Because France accepted me only to betray me later. Because country after country has refused haven to exiles, and declined to suffer their hungry homesickness. Because in all the world I found no country rich enough to give away freedom, no country with room for exiles from fatherlands, cultures, religions, and races – until I came here" (173–74).

The two accounts of Hoffmeister's exile experience: that of his seven-month incarceration in La Santé described in *Vězení*, and that of his flight halfway across Europe and North Africa told in *Unwilling Tourist*, differ substantially.

Nashledanou!
(*Sky-line New Yorku*)

Ill. 6. In: *Americké Houpačky*. Prague: Evropský literání klub 1937. P. 177.

His autobiographical report in *La Prison* is a highly reflective one, indicative of an inmate's sedentary situation in a notorious Paris jail, whereas the semi-autobiographical report of his escape from the Nazis narrates the dramatic events of his sojourn from Prague to New York, characterized by ongoing movement from staging post to staging post until the final destination America.[44] Hoffmeister quickly adopted Western democratic principles, despite ideological reservations (which had already found expression in his 1936-travelogue *Americké Houpačky*[45]), and became actively engaged in the fight against Fascism following his return to New York[46] after a brief stay in Hollywood in the second half of 1941. This political engagement – apart from his activities for 'The Voice of America' and journalistic work for the *New York*

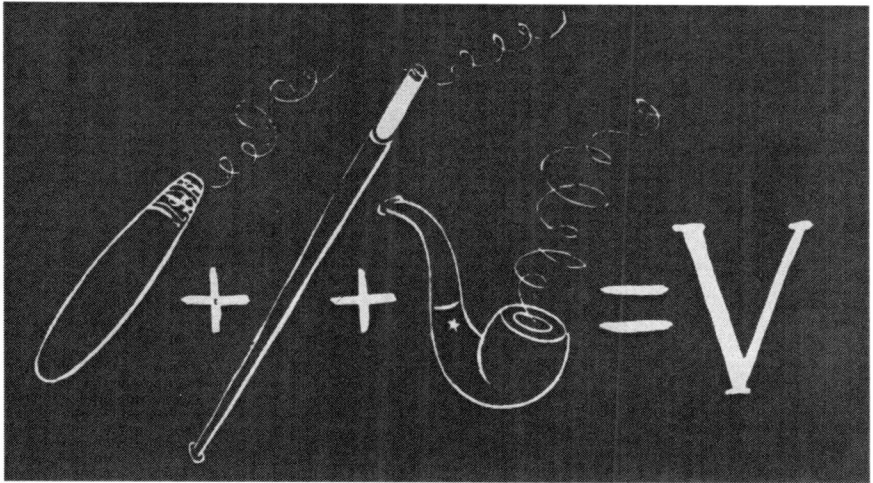

Ill. 7. Preface. In: *Jesters in Earnest. Cartoons by the Czechoslovak Artists Z.K., A. Hoffmeister, A. Pelc, Stephen, W. Trier*. Ed. by David Lowe. London: John Murray 1944. P. 3.

---

[44] See Srp: Svět Jako Smutek (n. 1). P. 184: "Mezi *Vězením* a *The animals are in cages* je podstatný rozdíl: zatímco v první knize stál na místě a propadal se svými úvahami dovnitř mysli, ve druhé popisoval vnější dramatický děj. Kniha *The animals are in cages* měla bezprostřední ohlas". Apparently, Egon Hostovsky commented similarly in a review of the travelogue in the Czech journal *Zítřku* (1942).
[45] See Srp: Svět Jako Smutek (n. 1). P. 177.
[46] He lived at 224 Sullivan Street, the Tribeca part of Greenwich Village. See Srp: Svět Jako Smutek. Ibid. P. 188.

Times and the British Sunday paper *The Observer* – found above all expression in two major exhibitions of anti-war caricatures: the first – and most famous – in the latter half of 1943 in New York's Museum of Modern Art (with the help of Alfred Barr, its then director, whose acquaintance Hoffmeister had made in the 1930s[47]), which subsequently went on tour across the United States;[48] and a second one 1944 in London, organized by David Low, entitled 'Jesters in Earnest',[49] which – apart from works by Hoffmeister – showed caricatures by fellow Czech artists Z.K., Antonín Pelec, Stephen,[50] and Walter Trier.[51] This exhibition also exhibited what arguably became Hoffmeister's most famous caricature: 'Roosevelt + Churchill + Stalin = Victory' (1943) from his series 'Antifašisické početnice' ('Topical Algebra').

---

[47] Alfred Hamilton Barr (1902–81) was founder-director of the New York Museum of Modern Art, which he ran from 1929 until 1943.
[48] See Srp: Svét Jako Smutek (n. 1). P. 190.
[49] See *Jesters in Earnest. Cartoons by Czech Artists*. Ed. by David Low. London: John Murray 1944.
[50] See Stephen Roth: *Divided They Fall*. London: John Murray 1943.
[51] See Srp: Svét Jako Smutek (n. 1). P. 200. See also: *The Pen is Mightier*. Ed. by J. J. Lynx: London: Lindsay Drummond 1946.

Laura Heins

Criss-Crossings of Robert Siodmak: The Time and Space of Cinematic Exile

This paper examines three phases in the career of exiled German-Jewish director Robert Siodmak: his late Weimar, Hollywood, and postwar German work. It argues that the exilic experience is reflected in a shift of temporal and spatial configurations in Siodmak's American film noirs and in his German films after his remigration to Europe after the war. This shift is visible in the differing treatment of modes of transport or spatial mobility and in alternative approaches to narrative progression.

As he assessed the damaged condition of the exiled intellectual, Theodor Adorno described the "annulled" past life of the involuntary émigré as memory driven out into the harsh glare of a false present tense. First at the border of the country to which the exile flees and then repeatedly at bureaucratic thresholds, lived life is forcibly transformed into the artificial and reified "background" of identification documents. The exile is forced into mobility, effecting the exposure and extermination of "anything that lives on merely as thought and recollection": "To complete its violation, life is dragged along on the triumphal automobile of the united statisticians and even the past is no longer safe from the present, whose remembrance of it consigns it a second time to oblivion".[1] It is perhaps significant that the means of reification, of sending authentic recollections into a void, is here pictured as the quintessentially American vehicle.

Shortly after this passage, Adorno reflected on the experience of seeing through the windows of the automobile onto the country of exile, describing travel through this vast country as an unsettling procedure in which the landscape itself appears yet again to threaten the life of the exile with cancellation: "[The American landscape] is uncomforted and comfortless. And it is perceived in a corresponding way. For what the hurrying eye has seen merely from the car it cannot retain, and the vanishing landscape leaves no more traces behind than it bears upon itself".[2] The open space of the road is not experienced as liberation from a confining civilization or as an expanse of possibility awaiting exploitation, but as a black hole of perception, identity, and affect. While attempting to visually grasp and contain the vanishing empty spaces, the anxious traveler reveals a fear of disappearing, uncomfortably and unheroically.

---

[1] Theodor Adorno: *Minima Moralia: Reflections on a Damaged Life*. New York: Verso 2005. Pp. 46–47.
[2] Ibid. P. 48.

This suggests that the vision of those unwilling emigrants exiled to America in particular might be marked by an agoraphobia that is at odds with the usual mythology of Western spaces. The more general experience of a past annulled by obligatory presentness also makes the exile want to rescue the multiple temporalities of memory, rather than following exterior ephemera and risking oblivion. And, indeed, such anxieties mark the vision of some German directors who were exiled to Hollywood after 1933, particularly in the film noir genre in which they excelled – a genre characterized by phobic spaces and discontinuous temporal structures. The exiles' films also evidence, as I would like to propose, a certain resistance to travel. Although similar observations might be made about the work of Fritz Lang, Billy Wilder, Edgar G. Ulmer, or Fred Zinneman, this essay will concentrate on Robert Siodmak, whose post-exile work evidences an altered relationship to spatial and temporal mobility.

Traitorous Traveling or Forced Mobility

Robert Siodmak may not seem the most obvious choice for examining the exilic style of film workers who fled the Third Reich. To many film critics and historians, Siodmak has generally appeared less damaged than many other German exiles, even among those fortunate few who managed to escape to Hollywood and continue their careers. Born in Dresden to a Polish-Jewish father who had obtained an American passport before marrying in Germany, Robert Siodmak was able, thanks to this background, to escape to the United States from France in 1939. He was consequently spared a few of the humiliations and existential crises of those refugees who were continually refused entry into the United States, and subsequently became one of the mostly highly paid directors in Hollywood and is particularly noted for his cycle of classic 1940s film noirs.[3] Despite his exceptional success there, he decided to depart from the American cinema after the war. His film career consisted thus of four major phases, the first in Berlin in the late 1920s and early 1930s, the second in Paris from 1933–1939, the third in Hollywood from 1940–1951, ending in a return voyage to European cinema in the 1950s through the late 1960s.

More than his international ties, it was Siodmak's adaptability and talent for assimilating new languages that allowed his directorial career to survive the repeated ruptures of exile. Since fame had not followed him from Berlin to Paris or from Paris to Hollywood despite his remarkable accomplishments in each of these locations, every new station of his exile required a completely

---

[3] Siodmak made nine mostly well-received film noirs in Hollywood: *Phantom Lady* (1944), *Christmas Holiday* (1944), *The Suspect* (1944), *The Strange Affair of Uncle Harry* (1945), *The Spiral Staircase* (1945), *The Dark Mirror* (1946), *The Killers* (1946), *Cry of the City* (1948), *Criss Cross* (1949).

new beginning. Over the course of a career in directing more than sixty films, Siodmak managed to move successfully among the modes of multiple national cinemas, differing production circumstances, and across a range of film genres. But unlike his fellow exile and postwar remigrant Fritz Lang, Siodmak generally failed to attract the attentions of auteurist film critics, largely because his visual language did not maintain an identifiable and consistently strong German accent. For Siodmak, survival in the film industry often required the relinquishing of a distinctive authorial voice; Siodmak was caught in the double bind of an emigrant film director in producer-controlled studio systems, where temporary survival came at the cost of a long-term legacy.

Not really qualifying for the title of intellectual, Siodmak has therefore been viewed primarily as a skilled craftsman of mass cultural wares. To look for evidence of a mutilated identity in Siodmak's work is to misunderstand his character, according to Lutz Koepnick: "to think of Siodmak's career simply in terms of unwanted dislocations underestimates what steered him to success in the first place... The exile's state of displacement was his home, and the migrant's desolation became the price for his relentless grasp for fame".[4] Admittedly, Siodmak's own narrative of his life in his autobiography *Zwischen Berlin und Hollywood* does not dwell for long on moments of dislocation, preferring instead to highlight his successful duels with producers and his original discoveries of future stars.[5] But the ideology of success should not be allowed to obscure entirely the distinctive struggle of any forced émigré. To view Siodmak as willfully *heimatlos* is to convert exile into opportunistic wandering and to overlook the evidence of undesired biographical and aesthetic detours in his films.

With Siodmak, critics have often been too willing to deny exile by attributing to the filmmaker an essentially rootless nature. According to his autobiographical account, however, travel was for Siodmak primarily more a means of escape from persecutions and strictures than a search for boundless adventure. The first escape that Siodmak narrates in his autobiography is his father's departure for Cuba (and later New York and Tennessee) in the 1880s, a flight from the internally and externally imposed restraints of an orthodox milieu:

> My father came from Austria, from the area around Krakow, which is now in Poland. He lived like all Jews in the ghetto of Podgorze on the other side of the Vistula, wore a caftan and a yarmulke... When my father was sixteen, he stole all the money he could find and went across the big sea to America. And so he escaped the ghetto.[6]

---

[4] Lutz Koepnick: *The Dark Mirror: German Cinema between Hitler and Hollywood.* Berkeley: University of California Press 2002. Pp. 168–169.
[5] Robert Siodmak: *Zwischen Berlin und Hollywood: Erinnerungen eines großen Filmregisseurs.* Ed. by Hans C. Blumenberg. München: Goldmann 1980.
[6] Ibid. P. 21.

As with the younger Siodmak, the father's flight from Europe to America ended in a return trip to Germany, where he married a culturally assimilated Jewish woman from Leipzig. Robert and his brothers were thus raised in a secular environment, yet with an awareness of a separate and often disadvantageous identity. Although born in Germany, Robert Siodmak never obtained German citizenship due to that nation's persistant *jus sanguis*, and was forced to remain a stateless non-citizen until the age of 38. Siodmak apparently also experienced some roadblocks in his career due to discrimination, as he reported having been denied the job of directing the film version of his brother Curt Siodmak's novel *F.P. 1 antwortet nicht* (*F.P. 1 Doesn't Answer*, directed by Karl Hartl in 1932) because the producers did not want a Jew to direct the film.[7]

After gaining fame in America, Siodmak's birth country was apparently willing to recognize him as a German, so long as his Jewish origins were obscured. As Karl Prümm has pointed out, Siodmak was generally well received upon his return to the German cinema in 1954/5, but commentators in the Federal Republic usually portrayed him as a voluntary traveler rather than an exile, thereby evading any historical responsibility:

> As if there were still censorship of language, no one called exile and expulsion by their names. Siodmak should appear as one who had left a long time ago in order to achieve "worldwide success" and then to gratefully return to his origins, having remained the same as before... The violence of expulsion was normalized as restless wandering and an adventurous career. No one wanted to speak about the Jewish identity or the life-threatening exclusion of Siodmak – no one faced up to the fact that his international successes arose out of a strategy of survival.[8]

If Siodmak has often been viewed as too flexible, as having no authorial character other than ambition, this view has served to conceal the conditions which required migrancy. Siodmak was not infrequently described in the German (as well as Swiss) press as a "cosmopolitan", "globetrotter" (*Weltenbummler*) or "wanderer",[9] rehearsing the old typecast notion of the eternally wandering Jew who has no culture of his own and only adopts the languages of so many host countries.

---

[7] Ibid. P. 57. There is some discrepancy in Siodmak's account here, as he suggests that *F.P.1 antwortet nicht* was scheduled to go into production in 1933 rather than 1932. It is possible that he misidentified the film and intended to refer to another scheduled UFA project that he was prevented from completing due to the Nazi seizure of power.

[8] Karl Prümm: Universeller Erzähler: Realist des Unmittelbaren. In: *Siodmak Bros.: Berlin-Paris-London-Hollywood*. Ed. by Wolfgang Jacobsen and Hans Helmut Prinzler. Berlin: Stiftung Deutsche Kinemathek 1998. Pp. 161–182. Here: p. 63.

[9] See for example Erwin Kreker: Weltenbummler Robert Siodmak. In: *Frankfurter Neue Presse* (March 9, 1959). Peter Motram: Kosmopolit der Leinwand: Plauderei mit Robert Siodmak. In: *Die Weltwoche*, Zurich (August 19, 1960). F. R.: Wanderer zwischen Welten. Robert Siodmak wird 70 Jahre. In: *Der Tagesspiegel* (August 8, 1970).

Such a regressive rewriting of exile as travel often hid the jealous sense among many Germans that those who had fled Hitler were actually traitors to their countries, since they had not stayed to suffer air raids and Soviet expulsion from eastern territories like their former compatriots. If Siodmak and other Hollywood exiles were given new identities as eternal tourists, then the guilty Germans could claim victim status and view themselves as the true refugees.[10] Not incidentally, perhaps, Siodmak's first successful film after his postwar return to Europe, *Die Ratten* (1955), concerned escapees from the GDR, as did his later *Escape from East Berlin* (1962). In none of Siodmak's locations of exile did audiences or producers call for representations of specifically Jewish displacement, although the rats in the title of his first postwar success certainly alluded controversially to the anti-Semite's imagination of the Jewish diaspora.[11]

European Time

Whether or not Siodmak was ultimately able to profit from the challenges of dislocation, he did apparently lose something on his own flight across stylistic and national boundaries. The gap between his Weimar films and his Hollywood and postwar work can be seen as etched with aesthetic damage, but one that ultimately did produce a few compelling examples of exile cinema, particularly his noir cycle. It is not possible to view any of Siodmak's films as pure products of auteurist intent or biographical expression, of course, not least of all because the cinematic production apparatus does not allow for the same measure of authorial control and direct expression of an exilic state as does literature. But some of his films were more autonomous than others, as he and his crew were given more freedom by producers, and it is particularly these ones that I will consider here. Furthermore, the exilic experience may be reflected even in non-auteurist, studio system productions if it is a collective experience of an era to which filmmakers and spectators alike would respond.

Perhaps the only film for which he and his collaborators (his brother Curt Siodmak, Billy Wilder, Edgar G. Ulmer, Fred Zinnemann, and Eugen

---

[10] For similar accounts of responses to the return of exiled film workers, see Maria Hilchenbach: *Kino im Exil: Die Emigration deutscher Filmkünstler 1933–1945*. München: K.G. Saur 1982. Pp. 219–221.

[11] This anti-Semitic image was used most notoriously in the Nazi pseudo-documentary *The Eternal Jew* (1940), in which a map depicting the Jewish diaspora in Europe was intercut with groups of rats. Perhaps due to such associations, Siodmak's producer and his distribution company insisted that he change the title of *Die Ratten*, calling it "repulsive" and upsetting to audiences. Siodmak insisted that the title remain, and the distribution company eventually capitulated. Siodmak: *Zwischen Berlin und Hollywood* (n. 5). P. 223.

Schüfftan) had complete artistic freedom was his first directorial effort, the 1929 low-budget, self-financed film *Menschen am Sonntag* (*People on Sunday*), which is now considered a landmark work of the avant-garde silent cinema. Influenced by Dziga Vertov's documentary exploration of one day in the life of a modern metropolis in *The Man with a Movie Camera*, Siodmak's semi-documentary narrative film takes the viewer along on a Sunday excursion of four young, lower middle class Berliners. Beginning on Saturday afternoon as the city's business week is winding down, the narrative follows a straight course until the main characters and the Berlin masses return to work on Monday morning. The excursionists – Erwin the taxi driver, Brigitte the record shop assistant, Christl the film extra, and Wolf the wine dealer, all non-professional actors playing themselves – travel out of the city to the Nikolassee, where they swim and flirt, until boarding trains and buses back into the city in the evening.

The dramatic plotting of the budding romances between the central characters is given somewhat subsidiary interest; instead, Siodmak and Schüfftan most often placed the camera at a distance from the human drama in order to record the ephemera of modern life. In particular, the film reveals a deep fascination for the visual sensations of travel, a reveling in the exhilarating speed and movement of city traffic. The opening shot of the film immediately announces this interest: it begins with a close-up of a license plate, opening to a wider shot as a car pulls away, followed by a dynamic change in screen direction as the taxi pulls up screen left onto a sunny Berlin street, until a passenger climbs in the back. The first character introduced in the film is thus Erwin, the most mobile of the non-professional actors. The next is Brigitte, viewed outside her record shop as she is setting up a window display of what was still very new media in 1929. A later shot of Brigitte's shop window shows an English-language advertisement for the Electrola gramophone company, founded only four years earlier. The film thus clearly embraces modernity in its most recent manifestations. The signs of Americanism in late Weimar culture are pictured as markers of youthful energy in this film, not as decadent or ominous, as might be expected from more Expressionist-influenced work.

The following sequences introduce Christl and Wolf, but maintain the heavy interest in the dynamic movement of traffic. High angle long shots show Wolf circling predatorily in front of the Zoo subway station, until he moves in on Christl, who is apparently waiting for a subway passenger who does not arrive. The two main characters are often barely distinguishable among distant framings cluttered with streetcars, horse carts, automobiles, and masses of boldly crossing pedestrians. The two characters appear amazingly unconcerned by the chaotic traffic, however, even as they are placed in the middle of the road and at the bottom of the camera's frame, allowing streetcars and automobiles to seemingly pass dangerously close to their heads. The scene is intercut several

Ill. 1 and 2: *Menschen am Sonntag/People on Sunday* (Filmstudio 1929). British Film Institute Video Publishing 2005.

times with a montage of shots of trains entering the station from different directions on an elevated track. The editing of the shots creates somewhat disorienting changes in screen direction as the scene is filmed from multiple axes. But the ultimate effect is not of a threatening destabilization of perspective, but rather of exciting dynamism. It is a non-paranoiac treatment of space that appears to predate the damaged relationship to spatial and temporal movement that Adorno described as the exilic state.

The visual cacophony in the shot composition of Siodmak's first Weimar film indicates an embrace of contingency rather than a desire for control and closure. *People on Sunday* is far removed from an Expressionist or an American film noir view of a threatening metropolis. Wolf and Christl are shot in a strong sunlight that casts high-contrast shadows, but these are not the shadows of *chiaroscuro* doom. The natural light instead gives a carefree sense of late summer heat and the joy of moving through both populated and open spaces. There are many traveling shots taken from the top floor of double decker buses that graze the tops of trees and buildings on the way out of and back into the city. The traveling camera also glances down onto the road,

Ill. 3: *Menschen am Sonntag/People on Sunday* (Filmstudio 1929). British Film Institute Video Publishing 2005.

taking delight in the clear view of motorcyclists racing against the trains and passers-by, a complete equality of movement. The hurrying eye stops for close-ups of faces and objects that it can grasp, and so the movement does not dissolve into vacant abstraction.

No one is being forcibly acted *upon* in these shots either, since the objects isolated in close-ups do not portend any certain narrative fate for the characters, unlike in Siodmak's post-exile films. Instead, objects in *Menschen am Sonntag* are viewed with relish for their photographic qualities of shape and surface. A particularly beautiful shot comes when Wolf and Christl go to an outdoor café next to the Zoo station. To entertain her, he performs a trick with a crinkled drinking straw wrapper. In a sparkling close-up, he lets a few drops of water fall onto the wrapper, and it begins to move and unfurl, the paper becoming like a live caterpillar. But this purely realist animating of objects has no metaphoric and little narrative value. It is a remarkable indulgence in momentary visual phenomena that underlines the pleasures of observation over the relentless subjugation to narrative containment. *Menschen am Sonntag*, as Siegfried Kracauer briefly noted, was an example of that type of episodic, semi-documentary realist approach that he championed in his *Theory of Film*.[12] It was a brand of cinema that served to "redeem physical reality" through an attention to the "material components of our world", and through an episodic temporality that emphasized and preserved the singular life of that which was captured by the camera.[13] It was a cinema that enjoyed its journeys, without worrying about arriving at a secure destination.

This brand of cinema embraced an approach to filmic time and narrative scripting that was generally at odds with industrial or studio system production. It was also, I would like to suggest, at odds with the experience of exile. After *Menschen am Sonntag* became a surprise hit, Siodmak was offered a regular studio contract. His first feature-length film for UFA, *Abschied: Ernstes und Heiteres aus einer Familienpension* (1930) initiated a recurring series of producer interventions into his work. Although the film was shot largely in a studio, it attempted to continue in the observational, *Neue Sachlichkeit* mode of *Menschen am Sonntag*, an interest in the facts and phenomena of daily life. It was criticized by UFA producers for having a lack of form, so a new and more conventionally conclusive ending was filmed by another director and added to the final release print without Siodmak's consent.[14]

In 1933, Siodmak's short but remarkable Weimar career came to an end when he left for Paris. Crediting a sixth sense for danger, Siodmak claimed in

---

[12] Siegfried Kracauer: *Theory of Film. The Redemption of Physical Reality*. New York: Oxford University Press 1960. P. 252.
[13] Ibid. P. 287.
[14] Prümm: Universeller Erzähler (n. 8). P. 83.

Ill. 4: *Menschen am Sonntag/People on Sunday* (Filmstudio 1929). British Film Institute Video Publishing 2005.

his autobiography that he escaped from Germany only one day after the Nazi seizure of power.[15] Since he never elaborated on the circumstances surrounding his departure, it is uncertain whether his journey to France was actually intended as an escape from the looming Third Reich or whether it began as a business trip that became an unforseen exile. The move was clearly not without its desolation, since Siodmak lacked financial resources and was only able at that point to obtain Nansen identification papers for stateless refugees issued by the League of Nations, but no national passport. Whether or not he had intended to relocate to France before January 1933, the experience of exile quickly became oppressive. In his autobiography, Siodmak described the initial period in France as "bitter years":

> I had no passport, and my wife only had a German one that could be declared invalid at any moment. My stay [in France] was only tolerated. No work permit. I can't even count the number of days that we spent in the courthouse. Hundreds and hundreds of us sat on wooden benches, people of all nations who, like me, didn't know if our residence permits would be extended. If they were denied, there was nowhere for us to go, since no country would take someone with a so-called Nansen passport. On the other side was Germany. Hitler was becoming more and more powerful.... One had to practically beg the few producers that knew us for a tiny salary. Sometimes I sent my wife, whom they couldn't refuse as easily, to do it. We were constantly worried about finding another job. We lived in a small hotel and always owed back rent to the owner Madame Guerin. So we had to eat the cheapest food there, always

---

[15] Siodmak: *Zwischen Berlin und Hollywood* (n. 5). P. 83.

afraid of being thrown out or reported to the police. The foreigner's police [*Fremdenpolizei*] kept watch over us.[16]

To escape the struggle of life as an only partially legal immigrant under the suspicious eyes of the French, Siodmak wrote that he barely ventured out of bed between his 1933 *Le sexe faible* (*The Weaker Sex*) and the aptly titled 1934 production *La crise est finie!* (*The Depression is Over!*).[17]

Siodmak ultimately endured by learning how to fulfill producer demands and filming in the local idiom. As Thomas Elsaesser has pointed out, Siodmak and a few of his fellow exiled German and Austrian directors made films which appeared "more French than the French themselves",[18] in an attempt to counter the resistance to what was perceived as an invasion of foreign film workers into an already depressed market for French cinema. Elsaesser added in regard to the position of exiles in France: "being a Jew meant being recognised not as a German anti-fascist but as a representative of German capitalism, an aggressive and more prosperous competitor".[19] Siodmak reported being subjected to personal attacks by native xenophobes, but he was ultimately able to make more films in France than any other exiled director.[20] His survival strategy was to sacrifice his late Weimar semi-documentary, observational mode and focus more on French qualities of acting. In France and later in America, Siodmak was conscious of avoiding the cliché of a German director by not adopting an authoritarian directorial style, and instead was noted for his comparatively cooperative and gentle handling of actors, unlike the famously tyrannical auteur Fritz Lang.

Instead of recording the more natural movements of non-professionals and making use of an episodic temporality and loose linear narrative plotting in the manner of *Menschen am Sonntag*, Siodmak's French work was marked by a divided aesthetic. Thomas Elsaesser noted what he calls the "two temporalities" or "two registers" of Siodmak's 1937 French film *Cargaison Blanche*/*Le Chemin de Rio* (*Traffic in Souls*), a film about two journalists' investigation of the transatlantic sex trade that is fractured by non-linear plotting and generic mixture. As Elsaesser notes, the film opens with an Expressionist scene of a death in a brothel and then moves to seemingly unrelated comedic scenes

---

[16] Ibid. P. 75.
[17] Ibid. P. 62.
[18] Thomas Elsaesser: The German Émigrés in Paris during the 1930s: Pathos and Leave-Taking. In: *Sight and Sound* 53: 4 (Autumn 1984). Pp. 278–283. Here: p. 283.
[19] Ibid. P. 281.
[20] According to Siodmak's account, the director Henri Chomette led a campaign against him motivated by xenophobia. Chomette reportedly protested in front of Siodmak's studio and wrote to the French justice ministry in an effort to have him deported. Siodmak: *Zwischen Berlin und Hollywood* (n. 5). P. 59.

which are treated with alternate pacing, *mise-en-scène*, and emotional effect. The disjointed and initially unexplained opening scene effects an intentional temporal division that underlines the artifice of the narrative plotting:

> [A girl] screams, backs away, throws herself over the balustrade and falls to her death. We then cut to a different location, different characters, a different time: it makes the opening scene violent, enigmatic, but in an odd sense undramatic because not part of the story's time-space continuum. The rupture is deliberate and unsettling: two temporalities – that of the intrigue and that of the *mise en scène* of each incident – contend with each other.[21]

The result of this contention is a somewhat unsettling non-synchronicity between story and plot, as the individual scenes appear to operate in a time frame that is independent of the entirety of the film's narrative.

Elsaesser concludes further that this dual temporality or "structural principle of counterpoint…[was] the German director's central contribution to the French cinema".[22] Whether a result of exilic trauma, of being forced to adapt to a new production system, or of the intercultural exchange of Siodmak's New Objectivity background with the poetic realism developing in the foreground of French cinema, Siodmak's treatment of temporality apparently underwent an initial shift in Parisian exile. But it was in America that Siodmak encountered the most significant aesthetic rupture.

The Interior Language of a Hollywood Polyglot

Again claiming an almost supernatural sense for danger, Siodmak reported that he obtained an American passport in the spring of 1939 and left for New York on August 30, 1939, just one day before the Nazi invasion of Poland.[23] The sense of menace had been building for weeks before he left, as Siodmak wrote:

> I still remember with horror how the general mobilization came in 1939 in the middle of August. The young men were called up. In the emptied stores of all of Paris, the old uniforms from 1914 were stacked up. They weren't cleaned and sometimes still had blood stains and bullet holes from the last war. The pants were red instead of field gray, and the shoes were completely dried out and hard as bone. The mobilized men were full of resentment. They simply did not want to fight, and it didn't matter to them if the German army rolled over all of France. It was impossible to utter a single

---

[21] Elsaesser: The German Émigrés (n. 18). P. 279.
[22] Ibid. P. 279–280.
[23] Siodmak: *Zwischen Berlin und Hollywood* (n. 5). P. 82. Since the Polish invasion was launched on September 1, 1939, Siodmak actually traveled two days before the outbreak of the Second World War.

German word at this time. Everyone had a deathly fear of a revolution or of falling into the hands of the Germans, particularly the Jews. It could start any minute.[24]

Many began to seek an escape route. The ship on which Siodmak booked was filled to more than three times its normal capacity, with panicked passengers sleeping in bathtubs and on billiard tables, as the blacked-out ship maneuvered through North Atlantic waters patrolled by German submarines and bombers.[25] Soon after arriving in New York, Siodmak drove across the country to Hollywood, with no contract and no concrete prospects of continuing his career.

Unemployed for two years after arriving in the U.S., Siodmak faced America as a place of renewed exile from his personal and professional past. Hollywood producers, as Siodmak soon realized, were utterly uninterested in Siodmak's European work and considered local box office statistics the only valid measure of quality. Despite the lively history of German-American cinematic exchanges of the 1920s and the difficulties that exiles encountered in establishing a new existence in France, many German-Jewish film workers found French cinema comparatively more familiar than classical Hollywood's studio system. (Speaking of his initial exile to Paris, Max Ophüls even claimed that French "emigration was not a hardship – it was a journey".[26]) For Robert Siodmak, it had also not been entirely foreign territory, since he had worked on two Franco-German co-productions in 1931, *Autour d'une enquête* and *Tumultes*, French language versions of his UFA films *Voruntersuchung* and *Stürme der Leidenschaft*. In contrast, his adaptation to the Hollywood language was more labored. As he confessed in postwar letters to his brother Werner Siodmak in Palestine: "here, a good director is someone who makes money for the company. I long for the old days when I could make the kind of films that I wanted to make... I have worked in Germany and France – and successfully – but I have to say that the path to success was never as difficult as it was here in Hollywood.[27] French film production, in Siodmak's estimation, was still commanded by directors and technicians who knew their craft, while Hollywood had become a thoroughly Fordist system dominated by dictatorial producers. By the time he tried to gain entry into it, American mass cultural modernity looked less positively dynamic to Siodmak.

In particular, he objected to the loss of control over editing, scripting, and casting decisions that accompanied his move to the Hollywood studios. His

---

[24] Ibid. P. 76.
[25] Ibid. P. 87.
[26] Maria Hilchenbach: *Kino im Exil: Die Emigration deutscher Filmkünstler 1933–45*. München: K. G. Saur 1982. P. 29.
[27] Robert Siodmak: Mein lieber Bruder Werner. Briefe 1931–1948. In: *Siodmak Bros.: Berlin-Paris-London-Hollywood* (n. 8). P. 53.

past production experience and visual language were annulled by a self-contained system that demanded assimilation, as he reported in regard to his first Hollywood film, the B-comedy *West Point Widow* (1941):

> The crew was mediocre and the actors were cast in about ten minutes, and no one dared to raise any objections. No one asked my opinion and no one had any respect for me. On the second day of shooting, [assistant director Charles] Coleman said to me in front of everyone: 'You should go to night school and learn English before you make films here!'... On the same day, my German cameraman, [Theodor] Sparkuhl, refused to do a shot as I requested. He said cynically: 'They do shots like that in Germany, but not in America!'[28]

Siodmak grudgingly accepted further low budget assignments in order to remain employed, such as the 1943 horror film *The Son of Dracula*. His breakthrough to somewhat greater creative autonomy and to a more "Germanic" *mise-en-scène* and shot construction came with the initiation of his noir cycle in 1944.

Noir was long considered by film critics to be chiefly a product of German-Jewish exile, a direct importation of early Weimar cinema's paranoid *mise-en-scène* into Hollywood studios, particularly of the fragmented spaces and *chiaroscuro* lighting of Expressionism. But scholars have recently called this genealogy into question. Some have noted that American cinema had a much longer history of using such lighting devices.[29] Furthermore, Robert Siodmak, the German director who made the most film noirs, showed no Expressionist tendencies in his Weimar work at all.[30] Lutz Koepnick argues, for example, that "Siodmak's success in film noir did not result from some kind of innate Germanness or authorial vision. Instead, it ensued from his competent immersion into studio filmmaking, his intuitive understanding of Hollywood production processes".[31] And it was not visual design, but rather asynchronous audio that marks Siodmak's fragmentary aesthetic, as Koepnick asserts.[32]

Although Siodmak's *Phantom Lady* and subsequent noirs may not be legitimately counted as direct descendants of *Caligari*, they may still be considered a product of exilic experience, as I would like to insist. The exilic shift may in fact answer the vexing question of how Siodmak became a leading director of

---

[28] Siodmak: *Zwischen Berlin und Hollywood* (n. 5). P. 98.
[29] Lutz Koepnick makes this point in reference to Marc Vernet's article: Film Noir on the Edge of Doom. In *Shades of Noir: A Reader*. Ed. by Joan Copjec. London: Verso 1993. Pp. 1–31. Koepnick: *The Dark Mirror* (n. 4). P. 167.
[30] See Edward Dimendberg: Down these Seen Streets a Man Must Go: Siegfried Kracauer, 'Hollywood's Terror Films,' and the Spatiality of Film Noir. *New German Critique* 89 (Spring/Summer 2003). Pp. 113–143.
[31] Koepnick: *The Dark Mirror* (n. 4). P. 167.
[32] Ibid. P. 168–170.

noir despite having shown little tendency towards the style in his Weimar work, only making use of Expressionist motifs after his flight to France. He, like other German-Jewish exiles, did not necessarily pack the style in his baggage. Rather, it was generated in transit and may be viewed as a common and recurring response to threatening circumstances. As Edward Dimendberg has proposed, film noir and Expressionist Weimar street films should be seen as "parallel representations of urban modernity", shared reactions to a form of insecurity that is "manifested spatially in a militarized physical environment that threatens psychic integrity".[33]

In their divergences from the spatial and temporal configurations of *Menschen am Sonntag*, Siodmak's noirs display characteristic elements of exilic style. A common feature of exile filmmaking, according to Hamid Naficy, is claustrophobic and agoraphobic spaces in which movement is restricted:

> These phobic chronotypes and paranoid structures take the form in the accented films of closed mise-en-scène and filming style and a receding structure of feelings. Small, dingy, and overcrowded immigrant apartments, prison cells, hotel rooms, buses, tunnels, and confining symbolic spaces such as the suitcase are favored. The claustrophobia of these settings is intensified by a dark lighting scheme that limits sight, by barriers in the shot that impede vision, and by tight shot composition, immobile framing, and a stationary camera...These phobic spaces and structures, along with panic-ridden plots, which create a sense of psychic narrowing, may serve therapeutic, strategic, and pathological purposes.[34]

Much of the above description fits the noir approach to the delineation of space, in which the already restricted spatial arrangements of classical Hollywood studio shooting become further limited by visual obstructions that externalize the fragmented and threatened psychic state of the persecuted protagonist.

For Naficy, of course, exile does not only and necessarily result in a pathology and aesthetics of restriction. The "interstitial mode" of contemporary small-scale, independently produced exile cinema instead allows for the constructive crossing of stylistic and cultural boundaries. Production outside of the studio system and entrenched national film conventions often encourages exiled filmmakers to develop strongly autobiographical, auteurist, and self-reflexive styles that provide compelling alternatives to commercial cinema. Furthermore, as Naficy argues, recent exile cinema addresses itself to a community of expatriates, transgressing hierarchical structures and stressing dialogic forms: "the alternative mode's collective enunciation and reception

---

[33] Dimendberg: Down these Seen Streets (n. 30). Pp. 122–125.
[34] Hamid Naficy: *An Accented Cinema: Exilic and Diasporic Filmmaking*. Princeton: Princeton University Press 2001. P. 191.

potentially blur the line that separates producers from consumers".[35] However, for exiled German filmmakers of the studio era, there was little possibility for developing such alternative modes of either production or reception. Hollywood's rigidly vertical system required film workers to relinquish most national accents and individual visions, in order to create a universal, internationally profitable cinema. The exiles' cross-cultural knowledge did give them an unusual sense for the menace lurking under everyday Americana, but personal experience could not generally be translated on the screen any direct manner. The *mise-en-scène* of phobic spaces and plots, as an extension and escalation of an already confining studio style, was one of the few options available to German-Jewish exiles seeking to express cinematically the shock of exclusion and the demands of renewed assimilation. Furthermore, a defensive posture of immobility rather than transgression may be seen as the logical result of an era of intensified mobilization against Germans on the one side and Jews on the other.

Whether or not they resulted from a distinct authorial vision, Siodmak's noirs are certainly marked by paranoid narrative and visual structures. One of his most well known films, the Hemingway adaptation *The Killers* (1946), is highly evocative of the experiences and aesthetics of exile. The opening shot of the film shows the two killers of the film's title in a car, with only their black silhouettes visible against back projected shots of a barely illuminated, desolate nighttime road and a jarring film score that announces a fatal outcome to this

Ill. 5: *The Killers* (Universal Pictures 1946). Criterion Collection 2003.

---

[35] Hamid Naficy: Between Rocks and Hard Places: The Interstitial Mode of Production in Exilic Cinema. In: *Home, Exile, Homeland: Film, Media, and the Politics of Place*. New York: Routledge 1999. P. 131.

shadowy car trip. It is a strikingly different vision than the opening sequence of *Menschen am Sonntag*, in which the taxi's jaunts on a sunny Berlin street portend no particular destiny. In the American film, the killers hunt their victim, the paradigmatic immigrant Swede, in the narrow dark corners of the small town to which he has fled. The first shot of Swede shows him in tight framing, stretched out on a dingy bed in a boarding house, his face obscured in a pool of darkness, awaiting his impending death with resignation. "I'm through with all that runnin' around", he explains, like a refugee mortally exhausted by the flight from persecution.

After Swede's execution, the rest of the film's panic-ridden situations are plotted in a complex series of flashbacks motivated by the memories of various protagonists involved in the murder. Since all of the film's excursions into the past end in death, the *mise-en-scène* mainly delivers signs of this predetermined outcome. Objects (a green silk scarf, a scarred hand) are no longer observed as units of physical reality, but rather as pieces of evidence. The settings are highly phobic, mostly small musty apartments and dark underworld bars filmed in tight and static shots, as well as the bureaucratic and disciplinary spaces of a prison cell, a hospital, and a police station. Almost all of the spaces of the film are carefully controlled studio set interiors, and even the few exteriors appear to be studio lot constructions. The restrained camerawork often restricts the spectator's view, since many scenes fade in on a close-up rather than offering a wide establishing shot of the entirety of the scene's space. There are few traveling shots in *The Killers*, much in opposition to the dizzying movements and long-range views of *Menschen am Sonntag*, which had been shot almost exclusively on location in Berlin streets and forests.

Missing from Siodmak's Hollywood films is also the type of time document achieved by the intense attention to the real and even accidental look of things in the particular moment of filming; the kind of cinematic realism which was advocated by Siegfried Kracauer rarely reappeared in any remarkable form after Siodmak's first exile from Germany. In large part, this is due to generic requirements and the conventions of classical Hollywood filming. But it is clear that the paranoiac style of noir meshed with Siodmak's own predilections after 1933. By the time that he moved to Hollywood, Siodmak began to favor the certainty of a constructed world over the ephemeral uncertainties of location shooting. Speaking to the interviewer about his 1948 *Cry of the City*, which made use of a few exteriors, Siodmak commented: "I thought it was good, but it's not really my type of film: I hate locations – there's so much you can't control".[36] Instead, Siodmak listed as his own favorite works *Phantom*

---

[36] Quoted in Russell Taylor: Encounter with Siodmak. *Sight and Sound* 28:3/4 (Summer/Autumn 1959). Pp. 180–182.

Ill. 6: *Criss Cross* (Universal Pictures 1948). Universal Studios Home Video 2004.

Lady, *The Spiral Staircase*, and *The Strange Affair of Uncle Harry*, all films about murder, pervaded by an atmosphere of suspicion and dread, and shot mainly in airless interiors. Siodmak had evidently developed a cinematic agoraphobia that extended beyond generic or studio system requirements.

Even when Siodmak did take his camera outside for his Hollywood films, they give evidence of a changed view of open spaces. Siodmak's 1948 noir *Criss Cross* has a few impressive exterior shots of Los Angeles streets and roads outside the city, as well as location shots of the main train station, but these public spaces are sites of entrapment rather than free movement. The train station becomes a hazardous place for the main protagonist, Steve, a man described by the script as a drifter who becomes involved in a fatal relationship with a group of gangsters. In one of a series of interior monologues that support another plot structured around recollections narrated in flashback, he imagines that venturing out of the safe confines of the home sealed his fate: "You know how it is – you don't know what to do with yourself. Travel, get away... If I hadn't been hanging around the Union Station that day..." In a subsequent scene that indicates an altered vision of travel as treacherous, Steve is shown in another dingy boarding house room with the gangsters, who are deceitfully planning his death. In the background of several of the shots, two criss-crossing tram cars (studio models rather than actual trains) are visible. Unlike the shots of dynamically crossing trains in *Menschen am Sonntag*, these rising and descending trams appear to be ominous indications of the protagonist's doom rather than the exciting sights of modern life.

Ill. 7: *Criss Cross* (Universal Pictures 1948). Universal Studios Home Video 2004.

After the ruptures of fascism and war, modernity looked perilous once again, and the physical environments of film noir seem to be a menacing system of potentially meaningful signs. In *Criss Cross*, the roads appear mined with war memories, from which the claustrophobic interiors are only a temporary refuge. In the climatic scene of the film, Steve is shown driving toward his eventual doom, in a militaristically evocative armored car. The open road induces paranoia, as tense point-of-view shots into the rear view mirror to look for the protagonist's pursuers build the sense of threat, while the interior monologue edited over the close-ups of his face suggest that his psychic integrity may be vanishing. The destination of Steve's journey is the factory yard where a robbery is to take place, but the scene of the crime quickly becomes the *mise-en-scène* of war: smoke bombs explode, a siren wails, a man in a gas mask emerges from the empty frame to fire shots and throw grenades. The car trip out of a sunny city ends in the disorienting fog of battle, open space becoming a void which threatens to annihilate the drifter. Siodmak's American landscapes may not have been as expressionless as Adorno's, but they held a parallel threat.

Return Voyages and Open Spaces

Consequently, it was not so much the decline of the studio system that motivated Siodmak's departure from Hollywood in 1951, as some scholars have suggested, but rather that system's departure from studio shooting.[37] Crediting

[37] See, for example, Lutz Koepnick: Doubling the Double: Robert Siodmak in Hollywood. *New German Critique* 89 (Spring/Summer 2003). P. 102.

a sixth sense about the imminent end of his preferred film language, Siodmak wrote in his autobiography, "I quit Hollywood and returned to Europe one year before the invention of CinemaScope".[38] The introduction of television as a competing culture industry would make film noir outmoded, as the cinema expanded into wide-screen formats, colors, and genres that television could not offer. Unlike with Fritz Lang, it was not any fear of failure and possible unemployment that motivated Siodmak's departure from Hollywood. Just before leaving, Siodmak refused the offer of a new seven-year contract with Universal, in order to go work for a much less lucrative European cinema. He could thereby hope to escape the Technicolor, wide-screen, optimistic, and often jingoistic tones of American cinema of the 1950s. In Germany, at least initially, Siodmak could continue working on the interiorized, psychological thematics that he had come to favor. Instead of the aggressive, expansionist visions of the newly popular American genres of the wide-screen Western and epic historical film, the exile craved the contained and knowable boundaries of a confined *mise-en-scène*.

For *Die Ratten*, Siodmak's first postwar German language film, his producer Artur Brauner promised Siodmak a level of creative freedom and control over casting decisions that Hollywood did not offer. He chose to film his tale of emigration in dark tones, as a "German film noir", offering a gloomy portrait of postwar Berlin tenements. The film's departure from the earlier vision of the lively city in *Menschen am Sonntag* testifies, according to Daniela Sannwald, to the "repeatedly ruptured vita of Siodmak".[39] His use of objects in the film underline a critique of postwar Germany, Sannwald argues: "Here, identification papers are more important than identity itself…the pen that lies waiting for a signature in a German government office become[s] under Siodmak's gaze [a] symbol of the meaningless, rigid traditions of a people that represses the past and fears the future".[40] Similar to Adorno's view, it seems, the obligatory present tense of the bureaucratized economic miracle cancels the lived past of the refugee in *Die Ratten*.

Siodmak's subsequent work, *Nachts, wenn der Teufel kam* (*The Devil Strikes at Night*, 1957), uses the figure of a serial killer to probe the Nazi era, as did Peter Lorre's single post-exile German work, *Der Verlorene* (*The Lost Man*, 1951).[41] As in the best of Siodmak's American work, this film maintains a

---

[38] Siodmak: *Zwischen Berlin und Hollywood* (n. 5). P. 83.

[39] Daniela Sannwald: Von Schatten und Ratten: Robert Siodmaks Neuanfänge in Hollywood und in der Bundesrepublik. *Film-Exil* 3 (November 1993). P. 36. I am relying on Sannwald's description of *Die Ratten* here.

[40] Ibid.

[41] On the earlier film, see Jennifer Kapczynski: Homeward Bound? Peter Lorre's *The Lost Man* and the End of Exile. *New German Critique* 89 (Spring/Summer 2003). Pp. 145–171.

mostly tight and static shot structure and a discontinuous elaboration of plot events. While most of the film takes place in interiors, it opens with a short scene of escape in a forest clearing. A man hides in a watery ditch to evade capture while a group of pursuers close in on him, the mostly immobile camera obscuring the action of the shot. This opening sequence at first appears disorientingly disconnected to those that follow, affecting a temporal rupture much like that of the beginning of *Cargaison Blanche*. The *mise-en-scène* of the first sequence of *Nachts, wenn der Teufel kam* refers to Siodmak's pre-exile work as well, since it is evidently staged in the same landscape as *Menschen am Sonntag*, the wooded lakes outside of Berlin. In the postwar film, however, it is no longer the unburdened site of Sunday excursions – as we later learn, it is the scene of strangulations. Towards the end of the film, as the murderer reveals to the police the exact locations of his killings, elliptical editing fragments the open space of the forest in a manner that evokes the confused panic of pursuit and death, shots structured by the sort of "discontinuity and fragmentation" that Naficy describes as integral to exilic style.[42]

Nachts, wenn der Teufel kam is set at the end of the Second World War, so its take on travel is necessarily fraught with the fatal outcome of much of that period's transports. A Jew in hiding unknowingly asks the murderer Bruno to take her along in his truck, so that she can escape the claustrophobic apartment where she has been since her husband's deportation to Auschwitz. A darkly lit

Ill. 8: *Nachts, wenn der Teufel kam*/*The Devil Strikes at Night* (Kirch Media GmbH 1958). Belle & Blade Studios 2002.

[42] Naficy (n. 35). P. 131.

train station hung with the ironically mocking propaganda banner "Räder müssen rollen für den Sieg!" is apparently the next-to-last stop before death for the film's hero, a police officer condemned to fight on the collapsing Eastern front. The camerawork is accordingly restricted to mainly static, shot-counter-shot constructions with few traveling shots, the camera only moving wildly when it alludes to the final moments of a woman's fatal suffocation at the hands of Bruno. Despite the citation of the propagandistic language of the period, the Third Reich is represented in Siodmak's film in strangely contemporary visual codes (especially in regard to costuming), so that it almost seems to be a Third Reich set in 1957 rather than in 1944. This anachronism was perhaps the result of the director's suspicion that the Adenauer era was not a complete departure from what had come before, as the subtle denial of his exile on the part of German film journalists and its conversion into cosmopolitan wandering certainly suggested.

Although Siodmak ultimately negotiated most of his (forced and unforced) migrations between countries and national cinemas successfully, one final cinematic border crossing seemed to cause him trouble: the importation of the wide-screen Western into German cinema. After agreeing to make the Karl May adaptation *Der Schut* (*Yellow Devil*) in 1964 and the Euro-Western *Custer of the West* in 1967, both of which were unsatisfying in aesthetic and financial terms, Siodmak told Artur Brauner that he did not want to make any more landscape films: "If you ever have an interesting film that isn't set only outdoors, then you can go ahead and write to me".[43] Siodmak's cross-cultural adaptability apparently stopped at the Western frontier, since the exile did not wish to be a conqueror of new territories, but rather to remain an explorer of interiors.

---

[43] Quoted in Wolfgang Jacobsen: Kann ich mal das Salz haben? In: *Siodmak Bros.: Berlin-Paris-London-Hollywood* (n. 8). Pp. 9–48. Here: p. 47.

W. Scott Hoerle

The Nazi Envoy: Travel Experiences of the Poet Hans Friedrich Blunck in Great Britain and France, 1935 and 1937

The infamous "blood and soil" poet, Hans Friedrich Blunck, was also a frequent traveler. As president of Die Stiftung des deutschen Auslandswerks, a Nazi-approved cultural embassy that promoted informal diplomatic links between Germany and its neighbors, he traveled far and wide during the five years before World War II. His goal: to build support for the "New Germany" and discredit the exiles. The following essay tells of his visits to London and Paris in 1935 and 1937. The paper highlights the genuine artistic struggle that preceded World War II for the hearts and minds of Europeans. It also exhibits the generally poor reception that Blunck received abroad, suggesting revulsion among many Europeans to Nazi artists.

The foreign travels of Nazi Germany's exile writers, or at least the fact thereof, are well known. Exile often required, particularly for the less celebrated among them, an endless search for acceptance, sustenance, and tranquility. Unfamiliar, however, are the international forays of Nazi writers – the regime's sponsored literary collaborators – who ventured abroad during this period. A number of them, too, traveled widely, visiting writers, giving readings, and meeting with government officials. Moreover, they, too, sought acceptance and recognition – though of a different kind.

Among them, none was more peripatetic than the Nazi *Literatus* Hans Friedrich Blunck. One of the most revered "blood and soil" conjurers, Blunck is best remembered for penning such literary gems as "der Morgen stand blutrot über der Erde",[1] "die Sonne ging … blutrot über den Hügeln zur Ruh",[2] and "wo die Heide rot blüht sickert Blut von uns an ihrer Wurzel".[3] Ruddy, earthy imagery coated his work. However, he was more than a master of poetic ostentation. Indeed, one might call him a frequent – even serial – traveler. Prior to the Third Reich, he traveled abroad regularly, not only throughout Europe but also to the United States, Central, and South America in 1928 and 1930. A brief perusal of his works betrays his fascination with far away places. *Land der Vulkane* and *Die Weibsmühle*, for which he took notes during his visits to

---

[1] Hans Friedrich Blunck: *Berend Fock*. In: *Werdendes Volk*. Hamburg: Hanseatische Verlagsanstalt 1938. P. 534.
[2] Hans Friedrich Blunck: *Märchen von der Niederelbe*. Jena: Eugen Diederichs 1923. P. 11.
[3] Hans Friedrich Blunck: *Von Geistern unter und über der Erde*. Jena: Eugen Diederichs Verlag 1935. P. 10.

the western hemisphere, tell of German settlers living in Central and South America, respectively. Parts of *Berend Fock* follow the story's protagonist through India and the Middle East. *Die große Fahrt* heralds the supposed discovery, before Columbus, of the Americas by the German Diderik Pining. Indeed, Blunck became indignant when the sobriquet *Heimat* was applied to him, for it ignored, he complained, his informed treatment of the exotic. Even the title of his memoir on the Third Reich, *Unwegsame Zeiten*, suggests rough paths, difficult terrain, and unfulfilled journeys through space and time. Aptly representative of the poet's life, these metaphors also betray the contorted and bumpy way in which the autobiography paved over his Nazi complicity, a point that is best reflected in his claim that he was an "anti-fascist" member of the Nazi literary elite.

Beginning in 1933, Blunck served as president of Joseph Goebbels' Reich Literary Chamber. Here, he clung to the perverse illusion that the Chamber was an "autonomous" cooperative that would somehow produce "freedom" and "autonomy" for writers. After leaving that office in 1935, he established *Die Stiftung des deutschen Auslandswerks* (DAW), a Nazi-approved cultural foundation that, along with its network of "friendship societies", promoted informal diplomatic links between Germany and its neighbors.

As the DAW's president, Blunck again traveled regularly, and it is here that he offers relevance to the exile experience. The following paper will tell of two journeys, the first to Paris and London in 1935 and the second to the same cities in 1937 (though each city will be dealt with in separate sections, for the sake of organization). Blunck's travels had a specific political agenda – to build support for the "New Germany" – and served as a foil to the wanderings of the "emigrants", as Blunck derided exile writers. Indeed, his travels composed a self-serving effort to discredit the exiles, to demonstrate to the world that Nazi writers, particularly he, were Germany's true poets, that their talent was real and their work legitimate. The fact that both traditional exiles and Nazi itinerants sought recognition, though from opposing ideological and artistic angles, lends an intriguing nuance to the story of Germany's wandering writers, both Nazi and anti-Nazi, during this period.

A central purpose of this volume has been to compare and contrast the meanings of "travel" and "exile" – to see, if one will allow a pun, where the terms arrive and depart. At first glance, Blunck's journeys offer nothing to the discussion. After all, he was no fugitive; his journeys were voluntary, and he had a welcoming home to which to return. Indeed, due to the enormous financial benefits he received from the regime in the late 1930s he was able to build a new, expansive house at his beloved Mölenhoff estate in Holstein, the point being that he was more at home in Germany than ever during the period after 1933. But the poet was most certainly a traveler, spending nearly a quarter of his time abroad between 1936 and 1939. As will be seen in this essay, he may also have been an "exile". Before the Third Reich, he had journeyed regularly and always found welcoming friends to host him. He liked to think of himself as just as comfortable abroad – particularly in England – as in Germany. As a Nazi poet, however, Blunck's search for recognition was mired in failure. No matter where he turned, the reception was cool and sometimes downright antagonistic. Blunck found himself a stranger in places he had previously called home – unwelcome in the stream of European culture and society in which, as a former member of the PEN-Club, he had once swum. Abroad, he had no home. Abroad – if one will allow for an admittedly broad definition of the word – he was an exile. During the period of the Third Reich for Blunck "travel" was "exile".

London: "For Old Sake's Sake"

Blunck's favorite destination was, and had always been, Britain. Only a brief review of his letters, diaries, and literary work exhibits a fascination with the "Germanic isle". Indeed, one might consider the DAW, though a sponsor of links throughout Europe, to have been principally British friendly. The hope was that the organization would foster informal cultural/political ties between Germans and Brits and that these ties would help inspire a formal military alliance – something that was coveted by Hitler and Blunck alike. But the poet's love for England was innate, for it originated in his northern German upbringing. Throughout his life, he harbored an exaggerated, mystical preoccupation, nurtured in childhood by his parents and in adolescence via his precocious reading of racist denizens like the English Germanophile Houston Stewart Chamberlain, with the racial, linguistic, and cultural ties between England and northern Germany. At the turn of the twentieth century, sympathy for England was quite common among northern Germans, who, like Blunck himself, were well versed in the ancient migrations of the Angles, Saxons, and Jutes across the channel and whose native dialect (i.e., *Plattdeutsch*) was closer to English than High German.[4] Blunck, however, was more enamored with these themes than most. He sometimes referred to himself as a "continental Anglo-Saxon", whose love for England was due to "old sake's sake" – an exaggerated reference to the aforementioned tribal connections but also to Hanseatic and other cultural bonds that Blunck argued had been established across the centuries.

In the 1920s, he had traveled to the island frequently. He gave readings at universities and other academic venues, met with writers of all kinds who were willing to receive him, and visited as much of the island as possible, from

---

[4] Gerwin Strobl: *The Germanic Isle. Nazi Perceptions of Britain*. Cambridge University Press 2000.

Sussex to Glasgow. In 1925, he joined the international PEN-Club, which was headquartered in London. Following the PEN-Club Congress of 1926, he visited the Club's president, John Galsworthy, at his home in Hampstead, and the two went on to organize a student exchange between the University of Hamburg and Oxford. In addition to Galsworthy, the poet cultivated a number of friendships in England with an eye towards the promotion of his books, which he believed should have special resonance on the island due to their thematic concern with the North Sea and Britain itself on occasion, but also in order to contribute personally to what he believed should have been a natural friendship between the two countries.

Through careful engagement, therefore, Blunck had established a "home away from home" in England by 1933. The question was whether this haven would remain welcoming thereafter. It was not until a blustery day in the middle of October 1935, when Blunck and his assistant at the DAW, Dr. Fiedler, boarded the ferry from Harwich to London, that he got the chance to find out. Blunck had always been an avid – obsessive is more accurate – searcher for traces of the racial and cultural connections between the English and the northern Germans. During previous visits, he had pondered such idiosyncrasies as "Saxon-like blond hair" on English women and the similarities between the "Germanic-Scottish way of speaking" and the "North Saxon linguistic forms".[5] Hence, it was only fitting that the first thing he noted upon boarding the ship was the resemblance between the English passengers and people from his region – "bis zum letzten die gleichen Gesichter, Spießer und Edelleute, wie an der Niederelbe...".[6] Here, in Blunck's eyes, was clear evidence of racial kinship.

The problem was that these "Germanic siblings" were now being turned against Germany by the media. Blunck picked up a couple of British newspapers on the ship and was horrified: "Man schlägt die 'Times' auf und schon schulmeistert sie und mengt sich in unsere Bekenntnisfragen ein (was begreift England von unserer Sehnsucht nach Einigkeit, es ist kein gespaltenes Volk)".[7] This was a preoccupation of the poet – that the press, not the broader population, polluted relations between Germany and its proper ally. The "people", if left alone, would naturally gravitate towards their racial and cultural kin across the channel. This was the mystical, messianic quality of Blunck's anglophilism writ large, and it gave him hope that the British might have begun to understand Germany's position and the calumny of Versailles: "Ob man in England nicht langsam spürt, daß es ein anderes ist ein besiegtes Volk zu verletzen und zu

---

[5] Blunck: *Tagebuch*. December 11, 1930.
[6] Blunck: *Tagebuch*. October 15, 1935.
[7] Ibid.

versuchen eine aufstrebende Nation zu verstehen. Nun, ich werde die Antwort hören in den zehn Tagen, die vor mir liegen".[8]

The day after arriving in London, the poet visited his old friend Hermon Ould, general secretary of the international PEN-Club. Ould and Blunck had become acquainted in the late 1920s via the PEN, in which Blunck (rather surprisingly, given his conservative and nationalist sympathies[9]) had remained active up until 1931. Indeed, both writers had tried to help one another get their respective works published in Germany and Britain, an effort that had accrued much better to Ould. In the late 1920s and early 1930s, they exchanged visits and corresponded regularly. Indeed, Blunck considered Ould, who was nearly the same age, a close friend.

That friendship was now frayed. After the *Machtergreifung*, conservative representatives of the German PEN division had stormed out of a PEN-Club gathering and subsequently dissolved their organization (which at any rate would have been forced upon them, given Nazi discrimination in the arts). Since then, Ould had taken the lead in building up the "German Exile-PEN", informally established the year before in Edinburgh at the PEN's annual meeting and formalized soon thereafter as a haven for German emigré writers. Many of Blunck's former enemies and the very same people he had helped eject from the Prussian Academy only two years before – Lion Feuchtwanger, Heinrich Mann, and Alfred Döblin – were members.[10]

Blunck nonetheless hoped that he could use his old ties to Ould to persuade him to change his mind and banish this new German division. Frustrated by the PEN's ostensible betrayal of Germany, Blunck refused to call upon PEN-Club offices, where Ould would have preferred a visit, so they met at the German embassy. Here, Blunck "urgently pleaded with [Ould] not to continue to receive refugees from Nazi Germany into the PEN-Club".[11] In the poet's mind, the exiles were a nuisance, an international fifth column that was undermining Germany's every attempt to establish critical military, cultural, and economic ties. If the exiles were denied a place in the PEN, a means could be established for the restoration of the old German PEN Division. This would help produce the greater cultural affinities between England and Nazi Germany that, he believed, would foster a formal military alliance.

---

[8] Ibid.
[9] Blunck's political and literary affiliations were eccentric. For a thorough discussion of the poet's ties, see my book, *Hans Friedrich Blunck. Poet and Nazi Collaborator, 1888–1961*. Bern: Peter Lang 2003. Particularly chapters 3, 4, and 5.
[10] Blunck was now vice-president of the hallowed (and recently sullied) Poetry Section of the Prussian Academy.
[11] Ould to Blunck. August 26, 1946. Blunck-Ould Correspondence # 65.

Ould was having none of it. In a discussion that immediately turned sour, he emphasized that it was "one of the PEN-Club's unchangeable rules that it only looked at quality with regard to writing and that Germany was required by duty to take writers of all political directions, if it were once again to become a member of the PEN-Club".[12] His position, underscored in a letter that he wrote to the poet two months later, was unyielding:

> You are quite wrong, when you assume that there is any official anti-German feeling in the PEN. In so far as Germany is concerned, the PEN has acted entirely according to the principles for which it was founded fifteen years ago. [...] As soon as the German Center admitted that it was excluding from membership writers of a certain race [or political orientation] the only honorable thing for the German PEN Center to do was to withdraw [...]. You are also mistaken in identifying the London PEN with the emigrant German Group. This group was founded at the International Congress in Scotland, and was no more the work of the London Center than of any other. It was the general opinion that, as a number of German writers, for reasons which were not our concern, found it impossible to live in Germany, but yet wished to be linked to the International PEN, a reasonable temporary solution would be the formation of a group of German writers outside Germany [...]. In conclusion, [...] it is not the PEN which has changed during the last four[13] years but Germany, and I am sure that if you will look at the matter objectively you will come to the same conclusion.[14]

Ould's reaction reflected the English mood that autumn. The additional contacts (Galsworthy was now dead) who agreed to meet with Blunck were similarly unyielding, and he returned home without success. He was bewildered, but not disheartened, shortly after his return sending off a letter to the *London Times* contesting its depiction of the RSK as an instrument of state control – an accusation he had heard repeatedly during his discussions.[15] In light of Nazi exclusionary policies, one might wonder how the poet could ever have imagined it possible to persuade a writer like Ould (who was of genuine character, intelligence, and humanity) to see the "New Germany" in a positive light and turn against the émigrés. But this would be to misunderstand Blunck. The poet was in the last analysis a "dreamer" (*Träumer*). His talent for self-delusion permitted him to view prospects of building European support, even among liberals, as plausible in the same way that it enabled him to see the Nazi regime as a promoter of "freedom". Jaded by the fairy-tale world of his literature and naïvely optimistic, he ignored reality when it turned against him. In his mind,

---

[12] Ould to Blunck. October (precise day unknown), 1935. Blunck-Ould Correspondence # 65.
[13] A seeming reference to the nationalistic/conservative influences in German arts and letters that grew rapidly after 1929, well before the Nazis actually took power.
[14] Ould to Blunck. January 16, 1936. Blunck-Ould Correspondence # 65.
[15] Blunck to the Editorial Staff of the London Times. RSK Briefwechsel IX (CB 92, 286).

the relationships he had established before 1933 would remain the same. The world had been turned upside down – only he refused to acknowledge it.

Possibly more important, Blunck approved of what was going on in Germany. Through his eyes, the country was experiencing a rebirth like never before – a sentiment that was reflected in his comment, later relayed to Thomas Mann, that "der neue Staat zum ersten Mal seit Jahrhunderten, ja vielleicht seit den Zeiten Walthers von der Vogelweide, die Würde der deutschen Kunst wiederhergestellt habe".[16] Because he supported the Nazi transformation, relished the supposed return of Germany's Classical and Romantic pasts, and quietly applauded the destruction of "Jewish influences" in the literary world, he found it puzzling that he had to defend the situation in Germany at all. In the end, he blamed England's misguided intellectuals: While the "common man on the street" loved Germany, Blunck wrote in his diary, English intellectuals "hated Germany. And England was ruled by its intellectuals".[17] The German exiles had, of course, become part of this intellectual juggernaut. Much to his dismay, they had gotten to Ould and Blunck's other friends.

The poet's return to Britain two years later, in 1937, was only slightly better. Although most of his schedule was filled with official meetings, particularly with the current ambassador to Britain, the infamous Joachim von Ribbentrop, he found time to take a sightseeing tour of London, visiting Guild Hall, the Tower of London, and the British Stock Exchange – places that he was seeing for the second and even third times. He also found a moment to view a London film, an experience that repelled his traditionalist sensibilities: "Es bringt einen in die Stimmung wie zwei Glas Bier am Mittag – so eine sanfte, süssliche Empfindsamkeit, die man ruhig einmal ertragen mag, wenn man dazu auch über sich selbst lächelt".[18]

His main efforts, however, were focused, as was to be expected, on promoting his coveted Anglo-German alliance. Although he claimed that the move was forced upon him due to his position at the DAW, Blunck had joined the Nazi party earlier that year. This made it impossible for him to maintain, as he had during his first visit, that he was an "unpolitical" and "purely cultural" figure. Not surprisingly, therefore, he avoided his old contacts, choosing instead to meet with pro-Nazi sympathizers whom he knew would inspire at least some optimism. Professor Convel Evans, a Germanist at the University of Liverpool and seeming Blunck sycophant, promised that he was on the verge of securing a parliamentary majority in favor of a declaration of peace between Germany

---

[16] Cited in a letter from Thomas Mann to Rudolf Blunck (Hans Friedrich's brother). November 19, 1945. Blunck-Mann Correspondence.
[17] Blunck: *Tagebuch*. October 15, 1935.
[18] Blunck: *Tagebuch*. June 30, 1937.

and England (something that never happened, of course).[19] Where Evans got this information – indeed, whether he was telling the truth at all – is puzzling, for there is no parliamentary record of anything of the kind. Evans added that he had recently attended a banquet, where a prominent member of the House of Lords, Lord Lothian, had commented that Britain had "either to allow Germany to buy back its colonies and spread to the east or be prepared to fight another deadly war".[20] According to Evans, at least half of the attendees, many of whom were MPs, agreed.[21]

Other comments were less heartening. Shortly after his arrival, the poet attended a dinner at the German embassy. Hosted by Ribbentrop, the proceedings included numerous Nazi sympathizers, not least the notorious Barry Domville, head of the "Anglo-German Link". A former submarine commander, Domville was bent on avoiding another war at all costs and became a leading English spokesman for a military alliance between Britain and Germany. Due to his fifth-column sensibilities (he attended a Nuremberg Party Rally in 1936), he was deemed a security risk and would wallow in a British gaol for the better part of the war. At the dinner, Ribbentrop stressed that he had "done [his] best and suggested some sort of formal demonstration whereby the four great powers could provide a show of good will. Nothing helped".[22] An English guest complained that the press was the biggest threat to peace between Germany and England, because "three-quarters" of the media were in the "hands of Jews" and "without the press" one could "make no politics even in England".[23] After retiring to his hotel room, Blunck noted that the situation regarding Jewish-influence in the media was "[a]uch hier wie in Paris".[24] This was an example of the anti-Semitism that suffused the outlook of both the poet and the Nazi sympathizers with whom he now surrounded himself. Relative to the effusions of a rabid Jew hater like Julius Streicher, the poet's was a much more subtle prejudice, which crept to the surface only on occasion and in opaque terms. Though less vulgar, his was no less sinister: if only the Jews were sidelined or somehow eliminated, he believed, the Anglo-German alliance would transpire.

After nearly a week in London, Blunck returned home without having made much progress. Although his alliance never transpired, his experiences nonetheless demonstrated that there were Britons with pro-German sympathies – first and foremost Evans, who was interested in "fair play" and "removing

[19] Blunck: *Lebensbericht*. P. 372.
[20] Blunck: *Tagebuch*. June 30, 1937.
[21] Ibid.
[22] Ibid.
[23] Ibid.
[24] Ibid.

misunderstanding of Germany",[25] but also others like Lord Lothian and Domville. Blunck appealed to appeasers. His gentlemanly, intellectual air contrasted with the crudity of most Nazi officials. Able to speak some English, he passed well in polite society. When he appeared at gatherings, Englishmen already favorable towards Germany could assure themselves that here, in this serious, but amiable poet was the country's true face. The media headlines about violence and anti-Jewish pogroms and the photos of black-booted storm troopers were but propaganda. Blunck was the international façade behind which the regime hid. Unfortunately, his cover was not good enough. The apparitions of Evans and Domville notwithstanding, Nazi sympathizers were too few and far between.

Paris: "Always a Disappointment"

Given the growing chasm between Germany's and Britain's artistic circles, Blunck's attitude to England was surprisingly positive throughout his trip in 1937. Upon arriving in Southampton, he noted how "schön" everything was: "durchaus nicht überladen, wie es nach den Bildern schien. Die gelben Schornsteine der Royal Mail, die rot-schwarzen der Cunard leuchten in der Sonne".[26] Similarly, the food was "ungewöhnlich sorgfältig" at the banquet following his arrival in London in June 1937 and the new German embassy "reichhaltig" and "mit guten alten Gemälden schön".[27] A few days later, Blunck and his wife dined with Evans at the Royal Empire Club, which "war gut, wohlausgerüstet mit einer vorzüglichen Bücherei über die Kolonien (und mit einem australischen Wein, der gut schmeckte)".[28] The "Germanic isle", united with Germany via the language and blood of the "Anglo-Saxons", shone brightly in the poet's eyes, regardless of circumstance.

The contrast to Paris could not have been starker. After arriving in June 1935 for the first of his two visits, the poet lamented his surroundings: "Rundgang Champs Elysées. Paris bleibt, vielleicht weil man seine Erwartungen hoch spannt, immer eine Enttäuschung. Die Kaffeehäuser, das 'Diane,' das Zeitungsviertel, der Triumpfbogen – alles etwas alt und allzuoft bestaunt".[29] So began his trip, and so remained his tenor. A subtle, yet pervasive anti-French sentiment – one that he seemed unable to suppress – colored his visits to the city.

Blunck's bias against France notwithstanding, friendships with writers and other figures in the country had always been important to him. France was the

---

[25] Collison to Blunck. May 31, 1934. Blunck-Collison Correspondence # 14.
[26] Blunck: *Tagebuch*. June 30, 1937.
[27] Ibid.
[28] Ibid.
[29] Blunck: *Tagebuch*. June 14, 1935.

strongest power on the continent, and this was cause enough for such an interest. However, Blunck also had a genuine attraction to international friendships of all kinds, not least in France, where his mother had once lived. Of course, this was especially the case, if these friendships were based on *his* Germanic-centered understanding of the world and helped achieve Germany's "rightful" place in Europe. In the late 1920s Blunck had organized exchange courses and trips for French students to the University of Hamburg similar to those for English students. Ironically, these courses attracted more attendees, and some two-dozen French students had joined the program in the summer of 1928.

Of the French PEN-Club members, Blunck was closest to Jules Romains. Like Blunck, Romains was interested in prehistoric finds, something that greatly impressed the poet. In conversations at PEN-Club meetings, Romains discussed the origins of his racial stock, the Celts, and Blunck covered the northern German foundations of the Germanic tribes. Another Frenchman whom Blunck befriended was Maurice Boucher, a Parisian Germanist who appreciated the historical significance of Blunck's native northern Germany.[30] Beginning in 1930, the two collaborated as editors of the *Revue d'Allemagne*, along with Romains. An additional colleague of Blunck was René Poupart, a young Germanist at the University of Bordeaux, whom Blunck befriended in 1928 when Poupart was working on his study, *Die Märchendichtung von Hans Friedrich Blunck*. Poupart became a disciple of Blunck – a French specialist in Lower-German fairy tales – and was his close comrade at PEN-Club gatherings.

Similar to his wishes in Britain later the same year, Blunck hoped that his old friendships in France would help smooth the way for his present incarnation as a "Nazi poet". That June of 1935, he and a number of other Nazi *Literati* were in Paris for an international gathering hosted by the French Academy of Writers. For the poet and his colleagues the visit had special importance. They aimed to showcase members of the "new" Prussian Academy, whose purge of the likes of Heinrich Mann and Arnold Zweig was still very much on the minds of European writers everywhere, not least the conference's French hosts. Blunck and his associates sought to legitimate themselves and demonstrate that the exiles – the most prominent among whom were the very same writers that had been ejected from the Academy – were not true representatives of German culture. This was, no doubt, a difficult task. Blunck's amity with Romains and Boucher (both of whom attended the gathering) notwithstanding, the French made it even more so.

Events irritated Blunck from the start. The "welcoming" speech of Archbishop Baudvillac of the Sorbonne (whom Blunck otherwise appreciated

---

[30] Maurice Boucher. Testimonial at Blunck's Denazification Trial, 1949. In: Blunck-Boucher Correspondence # 10.

for his racially striking "hartes Normannengesicht"[31]) on the "prépondérance Française en Europe" since the time of Cardinal Richelieu, who had founded the French Academy, horrified him: "ein ungeheurer, ein wilder, ein maßloser Chauvinismus von Anfang bis zu Ende, verklärend über die Gestalt Richelieus gebreitet. Das war eine Lehre. ... Es sei das wahre Herz Frankreichs, sagte man mir".[32] During the subsequent three days of meetings and talks, which Blunck complained were "sehr schlecht organisiert", everyone but the Germans was asked to give speeches. Blunck became so indignant that he began to view his hosts via the battle lines of the Great War (which was often on his mind): "Durch die Säle, hier etwas geredet, da etwas geredet. Trug wie tags zuvor als einziger mein einsames eisernes Kreuz durch die fünfhundert Gäste, die alle einst meine Gegner waren".[33]

Finally, Blunck's turn came ("Am dritten Tag unseres Hierseins erinnerte sich Frankreich plötzlich der Deutschen"[34]). However, he was only permitted a few hours to prepare and, unlike other guests, was required to give his talk in French: "Die französische Akademie verlangt die Ansprache heute, Donnerstag abend, in französischer Sprache. Wir werden beim nächsten Kongress in Berlin auch deutsche Ansprachen erbitten".[35] If this were not enough, the poet had to provide beforehand a copy of his speech to the president of the French Academy for review, to make sure that the president had enough time to read it, and to be mindful of the fact that the president needed time to write his own speech! The French were unwilling to risk a Nazi diatribe. As Blunck noted in his diary, the "Sonderbarkeit" of the situation was troubling, but he decided against making a fuss: "in diesen Tagen [wären] Erörterungen nicht gut".[36] To lend insult to injury, when Blunck went to take his assigned seat at the banquet where he was to speak, he discovered that it was occupied by the French Minister of Education. Embarrassed, he meandered through the tables, bumbling about until he found a free spot near the podium.

According to Blunck's diary, Boucher told him that his was one of the best speeches – that the applause was second only to that for the French Academy's president. However, Boucher, who genuinely liked Blunck, was probably just being polite. The whole experience left the poet saddened. As was his custom, he blamed the newspapers: "die Zeitungen sind entsetzlich. Man kann nicht an wirkliche Unkenntnis glauben, so plump und dumm und hoffnungslos roh sind

---

[31] Blunck: *Tagebuch*. June 17, 1935.
[32] Ibid.
[33] Ibid.
[34] Ibid.
[35] Ibid.
[36] Ibid.

die Vorstellungen über Deutschland".[37] His only consolation lay in the diplomatic isolation that France was now experiencing due to the recent Anglo-German Naval Agreement. With its stipulation that Germany's fleet could equal one third of the British, the pact granted Germany the right to build warships as fast as possible:

> Frankreich durchlebt seine schwersten Tage: Die Lösung Englands aus dem Schlepp. Es kann nicht begreifen. Vielleicht liegt seine neue europäische Mission in einer Zeit, wo es wieder gleich neben gleich steht, statt sich von der Trunkenheit der tausend Lobsprüche wiegen zu lassen.[38]

One of the things that irritated Blunck most during this trip was French ignorance of Germany's "new" literature – that is, the neo-Romantic, "blood and soil" kitsch now being promoted by the Nazi state. In a conversation with Boucher, he was shocked that this ostensible "Germanist" had "keine Ahnung von der neuen deutschen Literatur. Beumelburg, Ina Seidel – alles unbekannt".[39] Blunck had two villains for this oversight: The French press, which did nothing to promote Germany's authors, and the emigrants, who were doing everything in their power to spoil anything related to National Socialism. The formalities and shallow pleasantries of the conference were wearing on the poet, and he was happy when it ended.

Blunck's second trip, almost exactly two years later, was hardly better. Upon arriving in Paris in late June 1937, his mood darkened again: "Man muß in Paris immer die ersten Stunden überwinden. Die Stadt ist verstaubt, die Straßen brauchen Sonne, damit die graue und oft entblätterte Farbe freundlicher wird".[40] This time, Blunck should have had more reason to be optimistic. He and his Nazi friends were in Paris for a "German-French Congress" hosted by the *Comité France-Allemagne*. In 1935, as it became clear that the Nazi government was not going anywhere, a number of French writers, intellectuals, and officials – including Poupart and Romains – had decided that the time had come to establish informal ties with the "new" Germany and collaborate with Nazi writers. The *Comité France-Allemagne*, which was conceived as the French counterpart to the DAW's "German-French Society", was thus born.

After arriving on the train from Hamburg, Blunck hurried off to meet with Boucher. He had high hopes that his friend might have learned something about Germany's "contemporary" writers in the intervening two years. However, Boucher disappointed him – indeed, his knowledge of the subject had actually declined. The circumstance should have come as no surprise. The year

---

[37] Blunck: *Tagebuch*. June 14, 1935.
[38] Blunck: *Tagebuch*. June 17, 1935.
[39] Blunck: *Tagebuch*. June 23, 1935.
[40] Blunck: *Tagebuch*. June 26, 1937.

before, Boucher had dropped a plan (heavily promoted by Blunck) to translate the poet's fairy tales. Boucher's publisher complained that there was a "Nazi who hides behind the poet" (i.e., Blunck).[41] Thereafter, Boucher distanced himself from such material. Indeed, his friendship with Blunck threatened to ruin his academic career and would result in an unexpected transfer to a lesser position a couple of years later. In the hopes that he would take the time to read them, Blunck nonetheless gave Boucher a list of new Academy members. The circumstance tormented Blunck, since French bookstores were filled, as he complained, with emigrant works like Heinrich Mann's "sinnloses Haßbuch" *Der Tag kommt*.[42]

As president of the DAW, Blunck had by 1937 become one of the most prominent spokesmen for Nazi culture, and he gave a number of speeches at the gathering in Paris. In one, he criticized French "Hetzbücher" (agitation literature), a term that can be interpreted as meaning just about all publications critical of the Third Reich, and asked that his listeners help put an end to such "propaganda". He also called for increased sales of German books in France. German literature, in his view, was a seemingly objective bulwark against anti-German bias. In a speech two days later, he emphasized his main gripes regarding French neglect of the "new" German literature:

1) Daß die jungen Germanisten wenig von der heutigen jungen Literatur des Reichs erführen.
2) Die "Männer der Presse", die im Gegensatz zu der sorgfältigen deutschen Berichterstattung keine Ahnung von neuer deutscher Literatur hätten.

Blunck's characterization of reportage in the Germany of 1937 as "sorgfältig" spoke volumes about his talent for self-delusion.

In a notable (and from the poet's point of view incredibly irritating) coincidence, the international PEN-Club was having its annual meeting across town. A few of the "emigrants" were even staying at Blunck's hotel. Given that there is no record, one can only imagine the conversations or at least looks of mutual disdain that must have transpired in the lobby or halls of the hotel. The PEN-Club lambasted the "Nazi" Congress in its midst, and the French press ran stories exposing the German-French Society as an arm of the Nazi propaganda machine. Blunck and his colleagues found Paris staring down at them as a cabal of Nazi henchmen. In concluding comments before the German-French Congress, the poet lamented "[d]ie verlorene Fühlung mit dem französischen Schrifttum, das – und wir seien tief verletzt – in dieser Stunde unsere Emigranten im PEN-Club zu Gast habe".[43] In classic Blunckian hyperbole, he

---

[41] Blunck: *Tagebuch*. October 26, 1936.
[42] Ibid.
[43] Blunck: *Tagebuch*. June 23, 1937.

added: "Wir waren wegen der französischen Emigranten einst nach Valmy marschiert. Ob Frankreich wegen unserer Emigranten den gleichen Fehler machen wolle?".[44]

Complications of this kind proved the rule. Not long after the congress ended, France's Foreign Minister, Joseph Paul-Boncour, suppressed French organizations, like the *Comité France-Allemagne*, that collaborated with the German-French Society. In 1938, Communist delegates in the French National Assembly succeeded in having the main propaganda vehicle of the Society, the *Deutsch-Französische Monatshefte*, banned from public libraries and universities. In 1939, the French government prevented another "German-French Congress" from taking place in France.[45] Blunck's efforts to improve relations between the two countries via the DAW had proven fruitless.

Conclusion

Blunck did not return to France until 1940, in the wake of the German victory. Needless to say, this third visit proved more enjoyable. With the German army occupying the country and his antagonists silent or gone, he felt perfectly at home. Nazi writers were now as welcome as ever, and he toured Paris in a blissful mood: "Ich gehe, wie so gern, noch still für mich eine Stunde in den Sonnenschein der Champs Elysées, setze mich in ein Kaffeehaus [...]. Ein verrücktes Bild: Die Kaffees sind voll von 'Landsern' [*i.e.*, Landsherrn] aber ich bin in Paris! Ist es nicht alles ein Traum?".[46] His next visit to Britain did not occur until much later, in the 1950s. By this time, some of the enmities of the 1930s had started to wane, but the poet's old rapport with the island never truly re-emerged. Ould's death in 1951 left their friendship forever in disrepair. After the war, he had criticized Blunck harshly for his help to the Nazis.

Looking for respect and recognition, Blunck nonetheless continued to travel to other European countries after 1937, in the hopes of gaining a "fair" hearing for Germany's "new" writers and political interests. Copenhagen, Bucharest, Budapest. Prague, Sophia, Warsaw, Stockholm, Rome – these were but a few of the myriad metropoles he visited, some of them more than once. Rome was more receptive than Paris, Budapest more congenial than London, and he always received favorable responses from the numerous German expatriots he engaged – or *Auslandsdeutsche*, as he and Nazi officialdom called them. In the end, however, a certain discomfort plagued even these trips. He was now a Nazi ambassador, and, most places he went, the writers and other figures he had known before 1933 betrayed an air of distance. As a Nazi, he had changed, and

[44] Ibid.
[45] Vorstandssitzung of the German-French Society. January 26, 1939. German-French Society Correspondence (CB 92, 107).
[46] Blunck: *Tagebuch*. July 22, 1940.

therefore his old relationships had changed. When abroad, Blunck was an "exile" – at least from the associations he had enjoyed before 1933.

This sense of "exile" returned home with a vengeance after the war. Following his six-month internment in a British POW camp in 1945, the poet discovered that local farmers were vying to parcel his beloved Mölenhoff estate in Holstein. Many of them believed, not without some logic, that Hitler had given the farm to Blunck as a gift. He was also stripped of his publishing rights.[47] In 1947, British occupation authorities destroyed 30,000 volumes of his works being stored in warehouses. Blunck was also forbidden to give lectures and readings. In 1949, a denazification court, to which a number of former exiles sent testimonies, categorized him as a *Mitläufer* (i.e., one who attached his name to the regime and benefited significantly thereby) and fined him 10,000 marks. Although he was allowed to publish thereafter, newspapers that carried positive reviews of his books received barrages of complaints. Protests interrupted the few readings he was invited to give. As he noted in the unpublished third volume of his memoirs, "das große Verschweigen, der andere Teil der 'Entnazifizierung' begann".[48]

In an attempt to rehabilitate himself, Blunck sometimes characterized his DAW work as an effort to promote the German language abroad. The reaction of Thomas Mann was symptomatic of the response the poet received from numerous exiles after 1945 and is worth quoting:

> Is so much blindness possible? Is such a lack of perspective and feeling for the atrociousness that was going on permissible to an intellectual person? ... [T]he "Teaching of German Abroad"? Every child in the wide world knew what was meant by the euphemism, namely the undermining everywhere of the strength of the democratic opposition, its demoralization through Nazi Propaganda. Only the German writer did not know this.[49]

Although it is true that the DAW and associated organizations were involved in funding German language classes, the substance of Mann's commentary – that Blunck was complicit in a corrupt effort to gain international support for a murderous regime and weaken opposition to it, particularly that of the exiles – was spot on.

Some readers may take exception to the admittedly creative use of the term "exile" employed in this essay. However, if "exile" suggests "homelessness", if it embodies an endless search for acceptance, if it represents a dramatic transformation in social status, and, finally, if it implies – at least for some of the

---

[47] Actions against Blunck's books and publication rights were reported at his denazification trial. Sitzungsprotokoll. Captured German Documents Filmed at Berlin. Reichskulturkammer (T580). Blunck Reel. P. 1262.
[48] Blunck: *Lebensbericht.* 3 (unpublished). P. 513 and P. 529.
[49] Mann to Blunck. July 22, 1946. Blunck-Mann Correspondence.

less fortunate émigrés – constant travel, then a vast stretch of the imagination is not required, particularly in this post-modernist world, to understand why the term has been applied to Blunck here. The poet was not an "exile" in the conventional sense. However, his repeated sojourns abroad do intimate an acute estrangement, one that other Nazi writers may well have endured when traveling abroad during the period after 1933, though a great deal of more work needs to be done on the subject. The term "exile", particularly in the context of a volume on conventional exiles, can symbolize this outcast status. In this essay, it has intended to do so.

Blunck's trips exhibited important characteristics of the Third Reich. First and foremost, the Nazi government had a genuine interest in using culture to heighten Germany's international standing. The dissolution of the German PEN-Division, the emigration of some of Germany's greatest intellectuals and artists – these were all circumstances, Hitler and his cronies knew, that worked against Germany's international interests. Attempting to mend fences, to rebuild relations on the artistic level, to create new artistic organizations to replace those that had been lost – such efforts were no mere sideshow. As this brief essay has suggested, a subtle European-wide conflict preceded World War II, pitting the German exiles, or at least those who were sympathetic to them, against the efforts of a rising Nazi literary establishment to legitimize itself internationally and help validate the new German government. The key role Blunck played in this campaign was not surprising. His prior involvement in the PEN and numerous international connections meant that he had tools with which to fight the exiles. Although his reception in both England and France proved cool, particularly in the latter, this essay's documentation of individuals (Evans in London, Boucher in Paris, for example) and formal organizations (like the "Anglo-German Link" and the *Comité France-Allemagne*) willing to listen to the German point of view demonstrate that the Nazi effort was not one-sided. The fact that Blunck could engage numerous writers and other dignitaries in no less than a full-fledged "German-French Congress" in Paris in 1937 suggests at the very least that the experience of German arts and letters abroad in the 1930s has not been fully developed or understood.

Many of the attitudes Blunck exhibited during his trips were characteristic of Nazi affectations – the preference for England over France, the fascination with "Germanic" racial characteristics, the obsession with the battle lines of World War I, the belief that "Germanic" nations instinctively gravitated towards one another. In this sense, he represented the artistic embodiment of Nazi ideological pretensions. Certainly, he was not as crass as a Hitler, Himmler, Goebbels, or Rosenberg. Nor can he be directly implicated in the genocidal crimes of the regime. But he was fundamental to National Socialism, at least in its international apparition.

Primavera Driessen Gruber

Traveltalks in Music – Von Mahlers *Lieder eines fahrenden Gesellen* zu Eislers *Hollywooder Liederbuch* und darüber hinaus

Gustav Mahler's Lieder eines fahrenden Gesellen *and* Hanns Eisler's Hollywood Songbook, *both of which were inspired by Franz Schubert's famous song cycle* Winterreise, *stand in the romantic 'Lied' tradition. Focussing on these two song cycles, this article refers to some of the leading personalities of the reform movements in Vienna's musical life during the first half of the 20th century, encouraged by Gustav Mahler's presence and creative work in Vienna. Hitler's coming to power in Germany and the Austrian 'Anschluss' in 1938 brought the experiments of the musical avant-garde to an end – most of its protagonists had to flee into exile. But also Jewish composers and musicians rooted in late-Romantic tradition shared the same fate. A representative of this other group is the Lied-composer Eric Zeisl, who eventually was able to make a living in Hollywood writing music for a series of travel films, James FitzPatrick's* Traveltalks.

Examining these musical examples enables us to compare 'travel' and 'exile' as 'topoi' in music production. Both categories imply departure, crossing boundaries, transcultural experiences and the breaking of new ground. What distinguishes exile from travel is the mortal danger – also for relatives and friends left behind – that make people leave their home, their country, the hardships and existential fears that accompany this threat, and the doubtful prospect of returning home.

When there is no hope of return, other means of belonging, other ways of building a new identity are to be found, and in positive cases creative energy is set free and something new is created. But the profound rupture caused by nazi persecution and exile, both in the refugees' individual biographies and in Austrian cultural history, remains visible for many generations.

This essay explores how the composers mentioned here dealt with the experience of travel and exile, how it is reflected in their work and what consequences it had for the reception of their music.

Dr. Primavera Driessen Gruber, born 1951 in The Hague, Netherlands,
essayist and specialist in Austrian music exile, lives and works in Vienna, Austria.
orpheustrust@chello.at
www.orpheustrust.at

Prolog: *Die Novaks aus Prag*

In diesem Beitrag wird untersucht, wie einzelne Musikschaffende mit den Erfahrungen des Reisens und des Exils umgegangen sind, wie sich diese in ihrem Werk spiegeln und welche Folgen Reisen und Exil für die Rezeption ihrer Werke hatten. Als 'Ecksätze' dienen Gustav Mahlers *Lieder eines fahrenden Gesellen* und Hanns Eislers *Hollywooder Liederbuch*, dazwischen werden die Themen in mehreren miteinander verflochtenen Erzählsträngen variiert. Ein roter Faden bildet dabei die Ausstrahlung Mahlers auf die nachkommenden Generationen, die ihrerseits unmittelbar mit Vertreibung und Exil konfrontiert waren. Der Arbeit des Exilkomponisten Eric Zeisl für James A. FitzPatricks' Reisefilme *Traveltalks* in den MGM-Filmstudios in Hollywood, die den Komponisten in eine tiefe Depression stürzen sollte, verdankt der Beitrag seinen Titel. Dabei weist der – auf dem ersten Blick neutrale – Titel gleichzeitig voraus auf die Verzweiflung dieses Exilanten, der als Produzent von kommerzieller Gebrauchsmusik für Reisefilme sein Brot verdienen musste. Denn in der Gegenüberstellung der verwendeten Musikbeispiele werden sowohl das Verbindende als das Trennende der Topoi 'Reisen' und 'Exil' sichtbar: Beiden sind der Abschied und die Erkundung von 'Neuland' inhärent; beide implizieren Grenzüberschreitungen und sind mit transkulturellen Prozessen verbunden. Was das Exil jedoch grundlegend vom Reisen unterscheidet, sind die Lebensgefahr (auch für die zurückgebliebenen Angehörigen), die mit der Bedrohung einhergehenden existentiellen Ängste und die unsichere Aussicht auf eine Rückkehr.

Für die deutschsprachigen NS-Flüchtlinge in New York gehörte das Lied mit dem Titel *Die Novaks aus Prag* zu den Schlagern der Saison 1941–1942.[1] Die liebenswürdige Familie Novak aus Prag, wie sie vom Prager Universalgenie der Unterhaltungsbranche Kurt Robitschek (Prag 1890 – New York 1950, Exil USA) erfunden und vom Wiener Klavierhumoristen Hermann Leopoldi (Wien 1888 – Wien 1959, Exil USA) – "the world famous Viennese composer and Master of Songs at the piano" – und seiner in den USA geborenen Partnerin Helly Möslein – "sweet singer of sweet songs from Vienna"[2] – in 'Eberhardt's Café Grinzing' in New York besungen wurde, soll diesem Beitrag als kleine Vignette zu Reisen und Exil, zu Fern- und Heimweh, vorangestellt werden.

Die Novaks aus Prag[3]

Sie kennen die Novaks, die Novaks aus Prag, sie haben sie sicher gekannt:
Ein Gansl bei Novaks am Sonntag in Prag berühmt war im böhmischen Land.
Gewohnt hab'n die Novaks am Altstädter Ring, die Wohnung war stets aufgeräumt,
der einzige Fehler, den Novaks gehabt, sie waren so schrecklich verträumt.

---

[1] Christian Klösch und Regina Thumser: *From Vienna. Exilkabarett in New York 1938 bis 1950*. Wien: Picus Verlag 2002. S. 32.
[2] Programmzettel für Eberhardt's Café Grinzing, New York, nach 1941. In: Klösch und Thumser (wie Anm. 1).
[3] Die Novaks aus Prag. Text: Kurt Robitschek Musik: Hermann Leopoldi. Wien: Musikverlag Doblinger 1950. Bestell-Nr. 89086. Dem Wienerliedsänger Ingomar Kmentt danke ich für die rasche Zusendung, dem Verlag Doblinger für die Zustimmung zum Abdruck des Textes.

Es träumte der Leo
von Montevideo,
von Damen, die flüstern: "Seniore,
die Nacht ist gemacht für Amore"
die Tante, die Anna,
die träumt von Havanna.
Die Sehnsucht vom Jüngsten
ist ein Stierkampf in Lisbon zu Pfingsten,
die Köchin Marianka
träumt von Casablanca,
die Tochter, die Mali,
träumt von Tänzen in Bali,
von Shanghai und Bombay:
Wie schön ist die Welt!
Die Novaks, die träumen
in den eigenen Räumen
von einer Sehnsucht,
der herrlichen Welt.

Der Fußtritt der Zeit hat die Novaks gekickt, sie wurden aus Träumen geweckt
Man hatte den böhmischen Löwen verkauft, die Gansln, die hab'n sich versteckt
Marschierende Schritte, ein Führer ein Volk, da hat man im Schnellzug geseh'n
die Wrbas, die Krejčis, die Bilis, die Krčs, doch was ist mit den Novaks gescheh'n?

Es sitzt jetzt der Leo
in Montevideo
er denkt nicht mehr an die Senioras,
er hat jetzt ganz andere Zoras[4]
Die Tante, die Anna,
die sitzt in Havanna
und wartet auf Arthur, den Jüngsten,
weil der Dampfer von Lisbon kommt Pfingsten.
Die Köchin Marianka
sitzt in Casablanca,
die Tochter, die Mali,
hat kein Visum von Bali
nach Shanghai und Bombay,
und lang wird der Tag.
Die Novaks, die träumen
in gemieteten Räumen
von einem Ort nur,
sie träumen von Prag.

[4] "Zores haben": Jüdisch-Wienerischer Jargon für "Probleme haben".

Das Fernweh der gutbürgerlich-jüdischen Familie Novak im Prag vor dem deutschen Einmarsch wird in diesem Schlager kontrastiert mit der Exilsituation, die so gar nicht mit den früheren Träumen übereinstimmt. Aus den 'Reisen im Kopf' ist bedrückende Realität geworden. Leopoldis Publikum, die NS-Flüchtlinge in New York, konnten sich mit einem lachenden und einem weinenden Auge[5] mit diesen Novaks identifizieren. Hatte man nach einer abenteuerlichen Flucht den sicheren Hafen erreicht, so lebte man nun in einer fremden Umgebung, der nichts Exotisches mehr anhaftete, die aber auch wenig Vertrautes hatte, geplagt von Heimweh und Sorge um die Angehörigen. Zum Träumen blieb wenig Zeit: Aus Publikumslieblingen waren Bleistiftverkäufer[6] und Staubsaugervertreter, aus etablierten Komponisten Barpianisten und Notenkopisten, aus Söhnen und Töchtern 'aus gutem Haus' Laufburschen und Fabrikarbeiter geworden, die nun nebenbei versuchten, ihre im Heimatland erfolgreich angelaufene Karriere nicht ganz abreißen zu lassen. Und man hatte ja noch 'Glück gehabt', denn viele Familienangehörige waren zu Hause oder unterwegs stecken geblieben, wartend auf ein Visum, das sehr oft nicht mehr rechtzeitig kommen sollte.

Kurt Robitschek und Hermann Leopoldi wussten, wovon sie sangen. Der in Wien überaus populäre Klavierentertainer Hermann Leopoldi[7], der in Wirklichkeit Hermann Kohn hieß und Herschl genannt wurde, war kurz nach dem 'Anschluss' Österreichs an Hitler-Deutschland im März 1938 mit dem sog. 'Prominententransport' in das Konzentrationslager Dachau eingeliefert worden, später wurde er nach Buchenwald weiter deportiert. Er hatte noch rechtzeitig von seinem Ex-Schwiegervater ein Affidavit für die USA erhalten und war damit 'freigekauft' worden. Sein Bruder Ferdinand dagegen blieb als 'U-Boot' in Wien zurück und wurde 1944 verhaftet; nach einem Verhör durch die Gestapo starb er an einem Herzschlag. Dem Texter, Schauspieler, Regisseur und Gründer des berühmten 'Kabarett der Komiker' (KaDeKo) in Berlin, Kurt Robitschek (ab 1944 unter dem Namen Ken Robey), hatte es gleich nach der Machtergreifung Hitlers aus Berlin nach Prag und Wien verschlagen, wo er in den 'Kammerspielen' die 'Bühne des Lachens' gründete und bis Jahresende 1933 leitete. Bereits 1916 hatte er für Robert Stolz mit dem Text *Im Prater blüh'n wieder die Bäume* einen zeitlosen Werbeschlager für Wien verfasst. Nach Wien folgten mit Paris und London weitere Fluchtstationen, bevor er 1941 in New York mit dem ersten Auftreten des neugegründeten 'Kabarett der

---

[5] Vgl. Gerhard Bronner: *Tränen gelacht. Der jüdische Humor*. Wien: Amalthea 1999. S. 13.
[6] Zur Bezeichnung von Personengruppen, die beide Geschlechter umfassen, wird zur besseren Lesbarkeit des Textes nur die männliche Form verwendet.
[7] Informationen zu den im Folgenden erwähnten, vom NS-Regime verfolgten und aus Österreich vertriebenen Musikschaffenden stammen, wenn nicht anders erwähnt, aus der Forschungsdatenbank der Verfasserin: BioExil Datenbank Primavera Driessen Gruber.

Abb. 1: Hermann Leopoldi und Helly Möslein. © Ronald Leopoldi/Verein Orpheus Trust.

Komiker' im Mecca Temple wieder zu einem Fixstern des Show- und Varietébetriebs deutschsprachiger Exilantenkreisen in den USA werden sollte.

Lieder eines fahrenden Gesellen

"Ich gehe, weil ich das Gesindel nicht mehr aushalten kann".[8]

So erklärte Gustav Mahler Mitte Juli 1907 in einem Schreiben an den Physiker Arnold Berliner seine bevorstehende Abreise in die Vereinigten Staaten von Amerika, wo er ein Engagement als Dirigent an der New Yorker Metropolitan

---

[8] Gustav Mahler an Arnold Berliner, Mitte Juli 1907. Zitiert nach Gerhard Scheit und Wilhelm Svoboda: *Feindbild Gustav Mahler. Zur antisemitischen Abwehr der Moderne in Österreich*. Wien: Sonderzahl 2002. S. 9.

Opera antreten sollte. Die Schönberg-Schüler Anton von Webern, Karl Horwitz, Paul Stefan (Exil Frankreich – USA) und Heinrich Jalowetz (Exil USA) hatten per Post eine Einladung an die kleine Gemeinde der Mahler-Freunde und -Verehrer in Wien gesendet, "sich zum Abschied am Montag, 4.9. vor ½ 9 Uhr früh am Perron des Westbahnhofs"[9] zu versammeln. Von hier aus ging es nach Cherbourg, wo Mahler sich auf den Passagierdampfer 'Kaiserin Augusta Victoria' nach New York einschiffen sollte. Ungefähr 200 Personen hatten der Einladung Folge geleistet, darunter, wie der Musiksoziologe und Mahler-Forscher Kurt Blaukopf (Exil Frankreich – Palästina) schreibt, "wohl ein entscheidender Teil des österreichischen Geistesparlaments".[10] Als 'Gesindel' bezeichnete Mahler die weit größere Gruppe seiner Feinde in Wien, die nichts unversucht gelassen hatte, ihm das Leben als Direktor der Wiener Hofoper schwer zu machen. Wie Blaukopf andeutet, spielte dabei auch der Wiener Antisemitismus eine Rolle. In *Feindbild Gustav Mahler. Zur antisemitischen Abwehr der Moderne in Österreich*[11] wird diese Hypothese an Hand der Mahler-Rezeption in Österreich nach 1918 differenziert und überzeugend bestätigt.[12]

Aber es gab für Musikschaffende immer auch andere Gründe, zu reisen und 'Abschied zu nehmen'. So erfordert eine Musikerkarriere häufig bereits im Ausbildungsstadium einen oder mehrere Ortswechsel. Der Musikerberuf, ob im klassischen oder im Unterhaltungsbereich, ist in der Regel mit einem Nomadenleben verbunden. Sowohl in ländlichen Gebieten als im urbanen Umfeld, ob als Wandermusikanten oder im Opern- und Konzertbetrieb, Musiker waren und sind 'fahrende Gesellen'.[13] Der im böhmischen Kalischt geborene und in Iglau (Iglava) aufgewachsene Mahler absolvierte seine Musikstudien am 'Conservatorium für Musik und darstellende Kunst der Gesellschaft der Musikfreunde in Wien', bevor er als Kapellmeister die übliche 'Ochsentour' vom Kurort Hall, über Laibach (Ljubljana), Olmütz (Olomouc), Kassel, Leipzig, Budapest und Hamburg zur Wiener Hofoper antrat. Auch als Dirigent und Promotor eigener Werke war er gezwungen zu reisen. Zu den wenigen Kompositionen, die bereits zu seinen Lebzeiten, beziehungsweise bis 1938 regelmäßig in Wien zur Aufführung kamen,

---

[9] Kurt Blaukopf: *Gustav Mahler. Sein Leben, sein Werk und seine Welt in zeitgenössischen Bildern und Texten*. Wien: Universal Edition 1976. S. 256.
[10] Kurt Blaukopf: *Gustav Mahler oder Der Zeitgenosse der Zukunft*. 2. Auflage. München – Kassel: dtv und Bärenreiter 1980. S. 235.
[11] Scheit und Svoboda (wie Anm. 8).
[12] Ebd.
[13] Vgl. dazu Primavera Gruber: Schule der Wahrnehmung: Orpheus Trust – Verein zur Erforschung und Veröffentlichung vertriebener und vergessener Kunst. In: *Quasi una fantasia. Juden und die Musikstadt Wien*. Hg. von Leon Botstein und Werner Hanak. Hofheim: Wolke 2003. S. 159–168.

gehören die *Lieder eines fahrenden Gesellen*, welche um 1884 in Kassel entstanden und 1897 sowohl in einer Klavier- als auch in einer Orchesterfassung veröffentlicht wurden. Mahler, der die Texte für diesen Liederzyklus wahrscheinlich teils aus *Des Knaben Wunderhorn* entnommen, teils selbst verfasst hatte, schrieb an seinen Jugendfreund Friedrich Löhr: "Die Lieder sind so zusammengedacht, als ob ein fahrender Gesell', der sein Schicksal gehabt, nun in die Welt hinauszieht, und so vor sich hinwandert [...]. Sie[14] ist alles, was liebenswert auf dieser Welt ist. Ich möchte jeden Blutstropfen für sie hingeben. Aber ich weiß doch, dass ich fort muss [...]".[15]

Wenn es im vierten Lied heißt:

Die zwei blauen Augen von meinem Schatz,
Die haben mich in die weite Welt geschickt.
Da musst ich Abschied nehmen
Vom allerliebsten Platz!

fügen sich Text und Musik in eine romantische Liedtradition, in der das 'gehabte Schicksal' – Trennung nach schmerzvoller Liebeserfahrung, auf die Mahler im Schreiben an seinen Jugendfreund etwas voreilig, da es in Wirklichkeit doch noch ein 'happy end' geben sollte, hinweist – gleichzeitig Chiffre für ein 'in die Welt hinaus gestoßen sein', für Abschied und Einsamkeit ist.

Ich bin ausgegangen in stiller Nacht,
In stiller Nacht wohl über die dunkle Heide.
Hat mir niemand ade gesagt ...

Bekanntestes Beispiel für diese 'Reise- und Wanderliteratur' in der Musik[16] ist wohl Franz Schuberts Liederzyklus *Winterreise*, 1827 nach Gedichten von Wilhelm Müller entstanden, die dem jungen Mahler unüberhörbare Inspirationsquelle war. So ist es wohl auch kein Zufall, dass gerade das berühmte Lied

---

[14] Hier: Die nicht namentlich genannte, von Mahler verehrte Person.
[15] Gustav Mahler an Friedrich Löhr, Kassel, 1. Jänner 1885. In: *Gustav Mahler. Briefe 1879–1911*. Hg. von A.M. Mahler. Wien: Zsolnay 1924. S. 39. Zitiert nach Kurt Blaukopf: *Gustav Mahler. Sein Leben, sein Werk und seine Welt in zeitgenössischen Bildern und Texten*. Wien: Universal Edition 1976. S. 171.
[16] Der Terminus wird hier quasi 'avant la lettre' verwendet. Anders als in der Literatur findet sich im deutschsprachigen Raum in der Musik bisher ein Genre 'Reise- und Wandermusik' im hier verwendeten Sinne nicht. Weder sind das Kunstlied oder andere Formen der Kunstmusik, welche das Wandern und Reisen zum Gegenstand haben (so z.B. Franz Liszts *Années de Pélérinage* für Klavier) unter einem gemeinsamen Gattungsbegriff in die musikalische Formenlehre eingegangen, noch werden sog. 'Wander- und Fahrtenlieder', darunter die sog. 'Auswandererlieder' oder die neuere 'road music' zusammen mit oben genannten Formen unter einer solchen Gattung subsumiert.

Der Lindenbaum aus Schuberts *Winterreise* bei Mahler zitiert wird: In Mahlers Bild des 'schneienden' Lindenbaums scheint sich trotz der unterschiedlichen Jahreszeit die Reminiszenz an Schuberts 'Winterreise' poetisch zu verdichten und hoffnungsvoll in die Zukunft zu weisen.

> Auf der Straße stand ein Lindenbaum
> Da hab' ich zum ersten Mal im Schlaf geruht!
> Unter dem Lindenbaum, der hat seine Blüten
> Über mich geschneit, da wusst' ich nicht, wie das Leben tut,
> War alles, ach alles wieder gut!
> Alles! Alles! Lieb und Leid!
> Und Welt und Traum!

In der letzten Textzeile werden Reminiszenzen zum Liederzyklus *Dichterliebe* op. 48 von Robert Schumann, nach Texten von Heinrich Heine, geweckt:

> Ach, könnt ich dorthin kommen,
> Und dort mein Herz erfreun,
> [...]
> Ach! Jenes Land der Wonne
> Das seh' ich oft im Traum ...[17]

Auch hier findet sich die Sehnsucht nach Aufbruch in eine 'andere, bessere Welt', die nur im Traum zu existieren scheint, eines der Merkmale der Romantik. Im Lied lässt sie sich in der Verwendung poetischer Texte voller schroffer Gegensätze und einfacher, volksliedhafter Melodik festmachen. Wenn der Spätromantiker Mahler, dessen reiferes Schaffen bereits in die Zukunft weist, seine *Lieder eines fahrenden Gesellen* später als 'Burlesken' bezeichnet[18], so ist diese Bezeichnung nicht nur als nachträgliche Relativierung von frühen Kompositionsversuchen und jugendlichem Weltschmerz, sondern wohl auch unter dem Aspekt des 'unter Tränen Lachen' des jüdischen Humors zu verstehen,[19] getragen von der Hoffnung auf bessere Zeiten, auf ein 'Nächstes Jahr in Jerusalem'.

Die Orchesterfassung dieser Lieder wurde von den Wiener Philharmonikern und der Opernsängerin Selma von Halban-Kurz, von Mahler 1899 an die Wiener Oper geholt, bereits am 14. Januar 1900 zur Aufführung gebracht.[20] (Selmas Tochter Desirée, unter Mahlers früherem Assistenten, dem Dirigenten

---

[17] Aus: Heinrich Heine: *Lyrisches Intermezzo* (1822–1823). Nr. 43.
[18] Vgl. Therese Muxeneder: *Gustav Mahler: Lieder eines fahrenden Gesellen (1920). Bearbeitung für kleines Ensemble. Einführung.* http://www.schoenberg.at/6_archiv/music/works/no_op/compositions_Bearbeitungen_Mahler_notes.htm.
[19] Vgl. Bronner (wie Anm. 5).
[20] Kurt Blaukopf: *Gustav Mahler. Sein Leben, sein Werk und seine Welt in zeitgenössischen Bildern und Texten.* Wien: Universal Edition 1976. S. 223.

Bruno Walter (Exil USA) ebenfalls eine beliebte Mahler-Sängerin, hatte 1937 den niederländischen Kunsthändler Jacques Goudstikker geheiratet, der auf dem Weg ins Exil verstarb. Sie selbst erreichte über Großbritannien und Kanada 1942 New York). Gustav Mahler hatte als 'Symphoniker' im Ausland mehr Erfolg als in Wien: Zu seinen Lebzeiten wurden seine Symphonien in Deutschland, Frankreich, den Niederlanden, Finnland, den USA und Russland, in Budapest, Prag und Basel aufgeführt. In Amsterdam hatte sich unter dem Dirigenten des Concertgebouworkest Willem Mengelberg, der sich später dem Vorwurf der Kollaboration mit den deutschen Besatzern aussetzen sollte, eine begeisterte Mahler-Gemeinde gebildet. Nachdem Mahler 1903 seine *Dritte Symphonie* mit diesem Orchester in Amsterdam dirigiert hatte, und ein Jahr später seine *Vierte* sogar zweimal an einem Abend, einmal unter dem Komponisten selbst, einmal unter Mengelberg, im Concertgebouw aufgeführt worden war,[21] schien sich seine Musik durchgesetzt zu haben. Das in Amsterdam 1920 veranstaltete Mahler-Fest war dafür ein eindruckvoller Beweis.[22]

Wien war anders. "Die Euphorie über das Wien des fin-de-siècle und des frühen 20. Jahrhunderts soll uns nicht zu Illusionen verleiten: Das Wiener Publikum war immer reaktionär – und ist es noch immer", so der Museumskurator und Kunstsammler Dieter Bogner in einer Podiumsdiskussion anlässlich des 85jährigen Jubiläums der *Internationalen Gesellschaft für neue Musik* (IGNM; ISCM – Austrian Section).[23] So ist der Zusammenschluss zur IGNM in einer Linie mit den Reformbewegungen der Musikgeschichte der ersten Hälfte des 20. Jahrhunderts zu sehen, die auf das Wirken Gustav Mahlers in Wien zurück zu führen sind: Sie kann als eine der 'Nachfolgeorganisationen' der 1904 von Alexander Zemlinsky (Exil USA), Arnold Schönberg (Exil USA), Bruno Walter (Exil USA) und Karl Weigl (Exil USA) in Wien gegründeten *Vereinigung schaffender Tonkünstler*, deren Ehrenpräsident Gustav Mahler war, bezeichnet werden.

Dieser Verein mit dem Zweck, der zeitgenössischen Musik ein Podium zu bieten, war nur kurz aktiv; nachhaltiger konnte sich die Wirkung von Schönbergs *Verein für musikalische Privataufführungen* entfalten. 1918 gegründet, stellte sich jener Verein zum Ziel, "Musikwerke aus der Zeit 'Mahler bis jetzt' seinen Mitgliedern allwöchentlich vorzuführen".[24] Zwar musste die Konzerttätigkeit aufgrund finanzieller Schwierigkeiten bereits 1921 wieder eingestellt werden,

---

[21] Otto Glastra van Loon: *Onder de stenen lier. Het Concertgebouworkest. Lief, leed en luim in tachtig jaar samenspel van wereldberoemde muziekmakers*. Amsterdam: Ploegstra 1969. S. 58.
[22] Vgl. auch Scheit und Svoboda (wie Anm. 8).
[23] 85 Jahre IGNM. Musikfest IGNM Österreich 1.-7. Oktober 2007.
[24] Alban Berg in einem Brief an seine Frau Helene vom 1. Juli 1918. Zitiert nach: http://www.schoenberg.at/6_archiv/verein/verein_quellen.htm.

aber aus dem Mitgliederkreis (320 Mitglieder) hatte sich ein kompetentes und interessiertes Publikum gebildet. Die Wiederholung von Werken, bereits 1904 in Amsterdam von Mahler erprobt, der nichtöffentliche Charakter der Vereinskonzerte, das Verbot von Beifalls- oder Missfallensbekundungen, um "Künstlern und Kunstfreunden eine wirkliche und genaue Kenntnis moderner Musik zu verschaffen"[25] hatte Wirkung gezeigt. Am 6. Februar 1920 waren hier auch Mahlers *Lieder eines fahrenden Gesellen* in Schönbergs Bearbeitung für kleines Ensemble erklungen. Dass die Lieder, statt in der kostengünstigeren Klavierfassung von Mahlers Hand, in einer extra hergestellten Instrumentierung für kleines Ensemble zur Aufführung gebracht wurden, dürfte im Licht der selbst gestellten Aufgabe Mahlers Vermächtnis zu pflegen, zu werten sein. Auch die Initiative zur Gründung der IGNM, 1922 aus den Internationalen Kammeraufführungen zeitgenössischer Komponisten bei den Salzburger Festspielen hervorgegangen, ging ebenfalls von Schönberg-Schülern und Vereinsmitgliedern aus. Die Komponisten Bartók, Berg, Britten, Hindemith, Honegger, Janacek, Kodály, Krenek, Milhaud, Pisk, Prokofieff, Ravel, Respighi, Satie, Schönberg, Strawinsky und Varèse griffen die Idee auf, aber an der Wiege dieser heute weltweiten Organisation standen die Komponisten Egon Wellesz (Exil GB), Anton Webern (NS-Aufführungsverbot und innere Emigration) und Paul A. Pisk (Exil USA). Die Idee selbst stammte von Wellesz' Schulkollegen, dem Pianisten, Komponisten und Musikwissenschafter Rudolf Réti (Exil USA), der sich ebenfalls bereits in Schönbergs *Verein für musikalische Privataufführungen* engagiert hatte.[26]

Als Gustav Mahler während einer Probe am 21. Februar 1911 in New York zusammenbrach, kündigte sich die tödliche Krankheit an, die am 18. Mai sein Leben beenden sollte. Im April kehrte Mahler über Frankreich nach Österreich zurück.

"Nur wenige Personen erwarteten den Zug, der Mahler nach Wien brachte. Man hatte den Wunsch der Ärzte respektiert, um jede Aufregung von ihm fernzuhalten".[27] "Jetzt, da es schon sehr spät ist, sucht man die früheren Sünden gut zu machen. Adressen und Wünsche für Genesung werden dem Kranken zugewendet, der sie wahrscheinlich nicht liest. Jetzt erinnert man sich, dass er 'unser war'", so zitiert Karl Kraus in *Die Fackel* das *Neue Wiener Journal*, und fügt hinzu: "nachdem es die Mahler-Hetze organisiert hat".[28]

Eine Anekdote über den zum damaligen Zeitpunkt noch nicht zwanzigjährigen Komponisten und Pianisten und Schönberg-Schülers Max Deutsch (Exil

---

[25] Zitiert nach: http://www.schoenberg.at/6_archiv/verein/verein_quellen.htm.
[26] Programmheft Musikfest 85 Jahre IGNM, 1.-7. Oktober 2007 Wien.
[27] *Neues Wiener Tagblatt* vom 13. Mai 1911. Zitiert nach Blaukopf (wie Anm. 20). S. 279.
[28] Ebd. S. 279.

Frankreich), vermag die Mahler-Verehrung im Kreis um Arnold Schönberg zu illustrieren: "When Mahler died – that is something, that Max Deutsch told me – they walked two kilometers to sit outside the house of Mahler,[29] and all night they watched with the Jewish candles the death of Mahler".[30] Mahlers Tod läßt für kurze Zeit die Fronten zwischen 'Freund und Feind' verschwimmen, aber ab 1938 herrscht wieder Klarheit: Mahlers Musik ist nun auch in Österreich verboten. Arnold Schönberg ist bereits 1933 von Berlin über Paris in die USA ausgewandert; mit Ausnahme von Anton Webern, der sich nach dem Aufführungsverbot seiner Musik in die innere Emigration zurückzieht, und Alban Berg, der rechtzeitig verstarb, werden auch die meisten seiner Schüler vor dem Nationalsozialismus ins Exil fliehen müssen.

Exil

Das von Mahler in den *Liedern eines fahrenden Gesellen* vertonte 'Liebesleid', aber auch die in dieser süß-bitteren Musik, die vielen so 'österreichisch' in den Ohren klingt, so eindringlich evozierte Landschaft weisen voraus auf eine andere 'nachgetragene Liebe': Die Liebe der aus Österreich Vertriebenen zu einer 'Heimat', die ihnen keine sein wollte. Hier sollte sich ein Abschied vollziehen, der mit einem romantischen 'Aussteigen aus der Gesellschaft', einer Flucht vor der Leere des Alltags oder dem Bedürfnis nach Einsamkeit nichts mehr gemeinsam hatte, auch wenn das Künstlerbild des 19. Jahrhunderts – der am Leben leidende Künstler – in heutigen Künstlerbiografien nach wie vor seinen Nachhall findet.

An dieser Stelle möchte ich den österreichischen Komponisten Erich Zeisl (Exil USA) vorstellen. Zeisl stand nicht zuletzt durch seinen Lehrer, dem Komponisten, Bratschisten und Musikschriftsteller Hugo Kauder (Exil Niederlande – USA) in der Tradition Gustav Mahlers. Zeisl war kein 'fahrender Gesell': er wurde in eine in Wien ansässige jüdische Familie hineingeboren, und seine Reisen beschränkten sich auf die Sommerfrische am Wolfgangsee im Salzkammergut,

> wo der Musiker Erich, die Juristin Susi [Anm. der Verfasserin: Zeisls spätere Frau Gertrud Jellinek, Susi genannt] und die Malerin Lisel [Anm. der Verfasserin: Salzer] sich in verschiedenen Pensionen eingemietet haben. Das ist beruhigende

---

[29] Obwohl Gustav Mahler im Sanatorium Loew im 9. Wiener Gemeindebezirk verstarb, lautet die Eintragung im Totenprotokoll auf der Adresse Wien XIX Wollergasse 10, dem Haus seines Schwiegervaters Carl Moll. Vgl. Blaukopf (wie Anm. 20). S. 142.

[30] 'Oral history'-Interview Winfried Schneider mit Natika Yznaga, Stieftochter von Max Deutsch, 14. Juni 2001 Paris für den Verein Orpheus Trust, Orpheus-Archiv im Archiv der Akademie der Künste Berlin.

Abb. 2: Eric Zeisl im Trachtenlook. © Barbara Zeisl Schoenberg/Verein Orpheus Trust.

Gesellschaft. Tagsüber schwimmt, radelt und aquarelliert man am See, abends beschwört Erich auf dem verstimmten Klavier seiner Gastwirtschaft das ganze Instrumentarium der Pastorale herauf ...[31]

wie es seine Jugendfreundin, die Autorin Hilde Spiel beschreibt.

Zeisls Vater, Besitzer des Café Tegetthoff in der Nähe des Wiener Nordbahnhofs und des Tegetthoff-Denkmals, das an Österreichs einzigen Seehelden erinnert, hatte wie später sein Sohn Erich die Bürgerschule in der Vereinsgasse im zweiten Wiener Gemeindebezirk besucht, wo auch Arnold Schönberg, bevor er sechzehnjährig als Lehrling in das Bankhaus Winter & Co eintreten musste, zur

[31] Hilde Spiel: *Die hellen und die finsteren Zeiten. Erinnerungen 1911–1946.* München: Paul List 1989. S. 111.

Schule ging. Auch der Schriftsteller Joseph Roth hatte in dieser Gegend gelebt, als er 1914 nach Wien kam und dort seine journalistische Tätigkeit begann,[32] war doch die Gegend um den Nordbahnhof eine erste Anlaufstelle für die aus den östlichen Teilen der Donaumonarchie zugewanderten Juden. Wie Zeisls Tochter Barbara berichtet, war der Komponist durch das väterliche Caféhaus bereits seit frühester Jugend mit ostjüdischen Klängen vertraut.[33] Sein kompositorischer Weg bewegte sich zunächst aber in anderen Bahnen. Anders als Schönberg war er ein erfolgreicher Vertreter der gemäßigten Wiener Moderne; seine Kompositionen wurden zusammen mit Werken der Komponisten Richard Stöhr (Exil USA), Franz Mittler (auch als Klavierbegleiter von Karl Kraus bekannt, Exil USA) und Kurt Pahlen (Exil Argentinien) im Ehrbar-Saal und im Wiener Konzerthaus aufgeführt. Bis Februar 1938 hatte Zeisl neben Kammermusik, Orchesterwerken und einem Singspiel nach Büchners *Leonce und Lena* über 100 Lieder komponiert, darunter *Wanderers Nachtlied* nach Goethe und Vertonungen von Wunderhorntexten.

Die Uraufführung des Singspiels *Leonce und Lena*, das im Schönbrunner Schlosstheater in Wien hätte herauskommen sollen, wird nach dem 'Anschluss' abgesetzt: Musik von Juden darf nicht mehr aufgeführt werden. Zeisls letzte Monate in Wien sind von der ständigen Flucht vor der Gestapo und tiefer Depression gezeichnet. Kurz vor dem Einmarsch der Hitlertruppen in Österreich hatte er, nach einem unbekannten Text, ein letztes Lied komponiert: *Komm, süßer Tod*. Danach sollte er als Liedkomponist verstummen.[34] Seine Frau wird später sagen, sie hätte ihn "wie ein Postpaket verschicken müssen".[35] Kurz vor den Novemberpogromen gelingt es endlich, Wien zu verlassen. Am 10. November 1938 kommen Zeisl, seine Frau, die Mutter und sein Bruder Wilhelm in Paris an, wo die Familie nach einigen Monaten in einem kleinen Hotel den Sommer 1939 unter der symbolhaften Adresse 'Route de l'Asile 39' in Le Vesinet, etwas außerhalb der Stadt, verbringen sollte. "Also wir sind gerettet!", schreibt er seiner Jugendfreundin Hilde Spiel nach London.[36]

Da die Familie ohne gültiges Visum nach Paris geflohen war, gibt es auch keine Arbeitserlaubnis – das Geld ist knapp. Der französische Komponist

---

[32] Erste nachgewiesene Meldeadresse: Rembrandtstraße 35, zitiert nach Heinz Lunzer und Victoria Lunzer-Talos: *Joseph Roth 1894–1939. Ein Katalog der Dokumentationsstelle für neuere österreichische Literatur zur Ausstellung des Jüdischen Museums der Stadt Wien 7. Oktober 1994 bis 12. Februar 1995*. Wien: Dokumentationsstelle für neuere österreichische Literatur 1994. S. 160.
[33] Mündliche Mitteilung von Barbara Zeisl Schoenberg an die Verfasserin.
[34] Karin Wagner: *Fremd bin ich ausgezogen. Eric Zeisl. Biografie*. Wien: Mandelbaum 2005. S. 39.
[35] Mündliche Mitteilung van Barbara Zeisl Schoenberg an die Verfasserin.
[36] Eric Zeisl an Hilde Spiel, November 1938. Nachlass Erich Zeisl, zitiert nach Karin Wagner (wie Anm. 34). S. 11.

Abb. 3: Familie Zeisl im Garten der Route de l'Asile, Le Vésinet. © Barbara Zeisl Schoenberg / Verein Orpheus Trust.

Darius Milhaud (Exil USA), der viele jüdische Musiker auf der Flucht unterstützt, läßt Zeisl illegal kleine Arbeiten zukommen und verschafft der Familie damit ein wenig Einnahmen. Milhaud ist es auch, der mit einem Empfehlungsschreiben an den französischen Innenminister Albert Sarraut die Gefahr einer Abschiebung bannt. Damit kann das Haus in der Route de l'Asile noch eine Weile als Treffpunkt von Flüchtlingen aus Österreich, wie Alma Mahler (Exil USA) oder Marcel Rubin (Exil Mexiko), dienen. Aus der Begegnung mit dem österreichischen Film- und Theaterkritikers Hans Kafka (Exil USA, dort als Drehbuchautor John Kafka bekannt) im Pariser Exil entwickelt sich eine tiefe Freundschaft. Über Vermittlung von Erwin Piscator (Exil USA) wird Zeisl eingeladen, die Bühnenmusik für eine dramatisierte Fassung von Joseph Roths Roman *Hiob* zu komponieren. Er verliebt sich in den Stoff und fasst den Plan, daraus eine richtige Oper zu machen, Hans Kafka soll das Libretto schreiben. Sie wird leider niemals vollendet werden.

Die Pariser Aufführung von *Hiob* im Juli 1939 wird zu einer nicht unumstrittenen Gedächtnisfeier für den kurz zuvor verstorbenen Joseph Roth. Der Wiener Schauspieler Leo Askenasy (Exil USA, in Hollywood als Filmschauspieler Leon Askin bekannt) liest einführende Worte von Stefan Zweig (Exil Brasilien), Eric Zeisl hat Kompositionen beigesteuert und die

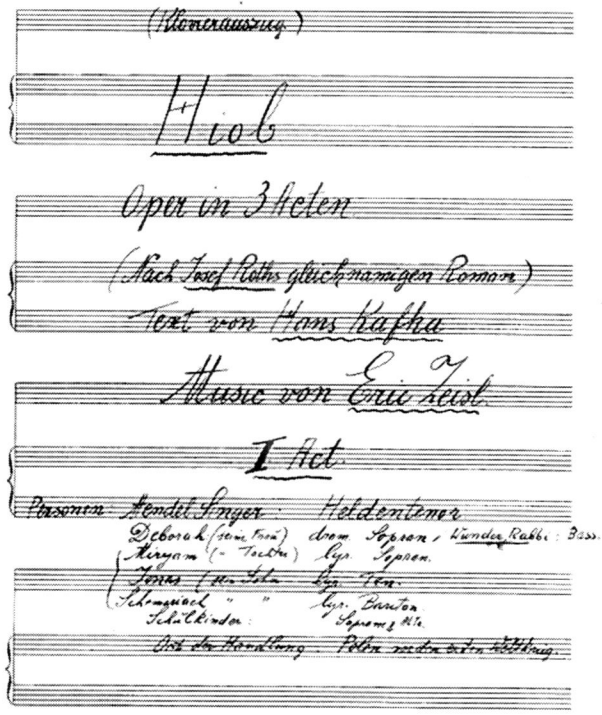

Abb. 4: Eric Zeisl: *Hiob*. © Barbara Zeisl Schoenberg.

musikalische Leitung übernommen, sein Bruder Wilhelm (Exil USA) spielt in einer kleinen Nebenrolle. In Zeisls Beschäftigung mit Roths *Hiob* fließen die Topoi 'Reise' und 'Exil' ineinander und bilden einen Wendepunkt für seinen späteren kompositorischen Weg, wie die Zeisl-Biographin Karin Wagner darlegt:

> Für Zeisl bedeutete die Auseinandersetzung mit Roths Romanstoff eine Konfrontation mit dem eigenen Schicksal: Sowohl Züge der eigenen Biographie als auch die Problematik der über Jahrhunderte währenden Vertreibung und Heimatlosigkeit der Juden spiegeln sich in Roths berühmtem Text wieder […]. War etwa Arnold Schönbergs Aufenthalt in Paris von seinem Denken um die Stellung des Judentums und von seinem Wiedereintritt in die jüdische Glaubensgemeinschaft als finale Konsequenz einer prozesshaften Ausbildung eines neuen jüdischen Bewußtseins geprägt und bedeutete somit die Pariser Zeit einen markanten Punkt in Schönbergs Biographie hinsichtlich der Frage nach der 'Sache des Judentums', so war auch für Eric Zeisl die Pariser Exilzeit gleich einer Neuorientierung bzw. gleich einer bewußten Hinorientierung zum Judentum. 'Innere Rückkehr' als Reaktion auf die Exilsituation, ein Zurückgeworfensein auf die jüdischen Wurzeln, ausgelöst

durch die Entwurzelung und den Bruch durch das Exil, und dabei gleichzeitig ein in der künstlerischen Arbeit auf die jüdische Identität gerichteter Fokus stehen seit der Zeit in Paris exemplarisch für Eric Zeisl. Was Zeisl trotz seiner zu Schönberg grundsätzlich verschiedenen Tonsprache nun mit diesem und auch mit anderen Exilkomponisten verband, ist das durch die geschaffene Musik im jüdischen Idiom nach außen getragene Phänomen einer 'inneren Rückkehr'.[37]

Auch für zahlreiche Schüler Schönbergs war Paris zur Zwischenstation auf der Flucht geworden.[38] Hanns Eisler, der als Zwanzigjähriger bei Karl Weigl am Neuen Wiener Konservatorium, anschließend bei Arnold Schönberg und Anton Webern studiert hatte, war 1933 gewarnt worden, dass die Gestapo in Berlin nach ihm fahndete und kehrte aus Wien, wo er auf Einladung von Webern weilte, nicht nach Berlin zurück, sondern fuhr zunächst in die Tschechoslowakei.[39] Von dort ging es mit einer Einladung des französischen Filmregisseurs Feyder 'auf gut Glück' nach Paris, wo er den österreichischen Kollegen Max Deutsch, der wie Eisler in Schönbergs 'Verein für musikalische Privataufführungen' aktiv gewesen war und in Berlin gleichfalls für den Film komponiert und sich politisch engagiert hatte, wieder begegnete.[40] Eisler sollte seine Musik für die französischen Filme *Dans les rues* (F 1933, Regie Victor Trivas, Buch Alexandre Arnoux, Victor Trivas) und *Le grand jeu* (F 1934, Regie Jacques Feyder, Buch Charles Spaak, Jacques Feyder) später für die *Suiten für Orchester* verwenden; die Filmmusik von Max Deutsch für Georg Wilhelm Pabsts *Die freudlose Gasse* (D 1925, nach Hugo Bettauer) ging im Spanischen Bürgerkrieg verloren. Deutsch hatte bereits für Pabsts Debütfilm *Der Schatz* (D 1923, Buch Willy Hennings, G.W. Pabst, nach Rudolph Hans Bartsch) – die älteste heute erhaltene Originalpartitur für einen deutschen Langspielfilm – die Musik geschrieben. Als er in den dreißiger Jahren in Madrid an der Universität Filmmusik lehrte und die Filmgesellschaft Casa Cinematografica Aranjuez leitete, hatte er seine Kompositionen mit sich, aber der Ausbruch des Spanischen Bürgerkriegs nach seiner Rückkehr nach Paris

---

[37] Karin Wagner: Eric Zeisl im Pariser Exil – Angelpunkt zwischen Alter und Neuer Welt. In: Michel Cullin und Primavera Driessen Gruber: *Douce France? Musik-Exil in Frankreich/ Musiciens en exil en France 1933–1945*. Wien: Böhlau 2008. S. 193–204. Hier: S. 198.
[38] Vgl. Primavera Driessen Gruber: *Douce France?* In: Cullin und Driessen Gruber (wie Anm. 37). S. 13–36 sowie S. 245–246.
[39] Louise Eisler-Fischer: Mein Leben. Autobiographische Skizze. In: *Es war nicht immer Liebe. Texte und Briefe*. Hg. von Maren Köster, Jürgen Schebera und Friederike Wissmann. Wien: Sonderzahl 2006.
[40] Albrecht Betz: In Frankreich bisweilen, in Frankreich konstant: Hanns Eisler und Max Deutsch. In: Cullin und Driessen Gruber (wie Anm. 37). S. 95–108.

ließ andere Prioritäten aufkommen. Mit Ausnahme von *Der Schatz* ist seither der Großteil seines kompositorischen Nachlasses verschollen.

Hollywooder Liederbuch

Für Eisler war Paris nur eine der vielen Zwischenstationen im Exil. Pendelnd zwischen Großbritannien, Frankreich und Dänemark, der Bürgerkriegsfront in Spanien und der Tschechoslowakei, entstand 1937 auf der Reise von Svendborg nach Prag seine *Sonate für Violine und Klavier*, der er den Untertitel *Reisesonate* gab, und die als "eines der luzidesten und vollendetsten Kammermusikwerke der ganzen Stilepoche"[41] gilt. Am 20. Januar 1938 landete er endgültig in New York, wo er an der New School for Social Research lehrte und ein Forschungsprojekt zu Filmmusik leitete. Seine Frau Louise (Lou) berichtet:

> Am 20. April 1942 fuhr Eisler nach Hollywood. Brecht war am 21. Juni [Anm. der Herausgeber Köster, Schebera und Wißmann: Juli] 1941 aus Finnland über die Sowjetunion und Sibirien wie der Reiter über den Bodensee dort angekommen. Seit Brecht da war, verlangte er nach Eisler und vice versa. Sie brauchten einander. Allein in New York hatte ich Zeit und Lust, wieder etwas zu schreiben [...]. Es kam nicht dazu [...]. Hanns Eisler brauchte mich, da hörte meine Emanzipation auf. Er hatte Arbeit gefunden, da war Not an der Frau – er brauchte eine Haushälterin, eine Sekretärin, vor allem aber ein Chauffeur. Ohne Auto konnte man in Hollywood nicht existieren, es gab keine andere Transportmöglichkeit ins Filmstudio oder in die Universität nach Los Angeles. Ich hatte nur zehn Tage Zeit, um chauffieren zu lernen. Stefan, der junge Sohn Brechts war mein Lehrer.[42]

Im August 1942 führte der Vertragsabschluß für die Musik zu *Hangmen Also Die* (USA 1943, Regie: Fritz Lang) auch Lou von New York nach Hollywood: Eisler hatte 'Arbeit gefunden'.

Bereits vor ihrer Ankunft hatte er mit der Arbeit am *Hollywooder Liederbuch* nach Texten von Bertolt Brecht u.a. angefangen. Die Texte waren größtenteils zwischen 1938 und 40 im skandinavischen Exil entstanden und wurden nun adaptiert und um die *Hollywooder Elegien* ergänzt.[43] Die Umstände der Entstehung, der Kontrast zur Filmwelt Hollywoods und das Wissen um den Krieg, der draußen tobte, gibt dem Liederzyklus eine abgrundtiefe Zerrissenheit, die bereits im Titel anklingt.

---

[41] Claus-Christian Schuster: *Hanns Eisler, Die Reisesonate*. In: Altenberg Trio Wien – Text: http://www.altenbergtrio.at/?site=text&textid=EIS_1937&lp=fr.
[42] Louise Eisler-Fischer (wie Anm. 39).
[43] Kerstin Piribauer: "Eine sehr seltsame und gelungene Arbeit". *Zum 'Hollywood-Liederbuch' von Hanns Eisler*. In: *Programmheft Wiener Konzerthaus*. 25. Oktober 1998. Konzert Hanns Eisler: *Hollywood-Liederbuch* mit Matthias Goerne, Bariton, Eric Schneider, Klavier, sowie einem Vortrag von Albrecht Dümling: *Hanns Eisler und das Exil*. Veranstaltet in Kooperation mit dem Verein Orpheus Trust.

Abb. 5: Hanns Eisler beim Schachspiel mit Rudolf Kolisch in Malibu. © Archiv der Akademie der Künste Berlin.

Hotelzimmer 1942[44]

An der weißgetünchten Wand
steht der schwarze Koffer mit den Manuskripten.
[...]
Auch die Masken sind da, und neben der Bettstelle
steht der kleine sechslampige Lautsprecher.
In der Frühe drehe ich den Schalter um und höre
die Siegesmeldungen meiner Feinde.

Die Stimmung dieses Liederzyklus erinnert an Schuberts *Winterreise*, aber die Person, die hier spricht, ist nicht mehr der an der Liebe oder am Leben leidende Künstler des neunzehnten Jahrhunderts. Albrecht Dümling bemerkt dazu:

> Die Jahreszeiten wurden dabei zu politischen Metaphern, so der *Frühling* zum Symbol der Hoffnung. In *Über den Selbstmord* klingt dagegen bei den Worten "Und die ganze

---

[44] *Hotelzimmer 1942*. Aus: *Hollywooder Liederbuch*. Text Bertolt Brecht, Musik Hanns Eisler. In: *Ausgewählte Lieder*. © Leipzig: Deutscher Verlag für Musik.

Winterzeit" melodisch das "Fremd bin ich eingezogen" aus dem Anfang von Schuberts *Winterreise* nach; zusätzlich verweisen das langsame Tempo und die kontrastreiche Dynamik auf den *Doppelgänger* [aus *Die Winterreise*, Anm. der Verfasserin].[45]

Im *Hollywooder Liederbuch* findet diese 'Winterreise' im schwärzesten 'Winter' des 20. Jahrhunderts statt, und so klingt sie auch: In Europa wütet der Krieg, die Deportationen in die Vernichtungslager beginnen und Millionen Flüchtlinge sitzen in der Falle.

Winterspruch[46]

Der Schnee beginnt zu treiben.
Wer wird denn dableiben?
Da bleiben wird, morgen wie heut'
die kalten Steine und die armen Leut'.

Im *Hollywooder Liederbuch* zeigen sich die grundlegende Unterschiede zwischen dem Reisen, wie es Mahlers *Lieder eines fahrenden Gesellen* zum Gegenstand haben, und dem Exil: Es sind die mit dem Exil verbundene Bedrohung, die ohnmächtige Wut, die existentiellen Ängste und die fehlende Möglichkeit der Heimkehr. Auch wem die Flucht gelungen ist, bleiben Angst und das 'Schuldgefühl des Überlebens' nicht erspart: Fast alle Exilanten haben in der Shoah ihre zurückgebliebenen Familienangehörige verloren. Eisler wird sich zuletzt in seiner Musik zum Film *Nuit et Brouillard* (F 1955)[47] mit der Vernichtung der Juden auseinandersetzen.

An den kleinen Radioapparat[48]

Du kleiner Kasten, den ich flüchtend trug,
dass seine Lampen mir auch nicht zerbrachen
besorgt vom Haus zum Schiff, vom Schiff zum Zug
dass meine Feinde weiter mit mir sprachen.

An meinem Lager und zu meiner Pein,
der letzten nachts, der ersten in der früh,
von ihren Siegen und von meiner Müh.
Versprich mir, nicht auf einmal stumm zu sein.

---

[45] Albrecht Dümling: Ins Paradies vertrieben. Zum 'Hollywooder Liederbuch' von Hanns Eisler. http://www.duemling.de/Hollywood.htm.
[46] *Winterspruch*. Aus: *Hollywooder Liederbuch*. Text: Bertolt Brecht, Musik: Hanns Eisler. In: *Ausgewählte Lieder*. © Leipzig: Deutscher Verlag für Musik.
[47] Regie Alain Resnais. Übertragung ins Deutsche: Paul Celan.
[48] *An den kleinen Radioapparat*. Aus: *Hollywooder Liederbuch*. Text: Bertolt Brecht, Musik: Hanns Eisler.
© Leipzig: Deutscher Verlag für Musik.

Die verzweifelte Beschwörung der letzten Zeile, deren Vertonung dem Text eine vervielfachte Aussagekraft verleiht, überträgt die Angst des Flüchtlings auf den Hörer. Es geht um mehr, als um das Verstummen des Radioapparates, es geht um das Verstummen der Widerstandskraft: drüben, auf den Schlachtfeldern Europas, und hier, beim Autor selbst. Und dennoch, im Lied *Frühling 1942:* "der Flüchtling nimmt sein schwier'ges Handwerk wieder auf: Das Hoffen".[49]

Im September 1939 war auch Erich Zeisl, der sich ab jetzt Eric nennen wird, mit der S.S. Volendam in New York eingetroffen. Zeisl schreibt an Hilde Spiel: "Wir sind sehr glücklich, dass wir hier sind! [...] Beruflich großer Erfolg. Die 2te Radiosendung 'Bitterlichsinfonie & Passacaglia' zugleich eine Sensation [...] Wenig Money und langsam auftretende Dollar".[50] Als die Tochter Barbara geboren wird, wird es finanziell knapp. Ein kahles Mietappartement ohne Heizung außerhalb von New York lässt Zeisl eine Übersiedlung an die Westküste ins Auge fassen. Über John Kafka, der als Drehbuchautor in Hollywood arbeitet, erhält Zeisl 1941 eine Einladung von MGM, mit der Familie nach Hollywood zu kommen und für den Film zu arbeiten. Brecht/Eislers *Unter den grünen Pfefferbäumen* vermag mit etwaigen Illusionen über eine 'Hollywood-Idylle' gründlich aufzuräumen.

Unter den grünen Pfefferbäumen[51]

Unter den grünen Pfefferbäumen
gehen die Musiker auf den Strich, zwei und zwei
Mit den Schreibern. Bach
hat ein Streichquartett im Täschen. Dante schwenkt
den dürren Hintern.

Kafka hat stellvertretend für Zeisl Vertragsverhandlungen geführt, und auch Hanns Eisler hat sich für Zeisl eingesetzt: "Ich habe eben mit Brunswick gesprochen. Die Sache schaut <u>gut</u> aus. Er hält es für durchaus möglich Sie plus Familie nach Hollywood zu verpflanzen [...] Gehen Sie sofort daran mit ihm zu sprechen [...]. Ich habe vorläufig einen <u>guten</u> Eindruck von der Angelegenheit. Also viel Glück!![52] "Ein Vertrag mit Metro-Goldwyn-Mayer

---

[49] *Frühling 1942.* Aus: *Hollywooder Liederbuch.* Text Bertolt Brecht, Musik Hanns Eisler. In: Eisler Lieder (1939): Fünf Lieder. Leipzig: Litolff 1952.
[50] Eric Zeisl an Hilde Spiel, 13. Februar 1940, zitiert nach Karin Wagner: "Ich bekomme für mein Leben gerne Post". Zu Eric Zeisls Korrespondenz im Exil. In: *Endstation Schein-Heiligenstadt. Eric Zeisls Flucht nach Hollywood.* Hg. von Werner Hanak, Michael Haas und Karin Wagner. Wien: Jüdisches Museum der Stadt Wien. 2006. S. 118–147. Hier: S. 127.
[51] *Unter den grünen Pfefferbäumen.* Aus: *Fünf Elegien. Hollywooder Liederbuch.* Text: Bertolt Brecht, Musik: Hanns Eisler. © Leipzig: Deutscher Verlag für Musik.
[52] Hanns Eisler an Erich Zeisl, vermutlich 1941, zitiert nach Karin Wagner (wie Anm. 34). S. 186.

kommt aber erst zustande, als Zeisl droht, Los Angeles mit seiner Familie wieder zu verlassen. Hanns Eisler, dessen Musik zu *None But the Lonely Heart* (USA 1944)[53] für den Oscar nominiert werden sollte, wird sich auch weiter um Zeisl bemühen. So schreibt er an Herbert Klein, Regisseur des Semi-Dokumentarfilms *The Forgotten Village*, für den Eisler die Musik komponierte: "May I introduce to you Mr. Erich Zeisl, composer (on the M.G.M. staff). He is a very gifted fellow and I think he would be splendid for your new picture. Listen to his music!".[54] Auch bei seinem ehemaligen Lehrer Schönberg wird Eisler vorstellig:

Hochverehrter Herr Schoenberg!
Herr Erich Zeisl, ein wirklich begabter Komponist (Refugee aus Wien) möchte gerne mit Ihnen arbeiten. Ich erlaube mir, ihn hiermit vorzustellen.
Ihr außerordentlich ergebener
Hanns Eisler[55]

Eine musikalische Zusammenarbeit kommt nicht zustande, wohl aber – viel später – eine Verbindung anderer Art: Die Eheschließung von Schoenbergs Sohn Ronald mit Zeisls Tochter Barbara.

Zeisl berichtet über seine Arbeit in Hollywood an Hilde Spiel: "I am since 10 Month in Metro M.G. and composing picture [...]. I have done until now 20 *Fitzpatrick travaltalks*. I was lately working on [...] Pictures mit (sic!) Franz Wachsmann together. One is *Journey of Margaret* a marvelous picture, the second is *Reunion*".[56] Die Arbeit an *FitzPatrick's Traveltalks*, Kurzfilme, die Landschaften oder historische Städte beschrieben, mit Titeln wie *Around the World in California, Calling on Costa Rica, Morning in Minnesota, Over the Andes, Romantic Nevada*, oder *Visiting Vera Cruz* erfordert eine illustrative Musik. Der so tief in Österreich verwurzelte Zeisl, dessen weiteste Reise ihn in das Salzkammergut geführt hatte, verdient nun seinen Lebensunterhalt mit Fließbandarbeit für die Filmindustrie und produziert Programmmusik für Reisefilme.

Die Filme haben immer geendet mit "reluctantly we take leave of" [...] und dann kam z.B. "beautiful Santiago Chile". Reisefilme. Und während des Krieges war das interessant, die Amerikaner konnten nicht reisen, und so sind diese Filme gezeigt

---

[53] Regie führte Clifford Odets.
[54] Hanns Eisler an Herbert Klein, 2. Juli 1942, zitiert nach Wagner (wie Anm. 34). S. 186.
[55] Hanns Eisler an Arnold Schoenberg, 194?. Nachlass Eric Zeisl. Eine Kopie befindet sich im Orpheus-Archiv des Archivs der Akademie der Künste Berlin.
[56] Eric Zeisl an Hilde Spiel, undatiert. Nachlass Eric Zeisl, zitiert nach Wagner (wie Anm. 34). S. 190. Der Film *Reunion in France* erschien 1942 in den USA. Musik: Franz Waxman, Mario Castelnuovo-Tedesco, Eric Zeisl.

worden [...]. Es gab zwei Komponisten, meinen Vater und jemand anderen, die das gemacht haben. Bei den anderen, den berühmten Filmen mit den berühmten Stars, war das eine ganze Fabrik.[57]

Barbara Zeisl Schoenberg versuchte Jahrzehnte lang, die Soundtracks zu finden.

> Der Sohn von Korngold [Erich Wolfgang, Komponist, Exil USA, Anm. der Verfasserin], Schurli wie wir ihn nannten [Georg, Anm. der Verfasserin], hat meiner Mutter gesagt, daß MGM die ganze Musik weggeworfen hat [...] und dass nichts mehr übrig geblieben ist, [von dem], was die Komponisten gemacht haben, die nicht den ganzen Film gemacht haben [...]. Ich wußte, daß mein Vater Musik für mehr als 50, 60 *FitzPatricks Traveltalks* geschrieben hat. Und eines Nachts habe ich für ein eigenes Filmprojekt im Fernsehen Filme gesammelt, und mir am nächsten Tag angesehen, was ich da hatte. Und da war ein solcher *FitzPatrick Traveltalk* [...]. Und da hab ich die Fernsehstation angerufen und hab gefragt [...]. Und sie haben mir dann einen Mann empfohlen, der fast alle Filme von meinem Vater gehabt hat, auch die conductor scores [...]. Und da gibt es auch zwei Minuten von *Lassie Come Home*, mein Vater hatte dafür die 'fight scene' geschrieben.[58]

Die Arbeit ist schlecht bezahlt und deprimiert ihn zutiefst, weil sie ihm weder Zeit noch künstlerische Freiheit lässt. Lukrative Angebote für große Filme mit anspruchsvoller Musik lösen sich in Luft auf. Zeisl schreibt darüber:

> Hatte einen großen Kampf im Studio, immer unnütze Besprechungen und am Ende lehnten sie meine Bitte nach einer kleinen Gehaltserhöhung ab [...]. So verhält sich eine Gesellschaft, welche eine Geschichte für 20.000 Dollar kauft und nie verfilmt [...] Da sitzen Dilettanten mit 500 Dollar in der Woche und meine Bitte um einen Gehaltserhöhung um 25 Dollar wurde schroff abgelehnt.[59]

Der Vertrag mit MGM wird nach achtzehn Monaten aufgelöst, Zeisls Frau sorgt nun als Lehrerin für Deutsch und Latein für ein regelmäßiges Einkommen. Auch die Schwiegermutter trägt als gelernte Juwelierin zum Haushaltsbudget bei. Der kleinen Familie gelingt es, finanziell zu überleben, aber Zeisl wird sich für immer entwurzelt fühlen. "Ich erinnere mich auch, dass ich des öfteren mit meinem Vater in der Nachbarschaft spazieren ging, und auf die Palmen kletterte, die ihm nie vertraut wurden. Die Wüstenbäume von Los Angeles konnten nie die dunklen, feuchten Wälder seiner Heimat ersetzen".[60]

---

[57] 'Oral history'-Interview Primavera Driessen Gruber mit Barbara Zeisl Schoenberg 14.03.2000. Orpheus-Archiv im Archiv der Akademie der Künste Berlin.
[58] Ebd.
[59] Herbert Martin: Österreichische Komponisten in Hollywood. In: *Österreichische Musiker im Exil – Kolloquium 1988*. Hg. von *Österreichische Gesellschaft für Musik*. Kassel: Bärenreiter Verlag 1990. S. 77.
[60] Barbara Zeisl Schoenberg: Kinder des Exils. In: Österreichische Musikzeitschrift (ÖMZ). 8/9 (2006). Sonderheft *Musik. Verfolgung. Freiheit*. S. 8–12. Hier: S. 10.

In seinen Kompositionen spiegeln sich die ostjüdischen Klänge, die er als Kind in Wien gehört hat, daneben schreibt er kleine Stücke für den Musikunterricht, den er nun erteilt. Ab 1946 bietet sich eine neue Existenzgrundlage: Als Nachfolger von Ernst Krenek wird er am Los Angeles City College in den Abendstunden Harmonie, Komposition und Kontrapunkt unterrichten.

Der nichtjüdische Komponist Ernst Krenek, dessen *Reisebuch aus den österreichischen Alpen*, ein Liederbuch in vier Bänden nach eigenen Texten, bereits 1929, also lange vor dem Machtwechsel im Nachbarland Deutschland, einen eigentümlich klagenden, im Text stellenweise satirischen Ton hatte anklingen lassen, war 1933 in Deutschland endgültig als 'Kulturbolschewist' denunziert worden; seine Werke, darunter die berühmte 'Jazz-Oper' *Jonny spielt auf* wurden als 'entartet' diffamiert und nicht mehr aufgeführt. Kreneks von Karl Kraus geteilte Hoffnung, daß sich im österreichischen 'Ständestaat' ein Bollwerk gegen den deutschen Nationalsozialismus entwickeln könnte, war rasch verflogen; nach dem 'Anschluss' traf ihn auch in Österreich das Aufführungsverbot. 1937/38 konnte er anlässlich einer USA-Tournee mit der Salzburg Opera Guild berufliche Kontakte in den USA knüpfen.[61] Er ging über Großbritannien ins Exil in die USA, wo ihm bereits nach einem Jahr eine Lehrtätigkeit am Vassar College, Poughkeepsie, New York eine gesicherte Basis für seine kompositorische Tätigkeit bot. In Poughkeepsie schrieb Krenek in seinem großen Essay über Gustav Mahler für die amerikanische Ausgabe von Bruno Walters Mahler-Buch: "Es werden uns einige Eigenschaften im Werk Gustav Mahlers erst dann verständlich, wenn wir uns im Klaren sind, dass er Österreicher war".[62] Als Krenek dies im Jahre 1941 schrieb, war Österreich bereits seit drei Jahren Teil des Dritten Reichs; die Exilanten aber fühlten sich als das 'wirkliche, das andere Österreich'. Krenek unterrichtete anschließend an der Music School of Fine Arts der Hamline University St. Paul, Minnesota, und schließlich an der Southern California School of Music bzw. am Los Angeles City College, wo Eric Zeisl seine Abendstunden übernehmen sollte.

Mit dem 1945 entstandenen *Requiem Ebraico*, "dem Gedächtnis meines Vaters und der anderen zahllosen Opfer der jüdischen Tragödie in Europa gewidmet", hat Eric Zeisl der Nachwelt ein berührendes musikalisches Zeugnis hinterlassen. Diese Vertonung des 92. Psalmes, in der sich Einflüsse jüdischer Kantoralmusik mit Stilelementen der christlichen Sakralmusik mischen, war

---

[61] Claudia Maurer Zenck: Ein Musiktheaterexport nach Nordamerika – die Salzburg Opera Guild. In: Peter Petersen und Claudia Maurer Zenck: *Musiktheater im Exil der NS-Zeit. Bericht über die internationale Konferenz am Musikwissenschaftlichen Institut der Universität Hamburg. 3. bis 5. Februar 2005*. Hamburg: Von Bockel 2007. S. 207–227.

[62] Ernst Krenek in: Bruno Walter: *Gustav Mahler*. New York: Knopf 1941. Zitiert nach Scheit und Svoboda (wie Anm. 8). S. 93.

wie Schoenbergs *Kol Nidre* eine Auftragskomposition von Jacob Sonderling, Rabbiner des Fairfax Temple in Los Angeles. Barbara Zeisl Schoenberg beschreibt das *Requiem Ebraico* in folgenden Worten:

> Die zwei Frauenstimmen schlingen sich ineinander wie Baumzweige – die Palme, repräsentativ für Israel, und die Zeder für die arabische Welt, als wollten sie immer höher bis Gott steigen. Gefühle der Versöhnung und Hoffnung werden nachhallend ausgebreitet, zwei verschiedene Kulturen und Glauben in Frieden zusammen geführt, symbolisch verbunden: 'Wie eine Palme blüht der Gerechte und wächst wie die Zeder des Libanon'.[63]

Nachklang und Aufbruch ins 21. Jahrhundert

Schreiben über Musik ist wie schreiben über Sex: es fehlt etwas. Musik soll gehört werden – die meisten der oben erwähnten Musikbeispiele sind im Handel erhältlich. Dieser Beitrag will nicht nur zum Lesen, er möchte auch zum Hören anregen.

Mit Ausnahme von Zeisls *Requiem Ebraico* liegt den untersuchten Musikbeispielen eine traurige Stimmung zu Grunde. Ist sie bei Mahlers *Lieder eines fahrenden Gesellen* durch jugendliche Lebens- und Liebeslust, die sich bisweilen auch in jubelnden Tönen Ausdruck verleiht, in Eislers *Hollywooder Liederbuch* durch das "Handwerk des Flüchtlings: Das Hoffen" – wie bei Schubert und Mahler mit der Metapher 'Frühling' verknüpft – und bei Leopoldis *Die Novaks aus Prag* durch das Sentiment des Wienerlieds gemildert, so überrascht das *Requiem Ebraico* nicht nur durch die Textauswahl, sondern auch in musikalischer Hinsicht. Der 92. Psalm, den Zeisl als Textvorlage gewählt hat, ist eine Lobrede auf den Schöpfer, und auch der Musik fehlt jegliche Resignation. Der Komponist, den die Verfolgung und Vertreibung durch die Nationalsozialisten, aber auch die Arbeit für die Filmstudios in Hollywood in eine tiefe Depression geworfen hatte, hat mit diesem 'Requiem' eine veritable Musik der Hoffnung hinterlassen.

Von den in diesen Ausführungen genannten Komponisten und Musikern lebt heute niemand mehr. Mit Ausnahme vom Hermann Leopoldi, Kurt Blaukopf und Marcel Rubin ist keiner der erwähnten Musikschaffenden 1945 definitiv nach Österreich zurückgekehrt. Sie wurden dazu nicht ernsthaft aufgefordert. Zwar dirigierte Bruno Walter Mahler auch wieder die Wiener Philharmoniker, zwar fühlte sich Krenek am Ende seines Lebens wenigstens wieder als 'Teilzeit-Österreicher', die nationalsozialistische Vergangenheit ließ man lieber ruhen. Wellesz' Posten am Institut für Musikwissenschaft der Universität Wien war eingenommen worden von Erich Schenk, einem Zuarbeiter für das *Lexikon der Juden in der Musik* von Theo Stengel und Herbert Gerigk, einer

---

[63] Barbara Zeisl Schoenberg (wie Anm. 59). S. 12.

Art 'Deportationsliste für Musikschaffende', und dabei blieb es auch nach dem Krieg.[64] Eislers Ausweisung aus den USA in der McCarthy-Ära brachte ihm zwar ein Wiedersehen mit Wien, eine Professur an der Wiener Musikhochschule (heute Universität für Musik und darstellende Kunst) wurde jedoch in Zusammenhang mit dem 'Brecht-Boykott' verhindert. Er kehrte in die damalige DDR zurück, und besuchte Wien nur sporadisch. Zemlinsky war bereits 1942 an einem gebrochenen Herzen verstorben, Schoenberg und Zeisl starben in den fünfziger Jahren in Los Angeles, Robitschek in New York. Max Deutsch blieb in Frankreich und wurde dort zu einem wichtigen Vermittler von Schönbergs 'Wiener Schule'; in Österreich setzte sie sich nur innerhalb eines kleinen Publikumssegments durch. Auch Mahlers Musik war 'im Exil' gewesen; eine breite Nachkriegs-Rezeption in Österreich kam erst wieder durch Leonhard Bernstein zustande. In der Forschungsdatenbank der Verfasserin, die Musikschaffende enthält, die Opfer des NS-Regimes wurden, finden sich allein 31 Eintragungen von Mahler-Biographen oder – Kommentatoren. Nur fünf von ihnen sind nach Österreich zurückgekehrt. Im Nachkriegs-Österreich herrschte langes Schweigen.[65]

Erst gegen Ende des vorigen Jahrhunderts haben sich Wissenschaftler, Komponisten, Interpreten und Publikum erneut auf die Traditionen, die 1938 abgerissen wurden, besonnen. Eine jüngere Generation hat sich daran gemacht, Brücken in die Zukunft zu schlagen ohne der verdrängten Vergangenheit auszuweichen. Pionierarbeit leistete dabei der Verein *Orpheus Trust*, der sich zum Ziel gesetzt hatte, die vom NS-Regime vertriebene Musik in das österreichische Musikleben zurück zu holen. Obwohl der Verein nach zehn Jahren seine Veranstaltungstätigkeit aus finanziellen Gründen – wie so viele seiner Vorgängerorganisationen – einstellen musste, schreitet die Dokumentation der NS-verfolgten Musikschaffenden, auch durch die Verfasserin, weiter voran.[66] Große Nachlässe, wie von Arnold Schoenberg, Ernst Krenek oder Hanns Eisler werden in Wien oder Berlin nicht nur verwahrt, sondern hervorragend gepflegt und der Öffentlichkeit zur Verfügung

---

[64] Vgl. Scheit und Svoboda (wie Anm. 8). S. 154–156.
[65] Vgl. Gruber: *Schule der Wahrnehmung*. In: Botstein und Hanak (wie Anm. 13). S. 159–160.
[66] Siehe dazu http://www.orpheustrust.at sowie Forschungsbericht FWF P15395 *Verfolgte Musik. Zur Geschichte der unter dem Nationalsozialismus ermordeten und vertriebenen Musikschaffenden aus Österreich – mit besonderer Berücksichtigung der Erfassung ihrer Werke*. Projektleiter Univ. Prof. Dr. Jürg Stenzl, Mitarbeiter Dr. Primavera Gruber, Dr. Gerhard Scheit, Dr. Evelyn Adunka, Mag. Sabine Reiter, Mag. Winfried Schneider, Mag. Dr. Irene Suchy. Die Fertigstellung eines 'Österreichischen Handbuchs der NS-verfolgten Musikschaffenden' durch die Verfasserin ist für 2012 vorgesehen.

gestellt. Heute reisen Künstler und Wissenschafter aus der ganzen Welt in das Arnold Schönberg Center in Wien, zur Ernst Krenek Stiftung nach Krems und nach Berlin in die Musikarchive des Archivs der Akademie der Künste Berlin. Eine breite Rezeption bahnt sich an.

Im gleichen Zeitraum ist ein verstärktes Interesse an zeitgenössischer Musik entstanden, das nicht nur dem kurzlebigen Zeitgeist verpflichtet ist. Das Festival Wien Modern, die Musikfeste der IGNM, aber auch das Wienerliedfestival 'Wean Hean' oder die jüdischen Film- und Musikfestivals in Wien – alle diese Initiativen stehen in einer Tradition, die in die Zukunft blickt. Sie sind eine Verbeugung vor dem Vermächtnis Gustav Mahlers und der zahllosen aus Wien vertriebenen Musikschaffenden. Das Exil dieser Künstler ist beendet, aber es ist nicht vergessen.

Lisa Hooper

Themes of Exile in the Music and Public and Private Writings of Arnold Schoenberg (1930–1945)

The years from 1933 to 1945 frame a period not only of national, political, and religious exile for Arnold Schoenberg, but they also connote a time of exile from musical academia and the larger listening public. In understanding Schoenberg's exile we must begin with the intuitive composition of his dramatic opera Moses und Aron *in 1930. This work not only foreshadowed Schoenberg's own political exile, first from Berlin, then from Vienna and finally from Germany, but it also becomes emblematic of Schoenberg's perception of himself working in the exile of a musical wasteland to give to the world an enlightened musical truth.*

This paper seeks to elucidate Schoenberg's psychological travels within, or without, society through an exploration of his public and private writings. Beginning with the prophetic composition of Moses und Aron *in 1930, the unfolding of events leading to his political exile are followed through personal correspondences conducted between Schoenberg and other musicians. His arrival in New York and Boston in 1933 provided historiographers with a wealth of letters, articles, and radio addresses documenting both his reception by Americans and his reaction to this new musical arena. We find throughout his writings not only descriptions of exile imposed from the outside, but also of a self-imposed exile that was both lamented and exalted in Schoenberg's own understanding.*

Through these documents Schoenberg's gradual acceptance by society and a corresponding rejection of society by Schoenberg can be traced. In exile both imposed and self-created, Schoenberg adopted a Moses-like role. As Schoenberg himself described it, it was his duty to develop a new and lasting music which, according to Schoenberg, could be accomplished only from the musical wasteland in isolation and exile. It is precisely this created path to exile that this paper explores.

> With the prophetic instinct of his race and his profound devotion to music he wished to explore unknown spheres, like atonality, with the object of finding out what could be done with it. His attitude was one of self-sacrifice – it consisted of putting on one side the 'known' methods […] in order to penetrate the 'unknown'. […][1]

This sense of self-sacrifice described by cellist Pablo Casals marks Arnold Schoenberg's journey into the musical and political unknown, a state of social limbo and exile. Schoenberg's awareness of his isolation, both political and cultural, is evidenced throughout his music and writings. As time progresses and the composer finds his place in American society, it becomes clear that Schoenberg's continuing sense of exile is self-imposed, created not by politics

---

[1] Pablo Casals: *Conversations with Casals*. Ed. by J.M. Corredor. New York (NY): Dutton 1957. Pp.169–171.

or cultural prejudices but, rather, by Schoenberg's adherence to an aesthetic ideal outside the commonly accepted bounds of musical society.

Schoenberg's path to an aesthetic exile began well before his flight from Germany in 1933. Approximately twenty years earlier, Schoenberg immersed himself in a new theory of pan-tonality and twelve-tone composition. In his new system of twelve-tone serialism, Schoenberg rejected the traditional, hierarchical theory of music for one which viewed the idea of 'dissonance' as a false concept. Dissonant pitch combinations once avoided and meticulously resolved into consonance were embraced in Schoenberg's new system of harmony. In an undated letter to Ferrucio Busoni, Schoenberg described the qualities of his theory:

> I strive for: complete liberation of all forms
> from all symbols
> of cohesion and
> of logic.
> Thus:
> away with *motivic working out.*
> Away with harmony as
> cement or building bricks.
> Harmony is *expression*
> and nothing else.
> Then:
> Away with Pathos!
> Away with protracted ten-ton scores, for erected or constricted
> towers, rocks and other massive claptrap.
> My music must be
> *brief.*
> Concise! In two notes: not built, but *expressed!!*
> [...][2]

With this simple explanation, Schoenberg effectively swept away centuries of music theory, providing impetus for the storm of outrage and exclusionism in which his contemporaries soon enveloped him.

Striking out against Schoenberg and his small but dedicated following was a much larger and far more vocal group fighting against the direction Schoenberg was taking his music. The world was introduced to pan-tonal music with the performance of *Pierrot Lunaire* in 1912. Those attending the

---

[2] Walter Frisch: Arnold Schoenberg to Ferruccio Busoni, undated. In: *Arnold Schoenberg. Self-Portrait: A Collection of Articles, Program Notes, and Letters by the Composer about His Own Works.* Pacific Palisades: Belmont Music Publishers 1998. P. 10.

performance were unequivocal in their response, erupting into riot at the concert hall. Similar protests, whether manifest in the violence of riot or words, followed each new composition. Despite eventually coming to enjoy conditional acceptance by some musicians, feelings of antagonism toward the composer lingered well after his 1925 appointment as professor of music at the Berlin Academy for the Arts. While a small number of students embraced Schoenberg's new style, many of his colleagues pushed the composer into an increasingly isolated state. This antagonism and isolationism certainly contributed to Schoenberg's 1930 article, "My Public":

> Called upon to say something about my public, I have to confess: I do not believe I have one. [...] There are many reasons why the great public makes little contact with me. Above all: the generals, who today still occupy the music directorates, are mostly moving along lines that my line does not fit, or else they are afraid to put before the public something they do not themselves understand. [...] I have seen countless times that, as regards the main point, it was not the public who hissed: it was a small but active 'expert' minority. The public's behavior is either friendly or indifferent, unless they are intimidated because their spiritual leaders are protesting. [...] It was characteristic that the loudest disturber of the [Italian premiere of *Pierrot Lunaire*] was identified as the director of the conservatoire.[3]

Despite the myriad voices advising Schoenberg to return to the traditions of harmony, Schoenberg continued in his own musical faith in pursuit of a new aesthetic ideal.

The aesthetic battle and growing isolation playing out in Schoenberg's life finds parallel expression in Schoenberg's dramatic opera *Moses und Aron*. Nearly completed by the time Schoenberg wrote "My Public", the work was composed, as was his wont, in his pan-tonal style. In using his own libretto and pan-tonal compositional methods to tell the story of Moses' encounter with the burning bush, the struggle to bring the people into a new aesthetic faith, and the people's continued and mistaken worship of symbols, Schoenberg was, in effect, telling his own story of social rejection and self-sacrifice in the cause of a musical and artistic aesthetic ideal. The parallels between the dismayed shouts of Schoenberg's critics and those of the disapproving priests are unmistakable. Just as the newspapers called for Schoenberg to return to harmonic reasoning and to return to the tonal style of his earlier works, the priests of Schoenberg's opera cried out to Moses and Aron: "Wahnsinnige! Wovon soll euch die Wüste nähren?". Schoenberg, in his writings and through the operatic voice of Moses, replied: "In der Wüste wird euch die Reinheit des Denkens nähren, erhalten und entwickeln..." Like the priests who failed to comprehend

---

[3] Arnold Schoenberg: My Public (1930). In *Style and Idea*. Ed. by Leonard Stein. Berkeley: University of California Press 1984 [1975]. Pp. 96–98.

the philosophical essence of the Biblical wasteland and worshipped symbol rather than idea, Schoenberg's contemporaries in academia worshipped music as style and symbol rather than as pure expression.

Though exile in his musical career began as a pressure from without, it quickly became a condition Schoenberg needed in order to attain his aesthetic goal. The Moses-like pureness of thought described by Schoenberg's libretto closely corresponds with what Schoenberg called the musical Idea. According to Schoenberg, the Idea is represented by the "totality of a piece", or "the method by which balance is restored" in a composition.[4] At its most elemental level, the musical Idea can be described as Music for Music's sake. Limited by what Schoenberg may have called the humanistic contraptions of style and symbol, conventional compositional practices obscured the purity of the Idea Schoenberg sought to express in each piece. His theory of twelve-tones, however, offered limitless possibilities of expression within a defined set of rules. In terms of *Moses und Aron*, Dominique Jameux astutely noted that the power of serialism lay in its ability to capture "the transcendence of thought in face of the contingence of action".[5]

Indeed, popular musical works of the early 1930's represent the philosophical antithesis of Schoenberg's musical aesthetic. Audiences eager for lighthearted, predictable music dramas depicting everyday life wanted little to do with music requiring active, analytical listening. Schoenberg remarked on this turn of taste in a brief article appearing in the *Berliner Börsen-Zeitung* on January 1, 1931:

> Today musical taste, as well as the public's ability to absorb musical works, is considerably hampered by Americanism in art, which to art's detriment, imposes upon it a mechanical cliché. The result is the public's acclimation to inferior musical production so that it is no longer able to distinguish between music of value and inferior kitsch. With a shrug, all masterpieces are declared outdated. That is the effect of the present on music. One cannot even claim that music is in a crisis. It is rather a crisis of public taste that we can observe today.[6]

Rejecting popular values, Schoenberg explained at length his own aesthetic ideal in a description of *Verklärte Nacht*, Opus 4:

> My composition was, perhaps somewhat different from other illustrative compositions, firstly, by not being for orchestra but for a chamber group and secondly,

---

[4] Schoenberg. In: *Style and Idea* (n. 3). P. 123.
[5] "Serialisme renvoit tout simplement au suject même de Moïse et Aaron: La transcendence d'une pensée face à la contingence d'une action". Dominique Jameux: Résonances de Moïse et Aaron. In: *L'Avant Scène Opéra* 167 (1995). P. 81.
[6] Schoenberg: Crisis of Taste. In: *Berliner Börsen-Zeitung* (January 1, 1930). In: *Schoenberg and His World*. Ed. by Walter Frisch. Princeton (NJ): Princeton University Press 1999. P. 291.

because it does not illustrate any action or drama, but was restricted to portray nature and to express human feelings. It seems that, due to this attitude, my composition has gained qualities which can also satisfy if one does not know what it illustrates, or in other words, it offers the possibility to be appreciated as pure music. Thus it can perhaps make you forget the poem which many a person today might call rather repulsive.[7]

Thus, Schoenberg's pursuit of the pure expression of the Idea led him further away from his contemporaries and deeper into his musical exile.

One final detail must be added to Schoenberg's isolation within academia and his conception of the musical Idea if his exile is to be fully comprehended. Namely, while protesting his isolation, both political and musical, Schoenberg just as often glorified his condition of musical exile. This point is perhaps best explained by Schoenberg himself in a 1931 radio lecture:

Far be it from me to question the rights of the majority. But one thing is certain: somewhere there is a limit to the *power* of the majority; it occurs, in fact, wherever the essential step is one that cannot be taken by all and sundry. That is my situation: I find myself in a minority, facing not only those who prefer light music, but also those who prefer serious music. It would be inconceivable to attack the heroes who make daring flights over the ocean or to the North Pole, for their achievement is obvious to everyone. But although experience has shown that many a pioneer trod his path with absolute certainty at a time when he was still held to be wandering half-demented, most people invariably turn against those who strike out into unknown regions of the spirit. […] We accept the activities of cave explorers, polar explorers and pilots as essential. So, if I say so in all modesty, are the activities of those who try to achieve something comparable in the spiritual and artistic fields. They, too, have rights. […][8]

What may have begun as a socially imposed isolation soon became Schoenberg's mantle in which he enveloped himself as he struggled for a new musical and artistic aesthetic. Schoenberg continued to refer to this struggle and to the resulting sense of isolation as he defended his compositional style well into his later years of life.

Paralleling his exclusion from academia, socio-political circumstances led to a political exile. Sensitive to the growing surge of anti-Semitism, the issue of nationality occupied much of Schoenberg's thoughts during the late 1920's and into the 1930's. In a letter to Wassily Kandinsky, Schoenberg wrote: "I have finally understood and shall not yet forget. Specifically, that I am no German,

---

[7] Schoenberg: Program Notes to a Recording (August 26, 1950). In: *Arnold Schoenberg. Self-Portrait* (n. 7). P. 119.
[8] Schoenberg: Variations for Orchestra, Opus 31. Frankfurt Radio Talk (March 22, 1931). In: *Arnold Schoenberg. Self-Portrait* (n. 7). P. 41.

no European, indeed perhaps hardly a human being (at least the Europeans prefer the worst of their race to me) but that I am a Jew".[9] Following the 1932 Nazi sweep of the German parliament, Schoenberg voiced his doubts about his national identity in a letter to Alban Berg:

> For here I'm constantly obliged to consider the question whether and, if so, to what extent I am doing the right thing in regarding myself as belonging here or there, and whether it is forced upon me... Of course I know perfectly well where I belong. I've had it hammered into me so loudly and so long that only by being deaf to begin with could I have failed to understand it... Today I am proud to call myself a Jew; but I know the difficulties of really being one.[10]

From this time forward, Schoenberg dedicated himself to securing safe passage for Jews trying to escape increasingly harsh persecution. During the three year period from 1930 to 1933, Schoenberg took time away from his composing in order to travel throughout Europe, working with various organizations to secure safe passages. It was likely during this time that Schoenberg began formulating his meticulous plan for an independent Jewish state, the creation of which Schoenberg anticipated throughout the wartime period yet was never invited to be involved in. At this time, however, when a Jewish state was yet a plan, Jewishness for Schoenberg meant not so much community and belonging as it did volition.

Schoenberg's emphasis on volition in religious practices became apparent following his conversion from Orthodox Judaism to Lutheranism in 1898. Jameux suggests that this apparent move away from Judaism was less an abeyance to social pressures and more a reaction against the highly structured form of religion he had been immersed in throughout childhood.[11] Though never fully explaining the conversion, Schoenberg implied throughout his biographical writings that he viewed himself as an atheist for a brief period around this date. Throughout the opening years of the 20th century, Schoenberg questioned his belief system, exploring one after another without fully committing to any. His metaphysical wanderings during this time became

---

[9] Schoenberg: Arnold Schoenberg to Wassily Kandinsky (April 20, 1923). In: Bluma Goldstein: Schoenberg's *Moses und Aron*. A Vanishing Biblical Nation. In: *Political and Religious Ideas in the Works of Arnold Schoenberg*. Ed. by Charlotte M. Cross and Russel A. Berman. New York: Garland Publishing 2000. P. 160.
[10] Allen Shaw: Arnold Schoenberg to Alban Berg (September 23, 1932). In: *Arnold Schoenberg's Journey*. New York: Farrar, Straus, and Giroux 2002. P. 223.
[11] Dominique Jameux: Résonances de Moïse et Aaron. In: *L'Avant Scène Opéra* 167 (1995). P. 81.

outwardly manifest in his 1901 draft for an opera libretto. Setting the stage for Act II, scene 3, Schoenberg wrote:

> In a third group people are going from the conversation on superstition to talk about God. THEODOR and EMMA are atheists. KONRAD polemicizes against atheism. The conversations are held in such a way that one alternately hears one group then the other. Finally one listens to the group around KONRAD, who is just saying: "The belief in God leads to culture and art. Unbelief, however, deprives man of any relationship to imagination, and thus of every basis for art".[12]

What Schoenberg was looking for in his metaphysical wanderings, then, was a cultural and artistic foundation for his own artistic endeavors. This search eventually led Schoenberg to the musical aesthetic described above in his letter to Busoni and was re-affirmed in such dramatic works as *Die Glückliche Hand* (composed 1910–1913), *Die Jakobsleiter* (begun 1915, unfinished), *Der Biblische Weg* (composed 1922–1923) and *Moses und Aron* (begun 1930, unfinished).

By the 1930's Schoenberg found himself at a crossroads in his personal life and professional career. If he were to choose the path of renunciation, Schoenberg must reject both his Jewish identity and his musical aesthetic. Despite having converted to Lutheranism, Schoenberg's social critics were yet unconvinced that Schoenberg had fully renounced his Jewish heritage. Even if Schoenberg had kept his concerns over the future of the Jewish condition in Europe silent, critics had only to look at Schoenberg's dramatic works on distinctly Jewish topics to confirm their suspicions. This choice, supported by the tentative endorsements of a few music critics,[13] would have theoretically secured his position in musical academia and German society. The other path,

---

[12] Joseph Auner: *A Schoenberg Reader. Documents of a Life*. New Haven: Yale University Press 2003. P. 31.

[13] "During the hour and a half [lecture by Schoenberg], they also may have learned how difficult it is at any given time to understand new art, and thus to judge it. They also may have learned how irresponsible it is to stroke it down with cheap arguments and thus to prejudice others against it. But for those who already knew something about new art, the most impressive aspect of the lecture lay in two things. First, that an artist equipped with the ability to communicate his ideas and goals in surprisingly simple verbal terms (and who not without humor and wit can distance himself from his work and its consequences) is still conscious that artistically he communicates only with difficulty. And finally, we see how much conviction and loyalty he nevertheless demonstrates as he searches for new values in this era of the inevitable reevaluation of old values". Karl Holl: A Musician Offers a Glimpse into his Workshop. In: *Frankfurter Zeitung* (March 23, 1931) cited in *Schoenberg and His World* (n. 6). P. 278.

down which Schoenberg could retain his Jewish identity and follow the path of his own musical aesthetic, would prove life-threatening, leave him without a national identity, and would assuredly end his teaching career in Germany. Schoenberg explained his choice as regards aesthetics in a retrospective article written in 1937:

> But then this happens: after having composed an extensive work [*Gurrelieder*], he visits a dear friend, his closest one and one whose judgment and musical knowledge seem to him perfectly indisputable. [...]
> Today it seems perhaps unbelievable that my friend did not recognize the melodies in songs like these two. [...] But knowing I had written melodies and feeling that they were not poor, I had the choice either of being discouraged or of doubting my friend's authority. I decided not to be discouraged. [...] I had had to fight for every new work; I had been offended in the most outrageous manner by criticism; I had lost friends and I had completely lost any belief in the judgment of friends. And I stood alone against a world of enemies. [...] While composing for me had been a pleasure, now it became a duty. I knew I had to fulfill a task: I had to express what was necessary to be expressed and I knew I had the duty of developing my ideas for the sake of progress in music, whether I liked it or not; but I also had to realize that the great majority of the public did not like it [...].[14]

This article, in which Schoenberg again glorified his isolation in defense of an aesthetic ideal, pronounces Schoenberg's decision. Accompanying his declaration of faith in his new musical theory, Schoenberg publicly reconverted to Judaism in July, 1933. The timing and public nature of this conversion could hardly be coincidental. According to Schoenberg's own accounts, he had privately returned to Judaism several years prior but decided nonetheless to make a very public reconversion just as antagonism towards Jews in Berlin ceased to be merely an undercurrent and transformed into an unavoidable fact of life.

Schoenberg sealed his fate with these decisions; the choices of 1933 became fuel for the fire soon to envelop the composer. Replacing the few cautious endorsements of only two years prior, critics now railed against Schoenberg the composer and Schoenberg the Jew. A February 1933 review of a lecture by Schoenberg marks the violent turn in sentiment:

> [...] Schoenberg, the intellectual creator of a compositional method aiming to destroy occidental music as it becomes a part of history – creator of a music whose style for the most part exists on paper anyway – has withdrawn as a theoretician as

---

[14] Schoenberg: How One Becomes Lonely (October 11, 1937). In *Style and Idea*. Ed. by Leonard Stein. Berkeley, CA: University of California Press 1984 [1975]. Pp. 39–40.

well into the loneliness of an art for art's sake ideology untouched by a creative and functional life.[15]

An even more vitriolic commentary shortly followed:

> [...] Here are the signs of such mental poverty that it does not even allow him to 'think up' something new, proving him to have become an absurdity to himself! Schoenberg's sick and desperate efforts to believe himself important, to lull his listeners with witticisms of a typically Jewish manner, his striving to cover an inner emptiness and lack of restraint with a deluge of words, all has to repel any person with healthy feelings. [...] If it was possible for Schoenberg to add to the negative image of his personal and musical appearance, he succeeded with this lecture.[16]

Coinciding with such socio-politically based criticisms of his music, the April, 1933, Law for the Restoration of the Professional Civil Servant launched a new threat against Schoenberg's career. The implementation of this law promoting the termination of employees unable to prove Aryan decent brought Schoenberg's career at the Berlin Academy to an abrupt end on September 20th, 1933. The following day he wrote the following letter to cellist and conductor Pablo Casals:

> Dear friend and grand maestro,
> Unfortunately, I am forced to ask you if it would be possible for you to play the first performance of the Concerto for Violoncello that I have dedicated to you in London, already on the 29th of November, 1933, at the Broadcasting. I have said "unfortunately", and that is, in this sense, almost ridiculous, because in reality I would be happy if it were possible: to give a first performance with a master without parallel as you are. But what is "unfortunately" is the cause that forces me to ask you to play this work, at a time which is perhaps not convenient to you. The reason, briefly, is: Yesterday I received a letter from the Arts Academy at which, as you know, I was the "Director of a class in composition". I was, because after this letter, I no longer am. I was dismissed yesterday the 20th of September, and it has been determined that I will receive on October 1 my monthly payment for the last time!! All of a sudden, without the slightest warning++) my contract has been voided, which, without this violation would have given me two years to establish a new life abroad.
>
> But now, all of a sudden, I am obliged to do whatever I can to earn money. [...]

---

[15] J.W.: Arnold Schoenberg's Idea. In: *Kölnische Zeitung* (February 11, 1933). In: *Schoenberg and His World* (n. 6). P. 279.

[16] Music-Ideas from Yesterday – A Lecture by Arnold Schoenberg at the Society for New Music, Cologne. In: *Völkischer Beobachter* (February 24, 1933). In: *Schoenberg and His World* (n. 6). Pp. 280–281.

++) I beg you not to publish these facts because the government takes revenge (as the case of Einstein has shown), and in my case, it would be my parents, who are still in Germany, who could serve as hostages![17]

After a brief stop in Paris, Schoenberg found himself in America by November of that year. With no other job prospects open to him, Schoenberg took a low-paying teaching position with the newly formed Malkin College, for which he traveled weekly between Boston and New York to fulfill his new obligations.

With his move to the United States, Schoenberg faced a new and unsettling form of isolation. Unlike his European experience, American audiences enthusiastically greeted Schoenberg, setting him at a level both above and apart from all others. Reflecting on the question 'who is the greatest living composer', the author of a January 7, 1933, article in the *Northwest Musical Herald* declared: "I nominate [Schoenberg] as a most likely candidate for the post of the world's most significant composer".[18] Perhaps with the opera *Moses und Aron* in mind, Nicolas Slonimsky wrote: "There is something biblical in Schönberg's spectacular martyrdom. Shuttling between Vienna and Berlin, revered by disciples, derided by scurrilous critics, he is the very picture of a prophet of the faith".[19]

Such overwhelming acceptance seemed unreliable to Schoenberg; he feared his music may be revered as a novelty object. Schoenberg expressed these fears in one of his earliest speeches in America:

> And allow me to say: in the same measure, as your acknowledgement enjoys me, in the same measure I am apprehensive. I fear now to be overestimated by you! Don't think, that I am saying that only for *modesty*! For in reality: I *know* my value; and I know also, which is my *work* and my merit. And, on the contrary, as I am knowing all that, I must consequently fear that, one day, you will have enough of such an appreciation, so as one has enough of certain foods of an extraordinary or extravagant character; so as human beings get enough of all that, what seems out of order, out of the daily regularity. And then, you shall *depreciate* me. [...] [A composer] who, on the contrary, has always and exclusively intended: to concentrate *all praise* to the *work*, such an author must fear to be overestimated as "caviar" and "creams"; and he must fear, that, one day, he could be depreciated, even as "caviar" and

---

[17] Schoenberg: Arnold Schoenberg to Pablo Casals (September 22, 1933). In: *Arnold Schoenberg Correspondence. A Collection of Translated and Annotated Letters Exchanged with Guido Adler, Pablo Casals, Emanuel Feuermann, and Olin Downes*. Ed. by Egbert M. Ennulat. Metuchen (NJ): The Scarecrow Press 1991. Pp. 175–179.
[18] Henry Cowell: Who is the Greatest Living Composer? In *Northwest Musical Herald* (January 7, 1933). In: *Schoenberg and His World* (n. 6). Pp. 315–317.
[19] Nicolas Slonimsky: Welcome for the Incoming Modern Master: Roundabout with Schoenberg Who Should Arrive in Boston Next Week. In: *Boston Evening Post* (October 28, 1933). In: *Schoenberg and His World* (n. 6). P. 318.

"creams". And therefore it is a burning desire of such authors, to get a place in the valuation of men, not as an extravagant, but as a daily food; to grow: *daily bread* of friends and art![20]

Schoenberg reiterated these concerns in 1937, retrospectively remarking on his German audiences:

> While the music proved to me lasting, these audiences were unstable. As suddenly as they had turned their favour to me and had procured me a popularity which was not consistent with my style, and which always seemed to me unsound, the same audiences made another turn and became hostile towards my music.[21]

This turn in public sentiment becomes all the more poignant by the parallel dramatic turn in events Schoenberg described in *Moses und Aron* ten years prior. With the amazement of the wonders Aron showed them, the people of Israel followed Moses and Aron into the wasteland to the foot of a mountain. Moses' followers remained below with Aron while he continued the ascent alone. In Moses' absence, however, the people began to doubt and grow fearful of a God that could not be seen and who existed as concept and belief, or Idea, rather than physical form. Seeking to calm their fears by demonstrating the powers of God, Aron created the golden calf. This symbol, around which the people rejoiced and descended into materialistic orgy, merely obscured the Idea for, as Aron himself had said earlier "Erwartet die Form nicht vor dem Gedanken! Aber gleichzeitig wird sie da sein!". Upon his return, Moses cast down the symbol, remarking "Vergeh, du Abbild des Unvermögens, das Grenzenlose in ein Bild zu fassen!". Without the golden calf or some other earthly symbol, the people dispersed, unable to comprehend the Idea. In Schoenberg's understanding, it was a similar fear that helped turn audiences against him:

> And we ask: How is it that such changes are perceived as upheavals; that they are called revolutions, that people become so excited over them? In reality, the obvious reason is this: that the effect of such changes within the work of art is equivalent to the change of course of a planet, at least as far as our perceptive faculties are concerned, which fear to find a new, un-known, and incomprehensible reality behind the new surface.[22]

---

[20] Schoenberg: For New York, delivered at the League of Composers' All-Schoenberg Welcome Concert and Reception, (November 11, 1933). In: *Schoenberg and His World* (n. 6). Pp. 292–293.
[21] Schoenberg: How One Becomes Lonely (October 11, 1937). In: *Style and Idea*. Ed. by Leonard Stein. Berkeley, CA: University of California Press 1984. Pp. 51–42.
[22] Schoenberg: A lecture about *Die glückliche Hand* (Breslau 1928). In: *Arnold Schoenberg Self-Portrait. A Collection of Articles, Program notes, and Letters by the Composer about his own Works*. Pacific Palisades: Belmont Music Publishers 1988. Pp. 32–33.

The turn against Moses and against the purity of idea represented in the scene of the golden calf unfolds yet again in Schoenberg's reality. In an article written in 1937, Schoenberg reflected on his relationship with his American audiences: "[...] As soon as the war was over, there came another wave which procured for me a popularity unsurpassed since. My works were played everywhere and acclaimed in such a manner that I started to doubt the value of my music [...]".[23]

The argument may be made that Schoenberg's exile was short-lived, as he found a new home within only three years of leaving Berlin. The welcoming endorsements Schoenberg received in New England upon his arrival in the country are certainly indicative of his new place within American society. Particularly following his appointment in 1936 to the faculty of the University of California Los Angeles, it may be argued that Schoenberg grew acculturated to American society as he settled into a new home where he remained for the rest of his life. Schoenberg also came to enjoy a large circle of friends within the Los Angeles intelligentsia, hosting gatherings at his home every Sunday with guests including Otto Klemperer, Eduard Stuermann, Artur Schnabel, Ernst Krenek, Edgard Varèse, Ernst Toch, Thomas Mann, and Alma Mahler-Werfel, among many others.[24] As time passed, Schoenberg's music made a marked return to more traditional forms of composition. These are all signs, as some suggest, of Schoenberg's acceptance into American society and the end of his exile.[25] Yet such a view fails to consider Schoenberg's broader place and work in America, which remained a constant struggle for him. While Schoenberg did find a position at UCLA, he was never afforded the latitude he expected, and his detailed plans for a curriculum for composition were never adopted during his lifetime. Perhaps it is ironic that his proposed requirements for a graduate program, including thorough knowledge of individual works, informing students of what to study for their oral examinations, inviting non-music faculty to participate on the oral examination committee, and a thesis on a problem of composition, have since been more or less adopted in many major musical institutions across the country.[26]

---

[23] Arnold Schoenberg: How One Becomes Lonely (n. 14). P. 51.
[24] Dorothy Lamb Crawford: Arnold Schoenberg in Los Angeles. In: *The Musical Quarterly* 86 (1). P. 19.
[25] Sabine Feißt is an advocate of this position. For further discussion see: Sabine Feißt: Zur Rezeption von Schönbergs Schaffen in Amerika vor 1933. In: *Journal of the Arnold Schoenberg Center* 4 (2002). Pp. 279–291; Sabine Feißt: Arnold Schoenberg and the Cinematic Art. In: *The Musical Quarterly* 83 (1). Pp. 93–113.
[26] Craword, Dorothy Lamb: Arnold Schoenberg in Los Angeles. In: The Musical Quarterly 86 (1). P. 24.

His struggle to have his educational philosophy adopted by UCLA was accompanied with an on-going struggle to have his works performed. Contradicting the numerous radio interviews that continued for some time after his arrival in America, performances of his works made a distinct decline: "Thanks to the attitude of most American conductors and under the leadership of Toscanini, Koussevitzky and [Bruno] Walter suppression of my works soon began with the effect that a number of performances of my works sunk to an extremely low point".[27]

Describing this new, popular isolation, Schoenberg wrote to Aaron Copland:

> But there is at least one man here in Los Angeles who goes around forbidding people to 'make propaganda' for Schoenberg, when they only speak about facts. And CBS has evidently intended to hit me, when they ordered 'no controversial music' to be broadcast – while they broadcast quite a number of controversial music from other composers. And you might know also about the attitude of "MY" publisher G. Schirmer, who if possible tries to counteract performances of my music... and many other similar facts.[28]

Schoenberg's apparent paranoia and sense of isolation were not entirely unfounded. Contemporary music critic Francis Perkins noted "that Mr. Schoenberg has reason for bitterness over the infrequency of the performance of his music in this country is suggested, so far as the New York orchestral field is concerned, by a look at a list which this department has maintained for twenty-five years".[29] Documentation of performances by the New York Philharmonic[30] reveals that the orchestra did not perform a single composition by Schoenberg from January 1932 until October 1935. From that time to the close of the 1945 concert season the New York Philharmonic included only four different pieces by Schoenberg in a matter of 20 total concerts. Schoenberg's earlier work, *Verklaerte Nacht*, Op. 4, accounts for just over half of these concerts. There was a similar situation in Chicago, where the Chicago

---

[27] Virgil Thomson: Schoenberg Celebrates Seventy-fifth Birthday with Attack on Conductors. In: *The New York Herald Tribune* (September 11, 1949). *Arnold Schoenberg Correspondence. A Collection of Translated and Annotated Letters Exchanged with Guido Adler, Pablo Casals, Emanuel Feuermann, and Olin Downes.* Ed. by Egbert M. Ennulat. Metuchen (NJ): The Scarecrow Press 1991. Pp. 260–261.
[28] Schoenberg: Arnold Schoenberg to Aaron Copland (February 21, 1950). In: *Arnold Schoenberg Correspondence* (n. 27). P. 271.
[29] Francis D. Perkins: Schoenberg and the Conductors: Record Bears Out His Position, in the *New York Herald Tribune* (October 2, 1949). In: *Arnold Schoenberg Correspondence* (n. 27). Pp. 260–261.
[30] Performance list compiled by philharmonic historian Richard Wandel (August 2006).

Symphony Orchestra performed only six works by Schoenberg between 1933 and 1945. Of these six selections, four were Schoenberg's arrangements of pieces by Bach, Brahms, and Handel. The remaining two works were *Verklaerte Nacht*, Op. 4, and *Five Pieces for Orchestra*, Op. 16. Slightly less than 90% of all performances by the Chicago Symphony Orchestra occurred between 1934 and 1938.[31]

Despite these difficulties, Schoenberg continued to defend his musical aesthetic. To pose the thesis that Schoenberg's return to tonal music during his final years is symbolic of his acculturation again neglects to look at the broader body of Schoenberg's intellectual output during his American years. In an article for the 1948 newsletter of the League of Composers, Schoenberg took the opportunity to remark upon the invasive and deleterious effects of commercialism on American composition, writing: "must one tolerate the moral and mental baseness of people who bow to the mere temptation of profits? [...] Is it aesthetically and morally admissible to accommodate the listener's mentality and preference?".[32] That Schoenberg explored the possibilities of American cinema, now perceived as an inherently commercial enterprise, in 1935 is less a matter of becoming bound by Americanisms and more a matter of exploring the artistic potential of a relatively new medium. In reflecting on the impact of his immigration to America on his music, Schoenberg remarked:

> If immigration to America has changed me – I am not aware of it. Maybe I would have finished the third act of *Moses and Aron* earlier. Maybe I would have written more when remaining in Europe, but I think: nothing comes out, what was not in. And two times two equals four in every climate. Maybe I had four times four times harder to work for a living. But, I made no concessions to the market.[33]

Schoenberg's exile was lasting. Physically speaking, it took little time for Schoenberg to establish a home and a dedicated group of friends after his arrival in America. His exile, however, was intellectually oriented, founded in Schoenberg's unbounded belief in the purity of the musical idea which could not bend to the whim of social or commercial materialism. It was in this manner that Schoenberg remained in a state of exile well after his arrival in America. Initially sent into social exile by music critics who reviled his musical aesthetic and by socio-cultural constructions determined against the rights

---

[31] Performance list compiled by philharmonic historian Frank Villela (August 2006).
[32] Schoenberg: Music and Morality. In: *The Composer's News-Record* 7–8 (Fall-Winter 1948–49). P. 306.
[33] Albert Goldberg: The Transplanted Composer. In: *Los Angeles Times* (14 May, 1950).

of Jewish heritage, Schoenberg's exile was later reinforced first by the 'greater-than-life' representations of his artistry, exclusion from popular media, and, finally, self-enforced as part of the mantel inherent to the role of aesthetic leader. His exile was complete and inescapable. As Casals noted, Schoenberg bore this weight "with an attitude of self-sacrifice". Schoenberg had, in effect, become Moses in the wasteland acknowledging his isolation and the driving need to toil for a musical truth from the space of exile. As did Moses, Schoenberg sought to bring a new language, a new musical 'religion' to the world. Schoenberg threw the final light on his relationship with exile:

> It should be discouraging to my suppressors to recognize the failure of their attempts. You cannot change the natural evolution of the arts by a command; you may make a New Year's resolution to write only what everybody likes; but you cannot force real artists to descend to the lowest standard to give up morals, character, and sincerity, to avoid presentation of new ideas.[34]

---

[34] Virgil Thomson: Schoenberg Celebrates Seventy-fifth Birthday with Attack on Conductors, in: *New York Herald Tribune* (September 11, 1949). In: *Arnold Schoenberg Correspondence* (n. 27). P. 261.

III. Narrating Exilic Travel

Patrick B. Farges

Transit/Transfer/Transgression: Das Erzählen von "Ent-Ortung" in Anna Seghers' Erzählungen (1924–1980)[1]

One aspect of Anna Seghers' work that has found relatively little resonance so far is the multicultural and international dimension of her oeuvre. Whereas Seghers scholars have largely dealt with the German problematic of her literature, the author also widely addressed issues of displacement – before, during, and after exile. Of course, it is no surprise that Seghers' 'excursions' (Ausflüge[2]) are closely linked to her exile after 1933: excursions in the upside-down and Utopian "Eleventh Empire" (Das Elfte Reich, 1939), *excursions in occupied France, the country that became a second home to her and her children (e.g. her novel* Transit*), excursions in the lost vs. in the new* Heimat (Der Ausflug der toten Mädchen, 1943/1944). *However, Seghers' taste for narrating stories of excursions had existed before and lasted long after the exilic experience* per se (Karibische Geschichten, 1962; Das wirkliche Blau. Eine Geschichte aus Mexiko, 1967; Drei Frauen aus Haiti, 1980). *This study shows that the confrontation of a genre (the short story) with a theme (displacement) was of particular importance to Anna Seghers.*

Begriffe wie "Ent-Ortung" oder *displacement* werden – jedenfalls im akademischen Diskurs – oft verwendet, um das postmoderne Dasein schlechthin zu charakterisieren. Es scheint aber notwendig, gerade diesen diskursiven Komplex ebenfalls zu dekonstruieren und die narrativen Strategien zu untersuchen, die jene aufgestellt haben, die selbst sozusagen "Ent-Ortung am eigenen Leibe" erlebt haben. Denn Ent-Ortung ist nicht nur eine postmoderne Erscheinung. Ent-Ortung ist keine einseitige Erfahrung, die nur mit Verlust und Abwesenheit verbunden ist, sondern eine komplexe und vielschichtige. Im Laufe des 20. Jahrhunderts, des Jahrhundertes der erzwungenen Massenmigrationen, hat sich zudem das Spannungsverhältnis zwischen "hier" und "da", "diesseits" und "jenseits", "Einheimischem" und "Fremdem" grundlegend verändert. Georg Simmels "Exkurs über den Fremden" (1907) kann hier als Ausgangspunkt moderner soziologischer Konzeptionen der Ent-Ortung oder des Entstelltseins gesehen werden. Simmel schreibt:

> Es ist hier also der Fremde [...] nicht der Wandernde, der heute kommt und morgen geht, sondern [...] der, der heute kommt und morgen bleibt – sozusagen der potenziell

---

[1] Anna Seghers: *Erzählungen 1924–1980*. 6 Bde. Berlin: Aufbau 1994.
[2] Hier beziehe ich mich natürlich auf die Segherssche Erzählung *Der Ausflug der toten Mädchen*. In: *Erzählungen 1934–1946*. Berlin: Aufbau 1994. S. 194–225.

Wandernde, der, obgleich er nicht weitergezogen ist, die Gelöstheit des Kommens und Gehens nicht ganz überwunden hat.³

Indem er sich wissenschaftlich für die "Wandernden" und "Fremden" innerhalb der industriellen Gesellschaften interessierte, gründete Simmel eine fruchtbare soziologische Tradition der Moderne, deren Resonanz sich transatlantisch z.B. innerhalb der "Chicago School" mit dem ehemaligen Simmel-Schüler Robert Park fortführte. Fortan würde der "potenziell wandernde" Migrant – ein Gleichnis für den scheinbar assimilierten Juden? – eine zentrale hermeneutische Rolle spielen, z.B. in den soziologischen Schriften eines anderen Simmel-Schülers, Siegfried Kracauer, oder in den verschiedenen Abhandlungen über den städtischen Flaneur. Auch der 1899 in Wien geborene Alfred Schütz griff das Thema "Ent-Ortung" auf, als er sich im amerikanischen Exil an der *New School of Social Research* befand, u.a. in seinen zwei berühmten Essays, "The Stranger" und "The Homecomer", die die Dialektik von Ent-Ortung und Heimkehr in subtiler Weise darstellen.⁴ Mit Simmel, Schütz und anderen wurden Fremdsein und Entortung also nunmehr als *relative* Sachverhältnisse gesehen. Und genauso sind Exil-Erfahrung und Exil-Gefühl auf komplexe Weise miteinander verflochten und stimmen nicht unbedingt genau überein. So kann z. B. die tatsächliche Exilsituation ein lang währendes Gefühl des Ent-Stellt-Seins auf den einzelnen *transferieren*, oder nur mit der Erinnerung an eine *transit*orische Ent-Ortung verbunden sein. Manche sprechen sogar von einer paradoxen "Heimat des Exils". Jedenfalls muss die Literatur zum Thema "Exil-Reisen" über die bloße Periode des *erfahrenen* Exils hinausgehen und andere Schaffensphasen mit einbeziehen.

Im Falle von Anna Seghers spricht Friedrich Albrecht von drei Gruppen von Gestalten: der "Gruppe der Verfolgten", der Gruppe der Aufbruchfreudigen und der Gruppe der "Einzelgänger" und "Außenseiter".⁵ Daran anschließend

---

³ Georg Simmel: Exkurs über den Fremden. In: *Soziologie. Untersuchungen über die Formen der Vergesellschaftung*. Berlin: Duncker und Humblot 1908. S. 509–512. Hier: S. 510.
⁴ Robert Park, Ernest Burgess, Roderick McKenzie: *The City*. Chicago 1925; Alfred Schütz: The Stranger, an Essay in Social Psychology. In: *American Journal of Sociology* 49 (1944). S. 499–507. Ders.: The Homecomer. In: *AJS* 50 (1945). S. 363–376. Zu Schütz, vgl. Helmut R. Wagner: *Alfred Schütz. An Intellectual Biography*. Chicago: University of Chicago Press 1983. Zur Genealogie der urbanen Soziologie, vgl. Olivier Agard: Contributions juives à l'ethnographie urbaine: Simmel, Kracauer et l'Ecole de Chicago. In: *Revue germanique internationale* 17 (2002). S. 127–146.
⁵ Friedrich Albert: "Die Unruhe, die in uns steckt" – Anna Seghers in ihren Gestalten. In: *Argonautenschiff. Jahrbuch der Anna-Seghers-Gesellschaft* 10 (2001). S. 90–108. Hier: S. 94ff.

möchte ich hier versuchen, drei Formen der Ent-Ortung bei Seghers hervorzuheben: Transgression, Transfer und Transit.

Ent-Ortung als Transgression?

Anna Seghers wurde 1900 unter dem Namen Netty Reiling in einer jüdischen Mainzer Familie geboren. Ihre erste Erzählung, *Die Toten auf der Insel Djal*, erschien 1924. Vier Jahre später trat sie in die KPD ein und erhielt im selben Jahr den Kleist-Preis für zwei Erzählungen: *Grubetsch* und *Der Aufstand der Fischer von St. Barbara*. Ende Februar 1933 – also nur wenige Wochen nach Hitlers "Machtergreifung" – ging sie als politisch Verfolgte und Jüdin mit Familie ins französische Exil, wo sie den Einzug der deutschen Truppen 1940 und das darauffolgende *exode* miterlebte. Im Januar 1941 fuhr sie von Marseille aus über die Karibik – die zur wichtigen Zwischenstation für sie wurde – und Ellis Island nach Mexiko, wo sie Ende Juni ankam. Dort blieb sie sechs Jahre, bevor sie nach Deutschland remigrierte und zur Vorzeige-Autorin in der DDR avancierte.

Zwischen 1924 und 1980 blieb Seghers, die im Allgemeinen keinen großen Wert auf Genreabgrenzungen legte, einer schwer definierbaren Gattung treu, mit der sie *große* gesellschaftliche, historische und politische Themen behandelte: der in eine Reihe sich einfügenden oder autonomen *Erzählung*, obwohl man vielleicht eher große *Sozialromane* von ihr erwartet hätte. Wie Hans Mayer urteilt, zeigte Seghers' schöpferische Kraft dann ihre Grenzen, als sie unter dem Einfluss ihres Freundes Georg Lukács versuchte, gerade diese groß angelegten Sozialromane zu schreiben. Und laut Mayer offenbare sich vielleicht gerade darin die Begrenztheit des realistischen Romans.[6]

Eines scheint Seghers immer wieder dazu bewogen zu haben, jene kurzen, begrenzten aber eine ganze Welt in sich bergenden Erzählungen zu verfassen: das Gefühl für die Begrenztheit ihrer Umwelt. Über ihre Jugend schreibt sie:

> Ich wollte überhaupt nur studieren, weil ich fürchterliche Angst hatte, in dem Nest Mainz hängenzubleiben.
> [D]as Eingesperrtsein [...] war mir so zuwider, dass der Drang in mir immer stärker wurde, so schnell wie möglich auszufliegen, wegzufliegen.[7]

Dazu meint die Seghers-Biografin Christiane Zehl-Romero:

> Sie selbst fühlte sich, wie das Tagebuch belegt – aber nicht direkt ausspricht oder diskutiert – als Frau, Jüdin und Künstlerin in ihrer eigenen großbürgerlichen, von

---

[6] Hans Mayer: *Der Widerruf. Über Deutsche und Juden*. Frankfurt/Main: Suhrkamp 1994. Kapitel 5.
[7] Achim Roscher: Im Gespräch mit Anna Seghers. In: *Positionen 1. Wortmeldungen zur DDR-Literatur*. Hg. von E. Günther. Halle – Leipzig: Mitteldeutscher Verlag 1984. S. 142–168. Hier: S. 143–144.

den sozialen Problemen um sie her isolierten und ihr inauthentisch erscheinenden Welt sowohl fremd als eingesperrt.[8]

Eine Reflektion dieses Gefühls taucht in ihren Erzählungen auf und die Kurzform wurde somit für sie zum privilegierten Medium des Ausfluges in die Ferne und Fremde – in ihren Frühwerken natürlich, aber auch dann, als sie sich in der DDR zwar reveriert sah, aber dennoch immer eingeengter fühlte. Bei Seghers ist also "Transgression" immer zunächst mit Mobilität verbunden, mit dem Überschreiten von Grenzen.

Die 1926 veröffentlichte Erzählung *Grubetsch* gehört zu den eindrucksvollsten Sozialtableaus der Autorin. Der Ort, aus dem die Figuren herauswollen, aber nicht -können, ist ein "böser", "gelber Hof", wo man Kinder "einsperrt", bis sie schließlich sterben, in dessen "vier Ecken" nur ein spärliches "Grubenlicht" hineinkommt und selbst die "schmierige Sonnenflut" "nach ranzigem Fett [riecht]".[9] In Seghers' Frühwerk symbolisieren der Hof – oder die Schenke – die Orte des Eingesperrtseins und des proletarischen Schicksals schlechthin. In diesem Hof vergeht die Zeit nur durch das unregelmäßige Wiederkehren der teuflischen Figur des Flößers Grubetsch, der zwar Abwechslung, aber gleichzeitig auch Unglück mit sich bringt, als käme jedwede Veränderung der Lage immer einer Verschlimmerung gleich. In dem Hof wächst auch die junge Anna bei ihrem Bruder auf: "Was ist das, ein Unglück? dachte Anna. Ist es wie der Hof dort unten und wie das Zimmer dort hinten? Oder gibt es auch noch andere Unglücke, rote, glühende, leuchtende Unglücke? Ach, wenn ich so eins haben könnte!".[10]

Sie, die nichts anderes als Unglück kennt, sehnt sich nach Fernem, nach dem Hinüberschreiten in eine andere Welt, nach Transgression. Leider bleibt ihr (vielleicht als Frau) das Wegfliegen enthalten, ganz im Gegenteil zu dem doppelgängerartigen kränklichen Vogel, den sie als Geschenk bekommt und den ihr Bruder eines Tages aus Bosheit, oder eher Gleichgültigkeit, freilässt. Sicher fühlt sich Anna nur *ein* einziges Mal in einem noch engeren Ort, nämlich im Keller bei Grubetsch: "Hier ist es so gut und dunkel", fuhr Anna mit heller, gar nicht heiserer Stimme fort, "niemand sieht einen an, lass uns hierbleiben, lass mich nie mehr heraus, mich nie mehr durch den Hof gehen!".[11] Doch ihre Befreiungswünsche bleiben dahingestellt: Anna wird zur tragischen Figur, die an den harten Regeln des *hic et nunc* scheitert. Ähnliches geschieht in der kurz

---

[8] Christiane Zehl-Romero: *Anna Seghers. Eine Biographie*. Bd. 1: 1900–1947. Berlin: Aufbau 2000. S. 189.
[9] Seghers: Grubetsch. In: *Erzählungen 1924–1933*. Berlin: Aufbau 1994. S. 13–74. Hier: S. 13, 17, 19, 26, 35 und 66–67.
[10] Ebd. S. 15.
[11] Ebd. S. 35.

darauf entstandenen Erzählung *Die Ziegler* (1927/28), die erneut in einem dunklen und armseligen Hof, "zwischen Wall und Mauer" stattfindet.[12] Hier denkt die junge Marie:

> Mochte doch hinter der Scheibe etwas ganz anderes sein, etwas ganz Unerwartetes. Einen Augenblick gehörte sie in das helle Kreisrund der Lampe hinein. Es wurde hell in ihr, ihre Wünsche, ihr Kummer, ihre Angst. Vor ihren Augen flimmerte etwas, was einem Himmel ähnlich war, Bergen und Bäumen [...]. Sie wünschte sich sehr, alles genau zu erkennen. Sie hatte nie geträumt, dass es solche Abgründe geben möchte [...]. Sie sehnte sich danach, alles genau zu begreifen.[13]

"Transgression" ist also für Seghers weniger moralisch als sozial besetzt: Es geht darum, Klassengrenzen zu überschreiten. Nebenbei sei hier auch bemerkt, dass bereits Seghers' Frühwerk davon zeugt, dass sie nicht nur große *männliche* Figuren dargestellt hat. Bei ihr sind weibliche Figuren genauso auf- bzw. ausbruchbereit, sie haben durchaus Wünsche und Vorstellungen, aber die harten sozialen und *gender*-spezifischen Verhältnisse erlauben ihnen nicht, diese zu verwirklichen. So verweist Seghers auch immer auf den Zusammenhang zwischen sozialer und intergeschlechtlicher Gewalt. Wie Christiane Zehl-Romero unterstreicht, sind es nicht die Männer, sondern die "Frauen und Kinder, die schneller und sicherer das 'Richtige' wählen".[14] Transgression ist also bei Seghers immer mit dem sozial verankerten Bewusstsein der Transgressions(un)möglichkeit verbunden. Vielleicht liegt gerade darin der Grund, weshalb sie immer wieder auf mythische und märchenhafte Stoffe zurückgreift, die im Laufe der Jahre immer weniger mit den Prinzipien des realistischen Sozialismus vereinbar waren. Sie, die eine faszinierte Leserin von Märchen aus aller Welt war, hatte ein ausgeprägtes Gefühl für die Fülle und "Farbigkeit von Märchen", die ganze parallele Welten beinhalten.[15]

Und so diente ihr der Rückgriff aufs Imaginäre und Märchenhafte zum Experimentierfeld für soziale Veränderung. In ihren Geschichten haben verkehrte oder utopische Welten eine Spiegelfunktion, die über einen bloßen Eskapismus hinaus gehen. Ein wichtiger Teil der im Exil entstandenen Erzählungen befasst sich mit mythisch-legendären Stoffen, die aber *realistisch* dargestellt werden, so z. B. *Die schönsten Sagen vom Räuber Woynock* (1936) oder *Sagen von Artemis* (1937). In diesem Sinne ist auch die 1939 entstandene Erzählung *Reise ins Elfte Reich* zu interpretieren, in der biographische Gegebenheiten – eine Rarität bei Seghers – und Utopievorstellung ineinander

---

[12] Seghers: Die Ziegler. In: *Erzählungen 1924–1933* (wie Anm. 9). S. 75–126. Hier: S. 81.
[13] Ebd. S. 86 und 109.
[14] Zehl-Romero: *Anna Seghers* (wie Anm. 8). S. 131.
[15] Seghers: *Aufsätze, Ansprachen, Essays*, Bd. 1. Berlin/Weimar: Aufbau 1980. S. 87.

fließen. Den ewig wandernden "Passlosen" in dieser Geschichte "wurde [bereits in zehn Ländern] die Einreise verweigert [...], trotz aller Bürgschaften und Bürgen und Zeugnisse und Empfehlungen". Also "reisten dann alle zusammen los, ein paar Dutzend Leute, und kamen schließlich auch eines Abends an die Grenze des Elften Reiches".[16] Im Elften Reich verliert der Neuankömmling all seine bekannten Wertvorstellungen, doch diese radikale Entfremdung wird als gute Überraschung dargestellt. Die Neuankömmlinge – jüdische Exilanten aus Deutschland? – weigern sich z. B., jegliche "Orden" zu tragen, die hier als ein Gleichnis für das Tragen des Judensternes interpretiert werden können:

> Wir hatten alle an einem Tag Strafmandate bekommen auf Grund von Anzeigen, die wider uns eingelaufen waren wegen unbefugten Ablegens von Orden. Von ihrem Standpunkt aus mit einem gewissen Recht, nahm die Bevölkerung daran Anstoß, dass wir kahl und undekoriert daherkamen, was trotz der größten Anstrengungen für Einheimische unerreichbar blieb [...]. Man ermahnte uns, rasch den Abstand aufzuholen, der uns von den Einheimischen trennte, die in jugendlichem Alter in die Sitten und Gesetze eingewöhnt waren.[17]

Hier zeigt Seghers ihr Gefühl für die Notwendigkeit, gar die Unumgänglichkeit der Adaptation und der Akkulturation, ganz im Sinne der Simmelschen "Wandernden", "die heute komm[en] und morgen bleib[en]". Sie vertritt also dezidiert keine "mit dem Gesicht nach Deutschland"-Haltung.

Transfer und Akkulturation – ein real existierender Internationalismus

Im Exil wird dann für Seghers das "Wegfliegen" zur existentiellen Alltagsrealität. Doch "Ent-Ortung" ist für sie keineswegs eine einseitige Erfahrung, die nur Verlust und Abwesenheit mit sich bringt. Darüber schreibt sie folgendes in dem Essay *Frauen und Kinder in der Emigration*, der vermutlich 1938 im französischen Exil entstand:

> Viele zur Emigration gezwungene Menschen glauben am ersten Tag, alles verloren zu haben. Später haben sie dann gelernt, dass sie vieles gefunden und vieles gewonnen haben, wovon sie früher nicht einmal wussten, dass es das gab. Für gar viele aus dem deutschsprachigen Kleinbürgertum emigrierte Familien ist die Emigration sogar das "Endlich" geworden.[18]

---

[16] Seghers: Reise ins Elfte Reich. In: *Erzählungen 1934–1946*. Berlin: Aufbau 1994. S. 76–89. Hier: S. 76–77.
[17] Ebd. S. 85.
[18] Seghers: Frauen und Kinder in der Emigration. In: *Anna Seghers-Wieland Herzfelde. Ein Briefwechsel 1939–1946*. Berlin/Weimar 1985. S. 119. Zur Entstehungsgeschichte dieses Textes, siehe insb. Hélène Roussel. Anna Seghers' Blick auf Frankreich in "Frauen und Kinder in der Emigration". In: *Argonautenschiff* (wie Anm. 5). S. 65 ff.

Seghers wertet die Entdeckung neuer Welten durchaus positiv: Das Exil eröffnet auch Möglichkeiten der sozialen, geographischen und ethnischen Horizonterweiterung, indem der Einzelne *de facto* de-zentriert ist. Und so heißt es auch am Ende der Erzählung *Wiedereinführung der Sklaverei in Guadeloupe* über einen Knaben, der zufällig über die tragische Geschichte des französischen Kommandanten Beauvais gehört hat:

> Die Ahnung von einer ihm unbekannten Welt machte ihn frösteln. Das war eine Welt, die von seiner eigenen vertrauten wie durch einen Vorhang getrennt war. Es gab also noch eine andere Welt. Dort wurde nach anderen Gesetzen gehandelt.[19]

Bei weitem nicht alle Exilanten teilten diese Anschauung. Hier sei nur an den verzweifelten und entwurzelten Stefan Zweig erinnert, der sich "überall" als "Fremder und bestenfalls Gast" fühlte. Und in ihrem Exilroman *Transit* lässt Seghers den Anti-Helden Seidler sagen: "Wie zäh ist die Zeit zwischen den Abenteuern! Wie langweilig das gefahrlose Leben!".[20] Aber im Gegensatz zu vielen Exilanten – und später auch Exilforschern – interessierte Seghers sich nicht lediglich für Flucht und Heimkehr, d.h. für die epischen Höhepunkte und Aventüren des Exils, sondern vielmehr gerade für die Zeitabläufe *zwischen* den Abenteuern. Denn dort geschahen die menschlichen Entwicklungen, von denen sie erzählen wollte.

Am Anfang der Erzählung *Crisanta*, die wahrscheinlich 1950 entstand, steht z. B.: "Ihr fragt mich, wie die Menschen in Mexiko leben? – Von wem soll man erzählen?". Seghers will nicht über die "großen Männern" berichten, die in Mexiko und anderswo *Geschichte machen*. Ganz im Gegenteil: "Ich erzähle euch von *Crisanta*".[21] Statt Heldentum und Personenkult zu unterstützen, wendet sich Seghers – *vor* der De-Stalinisierung – den kleinen Leuten und ihrem "gefährlichen und gewöhnlichen Leben" – wie sie selbst sagt[22] – zu. Nicht das Angekommensein und nicht die Verlustgefühle und Anpassungsstrategien der politischen und kulturellen Eliten interessieren sie, wenn sie schreibt, sondern die "ersten Schritte" der "Schwachen". Und mit dem Titel des 1965 veröffentlichten Erzählungsbandes *Die Kraft der Schwachen* machte Seghers das Zitat aus dem Zweiten Korintherbrief zu einem zentralen Begriff ihres Schaffens. Im *Mitmachen* lag für sie der wahre Internationalismus.

---

[19] Seghers: Wiedereinführung der Sklaverei in Guadeloupe. In: *Erzählungen 1948/1949*. Berlin: Aufbau 1994. S. 63–122. Hier: S. 122.
[20] Seghers: *Transit*. In: *Gesammelte Werke in Einzelausgaben*. Bd. 5. Berlin: Aufbau 1951–53. S. 172.
[21] Seghers: Crisanta. In: *Erzählungen 1950–1952*. Berlin: Aufbau 1994. S. 7–34. Hier: S. 7–8.
[22] Sonja Hilzinger: Nachwort. In: Anna Seghers: *Erzählungen 1924–1933* (wie Anm. 9). S. 213–222. Hier: S. 218.

Für Seghers bedeutete Ent-Ortung auch immer gleich ein Individuationsmoment, ein Augenblick der Selbstfindung, ganz im Sinne heutiger Überlegungen über Ent-Ortung und kulturelle De-Zentrierung. So schreibt Homi K. Bhabha in *The Location of Culture*:

> [E]ach position is always a process of translation and transference of meaning. The individuation of the agent occurs in a moment of displacement. It is a pulsional incident, the split-second movement when the process of the subject's designation – its fixity – opens up beside it, uncannily *abseits*, a supplementary space of contingency.[23]

Auch die Frage der Positionierung – der *subject-position* – ließ Seghers nicht unreflektiert, sei es in Briefen oder Erzählungen. Für sie hieß Ent-Ortung auch, dass sie da, wo sie sich gerade befand – ob in Deutschland, Frankreich oder Mexiko – *mitmachte*, sich engagierte und versuchte, ihr Umfeld so gut sie konnte zu deuten und es sich anzueignen. Akkulturation und Kulturtransfer waren also die Dimensionen ihres Ent-stellt-seins.

In der Erzählung *Post ins Gelobte Land* (1943/1944 entstanden) setzt sich Seghers ausführlich mit dem Problem der Assimilation aus, und zwar im Zusammenhang mit dem Judentum. Hier geht es um das Schicksal einer "ostjüdischen" Familie, die im Anschluss an ein Pogrom das "Städtchen L". in Polen verlässt und nach Westen migriert, zunächst nach Wien und dann nach Paris. Im Pariser "Pletzl" (d.h. im St. Paul-Viertel) passt sich die Familie schnell an:

> Sie hatten sich rasch in ihrem Quartier eingelebt [...]. Nathan Levi sprach bald ganz geläufig französisch. Der Sohn sprach es noch besser, obwohl an ihm ein paar russische und ein paar polnische Worte hängengeblieben waren, und etwas Hebräisch und Jiddisch.[24]

Nathan, der "jetzt mit Leib und Seele [...] dem Volk verpflichtet [war], dem er sich längst verbunden fühlte, dessen Sprache und dessen Gedanken längst in ihn gedrungen waren, vom Bastillesturz bis zum Dreyfusprozess", ist auch derjenige, der sich 1914 freiwillig zum Kriegsdienst meldet. Dadurch macht er die Erfahrung einer radikalen Assimilation: "Er hatte in einem Kriegswinter, in der Todesnähe, in der Kameradschaft, einen Weg zurückgelegt in Einschmelzung [...], den sonst Generationen brauchen".[25]

---

[23] Homi K. Bhabha: *The Location of Culture*. New York: Routledge 1994. S. 26 und 185.
[24] Seghers: Post ins Gelobte Land. In: *Erzählungen 1934–1946* (wie Anm. 16). S. 161–193. Hier: S. 167/168.
[25] Ebd. S.171–172.

Jede der drei Hauptfiguren – Salomon Levi, sein Bruder Nathan und dessen Sohn Jakob – verkörpert eine besondere Form der jüdischen Existenz in der Diaspora. Der junge Jakob Levi ist derjenige, der den Weg der Assimilation in die neue französische Heimat geht (genauso wie die Kinder Seghers' z. B.) und nunmehr heißt er "Doktor Jacques Levi". Doch nichtsdestoweniger sind sich alle Familienmitglieder der Peripetien des jüdischen Schicksals weiterhin bewusst: "Man lebte in der Verbannung, ob man in Paris oder in L. lebte, in Amerika oder in Wien, in der Verbannung, die Gott verhängt hatte".[26] Doch gerade dieses mythisch-religiöse Bewusstsein führt auch dazu, dass die Familienmitglieder – wie so viele Juden in Europa – die Zeichen der unmittelbaren Katastrophe nicht rechtzeitig ernst genug zu nehmen vermögen und somit höchst wahrscheinlich dem Holocaust zum Opfer fallen:

> Was Hitler beging, war nur ein Nachspiel von alten berühmten Untaten, die ihnen geläufiger waren als alles, was heute geschah, und ihnen traumhaft und zeitlos vorkamen [...]. Wenn ihre eigene Erinnerung versagte, fanden sie immer noch in der Bibel Vergleiche.[27]

Was ihnen fehlt, ist ein geschichtliches Bewusstsein. Doch dafür dürfen sie nicht gescholten werden. In dieser Erzählung zeigt Seghers nämlich ihre Sympathie für den schweren Weg der Assimilation und ihre kritische Distanz gegenüber dem Zionismus und a-historischen Denkschemen.[28]

Ewiger Transit oder die Unmöglichkeit der Heimkehr

Zugleich bedeutete aber ein "real existierender Internationalismus" auch eine permanente Entwurzelung. Dieses Gefühl schildert Seghers in der 1977 veröffentlichten Erzählung *Wiederbegegnung*, in der es heißt:

> Alle spanischen Emigranten [anti-Frankisten, P.F.], ob sie zu dieser oder einer anderen Gruppe gehörten, hatten an ihren Zufluchtsorten auf halbausgepackten Koffern gelebt. Die Koffer standen wie Möbelstücke in ihren Wohnungen. Sie hatten nicht mit Bleiben gerechnet, sondern mit Rückkehr.[29]

Für Seghers gab es nach der Exilphase keine eigentliche "Heimkehr" mehr. Als Remigrantin sah sie sich manchmal als "Marsbewohnerin", die "mit Sehnsucht und Schmerz an den Mars zurückdenkt, wo sie nun mal Kinder geboren hat für

---

[26] Ebd. S. 169.
[27] Ebd. S. 184.
[28] Das unterstreicht auch Erika Haas: Anna Seghers und das Judentum. Beschreibung eines schwierigen Verhältnisses. In: *Argonautenschiff* (wie Anm. 5). S. 79ff.
[29] Seghers: Wiederbegegnung. In: *Erzählungen 1967–1980*. Berlin: Aufbau 1994. S. 259–330. Hier: S. 272.

den Mars".[30] Immer mehr wurde sie – wie viele andere Remigranten – zur Außenseiterin im eigenen Heimatland. Etwas von diesem Gefühl ist sicherlich in die 1948/1949 entstandene Erzählung "Das Argonautenschiff" eingeflossen, in der der rückkehrende Jason seinen ehemaligen Landsmenschen als "bestürzend fremd" vorkommt: "Die Gäste stritten, in welcher Sprache ihnen der Fremde antworten könnte, denn unerträglich gleichmütig, unbewegt saß er da". Was seine Mitmenschen als Stumpfheit interpretieren, ist vielleicht eher ein Ausdruck der tief sitzenden Wehmut der Remigranten, die einem sowohl fremd als auch bekannt, ja verwandt, vorkommen. Bei Jasons Anblick "hatte jeder [...] das Gefühl, schon einmal irgendwo auf ihn gestoßen zu sein".[31] Nunmehr befand sich Anna Seghers wie Jason tatsächlich zwischen ewigem "Transit" und "Transfer" in der Position der simmelschen "potenziell Wandernden", die sich durch ihre gewonnene Erfahrung stets dialektisch mit den Begriffen "Fremde" und "Heimat" auseinandersetzen musste. So schreibt sie auch 1974 an ihre Freundin Lore Wolf:

> Ich habe keine richtigen Wurzeln mehr. Lateinamerika ist mir mindestens ebenso lieb wie Frankreich und Skandinavien. Ich wünsche mich oft in meine richtige Heimat, die ist aber so verändert – das weiß ich auch dass ich es keinen Monat aushalten würde. (Vielleicht).[32]

So sind diese beiden Pole auch sehr unterschiedlich (und manchmal widersprüchlich) besetzt. Am Anfang der Erzählung *Der Ausflug der toten Mädchen* (1943/1944 nach ihrem schweren Unfall entstanden) erscheinen Mexiko, seine Flora, Topographie und seine Einwohner als Verkörperungen des absolut Fremden. Darin meint die Erzählerin:

> Die Lust auf absonderliche, ausschweifende Unternehmungen, die mich früher einmal beunruhigt hatte, war längst gestillt, bis zum Überdruss. Es gab nur noch eine einzige Unternehmung, die mich anspornen konnte: die Heimfahrt.[33]

In einem Brief schreibt Seghers Ende 1947 hingegen: "[I]ch selbst habe das Land, das mir eine Art Adoptivmutter geworden war, von Herzen lieb gewonnen. Man kann es nicht beschreiben. Es ist wie ein anderer Stern, es hat nichts

---

[30] Brief von AS an Alix Guillain (16.12.1947). Zitat in: Zehl-Romero: *Anna Seghers*. Bd. 1 (wie Anm. 8). S. 14.
[31] Seghers: Das Argonautenschiff. In: *Erzählungen 1948/1949* (wie Anm. 19). S. 123–140. Hier: S. 123.
[32] Brief von Seghers an Lore Wolf (1974). Zitat in: Zehl-Romero: *Anna Seghers*. (wie Anm. 8). S. 270.
[33] Seghers: Der Ausflug der toten Mädchen. In: *Erzählungen 1934–1946* (wie Anm. 2). S. 195.

mit hier zu tun, wenig mit Europa".[34] Hier erscheint Mexiko also als exotisches und liebenswürdiges Land – keine "Stiefmutter" und kein "Vaterland", sondern eine "Adoptivmutter". Dieses Land entkommt ihr jedoch größtenteils. Wie Olivia C. Díaz Pérez bemerkt,[35] hat sich Seghers Mexiko-Auffassung nie ganz vom Klischeebild befreien können, das z. B. in der Beschreibung des stereotypischen müßigen Mexikaners mit großem Strohhut am Ende des "Ausfluges der toten Mädchen" kulminiert: "Mein Wirt hockte noch immer vor dem Haus, und neben ihm hockte ein Freund oder ein Verwandter, genau wie er, erstarrt von Nachdenken oder von gar nichts. Zu ihren Füßen hockten einträchtig die Schatten ihrer Hüte".[36]

In Briefen charakterisierte Seghers Lateinamerikaner manchmal pauschal als "so heftig, so leidenschaftlich".[37] Mexiko war auch der Ort, wo man noch "das Primitive", das Exotische schlechthin, treffen konnte. Und so unternahm Seghers gegen Ende ihres Aufenthaltes in Mexiko mit einer befreundeten belgischen Ethnologin eine Reise zu den "Eingeborenen-Urwalddörfern" in der Nähe von Manzanillo am Pazifik.[38]

Erst nachdem die Exilphase in eine gewisse zeitliche Distanz gerückt war, konnte Seghers dann diese "Exotik" gewissermaßen hinterfragen und sich in die Komplexität der Karibik vertiefen, eines Weltteils, den sie während der Überfahrt nach Mexiko nur flüchtig gesehen hatte. Gertraud Gutzmann hat diesbezüglich das "eurozentrische Welt- und Menschenbild" Anna Seghers' in den *Karibischen Geschichten* kritisiert.[39] Ich möchte hingegen argumentieren, dass sich das, was ihr für Mexiko nicht ganz gelungen war, in der Behandlung des karibischen Stoffes tatsächlich entfaltet: nämlich das Einblicken und Mitfühlen.

Als Frau, Kommunistin und ehemalige Exulantin konnte sie über diesen Erdteil nicht in der Art und Weise schreiben, wie sie die (männlichen) Kolonisatoren bevorzugten. Für Seghers war die Karibik keine kulturlose Fläche, die bloß darauf wartete, be-schrieben zu werden, sondern eine komplexe Umgebung, die erst einmal von innen und von unten verstanden werden

---

[34] Brief von Seghers an Kiki (16.12.1947). In: Seghers: *"Hier im Volk der kalten Herzen". Briefwechsel 1947*. Berlin: Aufbau 2000. S. 384.
[35] Olivia C. Díaz Pérez: Das Bild Mexikos und die Exilerfahrung im Werk von Anna Seghers. In: *Argonautenschiff* (wie Anm. 28). S. 85 ff.
[36] Seghers: Der Ausflug der toten Mädchen. In: *Erzählungen 1934–1946* (wie Anm. 2). S. 225.
[37] Brief von Seghers an Lore Wolf (01.11.1947). Zitat in: Zehl-Romero: *Anna Seghers*. Bd. 1 (wie Anm. 8). S. 24.
[38] Zehl-Romero: *Anna Seghers* (wie Anm. 8). S. 426.
[39] Gertraud Gutzmann: Eurozentrisches Welt- und Menschenbild in Anna Seghers' *Karibische Geschichten*. In: *Frauen, Literatur, Politik*. Hg. von Annegret Pelz u. a. Hamburg: Argument 1988. S. 189–204.

musste. Deshalb beruhte Seghers nicht bloß auf ihren ungenauen und fragmentarischen Eindrücken, sondern unternahm eine sorgfältige Forschungsarbeit über die historischen Entwicklungen in der Region. 1948 arbeitete sie in der Bibliothèque Nationale in Paris und nahm Kontakt mit Aimé Césaire auf, der u a. die *négritude* definiert hatte, jenes eigenbestimmte Verhalten der Schwarzen. Außerdem beschäftigte sie sich intensiv mit Land- und Seekarten. Das Ergebnis dieser Vertiefung in die Karibik sind die drei *Karibischen Geschichten*, die erstmals 1962 als unabhängige Erzählsammlung erschienen. Und am Ende ihres Lebens zeugte eine weitere Erzählsammlung – *Drei Frauen aus Haiti* (1980) – davon, dass die Karibik für die Autorin zum Zentrum ihres de-zentrierten Erzählblickes wurde.

Ein Mittel, um eine einseitige – koloniale – Schreibweise zu verhindern, lieferte ihr die ihr so geläufige Gattung der Erzählung, in der sie großen Wert auf Perspektivenwechsel und Kollektiverinnerungen legte. In ihren Erzählungen war Anna Seghers bemüht, eine *mittlere* Stimme zu finden zwischen der Subjekt- und der auktorialen Position. Gerade die Kurzform bot ihr die Möglichkeit dazu, vielleicht weil diese als literarische Gattung durch die Vielfalt an Formen, die sie annimmt, bestenfalls kaleidoskopisch ist. Und genauso wie Erzählungen mögliche Alternativwelten in sich bergen, so lieferte die Karibik mit ihren insularischen Verhältnissen den idealen Ort der erzählerischen Experimentierung: Hier stimmen Gattung und Stoff sozusagen überein. Außerdem gelang es ihr, trotz des geographischen Mikroblickes historisch-soziale Makroprobleme darzustellen: Rassenfrage, Kolonisierung und Dekolonisierung, usw. In den Antillen wurde ihr Blick auf Kulturen und Geschichten gerichtet, die von "farbigen" Untertanen und "weißen" Kolonisatoren gleichzeitig und dialektisch geprägt worden waren und die zu Widerstandskulturen und Subversionspraktiken geführt hatten.

In *Die Hochzeit von Haiti* z. B. wird die rassische und soziale Hierarchie der Insel höchst detailliert dargestellt und die komplexe Matrix der Farben erläutert:

[Die schwarze Hausbesorgerin des Gutes] verbeugte sich vor den Männern, weil sie ihnen als Schwarze im Rang unterlegen war, aber ohne Regung in ihrem ohnedies harten Gesicht, weil sie in diesen zwei jüdischen Händlern die kleinsten der "kleinen Weißen", ihrem Herrn an Rang tief unterlegen begrüßte.

[Nathan als Jude] wurde weder beachtet noch angesprochen, er wurde auch nicht deutlich gemieden, er gehörte zu keiner bestimmten Gruppe von Weißen und zu keiner Gruppe Mulatten.

[D]ie Mulatten [machten] alle erdenklichen Anstrengungen, ihre Gleichberechtigung mit den weißen Plantagebesitzern [...] durchzusetzen [...]. Sie setzten Kaffee und Zucker ab wie die Weißen. Sie hielten Sklaven [...]. Sie legten ja auf die Ebenbürtigkeit mit dem Weißen Wert, auf den Abstand von den Schwarzen.

Die Abneigung der Mulatten gegen die Schwarzen wurde von den Schwarzen erwidert. Sie arbeiteten sogar lieber unter den weißen Aristokraten, die an ihre selbstverständliche Macht zu sehr gewöhnt waren, um sie immerfort wie die neureichen Mulatten durch Willkür und Grausamkeit zu betonen.[40]

Hier stellt Seghers ein subtiles Spiel von Machtgefällen dar, das weit entfernt ist von der bloßen oberflächlichen Faszination für das Exotisch-Fremde. Als Vergleich und Gegenbeispiel sei hier nur ein Auszug aus Peter Gays Memoiren herangezogen, der mit seinen Eltern auf dem Weg ins amerikanische Exil auf Kuba kurz Zwischenstation gemacht hatte:

Es machte mir Spaß, lange am Hafen herumzuschlendern und mir die faszinierenden Exemplare der komplexen Rassenvermischung anzuschauen, die ich überall traf. Die Nachkommen spanischer Siedler, mittelamerikanische Indios, Schwarze von den karibischen Inseln und chinesische Einwanderer waren hier zusammengekommen und verschmolzen – man sieht, dass ich nahezu alles auf Deutschland rückbezog! – und waren eine farbenprächtige Widerlegung des Nazimythos der "reinen" Rasse. Gewiss hatte die kubanische Gesellschaft ihre eigenen Farbhierarchien, aber kaum jemand hier konnte überzeugend behaupten, irgend etwas Reinrassiges zu sein.[41]

Zwar ist Peter Gay im Nachhinein bewusst, wie eurozentrisch sein damaliger Blick war. In ihrem Falle nutzte Anna Seghers ihr ausgeprägtes Feingefühl für das Transitorische, um ganze parallele Welten zu rekonstruieren und *von innen* und *von unten* zu verstehen. Wie ihre Biografin schreibt, war für sie "der Schwebezustand von *Transit* und "Überfahrt" ein Raum der Phantasie und Selbstfindung, in dem die zwei Pole ihres Lebens zusammenkamen: das Bedürfnis nach Heimat und Realität und die Sehnsucht nach Ferne und Distanz".[42]

Schluss

Auf der Suche nach textuellen Materialisierungen von Entwurzelung, Zerrissenheit und Entstelltsein ging die Erzählerin Seghers mehrere "Metamorphosen" durch.[43] Was ihre Erzählungen am besten kennzeichnet, ist wohl, dass sie öfters Figuren in Übergangssituationen und Außenseiter – "Fremde" also – in Szene setzen. Hier war Seghers vielleicht die Vorläuferin

---

[40] Seghers: Die Hochzeit von Haiti. In: *Erzählungen 1948/1949* (wie Anm. 31). S. 7–62. Hier: S. 9, 12, 25 und 27.
[41] Peter Gay: *Meine deutsche Frage. Jugend in Berlin 1933–1939*. Übers. von U. Enderwitz, M. Noll und R. Schubert. München: C. H. Beck 1998. S. 177–178.
[42] Zehl-Romero: *Anna Seghers* (wie Anm. 8). S. 210.
[43] Vgl. Hans-Albert Walter: *Anna Seghers' Metamorphosen. Transit – Erkundungsversuche in einem Labyrinth*. Frankfurt/Main: Luchterhand 1984.

jener, die sich wie Edward Said um die Stimme der *dispossessed and dispersed* kümmern.[44] Gleichzeitig machte sie Gebrauch von der Simultan- und Montagetechnik, durch die eine Vielfalt an Perspektiven in den Text einfließen. Sie selbst sagte: "[M]an muss doch nicht, um etwas beschreiben zu können, es erst selbst erlebt haben. Man muss nur richtig hinsehen und intensiv mitempfinden".[45] Hier kommt ihr Empathievermögen und ihre Induktionskraft, aber auch ihr Idealismus zum Ausdruck. Aber dieser Idealismus war kein leerer: In ihren Figuren praktizierte sie, die Kosmopolitin, die zur Internationalistin geworden war, eine aktive und real existierende De-Zentrierung des Blickes.

---

[44] Edward Said: *After the Last Sky – Palestinian Lives*. Fotografien von J. Mohr. New York: Columbia University Press 1998. S. 20.
[45] Zehl-Romero: *Anna Seghers* (wie Anm. 8). S. 87. Dieses Zitat muss zusammen mit dem folgenden berühmten gesehen werden: "Denn wir schreiben ja nicht, um zu beschreiben, sondern um beschreibend zu verändern" In: Seghers: *Aufsätze, Ansprachen, Essays*. Bd. 1 (wie Anm. 15). S. 31–32.

Birgit Maier-Katkin

"Kahl und wild wie ein Mondgebirge" – Exile and Mind Travel in Anna Seghers' *The Excursion of the Dead Girls*

The novella Der Ausflug der toten Mädchen *describes three journeys which point to a curious dichotomy of physical and imagined trips. Analogizing the novella to Italian futurist paintings and drawing on critical frameworks on time and space by Siegfried Kracauer and Walter Benjamin, this essay explores the intricate and ambivalent experience of travel and otherness in Seghers' exile text.*

In 1944, toward the end of her exile from Nazi Germany, Anna Seghers finished the novella *Der Ausflug der toten Mädchen*. By this time, Seghers and her immediate family had lived outside of Germany for eleven years. In the beginning exile travels had taken her through Switzerland to France where she lived till 1941. With the military advances of the German army, she hoped for political asylum in America. When this was denied, she joined other émigrés in Mexico City. Her exile ended in 1947. Traveling through New York and Sweden Seghers returned to postwar Berlin. In the years that followed, she continued to travel, visiting China, Soviet Russia and Brazil, but this was no longer forced travel with its suffering and foreboding of persecution.

This essay explores Seghers' treatment of exile and travel in her novella *The Excursion of the Dead Girls*.[1] As the title foreshadows, the story connects the image of travel with premonitions of early death and catastrophe. Yet, contrary to the implications of the title, the novella does not recount "one" excursion but rather incorporates tales of numerous trips spanning different time periods and countries. While a major focus is on a group of girls, the narration is not explicitly limited to female travelers. Using the literary devices of *Rahmenerzählung* and *Binnenerzählungen* inherent to the novella the various accounts of travel in this story take place on two continents, South America and Europe, and span a time period from before World War I to the 1940s. The *Rahmenerzählung* describes a desolate Mexican landscape in 1943 where the protagonist Netty finds exile from Nazi Germany. Recuperating from severe illness, Netty undertakes a small excursion in the hot afternoon sun to satisfy her curiosity about a little Rancho with a white wall outside her village. Approaching the wall and

---

[1] Anna Seghers: Der Ausflug der toten Mädchen. In: *Der Ausflug der toten Mädchen und andere Erzählungen*. New York: Aurora 1946. Pp. 7–35. The novella was written in 1943–1944 in Mexico and published after the defeat of the Nazi regime by the Aurora publishing house. References are taken from the 1st edition.

feeling increasingly overcome with fatigue due to the heat and her unstable physical condition, Netty notices a green shimmer and begins to hear familiar voices as she enters through an old deteriorated archway into a small garden. Archway and wall divide the narration of the novella. The moment Netty crosses the threshold she enters into a different state of mind (i.e. into the realm of dream). If only mentally, she leaves the Mexican countryside and is unexpectedly back in Germany. Traveling through time and space, Netty finds herself in the midst of a group of friends reliving moments of a cheerful school excursion from before World War I in the years of the German monarchy when her class took a boat ride down the Rhine to a riverside café. The *Binnenerzählungen* contain numerous entangled events concerning Netty's former friends, classmates, teachers, family, and countrymen extending from her youth to 1943. Once Netty reawakens from her dreamlike state, she returns to the reality of her Mexican exile but remembers her teacher's request to create a written account of the school excursion.

Focusing on themes of exile and travel, this essay examines the depiction of exilic otherness which the protagonist Netty experiences during her travel, and points to a curious dichotomy of physical and imagined journeys. It explores this dichotomy by linking Seghers' narrative style to the paintings of Italian futurism and by drawing on critical frameworks put forth by Siegfried Kracauer and Walter Benjamin who explored the tension between actual experience and temporal endlessness where events do not follow a logic sequence or provide meaning that is self-contained. For clarity of discussion, Netty's travels are divided into three segments: 1) Mexican exile, 2) mind travel down the Rhine and through various time periods in Germany, and 3) her conscious travel through an in-between temporal realm (between actual and mind travel). At the center of all three journeys one finds intricate and ambivalent experiences of otherness. In the genre of *Reisebericht*, a traveler's sense of not belonging is often a central theme reflecting on the experience of *Fremdheit* in unfamiliar surroundings.[2] This is true for Netty's travel account which not only reveals her discomfort in an alien landscape and different cultural environment but also heightens her sensitivity to the possibilities and limits of the experience as traveler.

Travel into the Mexican Landscape

In the novella, Netty describes the utter strangeness she feels within the Mexican countryside. To her, the gray-brown mountain slopes seem "kahl und

---

[2] Peter J. Brenner: Die Erfahrung der Fremde. Zur Entwicklung einer Wahrnehmungsform in der Geschichte des Reiseberichts. In: *Der Reisebericht. Die Entwicklung einer Gattung in der deutschen Literatur.* Ed. by Peter J. Brenner. Frankfurt/Main: Suhrkamp 1989. Pp. 14–49. Here: p. 14.

wild wie ein Mondgebirge" (7). Trees glow rather than bloom, giant cacti form impenetrable walls around villages, and the air is filled with dust and stifling heat. The locals sit motionlessly against house walls and rest under the shade of broad-rimmed hats. Submitting to empty stupor they seem to contemplate "das vollkommene Nichts" (7). Olivia Díaz Pérez and others have noted that descriptions of Mexico and its people in the "Excursion" seem cliché-like, stereotyped, and display a Eurocentric perspective,[3] reminiscent of travel guides or scenes in Westerns without reflecting a deeper understanding of the culture. This is in sharp contrast to Seghers' personal experience. She was fascinated by Mexico, learned the language, familiarized herself with Mexican literature and culture, befriended Mexican artists and intellectuals, and thought of it as an enticing exotic country.[4] Nevertheless, in this novella Mexico and its people are reduced to their most barren, elemental and alien features.

Netty's descriptions of encounters with Mexicans reflect what is often found in travel writing: the otherness of foreign nationals becomes subject to the traveler's own sense of self. In this way, travel accounts tend to reveal more about the experience of the traveler's otherness than give a realistic account of the natives.[5] This focal point is already evident in the first two sentences of the novella in which Netty replies to the innkeeper of the Pulqueria, " 'Nein, von viel weiter her. Aus Europa' " (7). While the story leaves out the preceding question by the innkeeper, Netty's response hints at the man's inability to identify the exact geographic location of her home country and suggests that to him life and communities outside Mexico seem remote. Curiously, the conversation between Netty and the innkeeper ends here. There is no further inquiry or comment by either person about the politics or communal concerns of each country and continent. This gives the impression as if Netty's response is out of context or lost in a vacuum since neither the preceding question nor any additional clarifications are provided in the text. The only reaction that follows is a blank smile from the innkeeper which Netty interprets as, "Der Mann sah mich lächelnd an, als ob ich erwidert hätte: 'Vom Mond' " (7). With this last interaction the reader is not given any access to the mind of the native. Instead the text provides more insight into Netty's perceived experience of otherness. From the innkeeper's non-verbal reaction, she deduces that he sees her

---

[3] Olivia Díaz Pérez: Das Bild Mexikos und die Exilerfahrung im Werk von Anna Seghers. In: *Argonautenschiff* 11 (2002). Pp. 85–114. Here: p. 86. See also: Christiane Zehl Romero: *Anna Seghers. Eine Biographie 1900–1947*. Berlin: Aufbau 2000. Pp. 382–384.
[4] See Pierre Radvanyi: *Jenseits des Stroms: Erinnerungen an meine Mutter Anna Seghers*. Berlin: Aufbau 2006. P. 84. Also, Pérez (n. 3) and Zehl Romero (n. 3). Pp. 384–386.
[5] Brenner: Die Erfahrung der Fremde (n. 2). P. 15.

as an alien. For the remainder of the story the innkeeper acknowledges her existence but is non-responsive and the novella continues to give access only to Netty's story.

The lack of direct speech and scarcity of interactions between Netty and the natives establish an alien, almost fatalistic aura throughout the frame story. It is as if the mid-afternoon heat wears down everyone's ability to move, think, and converse. Netty shares a common space with the locals but not their community. By reducing to a minimum the contact between Netty and the people among whom she lives and by providing only her perspective, the focal point of the novella seems distant from the Mexicans and their country. In this story, the European traveler remains a stranger outside the intercultural contact zone.[6] The major focus is on Netty's impenetrable experience of otherness as she finds herself within the tension of forced exile and life in an unfamiliar place.

In Netty's descriptions of Mexico one finds certain characteristics of travel writing. A case in point is the protagonist; engaged with aesthetic self-representation her primary concern is the observing individual as subject.[7] The images of Mexican topography and people involve cliché-ridden descriptions. Yet, unlike travel guides that promote tourism to new and exotic locations,[8] this story inspires little excitement about the charms of Mexico. Instead, the novella conveys apathy and disinterest in the beauty and allure of this country. It is not that Netty is unaware of tourism or disinterested in international travel. She recalls earlier times when "Reiselust" was part of her life but the endless hardship of many years of exile has diminished earlier desires to explore the world. Netty writes, "Die Lust auf absonderliche ausschweifende Unternehmungen, die mich früher einmal beunruhigt hatte, war längst gestillt, bis zum Überdruß" (8). To Netty, the only trip that might spark her old desire to travel is "die Heimfahrt" (8). Yet, despite her aversion to travel there is one place in Mexico which does spark a sense of "müßige Neugierde" and that old desire to explore. Over the previous months when she recuperated from long illness and looked out from her roof garden she had become interested in a solitary Rancho with its white walls down in the valley. Her interest is heightened by the fact that no one can provide any information about this place.

---

[6] Mary Louise Pratt: Arts of the Contact Zone. In: *Ways of Reading. An Anthology for Writers*. 3rd edition. Ed. by David Bartholomae and Anthony Petrosky. New York: St. Martin's Press 1993. Pp. 440–457. Here: p. 444.

[7] Wolfgang Neuber: Zur Gattungspoetik des Reiseberichts. Skizze einer historischen Grundlegung im Horizont von Rhetorik und Topik. In: *Der Reisebericht* (n. 2). Pp. 50–67. Here: p. 50.

[8] See Wolfgang Reif: Exotismus im Reisebericht des frühen 20. Jahrhunderts. In: *Der Reisebericht* (n. 2). Pp. 434–462.

Mind Travel

As Netty sets out for her excursion into the valley and approaches the Rancho the local topography begins to play tricks on her mind. As if walking toward a Fata Morgana her judgment about distance becomes obscured "sodaß die Nähe entwich und die Ferne sich klärte" (8). As she draws near to the wall, Netty is overcome with exhaustion. She is aware of the oppressive afternoon heat which envelops everything within the Mexican dust, glimmering haze and sunlight. Netty arrives in complete solitude at the Rancho. Spotting a shimmer of green behind the white wall, she eagerly walks under a dilapidated archway into a garden. Much to her surprise she hears the squeaking noise of a seesaw followed by a familiar voice calling her name. As if entering a *locus amoenus*, Netty is enraptured by the paradise-like scene that welcomes her on the other side of the wall. She comments on the beautiful lushness of the garden, the fresh smell of green vegetation and the abundance of familiar German flowers and bushes. Netty immediately realizes that she has walked into the midst of her own school excursion on the banks of the Rhine. At this point in the novella, she begins her trip into the landscape of her mind where time and space turn topsy-turvy.

The instant Netty moves toward her classmates her thoughts are infiltrated by a multi-faceted spectrum of past and present images about their lives across time. As Mexico fades from her mind, Netty interacts with teachers and school friends and it appears that her earlier premonition about a Fata Morgana is coming true. Images that are far away in Germany appear close enough to touch while the presence of the Mexican Rancho becomes distant. In the inner stories of the novella, Netty's deepest desire – to travel back home – has materialized. While the mood of the Mexican countryside in the outer frame hints at the moon with its aura of alienation and strangeness, the experiences in the inner stories provide a sense of intimate belonging and the familiarity of shared national identity and culture. For Netty, Edward Said's words ring true, "Nationalism is an assertion of belonging in and to a place, a people, a heritage. It affirms the home created by a community of language, culture and customs; and, by so doing, it fends off exile, fights to prevent its ravages".[9] Throughout the stories of the *Binnenerzählungen*, Netty is reminded of a former sense of community. In contrast to the outer frame, she is known to the people around her and engages in conversation with them. She is intimately familiar with people's lives and aware of what happened to them over the years. Like Said, Seghers also knew that exile means being cut off from one's roots, land and past;[10] therefore in exile it is important to find ways to reconnect with the former homeland.

---

[9] Edward Said: Reflections on Exile. In: *Altogether Elsewhere. Writers on Exile*. Ed. by Marc Robinson. Boston: Harcourt 1994. Pp. 137–149. Here: p. 139.
[10] Ibid. P. 140.

To Netty, the experience of what it means to be home is most vividly described as she gazes at the Rhine landscape:

> Mich zog es zuerst dichter ans Ufer, damit ich die unbegrenzte sonnige Weite des Landes in mich einatmen konnte [...]. Die Dörfer und Hügel spiegelten sich in einem Netz von Sonnenkringeln. Je mehr und je länger ich um mich sah, desto freier konnte ich atmen, desto rascher füllte sich mein Herz mit Heiterkeit. Denn fast unmerklich verflüchtigte sich der schwere Druck von Trübsinn, der auf jedem Atemzug gelegen hatte. Bei dem bloßen Anblick des weichen hügeligen Landes gedieh die Lebensfreude und Heiterkeit [...]. (13)

Much to her surprise, Netty is immediately recognized and called by her childhood name. The familiar surroundings and presence of friends give Netty an instantaneous sense of relief and belonging. This does not mean that Netty's experience of exile travel and otherness has disappeared in the garden. To the contrary, the knowledge of travel and otherness remain part of her experience; however, it takes on a different significance than in the outer frame. In the same way that the Netty of the 1940s is not the same person as the schoolgirl she once was, the recent experience of exile and estrangement remains part of her inner self even while she re-connects with her homeland. As her reflections come from a distance removed in time and space, they reveal the simultaneous knowledge of exile and the passing of time since the school trip. The perspective of otherness has changed; it is no more the foreignness and strangeness of the outer frame, but rather the knowledge of being outside one's home country. This viewpoint permits a look at the course of events from a distance. Christiane Zehl Romero notes that it is the awareness of both: her foreignness in Mexico and her continued sense of belonging to Germany which gives Seghers "den doppelten Blick" that allows her to look at her home country, its history, and culture differently.[11] From her estranged perspective of mind travel and the lingering awareness of her exilic situation, Netty contemplates the history and current situation in Germany.

In the multiplicity of the inner stories, logic, time sequence, physical awareness, and topography adhere to a different realm of consciousness. There is no effort to report objectively or sequentially.[12] Instead, Netty's account of the school trip is disjointed and exposes a surreal infusion of conflicting memory flashes. When Else lines up together with the other girls before the class can leave for the boat ride home, Netty remarks, "Während die Else, fest und rund

---

[11] Zehl Romero: *Anna Seghers* (n. 3). P. 382.
[12] For a detailed discussion about the imagery in the "Excursion" see also Birgit Maier-Katkin: *Silence and Acts of Memory. A Postwar Discourse on Literature, History, Anna Seghers, and Women in the Third Reich*. Lewisburg (PA): Bucknell University Press 2007.

wie ein Knödelchen, durch nichts anderes zu zersplittern als durch eine Bombe, in ihre Mädchenreihe hineinsprang [...]" (23). Despite Else's robust figure during the school trip, she is revealed as fragile. This impression is created by interrupting the temporary sequence of the sentence. Instead of a series of motions in the present time describing how Else simply breaks into the line-up of her classmates, an announcement of her unusually cruel death is inserted as if to interrupt the girl's motion into the line. This narrative style reminds of cinematographic cutting-montage and gives the impression that the bomb is already present at this childhood moment. To the reader this imagery comes not entirely as a surprise since the preceding sentences had already revealed that during the Nazi years Else and her family were killed in an English bombing raid over Mainz.

Surreal images of early death and time conflation accompany the descriptions of most school children and bring Netty's experience of exilic otherness to a multilayered level of observation. This is evident, for instance, in Netty's precarious perspective when describing the older teacher Mr. Reiß who together with his class of boys took the same school excursion down the Rhine to the riverside café. Netty states: "Umgekehrt wie es sonst geschieht, erlebte der Lehrer das Absterben seiner jungen Schüler im folgenden und im jetzigen Krieg, in schwarz-weiß-roten und in Hakenkreuz-Regimentern" (24). The temporal sequence in this description has gone astray. Especially the words "folgenden" and "jetzigen" seem to have abandoned logic. In strict adherence to a time sequence World War I is the war which follows the event of the school excursion. However, from the teacher's perspective, the reference to the "jetzige" war is clearly out of place since it belongs to World War II which is still in the distant future. Hence, at the time of the school trip it would have been more appropriate for Netty to use the future tense "wird erleben" and not the past tense "erlebte" as she refers to events that Mr. Reiß has not yet experienced. The time convolution in this literary image makes sense only when seen from Netty's perspective at the time of her mind travel. In this way, the complex simultaneity inherent in this statement about the teacher conveys the focal point of Netty who – physically located in Mexico but mentally more attuned to former events on the Rhine riverbank – observes the teacher at the center of multiple events in which his pupils experience death and devastation in different times and locations. This imagery is akin to the paintings of Italian futurism in the early 20th century by artists such as Umberto Boccioni or Gino Severini. Capturing Netty at different locations and simultaneously adopting her gaze while engaged in mental travel, Seghers introduces with her writing a curious dichotomy between temporal standstill and simultaneous motion which portrays multiple aspects of one event. Similar to the multi-perspectivism of cutting-montage and the simultaneity of futurist art, the inner stories of the school excursion defy the common law of perception. Reminiscent of the Futurist Manifesto one notices in

Seghers' literary style that, "It is up to the artist to discover connections and set up relationships between remote, discontinuous, alien and dissimilar elements".[13] Like the futurist painter Gino Severini, Seghers sought to create art which "recognized the individual as both 'a centre of universal irradiation' and 'the point where centripetal forces converge', so that if all the lines of the universe converge on him, there is also a centrifugal expansion outwards from him".[14] This literary device allowed Seghers to convey novel perspectives on the relation between the individual and community as well as between individuals and a society's history through time.

By examining the structure of imagery in the inner stories of the "Excursion" one gets the impression that for each description of an individual there is a carefully crafted dichotomy at work which follows a pattern of contrasting childhood moments with later instants of adulthood. In this way the story conveys about Walter, "Jetzt waren die zu seinem Kummer noch kurzen Höschen zu stramm über seinem festen Hintern, später würde er, ein zwar schon ältlicher, aber noch äußerst ansehlicher SS-Mann, als Transportleiter Lenis verhafteten Mann für immer fortbringen" (24). In this image, the childhood and adulthood of Walter are set in temporal proximity even though in actuality these events are far apart. Through the banal imagery of clothing in youth and adulthood, Walter's childhood concern about tight little pants is subsumed in the well-dressed image of the adult Walter and member of the SS who directs the deportation of a classmate's husband. By juxtaposing child and adult interactions, the story reveals how Walter's relationships with community members and his moral concerns have transformed over time. During the school excursion no one would have predicted that Walter would one day transport Leni's husband to his death.

Other contrasting descriptions show how close and caring childhood friendships become shattered and suffused by tragedy. Observing gestures of genuine affection between Leni and Marianne during the school trip, Netty calls to mind how Marianne and her spouse precipitate the arrest of Leni and her husband. This results in the couple's death while their daughter is brought to a Nazi children's home. From her perspective of exile and otherness, Netty reflects:

> Mir kam jetzt alles unmöglich vor, was man mir über die beiden erzählt und geschrieben hatte. Wenn Marianne so vorsichtig die Schaukel für Leni festhielt und ihr mit soviel Freundschaft und soviel Behutsamkeit die Halme aus dem Haar zupfte, und sogar ihren Arm um Lenis Hals schlang, dann konnte sie sich unmöglich mit kalten Worten später schroff weigern, Leni einen Freundschaftsdienst zu tun. (12)

---

[13] Umbro Apollonio: Introduction. In: *Futurist Manifesto*. Ed. by Umbro Apollonio. London: Thames and Hudson 1973; *The Documents of 20th Century Art*. Ed. by Robert Motherwell and Bernard Karpel. New York: Viking Press 1973. P. 9.
[14] Ibid. P. 11.

The literary device of showing different moments of life in close proximity reveals how moral values, social behavior and individual conviction effect a community over time.[15] Unbeknownst to the characters themselves, the individuals in the "Excursion" are exposed as human beings trapped within slowly evolving socio-political circumstances which, especially during the Third Reich, demand decisive and often radically different moral judgments. As in the futurist paintings, Seghers reveals individuals who stand at the center of their universe while – through different moments and actions in their life – there is a centrifugal expansion outwards as well as centripetal forces converging from the outside. As a result of her observations, Netty is the only person who through her different position in space and time is aware of this phenomenon and able to reflect on it.

Netty had these insights neither during the original school trip nor during her previous excursion through the Mexican countryside. Instead, it is at the moment of re-awakening from her mind travel that Netty is able to see her previous life through the exilic perspective of otherness and contemplate on her own life and that of her classmates from a unique perspective. Therefore, at the point in the novella when Netty awakes and moves into a state of altered awareness, she finds herself in a third travel situation located "in-between" mind travel and actual travel.

Mindful Travel: Moving "In-Between" Dream and Reality

Netty's process of awakening begins toward the end of the *Binnenerzählungen* when she returns from the school excursion and enters her hometown Mainz. As she walks toward her family home a climax is reached. Netty's report of the school excursion is increasingly interrupted by thoughts of recent events which anticipate the total destruction of Mainz. Moving closer to the center of the city, she locates familiar landmarks and realizes with rising joy that her hometown is untouched by destruction. Simultaneous to these observations Netty becomes aware that she stands at the threshold between dream and reality. Images of the bombed out city reveal themselves as fixtures of her imagination. She realizes that they belong to a different reality than that of her vision. Finally, Netty's longing to embrace her mother is reduced to a final gaze at her mother's unharmed young face. Before the two can physically meet Netty is thrown back into lived reality and finds herself alone in the topography of Mexico and the time of exile. Throughout the inner stories Netty's awareness of exile infiltrates her judgment and observations about her classmates, but it is in

---

[15] Gertraud Gutzmann: Anna Seghers' Ausflug der toten Mädchen als ein Beitrag der Literatur zur Neugestaltung Deutschlands. In: *Das Exilerlebnis: Verhandlungen des vierten Symposiums über deutsche und österreichische Exilliteratur*. Ed. by Donald G. Daviau and Ludwig M. Fischer. Columbia (SC): Camden House 1982. Pp. 476–485. Here: p. 479.

the moments just before and after leaving her mind travel that she is most aware of her "in-between" position.

Netty's awareness of traveling through this "in-between" space links her two previous excursions: one into the Mexican countryside and the other into the German homeland. While Netty goes through a moment of transition twice, it is the second time of this experience that sharpens her ability to reflect on exile, her otherness, and the personal task that emerges from this new awareness. When Netty first moves from actual exile travel to mind travel, she has a premonition of a Fata Morgana. Without completely realizing what is happening to her she slides into a different state of consciousness and her experience becomes filled with spatial ambivalence and temporal distortion. When Netty moves back into the outer frame of Mexican exile, she is awake and aware that her thoughts and insights have been influenced by the images of the *Binnenerzählungen*.

At this point in the story, she experiences time and space in a different way and is aware that in her mind travel time had abandoned its clear forward motion and spun back and forth between past, present and future. Netty realizes that in the inner stories time and space were precious, but also chaotic and cut short by death and destruction. As with a pile of photographs, the events she looked at were not locked into a temporal succession but transmogrified through different locations and moments. Netty's "in-between" state of mind recalls Siegfried Kracauer's concept of "a citizen of two worlds".[16] In his essay "Travel and Dance", he asserts that a person is "simultaneously within space and at the threshold of a supra-spatial endlessness, simultaneously within the flow of time and in the reflection of eternity".[17] For Kracauer, awareness of the tension between actual experience and temporal endlessness exposes the fact that events never follow a logic sequence or provide meaning which is self-contained. Instead meaning is imposed on a succession of events and receives content and form from "that other realm" toward which the individual is oriented.[18] In the moment of transition between outer frame and inner stories in the novella – when the rushed impressions and temporal convolution of her school trip are still present in her mind – Netty comments how she experiences "einen unermeßlichen Strom von Zeit" (35). Time in exile seems unending and a challenge to the logical sequentiality of time; its sheer endlessness is only overcome by Netty's decision to use time wisely and describe a school excursion which to her has spun out of temporal sequence.

During the moment of transition from mind travel in Germany back to exile in Mexico, the experience of space and time in both locations is described as

---

[16] Siegfried Kracauer: Travel and Dance. In: *The Mass Ornament. Weimar Essays.* Ed. and transl. by Thomas Y. Levin. Cambridge (MA): Harvard 1995. Pp. 65–73. Here: p. 68
[17] Ibid. P. 69.
[18] Ibid. P. 69.

equally surreal. The anticipation of a bombed Mainz – which could have revealed itself as uninhabitable as the moon – and the return into the wild and barren Mexican countryside hints at the image of a *locus terribilis* with its intimations of melancholy, *Weltklage*, *Weltabkehr*, and innate sadness. In connection with the earlier suggestion of a *locus amoenus* (when Netty enters the paradise-like riverside garden) the topographical descriptions of Mexico and Germany take on special significance in the novella. Seghers, who earned a doctorate in art history, may have alluded to such stylized imagery in order to deflect attention from actual exile travel and concentrate instead on the experience of exile and otherness. It is only at the end of the novella – in the short moment of awakening when the memory of her dream is most vivid – that Netty is able to break through and overcome the desperate sense of estrangement in exile which marked the beginning of the story.

The moment of transition toward the end of the novella is suggestive of Walter Benjamin's 1929 essay on surrealism in which he states that at the threshold between "Wachen und Schlaf" one finds "wie von Tritten massenhafter hin und wider flutender Bilder".[19] Through the sheer flood of pictures during the moment of awakening, images and language fuse, become confused, and lose their initial precision and original meaning. Drawn to Marcel Proust's notion of involuntary memory, Benjamin attributes a special importance to the concept of "Erwachen". He argues that it is in the moment of surreal awareness, between dream and reality, that systematic labor is capable of recovering involuntary traces of memory that are otherwise lost to conscious remembrance. He writes, "Sollte Erwachen die Synthesis sein aus der Thesis des Traumbewußtseins und der Antithesis des Wachbewußtseins? Dann wäre der Moment des Erwachens identisch mit dem 'Jetzt der Erkennbarkeit', in dem die Dinge ihre wahre – surrealistische – Miene aufsetzen".[20] In the moment of transition from dreamlike vision to experienced reality, time for Netty seems frozen as in Benjamin's "Dialektik im Stillstand" in which past fragments begin to enter into present experience.[21] This is especially true for the moment when Netty awakens, a moment that Benjamin calls "Das Jetzt der Erkennbarkeit".[22] At this instant, the

---

[19] Walter Benjamin: *Der Surrealismus: Die letzte Momentaufnahme der europäischen Intelligenz*. Gesammelte Schriften. Vol. 2.1. Ed. by Rolf Tiedemann and Hermann Schweppenhäuser. Frankfurt/Main: Suhrkamp 1977. P. 296.
[20] Walter Benjamin: *N3a, 3. Aufzeichnungen und Materialien*. Gesammelte Schriften Vol. 5.1. Ed. by Rolf Tiedemann. Frankfurt/Main: Suhrkamp 1982. P. 579.
[21] For a discussion about similarities in the work and thought of Seghers and Benjamin, see also Birgit Maier-Katkin: Debris and Remembrance. Anna Seghers's 'Ausflug' and Walter Benjamin's 'Engel der Geschichte'. In: *German Quarterly* 79.1 (2006). Pp. 90–108; as well as Maier-Katkin: *Silence and Acts of Memory* (n. 12).
[22] Benjamin: *Aufzeichnungen* (n. 20). P. 579. See also, Benjamin: *N18, 4. Aufzeichnungen* (n. 20). P. 608.

many stories contained in the *Binnenerzählungen* burst out, like memory flashes, to the conscious state of the outer narrative. It is during this moment when Netty suddenly remembers the task set by her teacher Ms. Sichel who asked her to create a written record of this school trip. The last words of the novella are a promise to do the "befohlene Aufgabe" as soon as possible.

Implications of Exilic Otherness in Seghers' Diverse Travel Accounts

In her 1941 essay "Deutschland und wir" published in Mexico, Seghers claims, "Was hat unsre Freiheit für einen Sinn, wenn wir nicht immer wieder [...] reden und schreiben können [...] Deutschland: das ist die Sprache, die nicht nur für uns heute in der Fremde, sondern auch auf vielen Strecken der deutschen Geschichte die dichteste deutsche Wirklichkeit war".[23] Accordingly, Netty's diverse travel accounts in the "Excursion" are less concerned with the pressures of being the "exiled other" in a foreign country and more with a need to use one's experience of otherness as a position from which to look at history and the current situation of the home country. This is not to argue that Seghers is not interested in representing the problems of exile travel in her literature or that the awareness of exilic "otherness" might bar her characters from real engagement with the new surroundings. In fact in 1943, shortly before writing the "Excursion", Seghers completed a novel entitled *Transit* in which one finds descriptions of the overt perils and hardships of exile travel as well as the decision of the protagonist to make the place of exile his permanent home. In contrast, "The Excursion" grapples with the relationship between exile travel and the state of mind of an exile traveler. For Netty this means that her deepest desire is directed toward the trip home and toward the question of how an exile can be helpful during a time of crises. In the *Binnenerzählungen* the primary concern is with Germany's current socio-political transformations, the personal desire to remember former relationships, the urgency to help and be prepared (if only in imagination) for one's return. This places Netty's exile perspective within an inherent duality of forced travel and the desire to return home.

In many ways, Seghers' text about exile travel in Mexico carries a pedagogical impulse aimed at creating a written account which debunks the official Nazi mythos of blood and soil and exposes the Nazi destruction of "real" community.[24]

---

[23] Anna Seghers: *Aufsätze, Ansprachen, Essays 1927–1953. Gesammelte Werke in Einzelausgaben*. Vol. 13. 2nd ed. Berlin/Weimar: Aufbau 1984. P. 94.

[24] See, Gutzmann: Seghers. P. 478. Einhorn asserts that in her essay "Vaterlandsliebe" Seghers differentiates between a wholesome love for "Heimat" and the Nazi mythos of blood and soil. See Barbara Einhorn: Jüdische Identität und Frauenfrage im Werk von Anna Seghers. In: *Argonautenschiff* 6 (1997). Pp. 307–324. For a discussion on Seghers' essays "Deutschland und wir" and "Volk und Schriftsteller" (in the early 1940s) as important contributions to the socio-political discussion about Heimat, Volk and German guilt, see Zehl Romero: *Anna Seghers* (n. 3). P. 412.

In the "Excursion" one senses that Seghers is engaged in a process of grief and lamentation for the devastation of her hometown and family. The description of the school trip shows that her generation had been part of a relatively tolerant community during the monarchy, World War I, and the Weimar Republic, but in the Third Reich old values and former loyalties eroded.[25] After Hitler's rise to power the community of former classmates is slowly split into perpetrators and victims, friends and enemies, émigrés and those who stay home. Formerly meaningful and close relationships in families and communities break apart and are gradually destroyed along racial and political lines. By 1943, when Seghers began to write the "Excursion", it had become clear that Hitler's regime was drawing to an end. Outside of Germany, international discussion was turning toward the problem of how to re-integrate a defeated Nazi Germany in the world community. Exiles like Seghers not only began to contemplate their return but also joined the international discussion about the need to re-direct the Germans.

Seghers recognized that the German people were confronted with personal and political disasters and would need help from exiles and the international community to recover from the crisis. In the last years of exile, she called for the urgent redefinition of essential concepts of societal life. Seghers was most concerned about the German youth who had only experienced Nazi community, values, and structures. In her article "Die Aufgaben der Kunst", she writes "Die Künstler müssen die Begriffe von drei Werten in der deutschen Jugend neu erwecken: das Individuum, das Volk, die Menschheit".[26] Seghers' work and thought was concerned with the postwar task to redirect and reeducate the German community to a shared sense of "gemeinsame Arbeit, Kultur und Geschichte".[27] Zehl Romero states that for Seghers the answer lay in the significance of a new beginning, in the collaboration with a "transformation" of people, an expression which she preferred to the then more commonly used term "reeducation" because it involved a deeper contact and change concerning all of a person's personality.[28] As part of the text's pedagogy, the novella does not resolve any disaster but leaves it to the reader to work though various fragmented individual experiences and to reflect on their effects on the wider community. "It is left to her future readers to look into the circumstances under which individual human beings, groups, or an entire people become accomplices in acts of denunciation and betrayal, and of the persecution of others in

---

[25] See also Birgit Maier-Katkin: Writing for Memory: Anna Seghers, History, Literature, and Complicity in the Third Reich. In: *Clio* 31.4 (2002). Pp. 367–85.
[26] Anna Seghers: Aufsätze, Ansprachen, Essays (n. 23). P. 171.
[27] Ibid. P. 172.
[28] Zehl Romero. *Anna Seghers* (n. 3). P. 436.

their midst".²⁹ By giving examples of individual and community interaction which change over time, Seghers hoped to expose the immense brutality of the Nazi event and its devastating effect on the community.

As Netty contemplates interactions between individuals and community from her focal position of mind travel, she is shocked by the fact that her classmates have forgotten what it was like to experience community as they did during their school years. She states, "Nie hat uns jemand, als noch Zeit dazu war, an diese gemeinsame Fahrt erinnert. Wieviele Aufsätze auch noch geschrieben wurden über die Heimat und die Geschichte der Heimat und die Liebe zur Heimat" (28-9). Netty who is able to draw these connections through her altered perspective realizes the task set for her. She knows that under the Nazis the community has become devoid of assertive and strong voices that recall previous values of tolerance, respect and dignity for all kinds of human beings, and that it is her task to reassert and realign the memory of earlier times and relationships. Gertraud Gutzmann observes, "All that Netty has to offer her readers are uncertainties, hypothetical half questions, incomplete wishes, imagined alternatives to actual happenings".³⁰ For the participants in the school excursion prospects for survival are slim. They have little time for thoughtful decisions and reflections, therefore Netty leaves it up to the reader to take time and contemplate cause and effect in the various travel accounts and experiences.

Conclusion

At the center of Netty's three journeys one finds intricate and ambivalent experiences of otherness which span two continents and multiple time frames. It is the heightened awareness of all these experiences set in the curious dichotomy of physical and imagined journeys that allows Netty to make use of her exilic experience of otherness. Instead of self-pity about banishment from one's home and desperation about extreme foreignness in a place that seems as distant and barren as the moon, Netty uses her unique exilic vantage point. Through personal awareness of what it means to be the "other", she uses what Brenner calls a traveler's heightened sensitivity toward the possibilities and limits of one's experience to create a travel account that opens new constellations and experiences to readers at home.³¹ In the "Excursion", Netty expresses her sense of

---

²⁹ Gertraud Gutzmann: Literary Antifascism: Anna Seghers's Exile Writings 1936 to 1949. In: *Facing Fascism and Confronting the Past: German Women Writers from Weimar to the Present*. Ed. by Elke P. Frederiksen and Martha Kaarsberg Wallach. Albany (NY): State University of New York Press 2000. Pp. 85–102. Here: p. 91. Zehl Romero points out that Seghers wants to break down the distance between text and reader. Zehl Romero: *Anna Seghers* (n. 3). P. 314.
³⁰ Gutzmann: Literary Antifascism (n. 29). P. 91.
³¹ Brenner: Die Erfahrung der Fremde (n. 2). P. 14.

non-belonging in Mexican exile but also conveys the experience of otherness in regard to her home country. Looking at her beloved home country from the perspective of exilic experience, Seghers is able to reevaluate the importance of intimate relationships in her birth community, Mainz. For young people and future readers, Seghers hopes to provide a glance into the fragility of community, family, and friendships. With this novella, she conveys a new urgency and quality for those concepts of German culture that have been devalued by the brutality of the Nazi regime. In this way, she reveals the epicenter of a time of communal crises and points to new beginnings in which individuals work to reconnect to a community of shared culture, work and history at home.

Helga Schreckenberger

Aimless Travels: Deromanticizing Exile in Irmgard Keun's *Kind aller Länder* (1938)

The protagonists' restless travels across Europe shape Irmgard Keun's exile novel Kind aller Länder *thematically and structurally. Their movement is deformed by the experience of exile. Starting out as a voluntary decision to leave Nazi Germany, the protagonists' travels are increasingly determined by political, legal, and economic factors outside their control. Traveling becomes an end in itself, without destination or arrival. By focusing on the constitutive aspects of traveling, like class privilege, means of conveyance, agents, frontiers, documents and gender, the novel highlights the differences between the privileged voluntary travel of tourists and the forced wanderings of refugees. Moreover, the novel foregrounds the psychological difficulties of such an existence and its destabilizing impact on the identities of the adult protagonists. The ten-year old narrator's ability to navigate newness and her immunity to nationalism on the other hand suggests an ability to transcend traditional notions of exile.*

Irmgard Keun's third exile novel, *Kind aller Länder*, tells of the restless wanderings of a German émigré family of three from the perspective of the ten-year-old daughter. Published in 1938 by Querido in Amsterdam, the work never achieved the stunning success of the author's previous exile novel *Nach Mitternacht* which had come out with the same publisher only one year earlier.[1] While Keun's satirical depiction of life in Nazi Germany in *Nach Mitternacht* received critical accolades from her fellow exiles, the reaction to *Kind aller Länder* was rather subdued. Moreover, while *Nach Mitternacht* was quickly translated into many languages and remains one of the best known works of German exile literature, *Kind aller Länder* only saw one translation into Dutch. Even after Keun's rediscovery in the late 1970s, the novel has attracted little interest.[2] Keun scholars have focused primarily on the biographical aspects of the novel whose locations – Brussels, Ostende, Lemberg, Prague, Salzburg, Nice, Bordighera, Amsterdam, and the United States – correspond to Irmgard Keun's stops in exile. Consequently, these parallels have led to identifying the protagonists of the novel with the author and her acquaintances from the exile

---

[1] Keun's second exile novel, *D-Zug dritter Klasse*, also appeared with Querido in 1938.
[2] *Kind aller Länder* shares this fate with *D-Zug dritter Klasse*. The novel was translated into only one foreign language, Danish. Scholarship again focuses mainly on biographical details.

period.[3] Few scholars have considered the aesthetic quality of the novel and if so, they have judged it negatively. For example, Ingrid Machlewitz considers the open, often fragmentary structure of the novel an aesthetical failure, and views these formal shortcomings of the novel as a result of the pressures of Keun's life in exile, "als die Auswirkungen eines Produktions- und Erwartungsdrucks, dem die Autorin immer weniger gewachsen zu sein scheint".[4] Machlewitz misses a more nuanced, critical depiction of the countries encountered in this novel. She states: "Indem die Handlung jedes Bemühen um Seßhaftigkeit und somit die Probleme einer Immigration oder Assimilation ausspart, werden die besuchten Länder zu einer weitestgehend ohne gesellschaftskritische Wertung beschriebenen Kulisse reduziert".[5]

While Machlewitz recognizes that traveling itself is the main narrative focus ("der eigentliche Erzählgegenstand") (138) of Keun's novel, she fails to realize that all aspects of these travels are determined by the protagonists' status as exiles. They have little choice in the destination or duration of their travels. Thus, the novel is less interested in the encounter with foreign cultures than is the case in traditional travel accounts. Instead it focuses on the specific legal, economic, and psychological difficulties exile imposes on the travelers and its destabilizing impact on the identities of the protagonists.

The anthropologist and travel theorist James Clifford defines travel as "an inclusive term embracing a range of more or less voluntarist practices of leaving 'home' to go to some 'other' place".[6] Such a broad interpretation allows for subsuming experiences like exile, immigration, migration or other collective experiences of deterritorialization or displacement under the term of "travel." Clifford emphasizes the advantages of such an inclusive understanding of the term:

> I hang onto "travel" as a term of cultural comparison, precisely because of its historical taintedness, its association with gendered, racial bodies, class privilege, specific means of conveyance, beaten paths, agents, frontiers, documents, and the like. I prefer it to the more apparently neutral, and "theoretical," terms such as

---

[3] See Ingrid Machlewitz: *Irmgard Keun. Leben und Werk*. Würzburg: Könighausen und Neumann 1999; Irene Lorisika: *Frauendarstellungen by Irmgard Keun und Anna Seghers*. Frankfurt/Main: Haag und Herchen 1984; Gabriele Kreis: Schreiben aus eigener Erfahrung. Drei Schriftstellerinnen im Exil: Lili Körber, Irmgard Keun und Adrienne Thomas. In: *Zwischen Aufbruch und Verfolgung. Künstlerinnen der zwanziger und dreißiger Jahre*. Ed. by Denny Hirschbach and Sonia Novolseky. Bremen: Zeichen + Spuren 1993. Pp. 65–80.
[4] Machlewitz: *Irmgard Keun* (n. 2). P. 148.
[5] Ibid. P. 140.
[6] James Clifford: *Routes. Travel and Translation in the Late Twentieth Century*. Cambridge: Harvard University Press 1997. P. 66.

"displacement," which can make the drawing of equivalences across historical experiences too easy.⁷

Clifford argues for a deconstruction of "travel" in its historical context in order to shed light on less obvious conditions and experiences. This is also Keun's intention in *Kind aller Länder*. Her text focuses on all aspects that Clifford sees as constitutive of traveling: class privilege, means of conveyance, agents, frontiers, documents and gender. Her exiles are a non-Jewish German bourgeois family of three who are leaving Nazi Germany more or less voluntarily. They travel by train from one European capital to the next and navigate with differing success the various entry and residence permits. Traveling is indeed the narrative focus of the novel but it is travel that contrasts sharply with the privileged experience of the educational bourgeois tourist out for adventure. Rather it highlights the precarious political and economic situation of the emigrated family, their lack of self-determination, and the psychological price of permanent deterritorialization.

Initially, the exile of the family has the character of a family vacation rather than a permanent expulsion from their home. Kully, the ten-year-old narrator of Keun's novel, presents the emigration of the family as the voluntary decision of the father: "Wir sind aus Deutschland fortgefahren, weil mein Vater es nicht mehr ausgehalten hat, denn er schreibt Bücher und für die Zeitungen. Wir sind in die allgemeine Freiheit gewandert. Nach Deutschland gehen wir nie mehr zurück. Das brauchen wir auch nicht, denn die Welt ist sehr groß".⁸

Behind the child-like naive explanation of the reasons for the family's leaving of Germany, the more serious ones become visible: the government's censorship of authors and the media, the lack of freedom in Germany. The father wants to leave "weil eine Regierung Freunde von ihm eingesperrt hat und weil er nicht sprechen durfte was er wollte und auch nicht schreiben" (29). Still, the family starts their emigration not with a rushed flight but with a well-ordered departure at a time of their own choosing. The freedom and self-determination, which the departure from Nazi Germany was supposed to preserve quickly dissolve into illusion. The father's anti-Nazi publications make their return to Germany impossible: "[…] nach Deutschland können wir nicht zurück, weil uns dann die Regierung einsperrt, denn mein Vater hat in französischen und anderen Zeitungen und sogar in einem Buch geschrieben, daß er die Regierung

---

⁷James Clifford: Traveling Cultures. In: *Cultural Studies*. Ed. by Lawrence Grossberg, Cary Nelson, and Paula Treichler. New York: Routledge 1992. Pp. 96–112. Here: p. 110.
⁸Irmgard Keun: *Kind aller Länder*. Bergisch Gladbach: Lübbe 1983. Pp. 7ff. All page numbers refer to this edition and in the following will be cited in the text.

nicht leiden kann" (33). Soon their possibilities are further limited because of the Nazi's occupation of Czechoslovakia and Austria: "Jetzt können wir nicht mehr nach Wien [...], weil die deutsche Regierung alles besetzt hat" (42).

It becomes clear that the world is not as big as Kully initially had maintained. Moreover, the "general freedom" also has its limitation for it is not only the aggressive expansionist politics of Nazi Germany that severely impede the freedom of movement of the family. They also have to struggle with tightened immigration and residency laws that other European countries enacted in order to stem the waves of immigrants resulting from the occupation of Austria and Czechoslovakia. The family can no longer determine freely where they will travel and how long they will remain in any one country but they depend entirely on being granted the necessary visa and permits. Kully states: "Zuerst freuen wir uns immer schrecklich, wenn wir ein Visum bekommen haben und in ein anderes Land können. Aber dann fängt das Visum schon an, abzulaufen, jeden Tag läuft es ab – und auf einmal ist es ganz abgelaufen, und dann müssen wir aus dem Land wieder raus" (34).

The difference between traveler and immigrant is clearly marked. For the traveler, the temporal limits on visa and residency are inconsequential since she is merely a visitor, planning on moving on or returning home. For the immigrant, such restrictions can be life threatening.

Similarly, while passports and visa are also necessary for leisure travel, possessing them takes on existential importance for the immigrants: "Wenn man den Pass verliert, ist man für die Welt gestorben. Man darf in kein Land mehr. Aus einem Land muß man raus, aber in das andere darf man nicht rein" (32). For the immigrants, the loss of these papers not only means a restriction of their freedom to move (as it does for travelers) but also an extinction of their right to exist. They lose, as Sabine Rohlf puts it in her study *Exil als Praxis – Heimatlosigkeit als Perspektive?* "das Recht auf einen Ort in dieser Welt".[9]

Contrary to travel with its implied destination, exile is characterized by the impossibility of arriving. The incessant traveling of the family serves as a metaphor for their exterritorialism. Thus, the novel continually reverses the positive meaning which Kully conveys to traveling with remarks like "Und wenn wir woanders sind, sind wir wieder einen Schritt weiter und glücklich" (105). In the context of the novel, to travel does not mean to advance in the sense of progress and change. It is merely an escape from economical and political pressures and thus becomes static and circular:

"Glücklich sind wir eigentlich nur, wenn wir im Zug sitzen. Kaum, daß wir in einer Stadt angekommen sind, haben wir auch schon schreckliche Angst, daß

---

[9] Sabine Rohlf: *Exil als Praxis – Heimatlosigkeit als Perspektive? Lektüre ausgewählter Exilromane von Frauen.* München: edition text + kritik 2002. P. 148.

wir nie wieder fortkommen werden. Vor allem weil wir nie Geld haben, sind wir jedesmal in jedem Hotel gefangen und denken am ersten Tag schon wieder an unsere Befreiung (113).

For the exiles, traveling turns into an end in itself because the existential conditions of exile prevent them from settling down in any meaningful way. Kully and her family remain disconnected from their surroundings; they lose track of time and thus, any sense of orientation:

> Meine Mutter und ich wissen auch sonst oft nicht, in welchem Monat wir eigentlich leben, weil die Jahreszeiten in allen Ländern anders sind [...]. Wir haben auch sonst keine Zeiten, an denen wir uns festhalten können, manchmal erfahren wir nur ganz zufällig, daß Sonntag ist oder Weihnachten oder Allerheiligen [...]. Wir vergessen oft, wie lange wir aus Deutschland fort sind, in welchem Jahr wir leben [...]. Wir wissen auch oft gar nicht, wie lange wir an einem Ort sind (156f.).

Traveling in exile is a journey without destination. It suspends time by disrupting the familiar rhythm of life. Since Kully and her mother do not know the day or the date, they are also prevented from observing holidays that mark the passage of time. Their life has become a uniform series of waiting and fleeing. Estrangement from culture and place is accompanied by a loss of time causing alienation and disorientation.

Keun's novel also addresses the economical difficulties resulting from extended exile. Initially, the family acts like privileged tourists and stays in the best hotels enjoying the polite and courteous attention of the hotel employees. This predilection for luxury hotels and their voluntary emigration differentiates the family from other refugees. Kully reports: "Einmal sagte mir ein älterer Junge: 'Du bist ja gar keine richtige Emigrantin, ihr seid ja noch nicht mal Juden. Ihr seid Luxus-Emigranten'" (155). This difference quickly dissolves with the increasingly dire financial situation of the family. The novel depicts the painfully embarrassing, degrading circumstances in which Kully and her mother often find themselves because of their lack of money.

> Die Kellner im Hotel-Restaurant wedeln nicht mehr freundlich mit den Servietten, sie peitschen damit unseren Tisch. Meine Mutter sagt, das diene nur der Reinigung, aber es sieht aus, als schlagen sie nach uns wie nach Katzen, die einen Braten stehlen wollen. Wir wagen auch kaum noch, ins Restaurant zu gehen, meine Mutter und ich. Doch bleibt uns nichts anderes übrig, wenn wir nicht verhungern wollen. Denn wir haben keinen Franc mehr und können uns keinen billigen Käse kaufen, keinen Apfel und kein Brot, um heimlich im Zimmer zu essen [...]. Im Hotel-Restaurant wagte meine Mutter nicht, was Billiges zu bestellen, weil Kellner das nicht leiden können, und wir können es uns nicht leisten, die Menschen hier noch mehr zu verärgern (5f.).

Suspecting their inability to pay their bills, the hotel employees treat mother and daughter with disdain. While Kully's account does not lack comical aspects, it reveals the real financial and existential problems of the family which increase with the length of their exile. The combination of the restrictive immigration politics of the European countries and the financial straights of the family complicate the problems even further: "Es ist warm und wir haben Hunger. Wir können nicht abreisen, weil wir das Hotel nicht bezahlen können und weil wir in kein anderes Land können, aber wir dürfen auch nicht hierbleiben" (91). The movements of the family are no longer voluntary but are determined by the circumstances of their exile status.

The financial difficulties of the family result partially from the father's extravagant way of life. He is generous to a fault but also likes to enjoy the finer things of life and attempts to forget his monetary problems over champagne and caviar. The father cannot adjust to his new existence as an exile despite his demonstratively carefree attitude. More importantly, he no longer enjoys his success as an author in the new reality of exile since his novels don't find favor with the public any longer: "Herr Krabbe (the publisher) [...] sagte auch, daß mit dem letzten Buch von meinem Vater gar kein Geschäft gemacht worden sei, obwohl es doch sein bestes Buch sei" (148). Keun dispels the myth of the creative possibility which the experience of exile offers to the artists by foregrounding the economic realities of the exile situation. While the book is Kully's father's "best", it is not a financial success because of the lack of readership – the German-speaking market was largely inaccessible for the writers in exile. The money worries additionally interfere with the father's ability to concentrate on his work: "Mein Vater schreibt für unseren Lebensunterhalt. In Ostende hat er ein neues Buch geschrieben, das aber nicht fertig geworden ist, weil wir so viel Sorgen hatten" (9). Her father is forced to find other ways to make money. Since his novels are no longer financially viable, he attempts to write other genres like advertisements or theater plays which he deems more sellable. However, he mostly tries to support his family with advances from his publisher, without being able to deliver the promised manuscripts. The restless attempts of the father to find money turn him into a "Handlungsreisenden in Sachen Literatur" as Ingrid Machlewitz puts it.[10] He travels from one place to the other trying to interest someone in his projects or at least to be able to borrow money from them. Again, financial considerations determine the movements of the family albeit in different ways. While the father travels throughout Europe in search of money, Kully and her mother remain behind so that the hotel bill can remain open: "Wir bleiben als Pfand zurück, und mein Vater sagt: wir hätten einen höheren Versatzwert als Diamanten und Pelze" (5). This absurd situation turns mother and daughter into a possession that can be

---

[10] Machlewitz: *Irmgard Keun* (n. 2). P. 142.

pawned and degrades them to objects, underscoring the inhumane dimension of the exile experience where valid papers and ability to pay are more valuable than human life.

Loss of home, self-determination, security, and professional success that accompany the exile experience take their emotional toll and affect all members of the family in different ways. Annchen, the mother, is the least suited for a life in exile and thus the most negatively impacted. She embodies the traditional middle-class wife who never had a career of her own, and who lives her life through her husband. Annchen follows her husband into exile, and we never hear if she shares his political view. According to Kully, her mother's strengths lay mainly in her housewifely abilities.

> Sie kann für meinen Vater selbst Zigaretten drehen, dann kosten sie nur die Hälfte. Sie kann aus Tischtüchern Tintenflecke entfernen, die mein Vater reingemacht hat und Koffer packen, daß dreimal so viel reingeht, als wenn mein Vater sie packt. Der kauft dann einfach einen neuen Koffer oder schenkt die Sachen fort, die nicht mehr reingehen. Dann kann sie unsere Wäsche selbst im Waschbecken waschen und mit dem kleinen Bügeleisen bügeln, ohne daß im Hotel jemand was merkt. Und mein Vater darf es auch nicht merken, der will sowas nicht. Aber er hat es gern, wenn sie für mich und sich Mützen und Pullover strickt und wir schön darin aussehen (31).

Because of the exile situation and the father's aversion to menial tasks, the mother has little opportunity to act on her abilities. Staying in expensive hotels as her husband wishes does not allow her to practice her money saving, domestic virtues. She also cannot turn her abilities into gainful employment because of the immigration laws: "Meine Mutter möchte Zimmermädchen sein und arbeiten, damit sie Geld verdient. Aber die Länder erlauben ihr nicht, daß sie ein Zimmermädchen ist" (78). Annchen is emotionally and financially completely dependent on her husband who either "pawns" her when he cannot pay the hotel bill or uses her to manipulate his publisher to advance him more money. Annchen spends most of her time in hotel rooms waiting for her husband. The uncertainty of life in exile is cause for permanent fear and worries that escalate with the increasing threat of war. Her duty to her child alone prevents her from acting on her despair and taking her own life: "Meine Mutter will manchmal sterben, dann hat sie Ruhe und keine Angst mehr. Aber sie weiß nicht, was dann aus mir werden soll" (77f.).

Only one time Annchen manages to prevail over her husband. She convinces him to rent an apartment in Nice which she happily decorates and equips with the necessary household items. Kully reports: "Und wir wollten seßhaft werden und sparsam und weniger Sorgen haben" (145). Annchen is happy since she has recreated a domain where she can actively contribute to the financial survival of the family. While the constant traveling undermines Annchen's role as a contributing, autonomous member of the family, establishing something as a home, her "Reterritorialisierung im Haushalt"[11] restores her to a position of relative power as she can influence the financial situation of the family. However, the domestic bliss doesn't even last two days, when the father decides to take the family to the United States in order to pursue new financial opportunities.

Annchen's character embodies stereotypical femininity not only because of her domestic inclinations but also because of her appearance.

> [...] sie hat goldene fedrige Haare, eine runde weiche Brust wie so ein Vogel und ängstliche Augen, und immer sieht sie aus, als wollte sie gleich fortfliegen. Sie sitzt auch nie richtig breit und fest wie ein Mensch, sondern wie ein Vogel auf einem Zweig [...]. Und ihre Haare sind sauber gekämmt und hinten am Kopf sanft zusammengeknotet [...]. Meine Mutter ist viel schöner als ich, aber ich weine weniger (8).

Her femininity and beauty are her only weapons of survival in exile. She derives courage from her beauty when she has to beg for money: "Wenn sie schön aussieht, hat sie mehr Mut durch die Hotelhalle zu gehen und mit anderen Leuten zu sprechen, sie um Geld zu bitten" (41). Annchen's character shows little resemblance with the image of the courageous, capable women in exile whose ability to adjust to the new situation often makes them the sole supporter of their family in exile.[12] Consequently, Keun-scholars have criticized this character as unrealistic[13] or regressive when compared with the energetic, independent female protagonists of Keun's earlier novels.[14] Sabine Rohlf rejects this criticism and offers a different interpretation. She understands Annchen's character as a critique of the heterosexual economy of desire and dependency, of the power structures created and reproduced by the hierarchical gender binary. Rohlf states:

> Die Funktion und die Ortlosigkeit der Frau in einer sexistischen Ordnung werden in eine Erzählung gefasst, in der die Ökonomien der Identifizierung, des (Geld-)Wertes und des Begehrens sowie deren fatale Folgen für das weibliche Geschlecht höchst anschaulich werden. Die reduzierte, abgeschlossene und transitäre Lebenswelt der Hotelzimmer und -betten liest sich wie eine literarische Ausgestaltung der Metapher

---

[11] Rohlf: *Exil als Praxis* (n. 9). P. 152.
[12] See Helmut Pfanner: Die Rolle der Frau im Exil: Im Spiegel der deutschsprachigen Literatur in New York. In: *Analecta Heletia et Germanica. Eine Festschrift zu Ehren von Hermann Boeschenstein*. Ed. By Armin Arnold et al. Bonn: Bouvier 1979. Pp. 342–359.
[13] See Kreis: Schreiben aus eigener Erfahrung (n. 3). P. 77.
[14] See Machlewitz: *Irmgard Keun* (n. 2). P. 145; Ritta-Joe Horsley: Witness, Critic, Victim. Irmgard Keun and the Years of National Socialism. In: *Gender Patriarchy and Fascism in the Third Reich: The Response of Women Writers*. Ed. by Elaine Martin. Detroit: Wayne State University Press 1993. Pp. 65–117. Here: p. 95.

des "gender exile" und zeigt, dass die Frau sich nicht in einem undefinierbaren Außen, sondern in klar benennbaren Relationen zu einem männlich markierten Referenzpunkt befindet.[15]

Gender exile connotes in this context the effects of gender discrimination. Thus, Rohlf reads Keun's novel as an attempt to exemplify the double exile of women who experience cultural marginalization as well as a concrete loss of home.[16] Annchen is displaced by exile and marginalized by her husband who considers her his possession and has little consideration for her wishes. While Annchen may not be representative for women in exile after 1933, her story, so Rohlf, serves to illustrate a very real order which defines woman only in reference to man and always as the other.[17] Building on Rohlf's observation, I would like to suggest an additional reading. Annchen's "gender exile" can also be seen as a counter image to the modernist concept of exile as a prerequisite to (male) creativity, as aesthetic gain.[18] The fallacy and limitations of this understanding of exile are demonstrated through the figure of the father.

In contrast to his wife whose autonomy diminishes in exile, the free-spirited, decidedly anti-bourgeois father initially thrives. Exile promises to accommodate his desire for movement as well as his need for emotional distance and independence from his family. He initiates the family's emigration in the first place and Kully repeatedly emphasizes his restlessness: "Woanders hält es mein Vater nicht länger als vier Wochen aus, in Paris hält er es drei Monate aus, aber länger auch nicht" (113) and "Mein Vater wollte auch fort, er will immer fort" (73). However, this restlessness is not new, it existed already before emigration as Kully's description of an early Christmas celebration at her grandmother's house in Cologne indicates: "Mein Vater wurde unruhig und wäre gern in ein Lokal gegangen, um ein Glas Bier zu trinken, denn er ist nicht gern in Wohnungen eingesperrt" (110).

The father corresponds closely to the image of the anti-bourgeois, in most cases male, artist who feels restricted by middle-class conventions in his personal freedom as well as in his artistic creativity. Kully reports: "Ein regelmäßiges Leben stört seine Arbeit und ekelt ihn an" (9). Even his family bothers him at times: "Er hat uns auch oft fortgeschickt" (9). The father "von dem jeder sagt: dieser Mann hätte nie heiraten dürfen" (5) often appears

---

[15] Rohlf: *Exil als Praxis* (n. 9). Pp. 157f.
[16] Ibid. P. 52.
[17] See Ibid. P. 157.
[18] For a discussion of modernist discourses of exile, see Caren Kaplan: *Questions of Travel. Postmodern Discourses of Displacement*. Durham and London: Duke University Press 1996. Pp. 27–40.

emotionally absent and unavailable: "Wenn meine Mutter und ich meinen Vater mittags abholten, sahen seine Augen manchmal aus, als seien sie weit ins Meer geschwommen und noch nicht wieder zurück" (9). The suspicion arises that the father's frequent trips across Europe are not alone motivated by his search for new financial means but also by his need to escape his bourgeois family ties. One of his female admirers, the middle-aged Fräulein Brouwer who addresses him with "Meister", justifies his frequent leave-takings: "Ja, so ein künstlerischer Geist muß durch die Ferne schweifen, Familienbande dürfen ihn nicht hemmen" (38).

The father's anti-bourgeois stance, his need for distance and solitude reminds of the image of Edward Said's "solitary exile":

> The exile knows that in a secular contingent world, homes are always provisional. Borders and barriers, which enclose us within the safety of familiar territory, can also become prisons, and are often defended beyond reason or necessity. Exiles cross borders, break barriers of thought and experience.[19]

Said contrasts the solitary exile with the refugees: "Refugees [...] are a creation of the twentieth century state. The word 'refugee' has become a political one, suggesting large herds of innocent and bewildered people requiring urgent national assistance, whereas 'exile' carries with it, I think, a touch of solitude and spirituality".[20] In her discussion of Said's essay, Caren Caplan points out the similarities between Said's image of the exile and the modernist aesthetic understanding of exile.

> In "Reflections on Exile", Said draws upon images of refugees for inspiration, linking the solitary exile to mass, global experience of displacement. The distinction between earlier exile and those of today, Said argues, lies in the scale of the phenomenon [...]. Yet throughout the essay Said often abandons his reference to a global phenomenon and returns to a mystified figure – the solitary exile.[21]

Caplan points out that the modernist understanding of exile which still informs Said's image leads to a romantic vision of the exile that can be easily defined in aesthetic terms of loss and creativity. Refugees, however, do not belong in an aestheticized world. They are faceless, political constructs outside the sphere of literature and aesthetics.[22]

---

[19] Edward Said: Reflections on Exile. In: *Reflections on Exile and Other Essays*. Cambridge: Harvard University Press 2000. Pp. 173–186. Here: p. 185.
[20] Ibid. P. 18.
[21] Kaplan: *Questions of Travel* (n. 18). Pp. 119f.
[22] Ibid. Pp. 120–121. However, Kaplan points out that in the same article and in the body of his later work, Said does imagine the possibility of a poetics of "mass politics".

Keun's novel seems to anticipate this dual vision of exiles. Kully and her mother exist in a mundane reality fraught with hunger, coldness, and dependency on the mercy of others. The father, on the other hand, realizes his dreams of the romantic, exiled artist who preserves his freedom of movement to the detriment of his wife and child. While the anti-fascist, unconventional father certainly has positive aspects, his irresponsible behavior towards his family suggests a more critical evaluation of this figure. In the context of the novel, the reckless, selfish behavior of the father can be read as a criticism of the mystified, romantic figure of the solitary exile that dominates the modernist discourse of exile. While he pursues his freedom and lust for adventure, he leaves his family penniless at the mercy of strange people. In the face of the historic reality of exile from Nazi Germany which impacted women, children, and the elderly, the father's actions evoke little admiration.[23]

The limits of the father and his bohemian attitude toward exile become glaringly apparent when he moves beyond the familiar cultural realm of Europe. Escaping his wife's attempt to settle in the South of France the father whisks his family to the United States with promises of success and money. (However, he manages to leave his wife behind.) Already crossing the Atlantic on a boat brings about a strange change in the father. He spends his time in the cabin lying in bed "stumm und starr" (155), and refuses to take any part in the life on board of the ship.[24] The death-like immobility of the father underscores the enormity of the transition from the known European culture to that of the unknown America. It is especially the unfamiliar mode of transition – crossing the ocean on board of a ship – that immobilizes the father who only recovers when arrival becomes imminent. The father's insecurity suggests that his seemingly nomadic lifestyle is very much bound to the European realm. However, he shares this with most of the other exiles on board. Kully remarks:

> Mein Vater wurde wieder etwas fröhlich, die Leute auf dem Schiff wurden fast alle wieder gesund und lachten aufgeregter. Der Lunchroom war plötzlich voller Menschen, die man vorher nie gesehen hatte. Auch auf Deck nicht, wo kamen sie nur auf einmal her? (158).

---

[23] Sabine Rohlf advances a different interpretation of the father: "Kullys Vater verweist als durch und durch unsystematischer, nichtsesshafter, sorgloser und erklärt antifaschistischer Mensch auf die Verwandtschaft des unsteten Bohemien mit postmodernen Formulierungen des sich deterritorialisierenden, kontingenten, subversiven Individuums. Er lässt sich keine Grenzen setzen und schafft es selbst in der schwierigen Situation des Exils, seine Bewegungsfreiheit zu bewahren und einen scheinbar zwanglosen und lustbetonten Lebensstil zu verteidigen" (see Rohlf: *Exil als Praxis* [n. 9]. P. 166f.). However, he does so to the detriment of his wife and child.

[24] Kully, on the other hand, enjoys the worry-free period. She eats as much as she can, plays games and learns English from some of the sailors.

The expectation of leaving the strange transitional space of the ocean and going on land returns the father to his normal optimistic self. It also seems to restore hope in his fellow travelers and exiles who like him remained invisible during the ocean voyage.

However, arrival in the United States means entering a new world guided by unknown rules and customs. The experiences in the United States further underscore the father's deep rootedness in European traditions. It soon becomes evident that he cannot adjust to this new setting. He has difficulties with the American cultural traditions and ways of interacting. Language alone constitutes an almost insurmountable obstacle, especially on the telephone:

> Mein Vater telefonierte stundenlang. Danach brach er fast zusammen. Erst verstand die Telefonzentrale nie die Nummer, die er haben wollte, und später verstanden ihn die Leute nicht, er hatte dann zehn Verabredungen. Von keiner wußte er richtig, wann und wo. Amerika wuchs ihm über den Kopf (162).

The father, who in Europe was so successful in convincing people to advance him money solely on the merit of his ideas, fails miserably in the United States. Because of various confusions and misunderstandings he cannot realize his big plans to do business with Metro Goldwyn. The American publisher also loses interest and leaves town as do all other people whose patronage the father expected. Still, the father remains the generous, slightly irresponsible free spirit. He gives away the little money he manages to raise. He loses Kully at a rally, and she ends up wandering the streets of New York City until a policeman returns her to the hotel. However, the lack of success takes its toll: "Mein Vater würgte morgens vor dem Waschbecken, das tut er meistens, wenn die Zeiten mal wieder besonders aufregend sind. Ich brauche da schon gar nicht mehr zu fragen" (171).

Soon without money, the father seeks the help of a former childhood friend who immigrated to the United States many years ago. Driving to the friend's home in a borrowed car can be understood as a metaphor for the father's geographic and intellectual disorientation. He drives at a high speed, however without any sense of knowing where to go: "Wir fuhren auch oft rasend aber meistens falsch" (174). In addition, the car breaks down frequently. Since according to Kully her father cannot even repair a pen, they are stalled in the road until they receive help from other drivers. The father's mechanical shortcomings are an additional indication of his not fitting in the new world that represents the height of technological progress.

Moreover, the father cannot find common ground with the American population. In Virginia Beach where his childhood friend resides, he is repulsed by the petit-bourgois attitudes of his friend. Alternatively, he seeks the company of the black population. The African Americans serve as a counter image to the narrow-minded, straight-laced friend. While the friend is anti-alcoholic, boring, pompous, and money conscious, the African Americans are happy, spontaneous, like to drink, and are not concerned with financial security.[25] However, the African Americans prove too alien for Kully and her father. When the wife of one of them dies and he does not have the money to bury her, the father lends him the money for the burial. Four days later, Kully and her father see the man who asks them to his house in order to repay the money. When they arrive, they find the man's dead wife lying in bed. It turns out that the man did not pay for the burial but bought whiskey instead. The black undertaker not wanting to work without pay exhumed the woman and returned her to her bed.

Although Kully excuses the shoe cleaner for spending the money on alcohol – he had to console himself for his wife's death, she and her father are visibly shaken by the barbaric and irrational act of the undertaker. He not only showed a lack of respect for the dead woman but by digging up her body he did twice the work without getting paid. While Kully and her father condemn the act of the caretaker, their American hosts are more upset by the fact that the father loaned money to a black man, and went to his house. Keun underscores that the United States has nothing to offer to the German exiles. White society is too straight-laced and conformist, while their racism blinds them to the true horror of the situation. The African Americans however, are too barbaric and uncivilized to offer any true alternative to the bigoted American middle class. The father who navigated his European exile so successfully, flounders in the United States, because he remains culturally alienated. Yet, this alienation does not bring about artistic creativity as suggested by the modernist aesthetic discourse of exile.

The narrator Kully is the only protagonist who blossoms in exile. In contrast to her parents, she does not suffer from the uncertainties and unsteadiness of exile. The constant traveling provides her education. She learns to understand the nature of borders, visa, consulates, and immigration laws. She is very proud of her abilities to speak a number of foreign languages and to convert the different currencies. In contrast to her parents who mainly have contact with other exiles, Kully quickly befriends children in each new country, and is eager and

---

[25] In 1938, Irmgard Keun visited her friend Arnold Strauss who had immigrated to the United States in 1935. Strauss lived in Virginia Beach where he found employment at a hospital. Like the male protagonist of her novel, Keun was appalled by the narrow-minded, petit-bourgois attitude of Strauss and his new American acquaintances. It can be assumed that she incorporated some of her own experiences and observations in the novel. However, it is doubtful that she came in contact with the African-American population of the small provincial town, at least not to the extent that her protagonists do. The depiction of the African Americans has been rightly criticized as racist.

curious to explore her new surroundings. She seldom experiences fear, not even when she is lost in New York City. For her, the constant traveling, the staying in hotels, not settling at one place for any amount of time represent a new normalcy. As Sabine Rohlf emphasizes, Kully's well-adjustment and flexibility should not be read as a sign that she is a carefree child who does not comprehend the seriousness of the situation. Kully is well aware of her family's precarious situation and remains composed even when her parents' behavior does little to instill in her the feeling of safety.[26] Despite the childlike innocence with which she interprets the events unfolding around her, she acts maturely and is rather self-reliant. Often she takes on the role of the caretaker: she combs her mother's hair, organizes food for her, picks up the dropped curling iron, extinguishes the forgotten spirit lamp; she also packs her father's suitcase. While most of her schemes to contribute to the family finances remain fantasy, it is evident that exile has taught Kully to take on responsibility within the limits of her abilities.

Sabine Rohlf points out that Kully's exile experience combines that of both parents.[27] At times, she shares the waiting position of her mother, while at other times she accompanies her father on his travels. However, in both situations, Kully acts differently. She is much less passive than her mother because she interacts with her new environment, plays with the children, learns new languages and remains happy even if her father is not present. In her attempts to earn money for the family, and to take care of them, she assumes the role of the breadwinner which the father cannot fulfill. While Kully shares her father's adventurous and fearless spirit, she never underestimates or neglects the existential problems of life in exile. For Rohlf, Kully should not be seen as a mediator between the positions and experiences of her parents but as standing outside any gender order.

> Kullys Exil, ihr Außerhalb oder Anderswo im geographischen wie im geschlechtlichen Sinn lässt sich anders als das "gender exile" ihrer Mutter als eine Ortlosigkeit lesen, die sich darüber herstellt, verschiedene Orte zu durchqueren, ohne sich auf einen festzulegen. Ihr "Nomadenleben" zeigt sich nicht nur als ziellose Reise durch verschiedene Länder, sondern als Bewegung durch geschlechtlich markierte Räume.[28]

Rohlf refers to Kully's repeated refusal to conform to traditional images of girlhood by neglecting her appearance, and by rejecting the role of the "good" child.

---

[26] Kully does not panic when her father forgets her at a restaurant or loses her in New York City. When her mother breaks down mentally, Kully sends a telegram to notify her father.
[27] See Rohlf: *Exil als Praxis* (n. 9). P. 178.
[28] Ibid. P. 179.

More importantly, in addition to Kully's avoiding identification with gender expectations, she also refuses to identify with one geographic or rather national location. Like the title of the novel indicates, Kully becomes a child of all countries, a true cosmopolitan without national ties. " 'Hast Du nie Heimweh?' fragte mich ein alter Mann, und ich wusste zuerst nicht, was er meinte. Er hat es mir erklärt. Manchmal habe ich Heimweh, aber immer nach einem anderen Land, das mir gerade einfällt (190). For Kully, homesickness is not the result of longing for one single country but is caused by the beautiful memories she connects to all the countries she has visited:

> Manchmal denke ich an die singenden Autobusse an der Côte d'Azur, an eine Wiese bei Salzburg, die ein blaues Meer von Schwertlilien war, an die Weihnachtsbäume bei meiner Großmutter, an die Slotmaschinen in New York, an die Riesenmuscheln in Virginia und die Strohschlitten und den Schnee in Polen (190).

In contrast to her parents, Kully is able to cope successfully with exile and "Heimatlosigkeit". She is not rooted in any particular place or limited by specific cultural boundaries but has learned to find happiness and beauty wherever she is. Yet she does not represent the "solitary exile" of the modernist discourse. Kully recognizes the importance of community and family ties as the last sentences of the novel suggest: "Ich möchte aber nirgends hin, wenn meine Mutter nicht dabei ist. Richtiges Heimweh habe ich eigentlich nie. Und wenn mein Vater bei uns ist, schon gar nicht" (190).

With Kully's character, the novel suggests the possibility of a survival in exile, of a nomadic existence but without the gender specificity or the romanticization of solitude of earlier discourses of exile. Kully represents a new generation who is grounded enough in the past to have developed a sense of identity, yet is not weighed down by it and is thus capable to open up to new experiences.

Keun's novel *Kind aller Länder* succeeds in realizing James Clifford's call for a deconstruction of the conditions of travel that is historically precisely situated. In this novel, traveling loses its romantic, adventurous connotation since its conditions are determined by the political, legal, and economic realities of exile from Nazi Germany. Under these circumstances, traveling no longer produces the figure of the "solitary exile" or the "hero traveler", but the deterritorialized refugee. Loss of home, security and identity destabilize the adult protagonists of the novel. However, with the narrator Kully, the novel explores traveling and exile as possibilities to overcome national and cultural limitations in favor of an unconventional, fresh look at the world.

Margot Taureck

Exil und Reisen im Geiste – Rudolf Leonhards
Traumbuch des Exils

In 1927 the playwright, storyteller and essayist Rudolf Leonhard (1889–1953), one of the first German radio-play authors as well as a film writer, expressionist and pacifist, settled in Paris. After 1933 he became an increasingly ardent critic of National Socialism. He was the co-founder and organizer of the "League for the Protection of German Writers in Exile" and helped many emigrant friends. He was interned, an experience that resulted in over 600 poems, the tragedy Hostages *and the* Dream-Book in Exile. *The period from May 1941 to July 1944 is captured in dreams – the time of Rudolf Leonhard's internment in the* Le Vernet *camp on the edge of the Pyrenees and* Les Milles *near Aix-en-Provence, as well as his imprisonment in Castres, near Toulouse. This essay shows that the reality of Rudolf Leonhard's many journeys, part of his political and propagandist mission in his country of exile, France, surfaces in countless dream journeys. Exile and travel in spirit, journeys into the unknown, escapes, continuous traveling: descriptions of movement. Hotel lobbies, stations, and trains are the locations for many episodes. Secret arrivals are just as frightening as journeys to the underworld.*

Eintrag vom 29. April 1944: "Wir fahren in Jeans Auto. Jean fragt: 'Warum soll man reisen?" und ich preise die Ausdehnung der Weltkenntnis, das Welt-Gefühl, die Reisen uns geben".

In Rudolf Leonhards *Traumbuch des Exils*, einem der ungewöhnlichsten und erstaunlichsten Zeitdokumente der deutschen Exilliteratur, beherrscht das Thema Reisen ein knappes Viertel der brisanten Aufzeichnungen. Amerika, New York, England, Brasilien, Übersee heißen die Auswanderungsziele. Jedoch ist nur schwerlich ein größerer Gegensatz denkbar zwischen der aktuellen Situation des Autors, verdammt zur Illegalität, seit Jahren streng überwacht und in ständiger Gefahr, an die Gestapo ausgeliefert zu werden, und der Vorstellung des Reisens, die mit Freiheit, Offenheit, Entdeckungs- und Abenteuerlust, freiwilliger Entfernung vom Heimatort verbunden ist, manchmal auch mit Gefahren und Tod. Streng genommen schließen die Begriffe "Exil" – staatliche Unterdrückung, Zensur, Schreibverbot oder Verbannung zwangen unter anderen Schriftsteller, Künstler, Wissenschaftler seit frühesten Zeiten zur Emigration – und Reisen einander aus, denn:

> In der Verbannung zu leben, ist schwer, materiell und moralisch schwer. Der Gastgeber mit den besten Absichten vergisst nicht immer, dass sie in seinem Hause sind. Man darf nicht zur Last fallen und sich nicht leichtfertig zeigen. Man muss bescheiden sein, ohne sich zu erniedrigen, stolz, ohne sich aufzuspielen – würdig.[1]

---

[1] Maximilian Scheer: *Freunde über Rudolf Leonhard*. Berlin: Verlag der Nation 1958. S. 8.

Selten ist es möglich, eine Emigration unter den genannten Umständen wie eine Reise vorzubereiten. Reisen bedeutet hier Flucht, Preisgabe und im günstigsten Fall Lebensrettung. Das Reisevokabular, in beiden Fällen identisch – Ausreise, Anreise, Durchreise, Weiterreise gehören dazu, ebenso wie Visa, Pässe, Papiere, Kontrolle, Aufenthaltsgenehmigung, Ein- und Ausreiseerlaubnis, Hotels, und nicht zuletzt: Geld – erhält unter Exil-Bedingungen eine determinierende vitale Bedeutung.

Diese Wörter bilden den eisernen Bestandteil von Rudolf Leonhards zwar für eine Veröffentlichung vorgesehenem, jedoch über lange Jahre unbekannt und ungelesen gebliebenem *Traumbuch des Exils*. Der Autor wurde vermutlich seit dem 5. Oktober 1939 in einem der Pariser Sammellager, dem Stadion *Roland Garros*, ohne Haftbefehl und unter der Beschuldigung kommunistischer Propaganda gefangen gehalten, obwohl er ausgebürgert, jüdischer Herkunft, erklärter Antfaschist, seit 1927 in Frankreich lebend und mit einer Französin verheiratet war. Kurz darauf lernte er die Internierungslager *Le Vernet* und *Les Milles* sowie das Gefängnis *Castres* gründlich kennen, und schloss sich nach Ausbruch und Flucht aus diesem Gefängnis der französischen Résistance an. Wie durch ein Wunder hatte er fünf Jahre unmenschlichster Lebensbedingungen überstanden. Auch der größte Teil seiner Manuskripte aus dieser Zeit blieb durch die Umsicht von Freunden und den Mut seiner Frau Yvette erhalten. Seine letzte literarisch-politische Tätigkeit in Paris, bevor er den Status des "feindlichen Ausländers" im "Lager der Unerwünschten – dem Camp des indésirables" erlangte, war die Leitung des "Deutschen Freiheitssenders 29,8". Er galt als gefährlich für die innere und äußere Sicherheit Frankreichs, als überzeugter Kommunist, "stalinien convaincu", und wurde deshalb besonders eng und streng überwacht.

Rudolf Leonhard, auch Raoul Lombat, Roger Lehardon, Robert Lanzer, vier R.L., hinter denen ein Lyriker, Dramatiker, Erzähler, Essayist und Sprachphilosoph, Herausgeber und Übersetzer steht, im Frühwerk vom Expressionismus geprägt, später eher realistischer Gestalter, vor allem aber ein Kämpfer und Dichter gegen Unfreiheit, Unheil, Barbarei, Gemeinheit, Krieg und für das Leben.[2] Er wurde am 27. Oktober 1889 in Lissa (heute Polen) geboren. Die Eltern Levysohn, der Vater war Rechtsanwalt und Notar, ließen die Kinder evangelisch taufen; diese trugen den Namen Leonhard. Dem 1907 mit "glänzend" bestandenen Abitur folgte ein Studium von Germanistik und Jura in Göttingen, Berlin und München. 1914 wurde der Fünfundzwanzigjährige als Kriegsfreiwilliger zunächst abgelehnt, dann aber doch Soldat. Unter dem Eindruck des Ersten Weltkrieges und nach Verletzungen vollzog sich Rudolf Leonhards Wandlung zum Kriegsgegner. Sie brachte ihn wegen pazifistischer

---

[2] Rudolf Leonhard: *Ausgewählte Werke. Le Vernet*. Hg. von Maximilian Scheer. Berlin: Verlag der Nation 1961. S. 7.

Äußerungen vor ein Kriegsgericht, bescherte ihm ein Jahr der Internierung in vierzehn Lazaretten, bzw. Irrenanstalten, die in Lazaretten untergebracht waren,[3] und vor allem den Rückzug aus dem aktiven Militärdienst. Er schloss Bekanntschaft mit Martin Buber und dem Verleger Ernst Rowohlt, trat 1918 der USPD bei, war 1919 Mitglied der KPD und gehörte 1921 für ein Jahr der KPD-Splittergruppe KAPD (Kommunistische Arbeiterpartei Deutschlands) an. Als Anhänger Karl Liebknechts beteiligte er sich 1918 an der Novemberrevolution und im März 1920 an der Niederschlagung des Kapp-Putsches. Seit Beginn der 1920er Jahre Verlagslektor, nahm er an der Gründung und Leitung des Theaters *Die Tribühne* teil, war Mitarbeiter der *Weltbühne* und freier Schriftsteller.

Laut Steffen Mensching war Rudolf Leonhard

> ein kleiner Mann, Liebling der Frauen, Zahlenmystiker und Erotomane, ein Dichter, der auf das "image" des Dichters Wert legte, ein charismatischer Redner (der gern das Wort nahm), ein Dandy mit Stöckchen, Handschuhen, Seidentuch, Siegelring; korrekte Kleidung, Umgangsformen, regelgemäßer Ausdruck waren ihm selbstverständlich. Hinzu kam ein "hemmungslos hedonistischer" Zug.[4]

Wen es verwundern sollte, wie revolutionäre Einstellung und dekadentes Verhalten in Einklang zu bringen waren, der muss sich vor Augen halten, dass Leonhard "wie viele Zeitgenossen, die den Schlachten des Ersten Weltkrieges entronnen waren, eifrig in der Schule der freien Liebe studierte", keine Tabus gelten ließ und sozusagen über die Libido zum Sozialismus gelangte. Sinn des Lebens war für ihn nach dem Grauen des Massensterbens die Suche nach Schönheit. Je mehr Menschen daran teilhaben würden, desto größer der Genuss. Ein Gesinnungs-Ästhet also, der Politökonomie und marxistische Kategorien kaum in sein Werk integrierte. Ein Individualist, Einzelgänger und Eigenbrödler, der sich trotzdem in die Bewegung, in Parteidisziplin und Dogma einfügte. Vielleicht erkannte er aber, wie Mensching vermutet, in diesem "puritanischen Korsett eine rettende Maßnahme, die ihn vor Vereinzelung, Wahnsinn, Verzettelung im Rausch schützte". Viele Träume in Leonhards *Traumbuch des Exils* zeugen von dieser unbequemen Spannung.[5]

Seit 1927 lebte Leonhard – auf Einladung Walter Hasenclevers (Dramatiker, Lyriker, Romanautor, Wortführer des Expressionismus), mit dem er seit 1914 befreundet war – in Paris. Seine Wohnverhältnisse charakterisierte bis zu diesem Zeitpunkt und darüber hinaus ein gewisser "nomadischer Zug".[6] Ab

---

[3] Vgl. Bernd Jentzsch: *Rudolf Leonhard. Gedichteträumer*. München: Hanser 1984. S.14f.
[4] Rudolf Leonhard: *In derselben Nacht. Das Traumbuch des Exils*. Hg. von Steffen Mensching. Berlin: Aufbau 2001. S. 497.
[5] Ebd. S. 497f.
[6] Bettina Giersberg: *Die Arbeit des Schriftstellers Rudolf Leonhard im französischen Exil 1933 bis 1945*. Dissertation Berlin 2005. S. 26.

1933 verwandelte sich der frei gewählte Aufenthalt im Pariser Vorort Clamart zu einem obligatorischen. Leonhard änderte seine eher zurückgezogene Arbeits- und Lebensweise, engagierte sich tatkräftig für die deutschsprachige Emigration in Frankreich und zählte zu den zentralen Persönlichkeiten des Pariser Exils. Sein Einfluss öffnete deutschen Schriftstellern und Publizisten die Spalten französischer Zeitungen und er weckte das Interesse seiner französischen Freunde für die Probleme der deutschen Schriftsteller, die vor der Verfolgung nach Paris geflohen waren.

Er war Mitbegründer und Vorsitzender des "Schutzverbandes deutscher Schriftsteller im Exil" bis zum Krieg. Er hielt viele Reden, arbeitete in zahlreichen antifaschistischen Organisationen, arbeitete an der Vorbereitung einer deutschen Volksfront mit und war mehrere Jahre hindurch führend daran beteiligt, die zersplitterte Emigration durch Einheit und Volksfront dynamischer zu machen. Der französische Schriftsteller André Wurmser schrieb wie folgt über Rudolf Leonhard:

> Sein Geist leuchtete. Er geizte so wenig mit seiner Zustimmung wie mit seiner Freundschaft, so wenig mit seiner Kritik wie mit seiner Billigung. Er verstand. Verstehen heißt helfen. Er verstand die Absicht des Schriftstellers, seine Bemühung, sein Ziel, die Gründe der Unzulänglichkeit einer Erzählung, eines Kapitels, eines Romans. Darum wirkte sogar sein Tadel stärkend. Ich habe ihn als Verbannten gekannt. Ich habe ihn arm, sehr arm gekannt. Ich habe ihn in den schwarzen Tagen gekannt, als Hitler zur Macht kam. Er war oft sehr unglücklich; nie im entferntesten war er schwach. Ich habe viele Emigranten gekannt, die große Würde besaßen. Keiner war würdiger, blieb würdevoller ein Deutscher, besaß feinere Kenntnis Frankreichs und der Franzosen, bewies ihnen offenere und treuere Freundschaft, als mein Freund Rudolf Leonhard.[7]

Auf Einladung eines französischen Komitees fuhr er im August 1937 nach Spanien und veröffentlichte 1938 die *Spanischen Gedichte und Tagebuchblätter*. Der KPD nahestehend, aber nicht deren Mitglied, gelang es ihm, ein Netzwerk von Exilanten unterschiedlicher politischer Herkunft zu knüpfen. Da er auch in Deutschland als Gegner der Nationalsozialisten bekannt war, traute man seinen Schriften eine bedeutende propagandistische Wirkung zu, was wiederum ab 1939 seine Person zu einem wertvollen Pfand des Etat Français gegenüber den deutschen Besatzern machte.[8]

Während der Internierungswelle vom 1. bis 8. September 1939 ließ die Regierung Daladier die aus Deutschland stammenden Männer (etwa 20 000) als feindliche Ausländer internieren. Die zu "Indésirables" erklärten "politisch Verdächtigen" wurden in dem berüchtigten Lager *Le Vernet* zusammengefasst;

---

[7] Rudolf Leonhard: *Der Weg und das Ziel*. Hg. von Maximilian Scheer. Berlin: Verlag der Nation 1970. S. 18.
[8] Vgl. Giersberg: *Die Arbeit des Schriftstellers Rudolf Leonhard* (wie Anm. 6). S. 170.

die "unerwünschten" Frauen kamen in das Straflager *Rieucros*. Rudolf Leonhard wurde auch auf Grund seiner *activité politique*, der Leitung des *Deutschen Freiheitssenders 29,8* in Paris, Anfang Oktober 1939 im Stade *Roland Garros* interniert und traf am 12. Oktober 1939 im Männerinternierungslager *Camp du Vernet d'Ariège* im Département Ariège ein, wo er, unterbrochen von seiner Verlegung ins Lager *Les Milles* (November 1940 bis Mai 1941), schließlich bis Dezember 1941 blieb.

Alle die zahlreichen Bemühungen um seine Freilassung und den Erhalt einer Ausreiseerlaubnis scheiterten. Seit der Verhaftung Rudolf Leonhards im Herbst 1939 bemühte sich seine Frau Yvette Prost-Leonhard um seine Freilassung. Auch nach fast zwei Jahren engagierten, jedoch erfolglosen Bemühens arbeitete sie unermüdlich an der Rettung ihres Mannes weiter, reiste nach Vichy und zu ihm nach *Le Vernet*, schrieb an Roosevelt, an die Regierung in Vichy, an den Vatikan; vermutlich war auch sie als Kurier zwischen der kommunistischen Lagerleitung in *Le Vernet* und der KDP-Leitung in Toulouse tätig.

Ihr Einsatz führte zwar nicht zu Leonhards Freilassung, stärkte aber seinen Überlebenswillen und förderte seine literarische Arbeit in der Internierung. Ebenso lebenserhaltend wirkten die Sendungen der Sekretärin Lion Feuchtwangers, Lola Humm-Sernau, die sie von ihrem Wohnsitz in der Schweiz nach *Le Vernet* schickte. Auch der ebenfalls in der Schweiz lebende Schauspieler Wolfgang Langhoff sandte Quellenmaterial an Leonhard, das eine wichtige Grundlage für seine literarische Arbeit darstellte. Varian Fry, der das Centre Américain de Secours (CAS) leitete, unterstützte ihn als einen der von Auslieferung bedrohten Deutschen. Aber sein Name befand sich während der Vichy-Regierung auf einer Liste von Personen, denen das Ausreisevisum zu verweigern war, und spätestens Ende Januar 1941 stand fest, dass Rudolf Leonhard nach Deutschland ausgeliefert werden sollte.

Durch eine sehr persönliche Verbindung von künstlerischen – "Die Stacheln halten die Verse nicht auf", schrieb er im Gedicht *Le Vernet* – und praktischmenschlichen Überlebenstechniken gelang es ihm, diesen Zeitabschnitt, der Lager, Ausbruch, Wiederverhaftung und Gefängnis, Flucht, Illegalität und Todesdrohung umfasste und rund fünf Jahre dauerte, zu überstehen.

Die Entstehung von Literatur unter den Bedingungen eines Internierungslagers muss als ein besonderes Phänomen betrachtet werden. Sie ist den Lagerbedingungen abgetrotzt und als künstlerischer Prozess zum Überleben der Literaten in der Gefangenschaft wichtig. Allerdings ist die Fortsetzung der künstlerischen Arbeit nicht immer zwingend und möglich. Manchmal kann der dramatische Schnittpunkt von extremer Zeitgeschichte und einer die eigene Existenz gefährdenden individuellen Lebenssituation die psychischen und physischen Kräfte des Künstlers und Literaten übersteigen, so dass als einziger Ausweg nur noch der Freitod bleibt. Die Beispiele hierfür sind zahlreich. So stürzte sich Carl Einstein in Südfrankreich in einen Fluss, um der Auslieferung zu entgehen; Ernst Weiß legte in seinem Pariser Hotelzimmer Hand an sich wie Walter Benjamin in Port Bou an der französisch-spanischen Grenze; Ernst Toller erhängte sich in New York; Kurt Tucholsky nahm Gift im schwedischen Hindas wie Walter Hasenclever im französischen Internierungslager Les Milles und Stefan Zweig in seinem Haus in Brasilien. Rudolf Leonhard selbst äußerte sich dazu wie folgt in einer Tagebucheintragung vom 12. Januar 1944:

> Wieder musste ich daran denken: von Sieburg abgesehen, der den schlimmsten Selbstmord begangen hat, den moralischen, haben die paar Deutschen, mit denen ich in Paris am meisten befreundet war, alle durch Selbstmord geendet: Hasenclever, Tucholski, Toller – und schließlich hat sich ja auch Joseph Roth bewusst zu Tode getrunken. Warum habe ich mir nicht das Leben genommen, so groß oft genug die Verlockung war, ich, der ich mehr Grund und mehr Gründe gehabt hätte als sie alle? Sie waren mit mir ganz einig in der Ablehnung dessen, was ist, einig bis zur wirklichen Teilnahme am Kampfe, aber sie konnten sich nicht entschließen, am positiven Gestaltungswillen teilzunehmen. Sie kämpften tapfer und anständig, gegen etwas, aber nicht für etwas ganz Bestimmtes. Mich bewahrte die Kenntnis eines formulierbaren und formulierten Ziels, eine Methode, eine Philosophie. Ich konnte durch keine Not, Gefahr und Enttäuschung überrascht werden wie sie.[9]

Er beschrieb den Lageralltag und die miserablen Lebens- und Versorgungszustände in tagebuchähnlicher Lyrik. Diese literarische Form der Auseinandersetzung mit dem Alltag stellte in seinem Schaffen eine neue Form der künstlerischen Vermittlung dar. Fast täglich entstand außerdem ein Gedicht, zumeist in deutscher Sprache.[10] Vermutlich hat Leonhard bereits seit seiner Jugend ein Tagebuch geführt. Als junger Mann protokollierte er zudem regelmäßig seine Träume. Ignaz Jezover veröffentlichte in seinem *Buch der Träume* 1928 einige davon, die in den Jahren 1910–1924 entstanden waren. In der Monotonie und geistigen Kahlheit des Lageralltags wurden nun auch die Traumnotizen, die er sofort nach dem Erwachen, oft mehrmals im Verlauf einer Nacht niedergeschrieben hat, zur wesentlichen Strategie seines Überlebens. Das lyrische Diarium, das während der Internierung in *Le Vernet* entstand, war von Anfang an für die Veröffentlichung bestimmt. Es war der Versuch, trotz der demütigenden Situation die Menschenwürde zu bewahren, sollte Freunde und Mitgefangene erreichen, den künstlerischen und persönlichen Gesprächspartner ersetzen. Neben dem *Tagebuch* entstanden in diesen Jahren über 600 Gedichte, das *Traumbuch* und im Herbst 1941 die Tragödie *Geiseln*. Nur durch die Hilfe seiner Mitgefangenen und der Vertrauten außerhalb des Lagers konnte es gelingen, einen großen Teil der Arbeiten Leonhards aus dem Lager zu retten. So erschien im März 1940 im New Yorker *Aufbau* sein Gedicht *Nocturno im*

---

[9] Ebd. S. 224.
[10] Ebd. S. 94.

Lager, nachdem es von einem katalanischen Uhrmacher kopiert und aus dem Lager geschmuggelt worden war.

Das *Traumbuch* sollte ebenfalls veröffentlicht werden. Bei der späteren überstürzten Flucht aus dem Gefängnis in Castres musste Rudolf Leonhard sein Traumbuch-Manuskript schweren Herzens dort zurücklassen. Er glaubte das Manuskript verloren, aber Gefährten hatten es gerettet. Nach seinem Tod verwahrte es Maximilian Scheer, der jedoch nicht mehr als 25 Traumnotizen veröffentlichte. Seit 1986 war es im Archiv der Künste der DDR zugänglich, wurde dort schließlich 1999 durch Zufall von Steffen Mensching entdeckt, und im Jahre 2001 teilweise veröffentlicht.

Auffallend ist der relativ späte Beginn der Traumaufzeichnungen, am 28. Mai 1941, nachdem Rudolf Leonhard zum zweiten Mal im Lager *Le Vernet* eingeliefert worden war. Da er mehrmals über mexikanische Einreisevisa verfügte, hatte man ihn im Hinblick auf eine mögliche Ausreise am 28. November 1940 in das Durchgangslager *Les Milles* verlegt. Aus diesem Lager gelang ihm wahrscheinlich schon im März 1941 die Flucht. Wie aus seinen Gedichten herauszulesen ist, versteckte er sich in einem provençalischen Dorf, wagte sich allerdings auch, verkleidet, zu lebensgefährlichen Spaziergängen nach Marseille. Er wurde schließlich im Mai im Kohlenbunker eines Frachtschiffs mit Zielrichtung Nordafrika von der Marseiller Hafenpolizei entdeckt, wieder eingefangen und am 22. Mai 1941 erneut in *Le Vernet* eingeliefert. Viele der Freunde dort waren inzwischen abgereist.

Das *Traumbuch*, ein Konvolut von 2565 Seiten, bleibt einzigartig im Werk Rudolf Leonhards. Es ist "eines der eigenartigsten Dokumente der deutschen Emigrationsliteratur",[11] zugleich ein einmaliges, ganz außergewöhnliches Zeitdokument und gibt chiffriert über Leonhards Gedankenwelt im Lager Auskunft. Obwohl es sich um eine Traumwelt handelt: "die ganze Realität der Zeit ist – Goethe zufolge – auch im Traume".[12] Hier sind alle Beziehungen lebendig und möglich, Wiederbegegnungen mit Toten, wie das Wiederherstellen verlorener Freundschaften. In der Art von Videoclips unterschiedlichster Länge und Technik, die oft eine kafkaeske Atmosphäre heraufbeschwören – "Endlich findet, allerdings ohne Anschuldigung und nach sehr langer unaufgeklärter Haft, der Prozess statt" (13.2.42) –, erscheinen wichtige Stationen seines Lebens. Dabei ist der Haftalltag in den Kommentaren und Episoden allgegenwärtig. Der Formenreichtum von Leonhards Schöpfungen tritt auch hier zu Tage, in historischen Rückblenden, Elementen aktueller Nachrichten, romantisierenden Intermezzi, Gesprächsfetzen, Angstträumen und Wunschträumen, sachlichen wie surrealistischen Beschreibungen. So vielschichtig wie Rudolf

---

[11] Lothar Baier: Ist Gott ein Nazi? In: *Freitag*. 7. Juni 2002.
[12] Johann Wolfgang von Goethe: Briefe an Frau von Stein. 31. März 1776. Vgl. Leonhard: *In derselben Nacht* (Anm. 4). S. 501.

Leonhards Natur und seine Zeit finden sich neben alltäglichen Themen allgemeinen Interesses, publizistischen Fragen, Theaterarbeit, z.B. Gespräche über Pfeifenpflege, seine Arbeit in Berlin, die Wehrdienstzeit im Weltkrieg, die Schulzeit in Lissa, Hilfslieferungen ins Lager, die Zusammenarbeit mit Kollegen in Paris nach 1933, viele Freundschaften, Affären, reizvolle und detailliert beschriebene, erotische Begegnungen mit oft längst vergessenen Geliebten, Diskussionen über Homosexualität, mehrere Gespräche mit Magnus Hirschfeld, tägliche Basisverrichtungen, die oft in sehr direkter Sprache beschrieben werden. Die meisterwähnten Personen sind neben der Mutter seine Frau Yvette und seine Schwester Lotte. Großen Raum beansprucht zudem der Komplex seiner politischen Verwicklungen und der Intrigen innerhalb der KDP, wobei Willi Münzenberg eine bedeutende Rolle spielt.

Das Manuskript des *Traumbuchs* charakterisieren laut Steffen Mensching trotz der Lager- und Gefängnisbedingungen präzise Korrekturen, Stilsicherheit, exakte Rechtschreibung und Zeichensetzung. "So 'seelenbeladen' das Material, der Gestus der Erzählung ist nüchtern, analytisch, bezeugend".[13] Leonhard liefert auch theoretische Anmerkungen zu seiner Methodik des Erinnerns, zu den Stützen der Vorstellung und zu den Schwierigkeiten, vor allem zum Vergessen wichtiger Traumteile. Sicherlich kannte er Freuds *Traumdeutung*. Interessante Aufschlüsse über die Verbundenheit der Träume mit Tagesdingen und über die Fähigkeit, intellektuelle Leistungen im Traume zu vollbringen finden sich schon 1928 im Anhang des *Buchs der Träume*:

> Es kann ein äußerer Anstoß gewesen sein, der mich auf den Gedanken brachte, Träume regelmäßig aufzuzeichnen; soweit ich mich erinnere, war es die Lektüre der Traumaufzeichnungen Friedrich Huchs, lange vor der Lektüre von Traumberichten der Psychoanalytiker. Aber dieser äußere Anstoß hätte nicht die konsequente Beobachtung meines Traumlebens erreicht, wenn mir nicht meine Träume, die Vielfalt und Freiheit des Traumlebens, von Anfang an bedeutsam erschienen wären. Dieses Gefühl von ihrer Bedeutung wurde durch die Gewohnheit, Träume möglichst festzuhalten und zu fixieren, so gestärkt, dass ich fast Gewissensbisse verspüre, wenn ich […] das Aufzeichnen eines Traumes so lange verschiebe, dass ich ihn dann ganz oder zum größten Teil vergessen habe. Das Festhalten gelingt, wenn es sofort geschieht […].[14]

Auf einem knappen Viertel der Gesamtzahl der Eintragungen des *Traumbuchs* (in 90 von 393 veröffentlichten) mit Schwerpunkten auf den Jahren 1942 und 1943 ist die Rede vom Reisen. So finden sich 1941 sechzehn, 1942 einundvierzig, 1943 zweiunddreißig und 1944 nur eine Bemerkung zu diesem Thema. Nach der Massenflucht aus dem Gefängnis in Castres am 17. September 1943 befand sich Rudolf Leonhard bis zur Befreiung von Paris im August 1944 illegal in Marseille. Die letzte veröffentlichte Notiz ist auf den 1. Juli 1944 datiert.

---

[13] Ebd. S. 500.
[14] Ignaz Jezover. *Das Buch der Träume*. Berlin: Rowohlt 1928. S. 613.

Blickt man etwas genauer auf die *Traumreisen*, so ist festzustellen, dass die Notizen von 1941 noch zu einem erheblichen Teil von der Erwartung eines Ausreisevisums und Gedanken an Freilassung getragen werden. Dokumente sind wichtig, Geldsorgen präsent, ebenso wie die Angst, zu spät zu kommen. In den folgenden zwei Jahren dominieren 'Fehlleistungen' wie verhindertes Reisen, Reisen in falsche oder unbekannte Richtungen, Angstreisen. Erst der letzte 'Reisetraum' vom 24. April 1944 zeugt von einer Lösung der Spannung und enthält einen kleinen Hoffnungsschimmer in der optimistischen, fast amüsanten Beschreibung eines Fußmarsches durch den gesamten afrikanischen Kontinent. Stilistisch ist der Leser mit einer deskriptiven, fragmentarischen, fast stichwortartigen Darstellung konfrontiert, die nur die wichtigsten Informationen übermittelt und eine nüchterne, fast sterile Atmosphäre schafft.

Die folgenden Beobachtungen unterliegen nicht mehr der Traumlogik, sondern der des Wachseins, wobei das teilweise schon eingangs zitierte Reisevokabular wie Abfahrt, Ankunft, Reiseziele usw. wegweisend war.

Man findet im *Traumbuch* verschiedene Arten der Abreise: eher 'normale' wie der Spaziergang vor der Abreise mit einer geliebten Frau (23.4.43), ein Abendessen bei Freunden (24.5.43); beängstigende und zugleich beeindruckende 'Abreisen' aus dem Lager, vor allem Leonhards eigene. "Ich bin aus dem Lager weggebracht worden und komme im andern Lager an" (30.12.41). Es stellt sich die Frage, "wann wir abtransportiert werden" (7.1.42). Die Abreise wird mal als Spiel erlebt, "ich weiß, dass das ein Spiel ist und spiele mit, unter den Augen der andern", mal als Traum im Traum in quälender Unsicherheit widergespiegelt: "Ich weiß, dass dies alles ein Traum ist. Ich frage sie, sehr dringend, sehr gespannt, ob ich vor Beginn dieses Traumes noch nach Amerika gefahren bin?" (14.1.42). Oder als nackte Angst:

> Jemand führt mich vor ein an eine dunkle Tür geheftetes Plakat; soweit ich es verstehe, ergibt sich aus ihm, dass ich in La Seyne bin. Aber wie bin ich hergekommen? Ich muss also heimlich nach Frankreich geschafft worden sein, und nun wirken eine Ausweisung und viele feindliche Gesetze gegen mich (17.1.42).

Auch die Abreise der andern und der Freunde spielt eine wichtige, wenngleich weniger dramatische Rolle. Man spürt Rudolf Leonhards Solidarität und Anerkennung der Würde der anderen Internierten. Es gibt die Abreise von

> Leuten, die nach London fahren wollen (1.9.41), während die andern in die Provinz zurückreisen (12.11.41). Fast alle verreisen, manche noch vor mir (5.2.42). Mehrere werden morgen abreisen, [...] nach Moskau einige, und einige nach Paris. Auch eine Freundin reist; aber wer reist nach Moskau, wer nach Paris? (17.9.42).

Manchmal erhält man Auskunft über die Reisebedingungen: "Es sei im Zuge von Marseille sehr heiß gewesen, erzählt er" (3.4.43). Einmal wird der Vater

erwähnt: "Mutter erzählt, dass Vater, obwohl sein Plädoyer beendet sei, abgereist sei" (27.5.43).
Die Ankünfte bergen Mehrdeutigkeiten und tödliche Überraschungen. Ein Traum beginnt relativ harmlos mit der Feststellung:

> Ich will noch acht Tage in Zürich bleiben, [...] ich höre: "On les amènera d'abord à Toulon!" Ich stehe auf: ich bin doch in Zürich, und kann hingehen wo ich will? Ich sage das, und höre als Antwort ein hämisches Lachen [...] es ergibt sich, dass ich in La Seyne bin (17.1.42).

Ein Beispiel für die zahlreichen heimlichen Ankünfte: "Endlich komme ich, heimlich, in Lissa an, ich erschrecke tödlich, schon bin ich erkannt und erfasst. Die Reise ist schon zu Ende, und ich habe noch kaum etwas gesehn!" (23.3.42). Ebenso erfolgen verfehlte Ankünfte: "Ich steige auf einer hochgelegenen Hochbahnstation aus, muss einen Schritt falsch gemacht haben, und gelange statt ins Freie, in ein jüdisches Nachtasyl" (16.9.42). Oder: "Ich steige an der Station Gesundbrunnen aus. Ich stehe allein auf dem Bahnsteig. Ich verlasse den Bahnhof, ich bin ein wenig zu weit gefahren" (5.12.42). Schließlich ein Beispiel für das Mischgebilde eines Trauminhalts, ein Amalgam von Ankunft, Abreise und Politik:

> Ich bin aus Paris – in das Rundfunkhaus heimgekehrt. [...] Inzwischen ist nämlich die Scheidung unter den am Rundfunk Tätigen erfolgt. Viele sind schon zum Feinde übergegangen; es handelt sich um Gewinn und Organisierung der letzten, die noch widerstehn, das ist ein Teil meiner Aufgabe. [...] Ein Junge will Ernst machen und abreisen, nach Warschau. Ich selbst werde lieber gleich wieder nach Paris fahren. Ich will mich gar nicht erst an den Tisch setzen (11.10.42).

Nach einer Ankunft ist die Unterkunft von einiger Bedeutung. Hier fällt vor allem die Größe der bewohnten Traumräume auf, wobei vielleicht die Wunschvorstellung einer schriftstellerischen Bedürfnissen zumindest teilweise angepassten Wohnsituation mit einfließt. Dem Leser werden fast ausschließlich die Resultate vermittelt, nicht die Vorgänge geschildert, wie in den meisten Exilromanen. Nicht um die Zimmersuche, ein wesentliches Problem für Exilanten, geht es Rudolf Leonhard, sondern um das Angekommensein.

> Ich bin in einem riesigen fast leeren alten Zimmer einlogiert. (31.8.41) – Zu meiner Überraschung wird mir ein richtiges, sogar behagliches und komfortables Zimmer angewiesen, mit einem richtigen Bett, einem großen Bett, gutem Deckenlicht, fließendem warmem Wasser (30.12.41).
> Oder:
> Ich bin in einem großen gastlichen Haus (26.2.42).

In der folgenden, bedrohlichen und ambivalenten Traumnotiz befindet sich Leonhard in Posen:

> Ich bin in das Hotel Soundso umquartiert worden, das Nummer 16 der Galerie bildet. Ich suche den Eingang; es ist nicht der, den ich für den Eingang des Hotels

hielt, und hinter dem einige andre wohnen. [...] Jemand führt mich zu Nummer 16; er sagt, mit einem Ton des Mitleids, der mich erschreckt, ich werde wohl der einzige Mensch sein, der dort wohnt. Es ist überhaupt unheimlich, ganz allein in einem leeren Hotel zu wohnen (3.5.43).

Endlich liest man Anfang Oktober 1943: "Ich bin auf der Flucht. Mutter begleitet mich. Wir sind in Fraustadt angekommen. [...] Wir finden eine große, sehr belebte, sehr elegante, modern eingerichtete Pension" (8.1.43).

Eine dramatische Bedeutung erhalten insbesondere Reisepapiere und Protokolle, die Auslandsreisen zum Gegenstand haben. Ein einziges Mal, es ist der Eintrag vom 18.2.1943, formuliert Rudolf Leonhard dabei den Wunsch, es wäre ein Traum. Zum wiederholten Mal ist hier die Rückkehr nach Deutschland wesentlich. Viele Emigranten träumten über Jahre hinweg, sie seien noch einmal, ohne zu wissen wie, dorthin zurückgekehrt. Der Augenblick, in dem der Träumende erkennt, wo er sich befindet und dass er nicht wieder herauskann, ist vernichtend.

Ich bin heimlich nach Berlin gegangen. (Ich gehe mit einem Dokument in ein Behördenhaus [...].) Ich wünschte innigst, inständigst, inbrünstigst: Wenn das doch nur ein Traum wäre! [Da erwache ich, tauche ganz langsam hoch, und es war wirklich nur ein Traum. Eine Minute lang war ich glücklich, – nur hier im Gefängnis zu sein.]

Zum Reisen gehören Transportmittel, deren zum Teil recht amüsante Vielfalt die Traumnotizen beherrscht. An erster Stelle stehen Zug, Auto und Bus, gefolgt von Schiff und Flugzeug. Auch Reiten, Schwimmen, Schlitten fahren oder zu Fuß gehen, oder erdachte Fortbewegungsmittel wie die Erfindung, Schiffe über Land zu führen tauchen auf, und schließlich die charmante, dem Traum vorbehaltene Variante des eigenen Fliegenkönnens. Einzig das Fahrrad fehlt.

Ich fahre [...] durch die Stadt, in einer Trambahn. Sie ist aber auch Aufzug, und ich sehe den Wagen, mehrere Wagen übereinander, als Kabinen, von denen mein Wagen der letzte ist, im riesigen Stahldrahtschacht absteigen" (22.8.41). – Nachts fahre ich in einem kleinen Auto – es ist ein ganz billiges Taxi. (21.3.42) – Wir fahren in einem großen schönen Auto weg (1.10.42). "[...] als der Zug übrigens wie ein Autobus oder als Autobus anfährt (29.11.42).

Der Zug nimmt eine Sonderstellung ein und ist ein ambivalentes Transportmittel, das oft detailgenau beschrieben wird. Fehlleistungen wie Versäumnisse, Unkenntnis von Richtung und Ziel, sind auch hier zu verzeichnen. Waggons werden abgehängt, Züge haben sich schon vor dem Einsteigen in Bewegung gesetzt.

Ich denke an den dritten Transport, unsern, der nicht zu Schiff vor sich gehn wird, sondern mit der Bahn. (7.1.42). – Ich habe den 8h30 Zug in die Stadt versäumt, es scheint [...] kein zweiter Zug in absehbarer Zeit zu gehen, ich werde alles in der Stadt versäumen [...] (31.1.42). Ich fahre in einem Extrazuge, der mir gehört [...]

Der Zug wird hin und her rangiert. Er wird in den Bahnhof von Vichy hineingeleitet; unbehaglich fällt mir ein: wird nicht in Vichy eine besonders scharfe Kontrolle sein, werden nicht die Bücher scharf angesehn werden? [...] Da steht Yvette. [...] Yvette kommt mir nach und hilft mir (11.2.42). – In einer Straße, in der ich endlich ankomme, wird der Zug nach Paris formiert. Ich steige erleichtert ein. Aber diese ersten Wagen des Zuges werden gar nicht nach Paris gehn, sondern [...] abgehängt und nach Hamburg geleitet werden (23.7.42). – Der Zug steht schon da. [...] Mir fällt auch bald ein, dass ich überhaupt nicht einmal weiß, wann der Zug abgeht. [...] Ich suche nun meinen Zug; ich weiß gar nicht, wann er abgeht, und ob ich überhaupt noch Zeit habe (23.11.42). – Viele Züge fahren aneinander vorbei. Und diesen betrachten alle: es ist der Rom-Express, der sich gewaltig und elegant schlangenhaft zwischen die andern stößt, großartig; alle betrachten ihn, weil Verwicklungen mit Italien bestehn und weil der Krieg vor der Tür steht (15.5.43).

Die Traumnotizen verknüpfen mehrmals Bahnhöfe von riesigem Ausmaß mit fehlenden Visa und Passproblemen. Die Pass-Not war bekanntlich eine der schrecklichsten Nöte, denen Emigranten ausgesetzt waren. Auch hier erfolgt keine sehr differenzierte Darstellung, sondern die Beschränkung auf das Grundproblem. Im Gegensatz zu anderen Exilwerken sind die Züge in Leonhards Traumgedanken nie überfüllt, oft sogar leer.

Ich sitze mit vielen Menschen in einer amphitheatrisch bestuhlten Halle, nicht gerade einem Nachtasyl, aber einem Warteraum. [...] Wir haben schon den Bahnhof betreten. [...] Und nun fällt mir gar ein, dass wir vergessen haben, meinen Pariser Pass umändern, auf einen falschen Namen umschreiben zu lassen. Ich verlasse die Reihe vor der Bahnhofssperre, in die ich mich schon gestellt hatte (30.5.43).

Weniger bedrohlich und der Erfüllung des Wunsches nach Rettung näher scheinen Schiffsreisen zu sein:

Ich besuche ein Schiff. In einem halboffnen dunklen scheunenartigen Raume wohnen, übereinander aufgetürmt, Mitglieder der Internationalen Brigaden. Ich spreche mit ihnen. Plötzlich frage ich, ob ich nicht mitfahren kann. Ihr Führer nimmt mich sofort an. Ich gehe wieder auf das Schiff, ein Gewehr umgehängt. (Ich setze mich auf dem Schiff, auf dem alles dunkel ist, hin, und lese. Einige Interbrigadisten gegenüber unterhalten sich. An einer Stelle ihres Gesprächs erzähle ich hinüber, das ich über diese Sache – ihre Sache – zwei Bücher geschrieben hätte. Sie wissen es, oder es interessiert sie nicht.) [...] Das Schiff fährt ab (21.1.42).

Dennoch dominiert auch hier bald wieder die Unsicherheit:

Ich beschließe [...] weiterzureisen, morgen; freilich fällt mir bald ein, dass ich gar nicht weiß, ob morgen auch ein Schiff geht" (26.2.42). – Das Schiff soll draußen abfahren, am Kanal ist Bewegung, die Pforte geht auf, wir setzen uns in Bewegung (14.1.43). – Endlich kann ich abreisen, endlich geht das Schiff (28.1.43). – Endlich, endlich steht die Abreise nach Amerika bevor. [...] Nun, ich selbst werde diesmal fahren, das Schiff ist schon bereit, die Abfahrtzeit festgesetzt. Zwar bin ich, nach so vielen schlechten Erfahrungen, noch skeptisch; ich sage zu allem, was ich sage, wie abergläubisch hinzu "falls ich wirklich fahre! (4.7.43).

Die ständige Entfremdung und Verunsicherung der Exilexistenz äußert sich bei Leonhard selbst im Traum in Gerüchten und Zweifeln an den Fakten.

In der einzigartigen Funktion des Traumes als einer Wunscherfüllung erscheint der Freund Walter Hasenclever, der am 22. Juni 1940 im Lager *Les Milles* seinem Leben ein Ende gesetzt hatte. Rudolf Leonhard beschäftigte bis zum Schluss die Leere, die der Freund hinterlassen hatte. So liest man in den Tagebucheintragungen vom 7. und 9. Januar 1944:

> Immer wieder drückt der schwere Schmerz, dass ich nicht noch einmal, ein einziges Mal mit Walter sprechen kann. Ich weiß gar nicht, wie das Gespräch verlaufen würde, kaum was ich zu sagen hätte; aber das Gespräch würde schon gehn, und dass es nicht mehr sein kann ist entsetzlich. – An Walters Selbstmord muss ich immer wieder denken, und immer mit tiefster Bedrückung. Es ist nicht nur [...], dass damit ein großes Stück meines Lebens hingefallen ist. Es gibt Sachen, die nur er von mir wusste und die niemand in der Welt mehr erfahren oder wissen wird, die vor meinem Tode für immer verschollen sind. [...] es hätten noch ein paar Worte gesagt werden müssen, und alles wäre aufgeklärt worden.

Ergreifend und gleichsam, als ob er das Zerwürfnis, das zwischen beiden wohl wegen unvereinbarer politischer Haltungen entstand, ungeschehen zu machen versuchte, zitiert er den Freund nicht weniger als sechsundzwanzig Mal im *Traumbuch* – oft im Zusammenhang mit Reisen.

> Ich reise mit Hasenclever (23.8.41). – Ich stehe bei einer Gruppe um Heinrich Mann [...]. Ich rühre Walter Hasenclevers Schulter an und frage, ob er mit uns weiterreisen würde; er nickt und seine Bejahung erfüllt mich mit großer Freude (26.2.42). – Ich will mit Hasenclever nach Hamburg fahren (23.11.42). – Ich kenne das Schiff schon, ich habe es einmal mit Walter Hasenclever besucht (4.7.43).

Und die letzte, in ihrer Einfachheit bewegende Notiz: "Walter Hasenclever wird abreisen. Ich bleibe zurück; ich bleibe ohne Geld, ich weiß nicht, was ich machen werde" (9.11.43).

Den weitaus größten Raum beanspruchen jedoch die über dreißig unterschiedlichen Reiseziele, die im *Traumbuch* sehr oft im Sinne von neuen Fluchtwegen und möglicher Rettung auftauchen. Neben Südamerika, (hier eher Brasilien als Mexiko!), die USA (New York), Nordafrika, Italien, und Paris, reist er vor allem in deutsche Städte, sehr häufig nach Berlin, Hamburg und Lissa. So heißt es kurz nach seiner Einlieferung in Castres: "Ich frage, ob es bei der Abreise nach Südamerika bleibe". (25.12.41). Wenige Tage später:

> Eine Reise nach Italien oder die Ausreise aus Italien steht an (30.12.41). – Es scheint sich in unsrer Vorstellung um eine Fahrt nach Spanisch-Marokko, jedenfalls nach Afrika, zu handeln (21.1.42). – Ich fahre morgen, Sonntag, nachmittag um 5 Uhr nach Pyrmont. Ich erzähle es allen, voller Freude (5.2.42). – Wir sitzen in einem Zuge, der nach Russland fährt (18.2.42). – Ich bin in Brasilien, auf der Flucht oder auf einer Reise (26.2.42). – Wir fahren weit und noch weiter – Wir fahren von einer

Insel zur andern; weiß man unsre Adresse? – ich schreibe als Adresse unter ein Bild: St. Pierre-et-Miquelon (22.3.42). – Ich denke immer wieder und immer mehr an Flucht. [...] Ich muss nach England entfliehn, aber das wird sehr schwierig sein (8.5.42). – Endlich kann ich abreisen, endlich geht das Schiff. [...] Ich sage kurz, dass ich nach China weiterfahre (28.1.43). – Ich komme in New York an (18.4.43). – Ich bin nach Posen gekommen (3.5.43). – In Berlin findet ein großer bedeutender Kongress statt, [...] Ich bin dieses Kongresses wegen nach Berlin zurückgekommen (21.5.43). – Ich gehe in der Türkei hinter einer Beerdigung her. [...] Ich bin in Sofia, im Vorsaal einer Ausstellung [...] mein Name sei gefährlich, wird gesagt (31.5.43). – Ich bin eingeladen worden, in Italien (Rom) eine Rede bei einer Gedächtnisfeier zu halten. [...] Ich werde jedenfalls fahren (4.6.43). – Endlich, endlich steht die Abreise nach Amerika bevor (4.7.43). – Ich fahre über Berlin nach Moskau. Es wäre natürlich vorsichtiger gewesen, Deutschland zu umfahren, aber ich habe die Schnelligkeit und den Leichtsinn der Reise durch Deutschland vorgezogen. Ich übernachte in Berlin [...] Fremdenkontrolle – ich zeige meinen Sowjetpass. [...] Die Zeit der Gefahr, dass die Polizei mich vor einer Weiterreise finden kann, ist vorbei (12.7.43).

Das Transitäre der Exilwelt, in der jeder nur auf sich selbst zählen kann, die zahlreichen Angstträume vor der drohenden Auslieferung an die Gestapo, kompensiert Rudolf Leonhard häufig durch eine der kommunistischen Ideologie verpflichteten Hoffnung. In einem der Traumstücke berichtet er von einer wichtigen religiösen Disputation. Für ihn ist dabei die Entwicklung der Dinge so weit fortgeschritten, dass der Glaube erst kommen wird, am Ende. "Gott steht nicht am Anfang, sondern, zukünftig, am Ende! [Das ist ein Gedanke meines bewussten Lebens und meiner Wirklichkeit.]" lautet sein im wachen Zustand hinzugefügter Kommentar (21.7.1941). Daran schließt sich ein Traum an, der Leonhard im lebhaften Gespräch mit Göring zeigt.

> Im Verlaufe dieses Gesprächs sage ich: "Ich will theoretisch einräumen, dass es möglich ist, dass die Befreiung auf einem andern Wege geschieht als durch die Revolution, die ich will und wie ich sie will" – Ich meine und sage wohl auch: dass es nur in der Theorie möglich ist, und dass jedenfalls ein andrer tauglicher Weg noch nicht gezeigt und nicht versucht worden ist. [...] Dann bin ich in der Straße, ich habe Eile, ich muss mich retten. Ich kann nicht gerade fliegen, aber in der Luft gehn, sozusagen Luft treten, ich steige sogar ohne es zu wollen in die Höhe, daher kann ich nicht eingeholt und nicht – die Straße ist übrigens ganz leer – erfasst werden. Aber ich habe diesen Versuch des In-der-Luft-Gehens nie am hellen Tage gemacht, ich möchte nicht höher steigen als bis zu den Baumwipfeln [...], ich könnte abstürzen, ja ich habe Angst (23.7.42).

Ob im Traumbewusstsein der Reichsminister der Luftfahrt ironischerweise dem Verfasser die Idee des Fliegens als Fortbewegungsmittel eingegeben hat, bleibe dahingestellt. Das eigene Fliegen ist auf jeden Fall nicht nur einleuchtend, poetisch und sehr charmant, sondern auch höchst gefährlich. Es ereignet sich nur dreimal, obwohl man vermuten könnte, dass es den Wunsch nach Freiheit am einfachsten realisieren würde.

> Ich fliege leicht, ohne Angst vor den Verfolgern. [...] Flugzeuge gehn mich nichts an oder können mich nicht erreichen (13.6.41). – Während des ganzen Traumstücks

fliege ich. Es ist ganz selbstverständlich, dass ich fliegen kann, und es fällt auch den andern nicht auf, obwohl von denen niemand fliegt, so dass man glauben könnte, sie können nicht fliegen. Aber so sicher ich über Mauern fliegen, offnen Türen ausweichen und Ecken umbiegen kann, heute strengt mich das Fliegen an; und so sicher ich die Technik, die nur darin besteht, die Füße nach hinten zu stoßen (wie ein schräges Wassertreten, ein Schwimmen ohne Arme), handhabe, so fühle ich mich doch unsicher; ich denke, was sonst nie geschieht, dass ich an die Mauer stoßen, oder dass ich abstürzen könnte wie ein toter Vogel (31.5.42).

Gegenüber dem eigenen Fliegen ist das Reisen im Flugzeug eine zweischneidige und kontroverse Angelegenheit. "Ich kann mir nicht denken, dass das Flugzeug, in dem wir uns befinden, von einer Bombe getroffen werden kann" (21.10.42). – "Im Flugzeug wird Tabak verteilt. Es wird gleich danach abstürzen" (20.1.43).

Das Reiten, (in Amerika, nach der Flucht aus Castres), bietet Anlass zur Reflexion. Die Fußwanderung schließlich führt in die Heimat oder durch den gesamten afrikanischen Kontinent nach Asien, zur Entdeckung eines anderen Erdteils "als nur Europa" (24.4.44).

Stellt man einen Vergleich dieser imaginären "Traumreisen" mit der in der Reiseliteratur dargestellten realen Reisen an, die Referenzen auf den wirklichen Raum enthalten, so lassen sich zahlreiche Parallelen aufzeigen. Auch Reiseberichte bewegen sich oft zwischen Realität und Fiktion und werden trotzdem als zuverlässige Auskunftsquelle verwendet. Die Hauptdifferenz ist jedoch in den Gründen und Zielen der "Reise", in der Motivation der Ortsveränderung anzusiedeln. So gibt es einige Grundtypen je nach Zweck des Aufenthaltes an den Zielorten, wie Urlaubs- und Badereisen, Geschäfts- oder Handelsreise, Pilger- und Missionsreisen, wissenschaftliche Expeditionen, Entdeckungs- und Studienreisen, die Kavalierstour zur Ausbildung junger Adeliger vorwiegend des 19. Jahrhunderts und die modernere Bildungsreise. Während die traditionelle Reiseliteratur sowohl Ratgeber, Anleiter zum Reisen, Reiseführer und -berichterstatter ist, Landschaften, ferne, dem Leser unerreichbare Gebiete beschreibt, sie oft auch als Ersatz für diejenigen dient, die zu Hause bleiben müssen, ist die "Reise" der Exilierten erzwungen, unfreiwillig, Flucht, Folge des wiederholten Verjagtwerdens, "Irrfahrt" in fremde, oft ungastliche Länder. Eine meist fragmentarische Darstellung stellt technische Details, die das Überleben garantieren müssen, in den Vordergrund. Diese spezifische Exilliteratur ist auch ein Versuch, der Zerstörbarkeit des Ich Einhalt zu gebieten.

Die Traumnotizen Rudolf Leonhards legen in einem ganz eigenen Stil mehrere Facetten dieses Ich offen: Unsicherheit und Angst, – "Immer stehn welche vor mir" (7.1.42). "Ich verliere den Mut [...]" (25.3.42) -, Fragilität und Schutzbedürfnis:

> Ich bin sonderbarerweise allein in dem Waggon; er wird auf ein totes Gleis geschoben; ich will nicht vergessen werden (24.2.42). – Wer wird mich in Rom am

Bahnhof abholen? Wie wird er mich erkennen? Die Gestapo ist auch in Rom mächtig, wenn schon die Römer nicht direkt einem Böses wollen (4.6.43).

Edelmut, "Ich bin froh, darüber, dass sie nun reisen können, und traurig über Trennung und Zurückbleiben" (23.1.42). und Empathie. Auch Schläge, unter denen andere leiden, schmerzen den Träumer. Alles trifft ihn. Oft dominiert die Gewissheit, nicht erwartet zu werden, nicht erwünscht zu sein. Hingegen findet man keine Rache-Gefühle oder -Bilder. Im Vergleich zu anderen Exilromanen bleiben Leonhards Traumaufzeichnungen oft schemenhaft, auf eine plakative Darstellung beschränkt, in der man sehr genau die Umrisse sieht, der Leser die Plastizität aber selbst einbauen muss. Kurze, parallel gebaute Sätze in staccato-artigem Rhythmus, "gehetzte" Sätze, generelle Beschreibungen in der Art eines Notizzettels, übersetzen hier die Verdichtung, die die Traumarbeit zustande bringt. Sie ist enthüllend für die psychische Situation des Träumers, sie informiert den Leser und macht ihn betroffen.

Rudolf Leonhard schlug sich, nachdem er aus dem Gefängnis in Castres geflüchtet war, nach Marseille durch und lebte dort zwölf Monate versteckt und vogelfrei. Er schloss sich unter dem Decknamen Raoul Lombat der Résistance an und kehrte nach dem 25. August 1944 wieder nach Paris zurück. Durch eine lange Krankheit verzögert, übersiedelte er schließlich im April 1950 nach Berlin, wo er im Dezember 1953 im Alter von 64 Jahren starb; seine Heimkehr hatte sich, obwohl er weiterhin literarisch sehr aktiv blieb, allmählich in eine Abkehr verwandelt. "Auf dieser tragischen Kreisfahrt durch die deutsche Geschichte stieß", laut Maximilian Scheer, "Rudolf Leonhards dramatisches Lebensboot oft durch bewegte Gewässer und hielt manchmal in weltverlorener Bucht".[15]

Leonhard war sich der Brisanz seiner Aufzeichnungen, in die man sich ein-lesen muss, die einige prophetische Augenblicke, Zeitnähe und dichterische Visionen enthalten, bewusst. Sollte man sie als "Gekritzel" abtun, wie Klaus Harpprecht in seiner Kritik,[16] als rätselhafte, verworrene Schlafimpressionen, gestaltlos, unfassbar, ungreifbar und oft genug langweilig? Harpprecht bezeichnet die Herausgabe des *Traumbuchs* spöttisch als einen Akt der Wiedergutmachung, weist auf das begrenzte Interesse an Leonhards Werk hin mit dem hämischen Fazit – "so wird es wohl bleiben". Oder sollte man diese Aufzeichnungen als realistisches Geschichtenbuch lesen in Kenntnis der Aufgabe der Traumarbeit; als ein außergewöhnliches Zeitdokument?

Alfred Kantorowicz stellte gleich nach Leonhards Tod fest: "Wir sind ihm viel schuldig geblieben". Stephan Hermlin hat dieses Gedächtnis 1968

---

[15] Maximilian Scheer: Vorwort zu *Rudolf Leonhard. Segel am Horizont*. Berlin: Verlag der Nation 1963. S. 15.

[16] Klaus Harpprecht. Zwischen Kollaboration und Exil. In: *Die Zeit*. 4. Oktober 2001.

wiederholt: "Dann starb er, ganz schnell und allein, ohne, trotz allem, den Platz eingenommen zu haben, der ihm gebührte, der ihm noch immer gebührt".[17]

Richtig ist, dass seine Werke kaum erwähnt, nicht gewürdigt, geschweige denn ausgezeichnet wurden. Auch Hans Mayer urteilte: "An Leonhard ist viel versäumt worden. Hier bleibt viel gutzumachen". Er fügte noch hinzu:

> Nicht bloß um seinetwillen, sondern auch um unseretwillen. Unsere Literatur ist nicht so reich an Erscheinungen von ähnlicher weltanschaulicher Klarheit, moralischer Integrität, bester literarischer Handwerklichkeit (von allen Fragen des Talents einmal abgesehen), als dass wir darauf verzichten dürften, diese Hinterlassenschaft zu sichten und zu bewahren.[18]

Die Frage bleibt jedenfalls offen, ob es sich ganz einfach nur um einen Akt der "Wiedergutmachung" handelt, wie Harpprecht behauptet.

---

[17] Alfred Kantorowicz. Wir sind ihm viel schuldig geblieben. In: *Neues Deutschland*. 23. Dezember 1953. Vgl. Giersberg: *Die Arbeit des Schriftstellers Rudolf Leonhard* (wie Anm. 6). S. 241. Vgl. Jentzsch: *Rudolf Leonhard* (wie Anm. 3). S. 60.
[18] Hans Mayer. Ein deutscher Homme de lettres. Vgl. Scheer: *Freunde über Rudolf Leonhard* (wie Anm. 1). S. 105.

Karina Lindeiner-Stráský

"Jetzt stocke ich in zwei Zungen" – The Influence of Exile and Travel on Themes, Language and Literary Style in the Writings of Members of *Das Jüngste Deutschland*

This study investigates thematic, linguistic, and stylistic effects of travel and exile on young writers.[1] It looks in detail at the writings of three members of the Weimar Republic group Das Jüngste Deutschland. Klaus Mann, Peter Mendelssohn, and Herbert Schlüter are examples of young writers whose literary careers were profoundly influenced by their emigration, the politicization of their lives, and the loss of their native audience. The study first establishes common thematic and stylistic features in the writers' pre-exile works. It then traces their literary developments after 1933, in particular the introduction of the theme of travel and the politicization of their writings. This thematic expansion led to considerable stylistic changes, which are explored subsequently. Mann, Mendelssohn, and Schlüter, it appears, do not fit in at all with the common derogatory prejudice of simplistic, stylistically uninteresting literature in exile. Instead, this essay shows that the authors introduced a number of new narrative, linguistic, and structural changes in order to meet both the challenges of life abroad and the aims of writing in exile.

Exile and literature

There can be little doubt that the loss of their own culture and in particular their own language is one of the most uprooting events in the life of writers. While the challenge of living abroad and the intellectual exchange with foreign cultures and languages in itself may be an invigorating and stimulating experience, those who have fled or been expelled from their home country – unlike travel writers – have no possibility of enriching their native culture with the experiences made abroad. On the contrary, the cultural enrichment of the writer's own nation, one of the central aims of travel writing, is turned upside down in the case of political exiles. They, as can be seen in the case of many of the writers who fled Germany at the time of National Socialism, often aspire to introduce their host nations to what they believe is their true national culture in order to preserve it and to motivate and support political action against the regime that suppresses or abuses it.

[1] I wrote this essay as a Silvia Naish Postdoctoral Fellow at the Institute for Germanic and Romance Studies, London. I would like to thank the IGRS for funding my research, and Trinity College (Hartford, Connecticut) for supporting my attendance at the 2006 conference of the American Society for Exile Studies, where I presented an abridged version of my study.

At the same time, the loss of an audience from their own culture, and of a large proportion of readers of their native language, further deepens their sense of cultural uprootedness. Klaus Mann, one of the most outspoken German authors driven abroad by National Socialism, summed up the sense of isolation and disorientation of writers in exile: "nur in dem Lande, wo sie zu Hause waren, versteht man ganz die Reize und die Geheimnisse der Sprache, die das Material für ihre Produktion ist. Der emigrierte Schriftsteller hat mit seiner Heimat auch sein Publikum verloren".[2]

While the influence of political circumstances on the stories narrated in exile literature is comparatively well documented, the stylistic impact of exile, and especially traveling in exile, has all too often been neglected. Works written in emigration have even been outrightly dismissed as merely of historical interest, written for a political purpose and with an eye to political effect, and hence they have been categorized as stylistically unremarkable literature.[3]

However, the influence of exile on literary themes and style is not only one of the most interesting, but also one of the most complex issues of research on exile literature. Even though trends, particularly thematic ones, can be observed, it is hardly promising to attempt a definition of a particular, all-embracing exile style, or of one common formal development in émigré writings. Exile, Joseph Strelka claims, "was a stimulus that produced a variety of responses, depending on the idiosyncrasies of the individual author's character and personal history".[4] But while exile may not have triggered one specific stylistic alteration or innovation in modern literature, it is a fact that in many, if not the majority of cases, the literary approaches of writers changed considerably after their expatriation – notwithstanding that these changes were "by no means uniformly in one direction".[5] Hence it may well be possible also to observe stylistic exile trends, at least with regards to writers of a similar background and, more importantly, similarities in literary style. Such a group of authors may have developed in a similar direction when faced with the uprootedness of exile, and they might have come across similar problems and found similar approaches on their way to their individual literary responses to exile.

It is the aim of this study to investigate and explore central thematic developments and stylistic changes in the exile writings of a group of young writers. Young, not quite established writers provide a particularly promising field for

---

[2] Klaus Mann: PEN-Club. In: *Mit dem Blick nach Deutschland*. Ed. by Michel Grunewald. München: Ellermann 1985. Pp. 56–63. Here: p. 57.
[3] See for example Alexander Stephan: *Die deutsche Exilliteratur 1933–1945. Eine Einführung*. München: C.H. Beck 1979. P. 8.
[4] Joseph P. Strelka: The Novel in Exile: Types and Patterns. In: *Exile: The Writer's Experience*. Ed. by John M. Spalek and Robert F. Bell. Chapel Hill: University of North Carolina Press 1982. Pp. 24–31. Here: p. 29.
[5] Ibid. P. 24.

this observation, because they entered the literary scene before exile – in their case shortly before the Nazis seized power – but were still at the beginning of their literary careers. Hence the personal changes of exile might have left a greater mark on their writings than on those of more established writers who had already acquired a more distinct style and might have been familiar to their international audiences or even famous for a particular way of writing.

Das Jüngste Deutschland

A circle of writers famously known during the Weimar Republic as *Das Jüngste Deutschland* is such a group whose members were torn away from their newly established careers and had to make decisions regarding their personal, political, and most importantly artistic futures when the National Socialists seized power. Even though the writers commonly summarized under this name in fact denied forming a clearly defined literary circle, they wrote, acted, and in many instances also presented themselves as a group. They reviewed each other's work, dedicated their books to one another, portrayed each other in them, and co-published anthologies of prose and poetry, such as the *Anthologie Jüngster Prosa* (1928) and the *Anthologie Jüngster Lyrik* in two parts (1927 and 1929).[6] Furthermore, the renowned Reclam publishing house portrayed these writers in a group when it published a series of their novels and novellas under the common heading of "*Junge Deutsche*" from 1927 to 1931.[7] And, last but certainly not least, they were identified as a group "unbegabt und unjung, und leicht verschmockt" by critics such as Kurt Tucholsky, and mocked by more established writers such as Bert Brecht.[8]

At the heart of *Das Jüngste Deutschland* was one of the notorious black sheep of the literary scene of the Weimar Republic, Thomas Mann's eldest son Klaus. Klaus Mann, who was born in 1906, famously appeared on the literary radar aged only 19, when he published a volume of short stories, a novel and a play in the course of just one year. Soon, a loosely defined circle of young aspiring writers (poets as well as dramatists and prose writers) assembled around him and his sister Erika (born 1905), an equally aspiring actress. Amongst the better known of this group were Erich Ebermayer (1900–1970),

---

[6] *Anthologie jüngster Lyrik*. Ed. by Willi R. Fehse and Klaus Mann. Hamburg: Enoch 1927; *Anthologie jüngster Lyrik. Neue Folge*. Ed. by Willi R. Fehse and Klaus Mann. Hamburg: Enoch 1929; *Anthologie jüngster Prosa*. Ed. by Erich Ebermayer, Klaus Mann and Hans Rosenkranz. Berlin: J. M. Spaeth 1928.
[7] Among the published works were Klaus Mann's novella *Abenteuer* (1929), as well as Peter Mendelssohn's novels *Fertig mit Berlin* (1930) and *Paris über mir* (1931).
[8] Kurt Tucholsky: Allgemeine Leserempfehlungen. In: *Weltbühne* (1923). P. 290. See also Bert Brecht: Wenn der Vater mit dem Sohne mit dem Uhu. In: *Das Tage-Buch*. 14. 8. 1926. P. 1202–1203.

Willi R. Fehse (1906–1977), Peter Mendelssohn (1908–1982), Herbert Schlüter (1906–2004), and Wilhelm Emanuel Süskind (1901–1970). The National Socialists' seizure of power confronted these young writers with the choice either to leave the country or to compromise their personal and artistic lives. In the following, this study will focus on Klaus Mann, Peter Mendelssohn and Herbert Schlüter. Mendelssohn and Schlüter were prose writers who, like Klaus Mann, went into exile and also dedicated their lives as well as their literary writings to fighting the regime in Germany for years to come.

Peter Mendelssohn, who is also known by his self-adopted aristocratic name of Peter de Mendelssohn – like Klaus Mann – grew up in artistic surroundings, in his case in the colony of artists Hellerau near Dresden. He also went to a 'Freie Schule', an independent alternative school, where he was introduced to international literature and art. Moreover, he, too, was a cosmopolite long before exile. He lived in Paris in the early 1930s and even attempted to write in French. His novel *Paris über mir* (1931) deals with his experiences as an internationally-minded young intellectual in an increasingly nationalistic Germany and centers on his attempts to introduce French culture to his young German readers – experiences shared by Klaus Mann in his travel reports, short stories, plays, and essays on France and the USA.[9]

In contrast to Mann and Mendelssohn, Herbert Schlüter initially lived a middle-class life in his hometown Berlin, where he trained as a bank clerk. But he, too, abandoned his bourgeois life for a future of travel and literature, and in 1927 he published his first volume of stories entitled *Ein spätes Fest*.[10]

Themes and style in the writings of *Das Jüngste Deutschland*

In their early fictional writings the authors' cosmopolitan attitudes and their travel experiences only surface occasionally, for example in Klaus Mann's play *Gegenüber von China* which is set in the Unites States and confronts a young German exchange student with conflicting interpretations of the American way of life.[11] Yet travel and internationalism was not the dominating theme at this

---

[9] Peter Mendelssohn: *Paris über mir*. Leipzig: Reclam 1931. See also Klaus und Erika Mann: *Rundherum*. Berlin: S. Fischer 1929; Klaus Mann: *Auf der Suche nach einem Weg. Aufsätze*. Berlin: Transmare 1931. Klaus Mann: *Heute und Morgen. Zur Situation des jungen geistigen Europas*. Hamburg: Enoch 1927.
[10] Herbert Schlüter: *Ein spätes Fest*. Berlin: S. Fischer 1927.
[11] Klaus Mann: *Gegenüber von China*. First production in Bochum 1930. In his non-fiction writings, Mann's two travel books stand out. Even though these books rush through foreign countries and cultures in a rather unreflective manner, in many ways they follow the classical outlines of a travel report (*Rundherum*) and a tourist guide (*Das Buch von der Riviera*). See Erika and Klaus Mann: *Rundherum. Ein heiteres Reisebuch*. Berlin: S. Fischer 1929; Erika and Klaus Mann: *Das Buch von der Riviera oder was nicht im Baedeker steht. Reisebuch*. München: Piper 1931.

stage of their writings. Instead, it is their age that can be defined as the most common feature of these writers before exile. Because of it, Mann, Mendelssohn, Schlüter and most of the other members of *Das Jüngste Deutschland* shared formative experiences of their childhood. They had lived through the First World War as children and had spent their teenage years in the great confusions of the early Weimar Republic, the years of inflation, revolution, political radicalization, and the restructuring of society. Growing up in provincial Germany with disoriented parents, careers in Berlin, Paris or even Hollywood, the German youth movement, the questioning of hitherto established gender roles, contemporary art, sexual and political adventures were the issues on their minds – which fueled most of their writings. A number of similarities in their pre-exile literature reflect these common experiences.

Firstly, Mann, Mendelssohn and Schlüter – in a manner typical not only of their group, but also of writing in the Weimar Republic in general – put their own experiences, even themselves, into the center of their works. They made general examples of their individual lives, their feelings, and their problems. They created characters modeled after themselves and their friends. Mann's first collection of stories, *Vor dem Leben*, for example, consists of tales that tell of the author's barely disguised experiences at the 'Freie Schule', wrought with sexual and generational confusion, and with his discovery of his interest in art. Programmatically, the title tells us where the teenage writer and his characters stand: before life.[12]

Mendelssohn's *Schmerzliches Arkadien* is at least as much a tale of adolescence as Mann's collected stories. Its main character Vincent struggles to find himself and his position in society during his first year at a 'Freie Schule'.[13] In the course of this year, Vincent encounters an influential, free-spirited model teacher, his first love, and two opposing groups of students: the militarily organized, physically strong "Indianer" and the intellectual group of "die Alten". Vincent's father has died in the war. The outside world, which equals the world of grown-ups, is represented by his stepfather, a cavalry captain who is described in an estranging, slightly satirical way. Each and every one of these motifs (the teacher, the opposing groups of students, the dead father, and many more) can be found in stories of Klaus Mann, as well as in numerous other works of members of *Das Jüngste Deutschland*: Erich Ebermayer's *Nacht in Warschau* and *Kampf um Odilienberg*, both set amongst the pupils of a 'Freie Schule', spring to mind, as does Wilhelm Emanuel Süskind's first novel with its equally programmatic title, *Jugend*, in which he portrayed several members of *Das Jüngste Deutschland*.[14]

---

[12] Klaus Mann: *Vor dem Leben*. Hamburg: Enoch 1925.
[13] Peter Mendelssohn: *Schmerzliches Arkadien*. Berlin: Universitas 1932.
[14] Erich Ebermayer: *Nacht in Warschau*. Leipzig: Reclam 1929; Erich Ebermayer: *Kampf um Odilienberg*. Wien: Zsolnay 1929. Wilhem Emanuel Süskind: *Jugend*. Stuttgart: Deutsche Verlagsanstalt 1929.

The same can be said for Herbert Schlüter's early works, most notably for *Die Rückkehr der verlorenen Tochter*.[15] In this novel, Schlüter unknowingly anticipates Klaus Mann's suicide that was to happen in 1949: A gifted man kills himself with sleeping pills in Cannes. The novel's protagonist is the man's lover, a young, decadent and deeply unhappy woman, who returns to her father and grandmother in provincial Germany. The 'old ones' do not have bad intentions, but they are incompetent and unhappy themselves. Adultery, drugs, and the incompatibility of the modern youth with the world and values of their parents finally lead to the death of the young girl.[16]

Secondly, Mann, Mendelssohn and Schlüter's early works also show multiple similarities in style. Even though their stories were so closely inspired by real life and were put into a realistic framework in terms of time and chronology, the three authors did not necessarily narrate in a realistic way. Instead, their writings mixed elements of a neo-romantic style – dreams, fairy tales, poetic rhythm – with a kind of grotesque naturalism and the contemporarily popular objective style.[17] Altogether, the style of *Das Jüngste Deutschland* can be described as conservative. Their first works were published in the short period between Expressionism and *Neue Sachlichkeit*, but they seem to have modelled their works mostly on writers of the generation of their fathers, such as Hermann Bang, Knut Hamsun, Hugo von Hofmannsthal, Heinrich Mann, Walt Whitman, and Oscar Wilde.[18]

The style and structure of their works often mirror the contents very closely. Typical are, for example, short, breathless phrases and exclamations which draw attention to small, often emotional details that are embedded in longer rhythmic sentences. The style of the authors of *Das Jüngste Deutschland* reflects "die große Rat- und Hilflosigkeit, die Befangenheit, und Angst vor dem Leben in dem zarten, zitternden, traumhaft verwirrten Tonfall".[19] Particularly Klaus Mann's language

---

[15] Herbert Schlüter: *Die Rückkehr der verlorenen Tochter*. Berlin: Transmare 1932.

[16] Another example for these thematic correspondences in the works of authors of *Das Jüngste Deutschland* is Schlüter's collection of novellas *Ein spätes Fest* (1927), which, as Fredric Kroll has proven, shows considerable likeness in subjects, motifs and descriptions of milieu to Klaus Mann's first novel *Der fromme Tanz* (1924). Ed. by Fredric Kroll and Klaus Täubert. Hamburg: Männerschwarm 2006; *1906–1927. Unordnung und früher Ruhm*. Wiesbaden: Edition Klaus Blahak 1977 (Klaus-Mann-Schriftenreihe. Band 2). P. 179.

[17] See Herbert Schlüter: Klaus Mann. In: *Literarische Revue*. 4 (1949). Pp. 34–35. Here: p. 35.

[18] See Klaus Mann: *Der Wendepunkt*. Frankfurt/Main: S. Fischer 1952. P. 117.

[19] See *1906–1927 Unordnung und früher Ruhm*. Ed. by Fredric Kroll and Klaus Täubert. Wiesbaden: Blahak 1977. Pp.141–142 (Klaus-Mann-Schriftenreihe. Band 2).

erinnert an den müde und traurig dahingleitenden Rhythmus der Sätze Hermann Bangs [...] nur ist sie durch unendlich viele eingeschobene Partikel, die den starren Kontur des einzelnen Wortes, das starre Gefüge des einzelnen Satzteiles und Satzes immer wieder zaghaft verwischen und auflösen, noch unbestimmter, noch zaghafter, noch träumerischer gemacht.[20]

W.E. Süskind, to single out another member of the group, has been praised for a similar rhythmical style, "ein von Anaphern, Häufungen, Steigerungen mächtig geschwellter Rhythmus, in dem das dunkel schwellende, aber hoffnungslose Gefühl einer lebensunfähigen Kreatur nach dem Morgenlicht des Lebens, nach Klarheit, ergreifend sich ausdrückt".[21]

Mann, Mendelssohn, and Schlüter usually employed a classical omniscient narrator, occasionally mixing it with elements of more modern narration. This omniscient narrator, that seems surprisingly old-fashioned for prose writings of the 1920s, leads the reader through the story and the characters' feelings. Mendelssohn and Mann like to address their characters directly with sentences such as, "So öffnest du die Augen, Knabe aus der Fremde [...] Wo hast du dies schon gesehen?", whereas Schlüter's first-person narrators commonly speak to their readers and ask them questions such as "Kennen Sie das?".[22] At particularly important or emotional moments, all three writers change perspectives and even cross the borders into the minds of their characters. Mann, for example, changes into first-person perspective at the emotional climax of his novel *Der fromme Tanz*, and in his story *Sonja* he employs the considerably more modern technique of narrated monologues.[23]

In general, stylistic considerations were not at the heart of the Youngest Germans' literature. In his epilogue to the *Anthologie Jüngster Lyrik*, Mann even felt the need to mark the distance between *Das Jüngste Deutschland*'s interests and stylistic issues by putting the term itself in inverted commas: "Etwa einen neuen 'Stil' zu suchen ist [...] unsere Aufgabe nicht. Sind wir endlich unserer Richtung sicher, wird der neue 'Stil' bestimmt von selber kommen".[24] Unfortunately, the world around them agreed neither with their "Richtung" nor their "Stil". Schlüter's next novel *Nach fünf Jahren* was turned down by S. Fischer's publishing house for its "psychologisierenden Erzählstil"

---

[20] Walter Heinsius: Die jüngste Generation. In: *Der Kreis. Zeitschrift für künstlerische Kultur*. 3.8 (1926). P. 322.
[21] Ibid. P. 323.
[22] Peter Mendelssohn: *Schmerzliches Arkadien*. Berlin: Universitas 1932. P. 8; Schlüter: *Die Rückkehr der verlorenen Tochter* (n. 15). P. 8.
[23] See *1906–1927 Unordnung und früher Ruhm* (n. 16). See also Mendelssohn: *Schmerzliches Arkadien* (n. 22) P. 43.
[24] Klaus Mann: Nachwort. In: *Anthologie jüngster Prosa* (n. 6). P. 159.

in 1934.[25] The concerns and writings of *Das Jüngste Deutschland* were not welcome in Germany anymore.

Das Jüngste Deutschland Abroad: Klaus Mann, Peter Mendelssohn, Herbert Schlüter and Their Exile Writings

Mann, Mendelssohn, and Schlüter decided to leave Germany soon after the National Socialists' seizure of power: just when each of them had gained some critical approval though still far from being a continuously successful writer. This decision interrupted their literary careers just when they were taking off. Hence, the young writers were put on the verge of being remembered as either a one-off literary success or continuing their writing abroad, under rather different and more complicated circumstances.

It is well known that Klaus Mann outgrew himself in exile and became one of the most outspoken and active German émigrés who edited the journals *Die Sammlung* and *Decision* and lived in France, the Netherlands and the United States before he returned to Europe as an American soldier.

Peter Mendelssohn went to Austria, where he met and married the writer Hilde Spiel. Initially, he continued to publish in Germany, using the pseudonym Carl Johann Leuchtenberg. Together with his wife, he moved to London in 1935 where they lived until their return to Western Germany in 1945.

Herbert Schlüter's exile was less straightforward and financially more strained than that of his friends. He went to France in 1933 but, having suffered difficulties in adapting to life in exile, returned to Germany early the following year. However, he did not dare to fully enter the cultural life of the Third Reich. Instead, he lived almost hidden from the public and published one article only in a German newspaper. Yet his contact with Klaus Mann never ceased, and Mann accepted an article of Schlüter's for *Die Sammlung* even while the author was in Germany. In 1935, Schlüter changed his mind again and moved to Spain, where he lived in poor conditions with other artists on Mallorca. When the island was conquered by Franco's troops in 1936, Schlüter, with the financial aid of the Mann family, fled to Yugoslavia, and in 1938 he moved on to Italy. In 1941 he was caught by the Wehrmacht and was involuntarily enlisted as an interpreter.

Looking at the lives of Mann, Mendelssohn and Schlüter, it becomes apparent that they lived three variations of exile and that each of them is typical in his own way. All three of them had to cope with the problems that characteristically face writers in emigration: the aforementioned loss of a potential audience in their native language, an urge to focus on the current political situation,

---

[25] See Reinhard Andress: *'Der Inselgarten' – das Exil deutschsprachiger Schriftsteller auf Mallorca, 1931–1936*. Amsterdam – Atlanta: Rodopi 2001. P. 147.

general uprootedness, but also everyday problems such as the loss of passports and financial needs. Clearly, Schlüter had the toughest lot of these three, and this had an impact on his writings. During his years abroad, he only published one story and two poems in the exile journals *Silberboot* and *Die Sammlung*. In 1937/38, he submitted the manuscript of his novel *Vor dem Krieg* for the literary competition of the American Guild for German Cultural Freedom, yet his hope of winning the promised contract with a publishing house was not fulfilled. *Vor dem Krieg* was never published, and Schlüter destroyed its manuscript after the war. A second manuscript of a novel that was set in Dalmatia was lost in the disorder of war.[26]

Klaus Mann, in contrast, created the more renowned part of his oeuvre in exile. He published the three political novels *Flucht in den Norden* (1934), *Mephisto* (1936) and *Der Vulkan* (1939) as well as the biographical Tchaikovsky novel *Symphonie Pathétique* (1935) and the novella *Vergittertes Fenster* (1937) with the exile publishing house Querido in Amsterdam. Moreover, many of his works were translated and published by non-German publishers even before 1945.

Mendelssohn was similarily successful. His novel *Das Haus Cosinsky*, which had been published by Oprecht und Herbig in Zurich in 1934, was translated and published by Hutchinson's in London even before his move to the UK. He managed to follow up its success and in quick succession published three further novels with the same publishing house in 1938 (*All that Matters*), 1939 (*Across the Dark River*) and 1943 (*The Hours and the Centuries*) before shifting the focus of his work to non-fictional texts such as political analyses.

In order to adjust their writing to the demands and constraints of exile and a life of constant travel, the three writers undertook a number of changes. The first and perhaps most obvious of these is the shift in choice of subjects. We have seen that Mann, Mendelssohn, Schlüter, as well as other members of *Das Jüngste Deutschland*, often found their inspiration in their own lives. Hence it is unsurprising that after their emigration their writings reflected the very different experiences encountered in exile. This is a feature commonly seen in exile literature, and Loewy even claims that it was the principle aim of German exile writers to unite and motivate the émigrés in their struggle against fascism, and that they tried to achieve this by a "Thematisierung des Exils".[27] This can particularly be seen in two of the five novels Mann wrote in exile: both *Flucht in den Norden* and *Der Vulkan* are set amongst émigrés and discuss the problems and challenges of living in exile and fighting the Nazis. Schlüter initially felt, "über Emigration könnte ich nicht schreiben", but in fact he later chose a

[26] See Ibid. Pp.153–154.
[27] *Exil. Literarische und politische Texte aus dem deutschen Exil 1933–1945*. Ed. by Ernst Loewy. Stuttgart: Metzler 1979. P. 470.

similar topic for his *Vor dem Krieg*.[28] In addition, Mann's *Mephisto* as well as Mendelssohn's two novels *All that Matters* and *Across the Dark River* present variations of this topic. They are mainly set in the Third Reich and discuss fascism, the persecution of the Jews, and resistance from inside, as do, for example, some of Anna Seghers' novels. Schlüter planned a similar novel, which, according to his description, would have been counterpart to Mann's *Mephisto*: "Vielleicht schreibe ich einmal über die seelische Verfassung der Intellektuellen, die geblieben sind, <u>ohne</u> sich gleichgeschaltet zu haben. Sie sind ohnmächtiger und 'emigrierter' als die Emigranten, aber fast immer sehr anständig".[29]

This "Thematisierung des Exils" and its variations was a considerable change in the works of all three authors. Neither of them had focused on political topics before, but as their own lives became considerably more political, politics entered their literature. While writing his novel *Vor dem Krieg*, Schlüter expressed his ambiguity towards this politicization of his own work in a letter to Mann, who was already working on his third political exile novel:

> Einen Emigranten-Roman schreibst Du? Ich bin, schon aus moralischen Gründen, sehr dafür. Obwohl ich an dem, den ich selber schreibe, sehe, wie riskiert [sic] es ist. Ich kann nicht jeden Emigranten zu einem sittlichen Vorbild stilisieren, es wäre mir artistisch zu langweilig... Dieses Buch ist für mich ganz neuartig [...] es ist vor allem politisch ganz eindeutig, ein Bekenntnis zur Linken, zur Volksfront als den heute eigentlich bewahrenden Kräften der europäischen Civilisation [sic]. Es enthält entschiedene Angriffe auf das Nazi-Reich und auch auf die Auslandsgruppen dieser Partei. Ich bin glücklich, endlich eine artistische Möglichkeit gefunden zu haben, die private und stimmungshafte Überzeugung nun formulieren zu können [...]. Ich hätte nie geahnt, einmal Romane wie diesen meinen neuen schreiben zu müssen.[30]

Schlüter's letter points out one of the main concerns of political writing in exile: On the one hand, the author feels the need to use literature as a tool in the political fight. His belief in the power of the pen helps him to feel active and potentially effective in his fight against the oppressors at home. On the other hand, Schlüter's fear of being artistically boring, his declaration that he "muss" write political novels, and his expression of astonishment about his latest artistic development betray his ambiguity towards the genre of political literature and his desire to continue separating political from aesthetic concerns.

Parallel to the "Thematisierung des Exils" and closely related to it, another radical thematic change can be observed. It has already been mentioned that in

---

[28] Andress: "Der Inselgarten" (n. 25). P. 150.
[29] Ibid. P. 151. [Emphasized by Herbert Schlüter].
[30] See *1933–1937 Repräsentant des Exils: 1934–1937 Im Zeichen der Volksfront*. Ed. by Fredric Kroll. Hamburg: Männerschwarm 2006 (Klaus-Mann-Schriftenreihe. Band 4/2). P. 819.

their early works all three writers used their own broad travel experiences to promote foreign cultures and internationalism, but that neither international concerns nor the theme of travel was at the heart of their pre-exile writings. In exile, the paradigms of this promotion of foreign cultures and their occasional connections with travel writing shifted considerably. Indeed, by setting their novels amongst émigrés in the host towns of German exiles, and by describing the host countries, their inhabitants and political conflicts and the exiles' relationship to them, Mann, Mendelssohn, and Schlüter now hoped to go beyond simply providing a true depiction of life abroad. They aimed at furthering the cultural and political exchange between the host countries and the German émigrés and to put the "most distinguished representatives of European culture" that were running away from the Nazis into a "productive contact" with intellectuals and the politically active of the host countries.[31]

Indeed, the topoi of traveling and living abroad were now central in their writings, and they fulfilled different narrative and metaphorical roles. First and foremost, the act of traveling itself was presented as an act of survival. For most of the Jewish or outspokenly anti-fascist characters in Mann and Mendelssohn's novels, for example, traveling to leave their home country is the only chance to escape suppression and, ultimately, violent death in Germany. But once they are abroad, traveling also provides the opportunity to fight National Socialism. The refugees continue to travel in order to carry their "Sorge um Europa in die Welt hinaus", to propagate antifascism as well as German culture, and to network with other anti-fascists.[32]

Moreover, traveling is now used as a symbol for a character's development. This symbolism was not entirely new in their writings – in fact, Mendelssohn's narrator described Vincent's journey to himself in *Schmerzliches Arkadien* as "eine Reise sehr weit weg, in ein Ausland des Herzens" – but the personal development acquired through travel is now an act of political awakening, the development of a political conscience that influences both the characters' lives and works.[33] At the beginning of Mendelssohn's *All that Matters*, for example, the main character, a Jewish writer, lives in a completely apolitical, self-inflicted emigration in the French countryside and watches the rising National Socialism in Germany from afar. His transformation into an active antifascist and the different stages of denial and acceptance of his responsibility are reflected by his return to Germany and different stations during his travels through his home country. A short trip to the Northern German countryside towards the end of the novel is his last attempt at personal escapism and an apolitical life. In the end, however, he travels on to France, where he feels ready to

---

[31] Klaus Mann: Decision. In: *Decision* 1 (1941). P. 8.
[32] Klaus Mann: *Der Vulkan*. Amsterdam: Querido 1939. P. 495.
[33] Mendelssohn: *Schmerzliches Arkadien* (n. 22). P. 177.

accept both private happiness and his political responsibility as a writer, and takes up political activities in Paris.

The young communist heroine Johanna in Mann's *Flucht in den Norden* undertakes a similar trip. Her journey to Finland and the long trip on which she embarks with her lover until they are "nicht mehr richtig in Europa" (and hence away from European politics) is described as a 'journey into freedom' (as Rita Reil called the novel in her English translation) – the freedom from political responsibility and the freedom to find fulfillment in personal happiness.[34] But in the end Johanna, like nearly all other characters in Mann and Mendelssohn's novels, decides to join the fight against fascism and travels on to her comrades in Paris.

Mendelssohn's *Across the Dark River* combines these two aspects of the topos travel. Here, traveling is at the same time a means of survival and a symbol of political awakening: The main character is a stranger whose arrival in the village stirs the polical conflicts that, in turn, raise his political conscience. Yet whereas he guides the Jewish population of the village throughout several countries towards hope and survival, his personal journey towards political activism ultimately leads to his death as the angel of revenge for his friends.

In Mann's panopticum of exile, *Der Vulkan*, the two functions of travel as topos also occur in many variations: Most characters have to move from city to city in a quest to identify and accept their individual personal and political destinies. Whereas in his earlier novel *Flucht in den Norden*, as well as in Mendelssohn's *All that Matters*, a trip to the city equals the acceptance of political responsibility while a journey to the countryside equals escapism, Mann now takes this symbolism even further. He assigns different patterns of political awakening to individual cities, and the cities' patterns are usually closely connected to the author's own experiences. Paris, for example, was one of the most important centers of German exile before the war and home to many of Mann's personal friends. He presents it as the meeting point for young political intellectuals and artists of all nationalities that form a community in order to fight for a modern, international society, and the many storylines set in this city tell variations of this theme. In Amsterdam, the two most important publishing houses for German émigré writers were established and Klaus Mann founded the first of his two literary journals. Thus in *Der Vulkan*, it is the place where a character learns that only through antifascist writings he will finally gain acceptance as a part of the city's – and the émigrés' – community. Zurich, temporary home to the Mann family, was the place where Thomas Mann broke in public with the Hitler regime and where in 1936, after three years in exile,

---

[34] Klaus Mann: *Flucht in den Norden*. Amsterdam: Querido 1934. P. 268. See also: Klaus Mann: *Journey into Freedom*. Translated by Rita Reil. New York: Knopf 1936.

the Nobel Prize winner finally took on his responsibility as one of the most distinguished German émigrés. It is unsurprising, then, that the role his son assigns to this city is ambiguous. Zurich is presented as a family city in which true friendship between émigrés and natives can develop, but also a city whose inhabitants, both the Swiss and the German refugees, have to be awoken painfully in order to accept the challenges put upon their town by the threat of fascism. And, finally, in New York Mann edited his second journal and ultimately decided to continue his antifascist fight as a soldier. Here the tendencies of Paris, Zurich and Amsterdam, and hence all variations of an active émigré life, come together.

Interestingly, the inclusion of politics and the characters' inward and outward travels form another topic that is widely discussed in the novels. During his self-inflicted isolation in France, the main character in Mendelssohn's *All that Matters* attempts to flee politics and writes a "happy little thing [...] gay and carefree", a "very little book indeed, so small and weightless a thing".[35] But his growing political involvement leads to a second, much more political book that bears the programmatic title *Man of Decency* and is confiscated by the SA when its author is arrested the night of the Reichstag fire.[36] Mann told a number of variations of the same tale: the poet Sebastian in *Mephisto* has to learn to follow the "Gesetz des Kampfes" rather than the laws of art when writing his verses, and in *Der Vulkan* all five main characters, though not all of them writers, are subjected to similar artistic changes (which not all of them successfully master).[37]

In *Der Vulkan*, the importance assigned to the act of traveling as a means of survival as well as a symbol of personal and artistic politicization even cumulates in religious stylization. In order to connect the innumerable characters and plots, Mann uses the narrative device of "Engel der Heimatlosen [...] Engel der Entwurzelungs-Neurose [...] Schutzpatron der Expatriierten".[38] Unlike the émigrés, this angel can easily overcome all earthly boundaries. It is the angel's task "solche zu begleiten, die sich ohnedies schon rastlos unterwegs befinden", to observe the émigrés, protect them, and to report the details of their fight directly to "Der Herr".[39] Thus he enables the narrator to present a broad overview of the émigrés' activities all over the world. Yet there is more to the divine messenger than his structural importance for the plot. It is the angel's kiss that gives the escapist turned activist-character Kikjou the order and the

---

[35] Peter Mendelssohn: *All that Matters*. London: Hutchinson 1938. P. 114 and 121.
[36] Ibid. P. 251.
[37] Klaus Mann: *Mephisto. Roman einer Karriere*. Amsterdam: Querido 1936. P. 309.
[38] Mann: *Der Vulkan* (n. 32). P. 671 and 674.
[39] Ibid. P. 671 and 703.

strength to write an anti-fascist "Roman der Heimatlosen" and hence become the chronicler of exile.[40] The émigrés' fight, the angel claims, "geht um Leben und Tod, keiner meiner Schützlinge darf ihm ausweichen".[41] Thus, through the angel, Mann portrays the homeless travelers as chosen ones, whose political and artistic responsibilities have been assigned directly by god's "höchstes Gut, strengstes Urteil".[42] Their uprooted life of travel is in fact a religious mission. It is "Der Umgetriebene, Unbehauste, überall-Fremde" who has "vergleichsweise gute Chancen, dem Allerhöchsten Plan gerecht zu werden".[43] This is also reflected in the angel's appearance, which initially echoes the émigrés' difficulties and their exhaustion from being constantly on the move. His voice is tired and "er sah mitgenommen aus, beinah schäbig. Sein langer schwarzer Mantel war ramponiert und stellenweise zerrissen. Selbst die Flügel [...] wirkten zerzaust".[44] Yet when he predicts the potentially glorious future and the special role the émigrés will play in it, his coat is suddenly "nicht mehr abgenutzt, schadhaft und dünn; sein Stoff schien sowohl weicher als auch stärker geworden" and he now wears "ein[en] ritterliche[n] Mantel, ein fürstlich feines Kostüm".[45]

Moreover, both Mann and Mendelssohn also made another, more indirect choice of subject that is linked to the "Thematisierung des Exils". They turned to history as a means of expressing their opinion on the present. Mann described his feelings of uprootedness, loneliness and depression in the abovementioned novella that deals with the death of the Bavarian king Ludwig II and in the novel on the composer Tchaikovsky, who travels throughout Europe as a successful musician yet remains an outsider to society. Mendelssohn published a novel on the poet and knight Oswald von Wolkenstein. Beyond the metaphorical character of historical stories that closely relate to the present, Mann's and Mendelssohn's contemporary Wolfgang Cordan interpreted this turn to history as a "compilation of a cultural inventory"; again, it is a feature that frequently occurs in exile literature, such as in Heinrich Mann's novels.[46]

These considerable thematic shifts in the writings of Mann, Mendelssohn, and Schlüter reflect the writers' attempts to adapt their works to the demands

---

[40] Ibid. P. 681.
[41] Ibid. P. 674.
[42] Ibid. P. 677.
[43] Ibid. P. 707.
[44] Ibid. P. 671.
[45] Ibid. P. 673.
[46] Cor de Back: Die Zeitschrift 'Het Fundament' und die Deutsche Exilliteratur. In: *Zur Deutschen Exilliteratur in den Niederlanden 1933–1940. Ed. by Hans Würzner.* Amsterdam Rodopi 1977. Pp.183–213. Here: Pp. 196–197.

and needs of exile. Through the character Kikjou in *Der Vulkan*, Mann specified what he saw as the contemporary aims of literature:

> Die Nachwelt will doch Dokumente, Rechenschaft. Sie verlangt unsere Beichte... [...] Die Ereignisse und Zustände sollen verändert werden, darauf kommt alles an. [...] Wie soll man sie verändern [...] wenn man nicht einmal wagt sie zu benennen? [...] Das Verwirrte übersichtlich zu machen; den Schmerz zu lindern, indem man ihn analysiert [...].[47]

Unsurprisingly, a change of topics as radical as the one these writers undertook, the sudden usage of literature as a political instrument, the influence of constant travel and life abroad, the aim of giving "Rechenschaft" through literature, and the change of the potential audience influenced their style of writing as well. Mann and Mendelssohn – since Schlüter's manuscripts have been lost, it is more difficult to closely assess his works – introduce new stylistic features to adapt their writing to exile. Again, it is Mann's character Kikjou who voices the stylistic concerns raised because of political demands: "Vieles ist einzubeziehen, eine Menge von Themen machen die Symphonie. Ich darf nichts vereinfachen, auch nichts weglassen; umständlich und aufrichtig muss ich sein. – Wenn es aber langweilig würde? [...] Vielleicht sind Bücher nicht mehr zeitgemäß?".[48]

Clearly, the exile writers' books were now meant not to be exclusively aesthetically beautiful, but rather, as Schlüter put it in a letter to Mann, written in the hope that they were "politically effective".[49] To achieve such effectiveness, the three writers had to at least amend, perhaps even leave, the common paths of their pre-exile writings.

The most radical of these amendments is the writers' response to the loss of a large part of their native language audience. Mann, Mendelssohn, and Schlüter represent three rather different shades of reaction to this problem. Schlüter is not known to have written either fiction or non-fiction texts in a language other than German, despite his ability to speak several languages, his later work as an interpreter, and his postwar occupation as a translator of English as well as Italian literature. Mann, who spoke French fluently before exile and perfected his English while he lived in the United States, initially decided to defend his mother tongue against what he saw as National Socialist language abuse. He claimed: "kein Hitler kann mir meine Sprache nehmen".[50] However, confronted with the consolidation of the Third Reich, he began to

---

[47] Mann: *Der Vulkan* (n. 38). Pp. 679–80.
[48] Ibid. Pp. 678–79.
[49] See *1933–1937 Repräsentant des Exils* (n. 30). P. 817.
[50] Klaus Mann: *Ansprache vor deutschen Emigranten über Hitlers Politik nach dem Spanienkrieg*. München: Stadtbibliothek Monacensia, Literaturarchiv (KM 61).

attempt writing in English in the mid-1930s. He was soon able to write fluently and increasingly used the new language in his private letters and diaries. Yet a clear distinction can be made regarding his use of language: Even though he wrote and published articles and non-fiction books in English, such as his autobiography *The Turning Point* and the émigrés' Who's who *Escape to Life*, he did not manage to complete fiction in his adopted language, apart from occasional short stories which remained mostly unpublished in his lifetime.[51] Furthermore, Mann realized after the war that by now he felt at home in neither English nor German. Frustrated, he wrote to Schlüter: "Nun stocke ich in zwei Zungen. Im Englischen werde ich nie *ganz* so zuhause sein, wie ich es im Deutschen *war* – aber wohl nicht mehr *bin*".[52] His last (unfinished) novel *The Last Day* he outlined in English, but the linguistic problems may have played a considerable part in his description of the work's writing process as "mehr gekämpft als geschrieben".[53]

Mendelssohn, on the other hand, became what Alfred Döblin called a linguistic "Emigrationsgewinnler".[54] He believed that the Nazis would stay in power in the very long run and, immediately after his emigration, made every effort to become a full-fledged English-language writer. In January 1936, he was already able to start writing *All that Matters* in English. He quickly grew confident in his adopted language, and by 1943, had written three novels, of which the historical story *The Hours and the Centuries* has been judged as linguistically impeccable and as "the height of Mendelssohn's achievement as an English writer".[55] But his attempt to describe German matters in English caused linguistic problems for him as well. In *All that Matters*, for example, the Jewish names of the characters are used for a number of metaphorical allusions to their actual (German) meaning. Yet since Mendelssohn, probably in an attempt to keep the story as realistic as possible, uses German names throughout the novel, these allusions are in danger of being lost to the English reader. Hence, at several times in the book Mendelssohn lets his characters discuss these names and their meaning in English: "Schwarz is a Jewish name, just as

---

[51] See Klaus Mann: Speed. *Die Erzählungen aus dem Exil*. Reinbek bei Hamburg: Rowohlt 1992. See also Susanne Utsch: *Sprachwechsel im Exil. Die linguistische Metamorphose von Klaus Mann*. Köln – Weimar: Böhlau 2007.
[52] Klaus Mann: *Briefe und Antworten 1937–1949*. Ed. by Martin Gregor-Dellin. München: Ellermann 1975. P. 293. [Emphasis by Klaus Mann].
[53] Klaus Mann: *Tagebücher 1944–1949*. Ed. by Joachim Heimannsberg, Peter Laemmle and Wilfried F. Schoeller. Reinbek bei Hamburg: Rowohlt 1989. P. 214.
[54] See Stephan: *Die deutsche Exilliteratur* (n. 3). P. 147.
[55] Richard Dove: The Gift of Tongues. German-speaking novelists writing in English. In: *Between Two Languages. German-speaking Exiles in Great Britain 1933–1945*. Ed. by William Abbey, Charmain Brinson, Richard Dove, Marian Malet and Jennifer Taylor. Stuttgart: Hans-Dieter Heinz 1995. Pp. 95–115. Here: p. 105.

Weiß is [...] Black and White. Grün and Blau are Jewish names. Green and Blue".[56]

Another stylistic novelty in the writings of Mann and Mendelssohn is the emphasis the authors put on the close relation of their works to the reality of their exile situation. If their writings were to be political and historical chronicles of exile, their narrators needed to become chroniclers. Hence both introduced a number of precise geographical and historical markers that connect the private lives of their characters to the wider political situation. Sentences such as "That was in July, nineteen hundred and thirty-one" or "This happened in Barcelona, in March 1938" occur repeatedly.[57]

In an even more detailed way than in their pre-exile literature, both writers now included personal experiences in their stories and based their characters on real people. Mann, for example, used Herbert Schlüter's flight from Mallorca during the fascist invasion as a storyline for one of his characters in *Der Vulkan*. Events such as the conquering of Austria, the Czechoslovak crisis and the impending war form the background of *Der Vulkan* and of Mendelssohn's *Across the Dark River*. However, this often led to a considerable amount of sensationalism, particularly in the case of Mann's *Mephisto*, which can even be read as a roman à clef. Moreover, Mann as well as Mendelssohn used typical features of light fiction. Besides their political content, Mendelssohn's *All that Matters* and *Across the Dark River* tell exciting adventure stories of good versus evil, of lonesome manly fighters that defend their women against the Nazis, with shoot-outs, hide-and-seeks, and generally a high level of suspense. In Mann's case, all three political novels tell of drug abuse and feature rather sexually explicit moments – the most famous example being the sadomasochistic scene in *Mephisto* – and they also present a storyline that involves interaction between angels and humans and are in danger of being kitsch.

In all of Mann and Mendelssohn's political novels, the narration is mostly scenic, with a large amount of dialogue used to explain the characters' feelings and points of view. The above-mentioned use of phrases, typical for the language of *Das Jüngste Deutschland*, was being taken to the extreme. In *All that Matters*, Mendelssohn created cliffhangers at the beginning or the end of a chapter using short, often shocking sentences that clash with the preceding narration. In *Flucht in den Norden*, Mann used similar phrases especially to

---

[56] Mendelssohn: *All that Matters* (n. 35). P. 130. Another example is the German 'Schubhaus', a mixture of a shelter and a prison in frontier areas. Mendelssohn's first-person translator explains to the reader directly: "The Schubhaus, which means literally 'push-house', is an institution well known in all frontier districts and familiar to all tramps and persons without identity papers who happen to be picked up by the police". P. 222.

[57] Ibid. P. 54. See also Mann: *Der Vulkan* (n. 38).

increase the readers' emotional identification, whereas in *Mephisto* and in *Der Vulkan* they either draw attention to very important moments or direct the readers' sympathy for the characters.

Both in Mann and Mendelssohn's novels, this emotionalization was accompanied by an increasing closeness of narrator to characters. As in their pre-exile works, both authors preferred an omniscient narrator, but an increasing number of changes of perspective and inner monologues can be found. In *Across the Dark River*, Mendelssohn employed a first-person framework in which the narrator announces that he will tell a true story to the reader: "So I want you to sit still awhile and listen".[58] The actual story of the persecution of the Jews in an Austrian village is then told in third-person voice, but this narrative voice repeatedly enters the minds of several other characters, particularly when these characters are under emotional constraint.

Mann's narrators change perspective even more readily. Their function is almost evenly split between two tasks. First, in the manner of a commenting and summarizing chronicler, they emphasize the realistic elements of the story by showing consequences, discussing characters' actions and generally by being omnipresent. Second, they act as a kind of super-ego of several characters by slipping into their minds as well as addressing them directly to cheer them up or admonish them.[59] This change of narrative perspective creates an interaction between the subjective level of the plots and the objective, more general topics of the novels. The narrators combine the features of a journalist with those of a romancer. The characters' individual stories, often told simultaneously and from multiple perspectives, are constantly presented as part of a general framework. Their actions and feelings serve as comments on and criticisms of the general political situation that is narrated by the omniscient narrator.[60] In *Mephisto* and *Der Vulkan*, Mann took this double function of the narrator even further. He presents essayistic insertions that comment directly on the political background of the stories and are separated from the plot by the use of the present tense and a highly stylised language, for example the use of biblical metaphors: "Wehe, der Himmel über diesem Lande ist finster geworden. Gott hat sein Antlitz weggewendet von diesem Lande, ein Strom von Blut und Tränen ergießt sich durch die Straßen aller seiner Städte".[61] These insertions create a strong appellative and decidedly emotional effect.

Yet in one respect, Mann and Mendelssohn's political novels followed very different paths. Whereas Mendelssohn used to focus on one, chronologically

---

[58] Peter Mendelssohn: *Across the Dark River*. London: Hutchinson 1939. P. 11.
[59] See Nicole Schaenzler: *Klaus Mann als Erzähler: Studien zu seinen Romanen "Der fromme Tanz" und "Der Vulkan"*. Paderborn: Igel 1995. P. 115.
[60] See Ibid. Pp. 117–118.
[61] Mann: *Mephisto* (n. 37). P. 230.

told storyline, in Mann's novels, the inclusion of historical reality and the relentless exilic travel led to an increasingly complicated structure. Schlüter described this structural change in Mann's writings as a process of widening and claims that *Der Vulkan* "literarisch sein kühnster Versuch war, divergierende Darstellungsmittel in ein und demselben Werk [...] zu einer Einheit zu verbinden, Darstellungsmittel, deren Skala vom Realistischen bis zum Surrealistischen reicht".[62]

Schlüter's description alludes to Mann's attempt to find a literary equivalent for the increasingly chaotic, vast world of exile and constant traveling. Structural widening already takes place in his first exile novel, *Flucht in den Norden*: The main character, a young émigré, is surrounded by two groups of subsidiary characters that represent different types of apolitical bourgeois. In *Mephisto*, a larger group of subsidiary characters embody variations of resistance to the Nazis inside and outside Germany as well as forms of compromising and fellow traveling. *Der Vulkan*, finally, presents an exhaustive number of émigrés: the first chapter alone introduces twenty-six characters, of which five can be considered main characters. Their fates are told in innumerable episodes and storylines, which run parallel, join, or cross one another. Mann's first diary entry regarding this novel gives a good overview of the many fates he wanted to include into this panopticum of exile:

> Mein nächster Roman. Große Komposition aus Emigranten-Schicksalen: 'Die Verfolgten', oder so. Laufen nebeneinander her, jedoch durch irgendeine Klammer miteinander verbunden. In vielen Städten: Paris, London, Prag, New York, Hollywood, Zürich, Amsterdam, Palma, Florenz, Nice, Sanary u.s.w. Salzburg [...] Junger Prolet [...] Kommunisten, Katholiken. Gründung einer neuen Partei. Pass-Schwierigkeiten. Geldnot. Sexualnot. Der Hass. Die Hoffnung. Das Heimweh. Kriegsangst (und Hoffnung...) Politik: Saar; Spanien, Olympiade. Verbindung zu Illegalen im Reich. Melancholie. Les sans-patrie...[63]

Indeed, nearly all these motifs can be found in the finished work. These multiple storylines and their multiple connections suggest that Mann attempted to deal with the increasingly complex world of exile by presenting a grand panorama of many small exile worlds.

In his unpublished Mallorca novel, Schlüter seems to have aimed for a similar approach. The referee who judged his novel for the competition of the American Guild for German Cultural Freedom claimed that Schlüter's "offenbar autobiographische[r] Roman enthaelt eine grosse Menge von zum Teil gut

---

[62] Herbert Schlüter: Klaus Mann. In: *Literarische Revue*. 4 (1949). Pp. 34–35. Here: p. 35.
[63] Klaus Mann: *Tagebücher 1936–1937*. Ed. by Joachim Heimannsberg, Peter Laemmle and Wilfried F. Schoeller. Reinbek bei Hamburg: Rowohlt 1995. Pp. 69–70.

gesehenen Figuren, deren Vielheit der Autor aber nicht zu baendigen und zu lenken versteht; es ist, als ob ein Marionettenspieler seine Puppen immer wieder weghaengte".[64] Mann's *Der Vulkan* has been subject to similar criticism.[65] However, the disorientation of his characters in exile, the small part they play in the face of large social and political events, the increasingly complicated, polyphonic world can hardly be shown in a more radical style.

Conclusion

Alexander Stephan all too easily dismissed stylistic consequences of exile literature as an "ebenso buntes wie verwirrendes Kaleidoskop" that leads to contradicting results.[66] Yet a closer look at the thematic and stylistic developments in the exile writings of three members of *Das Jüngste Deutschland* has helped to separate this kaleidoscope into categories of changes and to identify typical problems of writing in exile as well as patterns of approaches to meet these challenges.

The three authors investigated in this study clearly modified their themes and stories to meet the political necessities of exile. Yet the example of the theme of travel shows that, notwithstanding considerable shifts in the focus of their writings, there are still thematic continuities from their pre-exile to their exile writings. International culture, cosmopolitanism, and traveling had always been present in Mann, Mendelssohn, and Schlüter's writing, but there is a clear transition from their pre-exile works to their exile writings, in which these issues move to the center of attention.

Moreover, these authors clearly did not neglect stylistic matters in favor of political messages. On the contrary, they considerably modified their style to meet the new difficulties of exile and of political literary writing. In the case of these young authors, the search for a politically effective narrative technique for the first time shifted stylistic concerns into the focus of their attention. By no means were all of their stylistic changes simplifications: Particularly the introduction of a more personal, 'modern' narrator and the increasingly frequent change of narrative techniques in the exile writings of *Das Jüngste Deutschland* prove that political writing does not have to be simple and stylistically one-dimensional.

Furthermore, the comparison of Mann, Mendelssohn and Schlüter's exile writings points out another key fact of writing in times of political crisis: the

---

[64] See Andress: 'Der Inselgarten' (n. 25). P. 155.
[65] See for example *1937–1942 Trauma Amerika*. Ed. by Fredric Kroll. Wiesbaden: Edition Klaus Blahak 1986 (Klaus-Mann-Schriftenreihe Vol. 5) P. 125–127. And Ilsedore B. Jonas: Klaus Mann im amerikanischen Exil. In: *Klaus Mann. Werk und Wirkung*. Ed. by Rudolf Wolff. Bonn: Bouvier 1984. P. 129.
[66] Stephan: *Die deutsche Exilliteratur* (n. 3). P. 206.

extraordinarily strong influence of life in exile on both theme and style of writing. The three writers may all exemplify typical émigré fates, yet they represent three very different versions of them: The political activist Mann who outgrew himself in exile and wrote his stylistically most challenging (and commercially most successful) works abroad, but lost the will to live and write after the war, contrasts with the well-adapted Peter Mendelssohn who became an acknowledged fiction and non-fiction writer in his host country and returned to be a similarly acknowledged intellectual in Germany, and with Herbert Schlüter, who suffered from the outward restraints of life in exile and whose literary ambitions were suppressed by his fight to overcome the daily challenges of a life in constant flux. It is even more significant, then, that when faced with a life spent as travelers with a mission to preserve their home country's culture, these authors still made similar decisions regarding the style and content of their writings.

Jacqueline Vansant

Involuntary and Voluntary Travel in Egon Schwarz's *Unfreiwillige Wanderjahre* and *Die japanische Mauer*

Recent scholars in a range of fields have argued for an expansion of definitions of travel, considering the subject positions of the travelers as well as the reasons for travel. Certainly the voluntary and the involuntary traveler share much as "bodies in transit" crossing borders and confronting the "other" in foreign lands. However, the impetus of the movement elicits different emotional and intellectual responses, shaped in turn by the traveler's gender, race, class, ethnicity, and age. This article focuses on three chapters of former exile Egon Schwarz's travel narrative Die japanische Mauer *in which he juxtaposes voluntary journeys with earlier involuntary travels into and in exile which also appeared in his autobiography* Unfreiwillige Wanderjahre. *The article furthermore examines where and how the experiences of voluntary and involuntary travel intersect, diverge, and merge for someone who has experienced both.*

Born in 1922 in Vienna to Jewish parents, Egon Schwarz was not yet sixteen in March 1938 when the National Socialists assumed power in Austria, turning his life upside down. He and his father fled the country in the summer to be reunited with his mother in nearby Bratislava (Pressburg), Czechoslovakia. After many harrowing experiences and via circuitous routes, the family arrived in South America where Schwarz spent a decade – from his late teens to his late twenties – in Bolivia, Chile, Ecuador, Peru, and Colombia. Schwarz writes of his travels as an exile during this period in his autobiography, which originally appeared under the title *Keine Zeit für Eichendorff. Chronik unfreiwilliger Wanderjahre* (1979) and most recently in a paperback edition as *Unfreiwillige Wanderjahre. Auf der Flucht vor Hitler durch drei Kontinente* (2005). Excerpts from the autobiography are included in his travel book *Die japanische Mauer. Ungewöhnliche Reisegeschichten* (2002).

While classical concepts of travel and exile are not usually associated with one another, recent scholars – from literary historians to anthropologists – have called for more differentiated definitions of travel. Using traditional definitions as their point of departure, the literary historian Susan L. Roberson and the anthropologist James Clifford argue against such narrow classifications. Roberson notes, "travel is traditionally seen as transformative and freeing, of promoting change for the individual and institutions because the traveler gains knowledge not only about the wider world but about the self, making the journey a double voyage of discovery".[1] And the anthropologist James Clifford writes that: " 'Travel' [...] is an inclusive term embracing a range of more or less voluntarist practices of leaving 'home' to go to some 'other' place. The displacement takes place for the purpose of gain – material, spiritual, scientific. It involves obtaining knowledge and/or having an 'experience' (exciting, edifying, pleasurable, estranging, broadening)".[2] Such definitions do not consider involuntary travel. Moreover, as Roberson and Clifford argue discussions of travel need to consider the traveler's subject positions. Roberson emphasizes, "Travel means different things to different people, depending on their reason for journeying, and their positions of gender, race, class, and ethnicity".[3] Clifford echoes Roberson with an eye to practices in cultural anthropology when he maintains:

> The long history of travel that includes spatial practices of "fieldwork" is predominantly Western-dominated, strongly male, and upper-middle class. Good critical and historical work is now appearing in the comparative domain, paying attention to political, economic, and regional contexts, as well as to the determinations and subversions of gender, class, culture, race, and individual psychology.[4]

Such assessments suggest that voluntary and involuntary travel can be seen as part of a continuum.

Just as Clifford and Roberson have made a case for a more sophisticated understanding of travel, the sociologist Erik Cohen argues that the concept of the voluntary traveler or modern tourist needs to be differentiated. He starts from a similar point of departure as Clifford and Roberson. For him, "Travelling for pleasure (as opposed to necessity) beyond the boundaries life-space assumes that there is some experience available 'out there', which cannot be found within the life-space, and which makes travel worthwhile".[5] In his preliminary phenomenology of tourist experiences, which he views as admittedly oversimplified (and which I in turn risk simplifying), he outlines five modes of tourism on a continuum. They range from the recreational to the existential mode.[6] The nexus of the traveler's center, i.e. the place from which the subject derives ultimate meaning and this place's relationship to the "life-space" determine the mode. On the one end of the scale is recreational tourism, where the tourist

---

[1] Susan L. Roberson: *Defining Travel. Diverse Visions*. Jackson: University of Mississippi 2001. P. xii.
[2] James Clifford: *Routes. Travel and Translation in the Late Twentieth Century*. Cambridge: Harvard University Press 1997. P. 66.
[3] Roberson: *Defining Travel* (n. 1). Pp. xiii-xiv.
[4] Clifford: *Routes* (n. 2). P. 66.
[5] Erik Cohen: Phenomenology of Tourist Experiences. In: Roberson: *Defining Travel* (n. 1). P. 29–55. Here: p. 33.
[6] Ibid. Pp. 33–46.

views travel as entertainment and a temporary escape from his or her center of meaning. On the other end, Cohen posits the existential mode where the traveler, alienated from the home culture, seeks meaning in an " 'elective' external centre".[7] Cohen underscores the fact that "the modes were separated for analytic purposes; any individual tourist may experience several modes on a single trip".[8] He also admits that travelers he terms "humanists" do not fit this scheme because they "entertain extremely broad concepts for 'their' culture [...]. For such people, there is no single principal 'spiritual' center: every culture is a form in which the human spirit is manifested".[9]

Certainly the voluntary traveler/tourist and the involuntary traveler share much as "bodies in transit" crossing borders and confronting the "other" in foreign lands. But if the voluntary traveler engages in travel for personal enhancement or some other "purpose of gain", the involuntary traveler or refugee leaves home as a matter of necessity and is very likely ill prepared for the journey. Consequently, the impetus of the movement elicits different emotional and intellectual responses, shaped in turn by the traveler's gender, race, class, ethnicity, and I would add age. While the voluntary or unencumbered traveler may experience the displacement as enriching, the involuntary traveler most likely experiences it at least initially as a diminishment of self.[10]

What then does voluntary and involuntary travel mean for someone who has experienced both? Where might such a traveler find himself within Cohen's phenomenology? Egon Schwarz's autobiography and his travel book provide a specific example. With the spotlight on the self in his autobiography, the author includes intense emotional reactions to different stages of the journey from "home" to exile, marking fundamental differences between voluntary and involuntary travel. Throughout he reflects on the profound influence that the exile experience had upon him. In contrast, in his travel book, which he contends is "ein 'leichtes' Buch", the author focuses on the act of traveling, situating his journeys as an exile within a larger complex of his travels over fifty years, playing down the (emotional) impact of involuntary travel.[11] By focusing narrowly on the author's juxtaposing of involuntary travels with later voluntary journeys in the chapters "Grenzüberschreitungen", "Schiffsreisen", and "Reisen in Latein Amerika" from *Die japanische Mauer*, I pinpoint and examine where

---

[7] Ibid. P. 42.
[8] Ibid. P. 45.
[9] Ibid. P. 45.
[10] See León Grinberg and Rebeca Grinberg: *Psychoanalytic Perspectives on Migration and Exile*. New Haven: Yale University Press 1989. They discuss exile as a traumatic experience.
[11] Egon Schwarz. *Die japanische Mauer. Ungewöhnliche Reisegeschichten*. Siegen: Carl Böschen Verlag P. 7.

and how the experiences of voluntary and involuntary travel intersect, diverge, and merge for someone who has experienced both. I consider the extent to which Schwarz's dual perspectives as refugee-traveler and pleasure traveler challenge traditional definitions of travel and fashion his depictions in the first three of sixteen chapters. I argue that Schwarz's exile experiences shaped him as a traveler, travel writer, and an intellectual and that his later travels influenced the ways in which he weaves his stories of travel as a refugee-traveler and pleasure traveler together, revealing him to be a "humanist" traveler.

Crossing Borders – Negotiating Boundaries

In both fiction and travel literature border crossings have been a frequent metaphor signifying inner journeys.[12] However, neither in his autobiography nor travel book does Schwarz view border crossings in metaphorical terms. The dangers that borders pose for the refugee are too immediate, the arbitrary annoyances facing the harmless traveler too trivial to use this trope. Schwarz reveals border crossings as places of negotiation between unequal power configurations – for the voluntary traveler it may bring frustration or mild satisfaction, for the refugee the success or failure of the interaction may be a matter of life and death.

In his autobiography Schwarz describes how he felt when he left Vienna in 1938 as he neared the border with Czechoslovakia – the first in his odyssey and he captures a fundamental difference between involuntary and voluntary travel. "Ununterscheidbar mischte sich in heiß aufwallenden Regungen die Liebe zu dem Verlorenen, die Scham und Empörung über den kläglichen Abgang, den einem die Heimat bereitete, und die Erleichterung, sich nun aus diesen lebensgefährlich gewordenen Verstrickungen lösen zu können".[13] The voluntary traveler may be nervous, somewhat uneasy before starting a longer trip, but she does not suffer the sense of loss and shame the youth felt as he left Austria. The young traveler's range of emotions also extends to fear and hope, both tied to the uncertainty of his position as a refugee:

> Aber auch die neue Zukunft [...] begann nun mächtig zu wirken, meldete ihr Herannahen durch Furcht und Hoffnung an. Die Hoffnung blieb nebelhaft undeutlich. Sie bezog sich auf ein 'besseres' Leben irgendwo in einem freien Land, wo unsereins geduldet war und unbehelligt seinen – sagen wir ruhig: Freuden nachgehen durfte. Die

---

[12] In the introduction to *Temperamental Journeys. Essays on the Modern Literature of Travel* (Athens: University of Georgia Press 1992), the editor Michael Kowalewski notes: "Travel writing involves border crossings both literal and figurative" (P. 7). See George Van Den Abbeele: *Travel as Metaphor from Montaigne to Rousseau*. Minneapolis: University of Minnesota Press 1992.

[13] Egon Schwarz: *Unfreiwillige Wanderjahre. Auf der Flucht vor Hitler durch drei Kontinente*. München: Beck Verlag P. 59.

Furcht war aber ganz konkret: Würde es gelingen, die Grenze zu überschreiten?! Denn uns fehlte das Lebenselixier, von dem damals – in einem den meisten heutigen Menschen unvorstellbaren Maß – Sein oder Nichtsein abhingen: ein Visum.[14]

For the refugee the hopes and fears of travel are not invested with any expectation of spiritual gain or knowledge the trip might bring. Rather they are immediate, having to do with physical survival.

The emotional impact of fleeing finds its expression in the opening of the author's travel book even it if is not obvious to readers unfamiliar with Schwarz's life story. By beginning his travel book with the chapter "Grenzüberschreitungen" and his emotions when crossing national borders, Schwarz intimates some earlier possible traumatic experience. "Wenn ich an eine Grenze komme, befällt mich ein Unbehagen, ein widriges Empfinden".[15] The complexity and intensity of Schwarz's emotions expressed in the autobiography are relativized by later border crossings described and the author appears less intensely emotional. What remains of the turmoil is a sense of ill ease which he confronts intellectually.

The experiences of Schwarz the refugee-traveler and Schwarz the pleasure or unencumbered traveler lead him to analyze the nature of borders and wish for utopian alternatives. Rather than tell readers why he feels uneasy crossing borders, Schwarz provides a short discourse on humiliations travelers suffer at borders and the ultimate futility of borders; he believes criminal elements will find ways of transgressing national boundaries and he arrives at the conclusion, "Nur harmlose Reisende und aus ihrer Heimat Vertriebene sind betroffen, nur ihretwegen ist der ganze Apparat aufgebaut".[16] Despite the extreme differences facing the voluntary and involuntary traveler at any border, Schwarz connects the experiences through exaggeration and he marks the two positions from which he will be narrating his tales of border crossings. Yet he once again defers sharing the reason for his ill ease before relating any stories of border crossings. Indeed, he introduces his philosophical stance towards borders and is simultaneously resigned to the status quo and forward-looking:

> Ich wüsste freilich nicht zu sagen, wie man die Grenzen abschaffen könnte, ebensowenig wie die Staaten, die ja die Ursache des ganzen Aufwands sind. Man muss sie einfach hinnehmen wie so vieles Ungemach, in das man hineingeboren wird, die Eiseskälten des Winters, die übermäßigen Sommerhitzen und überhaupt die vielen Unzuträglichkeiten der Natur, gegen die man sich durch Abhärtung und Anpassung, durch kleine Listen und Geduld schützt, so gut es geht.[17]

[14] Ibid. Pp. 59–60.
[15] *Die japanische Mauer*. P. 9.
[16] Ibid. P. 10.
[17] Ibid.

Schwarz's thoughts are rooted in his experiences as a transgressor of national borders as both a refugee and world traveler. Speaking from the position of the voluntary traveler, Schwarz shares his personal recipe, a practical solution for dealing with the frustration of crossing borders. He compares them to weather phenomena, which one learns to tolerate over time. Remembering his experiences as a refugee, he reminds us of the human agency behind the creation of borders, implying that the hope of change exists:

> Aber man sollte dabei nicht vergessen, dass es sich bei dem tyrannischen Firlefanz der Grenzen in bedeutsamem Gegensatz zu natürlichen Unbilden um Menschenwerk handelt. Indem man den Protest gegen das Unwürdige und Widersinnige lebendig hält und womöglich an die Kinder weitergibt, hilft man vielleicht doch den Tag vorbereiten, an dem die Willkür solcher Abkapselung verschwindet.[18]

From the melded perspective of voluntary and involuntary traveler, Schwarz maintains that if something is the creation of humans, we have the potential, and Schwarz might add, the duty to seek a change or at least imagine change. He suggests that the seeds to action and change lie in utopian thought:

> Die Lösung wäre das Zusammenleben von Menschen verschiedener Kultur ohne Staaten. Der Einwurf gegen solche Vorstellungen, das sei Utopie, der bei der neuen Utopiefeindlichkeit nicht ausbleiben kann, braucht einen nicht zu schrecken. Ohne Zukunftsentwürfe kommt die Menschheit nicht aus. Freilich sind die Grenzen noch das geringste Übel des nationalstaatlichen Prinzips, das die Welt schon mehrmals an den Rand der Vernichtung gebracht hat, und solange es seine Geltung behält, wird es auch Grenzen geben. Dass es dennoch nicht sinnlos ist, seine Stimme gegen die ärgsten Missbräuche zu erheben, dass Vereinfachungen und Erleichterungen beim Passieren von einem Land ins andere möglich sind, beweist der oft radikale Wandel, der sich in manchen Teilen der Welt abgespielt hat, wenn auch leider keineswegs überall.[19]

What begins as a resigned view evolves into a call for protest and finally a demand for a utopian perspective. In a world in which nationalism continues to be a threat to humankind, Schwarz views it as necessary to consider alternatives.

After his discourse on the nature of national demarcations the author turns to stories of actual border crossings. In his tales he highlights the arbitrary behavior of border guards he has experienced and provides examples of his or his companions' efforts to undermine the guards' authority. Sandwiching the story of his flight from post-Anschluss Austria and Europe between these tales, Schwarz underscores fundamental differences between negotiating national borders for the unencumbered traveler as opposed to the refugee. For example,

---
[18] Ibid.
[19] Ibid. P. 11.

having arrived by ship in Göteborg, the author and his wife were unpleasantly surprised when the Swedish border guards announced that they, the parents, could enter the country, but not their offspring as the children's photographs had been crossed out on the family passport. While the guards' pedantic commitment to rules seems ridiculous, it is ultimately little more than bothersome. "Zwei Tage waren verloren, es hatte Geld gekostet, man war in Sorge gewesen, hatte den Ärger verbeißen müssen".[20] Schwarz provides a counter example. In 1938, had the Czechoslovakian guards not been willing to break the rules – albeit because of bribery – the author might not be alive today. "Die Beamten waren mit Geld und guten Worten zur momentanen Versäumnis ihrer Berufspflicht gebracht worden und hatten gerade dadurch ihrer Menschenpflicht genügt".[21] Schwarz suggests limited possibilities of responding to the arbitrariness and the inhumanity of the borders by taking matters into one's own hands. While this may result in humorous tales in the case of the hapless traveler, it is a dangerous and chancy endeavor for the refugee. Later he and his parents escape from the no man's land between Czechoslovakia and Hungary when his mother's brother smuggles them out.[22] Had they been caught, they would most likely have been murdered or perished.

After relating any number of border crossings – annoying, humorous, and dangerous – the author closes the inaugural chapter of his travel book with a utopian moment reminding readers of his hopeful vision of a borderless world he voices earlier. He and his wife cross the border between Germany and the Netherlands on an evening walk with relatives without being aware of doing so. They experience the border as invisible and consequently lacking all the frustrations associated with border crossings. "Kein Zaun, keine Schranke behinderte unseren Weg. Wir hatten keine Ausweise mit, wir wurden nicht angehalten, mussten nichts vorzeigen, sind nicht befragt, nicht gezählt und nicht verzollt worden. Die Grenze war unkenntlich, geräuschlos, unsichtbar, nicht vorhanden. So sollten sie alle sein".[23] The placement of this story at the end of the first chapter of a travel book is hardly coincidental. While Schwarz does not relate his stories in chronological fashion, its position at chapter's close serves as a counterbalance to the opening and suggests that the crossing took place in a postwar democratic Europe. The virtual disappearance of borders within the European Union in recent times contrasts to the almost impenetrable borders of the Third Reich Schwarz "negotiated" as a youth with his parents.

---

[20] Ibid. P. 12.
[21] See *Die japanische Mauer*. P. 16; *Unfreiwillige Wanderjahre*. P. 60.
[22] *Die japanische Mauer*. P. 18.
[23] Ibid. Pp. 24–25.

The former refugee and world traveler, who has experienced borders as both an insidious manifestation and a bothersome invention of the nation-state, does not view the crossing of borders from one country to another as the marker of any type of personal transformation. By describing the shifting of national borders, their disappearance and appearance according to political exigencies, Schwarz points to their constructed nature. He also implies that their disappearance can only be viewed positively if they cease to be an expression of nationalism. The shifting and disappearing borders in 1938 resulting from racist and extreme nationalist policies naturally called forth fear. In contrast, the author hails the development of a democratic Europe and the borderless borders between countries.

Sea Travel – Contemplating Spaces

In contrast to national borders, which pose radically different challenges for the refugee-traveler and the pleasure traveler, the ship as a transitional space provided Schwarz the refugee-traveler and pleasure traveler with merging experiences. For him, sea travel creates a space removed from state boundaries with the potential to transform the traveler. For Schwarz the refugee-traveler the ship proved a temporary escape from his worries; the young exile's first ocean crossing brought relief from the disorienting displacement and alienation, and it opened up new worlds for him. For Schwarz the unfettered traveler, sea travel offers escape from daily obligations, room to think and write. Consequently, just as his feelings of ill ease when crossing national boundaries have their origins in his traumatic experiences as a refugee, so too does his positive attitude toward sea travel relate back to his first Atlantic voyage when he and his parents were fleeing Europe. Indeed, the two particularly memorable sea voyages Schwarz includes in his autobiography and travel book – his first sea voyage from France to Chile[24] and a later trip up the western coast of South America from Valparaiso to Guayaquil[25] – become the yardstick against which subsequent sea travel is measured. However, as in the first chapter, Schwarz does not relate his stories in chronological fashion nor does he immediately divulge the source of his positive feelings, but inserts them into a general discussion of sea travel and multiple ocean crossings.

If myriad border crossings appear to ameliorate the author's traumatic experiences crossing national borders as a refugee, the stories of his many sea voyages serve to underscore the author's positive attitude toward the mode of transportation in *Die japanische Mauer*. By juxtaposing trips on transatlantic carriers, freighters, and pleasure cruises with his first trip on a freighter for

---

[24] *Unfreiwillige Wanderjahre*. Pp. 78–83; *Die japanische Mauer*. Pp. 33–37.
[25] *Unfreiwillige Wanderjahre*. Pp. 162–163; *Die japanische Mauer*. Pp. 29–31.

refugees, the author amplifies his original impressions of the experience of sea travel. For him, the mode of transportation fosters the creation of a transitional space seemingly outside of time, a place where the refugee may find temporary relief from the worries associated with exile and the pleasure traveler can enjoy the escape from daily pressures. The author experiences the ship as an almost exterritorial space, neither here nor there, a space ideally suited for contemplation. "Nichts fördert meine Kontemplation mehr, als an der Reeling zu stehen, in den ewig gleichen, ewig wechselnden Gang der Wellen zu schauen, den Blick auf die endlose Weite des Ozeans und des Himmels zu richten oder dem steigenden, fallenden Horizont zu folgen [...]".[26] For the narrator who has experienced borders as both refugee-traveler and unencumbered traveler, the absence of borders, indeed, of any human marker is an invitation for the imagination to run free.

Yet Schwarz does not view sea travel as removed from human influence. "Jede Meerfahrt ist anders, je nach der Größe und Beschaffenheit des Schiffes, nach der Reiseroute und Jahreszeit, der Nationalität der Mannschaft und der Häfen, die angelaufen werden, nach der Lebensphase, in der man sie macht".[27] However, despite the microcosm of society recreated on board, being surrounded by the elements, removed from the confinement of any particular constructed national boundaries, the "borders" on the ship are much more permeable than their pendants on land:

> Ganz kann sich niemand dem Einfluss der veränderten Lebensbedingungen an Bord entziehen. Sich auf allen Seiten von den Elementen umgeben wissend, lassen die Passagiere manche von den Konventionen fallen, die sie an Land zum Schutz ihrer gefährdeten Gesellschaftsexistenz und verletzlichen Psyche aufgebaut haben, sie werden aufgeschlossener, mitteilungswilliger, und so kommt es, dass sich Bekanntschaften anbahnen und Beziehungen knüpfen, die oft weit über die Zeit der gemeinsamen Reise hinausreichen.[28]

Indeed, Schwarz views the absence of national and the occasional permeability of class borders as positive aspects of sea travel, particularly when he relates – not in chronological order – his flight to South America in 1939 and a voyage along the countries on the Pacific coast of South America from the 1940s. The journeys offered the poor young traveler the opportunity to meet people from all walks of life. Of the passengers on the refugee ship, he writes:

> Da waren die rauchenden, schnell schwatzenden Chilenen, die schachspielenden Kubaner, jeder ein kleiner Capablanca, und die wohlerzogenen jüdischen Matronen

[26] *Die japanische Mauer*. P. 28.
[27] Ibid. P. 29.
[28] Ibid. P. 28.

aus Köln und Frankfurt, die norddeutschen Doktoren und Universitätsdozenten, die sich des gepflegten Intellektuellenidioms bedienten, und bayrische Naturburschen mit ihrem breiten Dialekt, die, weiß Gott wie, mit den Nazis in Konflikt geraten waren, Ostjuden aus dem galizischen Städtel, verarmte österreichische Aristokraten, die sich noch an ein Restchen Vornehmheit klammerten, und Leute, die mit unsauberen Gefängnissen und der erbarmungslosen Fremdenpolizei aller Länder Bekanntschaft gemacht hatten. Und jeder wusste nicht nur einen, sondern viele Romane zu erzählen.[29]

The colorful group gathered on board must have been fascinating for the young Schwarz. As living novels, they provided the future literary scholar with the opportunity to observe and interact with a cross-section of society he might otherwise never have encountered. And on the trip down the South American coast he met members of a traveling circus as well as Juan Seoane, later known as the Peruvian Dostoevsky. Crossing the Atlantic a Spanish engineer taught him Spanish and on the trip up the South American coast, Schwarz slipped into first class where he played chess with a member of the Salesian Order. When he concludes his story of his first sea voyage, he asks, "Woanders als auf einem Schiff findet sich so vielfältige Gesellschaft zusammen?"[30] and when he closes the tale of the voyage down the South American coast, he comments, "Ich will nicht behaupten, dass solche Erlebnisse nur auf Schiffen möglich sind, aber die partielle Aufhebung der normalen Gesellschaftsordnung, die dort zuweilen statthat, erleichtern [sic] sie".[31] The ship as a vessel in transit has the potential for being a transitional and transformative space for both the refugee-traveler and pleasure or unencumbered traveler. Not only does the ship transport its contents from one place to another much of its time outside of national borders, but the situation on board promotes interactions which are less likely to transpire on land.

While Schwarz derives great personal pleasure from sea travel, he reminds readers of the long tentacles of humans' inhumanity. In contrast to the first chapter "Grenzüberschreitungen", which he concludes with a hopeful border crossing, the author closes the second chapter "Schiffsreisen" on a more ambiguous note – his flight from Europe to South America in a refugee ship. As he writes, "Nicht alle Schiffsreisen sind allerdings reiner Spass. Zu den weniger glücklichen gehörte schon meine allererste, und damit meine ich weder Sturm noch Seekrankheit, das meiste Ungemach auf Erden kommt von den lieben Mitmenschen".[32] Just as borders are a human creation, so was the reason for the existence of the refugee ship and the cruelty to which the refugee-passengers were subjected.

[29] Ibid. Pp. 36–37.
[30] Ibid. P. 37.
[31] Ibid. P. 31.
[32] Ibid. P. 33.

Consequently, in both the autobiography and travel book Schwarz underscores how one person can experience the same trip in multiple ways. In both he highlights the two very different subject positions from which he perceived his first trip. First, he relates how as a youth he experienced the trip as an adventure:

> Die Überfahrt, die einen ganzen Monat dauerte, setzte sich aus den verschiedensten Impressionen zusammen, die letztlich zwei Wahrnehmungssphären angehörten. Eine dieser Erlebnisschichten war die abenteuerliche Durchmessung zweier Weltmeere, aufgenommen mit der jugendlichen Erlebnisfreude eines Heranwachsenden, die erregende Insularität eines Ozeandampfers, winziges Molekül der Menschenwelt in einem fremden Element [...].[33]

Certainly, life on board opened up new vistas for the teenager. In spite of this, he does not fail to see it from a very different side, that of refugee:

> Die mehrwöchige Fahrt hatte aber noch eine zweite, der ersten ziemlich unähnliche Seite. Man befand sich, unverkennbar, auf einem Emigrantenschiff, das aus einem Frachter der plötzlichen Konjunktur zuliebe notdürftig zur Beförderung von großen Menschenmengen hergerichtet worden war. Wir fuhren in der untersten Klasse und durften das keinen Augenblick vergessen: das Essen war nahezu ungenießbar, die Schlafsäle und Kabinen waren tief im Schiffsbauch versteckt und, seit man in tropischen Gewässern fuhr, erfüllt von einer dampfenden Hitze. Das bedienende Personal beggenete uns mit unverblümter Verachtung. Der Kapitän soll gesagt haben, er bedaure die Länder, in die sich der menschliche Inhalt seines Schiffes entladen würde.[34]

Reflecting on the trip as a member of the refugee community, Schwarz highlights the physical discomforts and numerous humiliations which separated him and his fellow exiles from the crew. Nevertheless, these are outweighed by the adventure and the "worlds" the young traveler was exposed to. Indeed, his negative sentiments seem an intellectual response rather than emotional residue of the unpleasant side of the trip, for he closes this episode on a positive note, "So begann meine Freundschaft mit Schiffen und der See, und ich hoffe, dass sie noch manche Fortsetzung erleben wird".[35]

If human agency is highlighted in the author's feelings towards borders, the power of nature over human agency captures the author's imagination when discussing sea travel. In his autobiography Schwarz relates the story of the

---

[33] *Die japanische Mauer.* P. 34. The corresponding section in *Unfreiwillige Wanderjahre* is slightly different. See Pp. 79–80.
[34] *Die japanische Mauer.* P. 35. The corresponding section in *Unfreiwillige Wanderjahre* again varies slightly. See P. 81.
[35] *Die japanische Mauer.* P. 38.

storm he experienced when crossing the Atlantic for the first time. "Immer höher ging die See, im berüchtigten Golf von Biscaya tobte ein regelrechter Sturm, der das gewaltige Fahrzeug zur sprichwörtlichen Nußschale machte".[36] In his travel book the "proverbial nutshell" of his autobiography is transformed into a symbol of human civilization:

> Die sprichwörtliche Nussschale, die auf alle Launen des Meeres reagiert, die sanften wie die heftigen, wird einem zum gesteigerten Sinnbild der menschlichen Zivilisation, die ja aus nichts anderem besteht, als dem ewigen Versuch, sich teils durch vernünftiges Nachgeben, teils durch berechneten Widerstand gegen die fürchterliche, oft zerstörerische Gleichgültigkeit der Natur durchzusetzen.[37]

The image of the ship bobbing on the sea like a nutshell hardly seems comforting. But when seen within the context of the chapter and the recollections of the storm related in the autobiography, a positive connotation emerges. On the crossing in 1939 he was unaffected by the violent storm which overtook the ship. "Einsam, aber stolz thronte ich, von der Seekrankheit unangefochten, als einziger Eßlustiger in dem leeren Speisesaal".[38] The author who was able to ride the storm in the Gulf of Biscaya resembles the nutshell – he not only keeps afloat, but he does not suffer from sea sickness and rides the storm triumphant, enjoying the additional freedom to explore – this against all odds. If humans create nations and borders, the power of nature over human enterprise, while "terrifying", can nonetheless be comforting. For Schwarz, the sea is an equalizer treating the refugee-traveler and pleasure traveler alike.

Travels in South America – Experiencing Adventure and Confounding Difference

In the chapter "Grenzüberschreitungen", the author delineates between his earlier border encounters as a refugee and later ones as an unencumbered traveler. And in "Schiffsreisen" it is obvious that the author's first transatlantic voyage aboard a ship full of refugees favorably shaped his attitude toward sea travel. However, in the third chapter "Reisen in Latein Amerika" the exile experience disappears almost completely. When Schwarz turns his attention to trips taken in South America in his youth from 1939–1949 and later as a mature adult, only once does he explicitly mention the reason for his first encounter with the continent. Of a trip to Santiago, he writes:

> In Santiago hielt ich dann die Vorträge, um derentwillen wir nach Chile gekommen waren. Im Hause des Direktors des Goethe-Instituts fand danach ein Empfang statt.

---

[36] *Unfreiwillige Wanderjahre.* P. 80.
[37] *Die japanische Mauer.* P. 28.
[38] *Unfreiwillige Wanderjahre.* P. 80.

Es wurden Speisen angeboten, und ich war gerade dabei, ein Wachtelei aufzuspießen, als mir wie ein Blitz die Erleuchtung kam, dass ich auf den Tag genau vor fünfzig Jahren als halbwüchsiger Junge auf der Flucht vor dem europäischen Faschismus in Chile an Land gegangen war.[39]

The sudden recollection of his first arrival in Chile appears the ideal opportunity for the author to share reflections or knowledge gained. Though, even as he bites into his "madeleine", he is not overcome by a rush of emotions and lost memories, but only a sudden recognition of his first-time arrival in Chile. This suggests that on the one hand there is little to connect the ways in which the refugee turned émigré and the unencumbered traveler experienced South America and that on the other hand only the physical challenges of travel there remained the same.

A comparison between the author's descriptions of his travels in South America in the travel book with the related passages in his autobiography reveals the divergent perspectives of the exile and the tourist. Moreover, the placement in the respective texts and lack of discussion of the confrontation with the other in the travel book begs for a closer examination. In the introductory paragraph to "Reisen in Latein Amerika", Schwarz explains that the term Latin America is a "Sammelbegriff", a collective term for very different countries.[40] He then turns to Bolivia at "the roof of the world", where he arrived in the late thirties and proceeds to relate his first trip to La Paz, where everything appeared strange to him:

> *Alles kommt einem fremd vor*, sogar das Angebot auf den Märkten, mit den Chirimoyas, der Quinoa, einer Art Getreide, dem Chuño, gegorenen Kartoffeln, Tierembryos zu Kulturzwecken, den getrockneten Coca-Blättern. [...] *Fremd sind auch die Gerüche*, in denen sich die primitiven hygienischen Verhältnisse zu erkennen geben, sowie der Rauch der vielen offenen, mit Lamadung und Tundragehölz unterhaltenen Feuer; die Geräusche der melancholischen Indianermusik, die zuerst monoton und enervierend wirkt, die man aber nie wieder aus dem Organismus verliert, wenn man sie längere Zeit Nacht für Nacht gehört hat; [...] *Fremd sind vor allem die Menschen*.[41]

We learn only that the melancholy music of the indigenous peoples works its way into his being. The author does not elaborate on the foreignness, nor does he relate how he responded to it. Rather, he follows this with a brief description of the indigenous peoples and then begins with the stories of his travel adventures. And finally, the author closes the chapter with a brief summary of the countries visited:

> Bolivien, wildzerklüftetes Indianerland hoch in den Anden, Chile, Argentinien, Kolumbien, Perú, Ecuador oder eben Costa Rica. Vielgestaltiger Kontinent

---

[39] *Die japanische Mauer.* P. 50.
[40] Ibid. P. 39.
[41] Emphasis mine. *Die japanische Mauer.* P. 40; For the corresponding text in *Unfreiwillige Wanderjahre* see P. 86.

> Lateinamerika, welche Adjektive passen auf ihn? Exotisch, prähistorisch, zukünftig, traumhaft, brutal, verzaubert? Ich glaube, es passen alle. Mich zieht es immer noch hin, weil die neokapitalistische Dampfwalze dort noch nicht in alle Ecken gedrungen ist. Aber man muss sich beeilen, sonst kommt man auch hier zu spät.[42]

While this somewhat nostalgic description of South America is drawn from the autobiography, it contrasts significantly with the emotionally charged counterpart found in the author's life story. In *Die japanische Mauer* he emphasizes the countries' attraction in the oppositions and fears capitalism will level them. In contrast, when Schwarz, the autobiographer, introduces the "new world" to readers at the beginning of section III "Neue Welt" with parts of the same passage, he emphasizes the alienation and displacement he felt and observed in other émigrés:

> Bolivien, wildzerklüftetes Indianerland hoch in den Anden, in dem ich zum Mann herangewachsen bin, Chile, Ecuador, Perú, Kolumbien: Südamerika, vielgestalteter Kontinent, wo ich *in feindseliger Liebe und intimer Fremdheit* mehr als zehn Jahre zugebracht habe, welche Adjektive werden seiner Unvergleichlichkeit gerecht? Exotisch, prähistorisch, zukünftig, traumhaft, brutal, verzaubert? Wie *nichtssagend* sind doch alle diese Ausdrücke seiner unerschöpflichen Außerordentlichkeit, seinem überwältigenden Anderssein gegenüber. Wie begierig bin ich, Rechenschaft abzulegen und doch verzage ich vor dieser unlösbaren Aufgabe.[43]

What happened to the "feindselige Liebe" and the "intime Fremdheit" when the author turns to his travels in Latin America in *Die japanische Mauer*? Why do the adjectives once found inadequate to capture the place's otherness now suit? Why the change?

The difference in genre offers one explanation for the absence of introspection found in the autobiography. In keeping with the remarks in the introduction to *Die japanische Mauer*, Schwarz reveals little of his thoughts on the role of confrontations with the foreign other on personal change:

> Der Verfasser hat ein Jahrzehnt in der sogenannten Dritten Welt gelebt und weiß, was Elend, Ungerechtigkeit und Unterdrückung sind. Von diesen Dingen ist höchst indirekt die Rede. Über die sozialen Verhältnisse der erwähnten Länder kann der Leser aus mancherlei Bemerkungen seine Schlüsse ziehen, aber auf Reflexionen wurde bewusst verzichtet, es sollten in der Regel nur die unmittelbaren Erlebnisse des Reisenden zur Sprache kommen.[44]

If the travel writer sees a connection only in the adventurous nature of travel the absence of the mixed emotions of an earlier era makes sense. Indeed, the refugee turned émigré experienced the displacement very differently than the

---

[42] *Die japanische Mauer*. P. 57.
[43] Emphasis mine. *Unfreiwillige Wanderjahre*. P. 84.
[44] *Die japanische Mauer*. P. 7.

unencumbered traveler. I would argue that exactly because the confrontations with the otherness of South America had been transformational for Schwarz as refugee turned émigré that Schwarz the travel writer shows reserve in making pronouncements about his confrontations with the foreign other.

Looking back at an uncertain time of his life, Schwarz as autobiographer captures the alienation he and others felt:

> Nicht nur daran muß man sich gewöhnen, fast nichts ist, wie man es kennt, weder in der Gesellschaft noch in der Natur. Wer mitteleuropäische Maßstäbe an das Gesehene, Erlebte anlegt, wird es nie verstehen. Und dennoch bleibt einem nichts anderes übrig, als sich eines in Europa ausgebildeten Wahrnehmungs- und Erkenntnisapparates zu bedienen, Erwartungen und Vorstellungen einer völlig anderen Kultur auf das neu auf einen Zutretende anzuwenden. Darin besteht das Dilemma. Es wird Jahre dauern, ehe sich aus dem Mitgebrachten und dem Vorgefundenen ein übergreifendes, weitere Bereiche der menschlichen Erfahrung erfassendes Bewußtsein herausgebildet hat.[45]

Schwarz both understands the state of alienation he and many exiles felt and can examine it critically.[46] Among other things he gained the realization that a deeper understanding of the foreign other is the result of an extended process.

The different frames of reference between the travel book and the autobiography in the presentation of South America not only remind readers of the radically different experiences of the voluntary versus the involuntary traveler, but reveal much about the author as traveler and travel writer. Schwarz evolves into Erik Cohen's "humanist traveler" or tourist. Schwarz does not derive meaning from a particular place, but looks for the manifestations of the human spirit in every culture.[47] As he describes in his autobiography, his experiences have led him to feel at home nowhere and everywhere:

> So aber war ich weder das eine noch das andere, ich habe das eine nicht aufgegeben und das andere nicht erwerben können, und bin bis zur Stunde jemand geblieben, der im Grunde nirgends und in einem anderen Sinn wieder überall zu Hause ist. Auf dieser Doppeldefinition meiner Zugehörigkeit möchte ich aber bestehen, denn die Feststellung meines Mangels an Verwurzeltsein in einem religiösen, nationalen oder

---

[45] *Unfreiwillige Wanderjahre*. Pp. 85–86.
[46] See Leo Spitzer: *Hotel Bolivia. The Culture of Memory in a Refuge from Nazism*. New York: Hill and Wang 1998. In his introduction he writes, "the refugees' preconceptions brought from Central Europe impeded deeper cross-cultural exploration, cultural stereotypes also influenced perceptions of *mestizo* and 'white' Bolivians and affected their relations with immigrant Jews" (p. xiv). For an insightful examination of the role the European lens played in German and Austrian Jewish exiles' experiences in Bolivia, see particularly chapter 3: "Invisible Baggage".
[47] Paraphrase of Cohen: (n. 5). P. 45.

philosophischen Gefüge mit allen Nachteilen, die ein solches Fehlen und Freischweben in sich birgt, wäre einseitig ohne die ergänzende Erkenntnis der großen geistigen und emotionalen Vorzüge dieses Zustands.[48]

The author eschews any form of national identity and he feels Jewish in that he belongs to a community of people who shared a similar fate. In contrast, he views himself as a conglomerate. "Am richtigsten wäre es wahrscheinlich zu sagen, daß ich von allen diesen kulturellen und psychologischen Konfigurationen etwas in mir trage".[49] To Austrian, American, and Jew, we could add refugee-traveler, émigré, and unencumbered traveler, intellectual, husband and father. These meld together to form the humanist traveler, the narrator of *Die japanische Mauer*. The brief encounters of the pleasure traveler or humanist tourist with the other may result in awe of historical treasures (India), the recognition of the impact of colonialism (Latin America), the discomfort with social extremes (India), or awareness of racism (Israel). They may lead Schwarz, the travel writer, to reveal a general recognition of the richness of the human spirit. They, however, do not lead to a questioning or realignment of his center of meaning.

Conclusion

Schwarz's journeys as an exile shaped him as a traveler and a travel writer. His experiences resulted in his willingness to travel with little or no money, an ability to travel under extreme circumstances, a desire to see the peripheries and out-of-the-way places, and openness to trips with serendipitous experiences. However, in *Die japanische Mauer* Schwarz does not concentrate on the experiences of flight and exile, nor does he arrange the chapters in a strict chonological order. Nonetheless, the initial chapters of his compendium possess a logical progression tied to the author's experiences of travel into and in exile. Moreover, the juxtaposition of narrator's travels as the refugee- and émigré-traveler illustrates the importance of these years in his life as a traveler and intellectual. While Schwarz describes humorous adventures arising because of cultural differences, there is little room for analysis of them and reflection. As the former émigré, he realizes that to reach a deeper understanding he would need years to develop insight into the country. As the travel writer, his confrontations with the other often provide him cause for amusement or contemplation, and a means for poking fun at himself and cultural differences. And the juxtaposition of his voluntary and involuntary travels offer him the opportunity to restate convictions won in exile.

---

[48] *Unfreiwillige Wanderjahre*. P. 117.
[49] Ibid. P. 232.

Index

Abschied: Ernstes und Heiteres aus einer Familienpension (R. Siodmak), 209
Aciman, A., 12, 31
Adorno, T.W., 29, 31, 169, 201, 208, 219, 220
Albrecht, F., 284
Allemann, E., 118, 124, 129
Americké Houpačky (Hoffmeister), 180, 199
Améry, J., 73, 83–85, 87, 88, 90, 92–93, 173
"An American Soldier Visiting His Former Homeland" (K. Mann), 153, 170
Anders, G., 42, 172
Animals are in Cages, The (Hoffmeister), 177, 179, 183
Arendt, E., 45, 46, 131
Arendt, H., 42, 174
Argentinisches Wochenblatt, 118
Argonautenschiff, Das (Seghers), 292
Askenasy, L., 252
Assmann, A., 163, 173
Assmann, J., 156–157
"Aufgabe der Kunst, Die" (Seghers), 309
Aufstand der Fischer von Santa Barbara, Der (Seghers), 285
Ausflug der toten Mädchen, Der (Seghers), 49, 292, 297–311
Ausflüge (Seghers), 283
Ayguesparse, A., 79

Bachmann, I., 48
Bakhtin, M., 160–161
Bang, H., 352
Barr, D., 199
Barta-Mickl, E., 119
Bauchwitz, K., 70–72
Baudrillard, J., 26
Bäume am Rio de la Plata (Zech), 121

Belgischer Rundfunk., 74
Benjamin, W., 168, 169, 298, 307, 334
Benn, G., 93
Berend Fock (Blunck), 224
Berg, A., 249, 270
Berliner, A., 243
Berliner Börsen-Zeitung, 268
Berliner Kindheit um neunzehnhundert (Benjamin), 168
Betz, A., 77
Bhabha, H.K., 290
Blamberger, G., 102
Blaukopf, K., 244, 262
Bloch, E., 49, 169
Blunck, H.F., 223–238
Boccioni, U., 303
Bogner, D., 247
Borges, L., 130
Boucher, M., 232, 233, 234–235, 238
Bowles, P., 22
ter Braak, M., 40
Bradbury, M., 16
Brandt, M., 85
Brauner, A., 220, 222
Brecht, B., 24–25, 40, 42, 44, 45, 86, 255, 258, 349
Brenner, P., 181, 310
Breytenbach, B., 18
Brill-Czapski, A., 137–138, 148
Broch, H., 41, 42, 43, 87
Brod, M., 41
Bruckner, F., 40
Brüsseler Zeitung., 96
Buber, M., 331
Büchner, G., 251
Burkhard, H., 58n, 64n
Busoni, F., 266, 271

Caestecker, F., 74
Caplen, C., 322
Care, H., 87–88

Cargaison Blanche/Le Chemin de Rio
  (R. Siodmak), 211, 221
Carr, H., 88n
Casals, P., 265, 273, 279
Césaire, A., 294
Chiune, S., 62
Claudet, A., 81–82
Clifford, J., 11, 24, 314–315, 327, 369–370
Cohen, E., 370–371, 383
Coleridge, S.T., 15
Combat, 94
Comité France-Allemagne, 234, 236, 238
Comité de vigilance des intellectuals antifascists, 95
Copland, A., 277
Cordan, W., 360
Criss Cross (R. Siodmak), 218, 219
Cry of the City (R. Siodmak), 217
Czapska, I., 140–141, 147, 150

Darwish, M., 26
Decision, 354
Depression is Over, The (R. Siodmak), 211
Deutschland, Dein Tänzer ist der Tod (Zech), 120
Deutsch-Französische Monatshefte, 236
Deutschlandfunk, 83
"Deutschland und wir" (Seghers), 308
Deutsch, M., 248–249, 254, 263
De zomer van 1936, 78
Díaz, O.P., 299
Dichtung und Wahrheit (Goethe), 122
Dichterliebe (Schumann), 246
Direndberg, E., 215
Döblin, A., 38–39, 40, 41, 42, 43, 45, 49, 90, 180, 227, 362
Domville, B., 230, 231
Drach, A., 180
Dümling, A., 256–257

Ebermayer, E., 349, 351
Eckl, M., 134

Edschmid, K., 116
Elfte Reich, Das (Seghers), 283, 287–288
Elsaesser, T., 211–212
Englmann, B., 87
"Eine Theorie des Tourismus" (Enzensberger), 182
Ein spates Fest (Schlüter), 350
Eisler, H., 239–240, 254, 255–259, 262, 263
Einstein, C., 90, 93, 333
Enzensberger, H.M., 182–183
Escape from East Berlin (R. Siodmak), 205
Escape to Life (E. Mann and K. Mann), 154, 155, 362
Evans, C., 229–230, 230–231, 238
Evelein, J., 70
Exil im Exil, Das (Sahl), 48
Exkurs über den Fremden (Simmel), 283–284

Fackel, Die, 248
Fehse, W., 350
Feuchtwanger, L., 31, 40–41, 42, 43, 44, 45, 47, 180, 227, 333
FitzPatrick, J.A., 240
Flusser, V., 170
Frank, B., 41, 42
Frank, L., 41, 44
Frauen aus Haiti, Die (Seghers), 283, 294–295
Freccero, J., 28
Frei, B., 93
Freies Deutschland., 76
Freud, S., 173, 336
Friedrich, E., 80–81, 83, 95
Friedmann, J.I., 121, 129
Freytag, G., 41
Fry, V., 333
Fürst, P., 180
Fussell, P., 20, 22, 25

Galsworthy, J., 226
Gass, W.H., 12, 13

Gay, P., 295
Gegenüber von China (K. Mann), 350
van Gennep, A., 133–135, 150–151
Ghosh, A., 12
Glanz und Elend Südamerikas (Edschmid)., 116
Goebbels, J., 224
von Goethe, J.W., 122, 144, 157, 251
Goodman, D., 54
Görgen, H., 138–140
Göring, H., 342
Graf, O.M., 27, 45
Grenz-Echo., 98
Greverus, I., 162–163
grosse Fahrt, Die (Blunck), 224
Grubetsch (Seghers), 285, 286
Grünebaum, K., 74–75, 80, 83
grüne Flöte vom Rio Beni, Die (Zech), 115
Grunewald, M., 158
Gutzmann, G., 293, 310

Habe, H., 42
Hamburger, C., 136, 142, 144, 147, 150
Hamburger, H., 135, 136–137, 138, 144
Hamsun, K., 352
Harpprecht, K., 343, 345
Hasenclever, W., 331, 334, 341
Heidegger, M., 66, 67
Heine, H., 15, 246
Hellens, F., 79
Henner, H.B., 97
Herb, H., 117, 118
Hermlin, S., 344
Herzfelde, W., 117
Hewison, R., 192
Heym, S., 46
Hildesheimer, W., 99–113
Hiller, K., 40
Hiob (Roth), 252–253
Hirschfeld, M., 336
Hochheimer, W., 69
Hochzeit von Haiti, Die (Seghers), 294–295
Hoffman, E., 13–14, 19

Hoffmeister, A., 177–200
von Hofmannsthal, H., 352
Hollywood Liederbuch (Eisler), 239–240, 255, 262
Horwitz, K., 244
Hostovsky, E., 180
Huasipungo (Icasa), 117
Hübner, A., 116
Hugo, V., 74
Hulme, P., 23
von Humboldt, A., 120
Humm-Sernau, L., 333

Icasa, J., 117
Ich suchte Schmied . . . und fand Malva wieder (Zech), 121
In Stahlgewittern (Jünger), 97
Islam, S.M., 12, 22–23, 25
Israel, Nico., 16

Jalowitz, H., 244
James, H., 21
Jameux, D., 268
japanische Mauer, Die (Schwarz), 369, 371–380
Jehle, V., 102
Jewish Committee of Kobe, 62
Jezover, I., 334
Jünger, E., 97
Jüngste Deutschland, Das, 347, 349–367

Kafka, F., 20, 42, 48
Kafka, H (John)., 252, 258
von Kahler, E., 43
Kandinsky, W., 269
Kantorowicz, A., 343
Kaplan, C., 11, 13, 16–17
Karibische Geschichten (Seghers), 283, 293, 294
Katz, H.W., 40
Kauder, H., 249
Kaufman, A., 60
Kerr, A., 26–27, 30
Kesten, H., 41, 78, 81, 82, 93, 95
Keun, I., 40, 42, 78, 79, 313–327
Kiessling, W., 131

Killers, The (Siodmak), 216–217
Kind aller Länder (Keun), 79, 313–327
Kippenberg, A., 94
Kisch, E.E., 49, 78, 93, 131
Klein, H., 259
von Kleist, H., 124
Klemperer, O., 276
Knaben Wunderhorn, Des (Brentano), 245
Koepnick, L., 203, 214, 219n
Koestler, A., 42, 78
Kommunistische Arbeiter Partei Deutschlands (KDP), 331, 332, 333, 336
Kracauer, S., 30–31, 209, 217, 284, 298, 306
Kraft der Schwachen, Die (Seghers), 289
Kranzler, D.H., 54
Kraus, K., 248, 251, 261
Krebs, G., 54
Krenek, E., 261, 262, 263, 264, 276
Kreutzer, L., 66
Kühn, H., 76, 97
Kundera, M., 25
de Kusch, E., 118, 119

Landau, T., 137, 149–150
Landauer, W., 77
Land der Vulkane (Blunck), 223–224
Lang, F., 202, 203, 220, 255
Langhoff, W., 40, 333
League for the Protection of German Writers in Exile, 329, 332
Leed, E., 29
Leonce und Lena (Zeisl), 251
Leonhard, R., 329–345
Leopold III (King), 75
Leopoldi, H., 240, 242, 262
Le Rouge et le Noir, 81, 83
Lessing, G.E., 157
Liebknecht, K., 331
Lieblich, K., 135, 136, 138
Liederbuch eines fahrenden Gesellen (Mahler), 239–240, 245, 246, 248, 249, 257, 262
Ligeti, H., 85–87

Link, M., 181
Loewy, E., 355
Löhr, F., 245
London Times, 228
Lorre, P., 220
Lothar, E., 41, 44
Lotman, Y., 89–90
Low, D., 199
Löwith, K., 54, 64, 66–67, 68
von der Lühe, I., 167
Lukács, G., 41, 285
Luther, M., 157

Machlewitz, I., 314, 318
Mahler, A., 252
Mahler, G., 239–240, 243–249, 257, 261, 262, 263, 264
Mahler-Werfel, A., 38, 276
Maier, M., 142, 143, 144, 145
Maier, M.H., 144
Malouf, D., 14
Mann, E., 77, 82, 154, 155, 167
Mann, H., 17–18, 41, 43, 96, 227, 232, 235, 352, 360
Mann, K., 40, 41, 43, 47–48, 79, 153–174, 347, 349–367
Mann, T., 41, 42, 43, 44, 45, 95, 171, 229, 237, 276, 358
Marchwitza, H., 44
Marcuse, L., 40–41, 44
Martin, B., 56
Masanori, M., 54
Masante (Hildesheimer), 99–103, 108–113
Maul, H.E., 54
Marx, K., 15, 74, 116, 123
May, K., 120, 222
Mayer, H., 285, 344
McCarthy, M., 17, 30
McLeod, N., 57
Meisinger, J., 63–64
Mendelssohn, P., 347, 350–367
Mengelberg, W., 247
Menschen am Sonntag (R. Siodmak), 206–209, 211, 215, 217, 218, 220, 221

Mensching, S., 331, 335, 336
Meurer, E., 118, 119
Milhaud, D., 252
Mitscherlich, A., 174
Mitscherlich, M., 174
Mittler, F., 251
Morgenstern, S., 180
Moses and Aron (Schoenberg), 265, 267–268, 271, 274, 275, 278
Müller, W., 245
Musil, R., 41, 43n
Münzenberg, W., 78, 336
Mutter, Die (Brecht), 86
"My Public" (Schoenberg), 267

Nachdichtungen (Zech), 120
Nach Mitternacht (Keun), 313
Nachts, wenn der Teufel kam (R. Siodmak), 220–222
Naficy, H., 215–216
National Council of Jews in East Asia., 62
Nationalsozialistische Lehrervereinigung., 68
Neubert, W., 181–182
Neue Sachlichkeit, 352
Neue Verse von der Emigration (Zech), 121
Neue Weltbühne., 93
Neumann, G., 51n
Neumann, R., 27, 192
New York Times, 199
Nicholls, P., 17
Nietzsche, F., 157
Nobutaka, S., 57–58
Novaks aus Prag, Die (Leopoldi, Robitschek), 240–242, 262
Nussbaum, F., 79

Observer, The, 199
Olink, H., 93
Oliven, F., 135
Oliven, K., 135, 136, 138, 139–140, 142, 146, 148, 150
Ophüls, M., 213
Örtlichkeiten (Améry), 88, 92–93

Orpheus Trust, 263
von Ossietzky, C., 93
österreichische Heimatsfront, 85
Ould, H., 227–228, 229, 236
Ovid., 14

Pahlen, K., 251
Pansa, B., 53, 66–67
Paris über mir (Mendelssohn), 350
Park, R., 284
Parti Communiste de Belgique, 93
Paul-Bancour, J., 236
Penthesilea (Kleist), 124
Pérez, O.C., 293
Perkins, F., 277
Pethes, N., 169
Pfeffermühle, Die, 77, 82
Pierrot Lunaire (Schoenberg), 266
Pinthus, K., 129–130
Piscator, E., 252
Pringsheim, K., 61n, 66
Proust, M., 307
Pollak, R., 65
Post ins Gelobte Land (Seghers), 290–291
Poupart, R., 232, 234
Protokollen der Weisen von Zion, 59
Prümm, K., 204

Ratten, Die (R. Siodmak), 205, 220
Regler, G., 46
Remarque, E.M., 45–46
Renn, L., 46
Requiem Ebraico (Zeisl), 261–262
"Reunion Far From Vienna" (K. Mann), 153, 154, 158–166, 167
Revue d'Allemagne, 232
von Ribbentrop, J., 229, 230
Rilke, R.M., 157
Rites of Passage, The (van Gennep), 133–135, 151
Roberson, S., 369–370
Robitschek, K., 240, 242–243, 263
Rohlf, S., 316, 320–321, 326
Rolland, R., 95
Romains, J., 94, 232, 234

Roosevelt, F.D., 333
Rosenstein, P., 143, 146–147, 148–149
Rosenstock, J., 66
Roth, J., 41, 79, 87, 90, 251, 252–253
Rowohlt, E., 331
Rubin, M., 252, 262
Rückkehr der verlorenen Tochter, Die (Schlüter), 352

Said, E., 19, 301, 322
Sahl, H., 29, 42, 45, 48
Sammlung, Die, 354
Sannwald, D., 220
Schaevers, M., 78, 87
Schauff, K., 142, 145, 147, 149
Scheer, M., 335, 343
Schenk, E., 262
Schiff, ..., 56
Schiller, F., 41
Schlüter, H., 347, 350–367
Schmerzliches Arkadien (Mendelssohn), 351, 357
Schnabel, A., 276
Schoenberg, A., 244, 247, 248, 249, 251, 254, 259, 262, 263, 264, 265–279
Schoenberger, F., 44
Schröder, R.A., 94
Schubert, F., 239, 245–246, 256, 262
Schüfftan, E., 205–206
Schumann, R., 246
Schütz, A., 284
Schutzverband deutscher Schriftsteller, 93
Schwarz, E., 369
Schwesig, K., 95
Seghers, A., 29–30, 40, 41, 42, 46, 131, 180, 283–296, 297–311, 356
Seidel, I., 234
Seidel, M., 18
Senko, Y., 59–60
Severini, G., 303, 304
Sievers, M., 97
Simmel, G., 283–284
Simplicissimus, 179
Simplicus, 179

Singer, K., 67–68
Siodmak, C., 204, 205
Siodmak, R., 201, 202–222
Siodmak, W., 213
Slominsky, N., 274
Sontag, S., 23
Sopher, E., 137, 142, 148
Spaak, P., 75
Spanische Gedichte und Tagebuchblätter (Leonhard), 332
Spiel, H., 258, 259, 354
Spitta, A., 116, 129
Spitzer, L., 28
Stars and Stripes, 169
Stefan, P., 244
Stephan, A., 366
Sterne verlöschen nicht, Die (Ligeti), 85–87
Sternheim, C., 79–80
Stiefel, E., 68–69, 70
Stiftung des deutschen Auslandwerks, Die, 223, 224
Stöhr, R., 251
Stolz, K., 242
Stowe, W., 21
Streicher, J., 230
Strelka, J., 182, 348
Stuermann, E., 276
Südamerika. Alles und Nichts. Eine nicht ganz einfache Reise ins Blaue hinein (Zech), 119
Süskind, W.E., 350, 351, 353
Süss, P., 92
Swartz, M., 54

Tag Kommt, Der (H. Mann), 235
Tassin, J., 96
Theile, A., 119
Theory of Film (Kracauer), 209
Theroux, P., 14, 21–22
Timmermans, F., 94
Toch, E., 276
Tokayer, M., 54
Toller, E., 78, 90, 334
Transit (Seghers), 283, 289, 295, 308

Traumbuch des Exils (Leonhard), 329–345
"Travel and Dance" (Kracauer), 306
Traven, B., 46
Tucholsky, K., 334, 349
Turner, V., 134
Turning Point, The (K. Mann), 153, 154, 168, 169, 170, 174, 362
Tynset (Hildesheimer), 99–108, 109

Uhse, B., 46, 131
Ulmer, E.G., 202, 205
Unfreiwillige Wanderjahre (Schwarz), 369, 372–376, 380, 382–384
Universe of the Mind (Lotman), 89–90
Unwegsame Zeiten (Blunck), 224
Unwilling Tourist, The (Hoffmeister), 177, 179, 180, 182–191, 192–198

Vandervelde, E., 95
Vandervelde, J., 95
Varise, E., 276
Verein für musikalische Privataufführung, 247, 248, 254
Vereinigung schaffender Tonkünstler, 247
Verklärte Nacht, Opus 4 (Schoenberg), 268–269, 277, 278
Vertov, D., 206
von der Vogelweide, W., 229
Vom Friedens-Museum zur Hitler-Kaserne (Friedrich), 80
Vor dem Leben (K. Mann), 351

Walter, B., 247
Wagner, K., 253–254
Wagner, R., 15
Wahrheit, Die., 85
Walser, M., 48
Wander, F., 180
Weaker Sex, The (R. Siodmak), 211
von Webern, A., 244, 249, 254
Wedekind, P., 79
Weibsmühle, Die (Blunck), 223–224
Weigl, K., 247, 254

Weigel, S., 51n
Weisberger, L., 155
Weiskopf, F.C., 41, 45, 49
Weiss, E., 334
Wendepunkt, Der (K. Mann), 48
Werfel, F., 38, 42
Westheim, P., 93
West Point Widow (Siodmak), 214
Whitman, W., 352
Wiedemann, H., 141, 142, 143, 148, 150
Wilde, O., 352
Wilder, B., 202, 205
Wilkinson, J., 134
Winterreise (Schubert), 245–246, 256
Winder, L., 41
wirkliche Blau, Das. Eine Geschichte aus Mexiko (Seghers), 283
Wolf, F., 40
Wolf, L., 292
Wordsworth, W., 15
Wurmser, A., 332

"You Can't Go Home Again" (K. Mann), 153, 170

Zankin, M., 81
Zech, P., 46, 115–131
Zech, R., 117, 118, 119–120, 121, 122, 125, 129, 130
Zehl-Romero, C., 285–286, 287, 302, 309–310
Zeisl, E., 239, 240, 249–255, 258–259, 260–262, 263
Zemlinsky, A., 247, 263
Ziegler, Die (Seghers), 287
Zinn, A., 123
Zinneman, F., 202, 205
Zuckmayer, C., 36–37, 45
Zweig, A., 232
Zweig, S., 18, 26, 35–36, 42, 43, 78, 90, 117, 118–119, 131, 252, 289, 334
Zwischen Berlin und Hollywood (R. Siodmak), 203, 210–211, 212–213

CPSIA information can be obtained at www.ICGtesting.com
264722BV00002B/11/P